Lecture Notes in Computer Science 8016

Commenced Publication in 1973
Founding and Former Series Editors:
Gerhard Goos, Juris Hartmanis, and Jan van Leeuwen

Sakae Yamamoto (Ed.)

Human Interface and the Management of Information

Information and Interaction Design

15th International Conference, HCI International 2013
Las Vegas, NV, USA, July 21-26, 2013
Proceedings, Part I

Springer

Volume Editor

Sakae Yamamoto
Tokyo University of Science
Faculty of Engineering
Department of Management Science
1-3 Kagurazaka Shinjuku-ku
Tokyo 162-8601, Japan
E-mail: sakae@ms.kagu.tus.ac.jp

ISSN 0302-9743   e-ISSN 1611-3349
ISBN 978-3-642-39208-5   e-ISBN 978-3-642-39209-2
DOI 10.1007/978-3-642-39209-2
Springer Heidelberg Dordrecht London New York

Library of Congress Control Number: 2013941251

CR Subject Classification (1998): H.5, H.4, H.3, J.2

LNCS Sublibrary: SL 3 – Information Systems and Application,
incl. Internet/Web and HCI

Typesetting: Camera-ready by author, data conversion by Scientific Publishing Services, Chennai, India

Printed on acid-free paper

Springer is part of Springer Science+Business Media (www.springer.com)

Foreword

The 15th International Conference on Human–Computer Interaction, HCI International 2013, was held in Las Vegas, Nevada, USA, 21–26 July 2013, incorporating 12 conferences / thematic areas:

Thematic areas:

- Human–Computer Interaction
- Human Interface and the Management of Information

Affiliated conferences:

- 10th International Conference on Engineering Psychology and Cognitive Ergonomics
- 7th International Conference on Universal Access in Human–Computer Interaction
- 5th International Conference on Virtual, Augmented and Mixed Reality
- 5th International Conference on Cross-Cultural Design
- 5th International Conference on Online Communities and Social Computing
- 7th International Conference on Augmented Cognition
- 4th International Conference on Digital Human Modeling and Applications in Health, Safety, Ergonomics and Risk Management
- 2nd International Conference on Design, User Experience and Usability
- 1st International Conference on Distributed, Ambient and Pervasive Interactions
- 1st International Conference on Human Aspects of Information Security, Privacy and Trust

A total of 5210 individuals from academia, research institutes, industry and governmental agencies from 70 countries submitted contributions, and 1666 papers and 303 posters were included in the program. These papers address the latest research and development efforts and highlight the human aspects of design and use of computing systems. The papers accepted for presentation thoroughly cover the entire field of Human–Computer Interaction, addressing major advances in knowledge and effective use of computers in a variety of application areas.

This volume, edited by Sakae Yamamoto, contains papers focusing on the thematic area of Human Interface and the Management of Information, and addressing the following major topics:

- Interacting with Information
- Information Searching, Browsing and Structuring
- Design and Development Methods and Tools for Interactive Systems and Services
- Personalized Information and Interaction
- Cognitive and Emotional Aspects of Interacting with Information

The remaining volumes of the HCI International 2013 proceedings are:

- Volume 1, LNCS 8004, Human–Computer Interaction: Human-Centred Design Approaches, Methods, Tools and Environments (Part I), edited by Masaaki Kurosu
- Volume 2, LNCS 8005, Human–Computer Interaction: Applications and Services (Part II), edited by Masaaki Kurosu
- Volume 3, LNCS 8006, Human–Computer Interaction: Users and Contexts of Use (Part III), edited by Masaaki Kurosu
- Volume 4, LNCS 8007, Human–Computer Interaction: Interaction Modalities and Techniques (Part IV), edited by Masaaki Kurosu
- Volume 5, LNCS 8008, Human–Computer Interaction: Towards Intelligent and Implicit Interaction (Part V), edited by Masaaki Kurosu
- Volume 6, LNCS 8009, Universal Access in Human–Computer Interaction: Design Methods, Tools and Interaction Techniques for eInclusion (Part I), edited by Constantine Stephanidis and Margherita Antona
- Volume 7, LNCS 8010, Universal Access in Human–Computer Interaction: User and Context Diversity (Part II), edited by Constantine Stephanidis and Margherita Antona
- Volume 8, LNCS 8011, Universal Access in Human–Computer Interaction: Applications and Services for Quality of Life (Part III), edited by Constantine Stephanidis and Margherita Antona
- Volume 9, LNCS 8012, Design, User Experience, and Usability: Design Philosophy, Methods and Tools (Part I), edited by Aaron Marcus
- Volume 10, LNCS 8013, Design, User Experience, and Usability: Health, Learning, Playing, Cultural, and Cross-Cultural User Experience (Part II), edited by Aaron Marcus
- Volume 11, LNCS 8014, Design, User Experience, and Usability: User Experience in Novel Technological Environments (Part III), edited by Aaron Marcus
- Volume 12, LNCS 8015, Design, User Experience, and Usability: Web, Mobile and Product Design (Part IV), edited by Aaron Marcus
- Volume 14, LNCS 8017, Human Interface and the Management of Information: Information and Interaction for Health, Safety, Mobility and Complex Environments (Part II), edited by Sakae Yamamoto
- Volume 15, LNCS 8018, Human Interface and the Management of Information: Information and Interaction for Learning, Culture, Collaboration and Business (Part III), edited by Sakae Yamamoto
- Volume 16, LNAI 8019, Engineering Psychology and Cognitive Ergonomics: Understanding Human Cognition (Part I), edited by Don Harris
- Volume 17, LNAI 8020, Engineering Psychology and Cognitive Ergonomics: Applications and Services (Part II), edited by Don Harris
- Volume 18, LNCS 8021, Virtual, Augmented and Mixed Reality: Designing and Developing Augmented and Virtual Environments (Part I), edited by Randall Shumaker
- Volume 19, LNCS 8022, Virtual, Augmented and Mixed Reality: Systems and Applications (Part II), edited by Randall Shumaker

- Volume 20, LNCS 8023, Cross-Cultural Design: Methods, Practice and Case Studies (Part I), edited by P.L. Patrick Rau
- Volume 21, LNCS 8024, Cross-Cultural Design: Cultural Differences in Everyday Life (Part II), edited by P.L. Patrick Rau
- Volume 22, LNCS 8025, Digital Human Modeling and Applications in Health, Safety, Ergonomics and Risk Management: Healthcare and Safety of the Environment and Transport (Part I), edited by Vincent G. Duffy
- Volume 23, LNCS 8026, Digital Human Modeling and Applications in Health, Safety, Ergonomics and Risk Management: Human Body Modeling and Ergonomics (Part II), edited by Vincent G. Duffy
- Volume 24, LNAI 8027, Foundations of Augmented Cognition, edited by Dylan D. Schmorrow and Cali M. Fidopiastis
- Volume 25, LNCS 8028, Distributed, Ambient and Pervasive Interactions, edited by Norbert Streitz and Constantine Stephanidis
- Volume 26, LNCS 8029, Online Communities and Social Computing, edited by A. Ant Ozok and Panayiotis Zaphiris
- Volume 27, LNCS 8030, Human Aspects of Information Security, Privacy and Trust, edited by Louis Marinos and Ioannis Askoxylakis
- Volume 28, CCIS 373, HCI International 2013 Posters Proceedings (Part I), edited by Constantine Stephanidis
- Volume 29, CCIS 374, HCI International 2013 Posters Proceedings (Part II), edited by Constantine Stephanidis

I would like to thank the Program Chairs and the members of the Program Boards of all affiliated conferences and thematic areas, listed below, for their contribution to the highest scientific quality and the overall success of the HCI International 2013 conference.

This conference could not have been possible without the continuous support and advice of the Founding Chair and Conference Scientific Advisor, Prof. Gavriel Salvendy, as well as the dedicated work and outstanding efforts of the Communications Chair and Editor of HCI International News, Abbas Moallem.

I would also like to thank for their contribution towards the smooth organization of the HCI International 2013 Conference the members of the Human–Computer Interaction Laboratory of ICS-FORTH, and in particular George Paparoulis, Maria Pitsoulaki, Stavroula Ntoa, Maria Bouhli and George Kapnas.

May 2013   Constantine Stephanidis
                                          General Chair, HCI International 2013

Organization

Human–Computer Interaction

Program Chair: Masaaki Kurosu, Japan

Jose Abdelnour-Nocera, UK
Sebastiano Bagnara, Italy
Simone Barbosa, Brazil
Tomas Berns, Sweden
Nigel Bevan, UK
Simone Borsci, UK
Apala Lahiri Chavan, India
Sherry Chen, Taiwan
Kevin Clark, USA
Torkil Clemmensen, Denmark
Xiaowen Fang, USA
Shin'ichi Fukuzumi, Japan
Vicki Hanson, UK
Ayako Hashizume, Japan
Anzai Hiroyuki, Italy
Sheue-Ling Hwang, Taiwan
Wonil Hwang, South Korea
Minna Isomursu, Finland
Yong Gu Ji, South Korea
Esther Jun, USA
Mitsuhiko Karashima, Japan

Kyungdoh Kim, South Korea
Heidi Krömker, Germany
Chen Ling, USA
Yan Liu, USA
Zhengjie Liu, P.R. China
Loïc Martínez Normand, Spain
Chang S. Nam, USA
Naoko Okuizumi, Japan
Noriko Osaka, Japan
Philippe Palanque, France
Hans Persson, Sweden
Ling Rothrock, USA
Naoki Sakakibara, Japan
Dominique Scapin, France
Guangfeng Song, USA
Sanjay Tripathi, India
Chui Yin Wong, Malaysia
Toshiki Yamaoka, Japan
Kazuhiko Yamazaki, Japan
Ryoji Yoshitake, Japan
Silvia Zimmermann, Switzerland

Human Interface and the Management of Information

Program Chair: Sakae Yamamoto, Japan

Hans-Jorg Bullinger, Germany
Alan Chan, Hong Kong
Gilsoo Cho, South Korea
Jon R. Gunderson, USA
Shin'ichi Fukuzumi, Japan
Michitaka Hirose, Japan
Jhilmil Jain, USA
Yasufumi Kume, Japan

Mark Lehto, USA
Hiroyuki Miki, Japan
Hirohiko Mori, Japan
Fiona Fui-Hoon Nah, USA
Shogo Nishida, Japan
Robert Proctor, USA
Youngho Rhee, South Korea
Katsunori Shimohara, Japan

Engineering Psychology and Cognitive Ergonomics

Program Chair: Don Harris, UK

Universal Access in Human–Computer Interaction

Program Chairs: Constantine Stephanidis, Greece, and Margherita Antona, Greece

Virtual, Augmented and Mixed Reality

Program Chair: Randall Shumaker, USA

Waymon Armstrong, USA
Juan Cendan, USA
Rudy Darken, USA
Cali M. Fidopiastis, USA
Charles Hughes, USA
David Kaber, USA
Hirokazu Kato, Japan
Denis Laurendeau, Canada
Fotis Liarokapis, UK

Mark Livingston, USA
Michael Macedonia, USA
Gordon Mair, UK
Jose San Martin, Spain
Jacquelyn Morie, USA
Albert "Skip" Rizzo, USA
Kay Stanney, USA
Christopher Stapleton, USA
Gregory Welch, USA

Cross-Cultural Design

Program Chair: P.L. Patrick Rau, P.R. China

Pilsung Choe, P.R. China
Henry Been-Lirn Duh, Singapore
Vanessa Evers, The Netherlands
Paul Fu, USA
Zhiyong Fu, P.R. China
Fu Guo, P.R. China
Sung H. Han, Korea
Toshikazu Kato, Japan
Dyi-Yih Michael Lin, Taiwan
Rungtai Lin, Taiwan

Sheau-Farn Max Liang, Taiwan
Liang Ma, P.R. China
Alexander Mädche, Germany
Katsuhiko Ogawa, Japan
Tom Plocher, USA
Kerstin Röse, Germany
Supriya Singh, Australia
Hsiu-Ping Yueh, Taiwan
Liang (Leon) Zeng, USA
Chen Zhao, USA

Online Communities and Social Computing

Program Chairs: A. Ant Ozok, USA, and Panayiotis Zaphiris, Cyprus

Areej Al-Wabil, Saudi Arabia
Leonelo Almeida, Brazil
Bjørn Andersen, Norway
Chee Siang Ang, UK
Aneesha Bakharia, Australia
Ania Bobrowicz, UK
Paul Cairns, UK
Farzin Deravi, UK
Andri Ioannou, Cyprus
Slava Kisilevich, Germany

Niki Lambropoulos, Greece
Effie Law, Switzerland
Soo Ling Lim, UK
Fernando Loizides, Cyprus
Gabriele Meiselwitz, USA
Anthony Norcio, USA
Elaine Raybourn, USA
Panote Siriaraya, UK
David Stuart, UK
June Wei, USA

Augmented Cognition

Program Chairs: Dylan D. Schmorrow, USA, and Cali M. Fidopiastis, USA

Robert Arrabito, Canada
Richard Backs, USA
Chris Berka, USA
Joseph Cohn, USA
Martha E. Crosby, USA
Julie Drexler, USA
Ivy Estabrooke, USA
Chris Forsythe, USA
Wai Tat Fu, USA
Rodolphe Gentili, USA
Marc Grootjen, The Netherlands
Jefferson Grubb, USA
Ming Hou, Canada

Santosh Mathan, USA
Rob Matthews, Australia
Dennis McBride, USA
Jeff Morrison, USA
Mark A. Neerincx, The Netherlands
Denise Nicholson, USA
Banu Onaral, USA
Lee Sciarini, USA
Kay Stanney, USA
Roy Stripling, USA
Rob Taylor, UK
Karl van Orden, USA

Digital Human Modeling and Applications in Health, Safety, Ergonomics and Risk Management

Program Chair: Vincent G. Duffy, USA and Russia

Karim Abdel-Malek, USA
Giuseppe Andreoni, Italy
Daniel Carruth, USA
Eliza Yingzi Du, USA
Enda Fallon, Ireland
Afzal Godil, USA
Ravindra Goonetilleke, Hong Kong
Bo Hoege, Germany
Waldemar Karwowski, USA
Zhizhong Li, P.R. China

Kang Li, USA
Tim Marler, USA
Michelle Robertson, USA
Matthias Rötting, Germany
Peter Vink, The Netherlands
Mao-Jiun Wang, Taiwan
Xuguang Wang, France
Jingzhou (James) Yang, USA
Xiugan Yuan, P.R. China
Gülcin Yücel Hoge, Germany

Design, User Experience, and Usability

Program Chair: Aaron Marcus, USA

Sisira Adikari, Australia
Ronald Baecker, Canada
Arne Berger, Germany
Jamie Blustein, Canada

Ana Boa-Ventura, USA
Jan Brejcha, Czech Republic
Lorenzo Cantoni, Switzerland
Maximilian Eibl, Germany

Anthony Faiola, USA
Emilie Gould, USA
Zelda Harrison, USA
Rüdiger Heimgärtner, Germany
Brigitte Herrmann, Germany
Steffen Hess, Germany
Kaleem Khan, Canada

Jennifer McGinn, USA
Francisco Rebelo, Portugal
Michael Renner, Switzerland
Kerem Rızvanoğlu, Turkey
Marcelo Soares, Brazil
Christian Sturm, Germany
Michele Visciola, Italy

Distributed, Ambient and Pervasive Interactions

Program Chairs: Norbert Streitz, Germany, and Constantine Stephanidis, Greece

Emile Aarts, The Netherlands
Adnan Abu-Dayya, Qatar
Juan Carlos Augusto, UK
Boris de Ruyter, The Netherlands
Anind Dey, USA
Dimitris Grammenos, Greece
Nuno M. Guimaraes, Portugal
Shin'ichi Konomi, Japan
Carsten Magerkurth, Switzerland

Christian Müller-Tomfelde, Australia
Fabio Paternó, Italy
Gilles Privat, France
Harald Reiterer, Germany
Carsten Röcker, Germany
Reiner Wichert, Germany
Woontack Woo, South Korea
Xenophon Zabulis, Greece

Human Aspects of Information Security, Privacy and Trust

Program Chairs: Louis Marinos, ENISA EU, and Ioannis Askoxylakis, Greece

Claudio Agostino Ardagna, Italy
Zinaida Benenson, Germany
Daniele Catteddu, Italy
Raoul Chiesa, Italy
Bryan Cline, USA
Sadie Creese, UK
Jorge Cuellar, Germany
Marc Dacier, USA
Dieter Gollmann, Germany
Kirstie Hawkey, Canada
Jaap-Henk Hoepman, The Netherlands
Cagatay Karabat, Turkey
Angelos Keromytis, USA
Ayako Komatsu, Japan

Ronald Leenes, The Netherlands
Javier Lopez, Spain
Steve Marsh, Canada
Gregorio Martinez, Spain
Emilio Mordini, Italy
Yuko Murayama, Japan
Masakatsu Nishigaki, Japan
Aljosa Pasic, Spain
Milan Petković, The Netherlands
Joachim Posegga, Germany
Jean-Jacques Quisquater, Belgium
Damien Sauveron, France
George Spanoudakis, UK
Kerry-Lynn Thomson, South Africa

Julien Touzeau, France
Theo Tryfonas, UK
João Vilela, Portugal

Claire Vishik, UK
Melanie Volkamer, Germany

External Reviewers

Maysoon Abulkhair, Saudi Arabia
Ilia Adami, Greece
Vishal Barot, UK
Stephan Böhm, Germany
Vassilis Charissis, UK
Francisco Cipolla-Ficarra, Spain
Maria De Marsico, Italy
Marc Fabri, UK
David Fonseca, Spain
Linda Harley, USA
Yasushi Ikei, Japan
Wei Ji, USA
Nouf Khashman, Canada
John Killilea, USA
Iosif Klironomos, Greece
Ute Klotz, Switzerland
Maria Korozi, Greece
Kentaro Kotani, Japan

Vassilis Kouroumalis, Greece
Stephanie Lackey, USA
Janelle LaMarche, USA
Asterios Leonidis, Greece
Nickolas Macchiarella, USA
George Margetis, Greece
Matthew Marraffino, USA
Joseph Mercado, USA
Claudia Mont'Alvão, Brazil
Yoichi Motomura, Japan
Karsten Nebe, Germany
Stavroula Ntoa, Greece
Martin Osen, Austria
Stephen Prior, UK
Farid Shirazi, Canada
Jan Stelovsky, USA
Sarah Swierenga, USA

HCI International 2014

The 16th International Conference on Human–Computer Interaction, HCI International 2014, will be held jointly with the affiliated conferences in the summer of 2014. It will cover a broad spectrum of themes related to Human–Computer Interaction, including theoretical issues, methods, tools, processes and case studies in HCI design, as well as novel interaction techniques, interfaces and applications. The proceedings will be published by Springer. More information about the topics, as well as the venue and dates of the conference, will be announced through the HCI International Conference series website: http://www.hci-international.org/

General Chair
Professor Constantine Stephanidis
University of Crete and ICS-FORTH
Heraklion, Crete, Greece
Email: cs@ics.forth.gr

Table of Contents – Part I

Interacting with Information

Information Searching, Browsing and Structuring

Design and Development Methods and Tools for Interactive Systems and Services

Personalized Information and Interaction

Cognitive and Emotional Aspects of Interacting with Information

Table of Contents – Part II

Complex Information Environments

Health and Quality of Life

Mobile Interaction

Safety in Transport, Aviation and Industry

Table of Contents – Part III

Learning, Education and Skills Transfer

Art and Cultural Heritage

Collaborative Work

Business Integration

Decision Support

Part I
Interacting with Information

Estimation of Driver's Steering Intention by Using Mechanical Impedance

Takafumi Asao, Satoshi Suzuki, and Kentaro Kotani

Faculty of Engineering Science, Kansai University, Japan
{asao,ssuzuki,Kotani}@kansai-u.ac.jp

Abstract. We attempted to estimate a driver's steering intention by using human mechanical impedance, which changes as a result of muscle activity, because humans should be ready to act before moving. First, we verified the estimated accuracy of the impedance under a static condition. The estimation results showed good accuracy. Then, we tried to estimate the time-varying human impedance during a tracking task using the steering wheel. There were some instances where the stiffness became high before steering and became low after steering, but the occurrence rate was low.

Keywords: steering intention, mechanical impedance, dynamic identification, Kalman filter.

1 Introduction

Driving support systems have been developed to take the place of a portion of a driver's cognition, judgment, and operation [1]. However, there could be conflicts between the driver's intentions and those of the system if such systems become popular and cover various situations [2]. Drivers hope that such systems will not be bothersome, but will have properly designed support timing and functions.

The information required by these systems is divided into vehicle information, environmental information, and driver information. The vehicle information consists of dynamic data about the vehicle such as its position and slip angle. The environmental information includes the road alignment and the positions of other vehicles and pedestrians, as identified using various sensors. The driver information consists of the driver's operational and physiological data. Almost all of the existing systems utilize only vehicle and environmental information. However, using the driver information in addition to the vehicle and environmental information is necessary to ensure that such systems support drivers with appropriate timing, rather than becoming bothersome. If the driver's intention can be estimated, it will be possible to support the driver after determining the adequacy and safety of the driver's operation, while coordinating the vehicle, environmental, and driver information.

Some previous studies tried to estimate a driver's steering intention by using an electroencephalogram (EEG) and eye movements [3], [4]. Ikenishi et al. proposed an algorithm to estimate the steering intentions, which were going straight, turning right, or turning left, using the power spectrum (8 to 30 Hz) of a background EEG [3].

S. Yamamoto (Ed.): HIMI/HCII 2013, Part I, LNCS 8016, pp. 3–11, 2013.

Suzuki et al. attempted to estimate a driver's intention to change lanes (to the right) on a highway by using the driver's eye movements [4]. Performing EEG measurements in a moving vehicle has two problems. There is background noise in the EEG signals as a result of the body movements of the driver, vehicle vibration, and electric components of the vehicle. Drivers are constrained by the attached EEG electrodes. On the other hand, the eye tracking system, which has high resolution, is not applicable because of the cost.

Humans can move their arms, legs, and body in response to some task. They configure an appropriate mechanical impedance by adjusting their musculo-viscoelasticity before the movement [5], [6]. Impedance is a collective term for the inertia, viscosity, and stiffness, which constitute the motion resistance [5]. Humans raise the stiffness and viscosity of their hands in order to start moving quickly in the desired manner [6]. This study focused on the impedance in a driver's hands while grasping the steering wheel. The goal of this study was to estimate a driver's steering intentions by using the impedance. In this paper, we try to estimate the impedance dynamically and verify that the steering intention can be estimated from the impedance.

2   Identification of Impedance

2.1   Selection of Identification Technique

Studies on human impedance began with Mussa-Ivaldi, Hogan, & Bizzi (1985). They measured the stiffness of a human hand [7]. After that, impedance measurements were extended to include the viscosity and stiffness [8], [9], [10]. In these studies, perturbation was given to the hand for a very short duration in order to prevent changes in the impedance as a result of human voluntary reaction. This technique can only be applied to measure the impedance for static postures. Therefore, an ensemble method was devised, by which the impedance at any time could be estimated by using a large quantity of static single trial data [11], [12], [13]. In recent years, an online estimation technique has been developed in order to estimate the time-varying impedance during movements by using a frequency filter to remove the voluntary constituent [14], [15].

Shin et al. proposed a dynamic estimation method by using an electromyogram (EMG) and musculo-mechanics, in which an EEG was considered to represent the commands from the brain [16]. Hada et al. developed a dynamic estimation method by using a musculo-skeletal model and kinematics, in which muscular activations were estimated from measured sequential posture data [17].

The online method, muscular model method, and musculo-skeletal model methods should be suitable to estimate the steering intention, because the impedance is time-varying. However, the muscular model method is not recommended because of the restraints imposed by the EMG electrodes that have to be attached to the driver. The musculo-skeletal model method would also be unsuitable, because measuring driving postures is difficult at high resolution. Therefore, this study employed the online estimation method, with which the impedance could be estimated using only the steering wheel angles and torques.

2.2   Impedance Model for Human-Steering System

The equation of motion for a steering wheel is represented as

$$M_s \ddot{\theta} + B_s \left(\dot{\theta} - \dot{\theta}_e \right) + K_s \left(\theta - \theta_e \right) = \tau + \tau_h \tag{1}$$

where M_s, B_s, and K_s denote the rotational inertia, viscosity, and stiffness of the structural elements of the steering system, respectively. θ and θ_e denote the steering wheel angle and its equilibrium angle, respectively, and τ and τ_h denote the torques applied by a motor and human, respectively. The equation of motion for a human in relation to the steering wheel shaft is represented as

$$M_h \ddot{\theta} + B_h \left(\dot{\theta} - \dot{\theta}_e \right) + K_h \left(\theta - \theta_e \right) = -\tau_h \tag{2}$$

where M_h, B_h, and K_h denote the equivalent rotational impedance factors of the human. From Eqs. (1) and (2), the equation of motion for the human-steering system is represented as

$$M \ddot{\theta} + B \left(\dot{\theta} - \dot{\theta}_e \right) + K \left(\theta - \theta_e \right) = \tau \tag{3}$$

where $M = M_s + M_h$, $B = B_s + B_h$, and $K = K_s + K_h$ are the impedance factors for the human-steering system, which are time-varying because M_h, B_h, and K_h are time-varying.

A situation where a single perturbation is applied to the steering wheel by a motor connected to the steering shaft is considered. The torque changes from τ to $\tau + \Delta\tau$, and the angle changes from θ to $\theta + \Delta\theta$. Then, the following two conditions are assumed:

(1) The human arm posture and impedance do not change before and after the perturbation because the perturbation is small [7], [18].
(2) The human cannot change their impedance, equilibrium point, and force against the perturbation because the duration of the perturbation is short [18].

Based on these assumptions, the equation of motion for the human-steering system after the perturbation is represented as

$$M \left(\ddot{\theta} + \Delta\ddot{\theta} \right) + B \left(\dot{\theta} + \Delta\dot{\theta} - \dot{\theta}_e \right) + K \left(\theta + \Delta\theta - \theta_e \right) = \tau + \Delta\tau \tag{4}$$

If the frequency of human movement is considerably smaller than that of the perturbation, the human involuntary motion can be obtained, as shown in the following equation, by band-pass filtering the measured angle and torque [14], [15].

$$M \Delta\ddot{\theta} + B \Delta\dot{\theta} + K \Delta\theta = \Delta\tau \tag{5}$$

This equation can be applied to both a single perturbation and continuous perturbation.

2.3   Impedance Estimation Algorithm by Kalman Filter

This section shows the impedance estimation method. The time-varying variables from the previous section are represented with sampling number i as discrete variables. The impedance and variables are defined as vectors:

$$U_i = \begin{bmatrix} M_i & B_i & K_i \end{bmatrix}^T \tag{6}$$

$$\boldsymbol{\theta}_i = \begin{bmatrix} \Delta\ddot{\theta}_i & \Delta\dot{\theta}_i & \Delta\theta_i \end{bmatrix}^T \tag{7}$$

The parameter U is estimated using the following updating equations:

$$k_i = \frac{P_{i-1}\boldsymbol{\theta}_i}{\lambda + \boldsymbol{\theta}_i^T P_{i-1}\boldsymbol{\theta}_i} \tag{8}$$

$$P_i = P_{i-1} - k_i\boldsymbol{\theta}_i^T P_{i-1} \tag{9}$$

$$U_i = U_{i-1} + k_i\left(\Delta\tau_i - \boldsymbol{\theta}_i^T U_{i-1}\right) \tag{10}$$

where $k \in R^3$, $\lambda \in R$, and $P \in R^{3\times3}$ denote the Kalman gain, variance of the observation noise, and covariance matrix, respectively. ^{T} denotes transposing the vector or matrix. The initial values are set at

$$U_0 = 0 \tag{11}$$

$$P_0 = \mathrm{diag}\left(10^4, 10^4, 10^4\right) \tag{12}$$

where the diag operator indicates a diagonal matrix. λ is set at 0.8.

3   Verification Experiment for Estimation Accuracy

Before estimating the human impedance, an experiment was conducted to verify the estimation accuracy by using known parameters.

3.1   Apparatus

Fig. 1 shows an illustration of the apparatus. The outer diameter of the steering wheel (Nardi classic) was 360 mm. The steering wheel shaft was connected to an AC servomotor (SGMPH-08A1A41, Yasukawa Electric Corp.) via a high stiffness coupling. The torque of the motor was controlled by a PC via a D/A board and motor driver, which allowed it to generate perturbations. The steering wheel angle was measured using an incremental encoder in the motor unit (65536 pulse/rev). In this experiment, the equipment was placed on the floor because the rotational plane of the steering wheel was vertical. The steering wheel angles and command torque were measured by the PC at a 100-Hz sampling frequency.

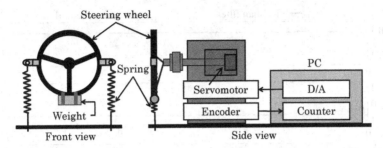

Fig. 1. Illustration of experimental system

3.2   Perturbation

The perturbation torque that was necessary for estimating the impedance was an M-sequence signal with the condition that a primitive polynominal was $x^7 + 1$. The 0 and 1 signals created by the M-sequence were assigned values of –0.5 or +0.5 Nm, respectively. The torque was changed at intervals of 30 ms because of the created signals. Thus, the cycle length of the perturbations was 3.81 s.

3.3   Experimental Conditions

Weights were attached to the bottom of the steering wheel, whose mass and shape were known. Two different weights were used, 0.5 and 1.0 kg, whose moments of inertia about the steering wheel axis were 1.9×10^{-2} and 4.1×10^{-2} kg·m^2, respectively. A set of two identical springs were vertically attached to the sides of the steering wheel, with their ends clamped to the floor. The spring constants of two different sets of springs were 114 and 458 Nm. The converted rotational stiffness values at the tangent of the steering wheel were 4.55 and 18.3 Nm/rad, respectively. There were a total of nine conditions for the various combinations of three weights (including no weight) and three springs (including no spring). The measuring duration for each condition was 15.24 s, which was four cycles of the M-sequence signals. Ten trials were conducted for each condition. Because the impedance of this system was invariant, the impedance was estimated using the least square method (LSM) from Eq. (5), in addition to the recursive Kalman filter method described in Eqs. (8) to (10). The measured data were preprocessed by using a fourth-order band-pass Butterworth filter whose cut-off frequencies were 5 and 20 Hz.

3.4   Experimental Results

Fig. 2 shows an example of the estimated results for the conditions of a heavy weight and weak spring. In the figures, the thick lines denote the impedance estimated by the Kalman filter, and the thin lines denote that by LSM. The impedances estimated by using the Kalman filter increased rapidly, because the initial values of the impedance were set to zero. On the other hand, the impedance estimated by the Kalman filter became the same as that by LSM over time. Therefore, in this section, the impedance found by LSM is discussed.

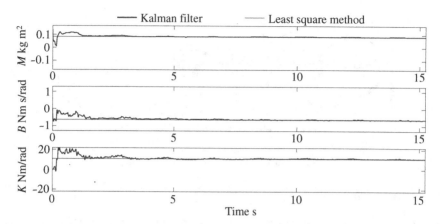

Fig. 2. Example of estimated impedances for condition of heavy weight and weak spring

Figs. 3 and 4 show the mean inertia and stiffness estimated by LSM with error bars for standard deviations, respectively. The structural impedance M_s and K_s could be obtained under the no weight and no spring condition. The structural impedance was subtracted from the values in the figures. The crossbars in the figures denote the given impedances. The estimated impedances increased with the given impedance. The estimated values were almost the same as the given ones. Therefore, the values estimated by the Kalman filter had good accuracy.

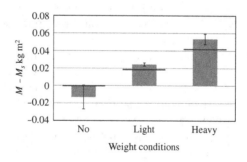

Fig. 3. Estimated inertia for validation

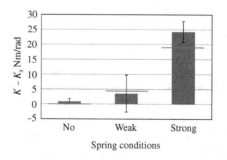

Fig. 4. Estimated stiffness for validation

4 Human Impedance during Steering Operation

4.1 Experimental Conditions

Fig. 5 shows a scene of the experiment. The subjects tracked a visual target using a steering wheel while sitting in the driver's seat. As shown in Fig. 6, a red square as the tracking target and operable black cross coupled to the steering wheel were shown on a CRT. The target moved laterally for a quarter cycle according to a sine wave. The subjects operated the steering wheel to prevent the operable target from deviating from the tracking target. The amplitude of the tracking target was set to 40, 80, or 120°. The frequency of the tracking target was set to 0.3, 0.5, or 0.7 Hz. The subjects were four healthy male university students.

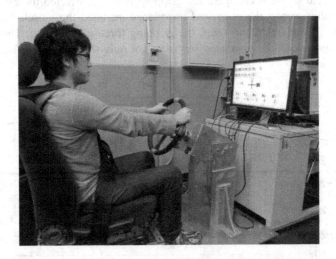

Fig. 5. Overview of tracking experiment

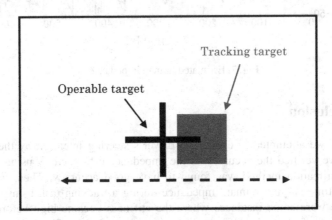

Fig. 6. Displayed screen image

4.2   Results and Discussions

Fig. 7 shows the estimated impedance for subject D under the condition of a 120° amplitude and frequency of 0.7 Hz. Each figure in Fig. 7 represents the steering angle, inertia, viscosity, and stiffness in order from the top. The red dashed lines cutting the figures longitudinally denote the moment at which the target started to move. The viscosity when the steering angle is almost at zero is higher than that for the other values. Moreover, as shown by the circles in the figure, there were some instances where the stiffness became high before steering and became low after steering. However, this did not occur in every case. This may have been affected by muscle contraction. Therefore, the muscle activity should be measured and validated. On the other hand, the pressure when gripping the steering wheel should not be constant. Whether or not the muscle stiffness changed, the gripping pressure affected the estimated impedance. In other words, the estimated impedance included the muscle stiffness and gripping state. If humans try to steer, the gripping force may change. Therefore, the steering intention could be estimated by using not only the muscle stiffness but also the gripping force.

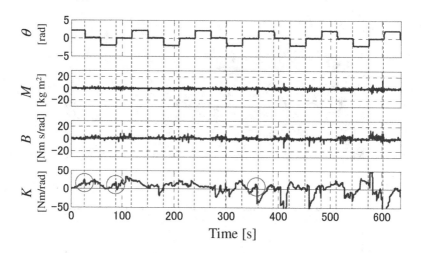

Fig. 7. Estimated human impedance

5   Conclusion

In this study, we attempted to estimate a driver's steering intention by their impedance. First, we verified the accuracy of the impedance estimated by using a Kalman filter. The estimation method was found to have good accuracy. Then, we tried to estimate the time-varying human impedance during a tracking task using a steering wheel. There were some instances where the stiffness became high before steering and became low after steering, but the occurrence rate was low. The factors that led to this occurrence were unknown. Therefore, in future work, we will verify the muscle activity and gripping force during the steering operation. Moreover, the estimation model, that is, the Kalman filter, will be improved in order to improve the estimation accuracy.

References

1. Tsugawa, S.: Current Status and Issues on Safe Driver Assistance Systems. Journal of Society of Automotive Engineers of Japan 63(2), 12–18 (2009)
2. Inagaki, T.: Humans understand machines; machines understand humans. In: Proceedings of 16th Annual Meetings of JSME Transportation and Logistics Division, pp. 7–10 (2007) (in Japanese)
3. Ikenishi, T., Machida, Y., Kamada, T., Nagai, M.: Estimation of Driver Steering Intention based on Brain-Computer Interface using Electroencephalogram. Transactions of Society of Automotive Engineers of Japan 39(6), 23–28 (2008)
4. Suzuki, M., Inagaki, S., Suzuki, T., Hayakawa, S., Tsuchida, N.: Estimation of Switching Point in Human Driving Behavior Based on Eye-movement and Bayesian Estimation. In: Proceedings of Industrial Instrumentation and Control Meeting, IIC-07-75, pp. 29–34 (2007)
5. Ito, K.: Bodily wisdom thesis as system, pp. 76–81. Kyoritsu, Kyoto (2005) (in Japanese)
6. Kim, J., Sato, M., Koike, Y.: Human arm posture control using the impedance controllability of the musculo-skeletal system against the alteration of the environments. Transactions on Control, Automation, and Systems Engineering 4(1), 43–48 (2002)
7. Mussa-Ivaldi, F.A., Hogan, N., Bizzi, E.: Neural, Mechanical, and Geometric Factors Subserving Arm Posture in Humans. Journal of Neuroscience 5(10), 2732–2743 (1985)
8. Tsuji, T.: Measurement of upper arm flexibility. Journal of Society of Instrument and Control Engineers 35(9), 689–695 (1996) (in Japanese)
9. Dolan, J.M., Friedman, M.B., Nagurka, M.L.: Dynamic and Loaded Impedance Components in the Maintenance of Human Arm Posture. IEEE Transactions on Systems, Man, and Cybernetics 23(3), 698–709 (1993)
10. Tsuji, T., Morasso, P.G., Goto, K., Ito, K.: Human Hand Impedance Characteristics during Maintained Posture in Multi-Joint Arm Movements. Biological Cybernetics 72(6), 475–485 (1995)
11. Bennett, D.J., Hollerbach, J.M., Xu, Y., Hunter, I.W.: Time-varying stiffness of human elbow joint during cyclic voluntary movement. Experimental Brain Research 88(2), 433–442 (1992)
12. MacNeil, J.B., Kearney, R.E., Hunter, I.W.: Identification of time-varying biological systems from ensemble data. IEEE Transactions of Biomedical Engineering 39(12), 1213–1225 (1992)
13. Gomi, H., Kawato, M.: Human arm stiffness and equilibrium-point trajectory during multi-joint movement. Biological Cybernetics 76(3), 163–171 (1997)
14. Xu, Y., Hollerbach, J.M.: Identification of Human Joint Mechanical Properties from Single Trial Data. IEEE Transactions on Biomedical Engineering 45(8), 1051–1060 (1998)
15. Deng, M., Gomi, H.: Robust Estimation of Human Multijoint Arm Viscoelasticity during Movement. Transactions of Society of Instrument and Control Engineers 39(6), 537–543 (2003)
16. Shin, D., Shimada, O., Sato, M., Koike, Y.: Arm stiffness estimation using mathematical model of musculo-skeletal system. Transactions of the Institute of Electronics, Information and Communication Engineers J87-D-II(9), 1860–1869 (2004)
17. Hada, M., Yamada, D., Miura, H., Tsuji, T.: An Equivalent Impedance Characteristics Analysis System for Human-machine Systems. Transactions of Society of Instrument and Control Engineers 42(9), 1083–1091 (2006)

The Relationship Between Handlebar and Saddle Heights on Cycling Comfort

Min-Chi Chiu[1,2], Hsin-Chieh Wu[3], and Nien-Ting Tsai[3]

[1] School of Occupational Therapy,
Chung Shan Medical University,
Taichung, Taiwan, R.O.C.
[2] Occupational Therapy Room,
Chung Shan Medical University Hospital,
Taichung 402, Taiwan, R.O.C
[3] Department of Industrial Engineering and Management,
Chaoyang University of Technology,
Taichung, Taiwan, R.O.C.
mcchiu@csmu.edu.tw

Abstract. This study aims to clarify the relationship between handlebar and saddle heights on cycling comforts by assessing the kinematics, kinetics, physiological loading and subjective perceived exertion rating. Twenty young adults with mean age 24.6 years (SD=0.1) were recruited to participate in this study. A commercial city bike with the adjustable handlebar and saddle had been set on the indoor cycling stands. All subjects were asked to ride randomly with 9 different postures (3 handle ×3 saddle heights) for continuous one hour. A 3-D motion analysis system (Zebris Medical GmbH, Germany) was used to collect the kinematic data. The body pressure measurement system (Body Pressure Measurement System, Tekscan, U.S.A) was applied to measure the pressure distribution, force and displacement of centre of mass (COM). A heart rate monitor (Polar RS-800, Kempele, Finland) was used to record the heart rate as the physiological loading. Moreover, a subjective perceived exertion rating scale (Borg CR-10) was used to assess subjective comfort around the body regions. The results of this study indicated that the lower handlebar with higher saddle cause greater ROM in wrist-ulnar deviation, wrist extension, trunk flexion and hip abduction. It also reveals more force on hand region, more discomfort around hand, ankle and back, and higher physiological loading. While cycling with higher handlebar and lower saddle, it has more ROM in wrist flexion, more body displacement on buttock region, little trunk forward, and more discomfort rating in buttock region. For handlebar and saddle adjustment, the considerations of body dimensions and characteristics, the relationship between handlebar and saddle heights might improve the cycling comfort and diminish musculoskeletal injury.

Keywords: cycling comfort, pressure distribution, range of motion, heart rate, subjective rating.

S. Yamamoto (Ed.): HIMI/HCII 2013, Part I, LNCS 8016, pp. 12–19, 2013.
© Springer-Verlag Berlin Heidelberg 2013

1   Introduction

With increasing awareness of lifestyles of health and sustainability (LOHAS) issues, more and more people ride bicycle as the means of transportation, exercise and the recreational activities worldwide. However, non-traumatic, chronic injuries, or called overuse musculoskeletal symptoms, are common in cyclists. It has been reported that up to 85% of cyclists have one or more overuse injuries, with 36% of these injuries were severe to warrant medical intervention (Dettori and Norvell, 2006). The general musculoskeletal symptoms for cyclists included the neck (48.8%), knee (41.7%), groin/buttock area (36.1%), hands (31.1%), and lower back (30.3%) discomfort (Schwellnus and Derman, 2005). Therefore, cycling posture and bike fit are closely related with performance, efficiency, safety and comfort for cyclists. For the basic components including frame, seat post, saddle, handlebar, crank arm, and pedals are used to compose across all bike designs. Saddle pressures are common to cause skin irritation and soreness in the groin regions for cyclists. Wilson and Bush (2004) indicated that vertical loads from seat were about 49~52% of body weight which were greater than shear loads during cycling. Proper handlebar and seat heights may be the most important adjustments when fitting a bicycle. Hence, this study aims to elucidate the relationship between handlebar and saddles heights on bicycle comfort. An understanding of bicycle design, fit, and function is important in treating the patient with an overuse injury.

2   Research Method

2.1   Subjects

Twenty young adults with mean age 24.6 yearswere recruited to participate in this study. None of them have history of cardiovascular and musculoskeletal disorder. Basic subject information, as well as anthropometric data, were collected and listed in Table 1. Men and women have significant difference in body height, weight, arm and leg length (p<.05). For the preferred height for saddle, men subjectively prefer to have higher saddle than women (p<.05). The preferred height for saddle was 104.4 (3.6) cm for men and 99.2 (3.4) for women, respectively.

Table 1. Subjects' information

Variables	Men (n=10)	Women (n=10)	P-values*
Age (years old)	24.7(0.4)	24.6(0.8)	0.21
Height (cm)	171.0(3.3)	160.2(2.6)	0.00*
Weight (kg)	63.7(5.9)	51.8(6.9)	0.00*
Crotch height (cm)	65.2(2.4)	65.1(2.1)	0.73
Arm length (cm)	68.2(3.3)	66.1(0.5)	0.00*
Leg length (cm)	92.7(3.2)	88.8(1.0)	0.00*
Preferred height for handlebar (PHH) (cm)	37.6(0.8)	37.9(1.5)	0.90
Preferred height for saddle (PHS) (cm)	104.4(3.6)	99.2(3.4)	0.00*

*Significant level at < .05.

2.2   Instruments and Response Measures

Motion Capture System. A ultrasound based, three-dimension motion analysis system (Zebris CMS-HS/Zebris Medical GmbH, Germany) was used to collect the kinematic data including the range of motion (ROM) of wrist ulnar-radial deviation, wrist flexion-extension, trunk flexion, hip adduction-abduction, knee flexion during exercise. Five markers were pasted on the hand back, forearm, upper arm, lower back and thigh. The hardware included two ultrasound sensors for measurement distance 2.5 meter. All data were recorded at a measurement frequency of 20Hz and processed using the software of Win Date (v.2.19.44) (Zebris Medical GmbH, Germany).

Pressure Measurement System. The body pressure measurement system (Body Pressure Measurement System/BPMS, Tekscan, U.S.A) was applied to measure and analysis the pressure distribution, force and displacement of centre of pressure (COP) on handlebar and saddle regions, respectively. Two pressure mats were placed on the hand and buttock. The data were recorded at a measurement frequency of 20Hz and processed using the software of CONFORMat (v. 6.20) (Tekscan, U.S.A).

Physiological Loading. A heart rate monitor (Polar RS-800, Kempele, Finland) was used to record the heart rate as the physiological loading. A resting heart rate (resting HR) was recorded while a subject was quiet for 1 min before the experiment. During exercise, the exercise heart rate (exercising HR) was collected with frequency of 1Hz and sustain for one hour. The physiological loading or exercise intensity was calculated by the formula: (Averaged exercising HR-Resting HR)/ [(220-age)-Resting HR].

Subjective Exertion Rating. A subjective perceived exertion rating scale (Borg CR-10 scale) was used to quantify and assess the overall perception of exertion. Subject rank fatigue level around the six body parts including wrist, upper back, lower back, buttock, knee and ankle from 0 (nothing at all) to 10 (maximal exertion), separately

2.3   Experimental Procedure

All participants were volunteers, and signed informed consent forms covering the experimental process, requirements and measurements. First, Basic subject information, as well as anthropometric data, were collected. A commercial bike (YS488 Gaint/ Gaint, Taiwan) had been set on the indoor cycling stands as a stationary trainer. The saddle and handlebar both were adjustable. At beginning, all subjects had to select the subjective preferred height for handlebar (PHH) and saddle (PHS) while cycling on this cycling trainer. Independent variables are 3 handlebars (PHH, 90% PHH and 110% PHH) and 3 saddle heights (PHS, 90% PHS and 110% PHS).The relationship between handlebar and saddle height was listed as table 2. All subjects were asked to ride randomly with 9 different postures (3 handle ×3 saddle heights) with the constant resistant, 80 rpm (revolution(s) per minute) for sustained one hour respectively. For the postures A to C, there are relative heights for handlebar and saddle but with different ratio, the conditions D to F are lower handlebar and higher saddle heights, the trails G to I are higher handlebar and lower saddle heights. The data of comforts were assessed by the measurements of kinematics, kinetics, physiological loading and subjective perceived exertion rating during the cycling.

Table 2. The relationship between handlebar and saddle heights

Postures	Definition*
A	90%PHH and 90%PHS
B	PHH and PHS
C	110%PHH and 110%PHS
D	90%PHH and 110%PHS
E	PHH and 110%PHS
F	90% PHH and PHS
G	110%PHH and PHS
H	PHH and 90%PHS
I	110%PHH and 90%PHS

*Preferred height for handlebar (PHH) and preferred height for saddle (PHS).

2.4   Statistical analysis

Statistical analyses were performed using SPSS version 14.0 statistical analysis software. Analysis of variance (ANOVA) was performed to analyze the effects of riding postures on the kinematics, kinetics, physiological loading and subjective perceived exertion rating. The level of significance was set as $\alpha = 0.05$. Duncan's multiple range tests was used to analyze the difference in between two levels of the variables.

3   Result

3.1   Handlebar, Saddle and Riding Posture

Table 3 displays the effect of cycling postures on range of motion (ROM) of wrist, trunk, hip and knee. Different riding postures influence the ROM on wrist deviation, wrist flexion –extension, trunk flexion and hip abduction-adduction ($p<0.05$). Table 4 shows the Duncan's multiple range tests for the ROM. It indicates that cycling with D, E and F postures require more ROM on wrist, trunk and hip joint and cycling with G, H and I have less ROM on these joints.

3.2   Handlebar, Saddle and Pressure Distribution

Table 5 reveals the effects of cycling postures on pressure distribution and the displacement of center of pressure (COP) on the hand and buttock region. It indicates that cycling postures have significant influence on the force on handlebar and COP displacement on buttock region ($p<0.05$). Table 6 displays he Duncan's multiple range tests for the force on handlebar and COP displacement on buttock. It shows that riding with D and E postures have higher force on handlebar and more COP displacement on buttock region ($p<0.05$).

Table 3. The cycling postures and joint range of motion of wrist, trunk, hip and knee

ROM[a] / Postures	Wrist deviation[b]	Wrist flexion-extension	Trunk flexion	Hip abduction-adduction	Knee flexion
A	14.5(1.1)	7.5(1.3)	38.10(1.2)	29.78(3.6)	55.4(16.1)
B	11.7(1.0)	-6.1(0.9)	37.75(1.2)	25.96(1.3)	58.7(17.6)
C	11.5(0.7)	8.3(1.2)	37.30(1.2)	45.97(8.9)	78.3(19.2)
D	15.9(1.4)	26.2(0.9)	57.35(4.6)	52.90(3.0)	77.3(21.0)
E	14.4(0.9)	24.7(1.8)	43.60(2.0)	46.16(2.2)	76.9(19.5)
F	14.0(0.7)	23.9(1.0)	44.15(1.5)	23.89(1.4)	57.5(17.2)
G	13.4(1.0)	-17.1(1.2)	18.25(1.6)	24.51(1.8)	58.0(18.1)
H	13.7(0.8)	-20.2(2.0)	27.95(1.7)	24.22(1.6)	57.9(17.4)
I	13.8(1.5)	24.1(0.7)	8.70(2.2)	25.43(1.8)	57.3(15.7)
F-test	12.82	8753.27	63.12	9.68	0.05
Significant[c]	0.00*	0.00*	0.00*	0.00*	0.99

a.　ROM: range of motion, units: degrees.
b.　Wrist deviation: ulnar deviation is positive (radial is negative),
　　Wrist extension is positive (flexion is negative),
　　Trunk flexion is positive,
　　Hip abduction is positive and Knee flexion is positive.
c.　Significant level is at $P < .05$.

Table 4. Duncan's multiple range tests for range of motion of wrist, trunk and hip

ROM[a]	Ranking[b]
Wrist deviation	DE> F > AGH > BCI
Wrist flexion- extension	D> EF > ABC > G > H > I
Trunk flexion	D > EF > ABC >H > G > I
Hip abduction- adduction	D > EC > A > B > FGHI

a.　ROM: range of motion, units: degrees.
b.　Significant level is at $P < .05$.

Table 5. The cycling postures and pressure distribution

Variables[a] / Postures	COP displacement on hand (cm)	Force on handlebar (N)	COP displacement on buttock (cm)	Force on saddle (N)
A	2.4(0.6)	4.9(0.6)	2.5(0.5)	15.5(1.9)
B	1.8(0.6)	4.7(0.8)	2.1(0.6)	15.8(2.4)
C	2.9(1.2)	4.6(0.8)	3.4(1.8)	15.3(1.9)
D	2.2(0.6)	6.0(0.8)	3.4(1.8)	14.1(1.1)
E	2.3(0.6)	5.7(0.8)	3.7(1.8)	14.3(3.3)
F	2.2(0.5)	6.1(1.0)	2.4(0.5)	15.4(2.2)
G	3.0(1.0)	4.4(0.8)	2.5(0.5)	15.8(1.7)
H	2.2(0.5)	4.6(0.8)	2.3(0.5)	16.8(3.3)
I	3.3(1.0)	4.4(0.7)	3.8(1.6)	16.8(3.1)
F-test	1.03	13.69	8.52	0.53
Significant[b]	0.39	0.00*	0.00*	0.72

a.　COP displacement on hand: displacement range of center of pressure of hand,
　　COP displacement on buttock: displacement range of center of pressure of buttock.
b.　Significant level is at $P < .05$.

Table 6. Duncan's multiple range tests for pressure distribution

Variable [a]	Ranking [b]
Force on handlebar	DF > E > A > BCGHI
COP displacement on buttock	CDEI > ABFGH

a.   ROM: range of motion, units: degrees.
b.   Significant level is at $P < .05$.

3.3   Handlebar, Saddle and Physiological Loading

Table 7 reveals the effects of riding posture on the physiological loading. Although cycling postures didn't affect exercising heart rate, but cycling postures have significantly influence on exercise intensity (p<0.05). Riding with postures of C, D and E demand higher exercise intensity.

Table 7. The cycling postures and physiological loading

Variables \ Postures	Resting HR	Exercising HR	Exercise intensity (%)
A	87.4 (0.3)	98.6 (7.4)	10
B	87.3 (3.0)	98.9 (3.6)	11
C	87.3 (1.9)	105.1 (2.7)	17
D	88.7 (2.2)	101.3 (10.6)	12
E	87.0 (0.9)	97.8 (8.6)	10
F	86.7 (2.6)	100.50 (5.9)	13
G	85.8 (3.3)	97.9 (3.8)	11
H	85.9 (2.5)	97.3 (8.9)	10
I	87.2 (0.4)	99.9 (2.6)	12
Significant [a]	0.7	0.3	0.00*

a.   Significant level is at $P < .05$.

3.4   Handlebar, Saddle and Perceived Exertion

Table 8 presents subjective exertion rating around the wrist, upper back, lower back, buttock, knee and ankle. It demonstrates that cycling posture have statistically influence on perceived exertion of wrist, upper back, lower back, buttock, and ankle(p<0.05). In general, the most discomfort region during cycling which were rated as higher scores were wrist and buttock areas. Table 9 shows the results of Duncan's multiple range tests for subjective exertion rating. Cycling with postures of D, E and F would have more exertion on wrist region and riding with postures of C, G, H and I would have more discomfort on buttock areas.

Table 8. The cycling postures and subjctive erxrtion rating

Postures \ Variables	Wrist	Upper back	Lower back	Buttock	Knee	Ankle
A	3.9 (0.7)	0.9 (0.7)	1.1 (0.7)	4.3 (0.2)	0.8 (0.6)	1.0 (0.5)
B	3.4(0.7)	1.3 (0.4)	1.5 (0.4)	3.9(0.7)	1.1 (0.5)	0.9 (0.6)
C	4.9(0.7)	1.1 (0.5)	1.5 (0.5)	5.3(0.2)	1.1 (0.5)	1.4 (0.5)
D	4.5(0.6)	1.2 (0.6)	1.5 (0.3)	4.4(0.5)	1.6 (0.3)	1.3 (0.3)
E	4.8(0.3)	1.2 (0.6)	1.6 (0.6)	4.8(0.3)	1.1 (0.5)	1.9 (0.6)
F	4.8(0.1)	1.1 (0.5)	1.3 (0.4)	4.7(0.6)	0.8 (0.5)	0.9 (0.4)
G	3.7(0.8)	1.1 (0.6)	1.4 (0.8)	5.3(0.4)	1.0 (0.6)	0.9 (0.7)
H	4.3(0.6)	0.8 (0.4)	1.0 (0.3)	5.0 (0.3)	1.0 (0.6)	0.9 (0.5)
I	4.4(0.6)	0.7(0.5)	1.1 (04)	5.2(0.2)	0.8 (0.5)	0.6 (0.2)
F-test	4.149	1.685	3.015	3.91	1.48	3.595
Significant [a]	0.00*	0.04*	0.00*	0.00*	0.07	0.00*

a. Significant level is at $P < .05$.

Table 9. Duncan's multiple range tests for subjective exertion rating

Rating of perceived exertion [a]	Ranking [b]
Wrist	DEF > ACGHI > B
Upper back	BDE > CFG > AHI
Lower back	BCDEFG > AHI
Buttock	CGHI > DEF >AB
Ankle	DEF > CABGH > I

a. Rating of perceived exertion, range from 0 to 10.
b. Significant level is at $P < .05$.

4   Conclusions and Recommendations

The main purpose of this study was to illustrate the relationship between handlebar and saddle heights on cycling comforts by assessing the kinematics, kinetics, physiological loading and subjective perceived exertion rating. For cycling with lower handlebar and higher saddle, it reveals more range of motion on wrist ulnar deviation, wrist extension, trunk flexion and hip abduction. Lower-handlebar riding might cause higher force on hand and wide displacement of center of pressure. Moreover, lower-handlebar cycling requires higher physiological loading and might induces more perceived exertion on wrist region. For cycling with higher handlebar and lower saddle, it presents less and natural range of motion on wrist, trunk and hip and less force on handlebar, reduced physiological loading, but more perceived exertion on buttock region. For adjustable-preferred handlebar and saddle, higher handlebar and higher saddle (C postures) leads more physiological loading and more perceived exertion rating than lower handlebar and saddle. For handlebar and saddle adjustment, the considerations of body dimensions and characteristics, the relationship between handlebar and saddle heights might improve the cycling comfort and diminish musculoskeletal injury.

References

1. Dettori, N., Norvell, D.: Non-traumatic bicycle injuries: a review of the literature. Sports Medicine 36, 7–18 (2006)
2. Schwellnus, M.P., Derman, E.W.: Common injuries in cycling: prevention, diagnosis and management. SA Fam. Pract. 47(7), 14–19 (2005)
3. Wilson, C., Bush, T.R.: Interface forces on the seat during a cycling activity. Clinical Biomechanics 22, 1017–1023 (2007)

Kanji Characters in Japan – Remaining Challenges

Toshihiro Enami

Fujitsu Research Institute
16-1, Kaigan 1-chome, Minato-ku, Tokyo 105-0022, Japan
enami.toshihiro@jp.fujitsu.com

Abstract. The Japanese Government has set its sights on becoming number one in the world in ICT, as seen in the announcement of an e-Japan strategy by the IT strategy organization established in 2000. However, according to the United Nations E-Government Development Index, Japan's ranking has remained low despite its progress in information infrastructure. The reason for this is that the Japanese government did not integrate the code and standardize the data which are needed to use ICT across the whole country. The government introduced the national ID bill into the Diet last year, but the issue of Kanji characters, i.e., how to define the Japanese Kanji character set, remains unresolved because this issue, especially as it related to Kanji characters of names, includes a complex problem of interface between human and machine. I think the current proposed solution will not be successful because it ignores the issue of human interface. I insist that the Kanji character issue should be viewed from the perspective of human interface, and I propose a solution whereby the government should regulate by law the range of Kanji characters used by ICT, rather than increasing the number of Kanji character used.

Keywords: e-Government, Character Code, Kanji Character.

1 Introduction

In recent years, countries around the world have introduced e-Government and it continues to spread its roots. EGDI (2012) shows the e-Government ranking of 190 countries, with an additional 3 countries having no online services at all. The Japanese government passed an ICT law in 2000, and the next year it announced that it would aim to become number one in ICT through its e-Japan strategy. Afterwards, high speed information infrastructure was built, but e-Government did not progress in terms of using ICT. Japan was ranked 11th in 2008, 17th in 2010, and 18th in 2011.

By contrast, Korea was number one in 2010 and 2011. The difference between Japan and Korea is increasing. Shimada, Enami, and Yoshida (2012) discuss this difference from many perspectives and conclude that Japan is caught in a vicious cycle and Korea in a virtuous one. The most critical point is that the Japanese government did not recognize the importance of building a legal system to optimize the whole country through ICT, especially by destroying the bureaucratic silos.

S. Yamamoto (Ed.): HIMI/HCII 2013, Part I, LNCS 8016, pp. 20–29, 2013.

In 2012, the My Number (national ID) bill, which would build a legal system to identify Japanese people, was introduced into the Diet. But Kanji character code, as another important legal system, remains unpromising. On the surface, the issue of Kanji characters seems to be a problem between technology and culture, but it fundamentally includes the issue of interface between human and machine. We must confront this issue from this point of view.

2   Methodology

I adopt the following methodology for this study.

2.1   The History of Japanese Character Code and the Issue of Kanji Characters in Names

I begin with a survey of the history of Japanese character code as mapped onto computer systems, followed by a look at its present state. I then describe the issues of Kanji characters in the field of administrative procedure and how the government would address this issue based on the reports of METI (Ministry of Economy, Trade and Industry)[1] and MIC (Ministry of Internal Affairs and Communications)[2] .

I identify 2 perspectives which the government overlooks in order to find a path towards solving this issue. I analyze the issue from these perspectives, as outlined in 2.2 and 2.3.

2.2   The Cost Perspective (People's Burden)

One perspective is that of cost. Japan uses different types of character sets, or Gaiji, which are defined broadly as a character not included in a character set and narrowly as a character outside of JIS level-1 and level-2. I will calculate the economic loss which results from using these in the field of administrative procedure and in the private sector. The Japanese people must cover any economic loss through taxes or the high cost of products, and we should discuss whether it is right or not to make the people pay for this loss.

2.3   The Recognition Perspective

Another perspective is that of recognition. I present data on the recognition of Kanji characters by Japanese people and show the big difference in recognition (speed and accuracy) between a standard range (JIS level-1 and level-2) and a broad range (includes Gaiji) of characters.

In addition, I would like to consider the recognition of seniors and foreigners because the population of these demographics is increasing in Japan.

---

[1] METI/IPA(2011).
[2] Fuji Xerox Co., Ltd.(2012).

2.4   The Proposal of a New Solution

I propose a new solution, as discussed above. In particular, I point out that the second perspective includes the issue of interface between human and machine, and therefore technological solutions would not work. I propose a solution using the legal system, rather than the technological solutions using UTF-16 and IVS (Ideographic Variation Sequence)/ IVD (Ideographic Variation Database) proposed by the government.

3   The History of Japanese Character Code and the Issue of Kanji Characters in Names

Let us first look at the history of Japanese character code as mapped onto computer systems. Japanese has 3 types of character: Kanji are based on Chinese characters; Hiragana are derived from certain Kanji; and Katakana are derived from a different set of Kanji. Hiragana is a syllabary which complements Kanji in expressing Japanese, and Katakana is a syllabary used to express imported words and mimetic/onomatopoeic words. Each syllabary includes about 50 characters and the set of Kanji includes more than 50 thousand.

From early on, Japan needed multi-byte character code systems mapped into its computer systems because Japanese must use these many characters. In Japan, JIS X0201 was defined based on ISO646 as a 1-byte code system. And JIS X0208, JIS X0212, and JIS X0213 are defined based on ISO2022 as multi-byte code systems. JIS X0208 was defined in 1978 and includes about 6000 Kanji characters (JIS level-1 and level-2). JIS X0213 was defined subsequently in 2000 and includes about 3700 additional Kanji characters (JIS level-3 and level-4). There are also Japanese character code systems which integrate character set and encoding scheme: EUC-JP for UNIX and Shift-JIS for PC. Mainframe computers have different proprietary Japanese character code systems depending on the vendor.

Later on, Unicode (ISO10646) was proposed as a universal character code system. This system adopts a separation of character set and encoding scheme. The popular Unicode standards are UCS-2, UCS-4, UTF-16, UTF-8, and UTF-32. Character set and encoding scheme are integrated in UCS, but UTF is an encoding scheme only. These standards include from 65,000 to 2 billion code points, which means that all the characters in the world can be used in this system. More importantly, this system can use a very broad range of characters, including old or historical characters for academic research.

In the field of Japanese administrative procedure, fewer than 10,000 characters (mainly JIS level-1 and level-2) have been used since mainframe computers could use Japanese characters. But the developing Koseki[3] system of the late 90's and the Juki[4] system of the early 2000's needed more characters. The Koseki character set was defined with about 56,000 characters and Juki with 21,000. In fact, not all characters

---

[3] Census registration system.

[4] Resident information system.

used in names were defined; undefined characters are managed using image data in the Juki system and with paper in the Koseki system.

The relationship among the JIS, Juki, and Koseki character sets is shown in Figure 1. These characters are used in the field of administrative procedure, mainly in names. This figure shows that the total number of characters is around 60,000, but each character cannot be identified correctly between character sets because each system has different definition rules, which are the way of defining differences between form and design in characters. The essential reason for this disparity is the inter-ministry bureaucratic silos. JIS is the jurisdiction of METI, Juki is that of MIC, and Koseki is that of MOJ (Ministry Of Justice). In addition, the Japanese language, including Kanji characters, is the jurisdiction of MEXT (Ministry of Education, Culture, Sports, Science & Technology).

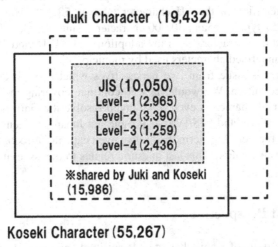

Juki Character (19,432)

JIS (10,050)
Level-1 (2,965)
Level-2 (3,390)
Level-3 (1,259)
Level-4 (2,436)

※ shared by Juki and Koseki (15,986)

Koseki Character (55,267)

(Number of Kanji Characters)

Fig. 1. Overview of JIS, Juki, and Koseki (based on data from METI/IPA(2011))

As the interconnectivity of society progresses, problems are occurring due to the current state of Kanji characters. Data exchange between government computers and other computers is not going well, data cannot be shared between public and private sectors or even among public sectors, and changing systems will be very costly.

Based on its "Report on Character Integration Infrastructure Project"[5] , METI integrated the 3 character sets to solve these problems and published the integrated character table (MJ character table). This report doesn't have a clear conclusion, but it seems to say that this problem can be solved in the future by identifying Gaiji with the MJ character table and implementing UTF-16 and IVS, as it says: "we are going to

---

[5] METI/IPA(2011).

use about 60,000 characters by encouraging the adoption of UTF-16 and IVS on top of the foundation of the MJ character table"[6].

However, I do not think the adoption of UTF-16 and IVS will solve the following challenges.

- Japan has no integrated, comprehensive set of rules, and no one has the authority to decide on and register new characters for IVS/IVD.
- Currently, there are about 60,000 characters which cannot be used on standard PCs, and the public electronic signature system accepts alternative characters instead of Gaiji. Will people accept these 60,000 characters?
- Even if standard PCs could use these 60,000 characters, can we (citizens and government) use them correctly in the field of administrative procedure?

In addition, the "Report on Gaiji used by Municipalities"[7] showed that the number of characters not identified in the MJ character table is 52,294. These characters are classified into 3857 types (around 30,000 characters cannot be classified) and include 2037 types of wrong character. Thus the adoption of UTF-16 and IVS cannot solve the challenge of undefined characters used by municipalities.

Let us look at this issue from two perspectives which have been ignored in the past: cost and recognition. We would have to continue covering the cost of using an enormous number of characters even if we could resolve the Gaiji issue with the MJ character table, UTF-16, and IVS/IVD. Is it right that Japan's citizens should continue to cover this cost forever? Furthermore, are we even capable of recognizing and using more than 10,000 characters? This last question relates to the issue of human-machine interface.

4   The Cost Perspective

Some say that the issue of Kanji characters is spiritual and cultural and should not be approached from an economical perspective. But the number of people whose names include Gaiji is very small (about 4-5% of the population). The rest of the population must cover this cost through taxes or expensive products. We must consider whether this burden is justified or not. What is the cost?

I have calculated the cost based on surveys in three cities, the results of which are shown in Table 1. By economies of scale, big cities are more efficient than small cities, and the average city population in Japan is around 73,000. Therefore, the national economic loss is estimated to be between 1.2 billion yen and 2.7 billion yen, or around 2 billion yen.

The above economic loss is only a simple computation. There are many incalculable economic losses when it comes to municipalities:

[6] METI/IPA(2011),p74.
[7] Fuji Xerox Co., Ltd.(2012).

- Local governments must run high cost computer systems because they cannot change computer vendors easily due to Gaiji.
- Local governments must outsource even easy processing to computer vendors because standard PCs cannot handle Gaiji.

As a result, Japan must bear the burden of more than 2 billion yen in economic loss due solely to the issue of Gaiji in municipalities.

Table 1. Cost of Gaiji in municipalities

Cities		C City	F City	K City
Population		959,000	136,000	50,000
Detail (yen)	Support for claim	245,000	94,500	17,500
	Input existing Gaiji	3,733,333	126,000	175,000
	Register new Gaiji	1,085,000	63,000	87,500
	Maintaining system	710,643	1,000,000	14,000
	Data exchange with external system	2,450,000		26,250
	Data exchange with internal system	1,087,500		750,000
	Others	61,250	70,000	0
Total Cost (yen)		9,372,726	1,353,500	1,070,250
Estimated national cost(yen)		1,237,903,563	1,260,546,397	2,711,157,300

※The cost of one person-hour for a public officer is 3500 yen. The national cost is estimated proportionally from the above cities' populations.

5   The Recognition Perspective

5.1   The Recognition of Standard Kanji Characters

Using UTF16 and IVS/IVD might reduce these economic losses, but this must not be the main solution of this issue because it includes the problem of character recognition capability of human beings. In cases of man-to-man or machine-to-machine, the problem can be ignored, but in the case of man-to–machine, it becomes a big issue which cannot be ignored.

MEXT's Agency for Cultural Affairs published the Joyo Kanji table, "a guide for written kanji when used in everyday life in Japan." This table contains 2136 characters, and combined with the Hyogai Kanji table (characters not in general usage) gives about 3000 characters. Thus around 3000 characters are enough in everyday life.

Now let us look at Japanese Kanji recognition ability in the range of JIS level-1 and level-2 (about 6 thousand characters). Below are data showing how many people can understand and use (read and write) the characters of this range. The Japan Kanji

Proficiency Test Foundation operates Kanji literacy certification examinations three times a year. This association provides certification from 1st level to 10th level, 1st level being the range of JIS level-1 and level-2 (about 6000 characters) and pre-1st level being the range of JIS level-1 (about 3000 characters).

Figures 2 and 3 are the pass rates and the successful candidates of 1st and pre-1st levels from 2007 to 2012. The figures show that the pass rate of 1st and pre-1st levels is less than 0.25%, which means that even among people interested in Kanji, not even 0.25% can handle JIS level-1 Kanji (about 3000 characters). Successful candidates of 1st and pre-1st levels total about 18,000 people, or only 0.014% of Japanese, or about 1 person per 10,000.

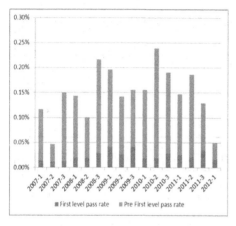

Fig. 2. Pass rate of 1st and pre-1st (left)   **Fig. 3.** Successful candidates of 1st and pre-1st (right)

Thus most Japanese people cannot understand and use even JIS level-1 (about 3000 characters) and only geniuses (2 persons per 100,000) can use JIS level-1 and level-2 (about 6000 characters). Why can Japanese use broader range of Kanji characters?

5.2   The Recognition of a Broad Range of Kanji Characters in the Field of Administrative Procedure

Next, to find out the Kanji recognition capabilities of Japanese people in the administrative range of Kanji (Juki and Koseki, about 60,000characters), I performed an experiment with check sheets. The check sheets were of two types: A used the range of JIS level-1 and B the range of Juki and Koseki. This experiment involved identifying pairs of Kanji characters arrayed in two lines of 12 in 2 minutes. The point of interest is the difference in recognition rates between A and B.

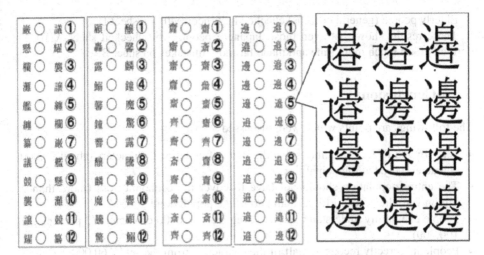

Fig. 4. sheet A (left)   **Fig. 5.** sheet B (right)

The examinees were of 3 types: private sector, local government, and general citizen. The level of education of each type was assumed to be higher than average. Elderly people were chosen to be general citizen examinees because the Japanese average length of life is 85 of female and 79 of male, and elderly examinees are likely to be active seniors who join lifelong learning courses. The results of the experiment are shown in Table 2.

Table 2. results of experiment on Japanese Kanji recognition

Group	Number of examinees (average age)	Sheet A (%)			Sheet B (%)		
		Right answer	Wrong answer	No answer	Right answer	Wrong answer	No answer
Local Government	96 (40's)	99	1	0	37	15	47
Private Sector	60 (50's)	98	0	2	33	27	40
General Citizen	47 (60's)	96	2	3	27	24	49

Table 2 shows the following:

- Most people recognized nearly 100% correctly on sheet A.
- People checked only one third correctly on sheet B.
- People checked 15-27% incorrectly on sheet B.
- People were unable to check 40-49% within the time limit on sheet B.

Elderly people (general citizens) checked half incorrectly on sheet B.

These results show that even those Japanese people who checked sheet A 100% correctly took much more time and made far more mistakes on sheet B.

6   Conclusion

The followings are points which were discussed above:

- UTF-16 and IVS/IVD cannot solve the issue of undefined characters (about 50,000 characters) used at municipalities.
- The entire population should not have to cover the economic loss (more than 2 billion yen) due to Gaiji for a small part of the population.
- People can hardly understand and use even a set of 6000 characters (2 persons per 100,000).
- People incorrectly recognize half of the characters from the set of 60,000 and need much more time to do so.

In the past, politicians and scholars said that the issue of Kanji should not be discussed from the perspectives of economy and efficiency because it is a spiritual and cultural issue. To the extent that Kanji is used between people, this might be true. But when Kanji is used between human and machine in a widely informatized society, a new problem occurs.

In the case of man-to-man interface, we accept the ambiguity of Kanji by negotiating with each other. But in the case of machine-to-machine, machines cannot accept ambiguity; even 1 bit of difference in the code causes a computer to treat characters as different Kanji. Even if we deal with similar Kanjis with IVS, humans must still decide which are variant characters and which are identical characters and register them to IVS using code. In the case of man-to-machine, we face a bigger problem: Our eyes cannot completely recognize the details in a character that a machine can. As shown by the above experiment, the recognition of 60,000 characters is beyond human ability. In this sense, we cannot communicate with machines.

Furthermore, it is important to note the fact that Japanese people cannot understand and use even JIS level-1 characters (about 3000 characters). The experiment above shows that Japanese people cannot use the sets of Juki characters (about 21,000 characters) and Koseki characters (about 56,000 characters) in everyday life, as seen in increased recognition time and a higher rate of incorrect recognition. Administrative procedures must always be carried out speedily and correctly, so we must limit the use of Kanji characters. Simply increasing characters and using IVS/IVD clearly will not solve the problem.

I propose the following two solutions:

- Solution 1

The use of Kanji characters for people's names and geographical name should be limited by law to the range of JIS level-1 and level-2 in the field of administrative procedure. The characters outside of JIS level-1 and level-2 which are used for people's names and place names must be mandatorily changed to similar characters within that range. Characters that cannot be so changed must be expressed with Hiragana or Katakana. Any use of Kanji characters outside of this range for people's names or geographical names should be punished by law.

- Solution 2

This solution involves adopting Solution 1 with the exception of Koseki procedures. Only Koseki procedures would allow people to preserve their identity by using Gaiji, while Juki and other administrative procedures would be subject to the rules of Solution 1. To identify a person between Koseki and Juki, the same Juki code (or My Number) would be attached to both their Koseki and Juki entries.

As a point of clarification, I do not insist that the effort to use more characters with computer is wrong. It is necessary to use several million characters when performing cultural research, for instance, old documents or unknown characters. I do insist, however, that using several million characters in daily life is wrong. We must consider the public interest, instead of oversimplifying the issue as one of technology versus culture.

References

1. EGDI, United Nations E Government Survey (2012),
   http://unpan1.un.org/intradoc/groups/public/documents/
   un/unpan048065.pdf
2. Tatsumi, S., Enami, T., Yoshida, K.: A comparative study of e-Government in Japan and Korea. In: Proceedings of International Conference on Business Management 2012, pp. 159–169 (2012)
3. METI/IPA, Report on Character Integration Infrastructure Project (March 25, 2011)
4. Fuji Xerox Co. Ltd., Report on Gaiji used by Municipalities (contracted by Ministry of Internal Affairs and Communications) (March 2012)
5. Japan Kanji Proficiency Test Foundation (2012),
   http://www.kanken.or.jp/index.php

A Study on Selection Ability in the 3D Space by the Finger

Junpei Fukaya, Yutaro Ooba, Hidetaka Kuriiwa, Ryuta Yamada,
Makoto Oka, and Hirohiko Mori

Tokyo City University, 1-28-1 Tamadutumi, Setagaya, Tokyo, Japan
g1281825@tcu.ac.jp, {ooba,kuriiwa,yamada}@ims.tcu.ac.jp,
{moka,hmori}@tcu.ac.jp

Abstract. Intuitive gestures are very effective for interactions. Pointing gesture with a finger would be used for interactions like pie menu selection. It has been researched as to the appropriate numbers of menu items being displayed in a pie menu. However, no research has been made for the case where menus are selected by using gestures. We got the ability of pointing gesture (selection ability) in the 3-dimentional space from the previous research. By combining the obtained resolution abilities of pointing gesture at the 2-dimensional surface of Pitch and Yaw, it is suggested that the selection ability of selection behavior in the 3-dimentional space is 22 areas. We will experiment in order to examine whether the subjects really point 22 areas without vertical guide. As a result, we found they can point 12 areas of 22.

Keywords: Gesture, Selection Ability, Menu, Pie menu.

1 Introduction

Intuitive gestures are very effective for interactions. In recent years, the researches on interactions, which operate various products and services such as music players and TV by using gestures, are being actively conducted.

It is difficult for computers to recognize the intentions of users from their natural gestures. Although it is relatively easy for computers to recognize standard gestures like sign language (commands), users need educations and trainings to be able to use them. Both have merits and demerits. Generally speaking, gestures are very effective for interactions if the use is limited to interactions like making selections from the displayed menu[1].

However, as the case now stands, there is no coherence between gestures and the allocations of interactions, and each application and service makes its own allocations.Products and services have become diversified and multifunctional, and there are more functions and interactions which need to be allocated to gestures, thereby the allocation has become difficult.

Therefore, pointing gesture with a finger would be used for interactions like menu selection. It is possible to select with simple gesture even when there are many menu items. In addition, pointing gesture is intuitive, thus users need no special education or training.

S. Yamamoto (Ed.): HIMI/HCII 2013, Part I, LNCS 8016, pp. 30–36, 2013.

Pie menu is a kind of GUI menus. It displays menu items in a radial fashioncentering on the mouse pointer. Users select a menu item by the direction to which they move the mouse pointer. Pie menu can be selected by the angles. It is suitable for interactions using pointing gesture.

It has been researched as to the appropriate numbers of menu items being displayed in a pie menu. However, no research has been made for the case where menus are selected by using gestures. In order to find it out, it is necessary to know human ability of pointing properly. Therefore, we will experiment in order to examine the ability of pointing gesture (selection ability) in the 3-dimensional space.

2   Related Research

Miyamoto et al. have discussed how they should allocate menu items to the extended pie menu[2]. They examined how the selection accuracy varied depending on the sizes and locations of each area within the pie menu so that they could discuss the most appropriate area pattern of the pie menu.

Saeki et al. have attempted to examine the selection ability of pointing gesture in the 3-dimentional space[3]. The experiment was conducted without posing restrictions on the arm joints of the test subjects, which allowed the free movements. Because each test subject had different pointing gestures, they were not able to conduct statistical analysis effectively.

Therefore, we thought it was necessary to examine the range of motion and the arthresthesia of joints of shoulder, elbows, wrists and fingers separately.

Yamada and Kuriiwa, they added a limit to point and examined the selection ability of the areas[4]. They found the selection ability for Yaw (horizontal) and Pitch (vertical) using the pointing at only using a point from a wrist limited rotary motion and did it with selection ability of the 3-dimentional space by putting them together. They got vertical selection ability, they pulled a board on the angle and demanded dividing any areas on the board. They obtained a result that selection ability using by pointing in the 3-dimentional space is 9 areas.

Oba, he found selection ability using the thimble which was in condition to have enabled the rotary motion of the wrist[5]. As a result, he found that it was distributed for 22 areas.

3   The Inspection Experiment of the Selection Ability

The experiment was conducted in order to find out the test subjects' selection ability of pointing gesture. With their forearms fixed horizontally, the selection ability for Pitch direction was obtained. The selection ability for Yaw direction was obtained for the each obtained selection ability for Pitch (Fig.1.). The below restrictions were added to the vision and arm joints of the test subjects

1. Visual feedback was eliminated.
2. The joints of arms and fingers, which were except for wrists, were fixed. (Fig.2.).

Pointing gesture in this research is by using the wrist and finger joints. In the previous research, pointing gesture is separated Pitch (vertical direction) and Yaw (horizontal direction) by vertical guide(2), but it isn't separated in this research. With the forearm fixed, the hemisphere centering on the direction from the elbow to the wrist was considered.

The test subjects were instructed to point at the center of a certain area, which was a part of the partitioned hemisphere. The accuracy of their pointing gestures was examined. We made the instructions area presentation device which really expressed the areas obtained in a study of Oba into a hemisphere in 3-dimentional space(Fig.3.). A subject pushes the switch, LED in the center of each area turns on and shows instructions area to him.

In order to obtain the pointing angles of the test subjects, 3D sensor module (9DOF RAZOR[6]) was attached on top of their index finger. 9DOF RAZOR is a sensor equipped with a triaxial acceleration speed sensor, a gyro sensor and a triaxial geomagnetic sensor. The test subjects were 5 males and females who were in early twenties and righthanded. All of them had normal wrists joints. It was defined that one trial consisted of the test subjects pointing at the center of an area as instructed one time. It was defined that one set consisted of one trial for 22 areas partitioned. Three sets were completed in the experiment. The order of the trials was random within one set. Each set had different order. The experiment took approximately 40 minutes.

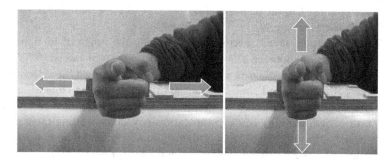

Fig. 1. Pointing Gesture by the finger(Left: Pitch, Right: Yaw)

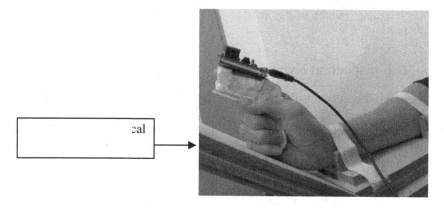

Fig. 2. The joints of arms and fingers were fixed

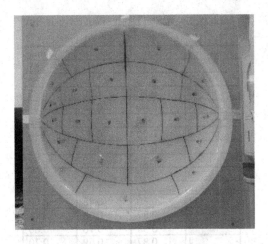

Fig. 3. The instructions area presentation device

3.1   Evaluation Method

The results of measuring the pointing angles of the gestures were analyzed. In the previous research, the pointing angles in one particular area of all the test subjects were assumed nearly normal distribution. So we let the average pointing angle in a particular area be μ and its standard variation be σ, assuming that they were able to point with the accuracy of approximately 68.3% if μ±σ was within the area.

However the pointing angles were not assumed normal distribution in this research. So we determine whether the subject can select right area using precision, recall and F-measure. I determine that the F-measure above 0.68 from previous works is possible to point at the area.

3.2   Results

We defined a area that could select correct is above 0.67 of F-measure from previous research result. We show a result in table 1. Furthermore, ending in a draw possibility refers to a judged area in the figure4. As a result, I found that we can point 12 areas in 22 areas of Oba.The area number is 1, 7, 8, 10, 12, 13, 14, 16, 17, 18, 20, and 21.

3.3   Discussion

We pictured the scatter diagram of the pointing angle to examine where subjects really pointed to when they pointed to the areas judged that they can't point(Fig.5.).

Meanwhile, we explain the conventional Pitch that previous work defined. It is an angle of the absolute coordinate system. By contrast, we get an Euler angle from a sensor. So we transform it from Pitch of Euler angle into Pitch of the absolute coordinate system. We can get the angle by using sine and cosine.

Table 1. Inspection result of selection ability

Area No.	Recall	Precision	F-measure
1	0.73	0.61	0.67
2	0.13	1.00	0.24
3	0.20	1.00	0.33
4	0.40	0.35	0.38
5	0.33	0.50	0.40
6	0.53	0.40	0.46
7	0.73	0.85	0.79
8	0.80	0.63	0.71
9	0.40	0.33	0.36
10	0.60	1.00	0.75
11	0.80	0.48	0.60
12	0.87	0.68	0.76
13	0.93	0.78	0.85
14	0.87	0.59	0.70
15	0.40	0.75	0.52
16	0.60	0.75	0.67
17	0.67	0.91	0.77
18	0.73	0.92	0.81
19	0.67	0.53	0.59
20	0.80	0.57	0.67
21	0.67	0.83	0.74
22	0.67	0.53	0.59

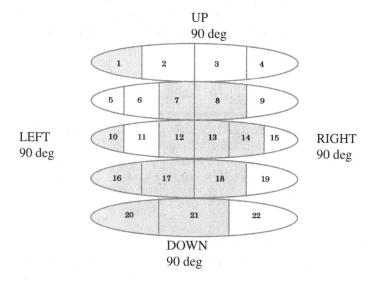

Fig. 4. Selection ability in the 3D space

As a Yaw angle becomes big, the vertical angle becomes big, and we point to upper area generally. Because when we convert a vertical angle to be provided from a sensor into the angle of the absolute coordinate system, as much as Yaw angle from a sensor becomes big, it has an influence on the angle after the conversion.

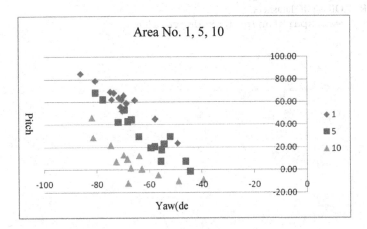

Fig. 5. Scatter diagram of area No. 1,5,10

4   Conclusion

From the result, we found that it is too difficult for pointing correct area without the vertical guide.

We think that previous research's selection ability which combining selection ability of pointing gesture at the 2-dimentional surface of Pitch and Yaw don't adupt to the selection ability by using pointing gesture in 3-dimentional space.

5   Future work

Combining selection ability of pointing gesture at the 2-dimentional surface didn't adupt to the selection ability by using pointing gesture in 3-dimentional space. So we need to get new selection ability adupted 3-simentional space by using pointing gesture.

References

1. Lenman, S., Bretzner, L., Thuresson, B.: Using Marking Menus to Develop Command Sets for Computer Vision Based hand Gesture Interface. In: NordiCHI, pp. 239–242 (2002)
2. Miyamoto, M., Terada, T., Tsukamoto, M.: An Area Allocation Algorithm for Hierarchical Pie Menu. In: Human Interface 2009, pp. 15–22 (2009)

3. Saeki, H.: A Study on Selection Ability in the 3D Space by the Finger, Graduation thesis of Musashi Institute of Technology (2008)
4. Yamada, R., Kuriiwa, H.: A Study on Selection Ability in the 3D Space by the Finger. Graduation thesis of Musashi Institute of Technology (2009)
5. Oba, Y.: A Study on Selection Ability in the 3D Space by the Finger. Graduation thesis of Musashi Institute of Technology (2010)
6. 9DOF RAZOR's pdf datasheet,
   https://www.sparkfun.com/products/10736

Empirical Evaluation of Multimodal Input Interactions

Sanjay Ghosh[1,2], Anirudha Joshi[2], and Sanjay Tripathi[1]

[1] Industrial Software Systems, ABB Corporate Research, Bangalore, India
[2] Indian Institute of Technology, Bombay, Mumbai, India
{sanjay.ghosh,sanjay.tripathi}@in.abb.com,
anirudha@iitb.ac.in

Abstract. With variety of interaction technologies like speech, pen, touch, hand
or body gestures, eye gaze, etc., being now available for users, it is a challenge
to design optimal and effective multimodal combinations for specific tasks. For
designing that, it is important to understand how these modalities can be combined and used in a coordinated manner. We performed an experimental evaluation of combinations of different multimodal inputs, such as keyboard, speech
and touch with pen etc, in an attempt to investigate, which combinations are efficient for diverse needs of the users. In our study, multimodal combination of
three modalities was found to be more effective in terms of performance, accuracy and user experience than that of two modalities. Further, we also inferred
the roles that each of the modalities play in a multimodal combination to
achieve the usability goals.

Keywords: Multimodal interaction, modality combinations, usability testing.

1 Introduction

The choice of a multimodal interaction depends on its interaction capabilities, the
nature of task, application context and users [1]. With a majority of these modern
interaction technologies achieving a level of maturity for reaching out to the mainstream mobile and computer applications, what would be the role of traditional
interaction methods like mouse and keyboard in the near future? In this study the
following research questions were under exploration –

- Which of the multimodal input combinations are efficient?
- Which modality contributes to which of the key usability goals?
- For multimodal combinations, are the usability parameters correlated?

Usability evaluation seems to be the logical method to investigate such questions [1].
In a multimodal setup, use of one interaction technology is also influenced by the co-
presence of the other interaction technologies. For such multimodal combinations,
"the total usability thus obtained is greater than the usability of each individual
modality" [2]. Therefore, for evaluation, combinations of multimodal interactions
must consider the as a whole, and not the sum of individual interactions. One of the

S. Yamamoto (Ed.): HIMI/HCII 2013, Part I, LNCS 8016, pp. 37–47, 2013.

objectives of this work is, to evaluate the multimodal interaction, especially for the commonly performed computer tasks. We considered two independent task sets, navigation and editing, to test users' performance. The evaluation was centered on measurement of *performance*, *accuracy* and *user experience* through the following four multimodal combinations; $K+S$, $K+T$, $S+T$ and $K+S+T$, where K stands for a keyboard, S stands for speech input and T stands for touch input with a pen or finger.

2   Related Works

Broad categories work related to the usability evaluation of multimodal interaction includes, multimodal evaluations through user questionnaires [3], user performance logs [4] [5], both performance logs along with questionnaires [6], Wizard of Oz technique [7] [8], eye tracking [9], model based formal verification methods with the use of Petri-nets [10] or Finite State Machines [11], etc. Ren et al. [5] reported empirical evaluation of Mouse, Keyboard, Speech and Pen for a prototype map and CAD applications. Metze et al. [6] used the post experiment user questionnaires to compare touch and speech modalities independently and their multimodal combination, for a wall mounted GUI based room management system. Similarly, Kaster et al. [12] evaluated the performance of the uni-modal combinations (only a single modality) and bi-modal combinations (two modalities) of mouse with speech, and touch with speech. Wechsung et al. [3] investigated the direct relationship between the bi-modal combinations and uni-modal interactions in terms of user experience based on user's rating on questionnaires. In contrast to these works, we considered only bi-modal combinations and tri-modal combinations (three modalities), because uni-modal interaction may be considered to be just a hypothetical situation without any practical use. Bernhaupt et al. [10] evaluated two mouse and speech, on an industry grade safety critical system by adopting the eye-tracking technique.

Almost all the earlier works did perform usability experiments on their custom developed prototype applications except for Beelders et al. [13], which used Microsoft Word to evaluate speech and eye gaze interactions as a replacement for the conventional typing. In the similar lines, our intent to use commonly performed tasks on computers for our experiments was, to evaluate multimodal combinations catering to a diverse group of users. Thus, our work is unique in terms of the multimodal combinations being evaluated and also the kind of tasks used for user experiments.

3   Method and Experiment Design

Experiments were conducted on IBM ThinkPad X230T, a touch screen enabled tablet computer, with an external keyboard attached. The users were allowed to use the handwriting recognition tool and Windows 'on screen keyboard'. For speech interaction, Microsoft Speech Application Programming Interface [14] was used. A good quality collar microphone was used to capture user's voice. The experiments were performed with ten participants within the age group of 25 to 30 years who were conversant in the use of computers. User recruitment was done using convenient sampling. Each participant was given speech training and a practice session of 3 hours. The experiment consisted of two categories of tasks, navigation and editing on Windows computer. The goal assigned for a navigation task was to navigate across the Windows help documentation to search for some information and to perform a calculation on the calculator tool. The goal assigned for the editing task was to document few sentences on the WordPad application, and then edit few words out of the text. Each user had to perform four such tasks using four different multimodal combinations as mentioned earlier. Participants were asked to work as natural as possible with the goal to complete the task quickly, with least errors.

Dybkjaer et al. [1] suggested the use of three usability parameters recommended by the ISO for such evaluations namely, efficiency, effectiveness, and user satisfaction. In our study, we renamed those as performance, accuracy and experience. Performance and accuracy were operationalized by the total time to complete a task and the number of errors committed, respectively. The objective was to evaluate the rankings of multimodal combinations in terms of their effectiveness for different tasks.

4   Results and Discussion

Statistical analysis was performed on low level captured data of user's events (screen captures, mouse clicks, pen movements and voice commands). We here present the results of the statistical analysis and our inferences on each of the research questions.

4.1   Which of Multimodal Combinations Are More Efficient?

We made a comparison among all the combinations of input modalities. The objective was to come out with the rankings of multimodal combinations in terms of their effectiveness for different tasks. Also it was investigated whether a combination of three modalities (tri-modal) is more effective than that of two modalities (bi-modal).

Performance. We observed the amount of time taken by the participants in completing the navigation and editing task using all the multimodal combinations one by one. Fig.1 shows the mean and standard deviation of the task completion times.

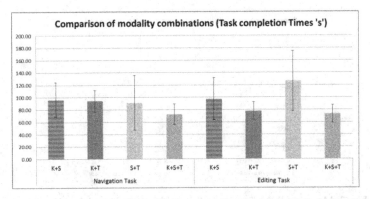

Fig. 1. Mean and S.D. of task completion times for all multimodal combinations

One way ANOVA was applied to analyze the performance variation among the four multimodal combinations. We found a significant variation among the multi-modal combinations K+S, K+T, S+T and K+S+T w.r.t. the task completion times for editing task (F(3, 36) = 5.949, p = 0.002), while this variation was not statistically significant for navigation task (F(3, 36) = 1.454, p = 0.243). Table 1 shows the result of paired sample t-tests comparing the multimodal combinations performance. For navigation task, K+S+T combination is significantly faster than K+S and K+T; for editing task, K+S+T and K+T combinations are significantly faster than K+S and S+T. All statistically significant values (p<α) are indicated by '*'. Additionally, by using t-test we compared the task completion times of bi-modal combinations (K+S, K+T and S+T) and the tri-modal combination (K+S+T). In terms of performance, the tri-modal combination was significantly better than the bi-modal for both navigation (t(29) = 2.786, 2-tailed test, p = 0.009) and editing tasks (t(38) = 3.215, 2-tailed test, p = 0.003).

Table 1. T-test results for multimodal comparison w.r.t. the task completion times

Multimodal pairs	Navigation Task			Editing Task		
	df	t stat	sig. '*p*'(2-tailed)	df	t stat	sig. '*p*'(2-tailed)
K+S vs. K+T	9	0.191	0.853	9	2.439	0.037*
K+S vs. S+T	9	0.476	0.645	9	-3.483	0.007*
K+S vs. K+S+T	9	3.586	0.006*	9	3.103	0.013*
K+T vs. S+T	9	0.194	0.850	9	-4.090	0.003*
K+T vs. K+S+T	9	2.867	0.019*	9	0.968	0.358
S+T vs. K+S+T	9	1.435	0.185	9	3.999	0.003*

Accuracy. We counted the number of errors committed by the participants, while performing the navigation and editing tasks using all the multimodal combinations one by one. Fig.2 shows the mean and standard deviation of the number of errors. One way ANOVA showed that, there is significant variation among the multimodal combinations K+S, K+T, S+T and K+S+T for navigation task (F(3, 36) = 5.594, p = 0.003), as well as editing task (F(3, 36) = 8.008, p = 0.000).

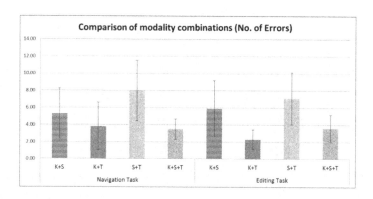

Fig. 2. Mean and S.D. of number of errors for all multimodal combinations

Further, table 2 shows the result of paired sample t-tests comparing the accuracy of the four multimodal combinations for navigation and editing task. Results of the t-tests showed that, for navigation task, S+T combination is significantly less accurate than all other combinations; for editing task, K+S+T and K+T combinations are significantly more accurate than K+S and S+T. Additionally, using t-test we also compared the errors committed by the participants using all the bi-modal combinations (K+S, K+T and S+T) as well as the tri-modal combination (K+S+T). We found that in terms of accuracy, the tri-modal combination is significantly better than the bi-modal combination only for navigation tasks (t(38) = 2.989, 2-tailed test, p = 0.005). In case of editing task this difference is not statistically significant (t(33) = 1.919, 2-tailed test, p = 0.064).

Table 2. T-test results for multimodal comparison w.r.t. the number of errors committed

Multimodal pairs	Navigation Task			Editing Task		
	df	t stat	sig. 'p'(2-tailed)	df	t stat	sig. 'p'(2-tailed)
K+S vs. K+T	9	1.649	0.134	9	3.592	0.006*
K+S vs. S+T	9	-3.304	0.009*	9	-0.937	0.373
K+S vs. K+S+T	9	2.529	0.032*	9	2.438	0.037*
K+T vs. S+T	9	-4.075	0.003*	9	-4.657	0.001*
K+T vs. K+S+T	9	0.331	0.748	9	-1.709	0.122
S+T vs. K+S+T	9	4.538	0.001*	9	3.312	0.009*

User Experience Level. We analyzed the user experience grades given by the participants using all the multimodal combinations one by one. Fig.3 shows the mean and standard deviation of the user experience levels.

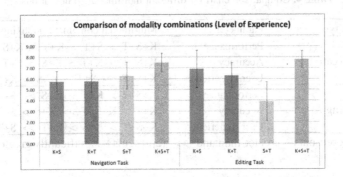

Fig. 3. Mean and S.D. of number of errors for all multimodal combinations

One way ANOVA showed that, there is significant variation w.r.t. the user experience levels among the multimodal combinations K+S, K+T, S+T and K+S+T for navigation task (F(3, 36) = 6.127, p = 0.002), as well as editing task (F(3, 36) = 13.629, p = 0.000). Further, table 3 shows the result of paired sample t-tests comparing the user experience level of the four multimodal combinations. Results of the t-tests shows that, for navigation task, the K+S+T combination has significantly higher level of user experience than all other combinations; for editing task, S+T combination has significantly lower level of user experience than all other combinations. Additionally, using t-test we also compared the user experience levels for bi-modal combinations (K+S, K+T and S+T) as well as the tri-modal combination (K+S+T). We found that in terms of user experience, the tri-modal combination is significantly better than the bi-modal combination for navigation (t(19) = -4.6208, 2-tailed test, p = 0.0002) as well as for editing tasks (t(37) = -4.7170, 2-tailed test, p = 0).

Table 3. T-test results for multimodal comparison w.r.t. the user experience level

Multimodal pairs	Navigation Task			Editing Task		
	df	t stat	sig. 'p'(2-tailed)	df	t stat	sig. 'p'(2-tailed)
K+S vs. K+T	9	0	1	9	0.818	0.434
K+S vs. S+T	9	-1.103	0.299	9	5.196	0.001*
K+S vs. K+S+T	9	-5.667	0.000*	9	-1.868	0.095
K+T vs. S+T	9	-0.921	0.381	9	3.145	0.012*
K+T vs. K+S+T	9	-3.431	0.748	9	-6.263	0.000*
S+T vs. K+S+T	9	-3.674	0.005*	9	-6.263	0.000*

Table 4 presents the summary of our analysis on effectiveness of different multi-modal combinations. We found that the tri-modal combination is more effective than the bi-modal combination. For a multimodal combination to be effective, the involved modalities should complement each other [4].

Table 4. Comparison chart for different multimodal combinations

Task type	Parameter	Multimodal combination ranking
	Performance	K+S+T > S+T > K+T > K+S
Navigation	Accuracy	K+S+T > K+T > K+S > S+T
	User Experience	K+S+T >> S+T > K+S = K+T
	Performance	K+S+T > K+T > K+S >> S+T
Editing	Accuracy	K+T > K+S+T >> K+S > S+T
	User Experience	K+S+T > K+S > K+T >> S+T

where, '>' represents – greater than and '>>' represents – significantly greater than.

4.2   What Are the Roles of Each Modality in a Multimodal Combination?

Here we made a comparison between multimodal combination pairs where, in one of the combination an input modality was present and in the other pair it was absent. This comparison gave us an idea about the role of each input modality towards usability goals, such as, performance, accuracy and user experience level.

Performance. Fig.4 shows the mean and standard deviation of task completion times, for the following multimodal combinations -

- With keyboard (K = K+S, K+T) and without keyboard (No K = S+T)
- With speech (S = K+S, S+T) and without speech (No S = K+T)
- With touch (T = K+T, S+T) and without touch (No T = K+S)

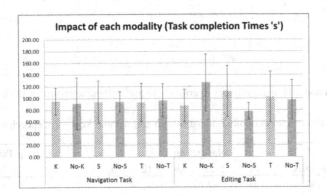

Fig. 4. Mean and S.D. w.r.t. task completion time with/without keyboard, speech and touch

Table 5 shows the result of t-tests comparing the performance of these multimodal combinations. Results shows that, for editing tasks, availability of keyboard significantly increases and that of speech significantly decreases the performance.

Table 5. T-test results of task completion times with and without keyboard, speech and touch

Multimodal pairs	Navigation Task			Editing Task		
	df	t stat	sig. 'p'(2-tailed)	df	t stat	sig. 'p'(2-tailed)
K vs. No K	11	0.281	0.784	12	-2.337	0.038*
S vs. No S	28	-0.036	0.972	26	3.175	0.004*
T vs. No T	21	-0.335	0.741	22	0.331	0.774

Accuracy. Fig.5 shows the mean and standard deviation of the number of errors, for the three pairs of multimodal combinations, i.e. with/without K, S and T. Results of t-tests shows that, for both navigation and editing tasks, a keyboard significantly increases and speech significantly decreases the accuracy of a user.

User Experience Level. Fig.6 shows the mean and standard deviation of the user experience levels graded by the participants, for the three pairs of multimodal combinations, i.e. with and without K, S and T. Table 7 shows the result of t-tests comparing the performance of the above mentioned multimodal combinations pairs for navigation and editing task. Results of the t-tests, showed that, for editing tasks, a keyboard significantly increases and touch significantly decreases the user experience.

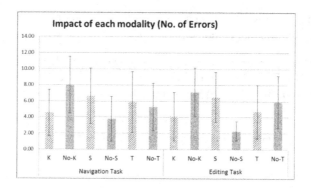

Fig. 5. Mean and S.D. w.r.t. number of errors with and without keyboard, speech and touch

Table 6. T-test results of number of errors with and without keyboard, speech and touch

Multimodal pairs	Navigation Task			Editing Task		
	df	t stat	sig. 'p'(2-tailed)	df	t stat	sig. 'p'(2-tailed)
K vs. No K	15	-2.676	0.017*	18	-2.560	0.020*
S vs. No S	22	2.435	0.023*	27	5.328	0.000*
T vs. No T	23	0.478	0.637	19	-0.946	0.356

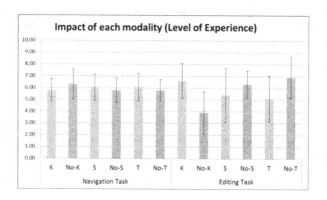

Fig. 6. Mean and S.D. w.r.t. experience levels with and without keyboard, speech and touch

Table 7. T-test results of user experience levels with and without keyboard, speech and touch

Multimodal pairs	Navigation Task			Editing Task		
	df	t stat	sig. 'p'(2-tailed)	df	t stat	sig. 'p'(2-tailed)
K vs. No K	14	-1.113	0.285	15	4.125	0.001*
S vs. No S	19	0.612	0.548	28	-1.424	0.166
T vs. No T	22	0.645	0.525	20	-2.591	0.017*

Our results showed that, the multimodal combinations with speech had low performance and accuracy. Few earlier works [5] [6] too reported similar results. Speech does contribute to the speed of task; however, due to less accuracy of speech this contribution is not achieved in a multimodal combination. Speech was found to be efficient for commanding and not for information entry. Keyboard was found to be efficient for information entry and not for commanding. Touch pen seemed good for pointing to entities which were easily located on the screen. In addition, it was found that the conventional interaction modality i.e. a keyboard has a significant role to play, even in the presence of non-conventional interaction modalities. Ren et al. [5] mentioned that mouse was useful and was more accurate than pen.

4.3   Are the usability parameters related?

Correlation was performed among the pairs of the three usability parameters used in the experiment, task completion times (representing performance), number of errors (accuracy) and user experience. Table 7 presents the Pearson's correlation coefficient 'r' and corresponding significance value 'p' between the pairs of usability parameters.

Table 8. Correlation among key usability parameters for multimodal combinations

(r, p)	Task completion times	Number of errors	User experience
Task completion times	1		
Number of errors	(0.626, 0.021)	1	
User experience	(-0.641, 0.009)	(-0.520, 0.041)	1

The results of correlation showed that, there is a strong correlation among the three usability parameters. This means, the multimodal combination having smaller task completion time (i.e. higher performance) is expected to have lesser number of errors (higher accuracy) and also higher user experience. Similar results were reported by Sauro and Kindlund, [15] who observed positive correlation between the direct data and indirect data from their experiments. Contrary to this, Hornbaek and Law [16] reported negative correlations between direct and indirect data.

5   Conclusions and Future Work

In this study, we have formulated few research questions on effectiveness of different multimodal input interactions, collected the user data through experiments, and performed analysis to answer those research questions. Speech input in general was observed to be the fastest input modality, but due to its low accuracy and uncertainty its performance gets compromised [17]. Speech input seems to be effective for commanding but not for information entry; unlike the keyboard which is more effective for information entry but not for commanding. Contrastingly, touch as well as mouse seems to be effective in pointing any visible GUI entity on the screen. Knowing such information related to the effectiveness of multimodal combination is crucial in designing multimodal interactions. For any application which requires extensive use of GUI but minimal use of text editing, speech along with touch would be the preferable multimodal combination. Similarly, for an application requiring more text editing and lesser navigation, speech together with keyboard would be preferable.

The work presented in this paper is an initial research in the direction of developing quantitative models of multimodal combination, which could guide in designing the multimodal interactions for different applications. Future work would involve inclusion of other non-conventional input modalities like hand or body gesture in the experiment. This work may also be extended for specific domain applications, and more involved user groups like bank teller, tele-caller, industrial plant operator, etc.

References

1. Dybkaer, L., Bernsen, N.O., Minker, W.: New Challenges in Usability Evaluation-Beyond Task-Oriented Spoken Dialogue Systems. In: ICSLP, vol. 3, pp. 2261–2264 (2004)
2. Bretan, I., Karlgren, J.: Synergy Effects in Natural Language-Based Multimodal Interaction. SICS Research Report (1994)
3. Wechsung, I., Engelbrecht, K.P., Schaffer, S., Seebode, J., Metze, F., Möller, S.: Usability Evaluation of Multimodal Interfaces: Is the Whole the Sum of Its Parts? In: Jacko, J.A. (ed.) HCI International 2009, Part II. LNCS, vol. 5611, pp. 113–119. Springer, Heidelberg (2009)
4. Oviatt, S.: User-centered modeling and evaluation of multimodal interfaces. IEEE 91(9), 1457–1468 (2003)
5. Ren, X., Zhang, G., Dai, G.: An experimental study of input modes for multimodal human-computer interaction. In: Tan, T., Shi, Y., Gao, W. (eds.) ICMI 2000. LNCS, vol. 1948, pp. 49–56. Springer, Heidelberg (2000)
6. Metze, F., Wechsung, I., Schaffer, S., Seebode, J., Möller, S.: Reliable Evaluation of Multimodal Dialogue Systems. In: Jacko, J.A. (ed.) Human-Computer Interaction, Part II, HCII 2009. LNCS, vol. 5611, pp. 75–83. Springer, Heidelberg (2009)
7. Bernsen, N.O., Dybkjær, L.: Evaluation of spoken multimodal conversation. In: 6th ACM International Conference on Multimodal Interfaces, pp. 38–45 (2004)
8. Serrano, M., Nigay, L.: A wizard of oz component-based approach for rapidly prototyping and testing input multimodal interfaces. J. Multimodal User Interfaces 3(3), 215–225 (2010)
9. Bernhaupt, R., Palanque, P., Winckler, M., Navarre, D.: Usability Study of Multi-modal Interfaces Using Eye-Tracking. In: Baranauskas, C., Abascal, J., Barbosa, S.D.J. (eds.) INTERACT 2007. LNCS, vol. 4663, pp. 412–424. Springer, Heidelberg (2007)
10. Bernhaupt, R., Navarre, D., Palanque, P., Winckler, M.: Model-Based Evaluation: A New Way to Support Usability Evaluation of Multimodal Interactive Applications. In: Maturing Usability: Quality in Software, Interaction and Quality, pp. 96–122 (2007)
11. Cohen, P.R., Johnston, M., McGee, D., Oviatt, S., Pittman, J., Smith, I., Chen, L., Clow, J.: QuickSet: Multimodal Interaction for Distributed Applications. In: 5th ACM International Conference on Multimedia, pp. 31–40 (1997)
12. Kaster, T., Pfeiffer, M., Bauckhage, C.: Combining Speech and Haptics for Intuitive and Efficient Navigation through Image Databases. In: 5th ACM International Conference on Multimodal Interfaces, pp. 180–187 (2003)

13. Beelders, T.R., Blignaut, P.J.: The Usability of Speech and Eye Gaze as a Multimodal Interface for a Word Processor. In: Speech Technologies, pp. 386–404 (2011)
14. Microsoft Voice Recognition System,
    http://www.microsoft.com/enable/products/windowsvista/
    speech.aspx (last retrieved on February 26, 2013)
15. Sauro, J., Kindlund, E.A.: Method to standardize usability metrics into a single score. In: ACM SIGCHI Conference on Human Factors in Computing Systems, pp. 401–409 (2005)
16. Hornbæk, K., Law, E.L.C.: Meta-analysis of correlations among usability measures. In: ACM SIGCHI Conference on Human Factors in Computing Systems, pp. 617–626 (2007)
17. Cohen, P.R., Johnston, M., McGee, D., Oviatt, S.L., Clow, J., Smith, I.: The efficiency of multimodal interaction: A case study. In: International Conference on Spoken Language Processing, vol. 2, pp. 249–252 (1998)

Usability Evaluation of the Touch Screen User Interface Design

Chih-Yu Hsiao, You-Jia Liu, and Mao-Jiun J. Wang

Department of Industrial Engineering and Engineering Management
National Tsing Hua University Hsinchu 30013, Taiwan, ROC
ede80899808@yahoo.com.tw

Abstract. With the advancement of ICT technologies, touch-screen interface mobile devices become a standard feature. This study aims to evaluate the Popover interface design under different age groups. The UI elements being considered for evaluation include location, window length and font size of the popover in three visual search tasks. The results show that there were significant differences in reaction time and accuracy rate between age groups. The worst performance was found in the older group. The best button position was on the bottom screen. In addition, significant performance differences between popover window length and font size were also found. Generally speaking, it is recommended to use the popover window with long cell length, and bigger font size for better readability, especially for the older age group users.

Keywords: Touch screen, iPad, User Interface Elements, Popover, Performance Measures.

1 Introduction

With the advancement of ICT technologies, the growth of mobile devices smart phones and tablets outpacing that of desktop systems in 2011. User interface design is becoming more and more important, especially for mobile devices with touch screen interface. These devices allow users to surf the web, read electronic documents, play games, send email and remain connected within their social networks [1].

Some usability studies showed that it is much more difficult to understand content when it is read on a mobile device than on a desktop computer. To encounter this problem, Steele and Iliinsky [2] recommended that the designers should identify the important content, and emphasize it visually by making it bigger, bolder, brighter and called out with circles, arrows and labels to help the users to understand the hierarchy of information on the screen.

Text direction, screen size and font size are the factors affecting user's search time and accuracy. Lin et al. [3] used the color LCD e-reader to investigate how legibility and visual fatigue are affected by different text directions, screen sizes, and character sizes. They found that the recognition performance was better for reading horizontal words than for vertical words. Screen size and font size were the factors affecting the

S. Yamamoto (Ed.): HIMI/HCII 2013, Part I, LNCS 8016, pp. 48–54, 2013.

user's search time. Wu et al. [4] used three different e-book displays to evaluate visual fatigue, reading performance, and subjective rating. The results showed that greater visual fatigue was found in smaller screen size and font size. Search speed is improved, when the screen size and font size are increased.

In general, the fingertip or touch pen is used as the input device for touch screen interface. As the primary input method, the interface design issues include touch target size, touch target layout, and tactile feedback. Since target size and layout are often restricted by screen size, users may be slower to type on devices with smaller target sizes and lacking of tactile feedback [5]. Budiu and Nielsen [6] indicated the fat-finger problem with the touch screen device, and it is difficult to precisely touch the small targets. Thus, some research has shown that the best target size for widget is 1 cm x 1cm for touch devices. Similarly, Wu and Luo [7] evaluated twelve touch pens including three lengths and four diameters, and recommended to use a smaller diameter and longer touch pen.

Due to the demographic change with an increasingly aging population, the usability issues of touch-screen interface devices for the older adults require high attention. With the increasing number of aged users on mobile devices, the issue of readability and usability are becoming more and more important. Ziefle [8] investigated the effects of font sizes and the size of the window on navigation performance with 40 elderly participants (55-73 years old). The results indicated that the optimal performance was found when the font size and the size of the preview window were large. Many usability issues regarding touch screen interface design needs to be addressed, especially for the older age groups. Hence, this study aims to evaluate the design of Popover UI elements including location, length and fonts size for different age groups.

2   Method

2.1   Participants

A total of 45 healthy participants (22 males and 23 females) involved in the experiments. Three age groups including, the younger group (8 males and 7 females) with age ranged 18-29 years old (Mean = 21.63 years; SD = 2.44); the middle group (7 males and 8 females) with age ranged 30-44 years old (Mean = 35.67 years; SD = 4.49) and the older group (7 males and 8 females) with age range 45-65 years old (Mean = 56.52 years; SD = 4.48). All of the participants were right-handed, and can understand and read traditional Chinese.

2.2   Equipment

The touch screen device used in this study was an Apple iPad based smart tablet device. It has a 9.7 inch screen with a resolution setting of 1024 x 768, and a portrait soft keyboard.

2.3   Experiment Tasks

The visual search tasks involved three levels of text length. In short text search task (2-5 words), the content can be the popular names and country names. In the middle (9-14 words) and long (at least 15 words) text searching task, the content can be the news headings and briefs.

According to the iPad Human Interface Guidelines, the width of the popover should be at least 320 points, but less than 600 points [9]. Thus, the width of a popover window for short text message was 320 points, the width of a popover for middle and long text message was 460 points and 600 points respectively, as shown in Fig.1.

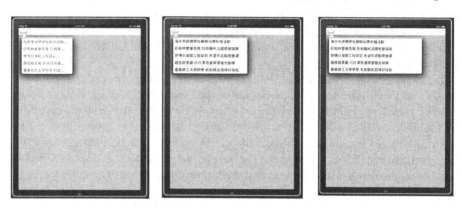

Fig. 1. The popover windows for the three visual search tasks

2.4   Experimental Design

The experiment design of this study was a nested-factorial design. The 45 participants were divided into three age groups (younger, middle and older). Each participant performed 180 trials, including 6 popover's button locations (upper left, upper middle, upper right, bottom left, bottom middle and bottom right), 6 popover window length (5, 7, 9, 11, 13 and 15 cell-length) and 5 font size (15, 17, 19, 21 and 23 pt). The dependent measures were reaction time and accuracy.

2.5   Procedure

Before the experiment, a training session was given to help the participants to familiarize themselves with the iPAD use as well as the visual search tasks. The participants used left hand to hold iPAD, and performed the touch screen task using right hand.

When the participants were ready, they have to press the "Start" button. A popover button would appear in one of the six locations randomly. They were then asked to press the button as quickly as they can.

After pressing popover button, participants were asked to perform visual search tasks. The visual search tasks have different popover window length and font sizes.

The three visual search tasks was given in random sequence. When participants located a target in the search field, they would touch the target and the target will be highlighted. A 3 min rest period was given between experiment sessions. Each of visual search tasks was given in random sequence.

3   Results

3.1   Reaction Time between Each Age Group and Locations of Popover Button

The results showed that there were significant differences in reaction time between 6 locations, $F (5, 210) = 13.619$, $p = .000$, and the interaction between location and age group was also significant, $F (10, 210) = 3.041$, $p = .001$. As shown in Fig. 2, the better performance was found in the middle bottom position and the worst performance was found in the upper left position. In addition, the younger and middle age groups showed no significant difference in reaction time. The older age group had the worst performance in all 6 locations.

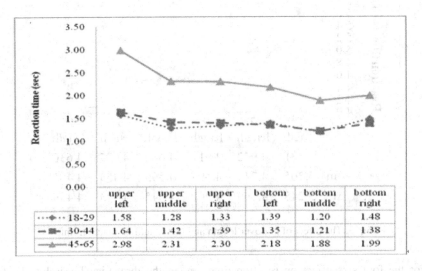

	upper left	upper middle	upper right	bottom left	bottom middle	bottom right
···◆··· 18-29	1.58	1.28	1.33	1.39	1.20	1.48
—■— 30-44	1.64	1.42	1.39	1.35	1.21	1.38
—▲— 45-65	2.98	2.31	2.30	2.18	1.88	1.99

Fig. 2. The effect of location and age group on reaction time

3.2   Accuracy and Reaction Time between Fonts Size and Popover Window Length

Accuracy
For accuracy measure, the results showed that there were significant interactions in age groups and font sizes in short text search task, $F (8, 168) = 2.623$, $p = .01$. And the worst performance was found in the older group, but the younger and middle age groups showed no significant difference in accuracy. The results showed that the older group had better performance with the font size of 23 pt.

Reaction Time

For reaction time, there were significant differences between visual search tasks, popover window length and fonts size. In short text search task, the significant effects were found in popover window length, F (5, 210) = 9.212, p = .000, fonts size, F (4, 168) = 7.235, p = .000, and the interaction between age group and popover window length, F (10, 210) = 4.321, p = .007. In middle text search task, there were significant differences in popover window length, F (5, 210) = 9.212, p = .000, and fonts size F (4, 168) = 7.235, p = .000. In long text search task, the significant effects were found in popover length, F (5, 210) = 10.510, p = .000, and fonts size, F (4, 168) = 4.785, p = .001. The worst reaction time performance was found in 5 cell-length popover length. In short text search task, the 5 cell-length popover window length had the worst reaction time performance. The better reaction time performance was found in the 13 and 15 cell-length popover in long text search task. Thus, the findings indicate that the reaction time decreased as the length of popover increased, as shown in Fig. 3.

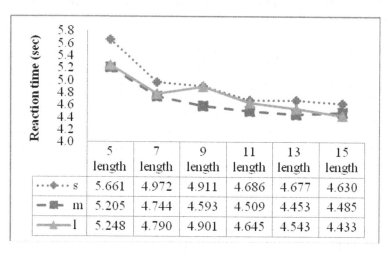

	5 length	7 length	9 length	11 length	13 length	15 length
···◆··· s	5.661	4.972	4.911	4.686	4.677	4.630
─■─ m	5.205	4.744	4.593	4.509	4.453	4.485
──▲── l	5.248	4.790	4.901	4.645	4.543	4.433

Fig. 3. The effect of popover length and text length on reaction time

For the font size effect on reaction time among the three visual search tasks, the worst performance was found in short text search task, and the best performance was found in middle text search task. In addition, for the middle and long text search task, the best performance was found in 23 pt font size, and the worst performance was found in 15 pt font size. In short text search task, the best performance was found in 21pt font size, as shown in Fig. 4.

In all three age groups, the worst reaction time performance was found in the 5 cell-length popover. For the older age group, the better reaction time performance was found in the 11, 13 and 15 cell-length popovers. Thus, this study suggests that the popover window length should have at least 11 cell-length for the older users.

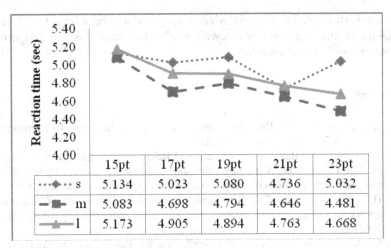

	15pt	17pt	19pt	21pt	23pt
···◆··· s	5.134	5.023	5.080	4.736	5.032
─■─ m	5.083	4.698	4.794	4.646	4.481
─▲─ l	5.173	4.905	4.894	4.763	4.668

Fig. 4. The effect of font sizes and text length on reaction time

4   Discussion and Conclusion

For the locations of the popover, the better performance in reaction time was found in the middle bottom and the worst performance was found in the upper left. In this study, the participants were asked to press the popover button when it appears. Since all the participants were right-handed, the upper left location of the popover had the longest hand movement distance. Thus, the hand movement time increases as the hand and target distance increases. Thus, it is recommended to position the button on the bottom of the screen.

For the font size effect, the results showed that the worst performance in reaction time was found in 15pt font size. Bernard [10] reported that reading 12-point size were faster than reading the 10-point size fonts. Lin et al. [3] also indicated that too small the font size tends to cause reading difficulty. Reading larger fonts had better performance than reading small fonts.

For the length of text message in visual search tasks, searching in short text message needs more reaction time than searching in long text message. In the small text search task, the participants were asked to perform word search task. McClelland and Rumelhart [11] indicated that perception of letters in words was actually lowered if the subjects focused on a single letter position in the word. In this study, the reaction time in long text search tasks (middle and long text message) were better than that of the short text search task. It seems that the user' ability to recognize a target in sentences is better than to recognize a target in words.

For the length of popover, the reaction time and accuracy performance was found to be better in the long cell-length popover than those in the short cell-length popover. Since the long length popover has more cell numbers, it can display more information, and reduce reaction time for target search and increase accuracy.

Considering the popover interface design for the older users, the findings suggest that the popover button is better positioned on the bottom of the screen. Font sizes should be at least 23 pt. The popover window length should be at least 11 cell-length. The findings of this study can provide very useful information for the design of popover interface to facilitate usability.

References

1. Chaparro, B., Nguyen, B., Phan, M., Smith, A., Teves, J.: Keyboard Performance: iPad versus Netbook. Usability News 12(2) (2010)
2. Steele, J., Iliinsky, N.: Beautiful Visualization. O'Reilly, United States (2010)
3. Lin, H., Wu, F.G., Cheng, Y.Y.: Legibility and visual fatigue affected by text direction, screen size and character sizeon color LCD e-reader. Displays 34, 49–58 (2013)
4. Wu, H.C., Lee, C.L., Lin, C.T.: Ergonomic evaluation of three popular Chinese e-book displays for prolonged reading. International Journal of Industrial Ergonomics 37, 761–770 (2007)
5. Lee, S., Zhai, S.: The Performance of Touch Screen Soft Buttons. In: The 9th Proceedings of the SIGCHI Conference on Human Factors in Computing Systems (CHI 2009), pp. 309–318. ACM, United States (2009)
6. Budiu, B.R., Nielsen, J.: Usability of iPad Apps and Websites, 2nd edn. Nielsen Norman Group, United States (2011)
7. Wu, F.G., Luo, S.: Design and evaluation approach for increasing stability and performance of touch pens in screen handwriting tasks. Applied Ergonomics 37, 319–327 (2006)
8. Ziefle, M.: Information presentation in small screen devices: The trade-off between visual. Applied Ergonomics 41, 719–730 (2010)
9. Apple Inc.: iPad Human Interface Guidelines: User Experience, United States (2011)
10. Bernard, M., Lida, B., Riley, S., Hackler, T., Janzen, K.: A Comparison of Popular Online Fonts: Which Size and Type is Best? Usability News 4(1) (2002)
11. McClelland, J.L., Rumelhart, D.E.: An Interactive Activation Model of Context Effects in Letter Perception: Part 1. An Account of Basic Findings. Psychological Review 88(5), 282–371 (1981)

A Study for Personal Use of the Interactive Large Public Display

Shigeyoshi Iizuka[1], Wataru Naito[2], and Kentaro Go[3]

[1] Kanagawa University, Japan
shigeiizuka@gmail.com
[2] Department of Education, Interdisciplinary Graduate School of Medicine and Engineering,
University of Yamanashi, Japan
naito@golab.org
[3] Interdisciplinary Graduate School of Medicine and Engineering, University of Yamanashi,
Japan
go@yamanashi.ac.jp

Abstract. In recent years, "digital signage" has been used for large screen displays in public spaces, such as stations or shopping malls. Some display terminals have used digital signage to dispatch information in an interactive format; thus, a user touches an electronic screen to obtain information, such as a map, store location, or advertisement, and receives it freely. Public systems commonly adopt user interfaces with touch panels on display terminals to facilitate interactive information exchange.

On the other hand, the popularity of personal computers and the explosive growth of the Internet now make it possible for users to handle a wide variety of information—regardless of location or time of day. Furthermore, users communicate not only information that may be seen by others but sometimes information not intended to be seen by others. In other words, even information of a highly confidential nature can be accessed anywhere and anytime. The information dissemination which cared about this point is desirable.

In this research, therefore, we will study information security and privacy as it pertains to large touch screens in public places. The goal of this research is to identify the variables associated with user safety when interfacing on large touch screens in public venues; additionally, we will propose a method for designing public space so that users can communicate interactively with reassurance of confidentiality.

Keywords: Information environment design, Public space, Large public display, private information, Reassurance.

1 Introduction

In recent years, "Digital Signage" has emerged where a large-screen display is installed in public spaces like a station or a shopping mall. Some display terminals used by digital signage have not only information dispatched to one direction, but also interactive interface. With such an interface, the user may freely access via touch

S. Yamamoto (Ed.): HIMI/HCII 2013, Part I, LNCS 8016, pp. 55–61, 2013.

various kinds of information, for example, a map, a store, or an advertisement. Many user interfaces which use touch panel for the display terminal, facilitating an interactive information exchange have been used in public spaces (Figure1).

The spread of personal computers and the explosive growth of the Internet now make it possible for users to access a wide variety of information, regardless of location or time of day. In using the Internet, users communicate both confidential and public information. From this, we see that even information of a highly confidential nature can be accessed and processed anywhere and anytime. Knowledge of the process of such information dissemination over the Internet is useful for those seeking to develop the confidential dissemination of information using public touch screen.

Therefore, in this research, we decided to study information security privacy for large, public touch screens in public spaces. The goal of this research is to clarify the facts regarding the safety of communicating confidential information using a large touch screen in a public space, and to propose the indicator and method or an environmental design of a large screen interface in a public space where users can communicate confidential information with the reassurance that the information will remain private.

Fig. 1. Large public display use image in public space

2   Related Works

The following materials are helpful to understanding this study:

- A comprehensive analysis of the design space that explains mental models and interaction modalities, as well as taxonomy for interactive public displays is presented by Müller et al. [4].
- A preliminary prototype of a personal display, which is deployed in a university context is presented by Böhmer et al. [1].

- A paradigm for measuring whether or not a user has read certain content is presented by Desney et al. [3].
- Two initial user studies investigating factors relevant to user acceptance and usability in the context of a deployed system that provides pedestrian navigation support through a combination of mobile devices and public displays are presented by Müller et al. [5].
- A crossmodal ambient display framework that supports multiple users simultaneously accessing information that contains both public and personal elements is proposed by Cao et al. [2].

A concept for personalized privacy support on large public displays is presented by Röcker et al. [6].

3   Concept

In order to promote the concept that users can safety disseminate information using interactive displays in public displays in public spaces, a design for a "shared terminal" and a "physical environment" must be developed with the user in mind. This research furthers the following three objectives:

- To clarify the characteristics needed to secure confidence in the means by which private information is conveyed by user's of large, public touch interactive displays in public spaces.
- To develop the indicator and method for the design of large, public touch screens in public spaces so users can feel reassurance in communicating information.
- To consider this proposal from two different designs: that of the graphical user interface (GUI) realized by software, and the solid user interface (SUI) realized by a physical component.

4   Proposal Method

We propose how to show private information on the portion of a large public display that is hidden by the body of the user, that is, the portion that is a dead angle to the surrounding people. By using this method, it will be possible to communicate private information securely in a public space. Moreover, it will also be possible to hide confidential information by a user's judgment by showing the user the portion of the display that cannot be seen by others.

However, it is insufficient to ensure safety merely to hide in the shade of user's body. Therefore we propose a method that makes the privacy of communicating information via a public interface more reassuring for the user of such an interface. This method will conceal information according to the level by which the user classifies it by hiding it in the "concealment domain." An image of this proposal is shown in Figure 2.

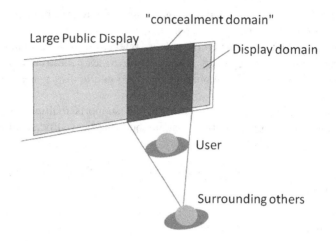

Fig. 2. Concealment domain

Thus, private information will be shielded from public view by being placed on the part of the screen blocked by the user's body. We call this the "concealment domain."

4.1 Theoretical Value of Concealment Domain

We made the trial calculation of the width of the display's concealment domain by realizing the proposal technique. The following conditions were applied to the trial calculation.

- user's shoulder width: 43.1 cm (Japanese average shoulder width)
- user's surrounding eyesight: 1.0
- user stands 35 cm away from a display (user can reach a display and can hide a screen domain to some extent)

We estimated that a user with surrounding eyesight 1.0 and who can read a 10 to 12 point font can see about 2 m~3 m. Then, we decided to divide the distance from a display into 3 points: 150 cm (clear,) 250 cm (visible), and 350 cm (not much visible).

The results of calculating the concealment domain based on these figures is shown in Table 1. From these results, we estimated that the range of abbreviation of 50–60 cm can be hidden.

Table 1. Width of the concealment domain on a display (trial calculation)

others' dis-tance (cm)	angle with a display(°)			
	90	75	60	45
150	56.22	56.83	59.00	64.33
250	50.12	50.41	51.41	53.74
350	47.89	48.08	48.73	50.20

4.2 Informational Privacy Level and Display

Using only the technique mentioned above, the concealment domain is not only restricted, but the view ability of the rest of the screen greatly depends on the position of a person behind the user (Figure 3).

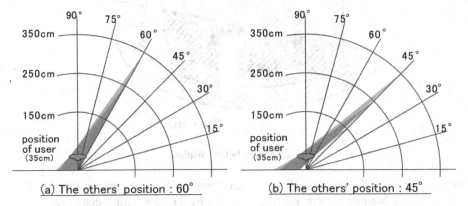

Fig. 3. The relation of the others' position and a concealment domain

In such a case, the two ideas below should be considered.

1. Gradually notify the user of the danger.
2. Hide information according to the privacy level that the user selects beforehand.

1. Gradually notify the user of the danger.

In order to gradually notify the user of the danger, it is necessary to divide the space in front of a display according to distance. Although the method for dividing the domain in front of a public display according to distance and changing an interaction is already proposed by Vogel and others [1], in our proposal, the interaction of the user using the domain before this display is not changed, and the divided domain is used as an index to notify of the user of the danger (Figure 4). According to the distance (domain) from a display, a system notifies the user gradually of the danger.

2. Hide information according to the privacy level that the user selects beforehand.

This method determines what kind of operation the system performs, and when the user's information will emerge from the concealment domain according to the privacy level that the user selects beforehand.

In a high level, contents are automatically moved into the concealment domain so that the user's information must remain within the concealment domain. Where the concealment domain does not exist, or where it does not effectively shield the user's private information, iconifying and minimizing information that appears on the screen

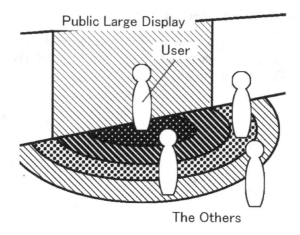

Fig. 4. Domain before display

directly in front of the user can prevent others from reading the contents (Figure. 5). In addition, the high level further protects privacy by hanging a filter that covers contents in the middle to low screen level. Thus, setting opacity in the filter and allowing the user to select the place on the screen where information can be read to some extent balances the competing goals of preserving safety of the information and allowing the user to see the showing information in a public space.

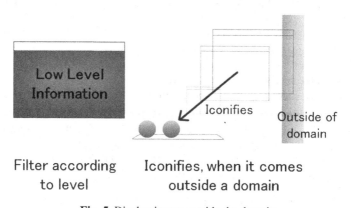

Fig. 5. Display image outside the domain

5   Conclusion

In this paper, in order to communicate private information on a large public display in a public space, we demonstrated how to display information on the concealment domain. From now on, we will investigate how someone's using a large public display in public spaces influences others to look at the display, and how many others do look. Based on those results, we aim to design a prototype for such a large interactive public display in a public space to maximize the privacy of communicated information.

Acknowledgements. This work is supported by KAKENHI（23500160.

References

1. Böhmer, M., Müller, J.: Users' Opinions on Public Displays that Aim to Increase Social Cohesion. In: 2010 Sixth International Conference on Intelligent Environments, pp. 255–258 (2010)
2. Cao, H., Olivier, P., Jackson, D., Armstrong, A., Huang, L.: Enhancing Privacy in Public Spaces Through Crossmodal Displays. Social Science Computer Review Archive 26(1), 87–102 (2008)
3. Desney, S.T., Czerwinski, M.: Information Voyeurism: Social Impact of Physically Large Displays on Information Privacy. In: Proc. CHI 2003, pp. 5–10. ACM Press (2003)
4. Müller, J., Alt, F., Schmidt, A., Daniel, M.: Requirements and Design Space for Interactive Public Displays. In: MM 2010, pp. 25–29. ACM Press (2010)
5. Müller, J., Jentsch, M., Kray, C., Krüger, A.: Exploring Factors That Influence the Combined Use of Mobile Devices and Public Display for Pedestrian Navigation. In: Proc. NordiCHI 2008, pp. 308–317. ACM Press (2003)
6. Röcker, C., Magerkurth, C., Hinske, S.: Information Security at Large Public Displays. In: Gupta, M., Sharman, R. (eds.) Social and Human Elements of Information Security: Emerging Trends and Countermeasures, pp. 471–492. IGI Publishing, Niagara Falls (2009)

Study on Haptic Interaction with Maps

Daiji Kobayashi, Anna Suzuki, and Nanami Yoneya

Chitose Institute of Science and Technology, 758-65 Bibi Chitose Hokkaido, Japan
{d-kobaya,b2080880,b2091930}@photon.chitose.ac.jp

Abstract. Although older adults' haptic interaction with a paper map (HIM) has been observed in our previous studies, the effectiveness of touch panel operation introducing HIM was not addressed. In this study, young adults' characteristic hand movements were observed, and the hand movements to understand the present location and directions to a goal by a walker as the HIM were defined. Hence, a digital map with three HIM functions was developed and the effectiveness of these functions was measured and experimentally clarified. Further, the effectiveness of a prompted HIM was experimentally investigated using a specific digital map that prompted various HIM on the walker's demand. Finally, the characteristics of HIM and the effectiveness of prompting HIM to the walker using a map were clarified.

Keywords: haptic interaction, paper map, digital map, touch panel, tablet PC.

1   Introduction

1.1   Background

Our previous research [1], [2] has shown that the Japanese elderly have an aversion to using personal computers (PCs). Therefore, we conducted a usability study of our specific digital evacuation-route map on personal digital assistants (PDA) with a touch panel for the Japanese elderly. Almost none of the older participants could get to the goal using the digital map, but they were able to do so using a paper map. Hence, we observed the participants' behavior using the digital evacuation-route map and compared this interaction with the behavior when they used a paper evacuation-route map. The results suggested that a participant's hand motion on the paper map is for route planning and understanding the present location [3].

The importance of object attributes for haptics and haptic exploration has been previously considered [4-6]. However, the hand movement on the paper map was not intended to explore the attributes of the paper map, such as smoothness or texture, but was for understanding the present location and visualizing the route toward a goal. Furthermore, the hand movement occurred either at the unconscious level or consciously with think-aloud protocols. Thus, we regard the hand movements as a type of haptics with paper map and we have named the meaningful hand movement for interacting with the map as *haptic interaction with map* (HIM).

S. Yamamoto (Ed.): HIMI/HCII 2013, Part I, LNCS 8016, pp. 62–71, 2013.

We assumed that HIM was useful for walking when checking a paper map for direction, and also that HIM would not be useful for a digital map on a PDA with a touch panel. Although the older participants knew how to use the digital evacuation-route map, they consciously or unconsciously tried HIM with the digital evacuation-route map. Hence, the older participants caused unintentional behavior of the digital evacuation-route map and confused themselves. It appeared to us that the confusion accumulated and the older individuals gave up walking to the goal using the digital map. However, the touch panel is a mainstream interface for portable information devices such as tablet PCs. Therefore, the style of digital map operation should be taken into account based on unintentional hand movements such as HIM for the Japanese elderly.

On the other hand, it is not clear that HIM is common for young Japanese individuals who have become familiar with smartphones. Further, how the HIM of young individuals using a digital map affects or effects their context of use is not clear.

1.2   Objective

The purpose of HIM is not to understand the physical properties of paper or a tablet PC touch panel, but for getting information from a paper map or the screen of a tablet. Although we can see that HIM is map-reading skill, we assume that the important characteristics of HIM for getting information by moving the hands, fingers, arms, and so on are similar to those using the haptic interaction with physical mattes. Thus, the aim of our study is to experimentally clarify the characteristics of HIM and its effect on users when reading a paper or a digital map. Although our previous studies [2] indicate that the Japanese people, especially the elderly, have very wide range capabilities when using information technologies, we focused on the HIM of young Japanese in this study.

2   Method

To clarify the characteristics of HIM in young individuals, our research was conducted according to the following steps.

2.1   Observing and Extracting HIM of Young Individuals

The hand movements of young individuals who tried to walk to a goal using a paper map were experimentally observed, and their HIM was extracted. The extracted HIM of the young was compared with that of the elderly we had previously investigated.

In the trial, four male and five female individuals who ranged from 20 to 22 years of age participated. The participants tried to walk using a paper map in a residential area. Two types of colored paper maps were prepared and used. One was A4-sized, printed on a scale of 1 to 3000, and easy to read, while the other was A3-sized, printed on a scale of 1 to 25000, and difficult to read.

The participants were given two tasks, i.e., to walk from different locations to the goal using the two maps, once each time. Each task had to be done within 40 min, after which the trial ended, regardless of whether the goal was reached or not. Further, we defined some roads to be impassable but told the participants to draw back only at the point when they tried to pass through it. As a result, the participant had to replan the route to the goal while referring the paper map.

Two investigators followed the participants and an investigator recorded the participants' behavior such as hand movement, expression, and think-aloud protocols using a video camera. The other investigator noted the remarkable hand movements and interviewed the participant about these hand movements after the trial.

The HIM of the participants was extracted from their various hand movements based on the experimental data such as the recorded and noted behaviors. In particular, we investigated the relation between the manner of hand movement and the participants' performance data such as the walking distance and the time taken to arrive at the goal.

2.2   Introducing HIM into Digital Map Operation

The extracted HIM of the young participants was introduced into the operation of the digital map by making specific digital software for the tablet PC (MSI Winpad 110W-017JP). The tablet PC ran Windows 7 Professional Japanese Edition and had a 10-inch display touch panel. Although the map on the tablet PC was made based on an easy-to-read map scale, the scale of the map could be changed by pinching in/out touch operation and it could be scrolled by running a finger on the touch panel. Furthermore, to express the HIM marks such as tracing along a road or applying pressure with fingers, we developed functions (HIM functions) that visualized HIM on the map in terms of lines and dots. The HIM functions were available when the user touched the center button. However, the map could not be rotated by the user.

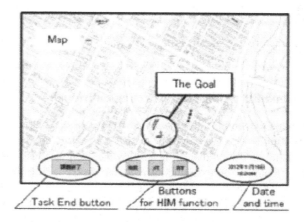

Fig. 1. Screen of specific digital map with touch panel

To observe HIM using our specific digital map, we conducted an experiment in a manner similar to the prior experiment using the paper maps. However, we made two versions of the digital map available on the same tablet PC to compare the participants' behavior and the performance for cases in two cases: (i) when the HIM functions were available and (ii) when they were not. The participants were three male and three female students who ranged from 19 to 22 years of age. We prepared two tasks (Task-A and Task-B) for the participants: to walk from two different locations to the goal using the two types of digital map, with or without HIM functions, once each time. Three participants tried Task-A using the digital map with the HIM functions, followed by Task-B using the digital map without the HIM functions; the other three participants tried Task-B using no HIM functions followed by Task-A using HIM functions.

The area for the experiment was a residential area in Chitose, Hokkaido, Japan, but different from the area used in the prior experiment. Each task had to be done within 30 min, after which the trial ended, regardless of whether the goal had been reached or not. Further, we defined some roads as impassable and told the participants to draw back only when they tried to pass through it. Consequently, they had to replan the route to reach the goal using the digital map.

Two investigators followed the participants and an investigator recorded the participants' behaviors such as hand movement, expression, and think-aloud protocols using a video camera. The other investigator noted the remarkable hand movements. Furthermore, the investigator interviewed the participant about the reason or meanings for characteristic hand movements, including touch operations, after the trial and if the participant could recall the particular hand movement.

The experimental data were analyzed and compared for both the cases by using and not using the HIM functions to clarify the relationship between HIM on the digital map and the participants' performance such as walking distance.

2.3   Investigation of HIM's Effectiveness Suggested by Digital Map

It seems logical that a user who confidently accesses a digital map by operations or manipulations, including HIM, will get the appropriate information required to walk toward a goal. This point gives rise to the hypothesis that prompting for HIM leads to a walker's successful decision-making and appropriate performance such as walking in the right direction without confusion. Hence, we experimentally confirmed this hypothesis using another specific digital map that prompted for the correct HIM on demand.

The specific digital map prompting HIM was made based on the prior specific digital map by adding the new feature that prompts the HIM on demand. If a walker became disoriented with the digital map, touched a "Need Help" button on the screen, and selected a context menu item from "Not certain of current position," "Lost all sense of direction," or "Planned route has been lost," then the digital map took into consideration the participant's situation and indicated a message prompting the applicable HIM, as shown in Fig. 2.

The effectiveness of the specific digital map with HIM prompting was tested by eight participants who ranged from 20 to 21 years of age. The participants were divided into two groups and the conditions for using the digital map with and without prompting the applicable HIM were tested based on the counterbalanced measures' design.

The area the participants walked in and the acquisition of experimental data were the same as the previous experiment.

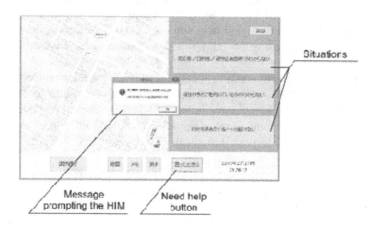

Fig. 2. Example of screen prompting the applicable HIM

3   Results and Discussions

3.1   Extracted HIM

From the data of the observational experiment for extracting the young participants' HIM, the meaningful hand movements recorded by video were extracted from the testing the effectiveness of the participant's map reading and/or route planning. Eight different hand movements were observed without any significant gender bias, as shown in Fig. 3.

From the participants' opinion, we assumed that four types of hand movements—"Turning," "Flipping," "Folding," and "Unfolding"—suggested managing the paper map to facilitate visualization, and the other four types—"Orienting," "Tracing," "Pressing," and "Writing"—were useful hand movements to decide the direction to reach the goal, understand the present location, and plan the route to the goal. Hence, we designated these three types of hand movement HIM to stimulate map understanding. The movement-type "Writing" was extracted from the behavior of a female participant who had a pen by chance; she wrote a line marking her planned route to the goal and also marked her location. Therefore, her aim when "Writing" was similar to the functions of "Tracing" and "Pressing."

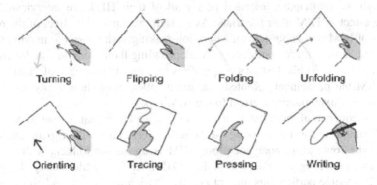

Fig. 3. Observed hand movements

Consequently, we extracted three different HIM for the paper map and applied them to the digital map operation to allow using the digital map as if the user manipulated a paper map. "Orienting" was made possible by the antirotation map on the screen; "Tracing," "Pressing," and "Writing" were made possible by the drawing function on the map when pressing or running a finger. With the exception of "Writing," the other three types of HIM were coincident with the older adult's HIM that we had observed in the previous studies, and we developed a digital map implementing these three types of HIM using a function. We then evaluated how the participant's performance was affected by the availability of the HIM function.

3.2 Effect of Digital Map Operation Including HIM

The participant's performance, measured by walking distance for Task-A and Task-B, was compared for the two cases: when the HIM function was available and when not available. The results showed that the minimum walking distance for Task-A was 878 m and that for Task-B was 737 m. From the statistical results of the one-side test, the walking distance for users having a tablet PC with the HIM function was significantly shorter ($p = 0.04$) than that for users who are unable to use the HIM function in Task-A (Fig. 4), but it did not differ significantly ($p = 0.41$) for Task-B. Although the results for Task-A suggested that the participants using the HIM function took some shortcuts to reach the goal and the walking distance is significantly shorter, the minimum walking distance for Task-B is 141 m shorter than that for Task-A. Therefore, we think that taking a shortcut by the participants is not a significant factor for the results on the right-hand side of Fig. 4.

According to the video-recorded behavior of the participants, two female students did "Orienting" on the digital map just as for a paper map. These students said that they did "Orienting" on the digital map to face in the direction they were going. One other female student and a male student also did "Orienting" unconsciously when they were confused on the way. On the other hand, all the participants did "Tracing" and "Pressing" by using the HIM function to draw tracks and mark the impassable road on coming across it. Further, two male students and a female student used the HIM function for drawing the planned route to the goal as necessary.

Although the participants recalled nearly all of their HIM, we interviewed them about the effect of HIM after the trials. As a result, we know the effect of the respective types of HIM on the participant's decision-making with respect to moving toward the goal and gaining more confidence in understanding their location and direction, as shown in Table 1. Table 1 shows a specific example of the effect of HIM and the related HIM the participants pointed out; the number shows how many participants relate a specific example of an effect to the HIM-type.

As a consequence of these experimental results, we know that the participants used the HIM function for memorizing or better understanding their path and/or the planned route toward the goal; therefore, HIM is useful for walkers with a map to some extent. However, the aim and style of HIM varied a little among the participants. In fact, some participants did not perform "Orienting" at all, and all the participants did not use the same types of HIM for the same purpose.

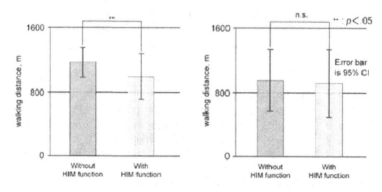

Fig. 4. Walking distance for Task-A (left) and Task-B (right) by the participants

Table 1. Specific example of the effect of HIM given by the participants

Specific example of the effect	Related HIM-type		
	Pressing	Tracing	Orienting
Understanding the present location, the goal, or the landmark well	6	2	0
Gaining more confidence in understanding the present location and/or the direction toward the goal	2	4	5
Planning the route to the goal	0	2	0
Understanding the path taken from the starting location	0	2	0

3.3   Effectiveness of HIM Suggested by Digital Map

We designed the digital map function prompting appropriate HIM in the user's context based on the knowledge about the HIM and its effect. Fig. 2 shows the three context menu items on right-hand side of the screen and the suggestion for the appropriate HIM based on the user's situation.

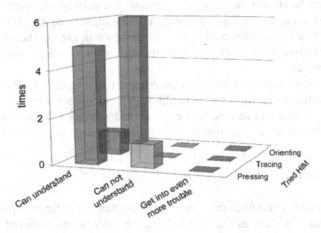

Fig. 5. The participant's situation after trying prompted HIM

The results show that the difference in the walking distance between two cases—(i) using the prompted HIM and (ii) without using the prompted HIM—was not statistically significant for the respective tasks; therefore, it can be said that HIM prompted by a message did not have a direct benefit on a walker's performance. Next, we focused on the participant's verbal protocol data when the participant was in trouble and tried the prompted HIM. Fig. 5 shows the outcomes of 13 situations when a participant was in trouble, touched the "Need Help" button, and tried the prompted HIM. The participants could grasp the key to adjust their understanding in almost all the cases by trying the prompted HIM.

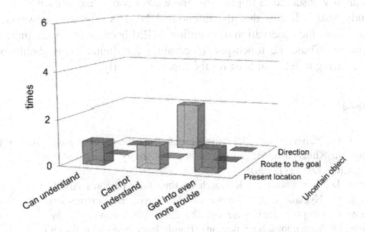

Fig. 6. The participant's situation after using the digital map without prompted suggestions

On the other hand, in five situations, we saw that participants were confused or were in trouble using the verbal protocol data on the digital map that prompted nothing; however, few participants could get help, as shown in Fig. 6. Therefore, prompting HIM is effective in difficult situations for walkers from the perspective of their cognitive processes.

Consequently, we conclude from this experiment that intentional HIM is useful for getting more information from the map, although haptic interaction is for getting the characteristics of physical mattes. In fact, we could see that HIM is a type of map-reading skill. Therefore, digital map operation should be designed based on HIM.

4   Conclusion

From the results obtained from this work, we know that the different types of HIM in young individuals is same as that of the Japanese older adults observed in previous studies; therefore, we may say that the three types of HIM including "Orienting," "Tracing," and "Pressing" are common in the Japanese people. However, the effect of these HIM types on decision-making for movements differed among the participants. From the experimental results, we assume that the effect depends on various factors such as the context of use rather than HIM, and therefore, HIM directly affects the performance measures such as walking distance.

Another question is whether or not intentional HIM and unconscious HIM lead to the same result. In this study, we focused on the intentional HIM rather than on the unconscious HIM because the latter is difficult to observe through experiments. However, some participants were pointed out as using their unconscious HIM by the investigators, and they said that the unconscious HIM was not effective because it was the result of a confused situation. Therefore, when unconscious HIM such as "Turning" is frequently observed, it implies that the walker could be confused.

This study also indicates that the intentional HIM is effective; however, digital maps do not allow the observation of intentional HIM because of the common style of touch operation. Thus, the touch-panel operation for digital maps should be redesigned by referring to HIM, at least for the Japanese elderly.

References

1. Kobayashi, D., Yamamoto, S.: Usability Research on the Older Person's Ability for Web Browsing. In: Kumashiro, M. (ed.) Prom. of W. Ability Towards Productive Aging, pp. 227–235. CRC, London (2009)
2. Kobayashi, D., Yamamoto, S.: Research on the Older Person's Ability for Touch Panel Operation. In: Nygård, C.-H., Savinainen, M., Kirsi, T., Lumme-Sandt, K. (eds.) Age Management during the Life Course, pp. 229–238. TUP, Tampere (2011)
3. Kobayashi, D., Yamamoto, S.: Study on a Haptic Interaction with Touch Panel. In: Khalid, H., Hedge, A., Ahram, T.Z. (eds.) Adv. in Erg. Mod. and Usability Eval., pp. 472–476. CRC, Boca Raton (2011)

4. Lederman, S.J., Klatzky, R.L.: Hand Movements: A Window into Haptic Object Recognition. Cog. Psy. 19, 342–368 (1987)
5. Lederman, S.J., Klatzky, R.L.: Sensing and Displaying Spatially Distributed Fingertip Forces in Haptic Interfaces for Teleoperators and Virtual Environment Systems. Presence 8, 86–103 (1999)
6. Lederman, S.J., Klatzky, R.L.: Haptic Identification of Common Objects: Effects of Constraining the Manual Exploration Process. Per. and Psy. 66, 618–628 (2004)

Relative Position Calibration between Two Haptic Devices Based on Minimum Variance Estimation

Masanao Koeda, Yuki Konbu, and Hiroshi Noborio

Osaka Electro-Communication University,
Faculty of Information Science and Arts, Department of Computer Science
Kiyotaki 1130-70, Shijonawate, Osaka 575-0063, Japan
koeda@isc.osakac.ac.jp

Abstract. In this paper, we propose a new method to estimate the relative positions of multiple haptic devices. As is the case in stereo camera calibration, the accurate measurement of the relative positions of haptic devices is difficult. The proposed method uses the acquired stylus positions of two devices and estimates the relative positions of two devices based on minimum variance estimation. In this method, the data acquisiton process has been improved to allow a large number of data points to be easily acquired. We conducted preliminary experiments to estimate the positions of two devices. The results showed the feasibility and reasonable accuracy of the proposed method.

Keywords: Haptics, Calibration, Positioning.

1   Introduction

In recent years, various haptic display devices has been developed and utilized in several practical applications such as surgical and dental simulators [1, 2]. We also constructed a smart but cheaper dental surgical simulation system [3]. In dental operations, dentists simultaneously use multiple tools such as a dental bar, mirror, pick, and vacuum. For this reason, our system is prepared for the use of multiple haptic devices in parallel. For effective and practical operation, it is preferable to allow the arrangement of devices to be changed based on the operation, working situation, or size of user's hand. However, the accurate measurement of the relative positions and attitudes of the haptic devices is a difficult and troublesome task, just as with stereo camera calibration. Therefore, once the device arrangement is initially fixed, it is rarely changed, but is continually as is, with the exception of some extraordinary circumstance.

In a multiple haptic device environment, it is important to know the relative positions and attitudes of the devices. We have been studying the calibration method in various situations [4, 5]. In our previous method [5], these properties were calculated by solving redundant simultaneous equations using data derived from several

S. Yamamoto (Ed.): HIMI/HCII 2013, Part I, LNCS 8016, pp. 72–79, 2013.

identical end-points of the two devices. It was found that the accuracy of the calibration was improved by increasing the quantity of end-point data that was stored. However, in the previous method, the data acquisition process was very complicated, and the maximum number of data points was only 24.

In this paper, we propose a new method to estimate the relative positions of multiple devices based on minimum variance estimation. In this new method, the data acquiring process has been improved, and a large number of data points can be easily acquired. The use of this new method is expected to improve the estimation accuracy. Preliminary experiments were conducted, and the results showed the feasibility and reasonable accuracy of the proposed method.

2   Methodology

p_{ri} and p_{li} are the position vectors of the end effectors of two haptic device in individual local coordination systems Σ_r and Σ_l, as shown in Fig. 1.

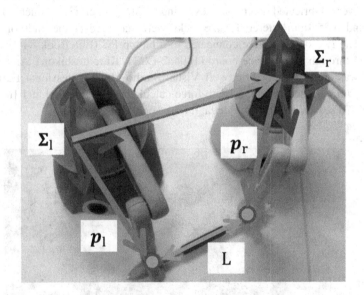

Fig. 1. Coordinate systems

$$p_{ri} = (x_{ri}\ y_{ri}\ z_{ri})^T$$
$$p_{li} = (x_{li}\ y_{li}\ z_{li})^T$$
$$i = 1, 2, 3, \dots, n$$

L_i is the distance between two end effectors in a world coordinate system. It can be calculated by

$$L_i = \|\, p_{ri} - p_{li} + p_d \,\|$$

where $\boldsymbol{p}_d = (x_d \ y_d \ z_d)^T$ is the relative position vector of both devices.
Here, V is defined as the variance of L_i,

$$V = \frac{1}{n}\sum(L_{ave} - L_i)^2$$

where L_{ave} is the average of L_i. In the world coordinate system, L_i should be the constant value because both devices are fixed; as a result, V becomes 0 in theory. Practically, V becomes close to 0. Then, under this constraint, $\boldsymbol{p}_d$ can be searched using a minimum variance estimation, $argmin(V)$.

3   System Setup

Two haptic devices (PHANToM OMNI, SensAble Technologies) were used for the following verification experiment. To acquire the position data $\boldsymbol{p}_{ri}$ and $\boldsymbol{p}_{li}$, the two devices were physically connected using a rigid connecting bar (Fig. 2). The connecting bars were fabricated from plastics using a 3D printer (3D Touch, Bits From Bytes), and 6.35 [mm] stereo female jacks were mounted at the ends of each bar (Fig. 3). The two devices were connected to a laptop PC (EliteBook 8440w, HP) by IEEE1394 through an interface board (1394a2-EC34, Kuroutoshikou). An estimation program was created using Microsoft Visual Studio 2008 Professional Edition. For the minimum variance search, a brute-force calculation was applied at 1 [mm] along each axis. To search a 100 [mm³] area, it took approximately 10 [s].

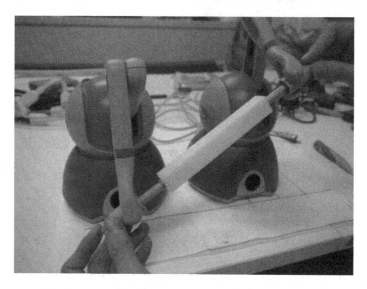

Fig. 2. Two haptic devices connected by connecting bar

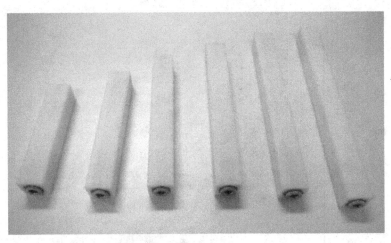

Fig. 3. Various lengths of connecting bars (100, 120, 140, 160, 180 and 200 [mm])

4   Experiment and Results

The horizontal displacement values x_d, y_d, and z_d were set visually to 250 [mm], [mm], and 0 [mm], respectively, by using a steel ruler (Fig. 4). The search range of p_d was set to $200 < x < 300, 0 < y < 100, -50 < z < 50$ for 1 [mm] sampling. By moving the connector randomly while measuring p_r and p_l, a large number of data points easily obtained. Fig. 5 shows the 3D plotted graph of p_r (red dots) and (green dots) when a 200 [mm] long bar was used. The number of data points for each experiment is shown in Table 1.

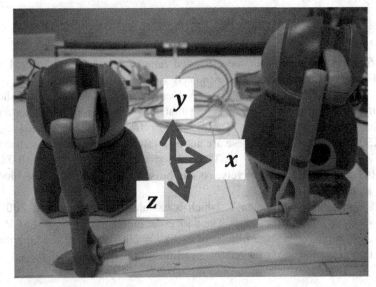

Fig. 4. Experimental condition ($x_d = 250, y_d = 50, z_d = 0$)

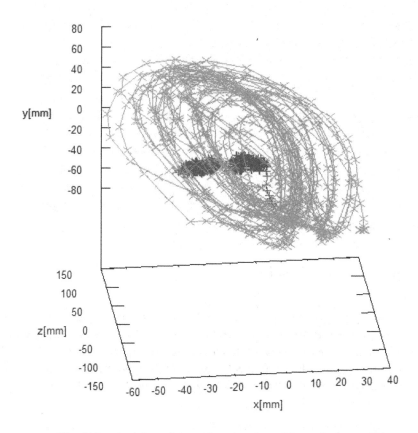

Fig. 5. Acquired data of $\boldsymbol{p}_r$ and $\boldsymbol{p}_l$ (number of data points n = 690)

Fig. 6 shows the results for the estimated relative position, and Table 1 lists the detailed values of the results. The estimated values are approximately the same regardless of the bar length, and all V_{min} values are quite low. This result shows the feasibility of the proposed method. Note that it is a matter of no importance that the estimated results shown in Table 1 differ from the experimental condition $(x_d = 250, y_d = 50, z_d = 0)$. These are not true values, but are only reference values.

Fig. 7 shows the variation in L_i. The red and blue lines show $\boldsymbol{p}_d = (0\ 0\ 0)^T$ and $\boldsymbol{p}_d = (241\ 51\ -7.0)^T$, respectively. As can be seen, the variance of the blue line is flat and almost exactly zero.

Fig. 8 shows the variation in V, which is calculated in the range of $200 < x_d < 300,\ 0 < y_d < 100,\ and\ z_d = 0$. The dark color indicates a low value of V. As can be seen, the graph has a local minimum of $x_d = 250, y_d = 50$, and the minimum point is the estimation result for relative positions of the two devices, $\boldsymbol{p}_{dmin}$.

Table 1. Results of relative position estimation

Bar length [mm]	argmin(V)			V_{min}	Number of data points
	x_d [mm]	y_d [mm]	z_d [mm]		
100	238	49	-3	0.144	773
120	240	50	-4	0.278	741
140	240	50	-7	0.163	745
160	240	50	-7	0.180	759
180	247	53	-8	0.166	770
200	241	51	-7	0.113	690

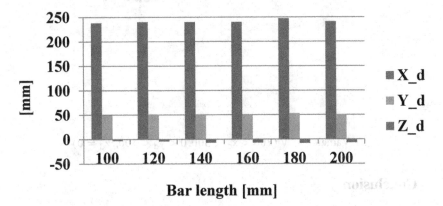

Fig. 6. Results of estimation

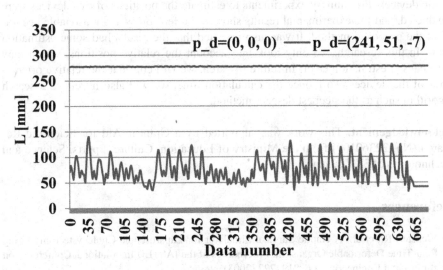

Fig. 7. Variation in L_i (blue: $\boldsymbol{p}_d = (0\ 0\ 0)^T$, red: $\boldsymbol{p}_d = (241\ 51\ -7)^T$)

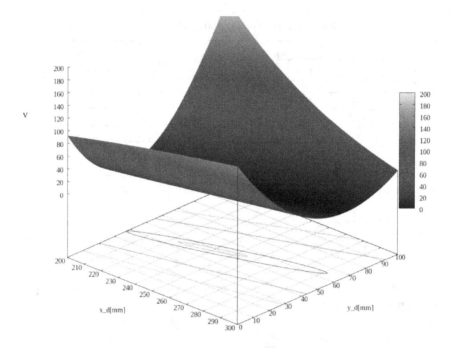

Fig. 8. Variation in V ($200 < x_d < 300, 0 < y_d < 100$, $z_d = 0$)

5   Conclusion

In this paper, we proposed a new method for estimating the relative positions of two haptic devices. Preliminary experiments to estimate the positions of two devices were conducted, and the experimental results showed the feasibility and reasonable accuracy of the proposed method. It was also revealed that the results had some estimation error. In this research, we only took into account the relative positions, which may have caused estimation error. In future research, we will consider the relative orientations of the devices. To reduce the calculation time, we will also introduce a search algorithm such as the steepest descent method.

Acknowledgement. This work was supported by a Grant-in-Aid for Scientific Research (No. 22360109) from the Ministry of Education, Culture, Sports, Science and Technology (MEXT), Japan.

References

1. Webster, R., et al.: A Haptic Surgical Simulator for Laparoscopic Cholecystectomy Using Real-Time Deformable Organs. In: Proceedings of the IASTED International Conference on Biomedical Engineering, pp. 219–222 (2003)

2. Kim, L., et al.: Dental Training System Using Multi-modal Interface. Computer-Aided Design & Applications 2(5), 591–598 (2005)
3. Noborio, H., Yoshida, Y., Sohmura, T.: Development of Human Interface Software in Our Dental Surgical System Based on Mixed Reality. In: Proceedings of the Workshop on Computer Graphics, Computer Vision and Mathematics, pp. 107–114 (2010)
4. Koeda, M., Kato, M.: Pen Tip Position Estimation Using Least Square Sphere Fitting for Customized Attachments of Haptic Device. In: Stephanidis, C. (ed.) Posters, Part II, HCII 2011. CCIS, vol. 174, pp. 340–344. Springer, Heidelberg (2011)
5. Koeda, M., Ninomiya, Y., Sugihashi, M., Yoshikawa, T.: Estimation Method for Relative Position and Attitude between Two Haptic Devices. In: Proceedings of the 12th International Conference on Human-Computer Interaction, pp. 446–450 (2007)

Optimization of GUI on Touchscreen Smartphones Based on Physiological Evaluation – Feasibility of Small Button Size and Spacing for Graphical Objects

Shohei Komine and Miwa Nakanishi

Keio University, Yokohama, Japan
bad-boc.jda.1991@a6.keio.jp, miwa_nakanishi@ae.keio.ac.jp

Abstract. Prompted by the increasing popularity of smartphones, we experimentally investigated how command button size and spacing influences users' operation and experience of the device. We measured user performance (input accuracy and operation time) and assessed physiological and psychological reactions. Tests were performed for a range of button sizes, spacing and handling modes. While large button size (9 mm) increased user comfort, a size of 7 mm aroused more user excitement, suggesting that user-interface design guidelines should be revised for uses such as games and amusement.

Keywords: GUI, touchscreen, smartphone, physiological evaluation, interest.

1 Introduction

In recent years, portable touchscreen terminals known as smartphones have experienced a global upsurge, which is expected to continue. Today, smartphones are used not merely as cellular phones but also in everyday online pursuits, such as SNS (Social Network Service) communication, browsing websites and gaming. In addition, a new role for smartphones is emerging for interface-control equipment in houses and home electronics.

Despite the diverse applicability of portable touchscreen terminals, structured GUI (Graphical User Interface) and corresponding design guidelines have yet to be established. In the UI guidelines of companies such as Microsoft and Apple, the recommended command button size is nearly 7 mm [1-3]. However, the optimal button size is expected to be purpose oriented; for example, controlling home electronics, creating a text message in SNS and repeatedly striking a game target should call for different button sizes.

Therefore, in this study, we experimentally investigated the effect of button size and spacing on both user performance (namely, input accuracy and operation time) and perception. The results will clarify whether user experience of smartphones could be enhanced by customizing button size to a particular task.

S. Yamamoto (Ed.): HIMI/HCII 2013, Part I, LNCS 8016, pp. 80–88, 2013.

2   Experimental Task

Prior to the experiment, participants rested with their eyes closed for two minutes. The assigned task involved repeated touching of command buttons on the touchscreen display of a smartphone (Android GALAXY S3, Samsung). The number of repeated touches was 20. The task was performed in the following sequence:

1. Participants were requested to press the central preparation button on the touchscreen display at arbitrary times.
2. At the time of touching the prepare button, a group of 9 (3*3) command buttons at random positions on the touchscreen display was shown. Among this group, participants were required to touch the centre button as quickly and precisely as possible. Touching point was determined as the first contact point of the fingers on the display. If the central button in the group was precisely touched, the detection was successful. If other points were touched, the detection was false.
3. Return to (1). A single task comprised 20 time repeats of sequences (1)–(3). Following a task, the participants evaluated performance usability on 100 levels and finally assessed the success rate of tasks.

The task was performed for different handgrips, button sizes and button spacings.

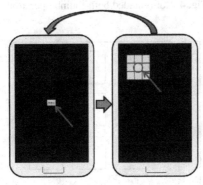

Fig. 1. Task sequence and display design used in the smartphone experiments

2.1   Experimental Conditions

Handgrips were dominant-handed dominant-thumb operation (Fig. 2), opposite-handed dominant-index-finger operation (Fig. 3) and ambidextrous thumb operation (Fig. 4). In the final case, participants also conducted thumb-free operations.

Four different button sizes were used: 3, 5, 7 and 9 mm. Button spacing was 0, 1 and 2 mm. Participants were given all 12 combined conditions in a perfect random order.

Fig. 2. Dominant-handed dominant-thumb operation

Fig. 3. Non-dominant handed dominant index finger operation

Fig. 4. Both-handed both-thumb operation

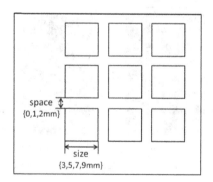

Fig. 5. Experimental conditions of button size and space

2.2 Measurements

The device was tested from performance, psychological and physiological viewpoints. Performance was assessed from input accuracy and operation time data. Input accuracy was defined as the probability of exactly touching the group central button in a single task; that is, the input accuracy measures the probability of successful touches per task. Operation time was the time difference between the fingers disconnecting from the prepare button and touching the next (arbitrary) position on the touchscreen display. As a measure of psychological impact, participants were asked the question "How easy was touching the command buttons in one task? Please valuate this task from 0 points (very easy) to 100 points (very difficult)" after task completion. Physiological measures were SCR (Skin Conductance Reflex) and re-rated human emotion; in particular, excitement and awareness. Measurement instruments were BIOPAC MP150 and GSR110C skin SCRamp (made by Monte System Corporation). Ag/AgCl electrode was placed on the index and middle fingers of the participant's non-dominant hand. Cutoff frequency was 0.05–1 Hz and sampling rate was 0.2 kHz.

2.3   Participants

10 male college male students (age 21–24) participated in the study. Participants had consumed no alcohol or caffeine since the previous day. All participants were right-handed. Eight of the participants used a smartphone in everyday use, while the remainder used a feature phone.

2.4   Ethics

We obtained informed consent from all individuals participating in this experiment.

3   Results

3.1   Task Performance

Accuracy as a function of size and spacing of command buttons was assessed using two-way analysis of variance (ANOVA). The results under dominant-handed dominant-thumb operations are shown in Fig.6. Size exerted a statistically significant effect on accuracy (Two-way ANOVA, $F (3,108) = 44.90$, $p < 0.01$), whereas spacing did not. Moreover, no interaction between size and space was observed. The above results were independent of handgrips.

Input accuracy decreased with button size. In particular, input accuracy declined from approximately 90% to 75% as the button size decreased from 7 mm to 5 mm, and reduced to below 50% when 3-mm buttons were used (Bonferroni multiple comparison). The accuracy achieved for a given button size was not affected by spacing between the buttons.

Next, operation time as a function of size and spacing of command buttons was analysed by two-way ANOVA. The results under dominant-handed dominant-thumb operation are shown in Fig. 7. Furthermore, button size exerted a significant effect (Two-Way ANOVA, $F (3,108) = 15.15$, $p < 0.01$) regardless of spacing, with no obvious interaction between size and spacing. These results were again independent of handgrips.

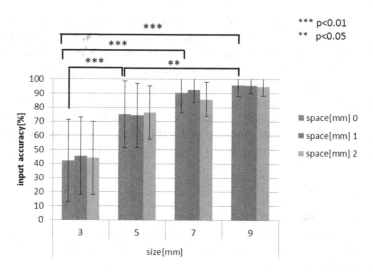

Fig. 6. Relationships between size, space and input accuracy under dominant-handed dominant-thumb operation

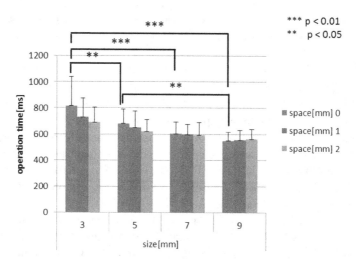

Fig. 7. Relationship between size, space and operation time under dominant-handed dominant-thumb operation

Operation time was inversely related to smaller button size. Operations performed on 9 mm buttons consumed less than 565 ms, whereas approximate operating times for 5 and 3 mm buttons were 651 and 746 ms, respectively (Bonferroni multiple comparison).

Meanwhile, spacing exerted no significant effect on input accuracy.

3.2 Subjective Evaluation

Two-way ANOVA was used to subjectively evaluate the ease of button touch for varying size and spacing of command buttons. Figure 8 summarizes the results under dominant-handed dominant-thumb operation. In this case, the effects of both size (Two-way ANOVA, $F(3,108) = 90.64$, $p < 0.01$) and spacing (Two-way ANOVA, $F(3,108) = 4.39$, $p < 0.05$) were statistically significant, but no interaction between size and spacing was detected. Similar results were obtained for other handgrips.

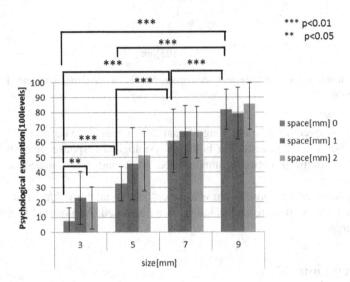

Fig. 8. Relationships between size, space and subjective evaluation points under dominant-handed dominant-thumb operation

Subjective evaluation points related to the ease of touch on command buttons increased with the button size (Bonferroni multiple comparison). Evaluation of the 3-mm buttons was especially low (around 20 points or less), with a significant increase as spacing was increased from 0 mm to 2 mm (Bonferroni multiple comparison).

3.3 Physiological Evaluation

It is known that physiological reactions markedly differ between individuals. Therefore, the SCR data were analysed as follows. The SCR of an individual was obtained as the average SCR during task performance minus the average resting SCR (measured prior to experiment). Also, the data measured from the same handgrip were standardized to satisfy average = 0 and variance = 1. In addition, because abnormal SCR measurements were obtained from three of the participants, the measured data are those from seven participants. SCR results, results under dominant-handed dominant-thumb operations, analysed by two-way ANOVA, are shown in Fig.8. Button size and spacing exerted no significant effects on physiological response, nor was any interaction between size and space detected.

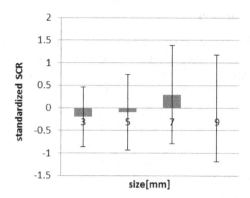

Fig. 9. Relationship between size and standardized SCR under dominant-handed dominant-thumb operation

Although no overall statistically significant differences were observed, on an average, 7-mm button size generated a higher physiological response than other button sizes. The relationship between standardized SCR and size showed an inverted U-shaped structure.

This physiological response curve was dependent on handgrip. Under the other two types of handgrip, SCR increased as button size decreased. An inverted U relationship did not emerge.

4   Discussion

The analysis of input accuracy and performance time revealed that users could operate exactly and quickly if command buttons were sufficiently large, consistent with a general hypothesis. Input accuracy was re-assessed for the eight participants in an ordinary manner using a smartphone (Fig.10).

In this sample, input accuracy was around 50% for the 3-mm buttons, but exceeded 80% and 90% for the 7-mm and 9-mm buttons, respectively. However, regardless of handgrip, the accuracy improvement as button size increased from 5 to 9 mm was not statistically significant. Therefore, we consider that most users can touch buttons over 7 mm 'exactly and quickly enough', whereas seasoned smartphone users can likely manipulate smaller buttons (5 mm) with an equally high accuracy.

However, we regard 9 mm as a suitable size for command buttons. With larger size buttons, the display has extra space and the 'ease of touch' judgment is maximized, as evidenced in the positive relationship between subjective evaluation points and increased size and spacing.

SCR analysis presents a different viewpoint. Ogawa et al. reported an inverted U relationship between 'interest' and information load (see Fig.11) [4].

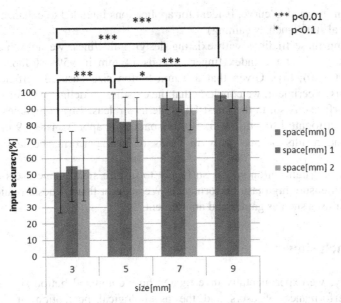

Fig. 10. Input accuracy as a function of size and space in smartphone users under dominant-handed dominant-thumb operation

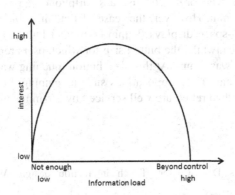

Fig. 11. Relation between 'interest' and information load (re-edited based on the chart presented by Ogawa, et. al. [4])

While the theory of Ogawa and colleagues is not entirely consistent with that of our study, it suggests that the inverted U-shaped relationship between load, which may be interpreted as 'difficulty to touch' and button size reflects a correspondence between the physiological response (SCR measurements) and psychological response, in particular, excitement and awareness. From the results of this experiment, the optimal size at which participants report exact and easy touching can be assumed as 7 mm. At this size, participants may conduct operations under the most active and excited psychological conditions. Therefore, a 7-mm command button, corresponding to the top of an inverted U curve, is ideal for applications intended to enhance the user's psychological state (such as gaming).

Comparing these findings with existing design guidelines, we note that the peripheral joint width of the index finger exceeds 14 mm in 95% of Japanese males (IOS9251-9(2000); [5]). Given that a 9-mm button size ensured sufficient performance in this experiment, we conclude that the existing guidelines are not suitable for modern interfaces. Also, in the latest UI guidelines released by companies, the minimum space allocated to button size plus spacing is approximately 9 mm, consistent with the results of our study in terms of task performance and subjective evaluation.

However, a 7-mm button size is sufficient to inspire smartphone users a sense of 'interest' and ensure high task performance. We suggest that UI design guidelines be reviewed for uses such as games and amusement.

5   Conclusion

In this study, we experimentally investigated how command button size affects the physical performance of users and the psychological perception of smartphone devices.

It was found that most users can easily and accurately touch command buttons exceeding 7 mm. Users who ordinarily use a smartphone can accurately manipulate buttons as small as 5 mm. However, the 'ease of touching' increases as button size increases. Thus, extra-space displays (9 mm command buttons) appear to offer the most user comfort. Meanwhile, the button size for which users reported 'not too difficult and not too easy' was 7 mm. At this size, button touching was accompanied with a rise in user excitement. Thus, applications such as gaming, in which users should feel excitement rather than relief, are well serviced by a 7-mm command button.

References

1. Microsoft: Windows Dev. Center: Touch interaction design (Windows Store apps) (January 13, 2013),
   http://msdn.microsoft.com/ja-jp/library/windows/apps/hh465415
2. Apple: iOS human interface guideline (2011)
3. Nokia: NOKIA Developer: S60 5th Edition C++ Developer's Library v2.1 (January 13, 2013),
   http://library.developer.nokia.com/
   index.jsp?topic=/S60_5th_Edition_Cpp_Developers_Library/
   GUID-5486EFD3-4660-4C19-A007-286DE48F6EEF.html
4. Ogawa, S.: Concept of playing—the basis of intent—the collection of treatises of economics research center, vol. 26, pp. 99–119 (2003)
5. ISO9241-9: Ergonomic Requirements for Office Work with Visual Display Terminals (VDTs) –Part 9, Requirements for Non-Keyboard Input Devices (2000)

Changes in Posture of the Upper Extremity Through the Use of Various Sizes of Tablets and Characters

Hiroki Maniwa[1], Kentaro Kotani[2], Satoshi Suzuki[2], and Takafumi Asao[2]

[1] Graduate School of Science and Engineering
[2] Faculty of Engineering Science
Kansai University,
3-3-35 Yamate-cho, Suita, Osaka 564-8680, Japan
k853884@kansai-u.ac.jp

Abstract. The aim of this study was to analyze the posture of the upper extremities during the use of mobile communication devices. Using various sizes of mobile devices and display characters, we examined subjective muscular loads, viewing distances, and joint angles in the head, neck, shoulder, elbow, and lower back. No postural differences were found between the use of 7-in and 10-in devices, whereas the head and neck were significantly flexed and the elbow angles were decreased during the use of the 13-in device. Character size significantly affected the viewing distance; however, no differences in body angles were found. Participants continually increased their muscular loads during the task by flexing the head and neck, despite their high subjective discomfort levels in the neck and upper arm.

Keywords: tablet devices, smartphone syndrome, upper extremity posture, angle analysis.

1 Introduction

The use of small mobile communication devices equipped with touch panels has become common. The resulting increase in the incidence of musculoskeletal disorders (MSDs) caused by extensive use of these devices (e.g., text messaging and viewing Web pages) has become a major concern [1]. Previous studies on MSDs associated with the extensive use of mobile devices have focused on subjective muscle loads on the upper extremities [2] and on the movement of the thumb during device operation [3]. The posture assumed during mobile device use has been reported to result in tensing of the upper extremities, which can lead to the development of MSDs [4]. However, no reports have addressed how changes in upper extremity posture during the use of mobile devices may affect MSDs risk. Moreover, no objective data have been reported regarding the pathology of smartphone syndrome, caused by extensive use of mobile devices, in relation to the size of the mobile device [3]. Although studies [5] have reported that the size of the characters on the display screen affects readability, the effect of character size on upper extremity posture has not been addressed.

Establishing guidelines to prevent MSDs caused by extensive use of mobile devices is important. To begin the establishment of such guidelines, we considered it

S. Yamamoto (Ed.): HIMI/HCII 2013, Part I, LNCS 8016, pp. 89–96, 2013.

important to objectively assess the posture of the upper extremities during the use of devices with different sizes of characters and display areas. In this study, we report the changes in upper extremity posture depending on the size of the mobile device used and the size of the characters displayed on its screen.

2   Method

2.1   Participants

Ten right-handed university students who used mobile devices regularly (5 men and 5 women) participated in the experiment. Their corrected vision was greater than 20/30.

2.2   Experimental Apparatus

In this study, video images were obtained while the participant was operating the mobile device to observe whether the posture of the upper extremities changed during device use. A digital video camera (PJ760V, SONY) was used, and the frame rate of the video was set to 29 fps. Three mobile devices of different sizes (7-in TOSHIBA REGZA AT570, 10-in AT700, and 13-in AT830) were used (Figure 1). Their weights were 332 g, 535 g, and 1000 g, respectively.

Fig. 1. Mobile devices used in the experiment
(7 in, 10 in, and 13 in, from left to right)

2.3   Experimental Procedures

Colored markers (diameter, 50 mm) were attached to the bodies of the participants to assist in the measurement of dynamic angular changes in upper extremity posture. The markers were attached to the body at the canthus, tragus, C7 vertebra, acromion, elbow, and lower back and at the center of the device, as shown in Figure 2.

In this experiment, 3 character sizes (small, 1×1 mm; medium, 3×3 mm; and large, 5×5 mm) and 3 display sizes (7 in, 10 in, and 13 in) were chosen as independent variables, giving a total of 9 combinations. The order of the trials was randomized.

Fig. 2. Location of the markers

To become familiar with the operation of the mobile devices used in the experiment, participants underwent practice sessions before the experiment. The input method was set to flick motion. Participants were instructed to use the left hand for grasping the device and the right hand for character entry. At the start of the trial, participants were asked to perform a simple text-editing operation for 5 minutes. In addition, they were instructed orally to enter the text message as follows: "There is no need to try to enter as fast as you can. Please focus on the work on your own pace." After 5 minutes, the instructor gave a signal to stop. After each trial, the participants filled out a questionnaire regarding the subjective muscular loads during operation of the mobile device.

3 Data Analysis

3.1 Video Analysis of Dynamic Angular Changes in Body Position

Dynamic angular changes were determined using an image processor (Labview, National Instruments). A still image was extracted every 30 sec (from 0 sec to 300 sec) for further analysis. Image analysis techniques were used to obtain the angles of the head, neck, shoulder, elbow, and lower back and the viewing distance. Angles were estimated using the reference markers, following the regimen reported by Sommerich et al. [6].

3.2 Range of Motion

The range of motion in the upper extremities, especially the head and neck, vary widely among participants [7]. Therefore, even if the same angle was obtained for different participants, the absolute range of motion could differ between participants. In this study, we used percentage range of motion (%ROM) as an index for normalizing the magnitude of the angle to represent the level of body flexion for each participant. Therefore, we defined "zero position" as the neutral posture assumed when relaxed. The %ROM was calculated as the absolute range of motion divided into the direction of extension and flexion and normalized by the maximum angles, as shown in Figure 3.

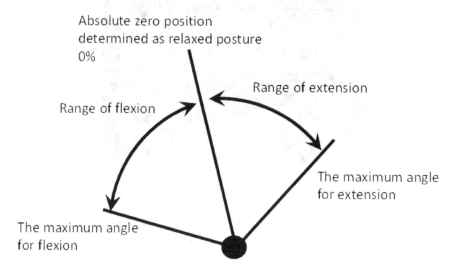

Fig. 3. Flexion and extension motions starting from a relaxed posture (absolute zero position)

3.3   Collecting and Analyzing Subjective Responses

Simultaneous with measurements of the upper extremity angle, the subjective discomfort level caused by the muscular load was assessed using the Borg Scale (CR-10). Subjective responses were recorded for eye fatigue and muscular loads of the upper back, neck, and upper left arm [3]. In addition, the participants were instructed to report any sense of muscular load in areas other than those about which we specifically inquired. For statistical analysis, ANOVA was used to analyze data on each body angle and viewing distance, as well as subjective responses, in relation to the independent variables of device and character size.

4   Results

4.1   Effect of Display Size on Upper Extremity Posture

The size of the mobile device was significantly associated with the viewing distance; flexion angles at the head, neck and elbow; and subjective muscular loads on the neck and left upper arm (Table 1). Multiple comparisons revealed that there were no significant differences between viewing distances for 7-in and 10-in devices. However, a significant difference was observed between the viewing distances for 13-in, 7-in, and 10-in devices. No significant difference was observed with respect to eye fatigue, the subjective muscular load on the upper back, or the flexion angle at the shoulder and lower back.

Table 1. Viewing distance, body angles, subjective muscular loads, and eye fatigue according to the size of the mobile device

$* *$; $p<0.01$

	7in	10in	13in	Significance
Viewing distance [mm]	252	251	328	**
Flexion at the head [%]	49%	48%	57%	**
Flexion at the neck [%]	38%	38%	52%	**
Flexion at the shoulder [%]	−1%	−3%	−3%	NS
Flexion at the elbow [%]	52%	53%	38%	**
Flexion at the lower back [%]	5%	4%	6%	NS
Subjective muscular load at the upper back [−]	3.63	3.83	4.27	NS
Subjective muscular load at the neck [−]	2.93	3.33	4.56	**
Subjective muscular load at the left upper arm [−]	3.67	4.33	5.41	**
Eye fatigue level [−]	2.36	2.33	2.73	NS

Table 2. Viewing distance, body angles, subjective muscular loads, and eye fatigue in relation to character size

$* *$; $p<0.01$

	small	mid	large	Significance
Viewing distance [mm]	258	284	288	**
Flexion at the head [%]	51%	52%	51%	NS
Flexion at the neck [%]	43%	44%	41%	NS
Flexion at the shoulder [%]	−2%	−2%	−2%	NS
Flexion at the elbow [%]	50%	47%	47%	NS
Flexion at the lower back [%]	5%	5%	5%	NS
Subjective muscular load at the upper back [−]	4.13	3.77	3.67	NS
Subjective muscular load at the neck [−]	3.89	3.56	3.37	NS
Subjective muscular load at the left upper arm [−]	4.78	4.48	4.15	NS
Eye fatigue level [−]	2.97	2.33	2.12	NS

A significant correlation was observed between viewing distance and character size. Multiple comparisons revealed significant differences in the viewing distance between the large (5 × 5) and small (1 × 1) character sizes and between the medium

(3 × 3) and small character sizes (1 × 1) (Table 2). No significant difference was found for any of the other variables.

4.2   Effect of Task Performance Time on Upper Extremity Posture

According to Lin et al. [4], people tend to unconsciously build up tension in the upper extremities, especially the neck and shoulders, during extensive operation of mobile communication devices. It is therefore likely that the posture of the upper extremities changes with the time of mobile device operation. To test this hypothesis, we compared the average flexion angles in each part of the upper extremities and the viewing distance after 30 and 300 sec of mobile device operation (Tables 3–5).

Table 3. Changes in flexion angles of the upper extremities and viewing distance with operation time of a 7-in mobile device

∗ ∗ ; p<0.01   ∗ ; p<0.05

	30[sec]	300[sec]	Significance
Viewing distance [mm]	258	239	∗∗
Flexion at the head [%]	43%	50%	∗
Flexion at the neck [%]	34%	40%	∗∗
Flexion at the shoulder [%]	-2%	-2%	NS
Flexion at the elbow [%]	49%	52%	∗∗
Flexion at the lower back [%]	3%	3%	NS

Table 4. Changes in flexion angles of the upper extremities and viewing distance with operation time of a 10-in mobile device

∗ ; p＜0.05   †; p＜0.1

	30[sec]	300[sec]	Significance
Viewing distance [mm]	258	245	†
Flexion at the head [%]	44%	49%	∗
Flexion at the neck [%]	34%	35%	NS
Flexion at the shoulder [%]	-3%	-3%	NS
Flexion at the elbow [%]	49%	51%	NS
Flexion at the lower back [%]	6%	6%	NS

Table 5. Changes in flexion angles of the upper extremities and viewing distance with operation time of a 13-in mobile device

∗ ∗ ; p<0.01   ∗ ; p<0.05

	30[sec]	300[sec]	Significance
Viewing distance [mm]	282	346	∗
Flexion at the head [%]	48%	67%	∗∗
Flexion at the neck [%]	38%	61%	∗∗
Flexion at the shoulder [%]	-1%	-3%	NS
Flexion at the elbow [%]	41%	26%	∗
Flexion at the lower back [%]	4%	6%	∗

The viewing distance significantly decreased and the flexion angles in the head, neck, and elbow significantly increased between 30 and 300 sec of mobile device operation (Table 3). The viewing distance decreased and the flexion angles in the head significantly increased between 30 and 300 sec of mobile device operation (Table 4). The viewing distance and the flexion angles in the head, neck, elbow, and lower back significantly increased between 30 to 300 sec of mobile device operation (Table 5). Therefore, the posture of the upper extremities changed with performance time; the flexion angles increased in the head, neck, and lower back and decreased in the elbow (with the viewing distance) for the 13-in device compared to the other devices.

5   Discussion

The viewing distance and the posture of the upper extremities changed with the size of the mobile device. A significant change was observed in the flexion angles of the head, neck, and elbow with the time of device operation of the 13-in device but not the 7- or 10-in device. In particular, a high subjective muscular load on the left arm was observed compared to the other parts of the body during operation of the 13-in device. This load may lead to the observed change in posture, most often the place-ment of the device on top of the thigh to support the weight of the device, causing hyperflexion of the head and neck. If the weight of the device exceeded the level that the participant could hold while in an upright position, they changed the viewing dis-tance and hyperflexed the head and neck. While the participants strongly felt that the subjective muscular load on the neck increased with increasing size of the mobile device, they tended to continue flexing the head and neck, with more neck flexion over time. A previous anatomical study [7] reported that flexing the head and neck affects hypertension of the trapezius, located in the upper back. However, no signifi-cant differences in the subjective muscular load in the upper back were observed, although the flexion angles of the head and neck significantly increased with increase in size of the mobile device. This observation is consistent with the report by Berolo et al. [2], suggesting that the subjective muscular load on the upper back does not necessarily lead to hypertonus of the trapezius from flexion of the head and neck.

Increasing the character size did not appear to change the angle of any part of the upper extremity, although the viewing distance increased. This observation suggests that the whole upper body cooperatively adjusted to decrease the viewing distance, not just one isolated part of the body. Enlarging the text on the mobile device actually produced a change in the posture of the upper extremities. A comparison of differenc-es in muscle strength and stature of participants is required to clarify whether text enlargement effectively reduces the risk of MSDs.

In this study, we observed that the flexion angles of the head and the viewing dis-tance changed significantly with the time of mobile device operation. Lin et al. [4] reported that muscle activity in the upper extremities changes under different working conditions (e.g., before work, during the first work break, during the second work break, and after work); however, studies regarding dynamic changes in posture during work have not been reported thus far. In our study, the flexion angle of the head in-creased with increasing time of mobile device operation. This observation indicates that the upper extremities remained tense throughout the task. Additional and more quantitative evaluation is therefore possible by studying the effect of muscular loads induced by different continual operation. Such information may help to clarify the relationship between mobile device use and the risk of developing MSDs.

6 Conclusion

This study aimed to determine whether changes in posture during mobile device use are related to the size of characters displayed on the screen or the mobile device size. No postural differences were found between the use of 7-in and 10-in devices, whereas the head and neck were significantly flexed and the elbow angles were decreased during the use of the 13-in device. We observed a tendency to support the subjective muscular load on the arm by resting the mobile device on the thigh. Character size did not affect posture but significantly affected the viewing distance; however, no differences were found in the body angles. Tension in the upper body increased with operation time of the mobile device; thus, operation of such devices for continuous stretches of time without breaks may be related to the risk of developing MSDs. Further research should focus on relating quantitative muscular loads recorded by electromyography to postural changes associated with the operation time of mobile devices.

Acknowledgements. Part of the present study was funded by Research Group Ecological Interface Design and Kansai University Kakenhi of the Japan Society for the Promotion of Science (24370143, 24657182).

References

1. Judith, G., Driban, J., Thomas, N., Chakravarty, T., Channell, S., Komaroff, E.: Postures, typing strategies, and gender differences in mobile device usage: An observational study. Applied Ergonomics 43, 408–412 (2012)
2. Berolo, S., Wells, R.P., Amick, B.C.: Musculoskeletal symptoms among mobile hand-held device users and their relationship to device use: A preliminary study in a Canadian university population. Applied Ergonomics 42, 371–378 (2011)
3. Gustafsson, E., Johnson, P.W., Hagberg, M.: Thumb postures and physical loads during mobile phone use - A comparison of young adults with and without musculoskeletal symptoms. Journal of Electromyography and Kinesiology 20, 127–135 (2010)
4. Lin, I.-M., Peper, E.: Psychophysiological patterns during cell phone text messaging: A Preliminary Study. Applied Psychophysiology and Biofeedback 34, 53–57 (2009)
5. Kubota, S.: Effects of character size, character format, and pixel density on subjective legibility of reflective liquid crystal displays for personal digital assistants. The Institute of Image Information and Television Engineers 55(10), 1363–1366 (2001)
6. Sommerich, C., Starr, H., Smith, C., Shivers, C.: Effects of notebook, computer configuration and task on user biomechanics, productivity, and comfort. International Journal of Industrial Ergonomics 30, 7–31 (2002)
7. Donald, N., Hirata, T., Hirata, S.: Kinesiology of the Musculoskeletal System Foundations for Physical Rehabilitation. Ishiyaku Shuppan Kabushikigaisha, 128–360 (2008) (in Japanese)

GUI Efficiency Comparison Between Windows and Mac

Eric McCary and Jingyaun Zhang

The University of Alabama, Computer Science Department
Tuscaloosa, Alabama 35487-0290
eamccary@crimson.ua.edu

Abstract. In present times, it is not uncommon to have a desktop with two or more monitors. How these operating systems perform in a multiple monitor environment is an interesting topic. In this work, we will evaluate the efficiency of and compare how two popular operating systems, Windows and Mac OS, perform in large and multiple monitor environments. In particular, we will evaluate the performance of menu bars in both operating systems as they serve a near identical purpose and have the same functionality while providing their offerings differently. It is well-known that Mac OS uses a menu bar at the top of the screen (global) and Windows uses a menu bar attached to the top of its respective application (local). The conducted user study shows that the overall performance of Windows menu bar was better than that of the Mac menu bar implementation in the conducted tests.

Keywords: Graphical User Interface (GUI), Menu Bar, Title Bar, Operating System, Locality.

1 Introduction

Graphical User Interfaces (GUIs) have become an integral part of the average individual's everyday activities even in instances where one may not be aware of its composition or of its existence. Modern operating systems normally come packaged with a graphical user interface, and these GUIs have continuously evolved over the years, and in most cases have extensively enhanced the user experience with every major release. For example, Windows and Mac have GUIs that are tightly integrated into their OS kernels and have made significant changes on nearly all of their versions. [1]

Window's and Mac's GUI implementation both support the use of large and multiple monitor environments. This functionality was eventually added due to the changing customer desire and the cheaper cost of display equipment. Support for these multiple monitor configurations was added to Windows in its Windows 98 OS, and Mac implemented this as a standard feature in 1987. [2]

A significant occurrence in GUI efficiency is the convergence of stylistic elements belonging to Mac OS X and Windows GUIs. This fact brings to our attention the amount of similarity found in these two operating systems, and upon observation beyond the "look and feel", there are more resemblances and likeness of functionality. With so little difference between core functionality, it is useful to understand the

S. Yamamoto (Ed.): HIMI/HCII 2013, Part I, LNCS 8016, pp. 97–106, 2013.

differing means of utilizing the functionality offered by the OS GUIs and how efficient and user-friendly these methods are. More specifically, how efficiently these two GUI styles will handle themselves in environments with large or multiple display screens.

Since these two operating systems implement their menu bars differently, it is useful to measure the disparity in efficiency among them in single and multiple display scenarios. This paper will evaluate the graphical implementation of the menu bar in the GUIs used by Microsoft Windows and Mac OS X.

2   Initial Analysis

An excellent tool to measure efficiency of interface design is Fitts' Law. Fitts' Law, as defined in [3] as a mathematical model of fine motor control which predicts how long it takes to move from one position to another as a function of the distance to and size of the target area. Although Fitts' model was originally formulated to project how quickly a human could point at a physical button, we can use the same set of rules to determine how quickly we can acquire specific points or objects on a screen. The law also states that the bigger buttons are the faster they can be accessed and should be used for more important functions. This law has been previously defined as:

$$\text{Time} = a + b \log 2 \, (2D \, / \, W + 1) \tag{1}$$

Mathematically interpreted, Fitts' Law is a linear regression model for a 2-dimensional space. [4] We will define D as the approximate distance of the impending movement and W is the width of the target. a *(intercept)* and b *(slope)* are empirical constants determined through linear regression which are device dependent.

The authors in [5] break the law down into two simple concepts:

- The farther away a target is, the longer it takes to acquire it with the mouse.
- The smaller a target is, the longer it takes to acquire it with the mouse.

For our purposes, Fitts' law will be used as a quantitative method of modeling user performance in rapid, aimed movements, where one's appendage starts at rest at a specific start position, and moves to rest within a target area while controlling a pointing device.

It is important to note the edges of a screen which ends the visible and tangible viewing area. These sections are thought of to be infinitely wide or tall because it is not possible to scroll or move past these areas. For example, it is not possible to scroll left past the leftmost boundary of a display. So we describe any object on the outermost borders as being infinitely wide or tall.

The authors in [6] explain how bigger targets are easier to click, and edge-adjacent targets are effectively infinitely big. This makes us aware of the fact that in order to improve user accuracy or acquisition speed, we can either make the desired object larger, or closer. To further examine this, we can inspect the equation that represents Fitts' Law with inputs from two hypothetical scenarios. These scenarios will demonstrate attributes that an infinitely large menu bar and a menu bar which has excellent proximity to its application would possess. If we maintain the values of a and b (which means the start and end locations lie on the same vector on a 2D plane, or in this case, the display screen), we can determine the disparity in *Time* which the equations will yield.

$$M1: Time = a + b \log2 [\ 2(1000) / \infty + 1] \tag{2}$$

$$M2: Time = a + b \log2 [\ 2(0.001) / 100 + 1] \tag{3}$$

M1 represents the equation with inputs from an infinitely large menu bar, while *M2* represents a menu bar which is attached to its application. We can see that the solutions to these equations will be very small in either case, and in reality, the value of D in M2 will likely be a very small number, making both *Time* values very close to zero.

There are many of such truths of interface that extend beyond what the user is used to or favors, and good interface design requires close attention to these. So familiarity has a lot to do with comfort and ease of use and users frequently prefer the familiar to the more usable.

Fitts' Law can be utilized to scientifically estimate the results of the experiment to be detailed later in the paper. This process can provide users with a definitive value which delivers the calculated efficiency of acquiring the menu bar in each of the GUIs being tested.

3   Effect of Screen Sizes

Screen size further complicates the efficiency in a GUI when dealing with differing methodologies of menu bar placement. This is important to consider as the technological trends seem to be incorporating larger and larger screens into the majority of environments where computers are used with exception to mobile devices.

Mac OS X is installed on a limited set of hardware. The smallest of these is an 11-inch MacBook air. Mac OS X works well in this environment, as the menu bar of applications is detached and resides on the top of the screen. This type of configuration maintains a shorter travel distance to the buttons belonging to the running program. This is achieved due to the small screen size of this specific laptop. So in this situation there is less work to be done by the user in order to access application controls. On the other end of the spectrum, in a situation where OS X is being displayed on a large screen or even multiple screens, this operating system's menu bar is sometimes located a great distance from the focused application.

As in both OS GUIs, a single instance of application control objects being located on a single screen culminates into a concept of a main screen. This basically means that objects such as the Menu Bar can only be located on this singular screen. The fact that the menu bar can only reside on this screen may create more efficiency difficulties. Considering that normally when one uses multiple screens to expand their workspace, this individual would like to move application and documents into windows other than the main screen. Moving back and forth between these screens may create more work for the user.

Windows software can be installed on a wide variety of devices with a wide range of screen sizes. This operating system also makes use of the main screen concept which will keep its taskbar on a single window when utilizing multiple monitors. However, Windows operates somewhat differently from Mac OS X with its menu bars for an application and allows for menu bars to be attached to their respective applications.

When dealing with single monitors of various sizes, Windows GUI configuration allows for universal locality of an application's control objects, including the menu bar. In this case, regardless of the screen size, the applications in use will still be relatively near to their respective controls and functional buttons.

We will be measuring efficiency of the GUI in part by the size and distance of objects that have an important relationship with each other. Many of the comparisons and tests will be evaluated with this premise in mind.

4   Application/Document Menu Bar

In an operating system, a menu bar is a horizontal strip that contains lists of available menus for a certain program. Windows and Mac OS X have different implementations of their respective menu bars which each of their dedicated followers seem to enjoy equally as much. In this section we will discuss each of the implementations.

Mac describes their menu bar as the semi-transparent bar that spans the entire width of the desktop at the top of the screen [7]. Their implementation is unique, in that is not attached to the application or document that it belongs to. For all of the applications running, there is a single menu bar that maintains the current application's menu options.

Varying Mac applications may have menu bars built onto them. Often these are open-source projects or java applications whose prime targets are not necessarily always Mac users. In addition to application specific menu options, Mac's global menu bar contains the Apple Menu, and it is always present, no matter which application you are using. It gives you quick access to a few essential system functions which are options Windows includes on its taskbar (which is comparable to Mac's Dock).

The placement of Mac's menu bar is important to consider. The top of the screen location is "infinitely tall". The acquisition of Mac's menu bar, according to Fitts' Law, takes advantage of its positioning and infinitely tall size. Also, multiple applications may be open simultaneously must also be addressed. These matters may occupy the current focus which will reassign the contents of the menu bar to the application currently in focus. When utilizing Fitts' Law to calculate the acquisition time of the menu bar, one would have to add the extra time to bring an application into focus which would be an inconvenience. Also, there may be multiple monitors in use. This will create in increase in total acquisition time as the time to navigate to the "main screen" must be added into the equation.

Windows menu bar is attached to whichever application it belongs to. This means that there can be multiple menu bars active simultaneously. This menu, much like Mac OS X menu bar menu, will be an interface to important functions offered by the application itself.

In Windows, there are no special cases when calculating the acquisition time for the menu bar. The reason for this is that the menu bar is attached to each application. This means no extra factors added in (screen navigation, focus...) as the application interface is uniform in Windows and there are no shared modules which may inconvenience the user. Also, the menu bar itself and its' buttons will be much smaller than those belonging to a Mac menu bar. Application control buttons and menus on Windows are of a fixed size based on the application while on a Mac they are "infinitely tall".

According to [3] Bruce Tognazzini, human computer interaction professional, claims the Mac OS menu bars can be accessed up to five times faster due to Fitts' law because the menu bar lies on a screen edge. The time to acquire a target is a function of the distance to and size of the target, with this knowledge Apple claims their pulldown menu acquisition can be approximately five times faster than Windows menu acquisition.

One can argue that any GUI offers the same "top of the screen" location if a window is simply maximized. Also, if one is utilizing an application and would like to close another, they would have to select the desired application to focus in Mac OS GUI while in Windows buttons grab the focus when the mouse hovers over it, and then close the application. Fitts' Law does not account for the time that this extra step consumes. The effectiveness of this technique is also reduced on larger screens or with low mouse acceleration curves, especially due to the time required to travel back to a target in the window after using the menu. [8]

It is also important to consider the menu bars proximity to the application, and that its positioning is based on logically sound reasoning. Another important fact to consider is that most operating system environments place the menus within the application window, and that is a familiar location.

5   Experiments

Experiments were conducted to test both of these GUI's efficiency. Each experiment yielded the time and distance it takes for a user to acquire several different control objects offered by the operating systems GUI.

Thirty participants were recruited to create the data necessary for this study. Twelve of the thirty expressed being familiar or expert users of Mac OS, while the others were primarily Windows users. The process was officially approved by the IRB at The University of Alabama and actions were consented to by the participants.

Each of the tests is comprised of a series of clicks with a pointing device which will each prompt the next step in the test. Upon the end of the testing session, the application will display the timing and distance results to the user. This test will record the time and distance traveled per task, and the deviation from the "best" possible route to complete the task (which will be a straight line).

5.1   Intuitive Impressions

The experiment is expected to gather data which will undoubtedly determine which of these two GUIs is more efficient in completing specific and common tasks. Initial impressions were based on most of the general population being more familiar with the Windows GUI environment, and environments fashioned like it. Since Windows' menu bar is based on locality to application that owns it, and excels in certain situations where the display is larger than normal or when multiple displays which span a large area are in use.

While Windows' menu bar has the locality advantage in all situations other than full screen mode, Mac's menu bar is infinitely tall and users have the ability to simply throw the pointing device to the corner of the screen and acquire their menu.

Taking these details into consideration, the initial assumption is that Windows GUI would be the better option when comparing distance traveled to acquire the menu bar, while Mac would dominate the acquisition time category. This premise takes into account the differing screen sizes in use today, and the skill level and ability of the average user.

5.2   Experiment Detail

A program was written that simulates the GUI environments (Mac and Windows), and will allow for the completion of identical tasks while recording the time and distance of each of the tasks. This program was built with java on Windows 7 and Mac OS X Lion.

To record data, the program will present the user with a window which simulates an application. A red square will serve as the starting point for the current task. The initial view of the application is the same in each of the tests, while the tasks in each test are in the same order and routine. Figure 1 displays one of the testing environments for a task. For this specific widow size there will be a total of seven separate tasks (represented by each of the red squares) which will generate new data about the user and the GUI which is simulated as a housing for this application in the specific task.

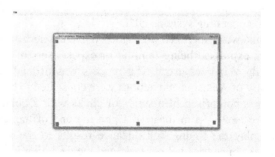

Fig. 1. Task start screen (Medium Window)

Once the starting point is clicked, the data from the actions which follow immediately will be recorded which should culminate with the user acquiring the File Menu in the simulated environment. The final data consists of distance per task, time per task, and each point the pointing device traverses over during the task session.

This data is recorded in three separate sessions where the participant will repeatedly acquire the menu bar in environments with different windows sizes. The largest windows size has nine points, the medium sized window has seven points, and the smallest window is host to a single point in the center. Each of these "start points" (red squares) will be acquired at the beginning of each task which upon completion (the user acquires the File Menu), will yield the desired result data.

6   Results

The data did not completely support the initial assumption that Mac's infinitely large menu bar would prove to increase acquisition rate. In fact, acquiring Mac's menu bar proved to be slightly slower on average in all but four of the tasks. These tasks were acquiring the menu bar from the bottom two corners of the medium sized window, and the top and bottom middle of the maximized window. Figure 2 shows the average time it took to complete a task during the tests below. This data is important to consider while misleading. Fast times could equate to the user being comfortable with the GUI (as suspected of the Windows users), or the ease of use and efficiency of the GUI.

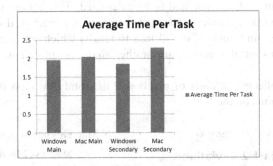

Fig. 2. Average Time per Task

When observing distance efficiency, it is obvious that Windows will likely require the user to move the pointing device the least distance with an acceptable amount of error. This premise was proven true as Windows was more efficient in all tasks. This data is represented in Figure 3. As is made understandable by the figure, Mac tasks took nearly twice as long as the Windows tasks. This is obviously directly affected by the environments locations of the features on the application which is determines the locality.

There is a very large disparity in this category with the advantage belonging to Windows. When comparing the distance traveled per amount of time, Mac more than doubles Windows in this category. This is partially a product of Mac's static menu bar position even though it is infinitely large. Windows menu bar is closer, but must move and resize itself as the window resizes and moves.

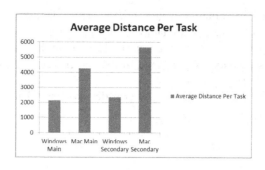

Fig. 3. Average Distance per Task

7   Faults and Error

To better understand the role of context in error inclusion and its adequacy, the deviation along the x-axis of the path that the participant took en route to completing each task was analyzed. This was accomplished by locating the start and end points of the task and every point directly between the two. In addition, the distance the participant's path is from each x-value had to be calculated. This data is very important to the experiment. While a normal amount of deviation is expected, if deviation is constantly above a certain threshold it will lead to results which are more defined by the ability and actions of the participants rather than the placement of objects and accessibility of the GUI.

This data is collected in units of pixels and the total deviation is the sum of the deviation of all points on the line.

Windows Deviation along x-axis: Mac Deviation along x-axis:

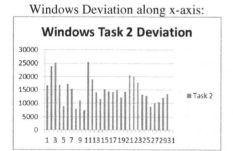

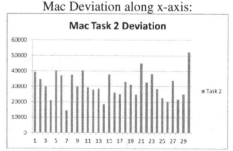

Fig. 4. Windows Task 2 Deviation   **Fig. 5.** Mac Task 2 Deviation

The numbers here are much more sporadic as they depend mainly on the participants' ability and focus. Each participant was encouraged to complete the tasks as they would in their most comfortable environment. It is understandable that the amount of deviation is greater on tasks executed in the Mac environment as the travel distance to complete the tasks is so much greater which creates more of an opportunity for error. With this method of error calculation, travel distance as well a precision plays a large role in the participants overall route efficiency. Taking all of these factors into account will help us to come to the best conclusion.

The deviation recorded for each task is displayed as a summation of the deviation at each point which the user traversed over during task completion. Understanding that the Mac tasks on average are several times more than that of the Windows tasks, we can calculate the exact ratio of time per unit of distance. This will make the deviation data more relevant and useful. For example, the distance ratio of the Mac to Windows tasks on the main screen is approximately 3.321467. This means if we divide each of the tasks in the Mac deviation by this amount, will have the amount of deviation per an equal amount of distance which makes the two categories comparable.

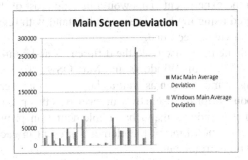

Fig. 6. Windows Deviation

Here, the Windows tasks have incurred more error in 5 of the 15 tasks. This can be attributed solely to the actions of the user, as the paths to complete tasks are all equally attainable.

The tasks set in the Windows GUI were completed slightly faster than the identical task in the Mac GUI. In terms of distance, the average distance per task in the Mac GUI is nearly double that in the Windows environment. When taking these facts into account, we see that the distance covered per unit of time is much more efficient in the Mac environment as the participants covered distance significantly faster here.

The experiment also calculated the deviation that the participants added in error to their routes along with the total time. In observing these details, we see that tasks completed in the simulated Mac environment were completed much more efficiently from a distance per unit of time standpoint due to the distance of the tasks being more the double the length of the Windows tasks while the deviation is relatively the same.

8   Conclusion

When determining the overall GUI efficiency, we must understand that the speed with which the participants completed the tasks reveals little about the efficiency of the environment whether it is of a small screen size or multi-monitor format. We must first weigh the value of the distance of the elements present on the interface as well as the time participants took to complete the tasks as the first line of assessment, then weigh the deviation results and other factors exposed in this study. This will render our final result.

The results from this study lead us to conclude that Windows menu bar presents a shorter travel distance in identical situations than Macs' menu bar. Although In certain situations, each GUI environment has its advantages. For example, Mac's GUI excels in scenarios where full screen mode is in use. The results yielded in these situations displayed that the time per task in a Mac environment is less, while the distances are relatively equivalent. In situations where small or overly large windows sizes are necessary, Windows excels. The amount of deviation introduced into the experiments makes it difficult to reach a clear cut victor but according to the overall results, Windows menu bar implementation is more efficient when completing tasks such as or similar to the ones in the experiment. This would include most of the everyday operations that are completed using the bar. These results stand with regard to the minimal amount of difference in values recorded.

This paper has evaluated and discussed the differences and similarities between the menu bars utilized by Microsoft Windows and Mac OS X. These aspects were evaluated while operating in multiscreen as well as large and small screen environments. The experiment introduced for the user study described in this paper, was used to help solidify and prove that Windows menu bar implementation provided for a shorter travel distance and acquisition time of the elements present in each of the operating systems simulated GUI environments.

References

1. Dale. E.: Operating Systems Uncovered: The Inside Scoops Are Revealed (March 2012)
2. Dunn D., Mikes. N.: Multiple Monitor Computing. 9X Media Inc.,
   http://www.9xmedia.com/PDFs/
   9X_Media_multiple_monitor_whitepaper.pdf
3. Tognazzini, B.: First Principles of Interaction Design,
   http://www.asktog.com/basics/firstPrinciples.html#fittsLaw
4. MacKenzie, I.S.: Fitts' Law as a Performance Model in Human-Computer Interaction. Ph.D. Thesis, http://www.yorku.ca/mack/phd.html
5. Harris, J.: Giving You Fitts,
   http://blogs.msdn.com/b/jensenh/archive/2006/08/22/
   711808.aspx (August 22, 2006)
6. Atwood, J.: Fitts' Law and Infinite Width,
   http://www.codinghorror.com/blog/2006/08/
   fitts-law-and-infinite-width.html (August 9, 2006)
7. Apple Inc.: http://www.apple.com
8. Leigh D.: "Mac" menubar as default,
   http://lists.kde.org/?l=kde-look&m=95705988431395&w=2
   (April 30, 2000)

Correction Method Based on KI-VPA Model for Changes in Vibratory Perception Caused by Adaptation

Yuki Mori[1], Takayuki Tanaka[2], and Shun'ichi Kaneko[2]

[1] RIKEN, Nagoya, Aichi, Japan
mori@nagoya.riken.jp
[2] Hokkaido University, Sapporo, Hokkaido, Japan
{ttanaka,kaneko}@ssi.ist.hokudai.ac.jp

Abstract. This paper describes a method for correcting differences in human vibratory perception caused by sensory adaptation. Humans feel a vibrational strength when a vibrating device is held in the hand. However when the vibrational frequency is changed, human perception of the new frequency is affected by the vibrational frequency experienced before the change. This is called sensory adaptation. The Katagiri–Aida model-based vibratory perception adaptation (KI-VPA) mode can estimate changes in vibratory perception caused bt adaptation. We have developed a correction method on basis of the KI-VPA model and tested the method on ten human subjects. The results indicate that the proposed correction method reduced the effects of adaptive changes to vibratory perception.

Keywords: Vibration, Vibratory perception, Tactile sense, Vibration alert interface.

1 Introduction

In recent years, a number of studies on information presentation through touch have been conducted; examples include tactile display, sensory substitution and virtual reality [1, 2]. We have been developing a vibration alert interface (VAI), which is a handheld vibrating that conveys information such as distance and degree of risk by changing the vibrational frequency. The current studies of informational presentation mainly focused on the configuration of the device and its vibrational patterns for conveying precise information. However, to convey precise information, it needs to consider disturbance which effect vibration perception. Yao, H.S. et al. have examined relation between weight of vibrating device and perceived vibration strength [3]. Morioka et al. have reported difference in perception threshold caused by vibration direction [4]. Thus it is known that vibration sensation varies with various factors other than vibration amplitude and frequency. The paper by J. F. Hahn has reported vibrotactile adaptation and recovery [5], M.Tommerdahl et al. have demonstrated frequency discriminative capacity after adaptation to vibration stimulation [6]. Our focus has been on adaptation to vibratory perception. We have experimentally found that human vibratory perceptions change by adapting to the sensations caused by

S. Yamamoto (Ed.): HIMI/HCII 2013, Part I, LNCS 8016, pp. 107–116, 2013.

vibrations. In particular subjects feel different vibrational strengths from the same frequency when that frequency is the result of a change from other frequencies. We have also proposed the Katagiri-Aida model-based vibratory perception adaptation (KI-VPA) model to predict changes in vibratory perception caused by changes in frequency. The model correctly shows changes in human vibratory perception.

In this study, we show that the KI-VPA model can be used as the basis for correcting changes in vibratory perception that are caused by adaptation. The KI-VPA model provides correction frequency on the basis of the vibratory perception to be conveyed by VAI; the model also considers duration of the frequency experienced before the change. In human tests, in accordance with the frequency before the change, subjects felt a precise vibrational strength from the correction frequency after the change.

This paper is organized as follows. Section 2 describes an experiment that examines how vibratory perception is affected by the frequency before the change. Section 3 explains the modeling of the change in vibratory perception described in Section 2. Section 3 also describes our method for correcting this change. Section 4 presents results obtained from experiments with human subjects that verify the effectiveness of the correction method proposed in Section 3. Section 5 states conclusions drawn from this work.

2   Changes in Vibratory Perception Caused by Changes in Vibrational Frequency

2.1   Experimental Method

Many devices use vibrations to convey information or issue warnings. When a user feels a vibration from a device, the user interprets signals on the basis of the vibrational strength. However, even when the vibrational frequency is the same, the user can feel the differences in vibrational strength. The user can misinterpret signals because of adaptation; when the vibrational frequency changes, the frequency before the change affects the user's perception of the vibrations after the change. In this section, we discuss experiments that show how vibratory perceptions after a frequency change are affected by the frequency before the change.

When that device's user feels vibration, user read information from vibration strength. Although vibration frequency is the same, user can feel different vibration strength. One of the causes is the adaptation to the vibration. When the vibration frequency changes, the frequency before the change affects vibration perception user feels after the change. Therefore this section examine experimentally how vibratory perception after the shift changes with the frequency before the shift.

Experiments were conducted to examine whether vibratory perceptions are changed by adaptation. In the experiments, vibrations were conveyed to subjects using VAI shown in Fig. 1. VAI had a diameter of 4 cm and a length of 10 cm. A vibration motor was mounted inside the device. The experimental procedure was as follows:

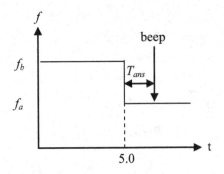

Fig. 1. Timing of the step change in frequency from the initial value f_b to the final value f_a. After a delay of T_{ans} s, the device beeps, signaling the user to record the perceived final frequency. On the abscissa, time is in seconds.

Fig. 2. Vibration alert interface. Length is 10cm, diameter is 3.5cm. A compact DC motor is mounted in the device.

1. Subjects grasped VAI. They were instructed to associate a relative vibrational intensity of 10 with VAI vibrations at 70 Hz and an intensity of 20 with vibrations at 150 Hz.
2. VAI vibrated for 5 s at one of these frequencies: 70, 90, 110, 130, or 150 Hz. This frequency was the one before the change, f_b, and its duration was T_{fb}.
3. Then, the frequency f_b was changed via a step function. The frequency after the change was represented as f_a and its duration was T_{fa}.
4. It beeped after another T_{ans} [s]. The values used for T_{ans} were 1.0, 2.0, or 3.0 s. At the beep, subjects reported their perceived vibrational intensities relative to the standard values 10 and 20. These reported vibrational strengths were represented by P_{va}.

The timings of events in steps 2–4 are illustrated in Fig. 2. In this experiment, T_{fb} and T_{fa} were both 5 s. Each subject repeated steps 1–4 20 times at five values of f_b and five values of f_a. Moreover, they repeated the steps three times using each of the allowed values for the interval to beep, T_{ans}. The test involved 10 subjects, both male and female, with an average age of 25.5 years. During the experiments, subjects wore eye masks and heard white noise through headphones to ensure that they were focused solely on their tactile senses.

2.2   Experimental Result

The experimental results are shown in Fig. 3. The plots in the figure show how the perceived vibrational strength after the change (P_{va}) relates to the frequency before the change (f_b). In Figs. 3(a), 3(b), and 3(c), the frequency after the change (f_a) is treated as a parameter. Each panel in Fig. 3 is for a different interval between the change and the beep. Figures 3(a), 3(b), and 3(c) had intervals of 1, 2, and 3 s, respectively. Each point in the figure is an average over the ten subjects, and the lines are linear approximations to the points.

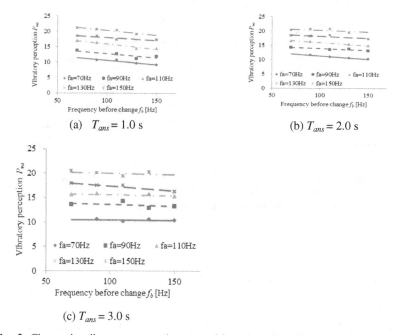

(a) $T_{ans} = 1.0$ s

(b) $T_{ans} = 2.0$ s

(c) $T_{ans} = 3.0$ s

Fig. 3. Change in vibratory perception caused by adaptation. Points are experimental values averaged over 10 subjects. Lines are linear fits to the points. T_{ans} of (a) 1 s, (b) 2 s, (c) 3 s.

Table 1. Slopes of the lines in Fig. 3 for P_{va} vs f_b

f_b [Hz]	$T_{ans} = 1.0$	$T_{ans} = 2.0$	$T_{ans} = 3.0$
70	-0.029	-0.023	-0.001
90	-0.027	-0.012	-0.007
110	-0.034	-0.021	-0.004
130	-0.018	-0.015	-0.020
150	-0.031	-0.012	-0.007
Average	-0.028	-0.017	-0.008

Since each line in each panel of Fig. 3 is at one final frequency f_a, each line should be horizontal if the perceptions of the subjects were consistent. However few lines in Fig. 3 are close to horizontal, and all have negative slopes. The slopes are tabulated in Table 1. The negative slopes indicate that higher the initial frequency f_b, weaker is the perceived vibration after the frequency change. This occurred irrespective of the final frequency f_a being greater or lesser than the initial frequency f_b. This implies that the perceived vibrational strengths depend on not only final frequency f_a but also the initial frequency f_b ; we interpret this as evidence for adaptive behavior.

Further note that the lines become more horizontal from Fig. 3(a) to Fig. 3(c), i.e., with increase in the interval of times after frequency changes. In Table 1, the slopes at $T_{ans} = 1.0$ s (Fig. 3(a)) are larger than those at $T_{ans} = 3.0$ s (Fig. 3(c)). This implies that the influence of f_b on P_{va} is large immediately after a frequency change but the influence decreases with time.

These experiments demonstrate that vibratory perception is affected not only by the current frequency but also by earlier frequencies. If the frequency before the change was low, subjects perceived strong vibrations after the change. But if the frequency before the change was high, subjects perceived weak vibrations after the change. Moreover, the influence of changes in frequency on vibratory perception decreased with time.

3   Correction Method for Change in Vibratory Perception by Adaptation

3.1   Adaptation Model

In this section, we model adaptive changes in vibratory perception using the KI-VPA model [7], which is based on the KI model shown in Fig. 3 [8]. The KI model consists of excitatory and inhibitory neuron firings and is represented as follows:

$$u_\pm(t) = \pm \frac{1}{2} Q_0 \frac{R\alpha_\pm}{\sqrt{\pi t}} \exp\left(-\frac{\beta_\pm}{\alpha_\pm^2} t\right) \tag{1}$$

where u is the potential for both excitatory (+) and inhibitory (−) responses, t is time, while α and β are parameters determined experimentally. Quantities Q_0 and R are constants; following [2], we set $Q_0 = 1.0$ and $R = 2.0$. Figure 4 displays the potential outputs of excitatory and inhibitory neurons. Excitatory neurons fire a positive pulse (Fig. 4(a)), while inhibitory neurons fire a negative pulse (Fig. 4(b)). The output from the KI-VPA model is represented as follows:

$$u(t) = a \sum_{i=1}^{N} \left[u_+\left(t - i\frac{1}{f(t)} + \tau\right) + u_-\left(t - i\frac{1}{f(t)}\right) \right] + b \tag{2}$$

where τ is the difference in firing times between excitatory and inhibitory neurons. An excitatory neuron fires when a vibrational stimulus is inputted, while an inhibitory neuron fires after a time lag. In the above equation, $f(t)$ is the vibrational frequency, and a and b are constants determined experimentally. To minimize the error between the model and the experimental results in Fig. 3, we set $a = 1.25$, $b = 4.42$, $\alpha_+ = 1.5$, $\alpha_- = 0.8$, $\beta_+/\alpha_+^2 = 3.6$, and $\beta_-/\alpha_-^2 = 2.0$. Figure. 5 shows the change in output of the KI-VPA model when frequency change to 110 Hz from 70-150 Hz. After 5 s, it is confirmed that vibratory perceptions are different even though frequency after the change are the same.

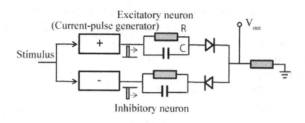

Fig. 4. Equivalent circuit for the KI model

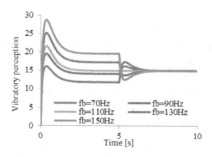

(a) Excitatory neuron   (b) Inhibitory neuron

Fig. 5. Pulse forms created by firing of two types of neurons

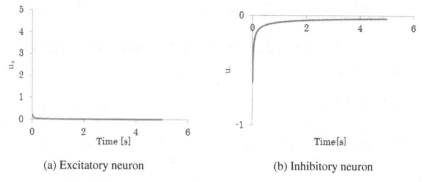

Fig. 6. Output of KI-VPA model when frequencies change to 110 Hz from 70-150Hz

The outputs from the KI-VPA model are shown in Fig. 6. In the figure, the lines are from the KI-VPA model, and the points are experimental data from Fig. 3. The figure shows that the KI-VPA model captures changes in vibratory perception with high accuracy.

3.2   Correction Method

With vibrational frequency as the input, the KI-VPA model outputs the vibratory perception felt by a user. Therefore, if the relation between the frequency and vibratory perception is known, VAI enables the user to feel the desired vibration by adjusting the vibrational frequency depending on the frequency before the change. We perform this correction using the schematic diagram shown in Fig. 6.

The KI-VPA model establishes a linear relation among the vibratory perceptions felt by subjects after the change (P_{va}), the frequency before the change (f_b), and the duration (T_{fb}):

$$P_{va} = g_1 f_b + g_2 T_{fb} + g_3 f_a + g_4 \tag{3}$$

where $g_1{\sim}g_4$ are non-linearly functions of T_{ans}. Especially g_4 is a function showing the relationship between P_{va} and T_{ans}. T_{ans} is time to report after it beeped. If T_{ans} is constant, P_{va} is given by

$$P_{va} = a_1 f_b + a_2 T_{fb} + a_3 f_a + a_4 \tag{4}$$

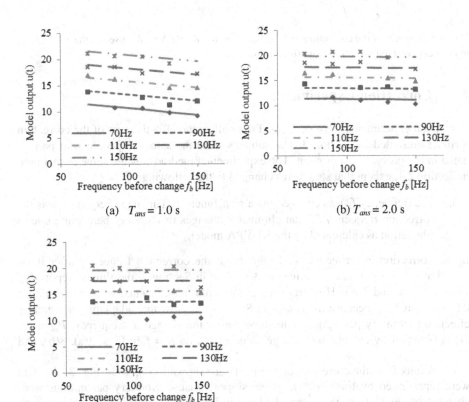

(a) $T_{ans} = 1.0$ s

(b) $T_{ans} = 2.0$ s

c) $T_{ans}=3.0$

Fig. 7. Output of the K I-VPA model (lines) compared with the experimental data in Fig. 3 (points). T_{ans} are the same as in Fig. 3.

where a_1–a_4 are constants. Therefore, the correction frequency f_a' that eliminates the effects of adaptation is calculated in the KI-VPA model by

$$f_a' = \frac{1}{a_3}(P_{va} - a_1 f_b - a_2 T_{fb} - a_4)$$

(5)

This equation provides the frequency that eliminates the influence of adaptation. It allows the VAI device to convey P_{va} by vibrating at f_a' after VAI has vibrated at an initial frequency f_b over a duration T_{fb}.

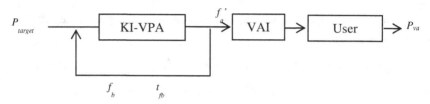

Fig. 8. Schematic of the correction method based on the KI-VPA model used in the VAI device to correct perceived vibrations for effects of adaptation

4   Correction Experiment

Correction experiments were performed to confirm the effectiveness of the correction formula presented in Section 3. The subjects were the same 10 people who participated in the previous experiment. The experimental method was the same as that used in Section 2.1, except that step 3 was changed to the following:

3.   The frequency f_b was changed via a step function. This new frequency was the correction frequency f_a' that eliminates changes in vibratory perception due to adaptation as calculated by the KI-VPA model.

In the correction experiments, VAI vibrated at the correction frequency after it vibrated at f_b for 5 s. In the experiments described in Section 2, the time to report T_{ans} were 1.0, 2.0, and 3.0 s. However, in the correction experiments, we reduced T_{ans} to 0.5, 1.0, and 1.5 s because the results in Section 2.2 show that adaptation has greater effects on vibratory perception immediately after the change in frequency. P_{va} in eq. (4) is obtained by calculating average value of P_{va} on $f_b = f_a$ in Figs. 3(a), 3(b), and 3(c).

The results from the correction experiments are shown in Fig. 8. In Fig. 3, the data were represented by lines with negative slopes because vibratory perceptions were changed by adaptation. However, the lines in Fig. 8 are nearly horizontal, i.e., with the correction model, VAI conveys precise vibratory perceptions without adaptive effects. Further, the correction model is effective at all times T_{ans} since all the approximated lines in Figs. 8(a), 8(b), and 8(c) are nearly horizontal. The slope of each line is shown in Table 2. Compared to the data in Table 1, the values in Table 2 are lower, confirming that changes in vibratory perception did not occur in the correction experiments.

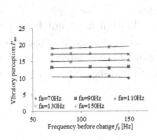

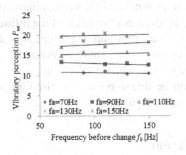

(a) $T_{ans} = 0.5$ s   (b) $T_{ans} = 1.$

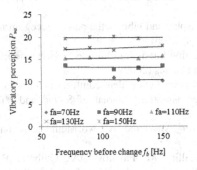

(c) $T_{ans} = 1.5$ s

Fig. 9. Results from the correction experiments. Points are experimental data and lines are linear fits to the points. Times to report of (a) 0.5 s, (b) 1.0 s, (c) 1.5 s.

Table 2. Slopes of lines in Fig. 8 from the correction experiments. MAV is the mean of the absolute values.

f_b [Hz]	$T_{ans} = 0.5$	$T_{ans} = 1.0$	$T_{ans} = 1.5$
70	0.0035	-0.0045	-0.0025
90	0.0000	-0.0079	-0.0019
110	0.0052	0.0040	0.0045
130	-0.0010	0.0101	0.0073
150	0.0075	0.0040	0.0005
MAV	0.0034	0.0061	0.0033

5   Conclusions

In this study, we used human subjects to experimentally measure changes in vibratory perception caused by adaptation. Then, we modeled those changes in vibratory perception using the KI-VPA model. The model provides a correction formula that eliminates changes in vibratory perception due to adaptation. We also performed additional experiments to test the correction formula; the experimental results verified the effectiveness of the correction model. In particular, correction frequencies calculated by the model can cancel the influence of adaptation.

To date, information presentation devices using vibration have not been able to convey precise information using changes in vibrational frequency, because vibratory perception is changed by adaptation. However, owing to this study, such devices should be able to convey precise information by vibrating at the corrected frequencies provided by our model.

References

1. Tsukada, K., Yasumura, M.: ActiveBelt: Belt-Type Wearable Tactile Display for Directional Navigation. In: Mynatt, E.D., Siio, I. (eds.) UbiComp 2004. LNCS, vol. 3205, pp. 384–399. Springer, Heidelberg (2004)
2. Jones, L.A., Lockyer, B., Piateski, E.: Tactile display and vibrotactile pattern recognition on the torso. Advanced Robotics 20(12), 1359–1374 (2006)
3. Yao, H.S., Grant, D., Cruz, M.: Perceived Vibration Strength in Mobile Devices: the Effect of Weight and Frequency. IEEE Transaction on Haptics (2009)
4. Morioka, M., Griffin, M.J.: Magnitude-dependence of equivalent comfort contours for fore-and-art, lateral and vertical hand-transmitted vibration. Journal of Sound and Vibration 295, 633–648 (2006)
5. Hahn, J.F.: Vibrotactile Adaptation and Recovery Measured by Two Methods. Jounal of Experimental Psychology 71(5), 655–658 (1966)
6. Tommerdahl, M., Hester, K.D., Felix, E.R., Hollins, M., Favorov, O.V., Quibrera, P.M., Whitsel, B.L.: Human vibrotactile frequency discriminative capacity after adaptation to 25 Hz or 200 Hz stimulation. Brain Research 1057, 1–9 (2005)
7. Mori, Y., Tanaka, T., Kaneko, S.: Design of Vibration Alert Interface Based on Tactile Adaptation Model to Vibration Stimulation. In: Smith, M.J., Salvendy, G. (eds.) HCII 2011, Part I. LNCS, vol. 6771, pp. 462–469. Springer, Heidelberg (2011)
8. Katagiri, Y., Aida, K.: Simulated nonlinear dynamics of laterally interactive arrayed neurons. In: Optomechatronic Technologies 2008 SPIE Proceedings (2008)

Non-contact Measurement of Biological Signals Using Microwave Radar

Hiroki Morodome[1], Satoshi Suzuki[2], Takafumi Asao[2], and Kentaro Kotani[2]

[1] Graduate School of Science and Engineering, Kansai University
3-3-35 Yamate-cho, Suita, Osaka 564-8680, Japan
k165069@kansai-u.ac.jp
[2] Faculty of Engineering Science, Kansai University
3-3-35 Yamate-cho, Suita, Osaka 564-8680, Japan
{ssuzuki,asao,kotani}@kansai-u.ac.jp

Abstract. The objective of this study was to develop a prototype system to monitor biological signals using microwave radar, without making contact with the body and without removing clothing. The prototype system has a microwave Doppler radar antenna with a 24-GHz frequency and approximately 7-mW output power. Experiments were conducted with a group of subjects. We found that the prototype system precisely captured the heart rate and the heart-rate variability (HRV). Our prototype system allows for the monitoring of biological signals, without placing any burden on the monitored individuals

Keywords: Non-contact, Microwave, heartbeat.

1 Introduction

To monitor the autonomic activation induced by mental stress without placing any burden on the monitored individual, we developed a non-contact autonomic monitoring method using a 24-GHz compact microwave radar. We have previously reported non-contact methods to monitor the heart and respiratory rates in experimental animals exposed to toxic materials or under a hypovolemic state to determine the pathophysiological condition of the subject, such as exposure to toxins or shock induced by hemorrhage [1, 2, 3]. Single photon emission tomography (SPECT) with a radioisotope (99mTe-FBPBAT) can successfully map the autonomic nervous system but is impractical for autonomic activation monitoring due to the need for large-scale equipment [4]. Using continuous electrocardiography (ECG) with conventional electrodes, rhythmic components of heart-rate variability (HRV) can be assessed using power spectral analysis, and modifications in autonomic activities induced by mental stress have been reported in the HRV power spectra [5, 6]. However, long-term electrocardiographic monitoring using electrodes places a heavy burden on the monitored individuals.

To determine human stress while driving or operating equipment, we monitored human autonomic activation induced by stressful temperatures using non-contact

S. Yamamoto (Ed.): HIMI/HCII 2013, Part I, LNCS 8016, pp. 117–125, 2013.

measurement of HRV with a 24-GHz compact microwave radar, which can easily be attached to the rear surface of the back of a chair without using either radioisotopes or electrodes.

2   System Design of a Prototype System Using Microwave Radar

The prototype system we designed consisted of a microwave Doppler radar antenna (TAU GIKEN Co., Yokohama, Japan), a device for controlling the power supply to this antenna, and a PC for analyzing the output data from the antenna. The frequency of this microwave radar antenna was 24 GHz, with a normal average output power of approximately (the maximum output power is less than 10 mW). The diffusion angle (θ_d) of the microwave radar antenna is approximately $40°$, the antenna gain is 10 dBi, and the electrical intensity is 0.7 mW/cm^2.

Damage caused by electromagnetic waves has been discussed in the literature, particularly in the case of human applications. At frequencies greater 3 GHz, the electrical field intensity limit is set according to the guidelines for radio waves established by the Telecommunication Bureau of the Ministry of Internal Affairs and Communication in Japan. The electrical field intensity of this microwave radar is 0.7; it is therefore in conformity with the guidelines. Furthermore, the 24-GHz frequency of our device is within the frequency band for normal use of radio waves, as approved by the Japanese law.

Before input into a PC for analysis, data were acquired at a sampling frequency of 100 Hz using an A/D converter (USB6008, National Instruments, Texas, USA). After digitization, the data were analyzed by a system that we developed using analysis software (LabVIEW, National Instruments, Texas, USA). In this analyzing system, in order to reduce noise and select data related to the motion associated with the heart rate, a band-pass filter was used for transferring data from the microwave Doppler radar antenna. This filter was set between 0.5 Hz and 3 Hz; this setting covers a range of 30–180 heartbeats per minute.

3   Experiment for HRV with Prototype System

3.1   Task and Settings

Experiments to measure the heart rate and changes in the HRV using the prototype system were conducted. At the same time, the ECG was measured by the contact monitoring system using normal electrodes. We compared the results for the ECG with the results acquired by the prototype system (see Fig. 1). The prototype system was tested with four healthy male subjects (mean age 22.00 ± 0.96 years; range 21–23 years). Each subject sat on a chair with a mesh back composed of 2 layers of polyester plastic (Baron-Chair, Okamura Co., Tokyo, Japan). The distance from the antenna of the prototype system to the chair back was 120 mm, and it was placed approximately 60 mm to the left of the spine at around the level of the fourth intercostal space.

Following a silent period of 120 s, a cold pressor test was conducted for 120 s. The cold pressor test was performed for 30 s, following which there was a break for 30 s. We performed this test for 2 min, repeating the cold pressor test twice over 120 s.

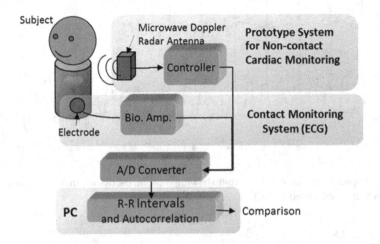

Fig. 1. Schematic diagram of apparatus for non-contact monitoring of autonomic activation

3.2   Analysis

The output signals from the prototype system and a reference precordial ECG signal from the V5 position were sampled by the A/D converter with a sampling frequency of 100 Hz. Band-pass filters were used for the prototype system outputs to reduce noise and interference. The band-pass filters were set at between 0.5 Hz and 3 Hz; this model band-pass filter covers a range of 30–180 heartbeats per minute. After filtering, the power spectra of heartbeat intervals at low frequency (LF) (0.04–0.15 Hz), high frequency (HF) (0.15–0.4 Hz), and LF/HF [7, 8] were calculated to monitor the HRV by using the maximum entropy method (MemCalc software, GMS Co., Tokyo, Japan); this method is normally used for medical research [9, 10].

The intervals of the peaks in amplitude in the outputs from the prototype system were assumed to correlate with the R-R interval for the ECG, and HRV was calculated by using peak-to-peak intervals in the output signal of the prototype system. The power spectra of the HRV (i.e., LF, HF, and LF/HF) for the R-R intervals derived by the ECG were also calculated by using the MemCalc software.

4   Results

When the subjects sat on a chair, the compact microwave radar output through the control unit showed a cyclic oscillation, corresponding to the ECG (Fig. 2). As can be seen in Fig. 2 (radar), cyclic oscillation synchronization with the occurrence of the R-wave of the ECG was confirmed.

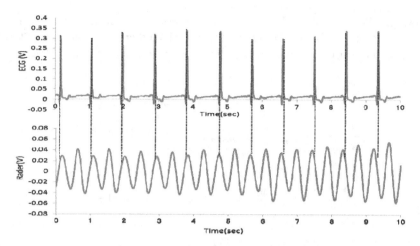

Fig. 2. A compact microwave radar output showing a cyclic oscillation that corresponds to the cardiac oscillation measured by ECG

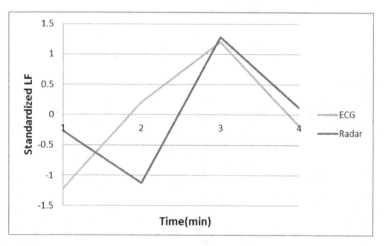

Fig. 3. In both non-contact and contact measurement, LF of a sbject (reflecting sympathetic activation) shows a peak during cold stimuli

In both non-contact (compact microwave radar) and contact (ECG as reference) measurements, the HRV parameter, LF of a subject, reflecting mainly sympathetic activation, showed a peak during cessation of the cold pressor test (Fig. 3). The mean LF of four subjects measured by non-contact and contact methods during cold stimuli increased, respectively, as compared with those of the silent period before cold stimuli.

The HF activity of the same subject, reflecting the parasympathetic activity, did not show any distinctive change during cold stimuli (Fig. 4), and the mean HF of the four subjects increased very little during cold stimuli in both the non-contact and the contact measurements.

The LF/HF activity of the same subject, reflecting sympathovagal balance, exhibited a peak during cold stimuli (Fig. 5). The mean of the four subjects measured by non-contact and contact methods during cold stimuli increased, respectively, as compared with that during the silent period before cold stimuli.

Without using radioisotopes or electrodes, stress-induced autonomic activation was monitored.

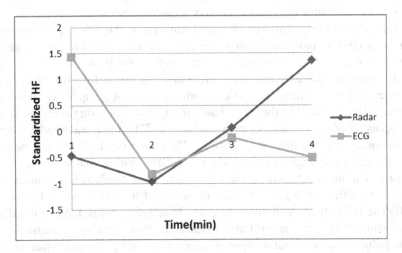

Fig. 4. In both non-contact and contact measurement, HF of a sbject (reflecting sympathetic activation) did not show any distinctive change during cold stimuli

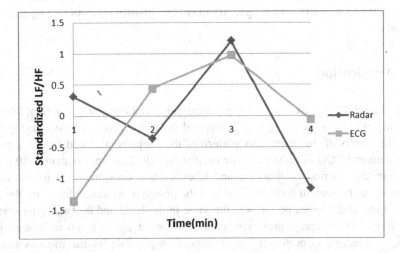

Fig. 5. In both non-contact and contact measurement, LF/HF of a sbject (reflecting sympathetic activation) exhibits a peak during cold stimuli

5   Discussion

We developed a prototype system using a 24-GHz microwave radar for non-contact cardiac monitoring. As compared with other noninvasive measurement methods (e.g., methods involving the use of strain gauges [11], pressure sensors [12], and PVDF sensors [13]), our method is completely non-contact and furthermore does not require the removal of clothing. We designed the antenna with relatively small dimensions to obtain high gain with high spatial resolution; the small size also reduces the possibility of signal absorption through the human body, which at 24 GHZ is more than that at lower frequencies. In addition, a high gain allows a smaller area to be analyzed. As a result, a small antenna at 24 GHz is easier to integrate into a monitoring system and is suitable for civil applications. The device can be produced at low cost, which makes it competitive, when produced on a large scale. On the other hand, the signal processing required is delicate, because there is a space between the body and the microwave radar antenna, and it is susceptible to other body motions. These disadvantages are compensated for by the relatively high antenna gain at 24 GHz, which enables better spatial resolution. The mean LF, which mainly reflects sympathetic activity during cold stimuli, is significantly higher than the mean LF of the silent period before cold stimuli. The HF indicating the parasympathetic activity changed very little during the cold stimuli. This can be attributed to the activation of the sympathetic nervous system induced by stressful temperature. Without using radioisotopes or electrodes, our system monitors sympathetic activation through the back of a chair. Mental stress affects the autonomic nervous system [5, 6]. Moreover, there is a relationship between mental stress and traffic accidents. By issuing auto nomic activation early warnings, it may be possible to prevent industrial accidents.

6   Application

We carried out the detection of abnormal breathing using a prototype system. Subjects simulating abnormal breathing were measured using the prototype system. Figure 6 shows the results of the respiratory pattern of the subjects, acquired from the prototype system and ECG as reference. The oscillation halted for approximately 30 s after continuing short-period oscillations, and Cheyne-Stokes respiration was confirmed. This trend can be seen in both the ECG and the prototype system. Moreover, the start and end time of the apnea period was the same in the ECG and the prototype system. These results show that a prototype system to detect apnea is possible with high accuracy. Therefore, a prototype system would be possible for the measurement of respiratory activity.

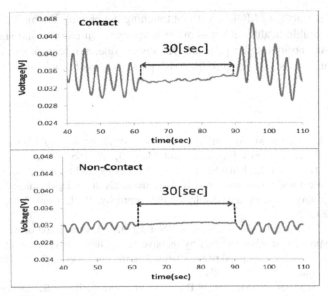

Fig. 6. The oscillation halted for approximately 30 s after a continuous short period, and Cheyne-Stokes respiration was confirmed

7   Conclusion

In this paper, we describe a novel prototype system using microwave radar for non-contact cardiac monitoring that requires neither direct contact with the body nor the removal of clothing. The antenna of our prototype system is relatively small and can easily be attached to furniture in the workplace. This means that the device is suitable for civil applications at a low cost. We will examine its actual use in various settings in the future.

We monitored human autonomic activation induced by a chilled water load through non-contact measurement of heart rate variability using a compact microwave radar. The results confirmed that the intervals captured by our prototype system are similar to the intervals captured by the ECG signal because the estimated heart rates determined by using the data captured by our prototype system are roughly in accordance with the actual measurements. Results confirmed that our microwave system can capture information similar to that obtained with the ECG system. In addition, the changes in the HRV measured by both methods were also similar, although there were some differences in the absolute values. These results mean that our prototype system can capture signals with sufficient accuracy to calculate the heart rate and HRV.

The long-term monitoring of HRV can be used as a diagnostic test for sepsis [14]. Moreover, it has been reported that a reduction in the HRV is useful in identifying septic patients at risk of the development of a multiple organ dysfunction syndrome (MODS) [15]. Our method of noncontact monitoring for HRV can thus be used not only for monitoring autonomic activation but also as a future diagnostic method for sepsis or as a predictor of MODS, without touching the patient. Zheng et al. [16] have proposed a wearable health care system for long-term continuous vital sign monitoring of high-risk cardiovascular patients. Our system does not require special gear and may be suitable for the screening of high-risk patients as part of a health check.

References

1. Kikuchi, M., Ishihara, M., Matsui, T., et al.: Biomedical engineering's contribution to defending the homeland. IEEE Eng. Med. Biol. Mag. 23, 175–186 (2004)
2. Matsui, T., Hagisawa, K., Ishizuka, T., et al.: A novel method to prevent secondary exposure of medical and rescue personnel to toxic materials under biochemical hazard conditions using microwave radar and infrared thermography. IEEE Trans. Biomed. Eng. 51, 2184–2188 (2004)
3. Matsui, T., Ishizuka, T., Takase, B., et al.: Non-Contact determination of vital sign alterations in hypovolemic states induced by massive hemorrhage: an experimental attempt to monitor the condition of injured persons behind barriers or under disaster rubble. Med. Biol. Eng. Compu. 42, 807–811 (2004)
4. Richter, S., Schaefer, A., Menger, M.D., et al.: Mapping of the cardiac sympathetic nervous system by single photon emission tomography with technetium-99 m-labeled fluorobenzylpiperidine derivative (^{99m}Tc-FBPBAT): result of a feasibility study in a porcine model and an initial dosimetric estimation in humans. Nucl. Med. Commun. 26(4), 36–368 (2005)
5. Ruediger, H., Seibt, R., Scheuch, K., et al.: Sympathetic and parasympathetic activation in heart rate variability in malehypertensive patients under mental stress. J. Hum. Hypertens. 8(5), 307–315 (2004)
6. Tuininga, Y.S., Crijns, H.J., Brouwer, J., et al.: Evaluation of importance of central effects of atenolol and metoprolol measured by heart rate variability during mental performance tasks, physical exercise, and daily life in stable postinfarct patients. Circulation 92(12), 3415–3423 (1995)
7. Singh, N., Mironov, D., Armstrong, P.W., et al.: Heart rate variability assessment early after acute myocardial infarction. Pathophysiological and prognostic correlates. Circulation 93, 1388–1395 (1996)
8. Carney, R.M., Blumenthal, J.A., Stein, P.K., et al.: Depression, heart rate variability, and acute myocardial infarction. Circulation 104, 2024–2028 (2001)
9. Clayton, R.H., Bowman, A.J., Ford, G.A., et al.: Measurement of baroreflex gain form heart rate and blood pressure spectra: A comparison of spectral estimation techniques. Physiol. Meas. 16, 131–139 (1995)
10. Suzuki, S., Sumi, K., Matsubara, M.: Cardiac autonomic control immediately after exercise in female distance runners. J. Physiol. Anthropol. 27, 325–332 (2008b)
11. Ciaccio, E.J., Hiatt, M., Hegyi, T., et al.: Measurement and monitoring of electrocardiogram belt tension in premature infants for assessment of respiratory function. Biomed. Eng. Online 6, 1–11 (2007)
12. Jacobs, J., Embree, P., Glei, M., Christensen, S., Sullivan, P.: Characterization of a novel heart and respiratory rate sensor. In: Conf. Proc. IEEE Eng. Med. Biol. Soc., vol. 3, pp. 2223–2226 (2004)
13. Wang, F., Tanaka, M., Chonan, S.: Development of a wearable mental stress evaluation system using PVDF film sensor. J. Adv. Sci. 18, 170–173 (2006)

14. Korach, M., Sharshar, T., Jarrin, I., et al.: Cardiac Variability in critically ill adults: influ-
    ence of sepsis. Crit. Care Med. 29, 1380–1385 (2001)
15. Pontet, J., Contreras, P., Curbelo, A., et al.: Heart rate variability as early marker of mul-
    tiple organ dysfunction syndrome in septic patients. J. Crit. Care 18, 156–163 (2003)
16. Zheng, J.W., Zhang, Z.B., Wu, T.H., Zhang, Y.: A wearable mobihealth care system sup-
    porting real-time diagnosis and alarm. Med. Boil. Eng. Comput. 45(9), 877–885 (2007)

Leaning Origami Using 3D Mixed Reality Technique

Atsushi Nakano, Makoto Oka, and Hirohiko Mori

Tokyo City University 1-28-1 Tamadutumi, Setagaya, Tokyo, Japan
{g1281820,moka,hmori}@tcu.ac.jp

Abstract. 3D Mixed Reality Technique is a kind of the AR (Augmented Reality). Using AR, we can reduce mistakes and can lead effective works. Especially, utilizing 3DCG will enhance the potential of AR. In the research of 3DCG, Non Photo Real rendering is proposed as a manner to understand structure of 3DCG easily. No researches have been done so far to verify whether the Non Photo Real technique works well in AR. This paper inspects whether the Non Photo Real technique is effective in utilizing AR to learning Origami (Japanese paper craft). We approach a way to rendering 3DCG animations in AR system and compare of works using each 3DCG animations. We got results accomplishment rate and easier to watch. As a result, we show that learning works using Non Photo Real in AR was improved understanding works.

Keywords: Leaning Origami, Mixed Reality.

1 Introduction

3D Mixed Reality Technique is a kind of AR (Augmented Reality) and, in 3D Mixed Reality Technique, 3DCG animation displays on the real world together. AR can display digital information in real world [1]. As, using AR, we can understand information more intuitively than watching a manual or a monitor separately from the targets, we can reduce mistakes and can work effectively. AR is increasingly being paid much attention in many fields such as the medical works and the maintenances of machines. Though 3DCG should be enhance the potential of AR because it cam represent more complexity information, no researches have been done so far to verify what kinds of rendering methods suit to AR.

3DCG can be classified into two types, Photo Real and Non Photo Real. Photo Real is a way to render objects in the manner to reflect the reality faithfully. On the other hand, Non Photo Real is a way of rendering objects for the purpose of easily understanding structure of 3DCG. Enhancing the outlines of objects is the most popular technique in Non Photo Real because it makes complex shapes clearer. In addition, it is also one of the effective techniques to give some simple shadows to represent the depth.

S. Yamamoto (Ed.): HIMI/HCII 2013, Part I, LNCS 8016, pp. 126–132, 2013.

Though, in this way, Non Photo Real renderings are be useful in 3DCG, the perspectives obtained in the researches in 3DCG may not be adopted in utilizing them in AR. For example, the enhanced shapes of objects may provide unnatural feelings in overlapping physical objects because some features of physical objects are deformed and some gaps may be appeared between physical objects and their 3DCG.

This paper aims to find some rendering manners suitable for the 3DCG mixed reality, and especially we focus on the Non Photo Real rendering. We investigate, in this paper, whether Non Photo Real rendering technique are suitable for the 3DCG mixed reality in making Origami.

Origami is one of the traditional plays in Japan and we transform one piece of paper into a complex shape such as animals and flowers by holding paper. Though there are many books with the illustrations, movies, and 3DCG to explain how to make Origami, it is difficult for the beginner to how to make origami correctly.

2   Related Works

Kitamura proposed a system which explains how to make Origami using AR [2]. The reason why Kitamura utilize the AR technique is that it is difficult for the beginners to comprehend the guidance because they should watch the paper and the instructions alternately and not to be able to understand where they hold the physical paper only watching the instructions. This system consist of a web camera and HMD (head mount display). When a web camera catches the AR markers on the paper, this system superimposes the line to fold on the paper through the HMD. Though the Kitamura's system could solve some problems of origami instructions, the users sometimes complicated the   lines on the paper.

Mitanni and Suzuki proposed a rendering manner of 3DCG for Origami 3DCG [2]. In general, it is difficult to understand how much paper is overlapped with 3DCG and even if the quality is improved. So, they proposed the Non Photo Real approach. Their approach represents a shape of origami in 3DCG as Non Photo Real like the illustrations used for the instructions in many books. In this approach, "Gap of Faces" and "Misaligned Overlap" were presented. Gap of Faces is the technique, to make easy to express which folded parts of the paper are overlapped, to render the paper of the top layer in thicker. In Misaligned Overlap, the overlapped parts of the paper are rendered in staggering positions even if they are overlapped precisely.

3   Using Origami 3DCG Animation

To investigate the Non Photo Real rendering animation is effective in 3DCG MR, we created two types of origami 3DCG animations. One is called "Normal Model", which is the animation of one of the traditional origami 3DCG renderings. The other is the one whose each frame are rendered by the Non Photo Real technique, called "Approach Model". To make these models to be superimposed on the physical paper, we utilize the ARToolKit [4].

3.1   Normal Model

Normal Model renders physical objects with the traditional manner to be realistic. Here, the outlines of the paper are rendered by the depth buffer rendering method (Figure 1), and, to clarify which part we should fold at the operation, green mesh lines are drawn on the surface we should fold the surface which no operations are done at that step are painted in blue.

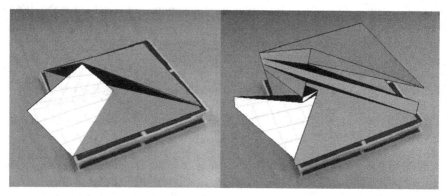

Fig. 1. Normal Model   **Fig. 2.** Approach Model

3.2   Approach Model

Non Photo Real rendering were developed to create a still CG. As the Approach Model requires their animation, we create the first frame and the last frame by Non Photo Rendering, and do the frames between them by tweening. The thickness of the paper in each frame is also tweened using the first and last frames to apply the "Gap of Faces" technique.

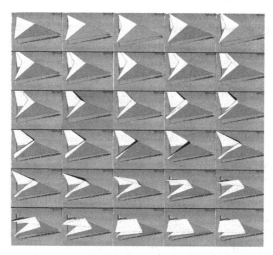

Fig. 3. Frame-by-frame playback of Approach Model

4   Experiment

In this system, we use the HMD for single eye to superimpose the 3DCG animations on the physical paper, and the WEB Camera to detect the special position of the paper (Figure 4). Several AR markers are printed on the paper. The subjects are 20 students who are not the expert of origami though they have a few experiments. 10 subjects were under the "Normal Model" condition and the other ten subjects are under the "Approach Model." After making Origami under their assigned condition, all subjects show the Origami CG animation of the other condition and filled out the questionnaires. Figure 5 is the steps of the task to be done in this experiment.

Fig. 4. Device NWEBcamera: Logicool 2-MP Portable Webcam C905m, HMD: SCALAR Teleglass-3 T3FCEMA

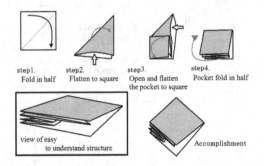

Fig. 5. Origami work illustration

5   Result

Figure 6 shows the rates the subjects accomplished each step. Though all subjects could accomplish the step1 and step2 with both of the Approach Model and the Normal Model because of too easy tasks, in the step 3 and step 4, the rate with the Approach Model is higher than the one with the Normal Model. By this result, it can be said that the Non Photo Real rendering also make special understanding easy even in animation and in overlapping physical objects. The subjective evaluation supports this result (Figure 7) Figure 7 shows the result of the question that the subjects felt easy to understand how to fold paper. Majority of the subjects answered that "the Approach Model is more understandable than Normal Model" and, interestingly, they also answered that "I feel real in the Approach Model than in the Normal Model", despite the Normal Model   represents physical objects more realistically.

However, all rendering ways of Non Photo Real do not have such effects. Figure.8 and Figure 9 show whether the subjects noticed each Non Photo Real techniques. Though most of subjects noticed the effect of the "Gap of Faces", only few subjects do not notice the effects of   "Misaligned Overlap".

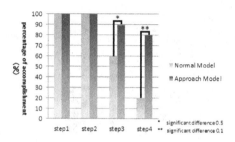

Fig. 6. Accomplishment rate

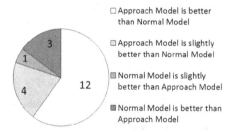

Fig. 7. Easier to watch

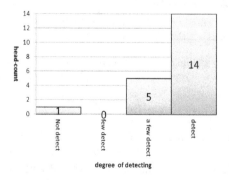

Fig. 8. Detected "Gap of Faces"

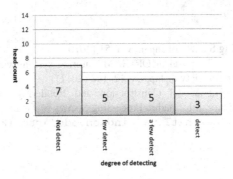

Fig. 9. Detected "Misaligned Overlap"

6   Discussions

The analysis showed Non Photo Real rendering is more understandable and human feel more realistic than the Photo Real rendering approach, even though the Photo Real technique reproduces physical situations. This may be caused by the nature of humans' internal image representation. It has been known that we do not represent external world in mind in just the way they are, but also in the manner of emphasizing their features. If the emphasis in rendering the feature coincide the human internal representation, we may feel realistic even if overlapped images have different external appearances from the physical objects.

All rendering techniques, however, do not allow human to be understandable. They feel "Gap of Faces" is realistic, while they do "Misaligned Overlap" is unrealistic. "Gap of Faces" is a technique to convey how to fold paper and to represents the internal structure. On the other hand, "Misaligned Overlap" is the one to depict how many layers of papers there are at one point and to represent the internal structure. It can be considered, therefore, the CG which represent the internal structure do not provide some sort of mismatch for human, even if it is unrealistic, while some sort of deformed CG such as depicting the external appearance provide it when they are overlapped on the physical object.

7   Conclusion

This paper investigated the effectiveness and the human feelings in overlapping the non-realistic 3DCG animation on the physical objects in Origami. The results show that human feels some non-realistic rendering more realistic than the realistic rendering and they allow human to understand the structure better, in spite of the gap between the CG and physical objects. We also showed that the rendering techniques to represent internal structure work well but the ones to emphasize the feature appearance do not well in overlapping physical object.

References

1. Information Processing Society of Japan, vol. 51 (2010)
2. Kitamura, Y., Oka, M.: Proposal of ORIGAMI tutoring system with Augmented Reality. Information Processing Society of Japan, 142–148 (2011)
3. Mitani, J., Suzuki, H.: Model Construction and Rendering for Understanding the Conformation of Origami. Information Processing Society of Japan 46(1), 247 (2005)
4. ARToolKit, http://www.hitl.washington.edu/artoolkit/

Basic Investigation into Hand Shape Recognition Using Colored Gloves Taking Account of the Peripheral Environment

Takahiro Sugaya, Takayuki Suzuki, Hiromitsu Nishimura, and Hiroshi Tanaka

Kanagawa Institute of Technology,
1030 Shimo-ogino, Atsugi-shi, Kanagawa, Japan
s0921071@cce.kanagawa-it.ac.jp,
{suzuki,nisimura,h_tanaka}@ic.kanagawa-it.ac.jp

Abstract. Although infrared cameras are sometimes used for posture and hand shape recognition, they are not used widely. In contrast, visible light cameras are widely used as web cameras and are implemented in mobile and smart phones. We have used color gloves in order to allow hand shapes to be recognized by visible light cameras, which expands both the type of background that can be used and the application areas. It is considered that the hand shape recognition using color gloves can be used to express many patterns and can be used for many applications such as communication and input interfaces, etc. The recognition performance depends on the color information of the color gloves, which is affected by the environment, especially the illumination conditions, that is bright or dim lighting. Hue values are used to detect color in this investigation. The relative finger positions and finger length are used to confirm the validity of color detection. We propose a method of rejecting image frames that includes a color detection error, which will, in turn, give rise to a hand shape recognition error. Experiments were carried out under three different illumination conditions. The effectiveness of the proposed method has been verified by comparing the recognition success ratio of the conventional method and with the results using the proposed methods.

Keywords: Colored Gloves, Visible Light Camera, Color Detection, Hue Value, Peripheral Environment.

1 Introduction

Communication is one of their largest barriers to independent living for hearing impaired or speech-impaired persons. Although most of people who are born with a disability have opportunities to study sign language or Braille, those who become handicapped later and non-handicapped people rarely learned such communication methods. Gesture recognition systems etc. have been developed in order to solve these problems [1]. A comparison between an inertia sensor based gesture recognition method and a vision based method has been reported [2]. In addition, a finger Braille recognition method using a special-purpose sensor has been reported [3].

S. Yamamoto (Ed.): HIMI/HCII 2013, Part I, LNCS 8016, pp. 133–142, 2013.

Gesture recognition using a 3D sensor has also been reported [4]. However, some problems remain with these methods.   The methods with a special sensor or devices [2-4] involve a high cost of introduction and this makes it difficult to expand the area of usage.   Locations where these systems can be used will also be restricted in the case of special purpose sensors.   Therefore, it is difficult to use these systems to achieve easy communication for handicapped people.

If we assume that a handicapped person can carry a computer system, we can achieve gesture recognition realize by using a camera and a laptop PC.   We have selected a vision-based recognition method, because it does not require sensor to be attached to the human body.   Although its range for satisfactory viewing is limited, this is not a problem because the distance between two persons when communicating is not great.   There are two kinds of approach as methods for vision-based gesture recognition.   One is a method using a color marker, such as a color glove, and the other is a method which does not use a color marker [5].   Of course, the recognition method that does not use a color marker is more user-friendly.   However, it is quite difficult to realize a highly reliable recognition system in an environment with a complex background color and under both, bright and dark light conditions without using a color marker.   We have given priority to use in a variety of environments.   Therefore, in this research we decided to use a color glove in which a different color was assigned to each finger.

In general, the use of color detection techniques alone cannot maintain high performance in an environment of varying light conditions, and as a result it is difficult to realize high recognition accuracy.   We propose a technique for recognizing hand shape with high accuracy under varying illumination conditions by taking additional features of fingers into account.

2   Proposed Color Gloves and Hand Shape

Color gloves have an advantage in facilitating the recognition of hand shapes in comparison with recognition by contour abstraction of hand shapes, especially when considering the background environment.   We have used colored gloves on each hand, with the fingers being identified with different colors.   Six colors were selected by considering the appropriate hue values, and the positions of the colored areas are the tip of each finger and the wrist as shown in Fig.1.   The viewing region of a single camera is divided into two separate regions and the crossing of hands during use is not allowed.   This makes it possible to distinguish between the two hands as right hand and left hand.

We propose a new set of finger patterns which is easy to memorize.   Some examples of these finger patterns are shown in Fig.2.   Each finger represents a binary number, where 1 means visible from the camera, and 0 means an invisible finger, that is a finger which is folded back and not extended.   The order of digits in a number follows the order of fingers, that is, the right hand digit is represented by the thumb, and the left hand digit by the little finger.   Since each finger pattern in each hand can represent different information, $2^5 \times 2^5$ different signals could theoretically be created.

In practice, $2^4 \times 2^4$ finger shape patterns are used, as some finger patterns are difficult to form.

Since the proposed finger patterns can be formed easily and quickly, the number of possible signal patterns is quite large, and this method seems to have many possible applications.   In addition, a high hand shape recognition performance can be expected, because each finger can be identified correctly by the color of the finger.

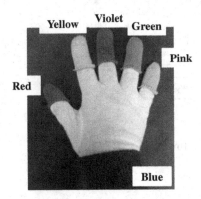

Fig. 1. Color glove

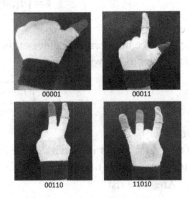

Fig. 2. Some examples of finger patterns

3   Recognition Methods

3.1   Hue Value Threshold Patterns for Color Detection

The hue value is used for color detection in this investigation, as this value corresponds to the color that we see.   Two hue value thresholds patterns are considered: one is the nominal threshold pattern which uses narrow regions to avoid color detection errors, as shown in Fig.3 (a), while the other uses broader regions as shown in Fig.3 (b).   This broader pattern is expected to provide high sensitivity for color detection in a variety of environments, especially under bright conditions.   However, this thresholds pattern might be more likely to cause color detection errors that result in finger pattern recognition errors as a side effect.

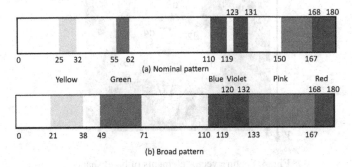

Fig. 3. Hue value threshold patterns for color detection

3.2   Recognition Model and Introduction of Features of Hand Shape

We used a nearest neighbor method for hand shape recognition. First, the distance between the center of the wrist and the tip of each finger is calculated by finding the center of gravity of each colored region. The feature vector $\mathbf{f}$ of a hand shape is defined as follows.

$$\mathbf{f} = \{d_1, d_2, d_3, d_4, d_5\} \tag{1}$$

where,

d_i : distance between the center of the wrist and center of the colored area at the tip of each finger as shown in Fig.4.

$$d_i = \frac{\sqrt{(fx_i - w_x)^2 + (fy_i - w_y)^2}}{\sqrt{S}} \tag{2}$$

where,

(fx_i, fy_i) : center of gravity of the tip of each finger $(i = 1, 2, 3, 4, 5)$
(w_x, w_y) : center of gravity of wrist
S : Area of wrist

S is used to normalize the distance so that the recognition is not influenced by the distance between the finger and the camera. The five elements of distance form a feature vector that represents a hand shape, where the element value of a colored region which is invisible due to a finger being bent is set to 0. The shape recognition result is obtained by selecting the hand shape which has the minimum distance between template feature vectors prepared in advance and the target feature vector which is to be recognized.

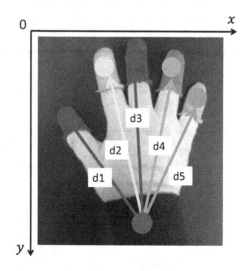

Fig. 4. Feature vector elements of hand shape

There exists a problem that the peripheral illumination affects the hue values that are used to distinguish each finger tips.   This change of values gives rise to a color detection error, which degrades the performance of the shape recognition.   We have therefore introduced a new operation of validation before the recognition process, which involves calculating the vector distance between a template feature vector and targeted feature vector to be recognized.   The relationships of the position of each finger, and the length of the fingers are taken into account when checking the validity of the color detection.   Figure 5 shows examples of color detection error.   Color detection errors may be of two kinds, an example of one being shown in Fig. 5(a). In this case, the color pink is detected in a different position to that it should be, on the little finger.   The other type of error, called, "over detection", as shown in Fig.5 (b).   The color yellow is found, but this color should not have appeared because the forefinger is bent.   We consider the relationships between each finger in order to guarantee the correct color detection.   Table 1 shows the judgment criteria for color detection error, taking the relative finger positions into account.   The intersection of the position of the column headings at the top and the row headings on the left indicates the position of the relationship between two fingers.   If the finger position relationship satisfies this Table 1, the frames are removed from recognition process as a frame including color detection error.   But this criteria cannot remove errors such as that in Fig.5 (b), which results from over detection.

However, the length of each finger also can be used to detect color detection errors. To detect color detection errors, the following conditions are applied, on the assumption that the finger length, d_i, is between 1.5 to 3.5 for correct color detection.   The color detection error as shown in Fig.6 in which the distance between the wrist and the tip of ring finger is abnormal can be detected by considering length of finger, with the following conditions assumed to indicate an error.

$$d_i < 1 \text{ or } d_i > 4 \tag{3}$$

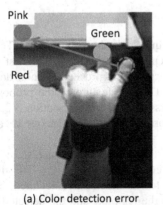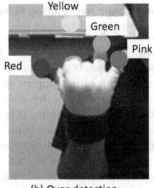

(a) Color detection error   (b) Over detection

Fig. 5. Examples of color detection errors

Table 1. Jugment criteria of color detection error

	Red (Thumb)	Yellow (Forefinger)	Violet (Middle finger)	Green (Ring finger)	Pink (Little finger)
Red (Thumb)	—	left	left	left	left
Yellow (Forefinger)	right	—	left	left	left
Violet (Middle finger)	right	right	—	left	left
Green (Ring finger)	right	right	right	—	left
Pink (Little finger)	right	right	right	right	—
Blue (Wrist)	Right or below	below	below	below	Left or below

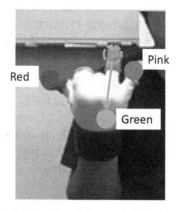

Fig. 6. Example of abnormal finger length

3.3   Hand Shape Recognition Sequence

The flow chart of the finger shape recognition sequence is shown in Fig.7.   Template feature vector files for each finger shape are prepared in advance.   The first step of the proposed sequence is to capture a camera image and to proceed to color detection to find the position of the fingers and wrist.   The key feature of the proposed sequence is the detection of color detection errors as described in section 3.2.   That means that any frame containing a feature vector that includes erroneous vector elements is rejected before the recognition process.

The Web camera captures hand shapes at about 30 frames per second, so, it is not a problem to remove any frames that include a color detection error.   The distance between the template vectors and the detected feature vector is calculated, and the hand shape with the minimum distance between the template and the detected vector is selected as the recognition result.   This sequence can enhance the recognition performance because frames that include a color detection error can be removed from the recognition process.

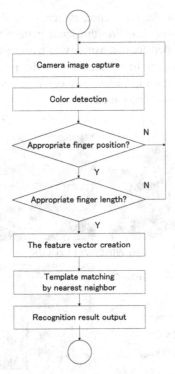

Fig. 7. Hand shape recognition sequence

4   Experiment and Evaluation

4.1   Experimental Environment and Conditions

The purpose of the proposed recognition methods is to maintain high recognition performance independent of the peripheral environment.   Therefore three different locations were selected for the experimental evaluation of the proposed method.   The experimental locations were, a place far from a window, a place at mid-distance from the window and a place near to the window, as shown in Fig.8.   The illumination conditions due to the room light and sun light from the window, which will affect recognition performance, are summarized in Table 2.   A Web camera (Logicool HD Pro Webcam C910, 5 million pixels, 30 frames/s) was used in this experiment.   The camera was mounted on the notebook PC as shown in Fig.8 and the distance between hand and camera was set to about 50 cm.

The recognition performance was evaluated using two methods, that is, with frame rejection based on considering the validity of color detection and without frame rejection, in order to clarify the effectiveness of the proposed method.   The following three experiment conditions, summarized in Table 3 were used to evaluate the proposed method.   Case1 is the base case, which used the conventional method. Case2 used the expanded color detection threshold pattern to confirm the effectiveness of enhancing the color detection sensitivity to avoid situations where detection was impossible.   Case3 was for full evaluation of the proposed sequence, that is, using the expanded color threshold pattern for color detection and the rejection of frames which indicated a color detection error.

Far from window (110Lux)

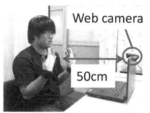 

Mid-distance from window (180Lux)

Near window (290Lux)

Fig. 8. Experimental environment

Table 2. Illumination conditions of experimental environment

Illumination	Position of room light	Influence of sunlight
110Lux	Above, Left slanting	Small
180Lux	Above, Back	Medium
290Lux	Above, Left slanting	Large

Table 3. Experiment conditions

	Threshold pattern	Frame rejection	Experiment purpose
Case1	Nominal	None	Base case
Case2	Broad	None	Enhancement of color detection sensitivity
Case3	Broad	Enabled	Evaluation of proposed sequence

4.2   Results and Evaluation

Experiments were carried out in each environment for each of the three cases.   6 typical hand shapes, as shown in Table 4 were used in each experiment.   The number of frames evaluated for each experiment that is for each light condition and each of the 3 Cases described above was 1800, that is, 100 frames, 3 times (each test was repeated three times), and 6 different hand shapes.   Table 5 shows the experimental results.   For each set of tests, the total of 1800 frames were classified into three types, frames rejected by color detection error (Case3 only), error frames and success frames (correctly recognized frames).   An evaluation factor was also calculated as the summation of the number of rejected frames (R) and 4×number of error frames (E).   The recognition success ratio was defined as follows.

Recognition success ratio = success frames / (total frames — rejected frames)   (4)

The following conclusions may be drawn from these results.   The effect of hue values expansions that is extending the hue threshold region is confirmed by the experiments carried out in a bright environment (290Lux), as shown in Case2 and Case3. The recognition success ratio was increased to 79.3% in a dark environment (110 Lux) by introducing both hue value expansion and frame rejection based on hand shape characteristics.   The average success ratio for the three cases, that is, Case1 (base case), Case2 (hue value expansion) and Case3 (hue value expansion and frame rejection) was 63.6%, 87.2% and 93.0%, respectively.   These results demonstrate the effectiveness of the proposed method.

Table 4. Hand shapes used in experiment

Finger pattern	00001	00010	00100	01000	10000	11111
Fingers extended	Thumb	Fore-finger	Middle finger	Ring finger	Little finger	All fingers

Table 5. Experimental results

Case	Illumination	Total frames	Rejected frames (R)	Error frames	Success frames (E)	R+4E	Recognition success ratio
Case1	110Lux	1800	N/A	619	1181	2476	65.6%
	180Lux	1800	N/A	18	1782	72	99.0%
	290Lux	1800	N/A	1327	473	5308	26.3%
Case2	110Lux	1800	N/A	663	1137	2652	63.2%
	180Lux	1800	N/A	27	1773	108	98.5%
	290Lux	1800	N/A	1	1799	4	99.9%
Case3	110Lux	1800	590	250	960	1590	79.3%
	180Lux	1800	11	0	1789	11	100.0%
	290Lux	1800	21	7	1772	49	99.6%

5   Conclusion

This paper presents a hand shape recognition method using colored gloves which takes into account the surrounding environment. Two methods are proposed to maintain a high recognition performance under different illumination conditions. The hue value threshold region is enlarged to enhance the sensitivity for color detection. In addition, image frame rejection is introduced to maintain recognition accuracy by considering hand shape features and finger length. A success ratio of 99.6% was obtained under bright illumination conditions, and 79.3% is under dark conditions. This verifies that the proposed method is effective in enhancing the recognition performance. To raise success ratio of 79.3% under dark conditions remains as one of further studies.

References

1. Khan, Z.R., Ibraheem, A.N.: Comparative Study of Hand Gesture Recognition System. In: Proc. of International Conference of Advanced Computer Science & Information Technology in Computer Science & Information Technology (CS & IT), vol. 2(3), pp. 203–213 (2012)
2. Baatar, B., Tanaka, J.: Comparing Sensor Based Techniques for Dynamic Gesture Recognition. In: The 10th Asia Pacific Conference on Computer Human Interaction, APCHI 2012, Poster 2P-21 (2012)
3. Matsuda, Y., Sakuma, I., Jimbo, Y., Kobayashi, E., Arafune, T., Isomura, T.: Development of Finger Braille Recognition System. Journal of Biometrical Science and Engineering 5(1), 54–65 (2010)
4. Jing, L., Zhou, Y., Cheng, Z., Wang, J.: A Recognition Method for One-stroke Finger Gestures Using a MEMS 3D Accelerometer. IEICE Transactions on Information and Systems E94-D(5), 1062–1072 (2011)
5. Yoruk, E., Konukoglu, E., Sankur, B., Darbon, J.: Shape - Based Hand Recognition. IEEE Transactions on Image Processing 15(7), 1803–1815 (2006)

Managing HMI Quality in Embedded System Development

Haruhiko Urokohara[1] and Naotake Hirasawa[2]

[1] U'eyes design Inc.,Yokohama, Japan
urokohara@ueyesdesign.co.jp
[2] Otaru University of Commerce, Hokkaido, Japan
hirasawa@res.otaru-uc.ac.jp

Abstract. We have developed HMI metrics to evaluate the usability of software products. System engineers who are not usability professional can design basic HMI software by using this metrics. The HMI metrics is expected to be applied for the Software Quality Auditing System in the future.

Keywords: HMI, Usability, Software quality metric, Knowledge management, Safety, Security and reliability.

1 Introduction

Today, a single system fault could cause a big disastrous turmoil, because many of functions in our modern society is operated by the collaboration of various information systems. The system fault could happen in wide range of field, such as from an embedded system in the smart phones to the social IT infrastructure. It is known that the many of the system faults were caused by software defects. In Japan, the "software quality audit system (provisional)" which audits systems in various fields by the third party has been considered to ensure safety, reliability, and usability. [1]

According to the previous research, the most causes of the software faults are software defects, problems in system planning and specification phase, and hardware defects. Especially, the first two already occupied more than 70%. [2]

In general, software defects are attempted to eliminate in software refinement phase. Especially, the development of the highly reliable software is aiming to eliminate all problems during software refinement phase. In such case, human-based activities are tended to minimize because the problems in software refinement phase are originated by human factors. On the other hand, problems in system planning and specification development can not apply this approach, because it is impossible to eliminate the human-based activity in those two processes.

Furthermore, the HMI (human-machine interface) specification makes the specification development more difficult. The performance and productivity of the system can be finally influenced by the HMI specification, because the operation or the use of the system is made by actual human. In the most case, even the safety of the system can be determined by it.

S. Yamamoto (Ed.): HIMI/HCII 2013, Part I, LNCS 8016, pp. 143–150, 2013.

Since this issue is widely recognized, one of the solutions is training and appointing specialists who have capability to deal with development of HMI. In fact, certifications systems of specialists in HMI design have been established in these years in Japan.

However, such certifications are well recognized by user-interface designers and web-designers, but not so well by embedded systems engineers. These engineers seem that introducing HMI design process has obstacles, such as overhead time and cost in development, not recognizable benefits for developers, and not urgent necessity [3].

For these reasons, system engineers with knowing the constraint of their development team without sufficient HMI design specialists, need to have to increase quality in use, and usability in their products, even in smaller steps, according to following requirements from the international market;

• Needs to provide a high-valued system
• Realized a system with high functionality and usability at the same time
• Ensure safety of a system

In this paper, authors attempt to clarify an approach to ensure the HMI quality that directly relates to marketability and safety of the products from the upper process of the development.

2   HMI Quality Issues in the Embedded System Development

In Embedded System Development Process (ESP) [4] by Information-technology Process Agency (IPA) in Japan, HMI design is done in the system architecture design process after the system requirement analysis process. (figure 1) In other words, HMI elements are decided, and the operational steps for each of them are designed according to required functions derived in the system requirement analysis process. And, incompletion of the basic design of HMI in this stage could cause a high risk of delay of the development.

On the contrary, it is said by HMI specialists solely the required function is not a sufficient input for HMI design. For instance, FACE method requires detailed information related to users.[5] Also practically, it is hard to design HMI without expert knowledge within the process of system requirement analysis and system architecture design.

In the case that the development organization includes HMI specialists, design guidelines and style guidelines are often provided to system engineers. System engineers often design HMI applying the style guidelines, since understanding and applying the design guidelines is too hard. Also experienced engineers develop patterns based on the style guideline and adds modifications according to given situations.[3]

However, this approach sometimes makes reviewing the HMI design properly within development process difficult.

And as a result, the HMI design solution without evaluation will be sent to the next process.

It is possible that HMI design solution without HMI quality tests will survive the final process of software development, if usability evaluation is not conducted within the whole development life cycle.

To avoid such situation, it is necessary to have a mechanism to check the HMI quality mechanism in the upper process of the system development. And, a method for quantitative evaluation of HMI quality has been studied. [6] This method, however, can not be applied to a single system development project to expect efficiency continuous basis, because the method requires the activities involving a whole organization, and requires the implementation of the quality management system and so on.

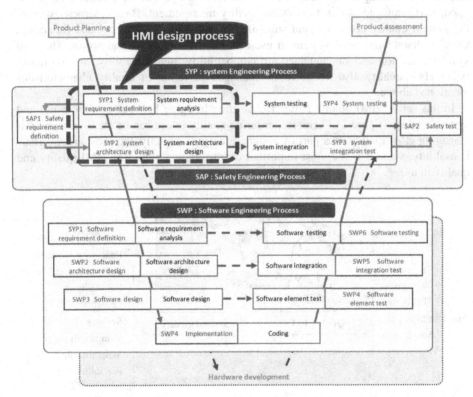

Fig. 1. HMI design process in the system life cycle   process (ESPR 2007)

3   HMI Quality Management

The HMI quality should be ensured within the framework of the quality management for the embedded system development. The product quality of system products has been schematized as ISO/IEC 25000 -Software product Quality Requirement and Evaluation (SQuaRE) series of international standards. [7] One of the merits of this series is that the quality management starts from the most upper process, and aims the quality improvement integrated with system development life cycle.

What kind of quality is required in HMI?

Firstly, the system enable for user to achieve what user is intended (user goal) efficiently. (Effectiveness and efficiency) And, risk for using the system such as the safety, economical efficiency, and ecological impacts is zero or minimized. (Freedom from risks) Additionally, satisfaction to use the system is required. (Satisfaction)

Those are all required as the overall quality by HMI, when user uses the system. Those are regarded as so-called "quality in use," and its quality characteristics are effectiveness, efficiency, freedom from risks, and satisfaction as mentioned above.[8]

From the viewpoint of developer, quality criteria for each system element are defined to meet during design process. Because HMI is a part of the system to be developed, it is managed within the system quality management. Basic characteristics of the system quality are functional suitability, performance efficiency, and reliability. Quality characteristics of system in use are usability, security, and so on. Those of system operation and maintenance are compatibility, maintainability, and portability.[8] HMI quality also needs to be managed in terms of quality characteristics mentioned above.

In this sense, HMI quality is one the position bridging between quality in use and system quality. (figure 2) Therefore, ensuring quality in use can be made efficiently if managing HMI quality as a part of system quality. Especially, the most critical issue is usability, since it is the most important characteristic connecting HMI quality and quality in use.

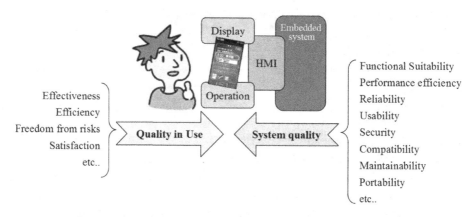

Fig. 2. HMI quality bridging between quality in use and system quality

And as previously mentioned, continuous improvement of HMI quality requires the implementation throughout development organization. HMI quality plan is developed, and HMI quality measurement criteria is set before the system development; quality is measured, and it criteria are verified toward the next development throughout the development lifecycle. (figure 3)

Implementing such management lifecycle for HMI quality ensures the continuous improvement of HMI quality.

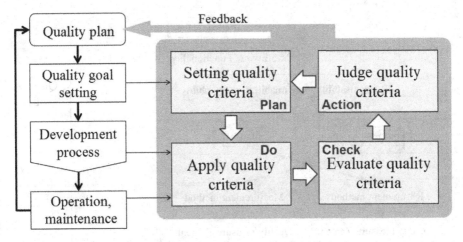

Fig. 3. Quality management lifecycle

4   HMI Quality Metrics

4.1   Introduction of HMI Quality Metrics

A quality metric indicates the measure of a quality characteristic and the method of measurement. The status of system quality is interpreted by the result of measurement. The relationship of HMI quality model and metrics is presented in Figure 4. As the figure shown, quality characteristics and metrics have many-to-many relationship, and the number of measurement indices will be uncontrollable to apply without proper management.

The objects evaluated by the measurement of HMI metrics are intermediate work products in HMI design process, such as HMI design specification, design solution (screen transitional diagram, screen layout, element design, and so on), and should be organized systematically.

HMI metrics rarely can be developed in logical way. Basically, they can be developed experts' knowledge and refined through development lifecycle. It is also possible that metrics to refer public metrics form standards and literature. And, systematical approach, such as the GQM method, can be done by clarifying measurement "Goal," clarifying the criteria if the goal is achieved by "Questions," and collect necessary "Merics". [9]

U'eyes Design Inc., with over 20 years experiences of development of HMI for embedded systems, has been developing over 150 metrics.

Those metrics will be redefined according to system development lifecycle for each client, and evaluated their validity through the operation in each development organization.

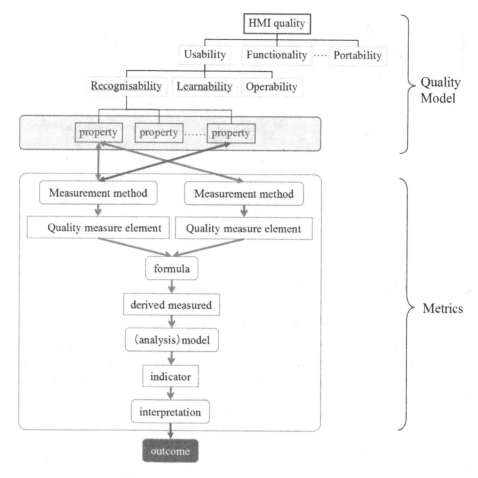

Fig. 4. Relationship of quality model and metrics

Also, by providing HMI metrics to organizations, the company helps them to implement HMI quality management lifecycle to ensure their continuous improvement in HMI quality.

4.2   Example of HMI Quality Metrics

Figure 5 shows an example metrics of counting the screen steps.[10]

And the upper half describes a count of screen steps of the original UI in the case from starting with choosing a reference mail address on Contacts to finishing with choosing a destination folder for 'create new message filter' process.

The original design, with the lack of the consideration for creating a message filter detecting multiple sender addresses, requires repeating same procedure many time if a user want to create a filter to collect messages from his/her family members. Then, the design solution can be very inefficient one for many cases.

The lower halt describes the improved UI design with positioning a "more" option to avoid such inefficiency on the original design. The new design requires fewer steps when creating a filter based on multiple sender addresses without going back to the first screen every time.

Although a drastic solution could be an operational flow requiring "done" operation after choosing multiple senders addresses, if the system is flexible enough for changing specifications.

Using such metrics can lead to create HMI designs with better quality in use by quantifying an attribute of usability, and leading efficient UI with less steps.

Here describes "'Steps for direct screen transition and indirect screen transition' on a smart phone" as an example of metrics for information architecture.

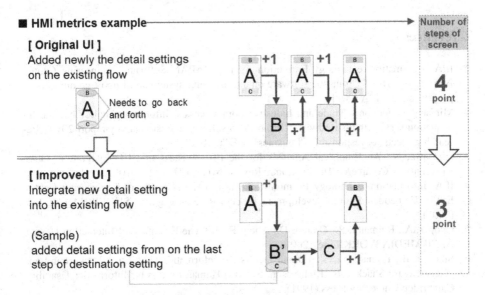

Fig. 5. The different number of steps by different flow structures in steps

5   Summary

This study discussed about the HMI quality which directly relates to the marketability and safety in the approach from the upper development process management. And also it is important to point out that the continuous measurement and evaluation of the quality to improve the HMI quality through the development life cycle. Therefore, it is essential to use HMI quality metrics.

And, it is important that the initial value of HMI quality metrics should be set according to the prior experiences, HMI metrics should be tailored through the system development process to confirm its validity.

For the basis of HMI metrics the following two are emphasized;

- HMI quality should be managed as a part of introduction of life cycle of system quality management.
- Development of the quality model covering a whole system, and metrics including HMI metrics based on of the model.

Finally, preparation of the metrics would be able to diagnosis of the HMI quality system, the safety in system operation as applications. Comparing to the filed software quality metrics, collecting and editing of empirical data rarely has done in HMI quality.

In order to ensure the safety in consumer products, improve the effectiveness in product development, and improve the competitiveness in international market, it is important to implement HMI metrics as a part of the social foundation.

References

1. IPA: Information-technology Promotion Agency, JAPAN Software Engineering Center, Activity reports of Group the software quality auditing system and Report commissioned project related, IPA (2011)
2. Ministry of Economy Trade and Industry, Commerce and information policy bureau, Information service industry division, Embedded software industry survey report 2010 - Research projects for responsible of business, METI (2010)
3. Hirasawa, N.: An Empirical Analysis for the Effectiveness of HCD Integration. Otaru University of Commerce The Economic Review 61(1), 127–139 (2010)
4. IPA: Information-technology Promotion Agency, JAPAN Software Engineering Center, ESPR: Embedded System development Process Reference guide. SHOEISHA Co., Ltd. (2007)
5. Cooper, A., Reimann, R., Cronin, D.: About Face 3 The Essentials of Interaction Design. ASCII MEDIA WORKS Inc. (2008)
6. Shackel, B., Richardson, S.: Human factors for Informatics Usability - Background and Overview. In: Shackel, B., Richardson, S. (eds.) Human Factors for Informatics Usability. Cambridge University Press (1991)
7. ISO/IEC 25000:2005 Software Engineering - Software product Quality Requirements and Evaluation (SQuaRE) - Guide to SQuaRE (2005)
8. ISO/IEC 25010:2011 Software Engineering - Software product Quality Requirements and Evaluation (SQuaRE) - System and software quality models (2011)
9. Basili, V.: Using Measurement to Build Core Competencies in Software. Data and Analysis Center for Software (2005)
10. Urokohara, H., Hirasawa, N., Kanda, S.: HMI guidelines and metrics for improving Quality in use. In: HCD Research Conference 2012 (2012)

Usability Evaluation of the Universal Computer Workstation under Supine, Sitting and Standing Postures

Hsin-Chieh Wu[1,*], Min-Chi Chiu[2], Cheng-Lung Lee[1], and Ming-Yao Bai[1]

[1] Department of Industrial Engineering and Management, Chaoyang University of Technology,
Taichung, Taiwan, R.O.C.
hcwul@cyut.edu.tw

[2] School of Occupational Therapy, Chung Shan Medical University,
Taichung, Taiwan, R.O.C.

Abstract. The purpose of this study was to evaluate the usability of the self-made universal computer workstation. The 9 handicapped and 10 healthy adults were recruited to participate in this study, in order to understand the performances of computer operation, ratings in comfort and satisfaction for using the tested workstation in different positions. This workstation can be successfully adjusted for standing, sitting, and supine postures. This workstation also allows easy access of wheelchair. No significant differences in performances were found among supine, sitting, and standing postures. All of the participants considered this workstation comfortable. Most handicapped participants preferred to adopt supine posture to use the computer. The experimental results revealed that supine posture lead to more comfort in the lower back without decreasing performances while using a computer. Further, the healthy participants had the mean rating in satisfaction of 3.7, which was similar to that of the handicapped. It indicates that the tested workstation satisfied both the handicapped and the healthy participants. The findings of this study can provide helpful information for further improvement of a universal computer workstation.

Keywords: universal design, workstation, usability, ergonomic design.

1 Introduction

The computer technology has greatly advanced in the world. No matter in life or work, the use of visual display terminals (VDTs) has been very popular and indispensable. Generally, the computer workstation is designed for sitting posture. Unfortunately, for the person with chronic low back pain (LBP), seated posture also has its share of risks. In fact, the traditional VDT workstations not only hinder the use by some people with chronic LBP but have been shown to cause LBP after prolonged use [1]. Some people with chronic LBP are able to relieve their discomfort by lying in

---

* Corresponding author.

S. Yamamoto (Ed.): HIMI/HCII 2013, Part I, LNCS 8016, pp. 151–156, 2013.

a supine or significantly reclined posture [2]. Alternative computer workstations have been designed to allow the VDT operator to access the computer from a significantly reclined or supine posture. These postures have been shown to relieve some forms of LBP [2].

Previous study found that lying supine can reduce the intradiscal pressure as much as 75% as compared to standing upright. Whereas sitting upright increases intradiscal pressure as much as 40% when compared to standing upright [3]. To adopt a supine posture not only can reduce the lumbar intradiscal pressure but also allow people who have difficulty in standing or sitting to use a computer. Although lying supine has the advantage of more comfort in lower back, someone may concern about that the operation performance may be decreased by the supine posture. Studies are needed to investigate whether or not body posture affects computer operation performance. Therefore, a universal computer workstation was made here for people to adopt different postures such as supine, sitting, and standing postures when using a computer.

The main purpose of this study was to investigate the effect of body posture on the performance and subjective comfort while using a computer. The handicapped and healthy adults were recruited to participate in this study, in order to understand whether these two groups lead to different results while using this universal computer workstation. We expected that this workstation can actually solve the problems of the handicapped and people with chronic LBP. Further, the users' recommendations this workstation were also collected, in order to improve the self-made universal computer workstation.

2   Methods

2.1   Subjects

Nineteen people, including ten healthy adults and nine young handicapped persons, participated in this study. The healthy adults all have no musculoskeletal disorders. The young handicapped persons have lower limb disabilities or spinal injuries, and need to rely on a wheelchair or crutches or other aids; but their mental abilities and hands are able to operate a computer. All of the subjects weekly use a computer for more than 10 hours. The entire participants are all right-handed, and must sign the written consent of the test.

2.2   Equipments

The self-made universal computer workstation was used here. This workstation had a base of electric lifting table, and it was designed to be adjusted for standing, sitting, and supine postures (as shown in Fig. 1). The screen can be adjusted from 0 to 90 degrees forward; keyboard adjustment range is from 0 to 50 degrees from the desktop plain.

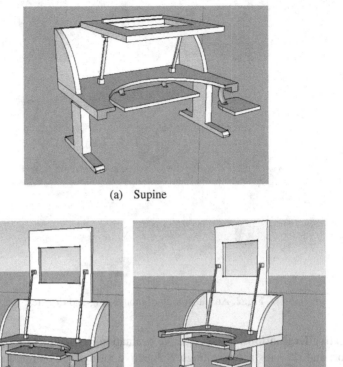

(a) Supine

(b) Sitting   (c) Standing

Fig. 1. Illustrations of (a) supine, (b) sitting, and (c) standing positions for using the tested workstation

2.3   Usability Test Protocol

Computer Operations. Subjects should type Chinese words in accordance with the articles shown on the computer display, and the article input time was ten minutes. After the Chinese typing test, the score and error rate were calculated as typing performances.

After the typing test, the mouse drag-and-drop test was required to perform by subjects. Each subject was required to select twelve objects evenly distributed on a circle surrounding a central box, and then drag each object separately into the box (Fig. 2). The program automatically record the completion time until all objects were moved to the central box. This test repeated three times, and the average completion time was the performance of the mouse operation.

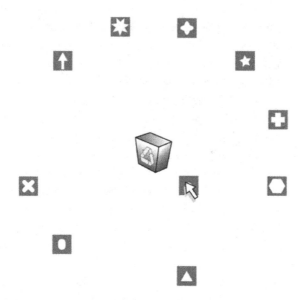

Fig. 2. An Illustration of mouse drag-and-drop test

Subjective Evaluations. The subjective evaluation included: (1) subjective ratings in comfort and (2) satisfaction ratings. Subjective ratings in comfort had a seven-point Likert scale, 1 representing 'very uncomfortable' and 7 representing 'very comfortable'. Eight body parts, including eyes, neck, shoulder, upper arm, forearm, wrist, upper back and lower back, were designed in the subjective comfort questionnaire. These data were collected after the use of the tested workstation.

In addition, subjects were asked to rate satisfaction of the tested workstation along eight items:

1. Workstations can be adjusted for standing, supine or sitting positions.
2. Various computer components can be easily placed in this workstation.
3. Can easily enter the workstation.
4. The tilt angle of the screen and viewing distance can be adjusted according to your needs.
5. Mouse and keyboard positions and tilt angle can be adjusted according to your needs.
6. Using the computer, operating the mouse and keyboard comfortably.
7. Can easily leave the workstation.
8. Can easily remove various computer components.

Each item had a five-point Likert scale, with 1 representing 'very unsatisfactory' and 5 representing 'very satisfactory'.

2.4   Experimental Settings

In order to reduce the interference of other variables, this study tried to control the following factors:

- The computer jobs, screen brightness and contrast were the same. The ambient illumination was controlled at 500 ~ 600 lux.
- The subjects were in good mental condition during the experiment. The input method taken by the participants was Microsoft New Phonetic, and the experimental room had no noise, so as not to affect the degree of concentration of the participants.

3   Results

3.1   Operation Performances

Table 1 shows the computer operation performances for the healthy adults and the young handicapped subjects in the standing, sitting, and supine positions. No data were available for the young handicapped subjects in the standing position because they were not able to adopt standing posture. The ANOVA results indicated that body posture had little effect ($p> 0.05$) on typing score, error rate, and mouse drag time. Further, it is obvious that the young handicapped subjects had worse operation performances than the healthy adults.

3.2   Subjective Evaluation Results

Table 2 shows the descriptive statistics (mean±SD) of subjective comfort ratings in eight body parts for the three different positions. No data were available for the young handicapped subjects in the standing position because they were not able to adopt standing posture. The ANOVA results indicated that body posture had a significant effect ($p< 0.05$) on the comfort ratings in lower back. Post hoc comparisons were then performed by Turkey method. The analyzed results revealed that supine posture had significantly better comfort ratings in lower back compared with standing and sitting postures. Further, it is obvious that the young handicapped subjects had similar comfort ratings as compared to those of the healthy adults.

Finally, the results of satisfaction ratings show that the healthy adults had the mean ratings in satisfaction of 3.7, and the handicapped also had the mean ratings in satisfaction of 3.7. It indicates that this workstation satisfied both the handicapped and the healthy participants.

Table 1. Computer operation performances in the standing, sitting, and supine positions

	The healthy adults			The young handicapped		
Performance	Standing	Sitting	Supine	Standing	Sitting	Supine
Typing score	516±168	500±169	435±141	N/A	51±77	44.4±74.6
Error rate (%)	5.3±10.4	1.6±1.6	2.2±2.8	N/A	18.5±18.2	32.4±37.5
Drag time (s)	13.9±1.4	14.1±2.0	14.9±1.8	N/A	58.9±22.4	52.1±15.7

Table 2. Subjective comfort ratings for the standing, sitting, and supine postures

Body part	The healthy adults			The young handicapped		
	Standing	Sitting	Supine	Standing	Sitting	Supine
Eyes	4.3±1.1	4.5±1.0	4.5±1.5	N/A	4.7±1.1	4.1±0.6
Neck	4.2±1.0	4.5±1.0	5.1±1.6	N/A	4.8±1.4	4.3±1.4
Shoulder	4.2±1.2	4.0±1.1	4.8±1.8	N/A	4.3±1.1	4.6±1.3
Upper arm	3.8±1.0	3.9±0.7	4.4±1.7	N/A	4.3±1.1	4.8±1.2
Forearm	3.7±1.1	3.1±0.9	3.5±1.6	N/A	4.1±1.3	4.6±1.4
Wrist	3.7±1.3	3.2±1.0	3.1±1.4	N/A	3.2±1.0	3.8±1.4
Upper back	4.1±1.4	4.4±0.8	5.4±1.4	N/A	5.0±1.2	4.9±1.4
Lower back*	4.0±1.3	4.5±0.9	5.6±1.3	N/A	4.6±1.6	5.1±1.1

PS: 1 representing 'very uncomfortable' and 7 representing 'very comfortable'.
* Body posture had a significant effect ($p < 0.05$) on the comfort ratings in lower back.

4   Discussion

The main purpose of this study was to evaluate the usability of the self-made universal computer workstation in three different body postures. Computer operation performances, subjective comfort and satisfaction were collected. Experimental results show that the participants had similar computer operation performances among standing, sitting, and supine postures. It implies that the tested workstation could be adequately adjusted for operating a computer in standing, sitting, and supine positions and inconsequently caused similar performances at different body postures. In addition, the comfort rating results show that supine posture had significantly better comfort ratings in lower back than those of standing and sitting postures. Therefore, it should be noted that supine posture can improve lower back comfort without decreasing operation performances while using a computer. However, the operation time of each trial was only 30 minutes in the current study. More studies are required to investigate whether the current findings can be applied in the prolonged VDT operation tasks.

Acknowledgments.   The authors thank the National Science Council of the Republic of China for financially supporting this research (Contracts No. NSC98-2221-E-324-013 and NSC99-2628-E-324-024).

References

1. Bendix, T.: Low back pain and seating. In: Lueder, R., Noro, K. (eds.) Hard Facts about Soft Machines- The Ergonomics of Seating, pp. 147–155. Taylor & Francis Ltd., London (1994)
2. Haynes, S., Williams, K.: Product review of alternative computer workstations as possible workplace accommodations for people with chronic low back pain. Technology and Disability 19, 41–52 (2007)
3. Nachemson, A.: The lumbar spine, an orthopedic challenge. Spine 1(1), 59–69 (1976)

Window Manager Designed for Cloud Services

Shizuki Yoshino, Tetsuo Tanaka, and Kazunori Matsumoto

Department of Information and Computer Sciences, Kanagawa Institute of Technology,
Atsugi, Japan
yoshinoshizuki@gmail.com,
{t-tanaka,matumoto}@ic.kanagawa-it.ac.jp

Abstract. Cloud services like web-based e-mail or hosted office suites are becoming widespread. With these services, PC users are likely to use several services and to visit several sites at once. As a result, several windows appear on the desktop, and their overlapping complicates access to hidden windows. In this study, the authors propose a window manager running on the browser. The proposed window manager employs a tiling style in order to improve the usability of multiple cloud services at the same time. It also employs a window placement method, implemented by drawing frame edges, and a window replacement method using drag and drop. It is user-friendly, even for unskilled PC-users. An experiment showed that the proposed window manager was effective in reducing the number of operations for window placement or replacement.

Keywords: window manager, cloud service, drawing frame edges, tiling style, window placement, usability.

1   Introduction

Cloud services, like web-based e-mail or hosted office suites, are becoming widespread. With such services, PC users are more likely to use several services and to visit several sites at once, e.g. document preparation while consulting a net dictionary, or Internet surfing while watching a movie. As a result, several windows appear on the desktop, and their overlapping complicates access to a hidden window. Reducing the cost of window operations is an important challenge. According to an analysis by Shibata [1], workers at an intellectual property management department spent 7.4–9.1% of time in window operations such as activating, moving, and resizing windows.

A window manager may be used to operate multiple windows efficiently. Window managers are classified into two categories, overlapping style and tiling style [2][3].

Most current window managers follow the independent overlapping window style. In this style the user manages a window's location and size in any way desired. When the location and size of a window changes, other windows may be obscured. When a window is hidden behind the front window, the user needs to move the window to the front in order to see the contents.

S. Yamamoto (Ed.): HIMI/HCII 2013, Part I, LNCS 8016, pp. 157–166, 2013.

The window manager of MS Windows 7 has a feature called Aero Snap[4]. Using this function, users can automatically resize the window to half the size of the display screen by dragging and dropping to the edge of the screen. But the size of the window is fixed at half of the screen. If there are three or more windows, windows overlap and rear windows are hidden. Moreover, users have to turn the function on or off in the control panel, and it is troublesome to re-enable the function if users have disabled it.

With the tiling style, any window is always fully visible, because windows are not allowed to overlap. It is easy to figure out where each window is. However in existing window managers like dwn[5] and so on, a user has to enter a numeric value in pixels to set the position and size of a window. It is not easy to use for unskilled users.

Shibata et al.[6][7] proposed a system that made it possible to construct workspaces consisting of multiple windows through a simple user interface of window docking. The system makes it possible to switch workspaces easily, and reduces the overhead of window operations within workspaces by use of a tiled window approach. Their experiment of a task-switching task showed that the system is 14% to 21% faster than a traditional window system. However, when using the system, the user builds a workspace by docking, after starting multiple windows for the task and so time is spent on the placement of the windows.

Meanwhile, there has been a wide introduction of cloud services, such as Google Drive[8], which lets you store all your files including documents, photos, videos and Google Docs online and access them from anywhere, Microsoft Office Web Apps[9], which is a web-based version of the Microsoft Office productivity suite, Facebook[10], which is a social networking service, and so on. As a result, a window manager for the cloud services is required. But existing window managers are designed for managing desktop applications. There are few designed for cloud services.

CEITON technology Inc. offers a window manager WinLIKE[11] running on a browser. With WinLIKE, web applications, websites and portals can contain real windows just like a normal desktop application. However, it adopts an overlapping window style, and so it suffers from the above-mentioned problems of overlapping windows. Moreover, it takes time to get used to using it, because its user interface is a CEITON proprietary one, and it requires users to enter a URL to launch cloud services.

In this study, the authors propose a window manager that is developed as a cloud service running on a HTML5 enabled browser, such as Chrome or Firefox. The proposed window manager employs a tiling style in order to improve the usability of multiple cloud services at the same time. It also employs a window placement method, based on drawing boundary lines, and a window replacement method, based on drag and drop. It is user-friendly, even for unskilled PC-users. In addition, it can save and restore a workspace consisting of a collection of multiple windows. Users can switch tasks smoothly.

2   Approach

2.1   Tiling Style Window Manager Running on a Browser

Cloud services such as Web-based office software and social networking services have become widespread.   In these cloud services, users don't have to download the application program; data can be stored on the server. Users can use them at any time, anywhere, on any PC or mobile device in the Internet environment. Leading companies like Microsoft and Google provide cloud services. These results suggest that the trend toward cloud services will continue to accelerate in the future.

In order to efficiently use multiple cloud services at the same time, we propose a window manager running on a browser. WinLIKE, described above, is a window manager for the cloud service, but because it uses an overlapping style, it requires a lot of operations for switching, moving, and resizing a window. There is a way to spread multiple browser windows over the desktop using the tiling window manager for the desktop, but with this approach, the proportion of the screen taken up with toolbars or menu bars at the top of each browser window increases, and the area available for the application body is reduced. In the proposed window manger, we adopt a tiled window manager that spreads multiple cloud service windows over a single browser window.

2.2   Intuitive Window Operation

In WinLIKE and dwn, because users must set the window size and position by means of numeric input, unskilled PC users do not really know where the window will be or how large it will be. For example, a user may need to modify the input number several times before succeeding in resizing the window to half the size of the desktop screen. It also takes time to move the cursor to the edge of the window to resize it by dragging the edge. If a user wants to swap a window, he or she must resize and reposition both of the two windows.

In order to overcome the difficulty of using the resize function by means of numeric input or dragging edges, this window manager provides three functions, namely adding and removing a window frame by drawing frame edges, automatic placement of the window, and moving windows using drag and drop. To add or to remove a window frame, the user draws frame edges in the window manager. The position and size of a window frame are determined by the frame edges. When a cloud service is invoked, the window is automatically opened at the size of window frame that has been set. If a user wants to swap the windows in the right half and the left half, this can be achieved by dragging the left half of the window, which the user wants to move, and dropping it into the right half of the window.

To use a cloud services, a user normally needs to enter the appropriate URL. To eliminate this operation, the window manager provides a menu bar at the top. The user clicks the cloud service menu item he or she wants to use, and the cloud service window will be displayed in the browser. The menu displays the cloud services that are commonly used. This makes it possible to launch a cloud service that the user wants to use in an instant, without entering the URL. At present these services are pre-determined in the window manager, so a user cannot change them, but this option may be possible in the future.

Fig.1 shows an example of a screen including windows of a word processing service, a dictionary service, and a video site. Items (a) are frame edges that have been drawn. Each window is resized to fit into the frame enclosed by the drawn lines. Items (b) are the drag and drop bars for moving or swapping windows. Item (c) is the menu bar; using this menu bar, users can start a cloud service with a single click, without having to enter configuration details in a dialog window.

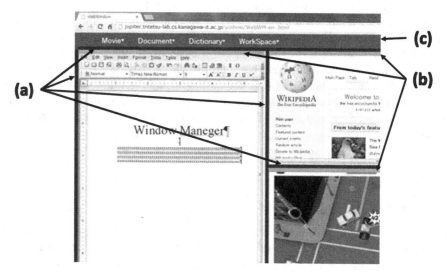

Fig. 1. Appearance of Window Manager

2.3   Operating Multiple Windows Collectively as a Workspace

When undertaking work, a user typically opens multiple application programs, and positions each application window in a place where it is easy for them to work. In other words, each user builds his/her own workspace specific to the job in hand. The applications which need to be open are different for each item of work. Therefore, users have to build a workspace to suit each job from scratch. Before users can start work on another job, it takes time if it is necessary to build a workspace from scratch. When a user suspends and then resumes his/her work, or when a user wants to use the same workspace many times, it is convenient if he or she can save and restore the workspace. This makes it possible to reduce the time spent on window operations.

This window manager is able to manipulate multiple windows collectively as a workspace in two ways: an operation on the browser window and a function of saving and restoring a workspace. Since the window manager runs on a browser, it is possible for users to manage a complete workspace containing several applications by a single operation on the browser window (resize, move, minimize, maximize). For example, for a brief interruption of work, the user only needs to minimize the browser window. In addition, to meet requirements of a longer suspension of work, the window manager provides functions to save and restore the workspace. This is done from the menu item "Workspace" on the menu bar. Using this function, the user can avoid having to rebuild a workspace from scratch.

3   Functions of the Window Manager

This window manager is written in JavaScript and HTML5, and has the following five functions: (1) cloud service launch, (2) adding or removing a window frame by drawing, (3) automatic placement of a window, (4) moving a window, (5) and saving and restoring a workspace. Details are described below.

3.1   Cloud Service Launch

Using the menu bar, as shown in Fig.2, users can invoke cloud services. In this window manager, users can invoke three types of services, i.e., office software, video sites, and dictionaries. In the current implementation, we use Hanscom's ThinkFree, which is compatible with Microsoft Office, as office software, Dailymotion as the video site, and Wikipedia, FreeTranslation and goo as dictionaries. Because the menu bar is similar to sites that have many users such as Google and Facebook, users can quickly grasp how to handle it. The menu has a hierarchical structure.

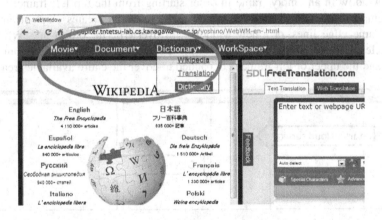

Fig. 2. Menu Bar

3.2   Adding and Removing a Window Frame by Drawing Frame Edges

In order to determine the position and size of the window, instead of a method of entering a numeric value in a dialog box, we have adopted a method of drawing frame edges. Users can determine the position and size of a window frame by drawing horizontal and vertical lines on the screen with a mouse click.

As shown in Figure 3, clicking point (a) on the frame edge (i), which is drawn in advance, a new frame edge line (iii) starting from point (a) is drawn. The frame edge line (iii) is deleted when a user clicks on the point (a) again.   A newly drawn frame edge (iii) can be manipulated in the same way, so clicking on point (b) will produce a new frame edge (iv). With this function, users can grasp the size of the window intuitively and visually. As a result, users can reduce the number of operations involved in resizing a window.

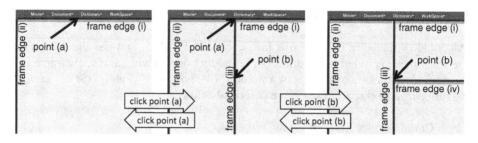

Fig. 3. Drawing frame edge lines

3.3   Automatic Placement of a Window

This function places the cloud service window to fit the drawn frame edge lines automatically. As shown in Fig.4, if the border lines have already been drawn, that is, if there is more than one empty window frame, the window manager displays the cloud service window in an empty frame in order starting from the top left frame. If there are no empty frames to display the window, the user can creates empty frames by adding frame edge lines, or a new window will overwrite the oldest one. When the user deletes a frame edge line, the frame on the extreme right or the bottom is removed, and the upper or left frame is expanded to cover the entire available area.

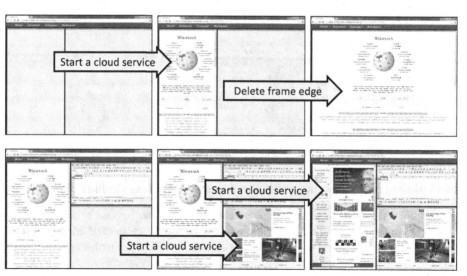

Fig. 4. Automatic Placement of Windows

3.4   Moving a Window

A window may be moved by the user dragging and dropping the window of a cloud service into another window frame. As shown in Fig.5, if a user wants to move the window in the frame on the left to the frame on the right, it is only necessary to drag the gray "drag and drop bar" at the top of the window and drop it onto the drag and drop bar on the right hand side. If another window is already displayed on the right, the positions of the windows are swapped with each other.

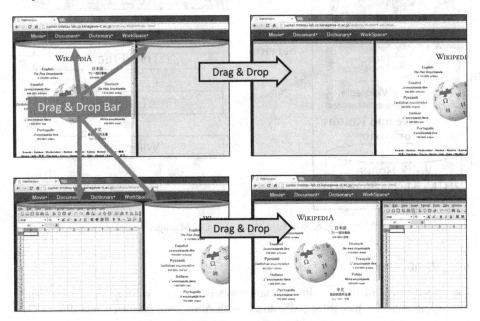

Fig. 5. Moving a Window

3.5   Saving and Restoring a Workspace

The list of window states that include position, size and the cloud service running on each window will be referred to as a "workspace". Workspaces can be saved or restored using the menu item "Workspace" on the menu bar. Using this function, the user can avoid having to rebuild a workspace from scratch.

4   Implementation and Evaluation

4.1   Implementation

In order to run the window manager on a browser, it was developed as a web application (as a cloud service) using HTML5, JavaScript as shown in Fig.6. The frame edge line drawing function is implemented using the Canvas feature of HTML5. The workspace store function is implemented by the Local storage feature of HTML5.

In addition, the moving window function is implemented by the drag and drop feature of HTML5. A window of a cloud service is embedded in the window manager by using the inline frame element of HTML.

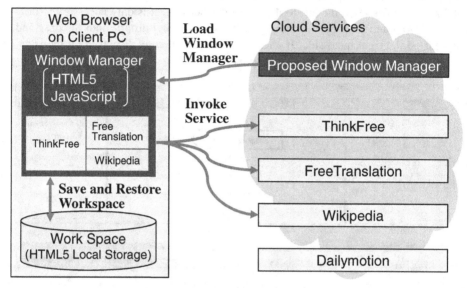

Fig. 6. Structure of the Window Manager

4.2   Evaluation

The effectiveness of this window manager was evaluated by comparison with Windows (with Aero Snap enabled), Windows (with Aero Snap disabled), and Win LIKE. In this experiment, we compared the number of mouse clicks and drags based on a scenario that consisted of the following seven steps:

1. Start the window manager
2. Launch three cloud services (i.e. a word processor, a presentation software, and a dictionary). Set the word processor window to be placed in the left half of the screen, arrange the presentation software window to be placed in the lower right quarter of the screen, and arrange the dictionary window to be placed in the upper right quarter.
3. Swap the word processor window with the presentation software window.
4. Save a document and a presentation, and save the workspace that has the current state of windows if possible.
5. Close the word processor and the dictionary, open a video site, set the video site window so as to be placed in the right half of the screen.
6. Exit the window manager and all cloud services.
7. Start the window manager again, start each cloud service and reconstruct window arrangement as it was stored in step 4.

Fig.7 shows the results of the evaluation. Thirty operations were required in Windows with Aero Snap disabled. When changing the window size by dragging, it was not possible to select the desired size with a single drag; it was necessary to make additional "tweaks" to the position when placing a tile, and in practice it takes thirty operations or more. In Windows, when Aero Snap is either enabled or disabled, the window manager does not remember the size and position of the window. Therefore, in order to reconstruct the window arrangement in step 7, the same operation as step 2 is required. WinLIKE requires a lot of operations to launch a new cloud service and to resize a window. This is due to the use of a dialog window to set the screen parameters when starting a new cloud service.

The experiment showed that the proposed window manager was effective, that is to say, it reduces by about half the number of operations for window placement or replacement compared with other window managers.

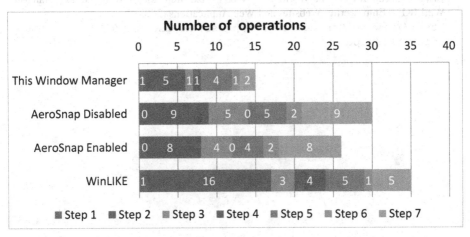

Fig. 7. Comparison of number of operations for different methods of managing windows

5   Conclusions

In this paper we have proposed a window manager designed for cloud services. The proposed window manager employs a tiling style in order to improve the usability of multiple cloud services at the same time. The main feature of the window manager is a window placement function based on drawing frame edge lines and a window replacement method by drag and drop. An experiment has shown that the proposed window manager reduces the number of operations for window placement or replacement.

References

1. Shibata, H.: Measuring the Efficiency of Introducing Large Displays and Multiple Displays. IPSJ Journal 50(3), 1204–1213 (2009) (in Japanese)
2. Bly, B., Rosenberg, J.: A Comparison of Tiled and Overlapping Windows. In: Human Factors in Computer Systems: CHI 1986 Conference Proceedings, pp. 101–106 (1986)

3. Myers, B.A.: Window Interfaces: A Taxonomy of Window Manager User Interfaces. IEEE Computer Graphics & Applications 8(5), 5–84 (1988)
4. Aero Snap, `http://windows.microsoft.com/en-US/windows7/products/features/snap`
5. dwn, `http://dwm.suckless.org/`
6. Shibata, H., Omura, K.: The support of multitasking through window docking. In: Proc. of IPSJ Interaction 2011 Conference Proceedings, pp. 391–394 (2011) (in Japanese)
7. Shibata, H., Omura, K.: Docking Window Framework: Supporting multitasking by docking windows. In: Proc. of the 10th Asia Pacific Conference on Computer Human Interaction, APCHI 2012 (2012)
8. Google Drive, `https://drive.google.com/`
9. Facebook, `http://www.facebook.com/`
10. Microsoft Office Web Apps, `http://office.microsoft.com/en-us/web-apps/`
11. CEITON technologies, The World Wide Web's Next Step Ahead: Web Window Manager WinLIKE – Empowering Websites and Web Applications (2003), `http://www.ceiton.com/CMS/EN/press/WinLIKE_pr_001_information.pdf`

Part II

Information Searching, Browsing and Structuring

Finders, Keepers, Losers, Seekers: A Study of Academics' Research-Related Personal Information Collections

Mashael Al-Omar and Andrew Cox

Information School, University of Sheffield, UK
{liq09ma,a.m.cox}@sheffield.ac.uk

Abstract. In conducting their research, scholars are not only information seekers, they are information keepers and managers as well. This paper describes a study of seventeen scholars from Education and Health disciplines (College of Nursing and Health Science College) in the Public Authority for Applied Education and Training (PAAET), Kuwait and their research-related personal information collections. A model explaining the size, diversity, hybridity and fragmentation of these collections to immediate and underlying causes is presented.

Keywords: Personal Information Management, Human Computer Interaction, Information Behavior, Information Practice, Information Retrieval.

1   Introduction

Within their research, scholars engage in "searching, collecting, reading, writing and collaborating" [25]. As a result of these information practices, they build and then have to manage significant Personal Information Collections (PICs) [23], [16]. Such materials accumulate over time [17] and collections can grow to be huge in size, diverse in nature and format [11]. They include books, published works, and web pages, emails and electronic files on a computer's hard drive [11]. Ensuring that information can be re-found when needed and so "exploited" [17], [27] is an information and data management challenge [10].

Investigation of these issues requires a holistic view of what are often separated out as different fields of study, i.e. Information Behaviour (IB), Personal Information Management (PIM) and Information Practice (IP). Research in this area should link information practices to the research process, and include investigation of the management of research data as well as secondary literature and other information. Studies often focus either on physical or electronic information collections [5], [15], [1], [13], [28] but both should be looked at together.

The purpose of this paper is to describe a study that was carried out to develop such in-depth understanding of scholars' research-related PICs. The study examined how research-related PICs are created, used and managed within the research process.

S. Yamamoto (Ed.): HIMI/HCII 2013, Part I, LNCS 8016, pp. 169–176, 2013.

It explored the factors that shape their management and sought to evaluate how successful scholars are at achieving the exploitation of information they collect.

2   Literature Review

Personal information management (PIM) is about how people "acquire or create, store, organize, maintain, retrieve, use, and distribute the information needed to complete tasks (work-related or not)" [12]. Researchers have investigated PIM in diverse ways such as to develop a system for information retrieval to facilitate information reuse [29] while others investigated information discovery and finding only [6], [7], [20], [4].

Relatively few studies to date have investigated scholars as information keepers and managers, rather the focus has tended to be on scholars information seeking behavior, in the context of their literature review [6], [24], [22]. One exception is Kaye et al. [18] who investigated forty eight scholars in multiple disciplines and ranging in seniority from graduate students to professors by touring their offices and conducting semi-structured interviews. The study found that academics not only store information for the purposes of information retrieval, but also for *"creating legacy, sharing resources, confronting fears and anxieties and identity construction"* [18]. The main uses were similar across disciplines and seniority. A great variety of storage strategies were uncovered in the research. Physical collections of information were stored in anything from custom-built offices to a mobile solution of bags and boxes stored in the back of a car. Digitally, academics developed their own individual way of archiving digital material rather than using available tools and solutions [18]. This is a relatively unique study.

Therefore, the aim of this research was to add to such relatively sparse literature by examining how research-related PICs are created, used and managed within the research process by answering main questions: What are personal information collections of scholars like? How do scholars use their personal information collections in their research? It also explored the factors that shaped their Personal Information Management (PIM) activities such as discipline, seniority, time pressure and the quality of support services.

3   Methodology

The study adopted an emergent design and an interpretive-qualitative approach based on in-depth, face-to-face interviews in order to understand the scholars' world and life [3] as they talk about their experience in their own words [21]. The focus of this paper is to present analysis of seventeen interviews of scholars in the Public Authority for Applied Education and Training (PAAET), Kuwait, from the disciplines of Education and Health preceded by tours of their personal space of information and observation.

In addition to interviews, photographs of scholars' personal space of information and their information collections were taken and treated as data complementing the interviews and achieve more understanding [26]. The interviews were transcribed then analyzed thematically with the photographs to produce a list of codes which were then integrated to produce the themes identified in the textual data [19]. Transcripts and photographs were sorted into broad categories known as "proto-themes" [8] in order to allow themes to emerge from the data by categorizing similar topics together. The transcribed interviews were re-read in order to refine the proto-themes into the actual themes [3], [8].

4   Findings

The study found that scholars' research information collections are large, diverse, hybrid, and fragmented (see figure 3 below). Scholars' personal space of information contained a massive quantity of information related to their research that is stored in different places at different stages of the research. The part of a scholar's desk where they were working usually contained an accumulation of information related to research, sometimes merged with non-research material such as for teaching, and management tasks. Research is an "off-on process" scholars said, so that when they are in an active research mood, the amount of the information on their desks is larger than when they are less active research mode. Within their working offices, the research collection accumulated in different storage places such as open shelves, drawers and closed cabinets in the form of piles, files, pile of files and randomly stored piles within a file. Information was stored in huge amounts electronically too. Electronic folders were found on scholars' desktops, external storage devices, and stored virtually in personal E-mail or websites of participants that were created in an effort to support their own research tools of management.

Fig. 1. Pile and files of diverse papers stored physically in different ways in the main setting working space

Fig. 2. Electronically stored diverse research related information collections

The research-related PIC was found to be typically diverse in type, including four main categories of material, namely: sources gathered for the literature review, research data, publications and administrative papers.

Even after publishing a paper, literature review sources were kept by many scholars. They said that they thought they would need the material in future research in the same subject. It was also kept to share with colleagues in their local network within the department or anywhere across Kuwait. The second type of information was research data. It was found that the original paper questionnaires, for example, were kept together with processed results. Electronic versions were stored on their personal computers. Some scholars found it enough to keep the summary of the data in SPSS or Excel tables, but others preferred keeping the data as originally collected in the form of paper questionnaires. Research publications were also part of the collection, again occurring in both traditional and electronic formats. The final category of material in the collection was paperwork related to the research project.

In addition to its size and diversity, the scholars' collection was hybrid in formats including a complex mix of physical and electronic content, and located in multiple locations that change at different research stages. There was typically no clear strategy of keeping print or electronic or even both. All what was found is a random mix of both with a large amount of redundancy. All four types forming the diverse collection were found in both print and electronic form. Some scholars prefer reading printed versions while others prefer reading electronic. Some would tend to start with one version and continue reading in the other.

The collection is also fragmented. Enormous piles of papers and files were stored in multiple spaces whether in the main or secondary setting, in addition to abundant external storage devices for saving electronic versions such as flash memory and hard disks. Working in different locations necessitated the existence of the collection in each of the locations either by carrying the collection between locations by a mobility solution or like in some case keeping multiple copies here and there. Scholars tried to build an identical copy of the collection in each location, however hard that was to achieve.

The causes for these collection features can be divided into two main categories namely immediate and underlying causes.

The immediate causes found were the need for research, time pressure, quality of space, technology opportunity, support services, English resources and display. Scholars were obliged to conduct research for their career development. Conducting multiple research projects at the same time, along with poor support services, created time pressure and affected the research collection size, hybridity and fragmentation. In order to overcome the time pressure, and accomplish their tasks, scholars tried to manage their time by taking uncompleted tasks to a secondary setting (usually home) rather than conducting all research activities at the workplace. The quality of personal space triggered the failure of management of the research collection. Shared or poor quality offices forced scholars to find different working spaces which encouraged information hybridity and fragmentation. Technology opportunities such as the facilities of internet and ease of tools with the currency of applications were also effectively challenging scholars to maintain control. Such opportunities helped create the

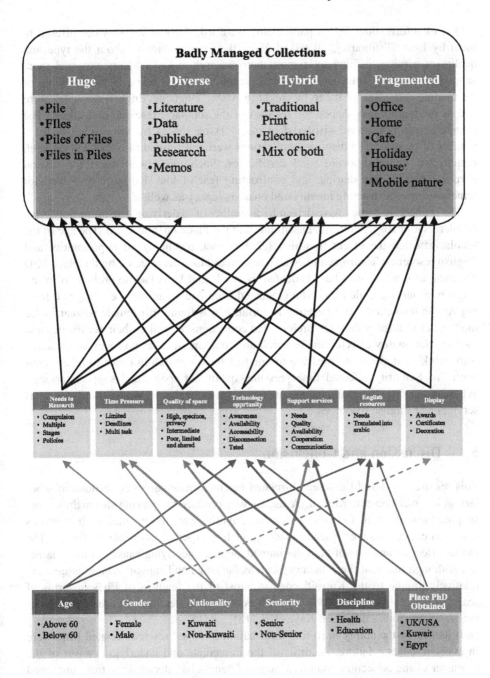

Fig. 3. Features and causes of research-related personal information collections

deluge of information. When participants were asked about the services offered to them by PAAET libraries, all talked about their dissatisfaction about the type and quality of services offered to support their research tasks. Scholars expected more support to aid their information finding, keeping and re-finding tasks. As some of the modules they teach have to be taught in Arabic language, English resources were one of the factors that shaped the features of the scholar's research collections. The research collections were displayed in the working spaces by some scholars for a number of reasons. The displayed collections were not limited to books and research output, but included awards and certificates. Such items were used for several purposes not for just sharing, and confronting fear of loss, but were displayed for remembering, constructing identity and creating legacy as well.

The immediate causes were driven by a number of underlying causes, namely Age, Gender, Nationality, Seniority, Discipline, and the Place PhD obtained. The age of the scholar affected the extent to which scholars took technological opportunities and English resources. Their need of Arabic resources also was affected by the place PhD obtained, as scholars who had graduated from UK and USA had no problem of using English resources, while those who graduated from Arabic universities struggled finding Arabic resources and translating material. It was found that female scholars were more eager to display their research related collections as well as their certificates and awards. Nationality affected the research and time pressure, as non Kuwaiti scholars were working under more pressure to conduct their research in order to renew their contracts. Seniority affected time pressure, quality of space, and support services. Whereas, the discipline affected the quality of space, technology opportunity, support services and English resources.

5   Discussion and Conclusion

This research explored the research-related personal information collections of scholars in a novel context, Kuwait. A model was produced capturing the main factors shaping the collection, and its size, diversity, hybridity and fragmentation. It identifies that such collections are typically made up of four types of information content. The model offers an analysis of both the immediate and underlying causes of this character. Although many of these factors (such as language and support related issues) are relatively unique to the Kuwaiti context, most of the features of PICs in terms of scale, fragmentation and hybridity as well as how the collections are used mirror findings from previous studies e.g. Kaye et al. [18].

If judged by the ability to re-find information scholars' research-related PICs were in many respects a failure. Analysis of the immediate and underlying causes of the character of the collection point to a range of beneficial interventions from improved space, technology support through to training in IM principles.

References

1. Boardman, R., Sasse, M.A.: Stuff goes into the computer and doesn't come out: a cross-tool study of personal information management. In: Proceedings of the SIGCHI Conference on Human Factors in Computing Systems, pp. 583–590. ACM (2004)
2. Bondarenko, O., Janssen, R.: Documents at hand: Learning from paper to improve digital technologies. In: Proceedings of the SIGCHI Conference on Human Factors in Computing Systems, pp. 121–130. ACM (2005)
3. Boyatzis, R.E.: Transforming qualitative information: Thematic analysis and code development. Sage Publications, Incorporated (1998)
4. Buchanan, G., Cunningham, S.J., Blandford, A., Rimmer, J., Warwick, C.: Information seeking by humanities scholars. In: Rauber, A., Christodoulakis, S., Tjoa, A.M. (eds.) ECDL 2005. LNCS, vol. 3652, pp. 218–229. Springer, Heidelberg (2005)
5. Dumais, S., Cutrell, E., Cadiz, J.J., Jancke, G., Sarin, R., Robbins, D.C.: Stuff I've seen: a system for personal information retrieval and re-use. In: Proceedings of the 26th Annual International ACM SIGIR Conference on Research and Development in Informaion Retrieval, pp. 72–79. ACM (2003)
6. Ellis, D.: Modeling the information-seeking patterns of academic researchers: A grounded theory approach. The Library Quarterly, 469–486 (1993)
7. Ellis, D., Cox, D., Hall, K.: A comparison of the information seeking patterns of researchers in the physical and social sciences. Journal of Documentation 49, 356–369 (1993)
8. Hayes, N.: Doing psychological research. Taylor & Francis Group (2000)
9. Henderson, S.: How do people organize their desktops? In: CHI 2004 Extended Abstracts on Human Factors in Computing Systems, pp. 1047–1048. ACM (2004)
10. Jones, W.: Finders, keepers? The present and future perfect in support of personal information management. First Monday 9 (2004)
11. Jones, W.: Keeping found things found: the study and practice of personal information management (2008a)
12. Jones, W.: Personal information management. Annual Review of Information Science and Technology 41, 453–504 (2008b)
13. Jones, W., Anderson, K.M.: Many views, many modes, many tools... one structure: Towards a Non-disruptive Integration of Personal Information. In: Proceedings of the 22nd ACM Conference on Hypertext and Hypermedia, pp. 113–122. ACM (2011)
14. Jones, W., Bruce, H., Dumais, S.: Keeping found things found on the web, pp. 119–126. ACM (2001)
15. Jones, W., Dumais, S., Bruce, H.: Once found, what then? A study of "keeping" behaviors in the personal use of Web information. Proceedings of the American Society for Information Science and Technology 39, 391–402 (2002)
16. Jones, W., Teevan, J.: Personal Information Management. University of Washington Press, Seattle (2007)
17. Kaye, J.J., Vertesi, J., Avery, S., Dafoe, A., David, S., Onaga, L., Rosero, I., Pinch, T.: To have and to hold: exploring the personal archive, pp. 275–284. ACM (2006a)
18. Kaye, J.J., Vertesi, J., Avery, S., Dafoe, A., David, S., Onaga, L., Rosero, I., Pinch, T.: To have and to hold: exploring the personal archive. In: Proceedings of the SIGCHI Conference on Human Factors in Computing Systems, pp. 275–284. ACM (2006b)
19. King, N.: Using templates in the thematic analysis of texts. Essential Guide to Qualitative Methods in Organizational Research, 256–270 (2004)
20. Kuhlthau, C.C.: Inside the search process: Information seeking from the user's perspective. JASIS 42, 361–371 (1991)

21. Kvale, S., Brinkmann, S.: Interviews: Learning the craft of qualitative research interviewing. SAGE Publications, Inc. (2008)
22. Marouf, L., Anwar, M.A.: Information-seeking behavior of the social sciences faculty at Kuwait University. Library Review 59, 532–547 (2010)
23. Meho, L.I., Tibbo, H.R.: Modeling the information seeking behavior of social scientists: Ellis's study revisited. Journal of the American Society for Information Science and Technology 54, 570–587 (2003)
24. Ocholla, D.N.: Information-seeking behaviour by academics: a preliminary study. The International Information & Library Review 28, 345–358 (1996)
25. Palmer, C.L., Teffeau, L.C., Pirmann, C.M.: Scholarly information practices in the online environment. Report commissioned by OCLC Research (2009), Published online at `http://www.oclc.org/programs/publications/reports2009-02.pdf`
26. Silverman, D.: Interpreting qualitative data: Methods for analyzing talk, text, and interaction. Sage Publications Ltd. (2006)
27. Whittaker, S.: Personal information management: From information consumption to curation. Annual Review of Information Science and Technology 45, 3–62 (2011)
28. Whittaker, S., Hirschberg, J.: The character, value, and management of personal paper archives. ACM Transactions on Computer-Human Interaction (TOCHI) 8, 150–170 (2001)
29. Whittaker, S., Sidner, C.: Email overload: exploring personal information management of email. In: Proceedings of the SIGCHI Conference on Human Factors in Computing Systems: Common Ground, pp. 276–283. ACM (1996)

EventLens: An Automatic Magazine Generating System for Social Media

Hao Chen, Han Tang, Zhiyu Wang, Peng Cui, Yingquing Xu, and Shiqiang Yang

Tsinghua University
Peter_chenhao@126.com, wonderwall1231@qq.com
zy-wang08@mails.tsinghua.edu.cn, cuip@mail.tsinghua.edu.cn
yingqingxu2004@hotmail.com, yangshq@tsinghua.edu.cn

Abstract. Social media has become the most convenient platform for news reading nowadays. In this paper, we introduce an automated digital magazine generating system—EventLens, which provides a platform to help the users get information more effectively through intelligent information selection and integration on social media. In our application, we not only design the functionalities, interface, and overall user experience to satisfy users' need in terms of information content and reading habits, but also propose the necessary solutions: an automated magazine layout method and a swift image retargeting method to solve the problems in the process of digital magazine auto-generation.

Keywords: magazine generating, layout, image retargeting, usability.

1 Introduction

Social media platforms, such as Twitter, are convenient channels for users to share experiences, discuss events, and read news. The big events are always the most trending topics on the micro-blog platforms. Such a platform provides not only a large quantity of rich media content but also gives users' different point of views of ongoing trending events. Besides, much more facets are also available from the third-party resources such as the news websites, which are good supplement for social media information. Adequate resources enable users to access the information presented comprehensively. However, information overload makes it very time-consuming to effectively find the useful content. Furthermore, the data retrieval of cross-platform usage is absolutely uncomfortable comparing to users' traditional reading habits. One of the possible solutions is to closely integrate the contents from multiple platforms into one medium like a digital magazine, to give a much more unified UI and centralized experience. However, how to provide the mechanism for auto-generate a magazine with aesthetic layout becomes a big challenge. In this paper, we introduce a novel digital magazine generation system—EventLens, that can automatically generate a digital magazine with a user-friendly and aesthetic layout.

S. Yamamoto (Ed.): HIMI/HCII 2013, Part I, LNCS 8016, pp. 177–186, 2013.

2 Related Work

Digital magazines have become more and more popular since 1980s; and it has been much evolved to be highly customizable. Many readers subscribing to digital magazines not only have desires to read their contents, but also tend to personalize their forms, such as selecting the layouts and appearances. With the rapid increasing of the mobile applications, now people can easily download many Apps from different platforms to create heavily customized digital magazines for personal or commercial purposes.

The apps that are currently available on different platforms mostly have slick user interface and enable the customization as their advantages. They classify the information into categories and let users to customize the categorization. For example, Flipboard lets user to have their own information resources registered as content provider, such as Twitter and Facebook, on the "board"—the main view in their UI. It is shown to be a generally accepted concept, from the huge success of Flipboard on iOS [1]. However, these apps are only categorizing the information in very restricted and limited ways, without being able to put the related news together automatically. Users cannot get any sort of linkage based on the semantic relevance of different pieces of information like Wikipedia does. The result is that user has to keep going in and out of different categories or even different apps, to manually search for more information about the same event he is interested in. We have developed EventLens system which is able to find the news related to a certain topic contextually and integrate them together.

In the digital magazine generating procedure, we faced two big challenges. The first is how to automatically generate the layout of the contents to deliver great legibility via well-designed presentation; and the second is how to do image-retargeting to make the reading experience conformable.

For the first challenge, there are some previous work but mainly focus on adaptive document layout via manifold content [2], and adaptive layout for dynamically aggregated documents [3]. These work give us great inspiration, but due to the different usage scenarios, it is hard to directly employ their methods to solve our problems. For the second challenge, many image retargeting methods have been studied [4], such as Non-homogeneous warping (WARP) [5], Seam-Carving (SC) [6], Scale-and-Stretch (SNS) [7], Multi-operator (MULTIOP) [8], Shift-maps (SM) [9], Streaming Video (SV) [10], and Energy-based deformation (LG) [11], but most of them were based on relatively complex computer vision algorithms. However, our foreground part based on Flash Actionscript3.0 that is not so strong in pixel level processing. So a fast image retargeting without complex computing is necessary.

3 System Design

To solve the information integration problem in social media, we propose our automatic event mining algorithm and layout management method. Our system (Fig.1) deals with a huge amount of micro-blog data by using the algorithm called "Bi-lateral

Correspondence Topic Model" [12] which mines the correlated data among the images, texts, and the related web news, to make each event containing more sufficient information. These correlated data consist of the unformatted texts, images, time, locations, persons, and articles. How to re-organize and make up such complex data in the digital magazine is a big challenge. There are three levels in our magazine generation system to form a top-down scope. The first level provides several trendy topics to make it easier to follow the popular events, since news readers are more likely to care about what is popular. On the second level, micro-blog keywords and related images provide users an overview of the whole event. The third level presents the detail of the news articles; the newsreader can access the links of the original news sources.

3.1 User Interface Design

A friendly user interface should match the product's function and the cognitive model from user's mind, as well as fitting the usage of a user. We first design the structure of our magazine. Traditional magazines usually attract people's attention with a shining cover, and then connect the contents together with an easy-read menu. Mostly there are two kinds of readers: some may read the magazine from the beginning to the end; and the others may find the special content that they are interested [13]. Actually, it is very similar to readers of websites, i.e., someone may browse the website from top to the bottom and the other ones may just do glance over on the site. So we design the structure of our magazine according to the habit of readers and the feature of the cognitive model of magazine. Based on our three levels system, we construct a flat and wide structure that can meet the easy-read need of user. A flat and wide structure of a website is that there are fewer levels but more pages in a level. So users can clearly find where they are and get more information at one time.

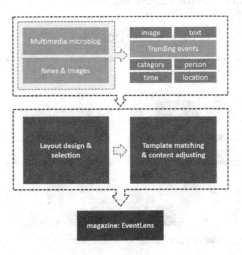

Fig. 1. Processing flow of magazine generation

Furthermore, we should propose a visual style to match our information structure. Based on the characteristics of our magazine—pushing news quickly and intensively, finally we use Metro UI design style for reference. Metro UI design style is a design language that is from Swiss graphic design [15] and focuses on presenting the information and pushes the information to user directly [16]. It provides a way that user can get the information immediately from background. What we need is to design the interface that is mush simple to just read the news. So we design the topic template into a color block just filled up with news' keywords and pictures, and then connect the pages with appropriate visual effect to enrich the magazine.

3.2   Auto-layout Based on Designed Templates

What does it mean to be beautiful? It is a difficult question. Artists always bring us beautiful sense which digital device cannot give us. We have tried some pure automatic layout methods, such as using Golden Ratio to divide the space to several parts, but none of the methods is good enough to satisfy the participants and even ourselves. For the traditional magazine, every page is well-designed by the editors and designers, so if we design some nice page layout template and find out what is the proper situation for each template, it may be helpful for solving the layout problem—since the human editors and designers are best at putting the proper contents into the right places and designing the best looking possible layouts of magazines, and our goal is to mimic what they do in an automated way. In order to have an aesthetic magazine that allows users to efficiently read the information, we carried out a user study that aimed to find out what kind of page layout are more reasonable for users' reading as well as more flexible for fitting texts and images with different scales. We firstly selected some news and images, then put them into the pre-designed template, and to ask the participants to vote which one they like the most. From seeing the results, we were able to find the most satisfied layout templates.

Layout templates

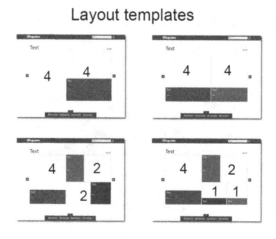

Fig. 2. The participants voted well-designed layout templates

The results show that when the templates contain 1 to 4 news blocks they will generally be accepted by participants. After calculating and analyzing the area division and arrangement of each layout, we found that if we define different values (large=4, medium=2, small=1) of each block, the layout template will fit the news with different size (Fig. 2). After layout templates design, our next step is how to put the real news into them. News on social media has not only texts and images, but also its time, location, type and popularity. The popularity always greatly affects the users' reading order, so we choose popularity as one factor for the news re-ordering. Popularity calculating is supported in our background algorithm, each piece of news is provided with its popularity. Firstly, the system will provide a popularity ranking, because users may pay more attention to more popular information. After popularity ranking, the system quantitates the news images by their resolutions into three levels (large=4, medium=2, small=1), while we think that the news with better image will take larger space and. Our system will separate the news to several pages firstly, each page contains 1 to 4 piece of news. Because the area summation of each layout template is 8, the system will computing how to group the news with different image levels to get a summation nearest to 8. Also, considering that adjacent pages should have slightly different layout to avoid repetition form which may influence the user experience, our system do not allow same layout form of news appearing in adjacent pages. After grouping the news by pages, we need to place each piece of news into the corresponding news block in the page.

3.3   Fast Image Re-targeting

In our system, every page of the magazine contains some news blocks, every news block have the news image as the cover (Fig. 3). However, if the images of the new have a different size from the block, it will be quite necessary to do extra work to fit the news image into the block size. Our images all come from micro-blog platform,

Fig. 3. Image retargeting result in our system

therefore the form factors and resolutions of the images are very different. In some extreme cases, pictures may even have a width-to-height ratio of 1/10 or less. And EventLens system is an automatic online magazine system, for one thing it will be a waste of time for traditional image retargeting methods to treat a large number of strange pictures by some complex pixel computing. For another reason the Flash Player platform is not very strong in image processing in pixel level. Thus, we need a fast and simple image retargeting method that can provide a generally acceptable result; maybe it cannot give the best result in quality, but getting the job done simple and fast is more important.

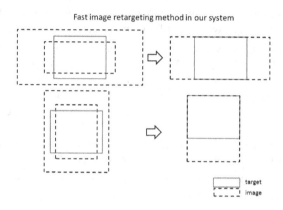

Fig. 4. Flow of fast image retargeting in our system

Considering the complexity of the social media images, we randomly selected 2000 images from Tencent Weibo as our sample pool. Then we manually retargeted the images to fit our templates with the best effort. During our work, we found that in the horizontal direction the main part of the image are mostly near the center, and we also found that in the vertical direction the main part of the image are mostly near the top. So we began to think how we can retain the main part of most of the images after a fast and simple treatment.

In order to retarget the images, we firstly compare the width/height ratio of the image with the re-targeting window. If the original image is wider than the retargeting image, we scale the original image without width/height ratio change until the height of the image and the retargeting image are equal, and then center-align the image to the retargeting window. If the original image is higher than the retargeting image, we scale the original image without width/height ratio change until the width of the image and the retargeting image are equal, and then top-align the image to the retargeting window(Fig. 4).

To validate the result of our image retargeting algorithm, we write a program, which aims to test whether the result will satisfy the users (Fig. 5). The program shows a random image from the dataset which contains about 20,000 images from Tencent Weibo (different dataset from the 2,000 sample images). We asked 20 average users and 5 artists to participate the experiment. The result shows our image retargeting algorithm has over 85% satisfaction (Fig. 6). So that we consider that the algorithm is an efficient method for our system.

Fig. 5. Image retargeting test program

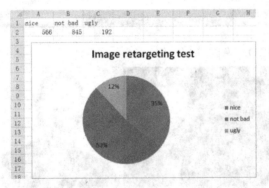

Fig. 6. Result of image retargeting test

4   Demonstration

To evaluate the effectiveness of our system, we have an online prototype of automatically generating a magazine by dealing with Tencent micro-blog data. Our system not only provides micro-blogs, images, and news of the hot events, but also allows users to search their interested events by keywords (Fig. 7). The keywords and images of a specific event give a more intuitive view (Fig. 8). For more detailed news or corresponding micro-blogs about the event, some hot news are also crawled from search engine and social pulses from micro-blogs. The page layout, the color selection, and the information structure are attentively designed. Our system and design have been recognized by ACM multimedia 2012 Grand Challenge. [17]

Fig. 7. Hot event detection in social network data by Bi-lateral Correspondence Topic Model

Fig. 8. Automatic layout based on designed template selection

5   Conclusion

Our EventLens system proposes a good solution of social network multimedia information integration, while it provides a platform that user can get social media

information about some events and topic more efficiently. Firstly, we designed and set up an automatic magazine generating system to make it more comfortable for users in reading information of events and topic on social media, because digital magazine form may satisfy the users traditional reading habits better. For more, the auto-system also reduces the human supervise editing cost. Thirdly, we developed a layout generation and designed templates selection method to make the magazine both automatic and aesthetic. Finally, we found a method to solve the problem of reducing the loss of semantic meaning and visual effectiveness when pictures sizes are not aligned well with the templates.

Acknowledgement. We must say thanks to all the people who contributed to the system testing. In particular, we wish to thank Lexing Xie,Wenwu Zhu, Mingdong Ou, Dan Xu, Shifei Jin, Chang Tu, Tao Cui, Yue Luo, Yunzi Qian, Menglin Ye for supporting us establishing the system and improving the user experience of the system.

This work was supported by the National Basic Research Program of China (Grant No. 2012CB725300), the National Natural Science Foundation of China (Grant No. 61232013), Project 973 under Grant 2011CB302206, and NSFC under Grant 60933013 and 61003097.

References

1. Indvik, L.: Flipboard: Behind Mobile's Most Beautiful News Reading Magazine, http://mashable.com/2012/06/05/flipboard-design/ (June 06, 2012)
2. Jacobs, C., Li, W., Salesin, D.H.: Adaptive document layout via manifold content. In: Second International Workshop on Web Document Analysis, WDA 2003 (2003)
3. Schrier, E., Dontcheva, M., Jacobs, C., Wade, G., Salesin, D.: Adaptive Layout for Dynamically Aggregated Documents. In: Proceedings of the 13th International Conference on Intelligent User Interfaces (2008)
4. Rubinstein, M., Gutierrez, D., Sorkine, O., Shamir, A.: A Comparative Study of Image Retargeting. SIGGRAPH ASIA 2010 (October 2010)
5. Wolf, L., Guttmann, M., Cohen-Or, D.: Non-homogeneous Content-driven Video-retargeting. In: Computer Vision, ICCV 2007 (2007) (WARP)
6. Rubinstein, M., Shamir, A., Avidan, S.: Improved seam carving for video retargeting. Transactions on Graphics (TOG) - Proceedings of ACM SIGGRAPH 2008 (2009) (SC)
7. Wang, Y.-S., Tai, C.-L., Sorkine, O., Lee, T.-Y.: Optimized scale-and-stretch for image resizing. ACM Transactions on Graphics (TOG) - Proceedings of ACM SIGGRAPH Asia 2008 (2008) (SNS)
8. Rubinstein, M., Shamir, A., Avidan, S.: Multi-operator media retargeting. ACM Transactionson Graphics (TOG)-Proceedings of ACM SIGGRAPH 2009 (2009) (MULTIOP)
9. Pritch, Y., Kav-Venaki, E., Peleg, S.: Shift-Map Image Editing. In: Computer Vision, ICCV (2009) (SM)
10. Krähenbühl, P., Lang, M., Hornung, A., Gross, M.: A system for retargeting of streaming video. ACM Transactions on Graphics (TOG) - Proceedings of ACM SIGGRAPH Asia 2009 (2009) (SV)

11. Karni, Z., Freedman, D., Gotsman, C.: Energy-Based Image Deformation. Computer Graphics Forum 28(5), 1257–1268 (2009) (LG)
12. Wang, Z., Cui, P., Xie, L., Chen, H., Zhu, W., Yang, S.: Analyzing Social Media via Event Facets. ACM Multimedia 2012 Grand Challenge (2012)
13. Hermes, J.: Reading Women's Magazines: An Analysis of Everyday Media Use (June 16, 1995)
14. Terror, D.: Lessons From Swiss Style Graphic Design (July 17, 2009), http://www.smashingmagazine.com/2009/07/17/lessons-from-swiss-style-graphic-design/
15. Hurlburt, A.: Publication Design: Guide to Page Layout, Typography, Format and Style (July 1976)
16. Mkruzeniski: How Print Design is the Future of Interaction (April 11, 2011), http://kruzeniski.com/2011/how-print-design-is-the-future-of-interaction/
17. ACM Multimedia 2012 Grand Challenge (2012), http://www.acmmm12.org/ntt-docomo-challenge-event-understanding-through-social-media-and-its-text-visual-summarization/

A User Driven Design Approach to Creating UGC Services – Challenging the Newspaper Industry

Esbjörn Ebbesson and Carina Ihlström Eriksson

Halmstad University, Sweden
{esbjorn.ebbesson,carina.ihlstrom_eriksson}@hh.se

Abstract. This paper presents a user driven approach to creating user generated content services together with newspaper representatives and researchers in a Living Lab setting. Two cases are discussed, one with creating city district blogs and one with creating a site for un-employed youth. In each case both situated and distributed design activities were conducted, and the paper discusses the challenges with this approach. As the newspaper industry traditionally designs their services in-house from their own ideas and thereafter tests them with their readers, a user driven approach by readers was very challenging. However, the newspaper representatives also found it rewarding to embrace their ideas. The participating readers were very active in the situated activities but only a few continued the same activity online. The paper concludes by proposing a model for how to view the changing role of a researcher or facilitator in these types of setting.

Keywords: user generated content, newspaper industry, user driven, co-design.

1 Introduction

Allowing readers to express their opinions has always been embraced by newspapers. However, in print media it has only been possible on a small scale, e.g. in the form of letters to the editor. Since the mid-nineties when most newspapers began their online journeys, the amount of material produced by readers increased substantially on their web sites.

User generated content (UGC) as a phenomenon has its origin on the Internet. New web services have empowered users to contribute in numerous ways by creating, customizing, developing, distributing, rating, commenting, and collaborating on internet content and applications (O´Reilly, 2007). Internet content includes video, sound, text and pictures that are created, elaborated on or customized by users. UGC has been a success in for example YouTube, Flickr, Wikipedia and The Huffington Post.

The newspaper industry has enjoyed a lucrative business over more than a century by bringing the news to the breakfast table. Revenues from subscriptions together with substantial income from advertisement made the industry prosper. However, this era is over and we are now witnessing a changing media landscape where newspapers

S. Yamamoto (Ed.): HIMI/HCII 2013, Part I, LNCS 8016, pp. 187–196, 2013.

struggle to keep their readers and to attract advertisers. They are seeking new ways of boosting their digital presence to attract both new readers and advertisers. One way of doing that is to innovate new interesting services based on UGC.

Traditionally, newspaper publishers work internally to innovate their business (Küng, 2008), and services are often evaluated with focus groups of readers. However, in order to develop new innovative services that are attractive to the end users i.e. their readers, it has been argued that a more open and user driven approach can be beneficial (see e.g. von Hippel, 2005); opening up in this manner is a challenging task for the newspaper industry.

In this paper we are presenting results from two cases in which we have taken a user driven approach to create UGC services at two different newspapers. In both cases the newspaper representatives (managerial, marketing and designer levels), readers and researchers worked together to: a) come up with ideas of new UGC services for the newspaper industry, b) design the services and c) evaluate the services. The readers should have a say in each decision regarding content and design.

We are discussing the challenges of conducting such an user driven design approach in a very traditional industry and illustrating reflections from all three involved parties.

2   User Influenced Design and Innovation Approaches

Recent phenomena, such as co-creation (Prahalad and Ramaswamy, 2004) and open innovation (Chesbrough et al., 2008), have popularized different types of co-design in the innovation process over many different industries. Co-design is nothing new within the design of IT products and services; we have a long history of engaging users of systems in the design process one way or another in for example the participatory design movement (Greenbaum & Kyng, 1991). However, much of the participatory design methods used for co-design between users and other stakeholders are developed for a situated face to face setting where the participants have the ability to meet (Danielsson Öberg et al., 2009). This has led to increasing interest in finding methods of how to engage users in a distributed fashion, where users from both inside organizations and outside organizations can engage in co-design design together (Obendorf et al., 2009). Distribution in this sense, regards both the physical space where people meet as well as the distribution between users and other stakeholders. This is challenging as the concept of the users has become a lot wider, and today the user can be engaged in a design process as a consumer and private citizen instead of a mere "system user".

These challenges are addressed by Living Labs (Eriksson et al., 2005). The concept of Living Labs according to Bergvall-Kåreborn et al. (2009) is built on openness, influence, realism, value and sustainability and puts the user in the center of the design process, through engagement. The openness promotes creation and validation of products and services in an as open fashion as possible, aligning itself with the thinking that users are the source of innovation (Thomke and Von Hippel, 2002). The view of the users as a vital part of the innovation process is also reflected in how the Living Lab sees the user as an essential resource when engaging them as active and competent domain experts (Bergvall-Kåreborn et al., 2009). To leverage value in shape of innovative IT products and services, the Living Lab methodology also calls for the involvement of other key stakeholders such as academia and private and public sector in the innovation process (Eriksson et al., 2005), thereby aligning itself with the open innovation thinking (Chesbrough et al., 2008).

The methods and techniques used within these heavily user influenced innovation processes to involve stakeholders vary widely from process to process due to obvious reasons such as different focuses of the processes and stakeholder needs, but also questionnaires, focus groups and observation are commonly used (Følstad, 2008). Others have mapped additional "traditional" participatory design or IT design techniques such as scenarios, mock-ups, image-boarding and brainstorming techniques into the innovation process of a Living Lab (Svensson et al., 2010). The challenges related to these methods and techniques in a Living Lab setting, for example to adapt or generate new techniques suitable for a distributed setting (Schumacher and Feurstein, 2007), is generic and shared by others in similar practices (Danielsson Öberg et al., 2009).

However, the actual facilitation of design work in these participatory settings has also been seen as very challenging. The inclusion of new types of users alongside other stakeholders such as public sector or firms presents challenges for the facilitator of the activities (Svensson et al., 2010). These challenges are related to the moderation of activities and to the balancing of perspectives (Svensson et al., 2010) in order to create a common ground where stakeholders with very different perspectives can meet to discuss, create and innovate together (Obendorf et al., 2009). These challenges not only illustrate how the changing landscape of design and innovation is changing our perspective on suitable methods and contexts, but also on the role of the user in these processes.

An additional level of complexity is found when looking at co-design processes where research is a vital part (Thomke and von Hippel, 2002, Bergvall-Kåreborn et al., 2009), as for example participatory design or Living Lab approaches. In these processes where researchers take an active part of the actual innovation or design activities, the role of the researchers has been noted to change from a more passive translator to a more active facilitator, with the ability to guide and help other stakeholders express their needs and creativity (Sanders and Stappers, 2008). This presents challenges for researchers, who may have to adapt their skillsets when working within multi-stakeholder settings.

3   The LoCoMedia Case

The two cases (Alpha and Beta) in this paper were part of a research project called The Local Newspaper 2.0 – with Engaged Readers (LoCoMedia) which was conducted between 2009 and 2011 in a Living Lab setting with seven Swedish newspaper partners.

In both cases, the researchers acted as facilitators between readers and newspaper representatives. The facilitation process included managing the design activities, experimenting with different types of technology that could aid the design process and helping the newspapers during the recruitment phase. The term reader will from now on be used to describe current readers of Alpha and Betas newspaper, but also the potential future users of the services that were developed in the two individual cases.

Both of the Alpha and Beta cases were designed to be user driven from the start, i.e. based on the initial area for a UGC service suggested by the newspaper, the readers should come up with ideas for the service and be a part of each decision regarding content, design etc.

Each case started with a pre-meeting with the project team at the newspaper to discuss the area for the potential UGC service and setup. Thereafter, readers were invited to participate in the project. They were recruited through ads in both the printed and online newspaper or from already established groups connected to a newspaper. A startup meeting with the invited readers and the project team was conducted at the premises of the newspaper. During this face to face meeting the readers and newspaper representatives participated in activities with the purpose of coming up with initial ideas and concepts for the service. Thereafter, the majority of the interaction between all participants was done through an online platform which functioned as a meeting place where design activities were carried out. At the end of these projects, which ran for 3-4 months, we interviewed members of the project team and participating readers. The projects were also evaluated through questionnaires. The projects were documented through notes from at least two researchers from the initial meetings, through all comments and questionnaires in the online platform, and through transcriptions of the recorded interviews. In Table 1, the different activities in the two cases are presented.

Table 1. Alpha and Beta case activites

Case	Readers	Activities and Data Sources
Alpha	13+34	1 face to face meeting, 32 threads and 266 comments in the online forum, 8 telephone interviews with readers, 5 interviews with newspaper project team, 1 interview with researchers.
Beta	10+35	2 face to face meetings, 24 threads and 86 comments in the online forum, 16 telephone interviews with readers, 2 questionnaires, design patterns, usability evaluation, 1 interview with newspaper project leader, 2 interviews with researchers.

The coding of the data was done manually by the researchers using the computer software HyperRESEARCH to manage codes and themes. Codes were applied to the empirical data in a grounded fashion to highlight the reader, newspaper representative and researcher perspectives in the individual cases. The empirical findings were then used to theorize on challenges, changing roles and perspectives in co-design processes involving readers, researchers and newspaper representatives.

3.1   The Alpha Case

The Alpha case was a multi-stakeholder design process that began in the end of 2009 and spanned over four months. In the pre-meeting it was decided along with the newspaper representatives that the aim of the project was to design and launch city district blogs to aid the coverage of local news through user generated content. Thereafter, readers in different age groups that either blogged themselves or were frequent readers of multiple blogs were invited through ads in both the printed and online version of the newspaper.

The design process was kicked off with a face to face start-up meeting between the newspaper representatives and the readers facilitated by the researchers. During this meeting the participants got to learn about the upcoming design process, for example why the design process had been initiated and what the limitations were. Thereafter, a workshop was conducted where the readers and newspaper representatives got to mingle and discuss the upcoming project and brainstorm ideas. The newspaper representatives were very impressed by what they learned from their readers at this first workshop and admitted that they have had some mistaken thoughts on what the readers wanted.

The workshop was finalized by an introduction of the online platform that was supposed to be used as a collaboration hub for the duration of the project. The initial transition to collaborating on the online platform went fairly smooth, and most of the initial users from the workshop registered on the platform and dove into discussions. It was however a challenge for the facilitators to make the switch to the online platform, as it was harder to engage the participants to collaborate online than it was in the face to face setting, especially the newspaper representatives.

The newspaper representatives claimed that part of the problem with the initially low activity from the newspapers side was that they had been very confused in relation to what their role in the process was. The collaboration with the readers and researchers was a completely new way of working for them, and they weren't completely clear on what they were supposed to do, as they have been told that they had to listen to the readers before making any decisions regarding the service. This is illustrated with a quote from the newspaper project leader:

"We are used to thinking about product development from an inside looking out perspective, and are not used to the outside looking in perspective, that's why this has been extra frustrating" (Rebecka, Newspaper representative).

The low activity from the newspapers side was however remedied over time and they became more and more active in the online discussions.

The majority of the discussions on the online platform throughout the project were initiated by the facilitating researchers, who picked up issues from the initial face to face meeting and ongoing threads to promote discussions. Some users, both readers and newspaper representatives, started up their own threads as well, but they rarely generated as many responses as the facilitators' threads. After the project ended some of the readers expressed that they would have liked the newspaper representatives to be more active and provocative, this was however not shared by all, and some thought that the newspapers engagement was well balanced. One of the readers said that:

"The newspaper staff should act as a partner that you can bring up ideas to, they shouldn't take up too much room, but always be there for discussions" (Nils, Reader).

The readers own commitment to the design process seemed to hail from a curiosity to explore new things, in this case to learn more about blogs and UGC, and some of them were interested in becoming bloggers themselves at Alphas blog platform when they were finalized. Another strong incentive seemed to be the ability or willingness to help shape the future services offered by Alpha. One of the more engaged readers stated that:

"I tried to be as active as possible, until the very end, I even managed to get the district I live in myself to become a city district blog, even though it initially wasn't supposed to be .. I was both active and managed to put my dedication into action, if I put it that way" (Mats, Reader).

After continuous discussions on issues such as ads in online media, what districts to cover, the design of the blogs, and who future bloggers could possibly be, the district blogs finally launched after 4 months of online collaborations. Some of the readers that participated in the co-creation process took the step to become bloggers, while the majority of the bloggers on the platform in its current state were recruited through advertising and voluntary sign ups.

The newspaper representatives primarily mentioned two areas when they reflected upon what they had learned from the design process; firstly that they had learned a lot about how to engage and work with users and secondly regarding how to think about user generated services and both the readers and newspapers role in the generation of such.

3.2   The Beta Case

The Beta case ran during the last quarter of 2009. In the pre-meeting it was decided that the aim was to create a service that could help unemployed youth in their job-hunting, which should consist of both UGC and material published by the newspaper. Invitations were sent to unemployed youth in the region (a province in mid-Sweden) who had attended an exhibition about youth unemployment organized by the newspaper earlier that year.

During the start-up meeting organized by the researchers where the newspaper representatives and the unemployed young adults (hereafter referred to as the readers, even though not all were day to day readers of the newspaper) engaged in a workshop. During this initial workshop, both newspaper representatives and readers were very enthusiastic and discussed a multitude of ideas and features for the upcoming service.

Towards the end of the workshop, two options were presented for the readers and newspaper representatives. To either use an already existing social network as a support platform for collaboration during the rest of the project, or a private community platform. Since not all users had an account for a social networking service, and not everyone was willing to give out that kind of information, it was agreed upon to continue the collaboration online using the private community platform.

Since all the participants had been so enthusiastic during the initial meeting, the team at the newspaper and the facilitators expected a smooth transition to the collaborative online phase of the project, especially since the readers stated that they were very active online. However, the second phase met many challenges. The researchers had a hard time getting the readers to register and sign on to the online platform, and when they did most of them did not interact with any of the other users. The most engaged newspaper representative was still very committed to the design process, even though it was very challenging to work with the readers in the online settings. The reasons for why this was challenging varied; some readers claimed that they had already found a job and thus their incentive to help build a job-hunting platform was lessened while others simply didn't want to be bothered with follow up activities. These opinions were however not shared by everyone; some of the readers were very active on the online platform, although not enough to create the critical mass needed to collaborate. One of the readers explained it like this:

"My engagement lessens when others aren't engaged. I want people to be engaged, I expected others that have accepted to be a part of this to give 100%. I was there every day [the online platform] in the beginning, but when others weren't as engaged, I just visited once a week. Everyone has to engage themselves!" (Anna, Reader).

After many, often fruitless attempts to stir life into the online platform, the facilitating researchers decided to change the approach and plan for more face to face meetings instead, since the initial meetings had been so successful. They decided to introduce techniques to the readers that made it easier to capture and communicate design ideas between the readers and the newspaper representatives. For example, design patterns and mock-ups were used during the face to face meetings to capture reader opinions, which later on were put on the online platform for other readers and newspaper representatives to feedback on. This feedback could then be incorporated into the design which eventually matured into a high-fi prototype that was evaluated with the group of readers.

The job-hunting service finally went live, and contained most of the features that the readers had wished for during the initial workshop, for example an "ask the expert" section, user blogs, tools to help market yourself and your skills etc. The service was deemed as a success from the project leader's perspective at the newspaper since it had allowed them to learn more about how to work with users, and also more about user generated content and the newspapers role in these kinds of processes. The project leader at the newspaper concluded that:

"UGC demands more resources than one thinks. The newspaper needs to have close relations with the readers that you have established a dialogue with. Those who had stated that they will contribute with material don't always deliver on their own" (Angela, Newspaper representative).

4   Discussion and Conclusion

We find that both of these cases are illustrative for user driven Living Lab activities, where the users could contribute on their own terms at the time of their choosing. However, as seen in the two cases this was not an easy task to achieve.

Both the newspaper representatives and the readers seemed to appreciate the new way of working; the incentives from the readers varied between the two cases and between the readers themselves, ranging anywhere from curiosity to more tangible rewards, like the hope of getting a job. The newspaper representatives seemed to appreciate learning about new ways of working with their readers, in some cases more than the actual service that was developed. This perspective might reflect a more long-term and process like thinking, which might not be that surprising since the majority of the newspaper representatives clearly expressed that they were all interested in trying out new ways of working along with readers, and that user involvement was here to stay in one way or another. The change of perspective on how to view the readers, and the acknowledgement of them as a competent resource that can be a part of future innovation processes also clearly reflects the key principles of the Living Lab.

Another important lesson learnt from the perspective of both the newspaper representatives and the readers was that user involvement takes time, and in some cases more time than expected. The newspaper representatives were used to brainstorm and develop first, and ask questions later; having the readers along for the ride made the processes a lot more time consuming. The slow pace was also reflected upon by some of the readers in the Alpha case that expressed interest in more face to face meetings and a faster process, to help sustain the engagement and enthusiasm.

Furthermore, an insight from the newspaper representatives was that UGC is much more complicated for the newspapers to handle than they thought. It is hard to try and "force" new innovative UGC services by involving the readers. UGC comes from the users by their own initiative, and sometimes a newspaper site is not the most preferred host for such services.

From the researcher point of view the difficulty of conducting design activities online was an eye opener. The insight is that it is essential to have a critical mass (a large sample) of users if choosing this path, as shown by the activity of the users in this project which maps the general activity of users in social media, i.e. only very few are actually contributing frequently, a larger mass contributes now and then, and some are only lurkers.

The two cases also clearly illustrate the shift of the role of the researcher in these types of processes. Sanders and Stappers (2008) have previously pointed out that the researcher that had more often acted as more of a translator in participatory design projects has to take the role of a more active facilitator. This can be illustrated by how the researchers had to take on an active role as mediator between Alpha and Alphas readers to help communication, and in the Beta case, had to spend much time trying to create more engagement amongst the readers. It is however interesting to note that the lower engagement from the readers in the Beta case increased the need for more translator-type work from the researchers where creative solutions aided the ability to translate needs between the readers and newspaper representatives, i.e. ad hoc planning of face to face workshops dedicated to design patterns and mock-ups. These findings indicate that even though the changing practice indeed has implications for a higher degree of commitment and facilitator skills from the researcher, the role as a translator is also still high in demand, but perhaps coupled with stronger facilitator skills. Figure 1 summarizes these findings and illustrates how the need for facilitation type changes based on commitment from the readers and organizational representatives Alpha and Beta.

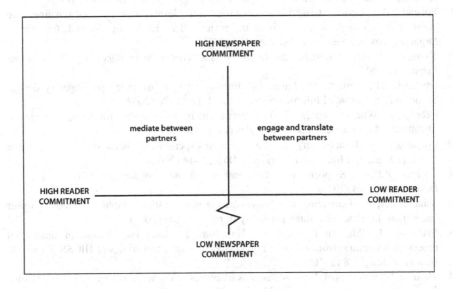

Fig. 1. Facilitator activities based on newspaper and user commitment

The empirical findings from the Alpha and Beta case do not suggest how facilitator activities change in innovation processes where the newspaper representatives commitment is low. Instead we suggest that as a possible future research area. Potential findings could help shed light on the changing practice of researchers, designers and facilitators, but could also provide managerial implications for how to manage innovation processes where users have a very high commitment but lack support from parts of the product or service developers.

Acknowledgement. This work was funded by the KK-foundation and the NordForsk LILAN programme through LoCoMedia and the SociaLL project.

References

1. Bergvall-Kåreborn, B., Ihlström Eriksson, C., Ståhlbröst, A., Svensson, J.: A Milieu for Innovation–Defining Living Labs. Presented at the 2nd ISPIM Innovation Symposium, New York City, United States, December 6-9 (2009)

2. Chesbrough, H., Vanhaverbeke, W., West, J.: Open Innovation: Researching a New Paradigm. Oxford University Press, Oxford (2008)
3. Greenbaum, J., Kyng, M.: Design at work: Cooperative design of computer systems. Lawrence Erlbaum Associates, Inc., Hillsdale (1991)
4. Danielsson Öberg, K., Gumm, D., Naghsh, A.M.: Distributed PD: Challenges and opportunities (Editorial). Scandinavian Journal of Information Systems 20(1), 23–26 (2009)
5. Eriksson, M., Niitamo, V.-P., Kulkki, S.: State-of-the-art in utilizing Living Labs approach to user-centric ICT innovation-a European approach. White paper, Center for Distance-spanning Technology, Lulea University of Technology, Sweden (December 2005)
6. Følstad, A.: Living labs for innovation and development of information and communication technology: a literature review. The Electronic Journal for Virtual Organizations and Networks 10(7), 99–131 (2008)
7. Küng, L.: Strategic Management in the Media: Theory to practice. Sage Publications Limited (2008)
8. Obendorf, H., Janneck, M., Finck, M.: Inter-contextual distributed participatory design. Scandinavian Journal of Information Systems 21(1), 51–76 (2009)
9. OReilly, T.: What is Web 2.0: Design patterns and business models for the next generation of software. Communications & Strategies (1), 17 (2007)
10. Prahalad, C.K., Ramaswamy, V.: Co‐creation experiences: The next practice in value creation. Journal of Interactive Marketing 18(3), 5–14 (2004)
11. Sanders, E.B.-N., Stappers, P.J.: Co-creation and the new landscapes of design. Co-Design 4(1), 5–18 (2008)
12. Schumacher, A., Feurstein, B.: Living labs - a new multi-stakeholder approach to user integration. In: Enterprise Interoperability II, pp. 281–285 (2007)
13. Svensson, J., Ihlstrom Eriksson, C., Ebbesson, E.: User contribution in innovation processes-reflections from a Living Lab perspective. In: Proceedings of HICSS 43, Kauai, Hawaii, January 5-8 (2010)
14. Thomke, S., von Hippel, E.: Customers as innovators: A new way to create value. Harvard Business Review 80(4), 74–81 (2002)
15. von Hippel, E.: Democratizing Innovation. MIT Press, Boston (2005)

A Novel Human-Computer Interface for Browsing Web Data by Leaping Up Web Pages

Che-Lun Hung[1,*], Cherng Chin[1], Chen-Chun Lai[2], and Ho Cheung Cheung[2]

[1] Department of Computer Science and Communication Engineering, Providence University,
Taichung, Taiwan
{clhung,cchin}@pu.edu.tw
[2] Lailab Computing Laboratory, Taiwan
{derek,ben}@lailab.net

Abstract. With the rapid growth of network technologies, various web services have been developed for providing information. Therefore, search engines become popular to obtain the useful data. It is critical to efficiently acquire the data from huge data pool in the Internet; especially the number of web pages is increasing dramatically. In this paper, we propose an efficient approach to browse web data by leaping up web pages. In addition, the proposed approach using web preloading and cache technologies to enhance the performance of accessing web page. The simulation results show the proposed approach can be useful for browsing and searching data in the Internet.

Keywords: Web Browser, Web Page, Leaping Up, Browser Interface.

1   Introduction

With the rapid growth of network technologies, network bandwidth has been enhanced dramatically. In the current generation of information explosion, an amount of data and information have to be abstracted and viewed in the limit time; especially on Internet. The number of web pages growth by billion each year. Not only the number of web pages is increasing, but also the complexity of web page is increasing. From 2003 to 2011 the average web page grew from 93.7K to over 679K, over 7.2 times larger [1]. During the same eight-year period, the number of objects in the average web page more than tripled from 25.7 to 85 objects per page. It is obvious that the web design is toward more complicated. Actually, the sitemap of a current web site is deeper and wider than former design. However, such complicated design leads to people browsing web page inefficiently. People may need to go through the whole page or several hyperlinks to retrieve the required information or reach the desired page. Browsing the content of a hyperlink, people have to click the hyperlink and wait to download the new page according the URL of the hyperlink. Therefore, it is inefficient if people need to reach the required page by click several hyperlinks.

---

* Corresponding author.

S. Yamamoto (Ed.): HIMI/HCII 2013, Part I, LNCS 8016, pp. 197–202, 2013.

In the past few years, web search engine has become the daily tool for people. People rely on such tool to retrieve information from Internet. However, the current web searching engines concentrate on improving the search accuracy, and the search results are listed as link by link according to the sequence of page ranking. In the duration of using search engine, the most of time is to check the web pages of the links. Sometimes, people have to click many links and view many pages to get to the page they need. It is time-consuming that people have to look at every hyperlink and the brief of the content of the web page linked by the hyperlink.

The user-interface design of current browsers, such as IE [2], Chrome [3], FireFox [4] and Safari [5], only present the web page by the URL. Therefore, user should view each web page by clicking hyperlink. These browsers are unable to provide efficient interface for uses to browse web pages. In addition, the web page has to be downloaded before showing on the browser. It is critical to decrease download times of web pages and reduce Internet traffic. To make document caching is a necessity for the increasing demand for World Wide Web (WWW) services [6, 7, 8]. To make efficient use of caching, an instructive conclusion has to be made as to which documents are to be ejected from the cache in case of cache saturation.

In this paper, we propose a novel mechanism to efficiently browse web pages by downloading web pages in parallel and leaping web pages. In this mechanism, the web pages are preloaded before browsing these pages. Otherwise, these preloaded pages are presented on the browser, and users can watch these pages by scrolling them. The simulation results show the proposed approach can be useful for viewing and searching data in the Internet.

2   Method

Nowadays, surfing on the Internet is the important part of life for most of human being. However, most of surfing time is wasted in looking for the real useful information. The huge amount of information exist on the Internet, also the huge amount of junk information exist as well. A search engine can be a filter at the first level to present the potential disserted data in first few pages. Generally, a well-designed search engine is able to decrease seeking time. However, more and more web designers have used the keyword skills to push their websites at the top of the searching results for specific search engines.   To reduce the download times of web pages and Internet traffic is a pivot for current web browser. Therefore, we propose a framework including a novel user-interface style and web caching mechanism to achieve this goal. The proposed user-interface, called "leaping-up", is to efficiently browse large amount of web pages by scrolling pages arbitrarily. The idea of leaping-up style is to present the web pages linked by the hyperlinks that are listed in the current web page. User can view these web pages without clicking hyperlinks. The web pages are presented as in a stack. Figure 1 demonstrates the web pages presented by leaping-up style. To implement the proposed framework, we use the agent server to pre-download the web pages. Then, these pages will be transferred to user from the agent server. User can go to next web page in the stack by scroll backward the scroll-wheel of mouse and vice versa. Therefore, user can exactly find the required web page without guessing among hyperlinks. Figure 2 shows the use of leaping-up style.

Fig. 1. Web pages are presented by leaping-up style

The leaping-up style consists of web cache mechanism and leaping-up presentation. In the back end, the web page linked by each hyperlink is been preloading by web cache technology when the main web page is loaded. In the front end, user is able to view the preloaded web pages by scrolling the scroll wheel even by fingers.

Only leaping up web pages cannot improve the performance of browsing data dramatically. The proposed web caching approach is used to enhance performance of leaping-up interface. Figure 3 presents this approach. When user input the key words and submitted the search request, the search results, such as hyperlinks and short contents, are listed in rows. Through leaping-up, all of these web pages behind hyperlinks can be viewed by scrolling mouse wheel. Hence finding the exact web page from huge amount of hyperlinks is easier than only text data. In addition, people sometimes only remember a specific picture in a web page, and people cannot find this web page by the links or short text. Leaping-up style is useful to present data in Internet and provide the efficient browsing performance.

3   Performance Evaluation

Without web caching technology, the behavior of the proposed framework in downloading web pages is similar to download pages in parallel but not smart. Actually, these related pages are downloaded simultaneously by following the sequence of hyperlinks shown in a page. The performance of the traditional browser is proportion to the network bandwidth which is shown below,

$$t_1 = \sum_{i=0}^{n} \frac{p_i}{b},$$

where p_i is the size of the ith page and b is the network bandwidth. The performance of the proposed framework can be evaluated for two parts: page preloaded time and the page download time for scrolling pages. The preloaded time is

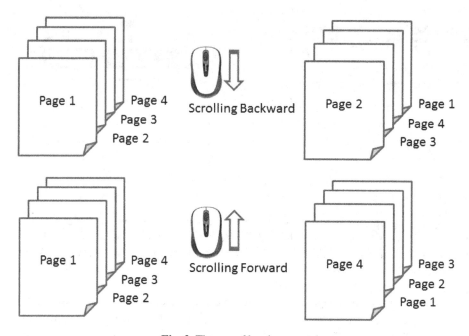

Fig. 2. The use of leaping-up style

$$t_{21} = \frac{\sum_{i=0}^{n} p_i}{B},$$

where B is the bandwidth of agent server. The page downloading time for the agent server is

$$t_{22} = \frac{p_{agent}}{b} \times m,$$

where p_{agent} is the size of the page from agent server and m is the number of the scrolling time. When the caching mechanisms is added in the proposed framework, the computing time is

$$t_2 = (1 - c_{hit}) \times \left(\frac{\sum_{i=0}^{n} p_i}{B} + \frac{p_{agent}}{b} \times m \right), c_{hit} = 0.8, 0.6, 0.4,$$

where c_{hit} is the cache hit rate. When B is xb and then the enhancement of the proposed framework is

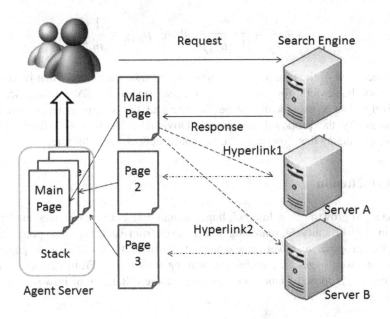

Fig. 3. Web caching technology for browsing results by using search engine

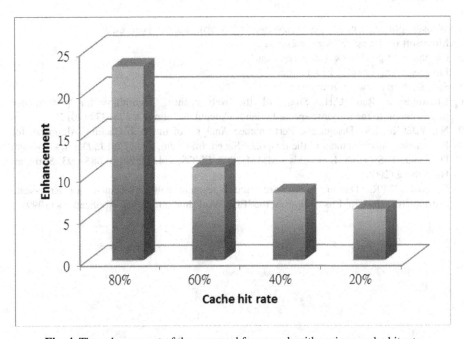

Fig. 4. The enhancement of the proposed framework with various cache hit rate

$$s = \frac{t_1}{t_2} = \frac{x}{\left(1 - c_{hit}\right)}, \text{ where } p_{agent} = \frac{1}{m} \sum_{i=0}^{n} p_i .$$

The enhancement of the proposed framework is illustrated in figure 4 that is based on the network bandwidth for end user and agent server is 10Mbps and 45Mbps, respectively. The x axis is the cache hit rate and the y axis is enhancement of performance by the proposed framework. Obviously, the proposed framework is useful for enhancing the browsing data, especially at 80% cache hit rate.

4   Conclusion

With the rapid growth of the Internet, huge amount data exist on the Internet. Thus, it results in the difficulty to searching information from such big data pool. In this paper, we propose a novel mechanism to efficiently browse web pages by downloading web pages in parallel and leaping web pages. From the performance evaluation, the proposed framework can enhance the efficiency of browsing data on the Internet.

References

1. Websiteoptimization, http://www.websiteoptimization.com
2. Microsoft IE, http://www.microsoft.com
3. Chrome, http://www.google.com
4. FireFox, http://mozilla.com
5. Safari, http://www.apple.com
6. Dhawaleswar Rao, C.H.: Study of the web caching algorithms for performance improvement fo the response speed. Indian J. Comput. Sci. Eng. 3, 374–379 (2012)
7. Na, Y.J., Ko, I.S.: Design and Performance Analysis of the Web Caching Algorithm for Performance Improvement of the Response Speed. In: Cham, T.-J., Cai, J., Dorai, C., Rajan, D., Chua, T.-S., Chia, L.-T. (eds.) MMM 2007. LNCS, vol. 4352, pp. 686–693. Springer, Heidelberg (2006)
8. Korupolu, M.R., Dahlin, M.: Coordinated placement and replacement for large-scale distributed caches. In: Proceedings of the IEEE Workshop on Internet Applications (1999)

Can a Clipboard Improve User Interaction and User Experience in Web-Based Image Search?

Leon Kastler and Ansgar Scherp

Institute for Web Science and Technologies
Universität Koblenz-Landau, Germany

Abstract. We investigate if a clipboard as an extension to standard image search improves user interaction and expèrience. In a task-based summative evaluation with 32 participants, we compare plain Google Image Search against two extensions using a clipboard. One clipboard variant is filled with images based on DCG ranking. In the other variant, the clipboard is filled based on gaze information provided by an eyetracker. We assumed that the eyetracking-based clipboard will significantly outperform the other conditions due to its human-centered filtering of the images. To our surprise, the results show that eyetracking-based clipboard was in almost all tasks worse with respect to user satisfaction. In addition, no significant differences regarding effectiveness and efficiency between the three conditions could be observed.

1 Introduction

A study on web-based multimedia search [10] revealed that 56% of all image searches have a follow up. On average, 2.8 queries are executed during an image search session [10]. Thus, multiple pages of query results are inspected and different images are reviewed and compared until the final decision is made. On the other hand, 90% of image search sessions last less than 5 minutes [10]. This raises the question for appropriate user interface designs to conduct image search tasks effectively and efficiently. Search engine providers constantly improve their information retrieval methods and add techniques like content-based filters to enhance the image search experience. However, selecting and using content-based features can be challenging to users. Our idea is to improve the user interaction and experience by extending standard web-based image search engines with the concept of a *clipboard*. A clipboard can be considered as overlay that is automatically filled with images during the users' search session. The users can open the clipboard at any time and view the selected images and review their details.

In this paper, we compare the unmodified Google Image Search with two variants using a clipboard. In the first variant, the clipboard is filled with the query search results of the users by applying an image ranking based on the discounted cumulative gain (DCG) algorithm. In the second variant, the user's gaze information provided by an eyetracking device is leveraged to identify relevant images. The eyetracking device is used without any specific interaction by the user. We have formulated the null hypothesis saying that there is no difference in the three

S. Yamamoto (Ed.): HIMI/HCII 2013, Part I, LNCS 8016, pp. 203–212, 2013.

conditions (plain Google Image Search, DCG-based clipboard, eyetracking-based clipboard) with respect to participants' efficiency, effectiveness, and satisfaction. We have conducted a sumamtive evaluation with 32 participants comparing the three different conditions. Each participant has conducted six different image search tasks of different complexity. The tasks have been taken from the top 20 queries worldwide of Google Insight in 2011. A natural assumption would be that the results show that the eyetracking-based clipboard with the human-centred filtering of the images will significantly outperform the other conditions. To our surprise, however, the results show that the eyetracking-based clipboard performed worse. The users' satisfaction with respect to the clipboard's support for conducting the image search tasks was in almost all tasks lower. In addition, there are no significant differences between the three conditions regarding efficiency and effectiveness in conducting the tasks.

2   Web-Based Image Search by a Clipboard

Using state of the art image search engines, we often encounter the problem that these systems are not suitable for more complex tasks. In situations where users are looking for multiple images to a specific topic with probably several queries, image search engines do not support them properly. Users have to keep a list of possibly interesting images. These are realized through saving images on the local machine or through opening images in different browser tabs. Both solutions need additional effort by the user. To handle this scenario, we introduce the concept of a clipboard to enhance traditional web-based image search.

Our approach of a clipboard is a session-wide, separated, automatically generated collection of interesting result objects as shown in Figure 1. It was designed in order to meet the needs of a multiple image search situation. Throughout a single search session, a user can formulate queries, e.g., different keywords or search engine specific filters, and look through returned result sets. During the search session, the user can open the clipboard. Here, the user receives a presentation of all images that were regarded as interesting by the system. Images are selected based on two different algorithms.

Fig. 1. Screenshot of clipboard within Google Image Search

One way to fill up the clipboard is an algorithm that only uses the result set of the image search engine. We use an algorithm based on the discounted cumulative gain algorithm (DCG). The DCG algorithm is normally used to evaluate information retrieval systems [6]. The function is shown in Equation 1. Here, $R_{B,i}$ is our selection function for image i, q_j is the j-th query of the complete query set Q, and $pos_q(i)$ is the position of image i in query q. If images are contained in several result sets, the system adds up the calculated values. The order of images is determined by the decreasing order of $R_{B,i}$ of all i. If the system calculates the same value for two images, it takes the first added image as higher ranked.

$$R_{B,i} = \sum_{q_j \in Q} \frac{1}{pos_{q_j}(i)} \tag{1}$$

The eyetracking-based clipboard is identical to the DCG-based clipboard in terms of user interface design. The difference lies in selecting interesting images for the user. The eyetracking-based clipboard decides based on the sum of gaze events and the total duration of fixations of an image, if it can be considered as interesting (see Equation 2). If two images have exactly the same total fixation time and numbers of events, the image that was fixated first will be ranked higher. $R_{C,i}$ is our selection algorithm for image i and $gazeEvents_q(i)$ are all gaze events in the result set of q for image i. $fixationDuration_q(i)$ is the total duration of all fixations of image i in query q.

$$R_{C,i} = \sum_{q_j \in Q} gazeEvents_{q_j}(i) + fixationDuration_{q_j}(i) \tag{2}$$

Since this algorithm is highly influenced by the user interaction, we face the following problem: it is necessary for our evaluation that the user does not know how images are added to the clipboard. Knowing how the selection algorithm works may lead to an explicit usage of the eyetracker by the participants, i.e., the eyetracker is applied as explicit input device. To prevent that the participants compare images in the clipboard with images outside the clipboard, we span the clipboard over the result set. This is done in both clipboard variants to keep them comparable.

3   Evaluation Design

To investigate the usefulness of a clipboard for image search, we designed a task-based, summative evaluation with three variants of a web-based image search engine. Our first variant, called variant A, uses the unmodified Google Image Search and acts as baseline. Variant B uses the DCG-based algorithm and variant C the eyetracking-based approach as introduced in Section 2.

Procedure: The evaluation consists of three phases. The introduction begins with a short welcome of the participant, followed by an explanation of the set-up, and

Table 1. Evaluation tasks of different complexity

Task	Description	Complexity
1	Good portrait of Michael Jackson	Simple
2	Beautiful, large image (min. 1200x900px) of the romantic rhine"	Filter
3	Five images of places of interest in Berlin	Composition
4	Good portrait of Lady Gaga	Simple
5	Clipart presentation of "Ampelmaennchen" (Icon of Berlin)	Filter
6	Three images about "Christmas" and "Loriot" (German Comedian)	Composition

the calibration of the eyetracker. The participant begins now with the machine-based evaluation process, starting with an overview of the system, the specific evaluation object and the task execution process. To ensure that the participant understands the task evaluation process, we give him an example task at the beginning, that is ignored in later data analysis. This helps to reduce curiosity in using the eyetracker. The task evaluation phase consists of a number of tasks that are executed by the participant. At the beginning of every task, the participant gets a short motivational description with a list of actions. When the participant clicks on the "next" button, a new window opens with the specific variant where the task is executed. Closing this window leads to a task-related questionnaire. When all tasks are processed, the participant is asked to fill in a final questionnaire with general questions about the evaluation. In addition, we encourage the participant to give a short free feedback, either written or oral.

Participants: For the evaluation, 32 participants (9 female) were randomly selected and assigned to the three different system variants. The average age was 25.7 (SD: 3.0). The majority, 28 participants, were students from our university. 20 of the students studied computer science, seven studied education and one participant studied in the field of humanities. The other four participants had a finished, non-academic training in one of the fields of economy, computer science, or physical therapy. All participants were asked to state their experience with Google Image Search on a five-point Likert-Scale. The average experience level was 3.78 (SD: 0.67). Concerning the question of their usage frequency of Google Image Search, eight participants reported that they use it on a monthly basis, 14 on a weekly basis, five on a daily basis and five participants use Google Image Search several times a day. Overall, we can say that all participants use Google Image search on a regular basis and are experienced in its usage.

Tasks: We developed three common scenarios with an increasing level of complexity, based on information from Google Insight[1]. Each scenario was translated into two tasks, rendering a total number of six tasks (as shown in Table 1) to be completed by participant. The first scenario was based on a simple image search task. The participant had to formulate a good query for the task, search through the result set, and select an image as his/her solution. The second scenario includes the usage of filters like specific image types or colouring. Here, the process of the first task was extended by either using a more complex query

---

[1] http://www.google.com/insights/search/

or filters of the search engine directly. The last scenario was designed to create a set of images given a specific topic where several queries were necessary.

Measurements: We recorded the same data for all participants: the duration of task execution, eyetracking events like gaze-in and gaze-out, mouse events like mouse-over and mouse-out, the number of queries, the number of filters used, questionnaire answers, and free feedback. Taking this measurement in all conditions A, B, and C ensures comparability of the groups and reduces the rule of error by bias.

Questionnaire: We have created two different questionnaires, a task-related (see Table 2) and a final one (see Table 3). The task-related questions aimed on the usability of the variant for the given task. The final questionnaire included questions about the evaluation as a whole. All questions were based on the

Table 2. Task-related questionnaire

Name	Group A	Group B/C
Q1	I can conduct the complete task with Google Image Search.	I can conduct the complete task with Google-Board.
Q2	Google Image Search offers me all things I need to conduct the task.	GoogleBoard offers me all things I need to conduct the task.
Q3	The results of Google Image Search meet my expectations I had during the formulation of my queries.	The results of GoogleBook meet my expectations I had during the formulation of my queries.
Q4	Too much input steps were needed to conduct the task.	Too much input steps were needed to conduct the task.
Q5	The presentation of results was suitable for the conduct of the task.	The presentation of results was suitable for the conduct of the task.
Q6	N/A	The GoogleBoard supported me in conducting the task.
Q7	N/A	The presentation of results in the Google Image Search was lucid.
Q8	N/A	The presentation of results in the Google-Board was lucid.
Q9	N/A	The images selected for the GoogleBoard were suitable for the task.
Q10	N/A	The ordering of images in the GoogleBoard was suitable for the task.

Table 3. Final questionnaire

Name	Group A	Group B/C
F1	The usage of Google Image Search is intuitive for me	The usage of Google Image Search with GoogleBoard is intuitive for me
F2	The presence of the eyetracker confused me during the task execution	The presence of the eyetracker confused me during the task execution
F3	I knew in every moment that Google Image Search was working	I knew in every moment that Google Image Search and GoogleBoard was working
F4	N/A	It is easy to switch between Google Image Search and clipboard
F5	N/A	The clipboard is a useful extension for the Google Image Search
F6	N/A	The usage of the clipboard was easy to learn
F7	N/A	There were system errors during my work with the clipboard

IsoMetrics Questionnaire Inventory for summative evaluations [3]. Group A was asked less questions in both questionnaires than for group B and C because several questions were related to the clipboard, which group A using the standard Google Image Search did not have.

4   Evaluation Wizard and System Architecture

To guide the participants through the evaluation, we have designed a browser-based evaluation wizard. With this wizard, we are able to create a seamless transition between the description, execution, and evaluation of the tasks. All data created during this session is recorded by the system. The answers in the questionnaires are given through a slider element. The limiting values on this scale are defined as "predominantly disagree" and "predominantly agree", taken from the standard Lickert scale. An important part for the evaluation is the absence of the slider handle at the beginning (Figure 2). The handle is only visible after the participant has decided for value on the scale (Figure 3). By this, no priming by a pre-selected value, e.g., a position of the handle on the scale is conducted.

| predominantly disagree | so-so | predominantly agree | predominantly disagree | so-so | predominantly agree |

Fig. 2. Slider element, initial state    **Fig. 3.** Slider element, after clicked on so-so

5   Evaluation Results

We measure the effectiveness by comparing the amount of images saved on the computer to the amount of images requested in the task description. To measure the efficiency, we mainly analyse the duration for every task per participant. We also analyse the number of gaze-in events on the images in the result set, number of mouse events, number of queries, and number of filter usages. We measure the user satisfaction by evaluating both questionnaires, the task-related and the final one. We had to remove two participants from the evaluation results. The first tried actively to manipulate the eyetracking-based selection algorithm. The second participant was removed because we lost the session data by a critical error during the evaluation process.

Effectiveness: For the other participants, we checked the images of all participants and verified, if they stored the amount of images as requested in the task description. We found out that one participant of group A and two participants of group C missed to store the correct amount. One participant of group A stored no image in task 1. In group C, one participant stored only one image in task 6, where three were requested and another participant in group C stored for task 3 one image less than requested.

Efficiency: For efficiency, we compared the durations of all three groups per task. Figure 4 shows an average-high-low diagram of these values. We analysed all three groups pairwise with the Mann-Whitney U-test at a significance level of $\alpha = 0.05$. These analyses show a significant difference between group A and C in task 1 ($p = .029$). In all other tasks, we had no significant differences. However, we could observe that variant C was on average slower than both other variants. Besides duration, we also investigated all other measured data as shown in Table 4, but no significant differences was inferable from it. To analyse the user satisfaction, we looked for statistically significant differences between the groups by using Mann-Whitney U-Test. For the task-related questionnaire, we tested every question for every task. The results are presented in Table 5. We found three significant differences between group B and C. Here, question Q6 ("The Clipboard supported me in the conducting the task.") and question Q9 ("The images selected for Clipboard were suitable for the task.") show advantages for variant B over variant C in task 3 ($p_{Q6}^{T3} = .021$) and task 5 ($p_{Q6}^{T5} = .027$, $p_{Q9}^{T5} = .045$). In regard of the final questionnaire, we compared the groups pairwise with each other, obtaining results that are presented in Table 6. Here, no significant differences could be found.

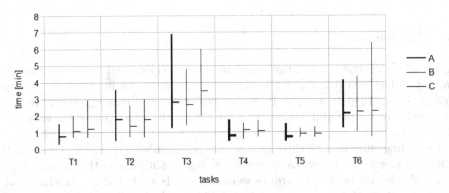

Fig. 4. Min-Max-Average diagram of processing duration per task and group

Table 4. Events sorted by task and group

		Task 1		Task 2		Task 3		Task 4		Task 5		Task 6	
		avg	SD	avg	SD	avg	SD	avg	SD	avg	SD	avg	SD
Duration [s]	A	45.15	21.08	94.35	65.34	153.91	103.7	49.36	26.84	44.57	21.5	134.51	65.12
	B	66.06	26.41	84.73	43.13	160.60	75.94	68.73	20.94	105.43	122.27	135.49	69.47
	C	74.69	39.56	108.06	52.69	207.91	75.64	66.10	17.77	55.16	13.73	138.81	101.55
Number of Gaze-In Events	A	34.5	58.44	73.4	31.49	143.8	155.41	25.5	58.44	20.67	31.49	109.71	155.41
	B	37.3	54.15	42.3	73.12	107.5	140.61	41	42.03	50.83	168.35	74	159.28
	C	50.4	68.7	58.1	105.12	113.8	140.76	40.88	50.01	25.71	28.93	84.5	179.36
Number of Mouse Events	A	20.8	15.19	74	50.62	112.2	68.21	20.38	10.39	17.88	9.25	97.86	79.86
	B	34	17.01	46	29.8	102.8	44.3	39.33	27.13	66.67	108.31	62.17	26.45
	C	36.9	23.69	59.5	54.11	148.3	88.84	36.38	22.36	36.63	30.3	86.38	86.38
Number of Queries and Filters	A	1	0	4	1.63	2.8	3.12	1.38	0.75	1.88	1.13	2.14	1.93
	B	1.3	0.68	2.1	0.32	1.7	1.06	1.17	0.4	2.5	1.76	1.17	0.4
	C	1.5	0.97	2.4	0.97	3.1	2.56	1.25	0.46	2.13	2.42	2.25	2.82
Images saved via GoogleBoard	B	0.6	0.52	0.4	0.52	1.6	1.58	0.17	0.41	0.67	0.52	.067	0.82
	C	0.1	0.32	0.3	0.48	1.2	1.69	0.38	0.52	0.25	0.46	1	1.41

Table 5. p-values of Mann-Whitney U tests of task-related questionnaire (significances marked)

Table 6. p-values of Mann-Whitney U tests of final questionnaire

		T1	T2	T3	T4	T5	T6
	A-B	.7	.82	.88	.9	.95	.8
Q1	A-C	.85	.55	.57	.75	.53	.6
	B-C	.76	.82	.65	.8	.8	.75
	A-B	.55	.88	.82	.9	.3	.85
Q2	A-C	.34	.6	.26	.6	.6	.14
	B-C	.94	.79	.14	.52	.8	.44
	A-B	.08	.41	.73	.12	.7	.52
Q3	A-C	.21	.14	.55	.6	.12	.29
	B-C	.6	.68	.68	.07	.3	.52
	A-B	.23	.5	.73	.44	.2	.18
Q4	A-C	.65	.97	.45	.4	.6	.29
	B-C	.29	.7	.97	.95	.65	.9
	A-B	.36	.91	.91	.52	.25	.52
Q5	A-C	.27	.4	.5	.67	.34	.46
	B-C	.7	.15	.27	.8	.24	.9
Q6	B-C	.07	.13	**.021**	.12	**.027**	.56
Q7	B-C	.26	.55	.6	.65	.9	.95
Q8	B-C	.57	.36	.43	.16	.8	.8
Q9	B-C	.5	.31	.07	.4	**.045**	.52
Q10	B-C	.31	.29	.15	.09	.7	1

	A-B	A-C	B-C
F1	.706	.880	.791
F2	.569	.620	.819
F3	.070	.791	.325
F4	N/A		.447
F5	N/A		.162
F6	N/A		.594
F7	N/A		.137

6 Discussion

In terms of effectiveness, all three variants can be considered similar. Although variant C has two participants with missing images, the interface for saving images is identical to variant B, where no image was missing. We have not observed any further differences with respect to the effectiveness between the three variants.

Regarding efficiency, all three variants are not significantly different from each other, besides for task 1 where group A was significantly faster than group C. In this task, the means of both groups were 15 seconds apart but due the fact that the task only took 30 seconds for A and 45 seconds for C at average makes it hard to derive further conclusions. As there are no further significant differences, we derive that the two different clipboard variants are equal to the Google Image Search and to each other. This shows on the one hand that the clipboard does not hinder users in executing tasks but also brings no advantages, what possibly indicates that the Google Image Search might be sufficient for most participants. Considering the average usage of Google Image Search of our participants, we can see that the group is familiar with this site.

The fact that the DCG-based clipboard (group B) got better results than the eyetracking-based (group C) is a surprise for us. For this, we investigated how often the clipboard was used in each task. For group B the average usage per task was 1.01 (SD: 0.36) and group C with 0.88 (SD: 0.42). Thus, the clipboard was only opened once or not at all in each task, although the participants were instructed to do so. This shows that the participants did only accept both clipboard variants to a minimum extent. We further investigated the amount of images shown in the clipboard when first opening it. We found out that group B had an average of 48.52 images in the clipboard (SD: 7.2) where group C had only 15.4 images (SD: 5.57). We also checked how many times the clipboard contained less than 20 images, which is the predefined maximum number of images stored in the clipboard. For group B, this occurred three times, for group C 19 times. Given this difference, the lower number of selected images for variant C might lead to a less satisfying selection as in variant B.

7 Related Work

This work is related to approaches that use eyetracking devices as input devices and approaches that receive implicit information from collected eyetracking data to improve ranking (relevance feedback). Cosato et al. [2] used eyetrackers as input devices for their so called Rapid Serial Visualization Presentation methods for large data sets of images. They compared their methods with a grid-based presentation of images. There are also many other applications that make use of an eyetracker as input device like for example drawing shapes [5] or composing texts [11,12]. A general problem of using eyetrackers as direct input device is that it was considered by participants as "unnatural" use of one's eyes in a focused way to control an application. By this, users get quickly tired using such a system. In contrast, in our approach we only collect normal gaze movements of the users while using an application they are familiar with. The users do not control the image search nor the clipboard by using the eyetracker as direct input device.

Another way to use eyetracking data is for implicit relevance feedback in information retrieval tasks. For instance, in textual information retrieval, Hardoon et al. [4] extracted implicit relevance feedback from eyetracking information. Another work is the Text 2.0 project from Buscher et al. [1]. They used eyetracking information to recognize text areas of interest and to provide additional content depending on these areas. Besides these text-based approaches, there are works like Pasupa et al. [9] that used eyetracking information to rank images. A work concerning the retrieval of relevance feedback from eyetracking data was published by Jaimes et al. [7]. They recognized different patterns of observation for images of different semantic categories. The system GaZIR, created by Kozma et al. [8], is an approach for visual image search engines using an eyetracker. In contrast to these systems, our approach aimed to use the feedback for filling the clipboard and so improving the usability of results, rather than improving the search itself. Also, prior work used predefined, closed sets of images, we use live data received from a popular web-based image search engine.

8 Conclusion

We have presented an approach to use eyetracking information in web-based image search engines. We have evaluated a baseline variant with two clipboard versions using different selection algorithms. To our surprise, all three system variants showed almost no significant differences ($\alpha < 0.05$). Comparing both clipboard variants, the selection algorithm using eyetracking information was overall less favoured by the participants than the one using the DCG-based algorithm applied on the Google image results. We identified and discussed several properties of both clipboard variants that explain why this unexpected result may have happened.

Acknowledgement. The research reported here was partially supported by the SocialSensor FP7 project (EC under contract number 287975).

References

1. Biedert, R., Buscher, G., Schwarz, S., Möller, M., Dengel, A., Lottermann, T.: The Text 2.0 Framework – Writing Web-Based Gaze-Controlled Realtime Applications Quickly and Easily. In: Proc. International Workshop on Eye Gaze in Intelligent Human Machine Interaction, EGIHMI (2010)
2. Corsato, S., Mosconi, M., Porta, M.: An eye tracking approach to image search activities using rsvp display techniques. In: Proc. Working Conference on Advanced Visual Interfaces, AVI 2008, pp. 416–420. ACM, New York (2008)
3. Günther Gedigaa, I.D., Hamborg, K.-C.: The IsoMetrics usability inventory: An operationalization of ISO 9241-10 supporting summative and formative evaluation of software systems. Behaviour and Information Technology 18, 151–164 (1999)
4. Hardoon, D.R., Pasupa, K.: Image ranking with implicit feedback from eye movements. In: Proc. Symposium on Eye-Tracking Research and Applications, ETRA 2010, pp. 291–298. ACM, New York (2010)
5. Hornof, A.J., Cavender, A.: Eyedraw: enabling children with severe motor impairments to draw with their eyes. In: Proc. Conference on Human Factors in Computing Systems, pp. 161–170. ACM (2005)
6. Järvelin, K., Kekäläinen, J.: Cumulated gain-based evaluation of ir techniques. ACM Trans. Inf. Syst. 20(4), 422–446 (2002)
7. Jeff, A.J., Jaimes, R., Pelz, J., Grabowski, T., Babcock, J., Chang, S.-F.: Using human observers' eye movements in automatic image classifiers. In: Proc. of SPIE Human Vision and Electronic Imaging VI, pp. 373–384 (2001)
8. Kozma, L., Klami, A., Kaski, S.: GaZIR: gaze-based zooming interface for image retrieval. In: Proc. International Conference on Multimodal Interfaces, ICMI-MLMI 2009, pp. 305–312. ACM, New York (2009)
9. Pasupa, K., Klami, A., Saunders, C.J., Kaski, S., Szedmak, S., Gunn, S.R.: Learning to rank images from eye movements. In: Proc. 12th International Conference on Computer Vision, pp. 2009–2016 (2009)
10. Tjondronegoro, D., Spink, A.: Web search engine multimedia functionality. Inf. Process. Manage. 44(1), 340–357 (2008)
11. Ward, D.J., MacKay, D.J.C.: Fast hands-free writing by gaze direction. Nature 418(6900), 838 (2002)
12. Zhao, X.A., Guestrin, E.D., Sayenko, D., Simpson, T., Gauthier, M., Popovic, M.R.: Typing with eye-gaze and tooth-clicks. In: Proceedings of the Symposium on Eye Tracking Research and Applications, ETRA 2012, pp. 341–344. ACM, New York (2012)

The Effects of Website Familiarity on Website Quality and Intention to Use

Scott McCoy[1], Eleanor T. Loiacono[2], Gregory D. Moody[3],
and Cristóbal Fernández Robin[4]

[1] Mason School of Business, Williamsburg, Virginia, USA
[2] School of Business, Worcester Polytechnic Institute, USA
[3] University of Nevada Las Vegas, USA
[4] Académico Departamento de Industrias,
Universidad Técnica Federico Santa María, Chile
scott.mccoy@mason.wm.edu, eloiacon@wpi.edu,
greg.moody@gmail.com, cristobal.fernandez@usm.cl

Abstract. Previous research has revealed that mere exposure to a website can positively influence a user's experience with that website. This research extends this line of investigation by looking into the influence of familiarity on ads that appear on a website as well as the website itself. The results revealed familiarity to have a significant impact on ad evaluation directly and website quality indirectly (through ad entertainment and informativeness).

Keywords: Website quality, WebQual, entertainment, online advertisement, Internet, experiment.

1 Introduction

Increasing the number of customers to a website and their use and reuse of that site has been a major focus of companies on the Web, since its inception. This has lead to numerous studies looking into website quality (Loiacono, et al., 2007) and usage (van der Heijden, 2003; van der Heijden et al., 2003).

Several factors that influence a consumer's satisfaction relate to the website itself (i.e., website quality) and have been studied in great detail (Loiacono, et al., 2007). These factors relate to the site's intrinsic components, which are both aesthetic and utilitarian in nature. Other factors, which have not received as much attention, are more extrinsic in nature. These aspects are outside of the website, but may still effect a consumer's decision to reuse it. First, the mere familiarity with a site may impact a consumer's perception of it (Zajonc et al., 1971; Kim and Malhotra, 2005). Additionally, external elements, such as advertisements (ads) that are placed on a website may influence the evaluation of that website.

The following research focuses on how these external factors impact a consumer's evaluation of a website and subsequent decision to reuse it.

S. Yamamoto (Ed.): HIMI/HCII 2013, Part I, LNCS 8016, pp. 213–220, 2013.
© Springer-Verlag Berlin Heidelberg 2013

2   Literature Review

Several theories have been put forth in psychology and communications to explain how individual perceive and react to entertaining phenomenon (Oatley, 1994; 1999; Vorderer, 2001). *Entertainment*, although difficult to define (Vorderer, 2004), is defined as stimuli that through interaction with the user produce a sense of enjoyment or pleasure (Moody et al., 2007). It is important to note that entertainment is perceived and experienced by the user and is not specifically an aspect of the system (Lowry et al., 2008a), even if a system is intended to produce entertaining outcomes or not (Klimmt and Vorderer, 2003; Moody et al., 2007).

2.1   Applying Entertainment to Websites

More recent research in information systems and consumer behavior has also attempted to explain how entertainment–related constructs aid our understanding of user intentions towards websites (Koufaris, 2002; van der Heijden, 2004). Koufaris (2002) applied the theory of flow, with further refining, and the theory of technological acceptance (Davis, 1989) to explain the intention to use a website alongside unplanned purchases on the website. They found that only the enjoyment of shopping and the perceived usefulness of the site were able to predict intentions to continue to use and return to the website.

Likewise, van der Heijden (2004) applied hedonic/intrinsic motivation in the form of perceived enjoyment of using a system to the technology acceptance model to explain intentions to use a system, which we extend towards websites. They found that the perceived ease of use of a website significantly increased the perceived enjoyment from using the website, which also increased the intentions to continue to use the website.

Both of these studies propose and show how entertainment is an important factor to consider when determining the intentions to use a website. Further, extent research on motivations within technology acceptance (TAM) literature (Lowry et al., 2008a) has shown that both intrinsic and extrinsic factors for usage should be considered. We thus build upon TAM to explain how entertainment, as an intrinsic motivator, is an important factor to consider in website design.

2.2   Website Quality

The literature on website quality is extensive. Many researchers have developed measures for evaluating a website's quality (Barnes and Vidgen, 2001; Schubert, 2002; Yoo and Donthu, 2001). None, however, have been as extensively tested and validated as WebQual (Loiacono, 2000; Loiacono, Watson, and Goodhue, 2007). For this reason, we chose WebQual as the website quality measure for this research.

According to WebQual, there are 12 key factors that consumers consider when determining a website's quality. They are: informational fit-to-task, tailored communication, trust, response time, ease of understanding, intuitive operations, visual appeal, innovativeness, emotional appeal, consistent image, online completeness, and relative advantage (See Loiacono, Watson, and Goodhue, 2007 for a complete explanation of these factors).

Extent research in e-commerce has also shown that cobranding is an effective mechanism for increasing perceived website quality (Lowry et al., 2008b; Stewart, 2003; 2006). Specifically, these studies have found that brand equity held by a brand advertised on a website can be transferred to the website. Given that online advertisements have already been shown to be influential in the buying process (Briggs and Hollis, 1997; Danaher et al., 2003; Ha and Perks, 2005), cobranding becomes an effective mechanism to quickly improve website quality by taking advantage of the advertised brand on the website.

3   Theoretical Model Development

We build on the underlying proposed by van der Heijden (2004) and the technology acceptance model (Davis, 1989) to build and propose our model to predict how cobranding attempts via online ads alters the perceived level of entertainment of the ad, and its level of informativeness, which are both increased on familiar websites. We then explain how the informativeness and entertainment of the ad impact its perceived website quality and intentions to use the website.

3.1   Predicting Entertainment and Informativeness of the Ad

Prior research, and the mere exposure effect[1] (Holden and Vanhuele, 1999; Lowry et al., 2008b; Zajonc et al., 1971), have long proposed that familiar websites are more likely to be viewed positively by its users (Lowry et al., 2008b; McKnight et al., 2002). Thus, building on prior research, and the mere exposure effect, we extend these findings specifically to the entertainment value of the online ad on the website, and propose:

H1: The familiarity of the website will positively influence the website user's perception of the entertainment value of an online ad placed on that website.

Familiarity of a website would serve as an indicator that the user has already deemed the website proficient enough to return and reuse (Beaudry and Pinsonneault, 2005). This positive impression is likely to spread to ads that are present on the website. This we propose that:

H2: The familiarity of the website will positively influence the website user's perception of the informativeness of an online ad on that website.

Finally, building on the spillover of affect as explained in psychology literature (Lowry et al., 2008b) and the theory of flow (Csikszentmihalyi, 1975; 1990), we posit that more entertaining websites ads will positively impact the users' perceptions of the ad's informativeness.

---

[1] The *mere exposure effect* refers to the consistent finding that through repeated interactions with an object, one's attitude the object is enhanced (Zajonc et al., 1971).

We thus propose:

> *H3: The perceived enjoyment of the online ad will positively influence the website user's perception of the informativeness of the online ad.*

3.2   Explaining Website Quality and Website-Related Intentions

We posit that the entertainment afforded by the website, via the online ad, will positively impact the perceived quality of the website, and intentions to continue to use the website. Thus building on the prior research linking motivations to attitudes and intentions (Feldman and Lynch, 1988; Jonas et al., 1997), we propose the following:

> *H4a: The perceived entertainment of the online ad on the website will positively influence the perceived quality of the website.*

> *H4b: The perceived entertainment of the online ad on the website will positively influence the user's intentions to continue to use the website.*

The perceived informativeness of the online ad on the website should also impact the perceived quality of the website and the users' intentions to continue to use the website. Thus, building upon the logic afforded by TAM, and the strong research stream that has shown the relationship between utilitarian beliefs and the attitudes and intentions formed from these beliefs (Davis, 1989; Venkatesh et al., 2003; 2013), we extend these findings to our specific belief of the perceived informative of the online ad on a website.

> *H5a: The perceived informativeness of the online ad on the website will positively influence the perceived quality of the website.*

> *H5b: The perceived informativeness of the online ad on the website will positively influence the user's intentions to continue to use the website.*

Previous research has longed predicted, shown and defended the relationship between the perceived quality of a website and users' intentions to continue to use the website (for example, Wells et al., 2013). Thus, we predict:

> *H6: The perceived quality of the website will positively influence the user's intentions to continue to use the website.*

4   Methodology

The study was conducted in an experimental setting to control the location and frequency of the advertisements, as well as to allow measurement of all of the outcome variables. The use of a real website and real ads allowed us to make the experiment as realistic as possible. The dependent variables were used as they appeared in previous research (for example, McCoy, et al. 2007; 2009; Galletta, et al. 2006). Four hundred and twenty volunteer students at a large South American university performed several search tasks under conditions chosen for them at random. The experiment was conducted in two closed rooms in the campus computer lab with each room containing 40 identical computers.

5   Analysis and Results

Data validation shows that our dataset exhibits strong factorial validity of the constructs, little multicollinearity, strong construct reliabilities, and the lack of any discernible mono-method bias. We used partial least squares (PLS) regression, using WarpPLS version 2.0, for the analysis of our theoretical model. We generated a bootstrap with 500 resamples to test the final model, which is shown in Figure 1.

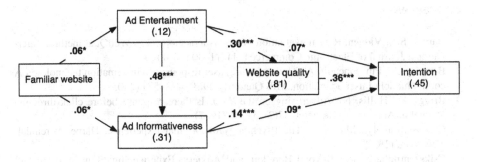

Fig. 1. Model Analysis Results

Analysis of the data supports our model. The results show strong explanatory power for website quality ($R^2 = 0.81$) and intention to reuse a website ($R^2 = 0.45$). The specific model relationships are strongly supported as well. We predicted that a familiar website would positively influence a user's perception of an ad's (H1) entertainment value and (H2) informativeness. The results support both hypotheses.

Further, it was predicted that the spillover of an ad's affect would impact consumers' perceptions of an ad's informativeness (H3), as well as the website's quality (H4a) and a consumer's intention to reuse the site (H4b). All three hypotheses were supported.

Extending the utilitarian concepts contained in TAM (Davis, 1989; Venkatesh et al., 2003; 2013), we predicted that an informative ad would positively influence a consumer's perception of a website's quality (H5a) and his/her intention to revisit that site (H5b). Both hypotheses were supported.

Finally, as Loiacono, et al. (2007) predict, the quality of a website is proposed (H6) to directly impact a consumer's intention to reuse the website. This hypothesis was highly significant. This is evident in the popularity and continued growth of websites like Amazon, Google, etc.

6   Conclusion

As outlined above, the results show strong explanatory power for website quality and intention to reuse a website with the model explaining over 80% of the variance in determining a website's quality and almost half of the variance for the intentions to continue to return to and use the website. In addition, the specific model relationships are strongly supported. It is important to note that ads can produce a negative feeling from website users. However, given the revenue they generate to the host site, they are often seen as a necessary evil. Our research shows that given the right ads, which are entertaining and informative, the result can provide positive feelings toward the overall website quality and intentions to return by users.

References

1. Barnes, S.J., Vidgen, R.: An evaluation of cyber-bookshops: The WebQual method. International Journal of Electronic Commerce 6(1), 11–30 (2001)
2. Beaudry, A., Pinsonneault, A.: Understanding user responses to information technology: A coping model of user adaptation. MIS Quarterly 29(3), 493–524 (2005)
3. Briggs, R., Hollis, N.: Advertising on the Web: Is there response before click-through? Journal of Advertising Research 37(2), 33–45 (1997)
4. Csikszentmihalyi, M.: Flow: The Psychology of Optimal Experience. Harper Perennial, New York (1990)
5. Csikszentmihalyi, M.: Beyond Boredom and Anxiety: Experiencing Flow in Work and Play. Jossey-Bass, San Francisco (1975)
6. Danaher, P.J., Wilson, I.W., Davis, R.A.: A comparison of online and offline consumer brand loyalty. Marketing Science 22(4), 461–476 (2003)
7. Davis, F.D.: Perceived usefulness, perceived ease of use, and user acceptance of information technology. MIS Quarterly 13(3), 319–340 (1989)
8. Feldman, J.M., Lynch, J.G.J.: Self-generated validity and other effects of measurement on belief, attitude, intention, and behavior. Journal of Applied Psychology 73(3), 421–435 (1988)
9. Galletta, D.F., McCoy, S., Henry, R.M., Polak, P.: When the wait isn't so bad: The interacting effects of web site delay, familiarity, and breadth. Information Systems Research 17(1), 20–37 (2006)
10. Ha, H.Y., Perks, H.: Effects of consumer perceptions of brand experience on the web: Brand familiarity, satisfaction and brand trust. Journal of Consumer Behavior 4(6), 438–452 (2005)
11. Holden, S.J.S., Vanhuele, M.: Know the name, forget the exposure: Brand familiarity versus memory of exposure context. Psychology & Marketing 16(6), 479–496 (1999)
12. InternetWorldStats (2010), http://www.internetworldstats.com
13. Jonas, K., Diehl, M., Bromer, P.: Effects of attitudinal ambivalence on information processing and attitude-intention consistency. Journal of Experimental Social Psychology 33(2), 190–210 (1997)
14. Kim, S.S., Malhotra, N.K.: A longitudinal model of continued IS use: An integrative view of four mechanisms underlying postadoption phenomena. Management Science 51(5), 741–755 (2005)
15. Klimmt, C., Vorderer, P.: Media psychology "is not yet there": Introducing theories on media entertainment to the presence debate. Presence 12(4), 346–359 (2003)
16. Koufaris, M.: Applying the technology acceptance model and flow theory to online consumer behavior. Information Systems Research 13(2), 205–223 (2002)

17. Loiacono, E.: WebQual™: A website quality instrument. Doctoral Dissertation. University of Georgia, Athens (2000)
18. Loiacono, E., Watson, R., Goodhue, D.: The effect of web site quality on intention to revisit and purchase. International Journal of Electronic Commerce 11(3), 51–87 (2007)
19. Lowry, P.B., Jenkins, J.L., Gaskin, J., Hammer, B., Twyman, N.W., Hassell, M.: Proposing the Hedonic Affect Model (HAM) to explain how stimuli and performance expectations predict affect in individual and group hedonic systems use. In: Proceedings of JAIS Theory Development Workshop, vol. 8(24) (2008a)
20. Lowry, P.B., Vance, A., Moody, G., Beckman, B., Read, A.: Explaining and predicting the impact of branding alliances and web site quality on initial consumer trust of e-commerce web sites. Journal of Management Information Systems 24(4), 199–224 (2008b)
21. McCoy, S., Everard, A., Loiacono, E.T.: Online ads in familiar and unfamiliar sites: Effects on perceived website quality and intention to reuse. Information Systems Journal 19(4), 437–458 (2009)
22. McCoy, S., Galletta, D.F., King, W.R.: Applying TAM across cultures: The need for caution. European Journal of Information Systems 16(1), 81–90 (2007)
23. Moody, G., Wells, T.M., Lowry, P.B.: A taxonomy of interactive digital entertainment (IDE). In: Proceedings of HICSS (2007)
24. Oatley, K.: A taxonomy of the emotions of literary response and a theory of identification in fictional narrative. Poetics 23, 53–74 (1994)
25. Oatley, K.: Meeting of minds: Dialogue, sympathy, and identification in reading fiction. Poetics 26, 439–454 (1999)
26. Schubert, P.: Extended web assessment method (EWAM): Evaluation of e-commerce applications from the customer's viewpoint. International Journal of Electronic Commerce 7(2), 51–80 (2002-2003)
27. Stewart, K.J.: Trust transfer on the World Wide Web. Organization Science 14(1), 5–17 (2003)
28. Stewart, K.J., Gosain, S.: The impact of ideology on effectiveness in open source software development teams. MIS Quarterly 30(2), 291–314 (2006)
29. Straub, D.W., Boudreau, M.C., Gefen, D.: Validation guidelines for IS positivist research. Communications of the AIS 13(24), 380–426 (2004)
30. van der Heijden, H., Verhagen, T., Creemers, M.: Understanding online purchase intentions: Contributions from technology and trust perspectives. European Journal of Information Systems 12(1), 41–48 (2003)
31. van der Heijden, H.: Factors influencing the usage of websites: The case of a generic portal in the Netherlands. Information & Management 40(6), 541–549 (2003)
32. van der Heijden, H.: User acceptance of hedonic information systems. MIS Quarterly 28(4), 695–704 (2004)
33. Venkatesh, V., Morris, M.G., Davis, G.B., Davis, F.D.: User acceptance of information technology: Toward a unified view. MIS Quarterly 27(3), 425–478 (2003)
34. Venkatesh, V., Thong, J.Y.L., Xu, X.: Consumer acceptance and use of information technology: Extending the unified theory of acceptance and use of technology. MIS Quarterly 36 (forthcoming)
35. Vorderer, P.: It´s all entertainment, sure. But what exactly is entertainment? Communication Research, Media Psychology, and the Explanation of Entertainment Experiences. Poetics 29(4-5), 247–261 (2001)
36. Vorderer, P., Klimmt, C., Ritterfeld, U.: Enjoyment: At the heart of media entertainment. Communication Theory 14(4), 388–408 (2004)

37. Wells, J.D., Valacich, J.S., Hess, T.J.: What Signal Are You Sending? How Website Quality Influences Perceptions of Product Quality and Purchase Intentions. MIS Quarterly (forthcoming)
38. Yoo, B., Donthu, N.: Developing a scale to measure perceived quality of an Internet shopping site (SITEQUAL). Quarterly Journal of Electronic Commerce 2(1), 31–46 (2001)
39. Zajonc, R.B.: Attitudinal Effects of Mere Exposure. Journal of Personality and Social Psychology Monograph Supplement 9(2) (1971)

Designing Effective User Interfaces for Crowdsourcing: An Exploratory Study

Robbie Nakatsu and Elissa Grossman

Loyola Marymount University, College of Business Administration, Los Angeles, CA
{Robbie.Nakatsu,Elissa.Grossman}@lmu.edu

Abstract. We investigate characteristics of the technology platform for different types of crowdsourcing initatives, as characterized by their task type—specifically we classify crowdsourcing applications by task structure, task interdependence, and task commitment. The method employed is to examine best practices of well-known crowdsourcing applications, investigating their user interface features, and characteristics that make them successful examples of crowdsourcing. Among the best practices uncovered were the following: easy searching for information; adaptive user interfaces that learned from the crowd; easy-to-use mobile interfaces; the ability to vote ideas up or down; credentialing; and creating sticky user interfaces that engaged the user. Finally, we consider issues for further study and investigation.

Keywords: Crowdsourcing, user interface design, open source design, online problem-solving platforms, distributed knowledge gathering, wisdom of the crowds.

1   Background on Crowdsourcing

Ever since Jeff Howe famously coined the term "crowdsourcing" in a 2006 Wired magazine article [1], the term has seeped into the public consciousness and become a popular buzzword for all things sourced on the Web. Well known crowdsourcing applications abound in the world today: A Netflix contest that offered a $1 million prize for coming up with the best movie recommendation algorithm; smartphone apps like Gas Buddy, which ask the crowd to report on the prices of gas stations in their area; crowdsharing web sites like AirBnB in which the crowd "rents out" their homes and apartments to others as a cheaper alternative to hotels. Howe's formal definition of crowdsourcing is "the act of a company or institution taking a function once performed by employees and outsourcing it to an undefined (and generally large) network of people in the form of an open call." [2]   More specifically, crowdsourcing can be viewed as a process that is made up of the following steps:

S. Yamamoto (Ed.): HIMI/HCII 2013, Part I, LNCS 8016, pp. 221–229, 2013.

1. A requestor (an individual or organization with a specific request—we do not limit the discussion to only organizations) identifies a specific task to be performed or problem to be solved.
2. The requestor broadcasts the task or problem online.
3. The crowd is asked to perform the task or solve the problem.
4. The crowd performs the task or submits solutions to the problem.

In some cases, it is necessary for the requestor to sift through the solutions to find the best one, or aggregate and synthesize the crowd output in some meaningful way, especially when there are numerous responses from the crowd.

Why crowdsource? What are the benefits of using the crowd to do something for you? There are a least three good reasons. First, crowdsourcing can lower costs to a much greater extent than hiring another organization to perform the task for you (as is the case in traditional outsourcing) because the crowd will often be willing to solve problems for little cost, or in some cases, for free. Second, companies can acquire firsthand insights into their customers or the marketplace by interacting directly with the crowd. Third, and perhaps most fundamentally, crowdsourcing enables companies to draw on a diversity of ideas and perspectives. By drawing on the crowd, companies may be able to more effectively tackle difficult problems that cannot be solved by their in-house staff.

2   A Taxonomy of Crowdsourcing: Fitting the Crowdsourcing Approach to the Task Type

After looking at over a hundred examples of crowdsourcing, we came up with a taxonomy that maps task characteristics to crowdsourcing approach. In [3] we report more fully on the classification scheme, but here only summarize the taxonomy. The taxonomy is presented in Table 1 on the next page.

Task structure refers to whether a task is well-structured or unstructured. Task interdependence refers to how tightly coupled the activities of the crowd are. If they are independent (Quadrants I and III), individuals perform work separately with little or no interaction with others. If they are interdependent either (1) the activites are still performed separately, but the outputs are aggregated into a more meaningful end product (Quadrant II) or (2) the individuals must problem-solve and collaborate to accomplish the task (Quadrant IV). Finally, task commitment refers to the amount of effort and resources that are required to perform a task or solve a problem. Low commitment tasks are relatively easy to perform while high commitment tasks would require more effort to perform. Although the three dimensions, taken together, would result in eight categories of crowdsourcing (2 X 2 X 2), we discovered in our analysis that Quadrant III tasks were almost always low commitment. Hence, our framework resulted in seven categories of crowdsourcing.

Table 1. A Taxonomy of Crowdsourcing Approaches by Task Characteristics[1]

	Independent Tasks (Solo)	Interdependent Tasks (Virtual Communities)
Well-Structured Tasks (The solution to the problem is well-defined.)	**I. Contractual Hiring** Low Commitment: • Human intelligence tasks • Crowdsharing marketplaces High Commitment: • Online employment platforms	**II. Coordination: Self-Organized Communities** Low Commitment: • Geolocated data collection • Distributed knowledge gathering • Crowdfunding
Unstructured Tasks (There is no known or well-defined solution to the problem.)	**III. New Idea Generation – Solo** Low Commitment: • Consumer-driven innovation High Commitment: • Online problem-solving platforms	**IV. Collaboration: Open Innovation Communities** Low Commitment: • Real-time idea jams High Commitment: • Open source software development • Open source design of hardware

3   Characteristics of the Crowdsourcing User Interface: Five Best Practices

We now look at user interfaces employed in five of the seven categories of crowd-sourcing (we do not consider the two categories in Quadrant IV: collaborative crowdsourcing, but leave this as an area of future investigation). Each of these user interfaces represents a successful crowdsourcing application, as evidenced by the long-term viability of the web site (or smartphone app) as a successful e-business model. Although each example is a well-known crowdsourcing application in the category, it does not represent all the user interface features that are possible or representative in that category: we acknowledge that there is more diversity within each category. This exploratory study is meant to illustrate what is possible in terms of user interface features across this limited sample of best practices.

3.1   Well-Structured Tasks Performed by an Individual: Contractual Hiring

Amazon's Mechanical Turk is a good example of a crowdsourcing platform that supports *low commitment tasks*. Through this web site, workers are paid for performing "human intelligence tasks" (HITs): these are simple rote tasks that are more

---

[1] This taxonomy does not address user-generated content in sites like Wikipedia, Yelp, and Youtube. Although an important form of crowdsourcing, we are primarily concerned with more novel forms of crowdsourcing in this paper.

effectively performed by a human than a computer. Tasks like selecting the correct spelling for search terms, choosing the appropriate category for products, and tagging images are all easily performed by a human problem solver but more difficult to automate using computers.

The user interface of Mechanical Turk is simple and relatively easy to learn. You first sign in and register as either a worker or a requester (the worker and requester user interfaces are different). As a worker you can search from over 200,000 HITs, and sort for an HIT by reward amount, title of task, expiration date, among other criteria. A requester can ask that workers fulfill qualifications, by taking a test. Once you have passed the test (e.g. knowing how to correctly tag a video clip) you satisfy the qualification, and can begin the task to earn rewards, usually a few cents per correct task performed. You can attain the status of Mechanical Turk Master when you have demonstrated an accuracy score on HITs across a wide variety of HITs. A dashboard tracks and shows what HITs you have performed and your earnings to date. Information on the site is easily tracked and monitored.

On the other end of the spectrum are *high commitment tasks* that are supported by web sites like **Elance**, one of the web's leading online employment platforms. The main idea behind this site is to find freelance jobs from companies that need programmers, mobile developers, designers, marketers, and the like. It is free to post a job or register as a freelance worker.

The user interface is well organized and easy to navigate through. You can click on categories of jobs like "IT and Programming" or "Design and Multimedia". You can also specify the job type, whether fixed price or hourly. Job postings feature a job description, together with desired job skills. One of the interesting features of the Elance user interface is that you can either self-rate your skills, meaning you evaluate yourself, or you can be tested in over 300 skill tests, which show how a candidate scored relative to all other individuals who took the same test. If you have posted a high score, you can share your results on your favorite social media outlet, or via email.

Like in Mechnical Turk, there are screens to manage your Elance account online. For example, you can view your transaction history: the Manage tab allows you to keep track of your account balance and scheduled transactions; you can also withdraw funds and deposit funds (to a bank account). Finally, Elance also has a ratings system where employers can rate the freelance workers they have hired in the past.

3.2   Well-Structured Tasks Performed by a Group: Self-organized Communities

Waze is a GPS app that enables a community of drivers to share real-time traffic and road information. The app is easy to use. Because it involves the reporting of geolocated data, it is most effective on a GPS-enabled mobile device such as a smartphone or tablet computer. All this real-time information is aggregated so that the GPS knows how to re-route you to a different route depending on traffic reports and other road alerts reported by the crowd. This is one important benefit of a crowd-sourced GPS application: it can learn about your travel times and adjust its navigational advice accordingly.

The Waze user interface enables you to very easily report events you see while driving. Because this is typically done on a small-screen smartphone, the driver (or the passenger in the vehicle) must be able to do this in a few short clicks. A report icon on the main screen quickly takes you to a Report screen, which contains a number of icons: traffic jam, police, accident, hazard, and so forth. An interesting feature is the Map Issue icon, which lets you report maps errors, and other driving errors as a result of receiving wrong driving instructions—hence Waze is able to update map errors in real time.

People using Waze, known as Wazers, are known to have a strong emotional connection to the app--as opposed to a run of the mill GPS device that are purely utilities. Because of the immediacy of the app, and its ability to detect real-time events, Wazers feel part of a community of drivers united by their mutual hatred of traffic. Through Waze, you can also connect to Facebook to arrange meet-ups with your friends. It allows you to see a live status of your friends and colleagues arriving to an event. Other features create a sticky app: map chat lets you chat with other Wazers, and a gas option shows the prices of gas around your area.

3.3   Unstructured Tasks Performed by an Individual: New Idea Generation

In term of a *low commitment task*, **My Starbucks Idea** is a good example of a web site that promotes customer-driven innovation. The idea of this web site is simple and straightforward: customers can share what they want from a Starbucks experience, everything from a new idea about coffee drinks and food to having waiters at Starbucks stores. The new ideas are neatly arranged into three categories—product ideas, experience ideas, and involvement ideas—so that it is easy to navigate through the different classes of ideas. Customers can vote the ideas up or down, and view the most popular ideas. There is a Top All-time list of ideas, as well as a section on "Ideas in Action" that showcases some of the customer ideas that have actually been implemented in some Starbucks stores.

Innocentive is a crowdsourcing platform that supports *high commitment tasks*. Using this web site, seekers can post challenges that are broadcast to a network of 275,000+ problem solvers. Oftentimes, these challenges involve difficult R&D questions that companies have been unable to solve internally. Challenges are categorized as brainstorm challenges, premium challenges, and grand challenges. Solvers can submit solutions to the challenges. If the seeker is satisfied with the solution, then the seeker provides the solver with a cash award in exchange for the IP rights to the winning solution.

The user interface for Innocentive is well-organized and provides navigational tools to search through the database of challenges posted. You can filter by discipline (e.g. business and entrepreneurship, chemistry, physical sciences, math/statistics, etc.), by award amount, by submission type (individual solver vs. team), as well as by keyword search. Registered users can enter their public profile, including bio information; external links to LinkedIn, Facebook, and Twitter; as well as professional qualifications including education, areas of expertise and publications. If the user becomes a winning solver, some of this information is displayed on the winning solvers page. There is even an Innocentive app that allows you to browse and read the latest challenges on your mobile device.

3.4   Unstructured Tasks Performed by a Group: Open Innovation Communities

Low commitment tasks include real-time "idea jams" that bring together a group of individuals to jointly solve problems and come up with new ideas. IBM's 2006 Innovation Jam brought together more than 150,000 people from 67 companies. Over two 72-hour sessions, participants discussed new business opportunities for IBM; as a result new IBM businesses were launched. [4]

The open source software development of Linux is a clear example of a successful application of crowdsourcing for a *high commitment task*. Linux was a game-changer in that something as complex as an operating system could be developed by huge numbers of programmers throughout the world. Quality control occurred not through a centralized organization, but rather through releasing a new version of the software every week, and getting feedback from programmers throughout the world. [5]

We did not investigate the user interfaces of either example above—this is a future area of investigation. However, we speculate that high commitment tasks would require a more sophisticated technology platform that would enable ongoing collaboration among individuals, and would include features like document/file sharing, wikis, and support for version control.

4   A Summary of Best Practices

The preceding discussion suggests a number of best practices for designers of crowdsourcing platforms to consider in the development of the user interface. Here we summarize some of the issues that emerged in our exploratory investigation.

Searchability of Information. In all best practices discussed above, information was very easy to find and search for. This is especially critical for crowdsourcing platforms containing numerous items that the crowd needs to search for: in Mechanical Turk, workers need to filter through thousands of HITs; likewise, in Innocentive, solvers need to be able to quickly zero in on what challenges are most suitable. Closely related to the issue of searching, is the categorization of information. For example, My Starbucks Idea categorizes new ideas into different topical areas, and prominently display these topics on their main page. The site would be far more difficult to use were it not for the categorization of ideas.

Simplicity of the Mobile App User Interfaces. It is important for a user interface to be simple and easy to use when it is delivered as a mobile app, and the task involves the reporting of real-time events. Waze is a case in point. Drivers need to be able to quickly access the appropriate screen of information. Through two direct clicks, a driver is able to immediately report an event, whether it is a traffic jam, road alert, or map issue.

The Ability to Vote Ideas Up or Down. To understand the pulse of the crowd—what it is thinking, what the most popular ideas are, and whether consensus has been reached—there needs to be a mechanism to vote ideas up or down. This is especially important when a crowdsourcing application becomes bombarded with a multitude of ideas. Voting and rating mechanisms allow one to quickly view what ideas have risen to the top. One example of this is My Starbucks Idea, which allows visitors to vote on their favorite ideas. The most popular ideas rise to the top, while the less popular ones can be filtered out.

Creating "Sticky" or Addictive User Interfaces. All of the best practices discussed in this paper employ techniques that engage the crowd, and make them more likely to stick around for more. Mechanical Turk has a dashboard that allows you to track your progress and money earned. Waze lets you chat with other Wazers, as well as check gas prices in your area. My Starbucks Idea uses Leaderboards so that creating the best idea becomes almost like a contest. Likewise their "Ideas in Action" give you incentive to create an idea that might actually be implemented. Innocentive has a mobile app that sends you real-time updates whenever a new challenge in your area of expertise has appeared. Many of these crowdsourcing initiatives also allow you to set up links to Facebook, Twitter, and other social media, further creating an experience that keeps you connected—e.g., Waze links up with Facebook to show you where your friends are.

Building Community. The most successful crowdsourcing platforms are good at building community. The immediacy of the real-time updates in Waze lets Wazers become part of a community united by driving and traffic; likewise the Map chat features allow Wazers chat with one another. Innocentive allows you to publish your public profile, and will publicize winning solvers. You become a community of problem solvers unified by your shared areas of expertise. My Starbucks Idea is about building a community of Starbucks customers, where you can share, vote, and discuss ideas about Starbucks.

Learning from the Crowd: Adaptive User Interfaces. User interfaces that adapt to crowd behaviors can be especially effective in creating an engaging interaction with the crowd. Waze aggregates information about traffic information and road alerts to dynamically generate a route to your destination. In the future, we foresee many more crowdsourcing applications that learn about you, and learn about the crowd, to deliver more effective advice tailored to your particular circumstances.

Credentialing. Before a worker is permitted to perform certain tasks, he or she must first take an online test to fulfill what they refer to as a qualification. The test usually involves the performance of a task, which must be successfully completed and verified by the requester. In a similar vein, but involving more complex skillsets, Elance offers over 300 online skill tests that prospective workers can take to demonstrate to prospective employers that they are capable of performing a task. Although online credentialing is imperfect—e.g., someone else could perform the task on your behalf—it offers one more way for others to verify what you are able to do.

5   Future Work

The exploratory study described in this paper will be the basis for a more extensive study on creating user interfaces for crowdsourcing. We will be looking more extensively at the 100+ examples of crowdsourcing that we have gathered in our own database and records. Some of our research questions will include consideration of the following:

- What types of user interface features are most appropriate for each different type of crowdsourcing?
- How do we support collaboration (Quadrant IV) types of crowdsourcing?
- How do we better support processes in managing more complex forms of crowdsourcing involving high commitment tasks—e.g., online problem-solving platforms that support the process for idea submission to payment, to intellectual property management.
- What can we learn from current efforts of crowdsourcing to developing user interfaces for new and emerging forms of crowdsourcing in the future? For example, what can we learn from open source software development that we can apply to the open source design of hardware and other products?
- What are some of the critical success factors of crowdsourcing? Conversely, why do some crowdsourcing initiatives die out and fail?

It is clear from our review of the literature, and this exploratory study, that crowdsourcing applications are very much on the rise today, and will continue to generate many more interesting applications in the future. We believe the study of the user interface is a rich area to pursue, one that is currently underserved in the literature.

References

1. Howe, J.: Crowdsourcing: Why the Power of the Crowd is Driving the Future of Business. Three Rivers Press, New York (2008)
2. Howe, J.: Crowdsourcing: A Definition (June 2, 2006), http://crowdsourcing.typepad.com

3. Nakatsu, R., Grossman, E., Iacovou, C.: Finding the Right Crowdsourcing Approach to Fit the Task. Under review in Sloan Management Review
4. IBM Invests $100 Million in Collaborative Innovation Ideas (November 14, 2006), http://www-03.ibm.com
5. Raymond, E.S.: The Cathedral and the Bazaar: Musings on Linux and Open Source by an Accidental Revolutionary. O'Reilly, Sebastopol (2001)

Trailblazing Information:
An Exploratory Search User Interface

Marcus Nitsche and Andreas Nürnberger

Otto-von-Guericke-University Magdeburg, 39106 Magdeburg, Germany
{marcus.nitsche,andreas.nuernberger}@ovgu.de

Abstract. When conceptualizing user interfaces (UIs) to support exploratory search, designers need to take into account various aspects. In contrast to ordinary information retrieval UIs, exploratory search user interfaces (XSIs) need to support users in a more complex and often long-term use scenario. Therefore aspects of Personal Information Management need to be taken into consideration. An XSI needs to provide a visually appealing overview over retrieved search results, it should offer simple ways to interact with the result set and offer easy ways of interaction to enhance the user's search experience by direct or indirect query refinement options. In this paper we propose a possible solution to address these requirements, implemented a fully functional prototype and present the results of a conducted usability study.

1 Introduction

Adhoc-searches are well supported by current web search engines. Beyond that, complex information needs or investigations which often rely on multi-session search processes are not very well supported [12]. There is a growing need of users to be supported in complex search tasks like exploratory searches.

Noël et al. [16] modelled the exploratory search process in general by providing three axes of freedom a user usually selects from in order to navigate in an (unknown) information space (Fig. 1). Thereby, an overview visualization of search paths (search trails) is identified as a crucial aspect to support the XS process. New concepts to satisfy such requirements are being developed and investigated under the term *exploratory search (XS)* [12,23]. It is based on advances in technology as well as novel insights from psychology. Ergonomically designed user interfaces (UIs) should support users by easy-to-use switches between overview and context views [20] since this is one of the key tasks an *Exploratory Search User Interface* (XSI) should support [23]. In this work we present a possible solution to address this requirement. Furthermore several novel interaction techniques and methods are proposed that were evaluated as useful enhancements to support exploratory search tasks.

2 State-of-the-Art

Modern search engines have been engineered and tested to be good in finding answers to relatively straightforward questions. However, if the user has a more

S. Yamamoto (Ed.): HIMI/HCII 2013, Part I, LNCS 8016, pp. 230–239, 2013.

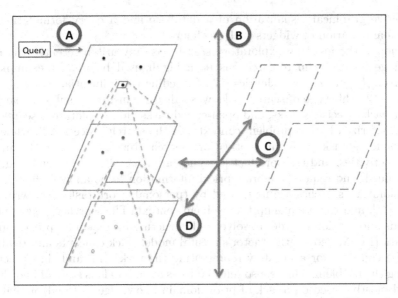

Fig. 1. 3D of movement in exploratory searches [16]: (A) query input, (B) vertical axis for filtering, (C) horizontal axis for similarity measures and (D) transversal axis

complex information need, traditional search engines can only partly - if at all - assist in finding sources that could satisfy the demand [8].

Beyond search user interfaces (SUIs) that are solely based on user queries, a myriad of systems to explore information spaces exist. One exemplary information exploration system is the dynamic queries interface by Ahlberg, Williamson & Shneiderman [1]. It is characterized as an interactive graphical visualization of a database and allows query formulation via direct manipulation of widgets such as sliders. While corresponding tasks differ in motivation, search objective, complexity, uncertainty, activities and task [6], exploratory search can be characterized by the problem context and the search process [23]. The searcher is aware that he needs information to solve an ill-structured problem or process [19]. Around 20-30% [18] of searcher's goals are undirected queries. Beyond knowledge acquisition, the search process yields higher-level intellectual capabilities of the searcher within a particular subject area [23]. The user experience suffers in these cases, as SUIs are not well equipped for exploratory behaviour, and thus users employ non-expedient strategies out of necessity [22].

"The goal of information exploration is the refinement of a vague information need that leads, through interaction with information objects and information resources, to a more thorough understanding of the problem" [21]. Further characteristics of this kind of exploration is a defined conceptual area [22] and the examination of metadata of information sources [7]. In this area, filtering techniques can be useful to reach the informational goals. Exploratory data analysis is an example for information exploration [22]. One exemplary information exploration system is the dynamic queries interface [1]. It is characterized by an interactive graphical visualization of a database and a query formulation via direct manipulation of widgets such as sliders.

Although the focus on exploratory search has only arisen recently, the need to change the focus in research has been highlighted before, for example by Ingwersen [10] or O'Day & Jeffries [17]. Preceding the influential paper of Marchionini [12], this type of search tasks was called for instance "subject searches, general tasks, decision tasks, and open-ended tasks" [6]. Exploratory search can be characterized by the problem context and the search process [23], while the corresponding tasks differ in motivation, search objective, complexity, uncertainty, activities, and task product [6]. They are generally "more engaging, less well-defined, and require[s] more a priori information to be known" [6].

Exploratory searches are motivated by (personal) work tasks, e.g. writing a report [24], and these make up the problem context. The searcher is aware that he needs information in order to solve an ill-structured problem for proceeding in this task [19]. Moreover, the "actor's mental models lack concepts and relations between concepts for accurately representing the task" [19] and thus precisely defining the problem. This is also referred to as an anomalous state of knowledge [3] and mostly based on a lack of prior domain knowledge [23] and/or that the target of the search may be (partially) unknown [21]. Nevertheless, "the user defines the problem internally as a task with properties that allow progress to be judged and a search strategy to be selected" [23]. According to Rose & Levinson [18], around 20-30% of searcher's goals are undirected queries.

The objective is mostly to "create a knowledge product or shape an action" [23], or to "collect information through a variety of means, and to combine the discovered information to achieve a coherent understanding of some topic" [8]. Beyond knowledge acquisition, the search process yields higher-level intellectual capabilities of the searcher within a particular subject area [23].

Aula & Russell [2] distinguish between measures of (procedural) complexity and explorativeness, where the latter can be measured with a goal abstraction level. Prior to that, for instance Byström & Järvelin [5] studied the task complexity in a conceptual sense and its implications for information need. Complex tasks require understanding and sense-making to process results from different sources. The complexity and difficulty of the task, or the imprecisely defined problem context can result in uncertainty [6]. This generally decreases as the search progresses [11].

A lot of innovative interface ideas have been developed over the last years, but only the most promising ones have found their way into major search engines [9]. Many features have also come up and disappeared again, as one can see observing the permanent minor and major changes and optimizations taking place in Google's[1] interface. While this is also motivated by company policy - e.g. the integration of Google+[2] and YouTube[3] in the starting page - most modifications focus on the *usability* and *user experience*.

---

[1] http://www.google.com (03.02.2013)

[2] https://plus.google.com (03.02.2013)

[3] http://www.youtube.com (03.02.2013)

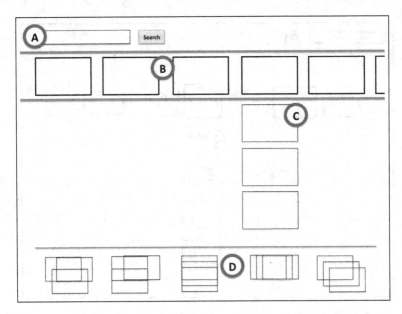

Fig. 2. Basic concept of "Trailblazer": A - text-based entry field, B - results ranked horizontal from left to right, C - orthogonal search trail (opens when result above is clicked), D - iconic representations of past search sessions

3   Trailblazer

In 1945, Vannevar Bush and Jingtao Wang described in their article "As we may think" the MEMEX system [4]. MEMEX (memory extender) is a theoretical system that was conceptualized to support users in "trailblazing": Trailblazing as a profession that establish "useful trails through the enormous mass of the common record" [4]. Since the proposed SUI here is also supposed to support users in trailblazing useful information out of the mass, we call the system "Trailblazer" in honor of Bush's early vision.

3.1   Concept

In our proposed solution, a domino metaphor (Fig. 2) is used to arrange single query results orthogonal to each other to visualize when and at which specific position a query refinement took place. Technically this happens by enhancing the original query with the secondary most representative term or multiple terms, derived from the actual selected search result. Thereby users become aware of their own search processes and firstly get the possibility to go back to a certain exploratory search step in order to choose an alternative path. This is realized (e.g.) by the design decision that path enhancements only take place in an orthogonal direction to the right or to the bottom. The such created search trails provide users with an interactive search history that can be easily enhanced.

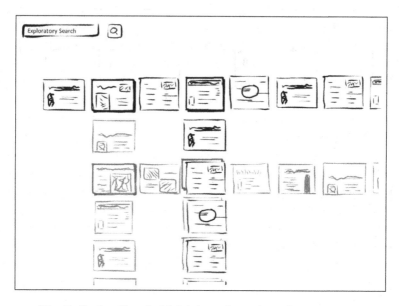

Fig. 3. Design Sketch: Multiple paths and overlapping issues

Using a domino metaphor, single query results will be arranged orthogonal to each other in order to visualize when and at which specific position a query refinement took place. Technically this might happen by simple enhancement of the original query by a representative term or multiple terms, derived from the selected search result. Thereby, users become aware of their own search processes and firstly get the possibility to go back to a certain exploratory search step in order to choose an alternative way, since path enhancements only take place in an orthogonal direction to right or to bottom, it is easy to navigate through and identify positions where query expansions took place. So-created search trails provide users with an interactive search history that can be easily enhanced.

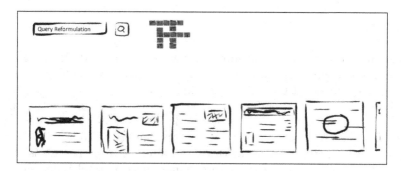

Fig. 4. Iconic representation of search trails. Here, the search trail of Fig. 3 is symbolized on top as a characteristic representation.

3.2   Design Follows Function

Following an old concept, the proposed XSI ...

- supports easy overviews of search results,
- shows interconnections between search results,
- provides users in keeping their focus while searching,
- provides easy ways to break out of known waters to explore unknown country (explore all three dimensions of exploratory search [16]),
- re-captures older researches in order to follow alternative paths,
- prevents users from switching between use modes (e.g. if PIM is necessary, directly support it in the XSI)

and

- supports easy query refinement / expansion.

3.3   Prototypic Implementation

The described concept has been implemented and features:

- horizontal instead of vertical result listing (Fig. 5),
- website preview in overview, interactive InFrame-Browsing [15] in detail view (Fig. 6),
- orthogonal layout of search refinements (implicit searches) - to right or to bottom to identify biunique starting points for the user's XS (Fig. 7),
- moving of whole research paths to the left upper corner of the UI, when new searches are started (easy resumption of previously started searches, Fig. 8),
- fading out non-followed paths to keep a clear UI design,

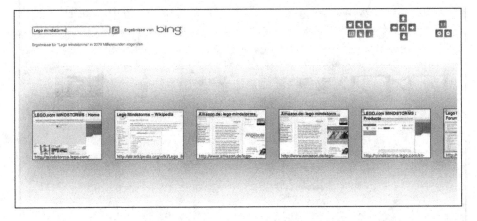

Fig. 5. Horizontal layout of first results as document previews

Fig. 6. Preview in context of other results (left and right) and InFrameBrowsing [15]

- automatic loading of further results if user reaches the right or bottom end of the display (infinite scrolling, no page turns necessary),
- support of explicit searches like user's expect of ordinary search user interfaces (in this case automatic archiving of previous search paths),
- saving & loading of search paths (supporting seamless switching between searches)

and

- enhancing search paths is done transparently (also in the implicit interaction mode) by showing the actual query send to the IR system.

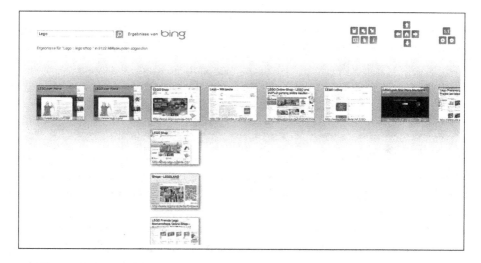

Fig. 7. Orthogonal layout of results retrieved by an implicit query expansion

We implemented the proposed concept using HTML5 and connecting to the Bing API[4] by Microsoft. The working prototype (see also Fig. 5, 6, 7 and 8) was tested by various users to evaluate its usability.

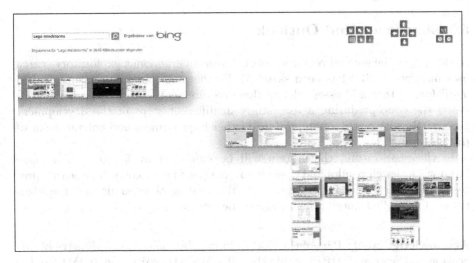

Fig. 8. Different searches: Selectable, reusable, comparably

4   Evaluation

Various studies have been conducted: A pre-study with a paper prototype to gain insights on the reception of the overall concept, a user study with a first running prototype and a final evaluation. In each study, different six participants were between 24 and 31 years old - with an average of 27.5 years -, three of them were female. The idea of search trails was received positive, even if it is a total new concept. Users liked the possibility to choose from alternative paths, but they suggested using the concept primarily for investigative tasks like exploratory searches, since it might overwhelm users when conducting simple look-up searches with this user interface concept.

Critic comments were to preserve clarity, let the interface be not so crowded, and provide only a minimum amount of animations and shifts. Another suggestion was to let the tool be a browser plug-in to ease integration into current practices. Five subjects would like most to test the system with a desktop computer or a laptop. Two would like to use a tablet. Many participants could imagine using the search interface on a regular basis. Four would use it daily instead of their current favourite search interface - not wanting to have separate systems to search. One test user stated, "if it provides more useful results than Google" as a reason, another one "if it's a customized perfect search engine".

---

[4] http://www.bing.com/developers (03.02.2013)

Three would use it for grounded specialist research, with one subject saying, "the system would be a good support, one only has to use one platform". Two of them would separate between their ad-hoc search system and a special tool for exploratory searches.

5 Conclusion and Outlook

In this paper the general requirements towards an ergonomic exploratory search user interface (XSIs) has been sketched. Furthermore, an XSI concept - called *Trailblazer* - that addresses a lot of these requirements was proposed. We evaluated the concept during a user study in different steps of the development process. Results reveal a potential for further improvement and enhancement of the concept.

In the near future, the system will be enhanced by features to manage in-between search results and options to save (parts of) exploratory search processes. Furthermore the performance while loading thumbnails and the algorithms for implicit query refinement will be improved.

Acknowledgement. Part of the work is funded by the German Ministry of Education and Science (BMBF) within the ViERforES II project (no. 01IM10002B). We thank Kathrin Scheil for further testing the proposed concepts during her Master's Thesis.

References

1. Ahlberg, C., Williamson, C., Shneiderman, B.: Dynamic queries for information exploration: An implementation and evaluation. In: Proceedings of the SIGCHI Conference on Human Factors in Computing Systems, pp. 619–626 (1992)
2. Aula, A., Russell, D.M.: Complex and Exploratory Web Search. In: Proceedings of Information Seeking Support Systems Workshop (2008)
3. Belkin, N.: Anomalous States of Knowledge as a Basis for Information Retrieval. Canadian Journal of Information Science 5, 133–143 (1980)
4. Bush, V., Wang, J.: As we may think. Atlantic Monthly 176, 101–108 (1945)
5. Byström, K., Järvelin, K.: Task Complexity Affects Information Seeking And Use. Information Processing & Management 31(2), 191–213 (1995)
6. Diriye, A., Wilson, M.L., Blandford, A., Tombros, A.: Revisiting Exploratory Search from the HCI Perspective. In: Proceedings of the Fourth Workshop on Human-Computer Interaction and Information Retrieval, pp. 2–5 (2005)
7. Golovchinsky, G., Belkin, N.J.: Innovation and Evaluation of Information. ACM SIGCHI Bulletin 31(1), 22–25 (1999)
8. Golovchinsky, G., Pickens, J.: Interactive Information Seeking via selective Application of contextual Knowledge. In: Proceeding of the Third Symposium on Information Interaction in Context - IIiX 2010, vol. 145. ACM Press, New York (2010)
9. Hearst, M.A.: Search User Interfaces. Cambridge University Press (2009)
10. Ingwersen, P.: Information Retrieval Interaction. Information Retrieval 246 (1992)

11. Kuhlthau, C.: Inside the Search Process: Information seeking from the users perspective. Journal of the American Society for Information Science 42(5), 361–371 (1991)
12. Marchionini, G.: Exploratory Search: From Finding to Understanding. Communications of the ACM 49(4), 41–46 (2006)
13. Nitsche, M.: User Interfaces for Exploratory Search - Towards generalized Design Patterns for complex Information Retrieval Tasks. Tagungsband der 1. Doktorandentagung Magdeburger-Informatik-Tage 2012 (MIT 2012), Magdeburg, Germany, pp. 43–50 (2012)
14. Nitsche, M., Nürnberger, A.: Trailblazer - Towards the Design of an Exploratory Search User Interface. In: Proceedings of the 6th Symposium on Human-Computer Interaction and Information Retrieval, Cambridge, MA, USA (2012)
15. Nitsche, M., Nürnberger, A.: InFrame-Browsing - Enhancing standard Web Search. In: Proceedings of the 6th Symposium on Human-Computer Interaction and Information Retrieval, Cambridge, MA, USA (2012)
16. Noël, L., Carloni, O., Moreau, N., Weiser, S.: Designing a knowledge-based tourism information system. International Journal of Digital Culture and Electronic Tourism 1(1), 1–17 (2008)
17. O'Day, V.L., Jeffries, R.: Orienteering in an Information Landscape: How Information Seekers get from here to there. In: Proceedings of INTERCHI 1993, The Netherlands, pp. 438–445. ACM, Amsterdam (1993)
18. Rose, D.E., Levinson, D.: Understanding User Goals in Web Search. In: Proceedings of the 13th Conference on World Wide Web, WWW 2004, p. 13. ACM Press, New York (2004)
19. Vakkari, P.: Exploratory Searching As Conceptual Exploration. Search, 3–6 (2010)
20. Ware, C.: Information Visualization. Morgan Kaufmann Publishers, San Francisco (2000)
21. White, R.W., Kules, B., Bederson, B.: Exploratory Search Interfaces: Categorization, Clustering and Beyond. ACM SIGIR Forum 39(2), 52–56 (2005)
22. White, R.W., Kules, B., Drucker, S.M., Schraefel, M.C.: Supporting exploratory search. Communications of the ACM 49(4), 37–46 (2006)
23. White, R.W., Roth, R.A.: Exploratory search: Beyond the Query-Response paradigm. In: Marchionini, G. (ed.) Synthesis Lectures on Information Concepts, Retrieval, and Services. Morgan & Claypool Publishers (2009)
24. Wilson, M.L., Elsweiler, D.: Casual-leisure Searching: the Exploratory Search scenarios that break our current models. In: Proceedings of HCIR 2010: 4th International Workshop on Human-Computer Interaction and Information Retrieval, pp. 2–5 (2010)

QUEST: Querying Complex Information by Direct Manipulation

Marcus Nitsche and Andreas Nürnberger

Otto-von-Guericke-University Magdeburg, 39106 Magdeburg, Germany
{marcus.nitsche,andreas.nuernberger}@ovgu.de

Abstract. When users search for information in domains they are not familiar with, they usually struggle to formulate an adequate (textual) query. Often users end up with repeating re-formulations and query refinements without necessarily achieving their actual goals. In this paper we propose a user interface that is capable to offer users flexible and ergonomic interaction elements to formulate even complex queries in a simple and direct way. We call this concept *QUEST* (Query User Interface for Exploratory Search Tasks). The proposed radial user interface supports phrasing and interactive visual refinement of vague queries to search and explore large document sets. The main idea of this concept is to provide an integrated view of queries and related results, where both - queries and results - can be interactively manipulated and influence each other. Changes will be immediately visualized. The concept was implemented on a tablet computer and the usability was stepwise evaluated during a formative and a summative evaluation process. The results reveal high usability ratings, even if the concept was completely unknown to our test users.

1 Motivation

When users try to handle complex information needs they often end up in conducting exploratory searches [11]. One of the main characteristics of exploratory searches is that users often do not know how to formulate their information need and that they are unfamiliar with the domain they search in [18]. Thereby learning and exploring aspects will be covered as well [18,11]. This concept of interactive visual filtering of relevant information in a more natural way that enables data processing in cases, where standard algorithms can not be applied since these algorithms might filter out relevant data.

In this work we like to tackle the problem of formulating appropriate queries by offering dynamic user interface (UI) elements that enable users to manipulate directly the UI elements by touch gestures. We introduced the concept of this paper back in 2011 [15], where we described the basic idea and did some pre-studies with a digital mock-up prototype. In [16] we first introduced a running implementation and a more detailed user study towards this concept. In this paper the latest results of conducted user studies the platform independent HTML 5 re-implementation of the proposed concept and newly designed UI elements are presented.

S. Yamamoto (Ed.): HIMI/HCII 2013, Part I, LNCS 8016, pp. 240–249, 2013.
© Springer-Verlag Berlin Heidelberg 2013

2   State-of-the-Art

Interactive filtering search user interfaces (SUIs) are not new: The VIBE-system
[10,17] also supports users in finding relevant information using magnets to attract relevant documents to specific screen points (Fig. 1). The principle of dust-
and-magnet was previously presented by Yi et al. [19]. Our proposed concept
uses this principle also - as one aspect of the interaction concept. In contrast
to VIBE we offer users an interactive visualization with less classical WIMP
(Windows, Icons, Menus, Pointer) UI elements. Thereby, no virtual mapping of
functions is necessary and users might be able to use the interface in a more
firm and reliable way. Cousins et al. [5] developed a system that follows a direct
manipulation approach like done here. In contrast to our proposed solution it
is divided into different UI elements and different views. It is less integrated in
a single view. Therefore user's work load might be higher since she or he needs
to face various mode switches. Commercial systems, like the Vis4you concept[1],
are more focused on visualization than on interaction (via direct manipulation).
Furthermore, their system is designed to be used on desktop computers with a
mouse (*single point and click principle*), no support for multi-touch, no platform
independent approach.

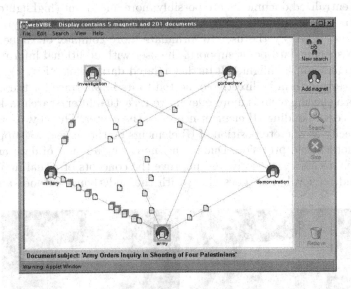

Fig. 1. webVIBE, a variant of the VIBE-system [10,17]

3   QUEST

Since users sometimes do not know what they are searching for, we like to support
them by the opportunity to formulate vague queries. The proposed solution

[1] http://www.vis4you.com/vis4you/ (accessed on 04.07.2012)

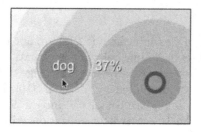

Fig. 2. Direct feedback: Relevance value next to the widget

is called QUEST (Query User Interface for Exploratory Search Tasks). Here, the user is asked to narrow the search results by dragging user interface (UI) elements, so called widgets, with its query terms (or objects), see also Fig. 2.

3.1   Concept

The concept follows the idea that more relevant data are centred. Note, this is equivalent to filtering an overcrowded desktop, cf. Fig. 3 (left picture), where the more centralized documents are possibly more important (highlighted in the right picture). Query objects (widgets) can be entered via a virtual keyboard and can also be dragged by the user to formulate more complex or vague queries. Selecting a specific data point supports the user with additional information on this data point and highlights all further related data points (Fig. 4). The distance of a certain term is directly connected to its importance for the user: If a user thinks a specific term is more relevant to its actual filter/search task, he positions the corresponding UI element nearer to the center. Thereby, users do not need to specify a concrete position of UI elements on the screen, we support this by a non-determined precision. Due to the increasing amount of data and complexity, it is necessary to apply and improve the concepts of visual information filtering and retrieval. This goes along with the underlying methods and tools.

Fig. 3. Crowded desktop: More relevant documents are centred[2]

---

[2] http://lawprofessors.typepad.com/ (accessed on 04.07.2012)

Considering clustering algorithms (e.g., k-means [3]), we thought about the concept of *vague query formulation*: Since users sometimes do not know what they are searching for, we like to support them by the opportunity to formulate vague queries. The system was designed to be a multi-user system. Therefore a number of multiple users need to be supported at the same time, also considering security aspects [14]. To offer each user the same possibility to interact with the system we use a radial form for the interface layout. Furthermore, an underlying multi-touch device is a hardware requirement, that enhances the combination of tool and application domain significantly. Another appealing advantage is, that multi-touch also supports users in a more natural way of interaction [9]. Other radial user interfaces for selecting or filtering often offers fixed places for items. In contrast to this our system is supposed to be more flexible since users are allowed to position their query widgets where they like.

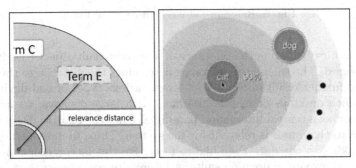

Fig. 4. Concept of relevance mapping (left) and corresponding results (right), visually highlighted to group them (e.g. highlighted results for the search term "cat")

We offer users a dimension merging according specified weights, similar to the result listing of search engines, where also different weights can be linked to specific query terms. Data points represent the data space. Query objects (widgets) can be entered via a virtual keyboard and can also be dragged by the user to formulate more complex or vague queries. Selecting a specific data point supports the user with additional information on this data point and highlights all further related data points.

The distance of a certain term is directly connected to its importance for the user. In other words, if a user thinks a specific term is more relevant to its actual filter/search task, he positions the corresponding UI element nearer to the center, which influences the weight of this term when computing its Term Frequency / Inverted Document Frequency (TF/IDF)-value [2], which in fact is a calculated weight to influence the ranking of the data space and this in return effects the visualization (Fig. 4). Thereby, users do not need to specify a concrete position of UI elements on the screen, we support this by a non-determined precision. The widget-induced relevance of a query term is calculated according to the formula in Fig. 5. Result elements are placed near to corresponding query elements.

$$R_{Widget} = \frac{d_{Center\ Point}}{r_{Search\ Area}}$$

Fig. 5. Widget-induced relevance of a query term

$$R_{Search\ Result} = \frac{\sum_{i=0}^{\#\ relevant\ widgets} R_{Relevant\ Widget_i}}{\#\ relevant\ widgets} - \left(\frac{\sum_{i=0}^{\#\ non\ relevant\ widgets} R_{Non\ Relevant\ Widget_i} + \sum_{i=0}^{\#\ relevant\ exclusion\ widgets} R_{Relevant\ Exclusion\ Widget_i}}{\#\ non\ relevant\ widgets + \#\ relevant\ exclusion\ widgets} \right)$$

Fig. 6. Relevance of a search result object

The formula for calculating the relevance of a SearchResult object (result dot) is shown in Fig. 6. The calculated relevance determines the distance to the center, considering further result objects. To address various types of end devices such as multi-touch desktops or mobile interfaces with large displays, we use direct manipulation as a central interaction paradigm. Only the relative distance of an UI element to the center is relevant for the system. Thus, we provide users with a direct linking to the data they like to filter. By this interaction concept, we propose to achieve more precise results. Additionally, we support users with the concept of *What-if*-queries, which supports a fault-tolerant interaction system, using a ghosting technique: Dragging an element and holding it on a specific position triggers the system to show the user how many items are in the center point of interest (POI) after releasing the element. Thereby, users are able to explore the impact of possible next steps.

Changes of the query configuration also effect the data points to provide the user with a direct link to the data (interactive visualization). By the underlying metaphor of magnets, we offer an integrated feedback, comparable to *Dust-and-Magnet* [19]: When users drag a specific UI element to a certain point, relevant data points follow this UI element. Data points that have the same TF-IDF value (equal relevance to a query configuration) are drafted with a minimal distance to each other to minimize the possibility of occlusions.

3.2   Features

The UI supports direct feedback since the relevance value is simultaneously shown while users interact with the widget (Fig. 2). Results, corresponding to a specific query object are visually highlighted and grouped to each other (Fig. 4 (right)). Detailed information on particular result objects, like a website preview, is provided after clicking on the result dot (Fig. 7).

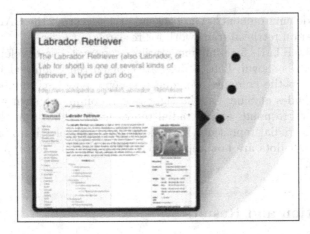

Fig. 7. Website preview popover, here a result for "Labrador Retriever"

4 Implementation

To proof the concept of the proposed user interface, a first prototype was implemented, using an Apple iPad (Fig. 8). This application was written in ObjectiveC

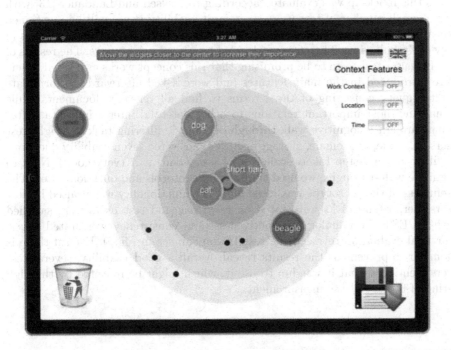

Fig. 8. Radial design of the iPad implementation

using the xCode environment[3]. The backend architecture is the CARSA system [1], an information retrieval framework for research purposes.

Currently, an HTML 5 re-implementation is going to be developed. In Fig. 10 the re-design is shown: Left, a drop area for currently unused UI elements is offered, on top the complex user query is represented by numbers and using different shades of blue. On the right side a common known result listing is shown that corresponds to the radial representation shown in the center of the screen. The radial representation follows the principles introduced in this paper. The result dots are now represented using favicons to support a better representation.

5 Evaluation and Results

Since this contribution is basically driven by fields of human factors and user interface design, we are using common methods from these research areas. Such as user centred design (UCD) processes [7], formative evaluation methods [12], questionnaires [6], think-aloud-protocols [8], and cognitive walkthroughs [4].

The evaluation concept followed a formative evaluation process where several usability testing were conducted. Several test users mentioned that it was fun to use it, which might is reflected by a high rating of joy of use measurings. Also in parallel to the development process: To identify at least 85% of all usability issues this mock-up was evaluated according to Nielsen and Landauer [13] with only a small number of test users since most usability issues will be mentioned repeatedly by users. The sixth tested user would report new usability issues in only 15% of all cases. Therefore we decided to ask only eight users. The results of this first user test seem to be promising that this concept works as desired. Users were introduced in the main features and were asked afterwards to formulate a filter query consisting of three terms to find all relevant documents while visualizing most important relations to other potential interesting data. After going through a cognitive walk-through of a movie filtering task our eight test users (six male, two female, average age: 23.4) answered seven usability questions by filling out a 7-step Likert scale from 1 (very bad) to 7 (very good). Next to cognitive walk-throughs, we used think-aloud-protocols and questionnaires. The usefulness of the prototype was rated high, the functionality was praised by test users, performing tasks were rated as *very easy* and test users were satisfied with QUEST. Terminology, attractiveness, and consistency were rated lower. Our final evaluation revealed the results you can see in Fig. 9. Even if there is room for improvement the results reveal overall a good usability, several test users mentioned that it was fun to use it, which might be reflected by the high rating of the *joy of use* measurement.

---

[3] `developer.apple.com/xcode/` (accessed on 04.07.2012)

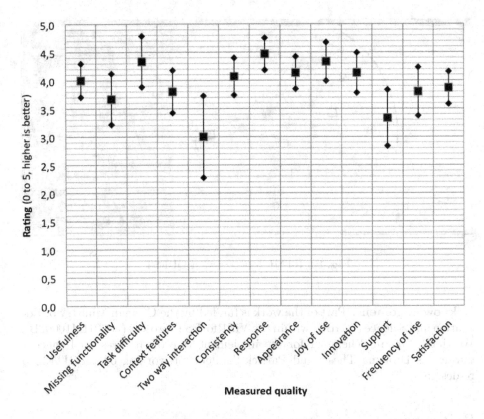

Fig. 9. Results of final usability testing

6 Discussion and Outlook

We described the newly designed UI concept *QUEST* for filtering, exploring and searching information via direct manipulation. The proposed concept is

– flexible: parameters can be adapted or enhanced by users
– context-sensitive: initial parameters are extracted from the current use case
– easy to learn: through work environment metaphor and direct manipulation

Currently, the system is about to be re-implemented using the upcoming web standard HTML 5 to provide a platform independent solution featuring enhanced UI elements such as visualising a result list in parallel to address users' expectations towards a standard search user interface and to provide a more smooth mapping to the proposed spatial design (see Fig. 10). In the near future, a more detailed and larger user study will be conducted.

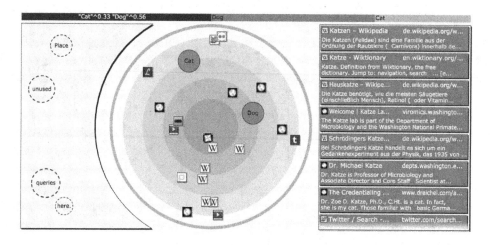

Fig. 10. HTML 5 re-design of QUEST

Acknowledgement. Part of the work is funded by the German Ministry of Education and Science (BMBF) within the ViERforES II project (no. 01IM10002B). We thank Martin Schemmer for the implementation of the presented concept during his Diploma Thesis and Patrick Saalfeld for working on the HTML 5 re-design.

References

1. Bade, K., De Luca, E.W., Nürnberger, A., Stober, S.: CARSA - an architecture for the development of context adaptive retrieval systems. In: Detyniecki, M., Jose, J.M., Nürnberger, A., van Rijsbergen, C.J. (eds.) AMR 2005. LNCS, vol. 3877, pp. 91–101. Springer, Heidelberg (2006)
2. Baeza-Yates, R., Ribeiro-Neto, B.: Modern Information Retrieval, pp. 29–30. Addison Wesley / ACM Press, NY (1999)
3. Bradski, G., Kaehler, A.: Learning OpenCV Computer Vision with the OpenCV Library, p. 479. O'Reilly (2001)
4. Busemeyer, J.R.: Choice behavior in a sequential decision-making task. Organizational Behavior and Human Performance 29(2), 175–207 (1982)
5. Cousins, S.B., Paepcke, A., Winograd, T., Bier, E.A., Pier, K.: The digital Library integrated Task Environment (DLITE). In: Proceedings of the 2nd ACM International Conference on Digital Libraries (DL 1997), pp. 142–151. ACM, New York (1997)
6. Czaja, R., Blair, J.: Designing Surveys. A useful resource for factual-style surveys, including material on interviews as well as mail surveys. Pine Forge Press (1996)
7. Eason, K.D.: User centred design for information technology systems. Physics in Technology 14(5), 219 (1983)
8. Ericsson, K.A., Simon, H.A.: Verbal reports as data. Psychological Review 87(3), 215–241 (1980)

9. Han, J.Y.: Multi-touch interaction wall. In: Proceedings of ACM SIGGRAPH 2006 Emerging Technologies (2006)
10. Koshman, S.L.: VIBE User Study. Technical Report LS062/IS97001, University of Pittsburgh (1997)
11. Marchionini, G.: Exploratory search: from finding to understanding. Communications of the ACM 49(4), 41–46 (2006)
12. Moxley Jr., R.A.: Formative and non-formative evaluation. Instructional Science 3(3), 243–283 (1974)
13. Nielsen, J., Landauer, T.K.: A mathematical model of the finding of usability problems. In: Proceedings of ACM INTERCHI 1993 Conference, The Netherlands, Amsterdam, pp. 206–213 (1993)
14. Nitsche, M., Dittmann, J., Nürnberger, A., Vielhauer, C., Buchholz, R.: Security-relevant Challenges of selected Systems for Multi-User Interaction. In: Detyniecki, M., García-Serrano, A., Nürnberger, A. (eds.) AMR 2009. LNCS, vol. 6535, pp. 124–134. Springer, Heidelberg (2011)
15. Nitsche, M., Nürnberger, A.: Supporting vague query formulation by using visual filtering. In: Proceedings of Lernen. Wissen, Adaption (2011)
16. Nitsche, M., Nürnberger, A.: Vague Query Formulation by Design. In: Proceedings of EuroHCIR 2012, The Netherlands, Nijmegen, pp. 83–86 (2012)
17. Olsen, K.A., Korfhage, R.R., Sochats, K.M., Spring, M.B., Williams, J.G.: Visualization of a Document Collection: the VIBE System. Information Processing & Management 29(1), 69–81 (1993)
18. White, R.W., Roth, R.A.: Exploratory search: Beyond the Query-Response paradigm. In: Marchionini, G. (ed.) Synthesis Lectures on Information Concepts, Retrieval, and Services. Morgan & Claypool Publishers (2009)
19. Yi, L.S., Melton, R., Stasko, J., Jacko, L.: Dust & Magnet: multivariate information visualization using a magnet metaphor. Information Visualization, 239–256 (2005)

Analytics on Online Discussion and Commenting Services

Sungho Shin[1], Sangkeun Park[2], Jinseop Shin[1], Sa-Kwang Song[1],
Sung-Pil Choi[1], and Hanmin Jung[1]

[1] Korea Institute of Science and Technology Information, Korea
[2] Korea Advanced Institute of Science and Technology, Korea
{maximus74,js.shin,esmallj,spchoi,jhm}@kisti.re.kr,
sk.park@kaist.ac.kr

Abstract. From the view of design claims for online communities, it is very crucial to take interactions among members in a community into account when starting and maintaining it. This means managers of online communities need to technically support their members through online discussion and commenting services. Online discussion and commenting service, so called, blog comment hosting service, helps communities to provide their members with feedbacks of others, since such feedbacks play much important role in starting and maintaining an online community. Through online discussion and commenting services, we can post a comment on the website using our own social network service account if the website uses a social comment platform. Whenever, whatever, and wherever users post a comment, every comment is integrated and managed by the social comment platform. One of most powerful social comment platforms is Disqus. It is the social comments platform or social discussion platform used in the world popular websites such as CNN, Billboard. Thus, we analyze it in various views and give a several suggestions to make the websites more active. Main findings reported in this paper include significant implications on the design of social comment platforms.

Keywords: Design Claims, Online Community, Disqus, Online Discussion and Commenting Service.

1 Introduction

Most online communities don't practically fail in their business. There are thousands of online community projects that have been created, and only the 10.3% of them have more than three members [1]. From the studies on boosting up online communities, many key words are extracted: motivation, incentive, Q&A, contribute, commitment, regulation, newcomers and so on. These are highly related to success of an online community. In other words, we need to take them into much account in analyzing an online community in order to start up and encourage it. Some of them such as motivation, incentives, Q&A are basically necessary to follow design claims to make an online community successful. The others directly guide it into being valuable. Based on design implications for the successful online community, their effects are simple and clear. Most of them are due to the increase of the members' motivation,

S. Yamamoto (Ed.): HIMI/HCII 2013, Part I, LNCS 8016, pp. 250–258, 2013.

contributions and commitments to a community, facilitating communications between the members, in particular, new members and existing members, regulating users' behavior to protect a community from trolls and manipulators, as well as the increase of new members and changing benefits for a community.

In terms of information organization and interaction with community members to encourage online communities, it is also important to technically support them with online discussion and commenting services such as Disqus, IntenseDebase, Livefyre, and Echo. Online discussion and commenting service, so called blog comment hosting service, helps communities to provide members with feedbacks of others. Feedbacks play much important role in starting and maintaining an online community. They can enhance motivation to perform community's tasks [2]. Moreover, discussing and commenting mean there are interactions between members including newcomers, which enables communities to be active and to make up a strong band their members. In this research, we introduce and analyze online discussion and commenting services, especially Disqus, in terms of online community design. Disqus is one of the most popular online discussion and commenting services for websites and online communities that use a networked platform. The platform includes various features, such as social integration, social networking, user profiles, spam filtering and moderation tools, analytics, email notifications, and mobile commenting. It is featured on many major publications, such as Engadget, CNN, Daily Telegraph and IGN. News sites and online communities including private blogs that allow the owners to change HTML tags can be applied Disqus services to. This absolutely makes online communities support members exchange their opinions and comments. Consequently, according to a March 2011 study by Lijit, Disqus is used by 75% of websites who use a third party commenting or discussion system.

The purpose of our research is to analyze how the online discussion and commenting service is actually used to boost up online communities and to give some design claims to make them better. For those purposes, we first review design claims to make online communities successful in section 2. Next, we analyze online discussion and commenting services including Disqus in section 3. Subsequently, some analysis on comments in Disqus will be covered in section 4. Finally, discussion on pros and cons of the Disqus service will be given as well.

2   Design Claims for Online Community

Online community is a group separated by space and time [3]. The other key concept behind online community is the use of networked technologies in one form or another to collaborate and communicate. It is also purposely designed by starters.

Starting and maintaining online communities should be much systematic and specialized to be successful. In order to start new online communities, Resnick et al. [1] suggest three major challenges. The first is to manage to obtain a position among online communities even though it is quite small. The second is to keep that position in the competing communities and to provide alternative ways that potential members can spend their time. We need to make strategic choices about the scope of the community and about its compatibility and integration with other communities to meet these two challenges. The third challenge is to get to critical mass. A new community must recruit members before it has become a kind of community that they will value. There are a number of design approaches to meet this challenge, including substituting a professionally-generated content for a user-generated content in the early stages, leveraging early participants to attract later ones, and setting expectations about the likely future evolution of the community. Here is some design claims mainly considered to begin new online communities, especially in terms of the interaction among members.

Single-user and small-group productivity, entertainment, or commerce tools can attract people to an online space before the community features are successful [1].

Many online sites with successful social content started by providing valuable services to their customers in the absence of a critical mass in the online community. Instead of offering a service that is individually valuable to one person, it is sometimes possible to offer a group service that is valuable to a small enough group that the group can collectively decide to join. For example, Yahoo! Groups, for example, is a community-hosting service that allows anyone to create a group (complete with e-mail list, discussion board, photo storage, calendars, and other tools). Amazon.com is another example of site that attracted initial users for shopping. It has a large collection of successful social content options within its site. It uses collaborative recommender technologies. Amazon amassed a critical mass of people and data by offering a distinctively non-social application.

Therefore, most design claims including one thing mentioned above emphasize on increasing members' motivation and commitment to communities, facilitating communications, and increasing new members. Online discussion and commenting services can't perfectly support all of them. These design claims, however, enable us to analyze how they are useful and helpful to manage online communities. Chua et al. [4] reveal in their recent study that based on the content analysis performed on a sample of 1,800 messages from six online discussion communities (ODCs), ODC users seemed to be engaged in a combination of online interactions to satisfy human sharing needs such as to share or acquire knowledge, establish a social presence and convey emotions. This implication represents how important online communities support a discussion and commenting service to their members. N.F.Ali-Hasan et al. studied on the social relationships on the blog through links and comments. They considered blogs as social networks and applied social network analysis method on the blogs to find out the way individuals share their information and how interact socially via blogs. They found out that many interactions occur in comments written by bloggers on a post of another blog [5].

3   Online Discussion and Commenting Service

Currently, there are several online discussion and commenting services such as Intense-Debate, Livefyre, Echo, and Disqus. [1]Many such services allow for users to log into a

---

[1] http://en.wikipedia.org/wiki/Blog_comment_hosting_service

blog comment hosting service using social network profile credentials, for example those of Facebook Connect, Yahoo!, Google, LinkedIn, MySpace, etc. Such services may also have an effect upon the instantiation of comment spam, as a prior registration to the comment hosts may be the only means by which to make comments onto many blogs.

Disqus[2] platform includes various features, such as social integration, social networking, user reputation, spam and moderation tools, analytics, email notifications, and mobile commenting (Figure 1). Disqus is featured on many major publications, such as Engadget, CNN, Daily Telegraph and IGN. The service offers a networked comment system used to foster engagement and connect audiences from around the web. It looks to make it very easy and rewarding for people to interact on websites using its system. Commenters can build reputation and carry their contributions from one website to the next. Using the Disqus' built-in network effects, bloggers and publishers can expect a higher volume and higher quality of conversations by using the comment system. Both the Disqus website and comment system are translated into more than 60 languages. Besides, it works in all major web browsers, including Internet Explorer, Firefox, Chrome, Safari, and Opera. On mobile devices, Disqus currently only supports browsers using the WebKit layout engine. Now, we will take more look at Disqus.

Fig. 1. Features of Disqus platform
(From the left, example screenshot of user reputation, email moderation, and analytics in a row)

Fig. 2. Discovery service of Disqus

The comment system of Disqus works hand-in-hand with a dedicated forum backend, so the conversations are never fragmented. It drives real engagement and traffic on websites[3]. The fully real-time Disqus is perfect for participation on breaking news, hot discussions, live events, and video content. No matter what platform people use,

---

[2] http://en.wikipedia.org/wiki/Disqus
[3] http://disqus.com/for-websites/

Disqus integrates seamlessly. It supports major platforms with easy-to-use plug-ins or copy-and-paste code. It also supplies wonderful UX. Its design is clean and intuitive, which makes users give comments and feedback fully real time. Developers and managers are all about encouraging quality discussions over one-dimensional comments. Everything is built into the Disqus system so that websites' visitors never have to leave websites. People can build loyalty with real-time social notifications and email notifications. It serves on phones and tablets with HTML5 design as well.

The Discovery service of Disqus helps people find new and interesting discussions and stories within Disqus (Figure 2). Discovery also helps publishers drive increases in internal recirculation and external referral traffic, resulting in increased advertising revenues. Users are very engaged when they arrive at the discussion thread because they are either engaging in the discussion or thinking through where they want to go next. However, this real estate is commonly underutilized by publishers because it's below the fold. By placing the Discovery box within the discussion thread, it enables a community's most engaged users to discover new content while also helping a community's users best optimize their audience monetization.

4   Analytics on Social Comments in Disqus

In Disqus, people do not need to make new account because Disqus supports social network login. For sure, it is possible Disqus account and people can connect their own SNS account to Disqus. Disqus supports a system of following and, follower such as Twitter. Using this function, we can subscribe the other users' comments. Moreover, votes, on like/dislike functions are supported in Disqus.

4.1   Data Gathering

Different from general web crawler systems [6], Disqus offers an Application Programming Interface (API) that is easy to crawl and collect data. We selected 10 websites which have high activity among many websites introduced in Disqus showcase[4]. The websites are CNN, The Week US, Washington Times, Wired, The Next Web, Billboard, People, AllKPop, BoingBoing, and MLB. We categorized those 10 websites into 4 types. CNN, The Week US, Washington Times were classified with News category. IT category was assigned to sites such as Wired and The Next Web. Billboard, People, AllKPop belonged to 'Entertainment'. BoingBoing and MLB sites were exclusive with others. For each website, we collected 100 most active threads (articles) with most 100 comments from each thread for recent 30 days on December 21th, 2012.

We made use of a Disqus API to collect data from the websites. Several Disqus APIs, however, are still running under beta version and even have a few limitations. For example, we could maximally obtain just 100 articles which users posted their comments on according to sorts of downloading purposes prefixed by the Disqus.

---

[4] http://disqus.com/showcase/

So we could download information on just 100 articles. Besides, the maximum number of comments on a article has the default limit of 100 to be downloaded. Even though a article has more than 100 comments, the Disqus API returns just 100 comments on the article. This limitation might be why there are few researches on analyzing Disqus data.

4.2   Analysis and Result

Comments. As mentioned before, we collected 100 most active threads (articles) with most 100 comments from each article. After that, additional information of the comments such as author, written time, message, etc was obtained as well. Total comments posted were 76,536 during the time. The number of comments by websites is shown in Table 1.

Users. We also obtained information of users with using URLs containing users' profile images who posted those comments. Furthermore, we downloaded all profile images to analyze how many users uploaded their own images. Total users were 21,006, but information of some users was not enough. Therefore, total valid users were 20,716. There are two default images provided by Disqus, and there might be additional default images depending on the websites. We checked out all default images from the websites. Finally, we extracted their color histogram and compared it with all profile pictures we downloaded. As a result, we had information on who changed their profile images from the default. The number of users by websites is shown in Table 1.

Table 1. Number of Users and comments by websites

Category	Websites	# of Comments	# of Users
News	CNN	10,000	2348
	The Week US	5,939	1717
	Washington Times	10,000	2619
IT	Wired	4,736	1769
	The Next Web	2,917	1305
Entertainment	Billboard	5,159	1838
	People	10,000	830
	AllKPop	9,697	4247
ETC	BoingBoing	8,088	2176
	MLB	10,000	1,867

User Profile. We found that there is an interesting feature in user profile. Some users upload their image file to change the profile picture from default to their own. According to our research, usually, almost half users uploaded their profile picture, and the others use one of default images as their profile picture. However, only 36.7% of users in 'News' category changed their profile pictures (Figure 3). We can assume that users in 'News' have low tendency to show their identity while users in the other categories usually want to show their identity. This happens more obviously on the list of top commenters of each category or website. For example, most top commenters in AllKPop uploaded their own profile pictures, but most top commenters in CNN do not have their own profile pictures.

There is less than 1% overlapped users between any two categories (Table 2). This is because users usually post comments on the websites they are interested in, which is proven by the result of analyzing the average number of forums mentioned above.

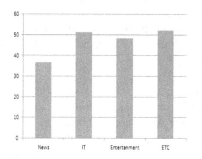

Fig. 3. User ration uploading their pictures by categories

Table 2. Overlapped users between two categories

Category	Total users	Overlapped
News & Entertainment	12502	21
News & etc.	11473	16
News & IT	10154	82
Entertainment & etc.	9120	0
Entertainment & IT	7860	7
IT & etc.	6797	36

5   Discussion and Future Work

Main services and functions of Disqus have been discussed so far. Some cons, however, are investigated through our review as well. In Disqus, users are sent notifications via email, and can also be sent replies via email simply by replying. But they receive nothing for notifications when other people like their comment. This may decrease intrinsic motivation and intangible incentive. Disqus provides real-time commenting, which means people don't have to refresh the page to view their new comment. But Disqus doesn't provide any real time counters for the number of comments or readers currently on the page. It also doesn't extend its real-time commenting service to mobile devices at this time. This may supports members' answering but finally can decrease intrinsic motivation and intangible incentive. Disqus has a community box that displays Disqus comment metrics for the website you're currently on. However, it is not sure that this feature is useful, and people can't share any individual comment with Disqus via Twitter or Facebook. This can decrease affective commitments of members. Disqus' Community Box contains metrics for the website people are currently viewing. The service tracks the likes people' comments have received. But these statistic numbers are scattered in different places and certainly don't look helpful for users. This can decrease normative commitments of members and members adherence to normative behavior at the same time because it is not efficient to show statistics of normative behavior. Disqus doesn't provide the service of tagging users' friends on Facebook and Twitter. This function is really attracting. So this problem can make it difficult to get to critical mass because of lacking of membership.

In contrast, one of the most attracting factors in Disqus for online communities is a user profiles management service. Disqus provides the full user profile via a pop-up. Pop-up profile includes full user profile, user bio, Twitter and Facebook account links, the number of comments and likes, a list of the communities associated with the user, and an activity stream(previous comments), so that people follow user's comments via Disqus by clicking 'follow'. This can increases bond-based affective commitment and membership in terms of the design claims.

We have some limitation in the analysis of Disqus data because the data provided by Disqus APIs is not enough. Moreover, we could not use the reputation scores of each user in this research because of reliability, although we collected them. We sent a Discus manager an email to ask how Discus generates the reputation scores. But their reply just said that the reputation is not perfect yet. What we only know is at this moment that the score is related with the number of likes and comments.

To make our study better, a comparative study is necessary such as how different the number of comments users post is between websites using an online discussion and commenting service and websites not using, or the analysis on how different the number of comments is between before a website starts using the service and after.

6   Conclusion

We have reviewed what design claims are important to start and to maintain online communities so far. Helping users in online communities to interact with other members is quite useful to make online communities successful through online discussion and commenting services. Some analytics on users and comments data from ten active websites have been also done to see how Disqus is used for them, and what we can do to make a website more active with using a discussion and commenting service.

Our analysis on Disqus data show the website that we selected can be classified mainly two types; news and the other. There are specific features and suggestions of websites. Firstly, interaction is more active by following and followers in 'News' category. The number of users who have their own followers and following is relatively higher in 'News' than in the other categories. Secondly, discussion is more active with thoughtful comments in 'News' category. This represents that the forums in 'News' are usually about hard topics such as politics, economics, etc. which are good for discussion.   Thirdly, users post comments in more various forums in 'News' category. Interestingly, they tend to post comments in the same type of forums which are mostly other news sites. Finally, users have low tendency to set their profile pictures in news type compared to the other websites.

References

1. Resnick, P., Konstan, J., Chen, Y., Kraut, R.: Starting new online communities. In: Evidence-Based Social Design: Mining the Social Sciences to Build Online Communities. MIT Press, Cambridge (2010)

2. Kraut, R.E., Resnick, P.: Encouraging contribution to online communities. In: Evidence-Based Social Design: Mining the Social Sciences to Build Online Communities. MIT Press, Cambridge (2010)
3. Johnson, C.M.: A survey of current research on online communities of practice. Internet and Higher Education 4, 45–60 (2001)
4. Chua, A.Y.K., Balkunje, R.S.: Beyond knowledge sharing: interactions in online discussion communities. International Journal of Web Based Communities 9(1), 67–82 (2013)
5. Ali-Hasan, N.F., Adamic, L.A.: Expressing Social Relationships on the Blog through Links and Comments. In: The IEEE International Conference on Web Services (2007)
6. Seo, D., Hwang, M.N., Shin, S., Choi, S.P., Jung, H., Song, S.K.: Development of Crawler System Gathering Web Document on Science and Technology. In: The 2nd Joint International Semantic Technology Conference (2012)

Incentive Structure of Participation in Community Activity

Yurika Shiozu, Katsuhiko Yonezaki, and Katsunori Shimohara

Faculty of Economics Doshisha University, Karasuma-Higashi-iru, Imadegawa-dori,
Kamigyo-ku, Kyoto, 602-8580, Japan
Graduate School of Science and Engineering Doshisha University, 1-3 Tatara Miyakodani,
Kyotanabe City, 610-0394 Japan
{yshiozu,kyonezak}@mail.doshisha.ac.jp,
kshimoha@mail.doshisha.ac.jp

Abstract. In this paper, we disassemble community mutual aid into two components: providing local public goods and everyday associations with neighbors. If the OFT (Out-For-Tat) strategy is taken, and the benefit of everyday associations with neighbors exceeds the cost, cooperation was demonstrated not only in associations in everyday life but through providing local public goods. To fulfill this condition, it is necessary to lower the participation fees in associations with neighbors, and for all the members to choose the local public goods that receive the benefit. When using ICT (Information Communication Technology) especially, cost cutting for associations with neighbors is expected.

Keywords: Incentive structure, Community activity, OFT strategy.

1   Introduction

It is said that relationships raise an individual's feeling of happiness. However, relations with the neighborhood have weakened over time, and the community's role as a safety net has also diminished. In this paper, we have clarified, using game theory, the structure of inducements for local residents to join community activities. Using the framework of game theory, we analyzed the conditions for participation in community activities that are possible in the new towns and the surrounding area that have developed during Japan's period of high economic growth.

2   Previous Studies

2.1   Factors for Happiness

The notion of subjective well-being (SWB) was introduced as an approach from psychology. According to this theory, income and interpersonal relations raise the subjective feeling of happiness. Social capital, an approach from sociology, is the idea of

S. Yamamoto (Ed.): HIMI/HCII 2013, Part I, LNCS 8016, pp. 259–268, 2013.

increased happiness. It is often said that financial relationships with family, companions, the neighborhood, etc. contribute to happiness. Also, from economics, the significance of social relations is pointed out based on the capability approach. Every theory shows that relationships increase the feeling of happiness.

2.2   Game Theory and Social Network Analysis

Previous research shows that association brings about a feeling of happiness. And if the player recognizes that human relations for him/her are being materialized over the long term, this will become a move in an infinitely repeated sequential game. Unlike a one-time game, each player chooses concerted actions from the beginning all the time.

Greif (2006) shows that in the history of trade around the Mediterranean Sea cooperative action occurred when a company began business. This reveals an infinitely repeated game structure of sequential moves in an exclusive network, if a player's traffic is limited within the network, and even if there is a spread spatially. Furthermore, first-time players will care about a subsequent repute and take concerted action.

Aoki (2001) explained concerted action in a rural community in modern Japan using game theory. Homogeneous farming households in Japan have been living for a long time in rural villages. The formation of long-term human relations makes these closed networks. It   performs infinitely repeated game in an exclusive network. Using folk theorem, a cooperative relationship is achieved in such a game. However, once somebody betrays deviates, , other villagers stop the association using an Out-For-Tat (OFT) strategy. For many farming households, since a lost association was a matter of life or death, these became societies that supervised, as there were no mutual deviations. Aoki (2001) examined the potential for cooperation under the status of the social dilemma by connecting a joint-work game (social exchange game) and a fellowship game (commons game). Where, since the benefits obtained from joint work were a characteristic of public goods, the member who does not participate in an operation can also enjoy benefits.   There exists the joint work which requires the expense, C_i from each member. By participating in these operations, all the members can acquire sufficient results and can get the benefit[1] B_i . However, whenever there is a member who does not participate in an operation, the benefit decreases only by d_i .

In this game, although the cost for mutual help including association with neighbors must be paid, C_s , if N players participate, they can obtain the benefit, $B_s(n)$. However, to do joint work is a requisite for this game. Therefore, if someone does not perform joint work, other players will lose the benefit annually from the following year, $z = B_s(n) - C_s$ .We summarize this in Figure 1.

---

[1] For example, m persons expense the cost, benefit will be expressed as $B_i - (N - m)d_i$.

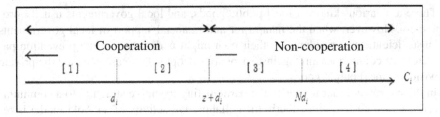

Fig. 1. Relationships in the solution for the game

Sphere [1] and [2] show cooperating cases, and sphere [3] and [4] express non-cooperative cases. As the conditions are originally satisfied, in sphere [1] cooperation is carried out. On the other hand, in sphere [2] by connecting games, cooperative behavior occurs. Since the benefit obtained by linking a game is less than the sphere [3] from the cost cutting on which I depend non-cooperative, cooperative behavior does not break out. Since the incentive which I depend non-cooperative exists and a benefit serves as the maximum under the behavior, sphere [4] is a sphere where social dilemma does not exist.

Therefore, even if a social dilemma exists, Aoki has pointed out that there is the potential that cooperative behavior will be performed, when social capital exists. These models assume that society consists of brethren groups, such as trading merchants or farmers only. As a result, social composition members have long-term relationships, and maintain the workplace environment together. Thus, these models are based on a strong relationship of interdependence.

3   Model

3.1   Features of a Current City Suburb

In current city suburbs, since they are easier to move into than modern rural communities, suddenly an unknown person becomes a neighbor. It is an open network. Since current city suburb inhabitants' vocation and family structure are diversified, community activity consists of the following two types.

Private Provision of Local Public Goods. For local residents, broadening sidewalks, and a crime prevention patrol, etc. are common subjects. Two or more persons can improve sidewalks and simultaneously take countermeasures against a suspicious person. However, they cannot completely eliminate [remove] someone who does not pay the cost. Based on these two characteristics, broadening a sidewalk and taking countermeasures against a suspicious person, etc., can be called public goods. In addition, peripheral [other] people can use the sidewalk daily, or can expect crimes to be prevented by the patrol of a specific area. Therefore, broadening sidewalks and countermeasures against a suspicious person can be called local public goods.

There are various kinds of local public goods, and local governments usually provide them. However, when the manpower and financial support of local governments are insufficient, local residents on their own might undertake a crime prevention patrol, etc. as a countermeasure against suspicious people. This case is called the private provision of local public goods.

In this paper, in order to clarify the participating incentive structure to a community activity of a current city suburb, the collaborative activity of an Aoki model is replaced with the private provision of local public goods. But since there is a conflict of interest for local residents about the provision of local public goods, a model is made about this section using the tie-up formation on the basis of a negotiation model.[2]

Association with Neighbors. According to Ishida (2011), in the past in Japan, the gender division of labor was not clear, and there was mutual help for nursing, patient care, etc. by the neighborhood. The benefit of the community game in an Aoki model assigns merit to the mutual help of such a community.

In Japan after modernization, with the emergence of an industrial structure, gender division of labor advanced and the number of employees increased. As a result, companies and households started to offer the mutual help function that the community had so far borne. The benefit of association with neighbors assumed by the model of this paper is a residual part of the mutual help which neither the household nor the company can cover. Specifically mentioned are people talking to one another in a neighborhood, confirming their safety following a disaster and taking refuge together, etc. It is assumed that the cost of association with neighbors is dependent on the number of interveners. This is because various types of effort are required in an open network in order to have interpersonal relations.

3.2   Model Building

Regional community activities consist of two stages: At the first stage, the members of the community determine by negotiation the type of local public goods that they will provide privately. The model of the game is the sequential style negotiation model of Rubinstein (1981). The second stage is the game where someone communicates with neighbors or does not.

The model consists of two stages: First by an OFT strategy, where only when the participation right to the negotiation of the private provision of local public goods in the first stage is acquired. Also examined is the case where there is participation in association with neighbors at the second stage. Later, when an OFT strategy is not being achieved is also analyzed.

First Stage: Negotiation/Tie-Up for the Private Provision of Local Public Goods.
We assume the inhabitants of a community, $N = \{1, --, N\}$. Cooperative relations is

---

[2] Aoki (2001) also points out the importance of negotiation as another side of economics.

expressed as the tie-up S. The structure of this tie-up is denoted by $\Pi = \left\{ S^k \right\}_{k=1}^m$.
Moreover, Π is a split ups (partition) of N= $\{1,--.,N\}$ (i.e.
$S^k \neq \varnothing$, $S^k \cap S^{k'} \neq \varnothing$, for k $\neq$ k', and $\cup_{k=1}^m S^k = \{1,...,N\}$). Each inhabitant
supplies local public goods privately. z is the social marginal benefit from the player
or inhabitants who cooperated in the private provision of local public goods arbitrarily, and sets the cooperation cost to c(z). When Z is made into the total benefit from a
private provision of all the inhabitants' local public goods, a certain inhabitant's gain
is defined as Z-c(z).

If it is assumed that when all the people that belong to the tie-up S contribute at the
same level, the total of the gain of the tie-up S will become like $s[sz - c(z) + Z_{-i}]$. s
is the number of member participants of the tie-up S, and Z_{-i} is the total of inhabitants' contribution that is not included in S. Therefore, the participant in a tie-up will
solve the following questions:

$$\max_z sz - c(z)$$

This expresses the kind of cooperation organization on the basis of the private provision relationship of local public goods using a tie-up formation model. The sequence
of the suggestion and the response is decided exogenously and the negotiation process
of a tie-up formation performs the game according to the sequence. When people of
the initiative propose a formation of the tie-up S to which self belongs, a game starts.
In proposed tie-up S, each person who has participated answers the suggestion according to the sequence decided. If one refuses a suggestion, the person has to propose S', a counterproposal. A tie-up will be formed if a suggestion is accepted by all
the people contained in the tie-up S. And when all the people in the tie-up S are away
from the game, the inhabitants of the initiative begin a suggestion out of a set of the
inhabitants of N/S which remain. Time is denoted by t=1,2,.... Each inhabitant's strategy, tie-up size which may happen at each term if it is a proposer and which contains
self for every history. It proposes, and if it is a response person, it is an acting program which may happen and which opts for "acceptance of order" and "veto" for
every history.[3]

A stationary subgame perfect equilibrium (SSPE) is a strategy profile
$\Gamma = \{\Gamma_1,...,\Gamma_m\}$ that fulfills the following two conditions: (1) About all inhabitants,
Γ_i is a stationary strategy. (2) A strategy is an optimum strategy to other inhabitants' strategy in all the histories in which each acted about all inhabitants.

A strategy profile means that it is dependent only on a suggestion while each inhabitant is running, and the already formed tie-up. That is, in a stationary strategy, inhabitants' behavior is dependent only on the factors relevant to gain. In the game of this
paper, this corresponds to the already formed tie-up and the left-behind inhabitant
player. In other words, a stationary subgame perfect equilibrium is the profile of a

---

[3] We call what happened in the past history. So, the history of time t is all the list of behavior.

stationary strategy with the history that inhabitants do not exist for whom gain goes up from the strategy determined by one-sided deviation.

Second Stage: Association with Neighbors. The second stage is based on the commons game by Aoki (2001), which is a part of community game connecting the social exchange game and the commons game by Aoki (2001). The participant has to pay the cost C_s for association with neighbors, as in the preceding paragraph. The benefit $B_s(n)$ can be obtained if n person has participated in it among the inhabitants of a certain region.

When the OFT Strategy Is Achieved. We calculate the solution of the game by backward induction from the second stage to the first stage. First, we reason from the second stage (association with the neighbors). When an OFT strategy is taken, in association with the neighbors, it will be a requisite that the negotiation for private provision of local public goods has been achieved.

If it is a game only for one time and is $B_s(n) > C_s(n)$, it participates in an association with the neighbors, and mutual help is performed. If it is $B_s(n) < C_s(n)$, it will not participate in an association with the neighbors' game.[4]   But since the social interaction in the region is not a one-time limitation, it usually considers repeating a game.

A benefit at each time and the slippage of the cost serve as $B_s(n) - C_s(n)$. Total benefit which will be obtained by participating in association with the neighbors if the discount rate to the future is set to δ_S is below. It is set to (1).

$$B_{SC} = \frac{\delta_S}{1-\delta_S}(B_S(n) - C_S(n)) \tag{1}$$

Because the benefit that eq.(1) expresses is considered to also be the benefit obtained only by doing the private provision of local public goods, this can be interpreted as social capital which associates   neighbors with each other. So,

$$B_s(n) > C_s(n) \text{ or } B_{sc} > 0 \tag{2}$$

As long as it is (2), participate in association with the neighbors at the second stage. Eq.(2) is the participating incentive compatibility condition (IC 1) for association with neighbors.

We consider that, at the first stage, the cooperative relationship to the private provision of local public goods includes the results of the second stage. Each inhabitant's utility function serves as the shape where the gain of the first stage and the second stage was united, and is the following:

---

[4] We call what happened in the past history. So, the history of time t is all the list of behavior.

$$u = \begin{cases} sz - c(z) + Z_{-i} + B_{SC} & i \in S \\ Z - c(z') & i \notin S \end{cases}$$

(3)

Proposition 1

1. If $Z - c(z') > sz - c(z) + Z_{-i} + B_{SC}$, the tie-up structure will serve as Singleton.

2. If $Z - c(z') < sz - c(z) + Z_{-i} + B_{SC}$, the tie-up structure will serve as a totality tie-up.

<Proof> Here, we use the theorem written by Bloch (1996). "When a player is symmetrical, as for the regular subgame perfect equilibrium of a tie-up formation game, the player 1 chooses whole-number k_1 from interval [1,n]. Then player $k_1 + 1$ chooses whole-number k from interval $[k_1 + 1, n]$. The game agrees with the part game perfection balance in the limited procedure game that continues until a style line of the integer $(k_1, k_2, ..., k_n)$ satisfies $\sum k_j = n$.

If $Z - c(z') > sz - c(z) + Z_{-i} + B_{SC}$ is always formed, they are all the suggestions, everyone does not propose several tie-ups, but one proposes the cooperation with only oneself, and it is achieved. For the opposite case, the first proposer proposes totality tie-up, and it is achieved.   ∎

If the inhabitants who do not cooperate in a tie-up assume that private provision of local public goods is not carried out at all, the conditional expression in which the totality tie-up is achieved will be set to $Z < sz - c(z) + B_{SC}$. Since Z=sz here, it is set to $c(z) < B_{SC}$ and the measurement of the private provision cost of the gain of the second stage of association with neighbors and the local public goods of the first stage serve as a key to whether it is able to produce a cooperation system. But since the cost of association with the neighbors is dependent on the number of people participating in the game, the following corollary is drawn.

Corollary

When the number of players who participate with neighbors becomes N→∞,

1. If $B_s(\infty) > C_s(\infty)$, a tie-up structure is the totality tie-up.

2. If $B_s(\infty) < C_s(\infty)$, a tie-up structure is Singleton.

When the cost of association with the neighbors exceeds the benefit, $B_s(\infty) < C_s(\infty)$, or the cost for cooperating in the private provision of local public goods exceeds the gain of association with the neighbors, $c(z) > B_{SC}$, it is difficult to do private provision of local public goods over the long run.

When the OFT Strategy Is Not Achieved. We examine the case that even if someone does not cooperate for the private provision of local public goods they still associate with neighbors. In order to find a long-term relationship (following the preceding paragraph), we examine an infinite time repeated game.

Theorem. If the following conditions are satisfied when the OFT strategy is not taken, someone who does not cooperate in the private provision of local public goods and participates in association with neighbors. However, this strategy is not a dominant strategy.

$$c(z) > c(z') - B_{sc} + C_s(n) \tag{4}$$

<Proof>   When the OFT strategy is not taken, the first stage and the second stage become independent. Therefore, the utility function of each inhabitant of eq.(3) becomes only a benefit of the first stage.

$$u = \begin{cases} sz - c(z) + Z_{-i} & i \in S \\ sz - c(z') & i \notin S \end{cases} \tag{3'}$$

Proposition 2 is obtained like proposition 1.

Proposition 2
1. If $Z - c(z') > sz - c(z) + Z_{-i}$, a tie-up structure will be Singleton.
2. If $Z - c(z') < sz - c(z) + Z_{-i}$, a tie-up structure will be totality tie-up.

<Proof>   which can be proved like proposition 1   ∎

The condition is that it is non-cooperative in both of the games to become a dominant strategy when an OFT strategy is not taken is $c(z) > c(z') + \delta_s B_s(n) - C_s(n)$. However, if the participating incentive compatibility condition (IC 1) to association with neighbors of eq.(2) is satisfied, an association with the neighbors nonparticipation will be the dominant strategy, irrespective of a strategy selection for the private provision of local public goods.

4   Considerations

When thinking of present-day Japanese society, a community consists in many cases of households that have only an aged single person or an aged couple, especially in the new town of a big city suburb. Because an increase in the aged population will continue and the inhabitants from the former will die in time, the number of private providers of local public goods, like crime prevention patrols and so on, will decrease. If new inhabitants do not come from other places and they try to carry out a crime prevention patrol like before, one's cost of private provision of local public goods, $c(z)$, will increase. Moreover, if it becomes troublesome at an advanced age to go out, going to talk with a person will also become laborious. In this way, cost of association with the neighbors, $C_s(n)$, cannot but go up. Then, the case that the cost of association with the neighbors exceeds the benefit of association with the neighbors or the case where the cost of private provision of local public goods exceeds the benefit of association with the neighbors will occur. As a result, the continuation of a community activity can become impossible from the propositions and corollary.

Of course, a working population also resides in the region. Considering deleting the time of an occupation or holidays and going out for a crime prevention patrol for the aged (the cost of private provision of local public goods), and the aged's talk (the cost of association with neighbors), $C_s(n)$), they may sometimes feel more satisfaction is obtained from an occupation, housewifery, and leisure than the sense of security that there is a companion nearby. Today, since NPOs or volunteers carry out crime prevention patrols in the region, they take over the cost of private provision of local public goods (c (z')). In this way, if the OFT strategy is achieved, the strategy of cooperation will realize only the private provision of local public goods. Otherwise, the strategy of participating in no community activities is realized. In fact, there are many cases where people only associate with neighbors and are exempt from cooperation in the private provision of local public goods for reasons of being aged or by paying a fee. These are considered to be the cases where the OFT strategy is not achieved.

For the private provision of local public goods at the first stage, the problem is the selection of the kind of private provision of local public goods. In many cases, long-time inhabitants and subjects who have already performed the community activity act as the proposers of the initiative. If the OFT strategy is achieved, from proposition 1 and the corollary (when new inhabitants cooperate in private provision of local public goods), only the old inhabitants form a tie-up and a situation without friendships developing with new inhabitants may also occur in a new residential area.

5   Conclusion and Remarks

Two procedures can be considered as solutions to the question raised as the subject in the preceding sections. One is decreasing the cost of the private provision of local public goods or association with neighbors. Another is that the new and the old inhabitants will cooperate to equally enjoy the benefit of community activity.

First, we concretely consider the ways for decreasing the cost of private provision of local public goods or association with neighbors. If you meet and talk with your neighbors, your time with an occupation, or housewifery and leisure will decrease. However, there's some possibility to reduce the troublesomeness of association with neighbors. That is, by using ICT such as a virtual common space composing of virtual plants as users' avatars, a person's movements may be visualized as a plant on a screen, and another person may send a certain signal at his/her slit time.

Similarly, appeals for participation in a crime prevention patrol, etc. by an electronic bulletin board or a discussion in an electronic conference room might also decrease the cost of private provision of local public goods. But, according to the social trial run that Hampton (2007) studied in the Boston suburbs, a big slippage was seen by the occupancy rate of an electronic conference room or an electronic bulletin board by individual ICT skill and life stage. Kimura (2012) has indicated that a survey in Japan like Hampton's has not been conducted yet but such a measure is required.

Another is that new inhabitants and old inhabitants will enable participation to equally enjoy the benefit of a community activity. What is necessary is, theoretically, just to suppose that a sequential move game with an entry and recession is repeated, in order to raise the benefit of private provision of local public goods. In fact, there is a way to do that. For instance, by using an electronic conference room, everyone could easily make suggestions or confirm participation in activities. Considering regions where the OFT strategy has not already been achieved, this is one of the ways to reduce inhabitants' opportunity cost by collecting the cost of private provision of local public goods in money, and to outsource this to NPOs and so on.

We will do a future trial run to solve these two questions in a specific community by utilizing ICT. The purpose of the trial run will be to see whether or not this contributes to improving the happiness of local residents.

Appendix. When the private provision of local public goods and association with the neighbors are restricted only once. Since the benefit to the non-cooperative person of private provision of local public goods is $B_i - (N - n)d_i$ and if it is a game with limitations, un-cooperating is chosen once. Since participation in association with neighbors is refused by an OFT strategy, if one does not cooperate in the private provision of local public goods, the gain from association with neighbors is set at 0.

Suppose all the members other than oneself participate in association with neighbors in cooperation on the private provision of local public goods (n=N-1), the gain for the non-cooperative person of the private provision of local public goods will be $D(N - 1) = B_i - (N - N + 1)d_i = B_i - d_i$. The gain of association with the neighbors is set to 0, as mentioned above.

Similarly, the gain for the cooperation of the private provision of local public goods is $C(N - 1) = B_i - (N - N + 1)d_i - C_i = B_i - d_i - C_i$. In addition, when all other members cooperate in association with neighbors, an association with the neighbors participant's gain is $B_s(N - 1) - C_s$.

References

1. Aoki, M.: Toward a Comparative Institutional Analysis. MIT Press (2001)
2. Bloch, F.: Sequential Formation of Coalitions in Games with Externalities and Fixed Payoff Division. Games and Economic Behavior 14, 90–123 (1996)
3. Grief, A.: Institutions and the Path to the Modern Economy: Lessons from Medieval Trade (Political Economy of Institutions and Decisions). Cambridge University Press (2006)
4. Hampton, K.N.: Neighborhoods in the Network Society. Information, Communication & Society 10(5), 714–748 (2007)
5. Rubinstein, A.: Perfect Equilibrium in Bargaining Model. Econometrica 50, 97–109 (1981)
6. Ishida, M.: Sociology of Loneliness, Keiso-shobo. Koritsu-no-syakaigaku (2011) (in Japanese)
7. Kimura, T.: A desire to Community Network is disassembled. Senri Ethnological Reports 106, 41–60 (2012) (in Japanese)

Are the Intrusive Effects of SPAM Probes Present When Operators Differ by Skill Level and Training?

Hector I. Silva[1], Jason Ziccardi[1], Tristan Grigoleit[1], Vernol Battiste[2], Thomas Z. Strybel[1], and Kim-Phuong L. Vu[1]

[1] Center for Human Factors in Advanced Aeronautics Technologies, Department of Psychology, California State University Long Beach, 1250 N Bellflower Blvd, Long Beach CA 90840
[2] San Jose State University Foundation and NASA Ames Research Center
hector_silva91@yahoo.com, jbziccardi@gmail.com,
t_grub@msn.com, Vernol.Battiste@nasa.gov,
{Thomas.Strybel,Kim.Vu}@csulb.edu

Abstract. The Next Generation Air Transportation System (NextGen) plans to implement a series of automated tools into the National Airspace System to aid air traffic controllers (ATCos) in managing a two to three times increase in air traffic density. However, introducing automated technologies into a system like air traffic management (ATM) changes the responsibilities of the ATCo from an active controller to a passive monitor, which can result in lower levels of situation awareness (SA). To measure SA objectively in such a dynamic task as ATM, the Situation Present Awareness Method (SPAM) is often used. SPAM provides the operator with SA probes while the operator is performing the task. Some studies have shown that the use of SPAM to measure SA is intrusive because it provides the operator with a secondary task. The present study examines whether these intrusive effects of SPAM are present when the operator has achieved a high skill level at the time of test, and whether training operators to rely more or less on NextGen automated tools influence their performance when SPAM queries are presented as a secondary task.

Keywords: situation awareness, online probe methodology, situation present assessment method.

1 Introduction

The Next Generation Air Transportation System (NextGen) plans to implement a series of automated tools into the National Airspace System in order to aid air traffic controllers (ATCos) in managing a two to three times increase in air traffic [1]. NextGen seeks to accommodate this increase in traffic efficiently and safely, and at the same time reduce its impact on the environment. To do this, NextGen will implement a series of automated tools into air traffic management (ATM) systems that will aid ATCos in managing the increased number of aircraft (AC). Some of the tools that NextGen seeks to implement will aid controllers with conflict detection and resolution [1].

S. Yamamoto (Ed.): HIMI/HCII 2013, Part I, LNCS 8016, pp. 269–275, 2013.

However, the lack of attention on the part of the operator when a system is highly automated is likely to cause detrimental effects. For example, introducing automated technologies into a system like ATM changes the responsibilities of the ATC from an active controller to a passive monitor [2], which can result in lower levels of situation awareness (SA), and out-of-the-loop syndrome. With highly automated tasks, the operator is less vigilant, and, as a result, will have a harder time regaining awareness should something go wrong [3-4].

The most common real-time probe method used to measure SA in a dynamic task such as ATM is the Situation Present Awareness Method (SPAM). With SPAM, operators are presented with a "ready" prompt to indicate that a probe question is ready to be administered. If the operator's workload is low enough for him/her to be able to take a question, the operator will indicate that s/he is ready (typically by pressing a designated button). The time between the presentation of the ready prompt and the operator's response is a measure of workload. The time needed to answer the SA probe question, and the accuracy of the answer, is taken to be a measure of SA. Participants who show shorter SA probe latencies and higher SA probe accuracy are considered to have higher SA. Using SPAM to measure SA has many benefits over other methods by providing a more sensitive measure of SA (i.e., providing latency data as well as accuracy data), being a method that can be applied in the field while the operator is performing his or her task, and by being consistent with theoretical notions of SA, such as the distributed approach where the user off-loads information into the environment or displays [5-9].

Besides the benefits of using SPAM, it is important to note the drawbacks of using this method. Despite the use of the ready prompt, SPAM does not eliminate all effects of workload, which makes the method somewhat intrusive. Answering probe questions is a secondary task which could cause negative effects on the primary task [9]. Pierce [10] had participants perform an air traffic management task in conjunction with a secondary task that consisted of answering SPAM queries, or one that involves a high or low cognitive load. Pierce reported that use of SPAM queries resulted in greater disruption in performance compared to other secondary tasks. In addition to this, asking the operator questions may change the information that the user is paying attention to and therefore can affect the user's attention post-query [9, 11]. On the other hand, Bacon and Strybel [12], in a simulation designed to manipulate the operators' attention to off nominal events, found no evidence that SPAM SA probes affected the operator attention.

The present study examines whether these intrusive effects of SPAM are present when the test participants are given extensive practice with the task, and whether the effects of SPAM differs depending on the operator's skill level at the time of test. In addition, we wanted to determine if there were differences in the effects of administering SA probe questions using SPAM when operators were given different types of training. The data reported in the present study comes from a larger study examining the effects of training participants to rely more or less on NextGen automated tools. It could be that being trained to rely more on automated NextGen tools would lower workload enough and thus allow the operator the cognitive resources to be able to complete the secondary task of answering probe questions without disturbance to the primary task. Conversely, it could also mean that training to rely on the harder-to-learn manual skills provides a strong foundation, which could lead to the development of multi-tasking skills that can lead to successful completion of both primary and secondary tasks. In addition, highly skilled ATCo students may have gained multi-tasking skills and be efficient enough to allow them to complete a secondary task without much interference to the primary task.

2   Method

2.1   Participants

Fourteen students enrolled in Mount San Antonio College, a Federal Aviation Administration Collegiate Teaching Initiative school, were recruited to participate in this study. The students were seeking an Aviation Science degree and took part in a 16 week internship at the Center for Human Factors in Advanced Aeronautics Technologies at California State University, Long Beach.

2.2   Measures

To measure mental workload, the NASA Task Load Index (TLX) was administered after each scenario. The TLX is a questionnaire that measures workload on six dimensions: Mental Demand, Physical Demand, Temporal Demand, Performance, Effort, and Frustration. The scores on these dimensions can be added and multiplied by 1.11 to yield a combined score on a 100 point scale. The combined score of these dimensions were used for data analysis.

Measures of air traffic controller task performance were also recorded. Performance as a measure of safety was recorded as the number of losses of separation (LOS) that occurred. A LOS occurs when two aircraft come within 1,000 feet vertically or 5 nautical miles laterally of each other. The lower the number of LOS, the safer the controllers were in managing the sector. Along with safety, two measures of efficiency were recorded. The average time and distance that aircraft took to fly through a sector show how efficient the student controllers were in maneuvering the aircraft through the sector.

2.3   Simulation Environment

The simulation environment was presented using the Multiple Aircraft Control System (MACS), a medium fidelity simulation software [13]. The program simulated Indianapolis Center, Sector ZID-91, where traffic consists of en-route flights and arrivals/departures to Louisville airport. Highly trained "pseudopilots" maneuvered all the aircraft in the sector and communicated with the ATCo students. Verbal radio communications were achieved with push-to-talk headsets and a voice IP server between the ATCo students and pseudopilots.

The NextGen equipped aircraft had Integrated Controller-Pilot Data Communication (Data Comm) to allow ATCo to issue clearances and request information digitally, Conflict Alerting, which alerts the ATCo of conflicts between NextGen equipped aircraft 6 minutes before a loss of separation (LOS) occurs, and a Trial Planner with Conflict Probe, which allows ATCos to modify aircraft routes by clicking and dragging them on the screen, while simultaneously probing for potential conflicts with other aircraft.

2.4   Training Procedure

The students that participated in the internship were separated into two groups. Both groups were trained to manage traffic in a mixed equipage airspace where some aircraft were equipped with NextGen technologies and others were not. One group trained with 25% equipped and 75% non-equipped aircraft, and thus trained to rely mostly on their manual skills to manage aircraft for the first 8 weeks. Because this group only had a few equipped aircraft, the students were much less likely to benefit from NextGen technologies.

The second group was trained in 75% equipped aircraft and 25% non-equipped aircraft for 8 weeks, which had the students rely heavily on NextGen technologies. Seventy five percent of the aircraft in the sector are equipped because prior research has shown that at least 50% of the aircraft must be equipped in order for the benefits of NextGen to be realized [14]. By having mostly equipped aircraft in their sector, the students were able to benefit from NextGen technologies as well as have much more opportunity to use them.

Both groups were trained to identify and resolve conflicts between aircraft using manual and NextGen tools before a LOS occurs. To resolve and/or avoid these conflicts, the students were trained in four separation techniques. One skill is vectoring aircraft, where the ATCo changes the flight plan or heading of one or more aircraft. The ATCo must assess the current heading of the aircraft and be able to calculate the safest heading change. The ATCo may change the heading angle in which the aircraft is traveling (determined by the degrees on a compass), or by having the aircraft move a number of degrees to the left or right of its present course. Another skill is altitude separation, where the altitude of the aircraft is manipulated. If two or more aircraft are at the same flight altitude and their paths will converge, the ATCo can issue clearances to one or both of the aircrafts to climb or descend from their current altitude to maintain separation between the aircraft. The students can also use speed separation, where the speed of the co-altitude aircraft is increased or reduced to maintain lateral separation. Lastly, the students were trained to use structured traffic flows, where the controller can create a "highway" for aircraft at certain altitudes, headings, and speeds. This helps the ATCo by grouping aircrafts together in a structure that will maintain separation. The students had to complete a full scenario using only one of these separation methods to successfully move to the next technique. Upon successful completion of all four techniques, the student was awarded "Journeyman" Status by the instructor. Skill level was determined by whether or not the students had earned Journeyman Status by the time testing occurred after the 8th week. Seven out of the 14 participants earned Journeyman Status by the time of the midterm testing.

2.5   Testing Procedure

As noted earlier, the data for this report is a small part of the larger study. The present study included data obtained after the first 8 weeks of the internship when the students completed a midterm examination. The scenarios used in the midterm test varied in the percentage of equipped aircraft, with participants completing scenarios with 0%, 100%, and two 50% equipped aircraft scenarios. The order of the scenarios was counterbalanced between all participants using a partial Latin square. The Situation Present Awareness Method was employed during only one of the two 50% scenarios. To establish a baseline measure, no SPAM queries were presented during the other 50% scenario. This allowed us the opportunity to directly compare the effects of SPAM query presentation.

When administered, SPAM queries operators with questions about their task as the task is ongoing and all displays remain visible and active. Therefore, SA is measured in response time to answering correct questions (with lower response times indicating greater SA) and with accuracy to answering the probe questions (with higher accuracy indicating greater SA). Before a query is presented, the operator must first accept it. Although more realistic in terms of real-world performance than many other freeze-probe methods, answering probes is still a secondary task that may disrupt the primary task of air traffic management. In the present experiment, a query was presented on a touch screen computer approximately every 3 minutes for the complete duration of the scenario. The ATCo students responded to these questions by touching one of the multiple choice responses on the touch screen monitor.

3   Results

Because we are mainly interested in whether the effects of using the SPAM probes are intrusive, we report data from the two 50% scenarios. The performance measures of interest were analyzed using separate 2 (training emphasis: manual/NextGen) × 2 (Journeyman Status: yes/no) × 2 (probes presented/not presented) ANOVAs. NextGen training emphasis and earning Journeyman Status were between subjects factors, and use of SPAM probes (presented or not presented) a within-subjects factor.

3.1   Workload

For workload as measured by the NASA TLX, a main effect of Journeyman Status was present, $F(1, 9) = 13.783$, $p = .005$, $\eta^2 = .605$. Air traffic control ATCo students who achieved Journeyman Status experienced significantly lower workload ($M = 45.18$, $SE = 3.14$) than ATCo students who had not achieved Journeyman Status ($M = 62.79$, $SE = 3.56$). We did not find any differences in workload as a function of whether the SPAM queries were presented, and the use of SPAM probes did not interact with any other variables.

3.2   Performance

Only the main effect of Journeyman Status was found to be significant for time and distance through the sector, $Fs(1, 9) = 11.00$ and 12.66, ps < .010, $\eta^2s = .550$ and .585, respectively. Students who achieved Journeyman Status managed their aircraft in less time ($M = 652.78$ s, $SE = 3.52$ versus $M = 670.45$ s, $SE = 4.00$), and had their aircraft travel a shorter distance ($M = 78.65$ nm, $SE = .42$ versus $M = 80.89$ nm, $SE = .47$) through their sector, than students that were not awarded Journeyman Status.

The analysis on the number of losses of separation revealed a marginal main effect of Journeyman Status, $F(1, 9) = 3.57$, $p = .079$, $\eta^2 = .303$, where students awarded Journeyman Status tended to commit fewer LOS ($M = .60$, $SE = .26$) than those who were not ($M = 1.375$, $SE = .29$). In addition, a main effect of training emphasis was also found, $F(1, 9) = 5.280$, $p = .047$, $\eta^2 = .370$. Students trained to rely on manual skills committed fewer LOS ($M = .542$, $SE = .26$) than students trained to rely on NextGen tools ($M = 1.438$, $SE = .29$).

We did not find any differences in performance as a function of whether the SPAM queries were presented, and the use of SPAM probes did not interact with any other variables.

4   Discussion

The results showed that the main factor determining whether the student ATCos experienced less workload and better performance was their individual skill level—that is, whether they were awarded Journeyman status by the time they were tested. There was no evidence in the present analysis that SPAM probes were intrusive to performance or affected operators differently as a function of their individual skill level or training method. However, the lack of significant effects involving the use of SPAM queries may be a result of the low observed power observed in our analyses. Upon closer look of the analyses executed, we see modest values of observed power for the significant effects reported above (0.91 for Journeyman effect of TLX scores; 0.84 and 0.89 for Journeyman effect on time and distance through sector, respectively; 0.54 for training effect on LOS, and 0.42 for Journeyman effect on LOS). However, we see relatively small observed power values for all other effects that were expected (all < 0.35). Thus, although our sample of 14 participants allowed us to detect some effects, it may not have been sufficient to capture the intrusive effects of SPAM probes, if any were evident.

Acknowledgments. This project was supported by NASA cooperative agreement NNX09AU66A, Group 5 University Research Center: Center for Human Factors in Advanced Aeronautics Technologies (Brenda Collins, Technical Monitor).

References

1. Joint Planning and Development Office. Concept of operations for the next generation air transportation system version (2010),
   http://www.jpdo.gov/library/NextGenConOps.pdf
   (retrieved January 10, 2012)
2. Parasuraman, R., Sheridan, T.B., Wickens, C.D.: A model for types and levels of human interaction with automation. IEEE Transactions on Systems, Man, and Cybernetics – Part A: Systems and Humans 30(3), 286–297 (2000)
3. Wickens, C.D., Dixon, S.R.: The benefits of imperfect diagnostic automation: a synthesis of the literature. Theoretical Issues in Ergonomics Science 8(3), 201–212 (2007)
4. Kaber, D.B., Onal, E., Endsley, M.R.: Design automation for telerobots and the effect on performance, operator situation awareness, and subjective workload. Human Factors and Ergonomics in Manufacturing 10(4), 409–430 (2000)
5. Chiappe, D., Strybel, T.Z., Vu, K.-P.L.:   Mechanisms for the acquisition of Situation Awareness in situated agents. Theoretical Issues in Ergonomic Sciences 13, 625–647 (2012)
6. Durso, F.T., Dattel, A.: SPAM: The real-time assessment of SA. In: Banbury, S., Trembley, S. (eds.) A Cognitive Approach to Situation Awareness: Theory, Measures and Application, pp. 137–154. Aldershot, New York (2004)
7. Durso, F.T., Hackworth, C.A., Truitt, T.R., Crutchfield, J., Nikolic, D., Manning, C.A.: Situation awareness as a predictor of performance for en route air traffic controllers. Air Traffic Control Quarterly 6, 1–20 (1998)
8. Jeannot, E., Kelly, C., Thompson, D.: The development of situation awareness measures in ATM systems. EATMP Report, HRS/HSP-005-REP-01 (2003)
9. Salmon, P.M., Stanton, N.A., Walker, G.H., Green, D.: Situation awareness measurement: A review of applicability for C4i environments. Applied Ergonomics 37, 225–238 (2006)
10. Pierce, R.S.: The effect of SPAM administration during a dynamic situation. Human Factors 54, 838–848 (2012)
11. Langan-Fox, J., Sankey, M., Canty, J.: Human factors measurement for future air traffic control systems. Human Factors 51, 595–637 (2009)
12. Bacon, L.P., Strybel, T.Z.: Assessment of the validity and intrusiveness of online-probe questions for situation awareness in a simulated air-traffic-management task with student air-traffic controllers. Safety Science (in press)
13. Prevot, T.: Exploring the many perspectives of distributed air traffic management: The Multi-Aircraft Control System MACS. In: Chatty, S., Hansman, J., Boy, G. (eds.) HCI-Aero 2002, pp. 149–154. AIAA Press, Menlo Park (2002)
14. Hah, S., Willems, B., Schulz, K.: The evaluation of data communication for the future air traffic control system (NextGen). In: Proceedings of the 54th Annual Meeting of the Human Factors and Ergonomics Society, Santa Monica, CA, pp. 99–103 (2010)

Persuasive Narrative via Digital Storytelling

Kaoru Sumi[1] and Mizue Nagata[2]

[1] Future University Hakodate,
Department of Media Architecture
041-8655 Hakodate, Japan
kaoru.sumi@acm.org
[2] Jumonji University,
Department of Child Education
352-8610 Saitama, Japan

Abstract. This paper describes an experiment on conveying the messages of stories to users. We investigated what kind of story and what kind of character, in terms of the level of abstraction, should be applied to convey a story's message. The animated stories used in the experiment were created using WordsAnime, a software tool for creating animation content easily from an input scenario. The experiment was then conducted by showing subjects animated stories with varying levels of abstraction for the story and the central character.

Keywords: Persuasion, digital storytelling.

1 Introduction

Recently, storytelling has attracted much attention in a variety of areas. Among various benefits, stories have emotional appeal, generate deep understanding, shape the subconscious mind, and motivate action [1]. In particular, applications for marketing and management using storytelling have been an important research target. The medical field is developing the method of narrative therapy [2], in which patients receive psychological treatment by telling their own life stories. In the area of developmental psychology, studies on child development have examined the process by which children generate stories [3]. In social psychology, studies of people's life stories [4] have indicated the possibility of understanding human identity, life, and society by recording and analyzing such stories.

In all of these cases, the key requirement is that storytelling should make an impression on the target person and convey a message to him or her. Hence, in this paper, we describe an experiment investigating the conditions under which the message of a story is best conveyed to a user. We conducted the experiment by showing subjects animated stories that varied in the level of abstraction of both the story and the central character.

S. Yamamoto (Ed.): HIMI/HCII 2013, Part I, LNCS 8016, pp. 276–283, 2013.

Fig. 1. Two axes of abstraction

2   Axes of the Abstraction

What is required for a storytelling system to convey the messages of stories to users? For the work described here, we considered four types of conditions based on two factors for a story and its central character. As Figure 1 shows, there are two axes corresponding to the two factors: the x-axis represents the central character's level of abstraction, while the y-axis represents the story's level of abstraction. For each axis, the level of abstraction ranges from abstract to concrete. The four conditions are thus as follows.

- Myself: This is a condition based on a user's real story. The main character is the user himself or herself. In this case, the story and character are both concrete.
- Fairy tale: This is a condition based on a traditional fairy tale. The story and character are both abstract.
- I play a fairy tale character: This is a condition based on a fairy tale but with the user playing the central character. Here, the story is abstract but the character is concrete.
- A fictional character plays my role: This is a condition based on a user's real story but with someone else playing the central character.

A storytelling system can change the central character's face to the user's face, his or her friend's face, or someone else's face according to the level of character abstraction. The user's face is very concrete, a friend's face is somewhat less concrete, but an unknown person's face is abstract. In this case, therefore, the story is concrete but the character is abstract.

We might use a storytelling system to persuade users via abstract stories with a message, or via concrete stories. We might also persuade via the story of a friend's failure. An experimental storytelling system should be able to change conditions as described above. Hence, we devised an experiment using WordsAnime [5][6], a software tool that can create animation content easily from an input scenario. WordsAnime uses the animation database of Anime de Blog [7], in which animation data is linked to verbs or nouns.

3   Experiment

We conducted a comparative experiment to examine what kind of content is more persuasive [12] for a user, a concrete or an abstract story. In the experiment, subjects viewed concrete or abstract characters according to a character's level of abstraction, and concrete or abstract stories according to the story's level of abstraction.

Experimental Method

To perform this comparison between types of content, we varied two factors—the character condition (myself or someone else), and the story condition (realistic or fairy tale)—and showed corresponding animated content to each user. A total of 34 undergraduate student subjects were assigned each of the four condition combinations.

Experimental Content

1. Content

The animation content was created using WordsAnime. The subjects were shown Aesop's fable of "The Ant and the Grasshopper" for the fairy tale condition, or an original story called "Job Hunting" for the realistic condition. "The Ant and the Grasshopper" suggests the virtue of not being lazy, while "Job Hunting" gives the same message in a student's real world environment. In addition to the meaning, the number of scenes in each story was also the same.

For character condition, when the condition was "myself" the system showed a picture of the user's face on the face of the main character, and also the name of the main character in the sentence was changed to the user's name. When the condition was "someone else" the system showed the picture of an unknown person's face on the face of the main character (Figure 2), and also the name of the main character in the sentence was changed to the unknown person's name.

The two stories and the scenarios were as follows (Figure 3).

The story of "The Ant and the Grasshopper":
During the summer, the ant worked to store food for the winter.
On the other hand, grasshopper played his life away.
Winter came; the grasshopper had nothing to eat and was hungry.
The grasshopper asked the ant for food, but he refused.
The grasshopper died of hunger.

Fig. 2. "Someone else" face is pasted to the main character

The scenarios for "The Ant and the Grasshopper":

1. The ant worked hard in the summer.
2. The grasshopper played a lot in the summer.
3. The grasshopper was hungry in the winter.
4. The grasshopper asked the ant for food, but the ant said "no".
5. The grasshopper died.

The story of "Job Hunting":

During the summer, my classmates worked hard at job hunting.
On the other hand, I played my life away with my friends during this time
Winter came; I panicked because I had no job offers, though my classmates had all found jobs.
I asked my father's acquaintance for a job, but he refused.
I was very disappointed, because I could not find a job.

The scenarios for "Job hunting":

1. My classmates worked hard in the summer.
2. I played a lot with my friends in the summer.
3. I panicked because I had no job offer in the winter.
4. I asked a businessperson for a job, but he said "no".
5. I was very disappointed.

Procedure

The subjects followed the procedure below:

1. Submit user information and upload a picture.
2. Choose a friend's face.
3. Choose an acquaintance's face.
4. Respond to an initial questionnaire.
5. View the selected content.
6. Respond to a follow-up questionnaire.

Fig. 3. Stories of "The ants and the grasshoppers" and "Job hunting"

First, the subjects submitted their information and pictures of their faces. Next, they each selected a friend and an acquaintance. Depending on their answers to an initial questionnaire, the system chose their stories. As described above, we offered two stories with the same message. After viewing the selected content, the subjects answered a follow-up questionnaire.

The follow-up questionnaire contained the following questions:

Question 1: Was the story impressive?
Question 2: Was the story interesting?
Question 3: Did you know the story?
Question 4: Did you understand the message of the story?
Question 5: Are you in the same situation as the person in the story?
Question 6: Is the story relevant to you? (i.e., could you learn from the message?)
Question 7: Did you learn a lesson from the story?
Question 8: Did you improve yourself by watching the story?

We found the average evaluation values on a five-point scale for each of the eight questions. We then conducted a two-factor analysis of variation among the subjects, consisting of the central character (2: myself/someone else) and the story (2: concrete/abstract). The following questions were of particular interest.

- *Question 1*: This question reflected the trend of interaction between the central character and the story ($F(1, 30)=3.65$, $p<.10$). Specifically, when the central character was another person, the realistic story was more impressive than the fairy tale. It also reflected the trend that when the story was a fairy tale, the central character as "myself" was more impressive than as "someone else".
- *Question 3*: The main effect of the story was significant ($F(1, 30)=88.24$, $p<.01$), confirming that a realistic story was more unfamiliar than a fairy tale. The main effect of the central character was also significant ($F(1, 30)=3.57$, $p<.10$), confirming that the "myself" central character was more familiar than "someone else". This question also reflected the trend of interaction between the central character and the story ($F(1, 30)=3.53$, $p<.10$). Specifically, when the story was a fairy tale, the "myself" central character was more familiar than "someone else".
- *Question 8*: The main effect of the story was significant ($F(1, 30)=4.23$, $p<.05$), indicating that the fairy tale was more suggestive of self-improvement.

According to cross tabulation, when the story was a fairy tale, if the central character was "someone else", subjects tended to think of improving themselves, whereas if the central character was "myself", subjects tended to answer "no opinion".

By analyzing the correlation factors of the questions, we obtained several findings.

- Typical positive correlation when the central character was "myself":

When the subject associated the central character with himself or herself, the impression of the content was related to understanding its meaning, and the amusingness of the content was related to whether it was helpful or not. If the subject considered the content relevant to himself or herself, then he or she considered self-improvement.

- Typical positive correlation when the story was "concrete":

When the story was concrete, if the user understood the message, then he or she considered it a good lesson.

- Typical positive correlation when the central character was "someone else" (equivalent to the case when the central character was "myself" and the story was "abstract"):

It was difficult to understand the message and to learn from it.

- Typical positive correlation when the central character was "myself" and the story was "concrete", or when the central character was "someone else" and the story was "abstract":

Whether the condition that was realistic or had little relevance to the real world, it was interesting and provided a good lesson.

4   Discussion

In the experiment, we used two kinds of content and two conditions for the central character, according to the level of abstraction for both the story and the character. When the story was a fairy tale, the condition when the central character was "myself" was more impressive to the subjects than when the central character was "someone else". Furthermore, in the case of a fairy tale, the subjects knew the story. In general, when the central character was "myself", they knew the story better than when the central character was "someone else", but this was especially so for the fairy tale case.

The experiment indicated that a fairy tale encouraged subjects to improve themselves more than a realistic story did. According to this result, when a subject was shown a fairy tale, if the central character was "someone else", he or she tended to think about self-improvement; while if the central character was "myself", the subject tended to answer "intermediate".

As for the subjects' impression of the story, a greater impression was created when the central character was "myself" than "someone else". Moreover, the subjects thought more about improving themselves when the central character was "myself" than when it was "someone else". According to this result, the combination of an abstract story and an abstract character was effective in prompting subjects to reflect on themselves.

Finally, we can summarize our statistically significant results as follows. First, regarding the ease of creating an impression through a story, if the central character is "someone else", a realistic story is more impressive. This means that a real story with an unknown person as the central character would be impressive. Next, regarding message transmission via a story, a fairy tale encourages people to be more careful than a realistic story does. This means that people simply accept the message of a fairy tale. This suggests that a game with sententious messages should consist of a fantasy story, like a role-playing fantasy adventure, rather than a realistic story.

Our experiment suggests that in the fairy tale case, if the central character is "someone else", people take heed of the message; on the other hand, if the central character is "myself", people do not apply the message to themselves. That is, a fairy tale better conveys its message when the central character is an unknown person, and the same consideration applies for such as fantasy role-playing games.

Note that in this experiment, the subjects were all freshmen and thus a few years from searching for work, so they did not take job hunting seriously. If we had used junior or senior students as subjects, the results might have been different.

Given that users have no idea of the conditions of their characters (e.g., honest/dishonest), we will have to investigate the effectiveness of persuasion on multiple personal characters and their conditions on a case-by-case basis.

5   Conclusion

In this paper, we have described an experiment investigating what factors in story content, as in role-playing games, are persuasive to people in the case of showing an animated story. The specific factors were the levels of abstraction for both the story and the character.

References

1. Yamakawa, S.: Jirei de wakaru monogatari marketing, nihon nouritu management center (2007) (in Japanese)
2. Brown, C., Augusta-Scott, T.: Narrative Therapy: Making Meaning, Making Lives. Sage Publications (2006)
3. Uchida, N.: Kodomo no bunsho: Kaku koto kangaeru koto (Shirizu ningen no hattatsu), Japanese edn. Tokyo Daigaku Shuppankai (1990)
4. Atkinson, R.: The Life Story Interview. Sage Publications (1998)
5. Sumi, K.: Animation-based Interactive Storytelling System. In: Spierling, U., Szilas, N. (eds.) ICIDS 2008. LNCS, vol. 5334, pp. 48–50. Springer, Heidelberg (2008)
6. Sumi, K., Nagata, M.: Interpersonal Impressions of Agents for Developing Intelligent Systems. In: Prendinger, H., Lester, J.C., Ishizuka, M. (eds.) IVA 2008. LNCS (LNAI), vol. 5208, pp. 496–497. Springer, Heidelberg (2008)
7. Sumi, K.: Anime Blog for collecting Animation Data. In: Cavazza, M., Donikian, S. (eds.) ICVS-VirtStory 2007. LNCS, vol. 4871, pp. 139–149. Springer, Heidelberg (2007)
8. Fogg, B.J.: Persuasive Technology –Using Computers to Change What We Think and Do-. Elsevier (2003)

Prediction of the Concern of People Using CGM

Yusuke Ueda and Yumi Asahi

Shizuoka University

1   Introduction

It is that the spread of CGM(consumer generated media) is been noticed in recent years. There are 42,890,000 Japanese SNS users at the end of 2011, and it is say that 56,430,000 people will be user of it at the end of 2014. The month-long user of a buzz marketing site has reached to 83,560,000 people, and it being increasing. Recent market scale is 200,500 million yen in Japan. This will be expanded 396,300 million yen in 2013. It originates in the background of growth at (A), (B), and (C). (A) It can use for free. (B) Not only a general user but a company can do promotion and communication. (C) Receiving physical restrictions, such as a place and time, are decreased by development of a communications infrastructure and a portable terminal. On the other hand, pretending to be it a negative campaign and false rumor information by the anonymity of the sender occurs a lot. This becomes the inveterate problem that the net literacy of users is asked. Still ,CGM is becoming indispensable to our life up to everyday communication and interchange, purchasing activity [1]. We show some concrete example. It is used for Web promotion activity or the questionary survey. Because its give a user easiness of friendly feeling and get the true intention. Subsequently, we give an example of the further possibility of CGM. kabu.com Securities Co. Ltd develop a system that collect and analyze the huge information from SNS such as Twitter or mixi. It may be said that this is one of the big data business. And we expect further value of CGM. This time, we select Twitter from CGM and I build a model to observe the interest of people, and to estimate and inspect it. Twitter is SNS site to contribute the short sentence within 140 characters to. The user reach 13,920,000 people, it is the second scale next to Facebook in Japan. Also it has four characteristics. First, it holds the organization which can be connected without needing each other's approval. Second, it is easy to aim the opinion leader from the number of the followers and the number of retweet. Third, full retrieval service. Last, observation of the number of tweet is easy, and it is easy to treat it as quantitative data. Thus, We paid attention to Twitter.

The goal of this researches to prediction in transition of new objects (a product and a phenomenon).For that purpose, we build a model to express a change of the interest, and carry out numerical value simulation. From a simulation result, I examine to grouping the tendency of research object.

2   Concern Shift Model

The model is built based on "ON A DIFFERENTIAL EQUATION MOEL OF BOOMS" [3]. This model is built by paying attention a boom. A boom is said

S. Yamamoto (Ed.): HIMI/HCII 2013, Part I, LNCS 8016, pp. 284–292, 2013.

"A product and a phenomenon spread among people instantly, and it is forgotten afterwards during a short term." The interest of people greatly changes by a boom. In a word, it is easy to read a change if it greatly works, and is suitable for surveying a change of the interest. In the construction of the model. I use the number of tweet to measure interest for numerical value. The existing model collects the number of the words and target consumers population from various information media (ex Newspaper, data yearbook ,statistics data on web). And it estimates condition of consumption and the recognition. The change of the number of tweet before the boom does not consider. Because, there is more Twitter in the appearance number of the word after boom than these information media.

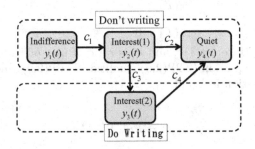

Fig. 1. concern shift model

From fig. 1, State of the user

Indifference : State of the user who does not recognize to an object

Interest(1) : State of the user who has not surfaced although it is interested to an object

Interest(2) : State of the user who it is interested and has surfaced to an object

Quiet : State of the user for whom the concern about an object settled down

I assume the ratio of user belonging to each state $z_1(t)$'$z_4(t)$ in parameter of the time t

$$z_1(t) + z_2(t) + z_3(t) + z_4(t) = 1 \qquad (2.1)$$

Expression of the state change of the user

$$\acute{z}_1(t) = -c_1 y_1(t) \qquad (2.2)$$

$$\acute{z}_2(t) = c_1 y_1(t) - (c_2 + c_3) y_2(t) \qquad (2.3)$$

$$\acute{z}_3(t) = c_2 y_2(t) - c_4 y_3(t) \qquad (2.4)$$

$$\acute{z}_4(t) = c_3 y_2(t) + c_4 y_3(t) \qquad (2.5)$$

Parameter to be given $c_1 {}^{\backprime} c_4$

c_1 : Percentage of the users who begin to get interested

c_2 : Percentage of the users who occur surfaced concern

c_3 : Percentage of the users who settle down before surfaced concern

c_4 : Percentage of the users who cool down gradually after surfaced concern

The value that is in each state at the time of the boom

$$z_1(T) = (1 - l - m) \tag{2.6}$$

$$z_2(T) = l \tag{2.7}$$

$$z_3(T) = m \tag{2.8}$$

$$z_4(T) = 0 \tag{2.9}$$

l is ratio of user of "Interest(1)", and m is ratio of user of "Interest(2)".

Give differential equation $(2.2)'(2.5)$ condition $(2.6)'(2.9)$, and the solution of the differential equation is found.

$(T \leq t)$

$$z_1(t) = P e^{-c_1(t-T)} \tag{2.10}$$

$$
\begin{aligned}
z_2(t) = {} & \frac{c_1 P}{C_1}(-e^{-c_1(t-T)} + e^{-(c_2+c_3)(t-T)}) \\
& + l e^{-(c_2+c_3)(t-T)}
\end{aligned} \tag{2.11}
$$

$$
\begin{aligned}
z_3(t) = {} & \frac{c_1 c_3 P}{C_1 C_2}(-e^{-c_1(t-T)} + e^{-(c_2+c_3)(t-T)}) \\
& + \frac{l c_3}{C_2}(e^{-(c_2+c_3)(t-T)} - e^{-c_4(t-T)}) \\
& + \frac{c_1 c_2}{C_2(c_1 - c_4)}P(e^{-c_1(t-T)} - e^{-c_4(t-T)}) \\
& + m e^{-c_4(t-T)}
\end{aligned} \tag{2.12}
$$

$$
\begin{aligned}
z_4(t) = {} & \left(c_3 + \frac{c_2 c_4}{C_2}\right)\left(\frac{P}{C_1(c_2 + c_3)}\right)E_2 \\
& + \frac{l c_2}{C_2(c_2 + c_3)}\left(-c_4 e^{-(c_2+c_3)(t-T)} + (c_2 + c_3)e^{-c_4(t-T)}\right) \\
& + \frac{c_2 P}{C_2(c_1 - c_4)}(-c_4 e^{-c_1(t-T)} + c_1 e^{-c_4(t-T)}) \\
& - \frac{l c_3}{c_2 + c_3}e^{-(c_2+c_3)(t-T)} - m e^{-c_4(t-T)} \\
& + \frac{c_2 P}{C_2}\left(1 + \frac{c_4}{c_2 + c_3}\right) + \frac{1}{c_2 + c_3}\{c_3 P - c_3 l + c_2 l\} + m \\
P = {} & (1 - l - m), C_1 = (c_1 - c_2 - c_3), C_2 = (c_4 - c_3 - c_2) \\
E_2 = {} & (c_2 + c_3)e^{-c_1(t-T)} - c_1 e^{-(c_2+c_3)(t-T)}
\end{aligned} \tag{2.13}
$$

3   Data Analysis

3.1   Analysis Method

The process of analysis method is as follows.

1. The numbers of the tweet containing the name of investigation contents are observed and collected.
2. Simulation result has been compared with collected data. We value it at the eye measurement of graph and the coefficient of determination decided by regression analysis.
3. The potential concern of the user who cannot measure from the number of the tweet is predicted. (The user's concern makes the number of the tweet the index.)
4. It is inspected whether a tendency is looked at a user's concern predicted transition of the number of the tweet.

There is not the numerical index to measure usefulness in procedure 4. Thus, we judge it from the user reaction (The number and contents of the tweet) and the environment of the target word. The target word elects from upswing in Google searching search word ranking in the first half in 2012. In the election of the word, it is thought that a thing collecting much tweet is desirable as subjects of survey. The thing which greatly collected the interest of the user showed sudden growth during a short term. Understood that it was similar to a boom.

Target words are "genpatsu (nuclear power generation), sutema (stealth-mareting), siri, kinkan-nissyoku (annular solar eclipse), kinkansyoku (Synonym of kinkan-nissyoku), hikarie (One of the shopping centers), nottv (net media), sky-tree, comp-gacha (complete-gatya)". The investigation period is Jul-2011 - Sep-2012. The use site is TOPSY [2].

3.2   Setting of the Parameter

We set the parameter to perform the simulation by the model. The setting of the parameter uses least squares method by the Solver of Excel. When we set it, set the number of tweet per unit time of $Tw \times z_3(t)$ Tw expresses the number of total tweet per unit time. We suppose the number of tweet per month to be 1,200 million and analyze.

4   Result of Analysis

We perform inspection and consideration of the analysis. $Tw \times y3$ is indicated estimated value, *data* is indicated measured value. The number of tweet of the target word and change of the interest state of the user are provided than simulation. We can classify it in three cases from them.

Continnuation

The case which continues keeping the interest of the fixed quantity after a boom. The fixed quantity is that the interest of the standard is higher than before boom. The revival that the number of tweet increases again is classified in this case too. In the change of the interest, Interest(1) continues lengthening after a boom.

The Second Boom

The case which shows sudden increase again when a change calmed down. The increase and decrease of the number of tweet is confirmed before a boom. The change of the interest is similar to continuation.

One - Shot

The case which suddenly falls in when a boom is over. After a boom, there are few signs that interest rises to. It is supposed that the phenomenon that has concluded without what is used on Twitter is just forgotten. The number of tweet decrease, and the interest of the user calms at the same time.

Table 1. Positioning of the target word

	Target word
CONTINNUATION	genpatsu , sutema hikarie , nottv
THE SECOND BOOM	siri sky-tree
ONE - SHOT	kinkan-nissyoku kinkansyoku comp-gacha

Inspect the precision of the model as a specific example from three cases which were classified.

4.1 STUEMA

An official name is called stealth-mareting with sutema. Point to publicizing it with an article so that it is not noticed with an advertisement by consumers. The words existed than before. However, it became if in late years it would be used frequently led by a net user.

It is said that the simulation result is good from Fig. 2 and R^2. But it did not come true to reproduce the increase and decrease of the number of tweet fully. It is necessary for precision of the simulation to give a thought to a standard to what extent.

The change of the user who is in each state becomes Fig. 3.

The user of the state of Indifference occupies most in a change . In this situation, the user of other states is uncommon. I will omit a change of Indifference

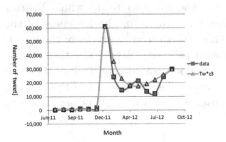

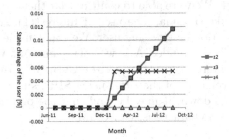

Fig. 2. Change of the number of tweet (sutema) ($R^2 = 0.877$)

Fig. 3. State change of the user (sutema)

in a similar case from notation in future. When we pay attention to a change of Fig. 2, Interest(1) increases steadily, and Quite shows presence of mind. When interest gradually penetrates from there, we can read it. On the other hand, it is thought that this is supported only by a digital native and youth good at net slang.

4.2 SIRI

SIRI is secretary function applications software for iOS. It provides a reply and the Web Service for the question of the user by the sound recognition. It was put on iPhone 4S on October 4, 2011, came to support Japanese on March 8, 2012, and attracted attention by announcement of iOS6 of September, 2012 again.

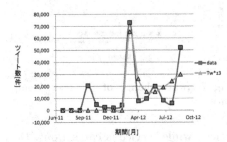

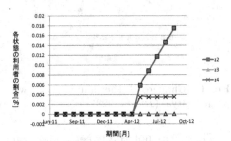

Fig. 4. Change of the number of tweet (siri) ($R^2 = 0.718$)

Fig. 5. State change of the user (siri)

We set March, 2012 when a Japanese edition was released with a boom start from Fig. 4. We have ignored the big upsurge at the time of the announcement in the previous year in October. Not having been able to follow a rapid increase of the number of tweet of September, 2012, it may be said that it is the factor that a value of R^2 has lowered. These will become the future problem.

The change of the user who is in each state becomes figure 5.

We were able to confirm that there was not the influence to the whole Twitter like stemma. The user of Interest(1) shows big growth for the littleness of the ratio of a tweeting user. We can consider this growth from contents of the tweet. For example "A new story came out when I said that I told siri that it was interesting. http://t.co/4zC6BpBF". He(she) does not merely declare the convenience of the verge using SIRI, suggests play to let the interest of the partner go down. It may be said that the organization where a user offers new value to is a characteristic of CGM.

4.3   Comp-Gacha

Comp-gacha calls an official name complete-gatya. (The meaning of gacha is capsule toy.) It is one of the charging methods of the social game for cell-phone, smartphones. It purchases an item by a lottery method like a capsule toy. And complete several kinds of decided items. The system what obtain a rare item by doing so it. Consumer Affairs Agency forbade comp-gacha by the charging large amount request of the social game on May 5, 2012. The contents that accounted for important weight in the profit of the industry were abolished. Therefore a social game-related brand of the Tokyo business market makes a sudden drop. DeNA and GLEE of industry major became the stop-low, and aggregate market value of 200 billion yen became extinct in a day.

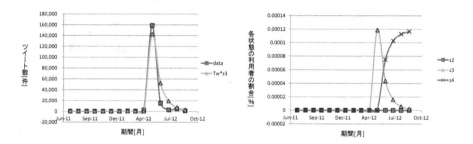

Fig. 6. Change of the number of tweet **Fig. 7.** State change of the user (comp-(comp-gatya) ($R^2 = 0.928$)   gatya)

There was not the tweet about comp-gacha while service is carried out. Detailed structure was transmitted many users after Consumer Affairs Agency decided it illegal. In that way we understand that it followed that collect big interest. The stock plunge acts as a cause to attract interest. Change of the user who is in each state is Fig. 7

We collect interest at the time of the outbreak of the phenomenon, but calm if a boom is over because there is not an additional impact. The case concluded early, It is thought that it becomes the aspect like this time.

4.4   Observations

Cf. analysis, If the pattern of continuation and pattern oh one-shot, An estimate of the precision that R^2 is high in like about 0.9 is possible. The problems that the model had became clear from the second boom.

Specially, because the control of the boom is early as for the single-engine pattern, a stable estimate is possible. Conversely, Interest(1) continues lengthening, and do not get control in other cases. Thus, it is necessary to build the structure which can be equivalent about a future prediction.

About a Change of the Interest

It may be said that the judgment of the right or wrong of the purpose "visualization of size and the change of the interest" is difficult. Realy, the proof of the estimated result is poor just method to consider it from contents of the tweet, and to plan adjustment. The measures thought about are qualitative investigations using the questionnaires at the very beginning. It is thought that sequential adjustment is difficult by Twitter observing a continuous change and the questionnaire to capture a change discretely. In other words We cannot assert with the interest of the user by an estimated result as now. However, it is a fact that one featuring it of the target words became clear by digitizing a process before leading to the estimate of the change of the number of tweet.

Corectively, We was able to visualize invisible interest. A problem is left in the proof of the result, and the right or wrong is divided by how to receive estimate results. In a future study, you must define it some other time how you treat it.

Text Mining

We examine qualitative analysis by the text mining. In this reserch, we express the influence that the qualitative elements such as contents of tweet used for only the proof in the change of the interest give.

The factor that comp-gatya is classified in a single-engine case is "lacked versatility of word" and "stamina of the topic is short". In the case of nuclear power generation, number of tweet and volume of interest are bigger than other target words. Not only because this is derived from interest of the nuclear power generation in various elements, it is explained, but also it is pointed to be problem connected directly with our life. It is thought with the example that a sense of impending crisis supports than interest. We can ask about size of the influence that the qualitative factor and background in the target word. Then, we give the tendency of the word to classify from contents of the tweet.

1. Sutema, siri, kinkansyoku, kinkan-nissyoku, sky-tree and comp-gacha are liven up by user.
2. Hikarie and nottv are liven up by user and service-provider. They work hard not to run out of interest.
3. Genpatsu is liven up by user, the media, learned men and society as a whole.

We can classify these with volume of growth of Interest(1). The case to write in with the service-provider has a bigger surge of the interest than the case to write in with user. Furthermore, we understood size of the influence by the media and learned men. From the above, we derive a tendency from contents of the tweet about the target word. And we promise improvement of the precision by it. K

5   Conclution

Express the thing that became clear and the consideration about the inflection method of the model in this reserch.

- The simulation result by the model left a problem in the second boom, but appearance of the graph, decision coefficient R^2 were good together.
- In Twitter, there was a big difference in the number of tweet before and after a boom. Thus, it worked to have built a model based on an existing model.
- There is a tendency in the number of tweet and the interest of the user each and can sort it. In addition, We seemed to be able to grasp a tendency from an attribute derived than consideration by contents of the tweet.
- There is not a numerical index about the proof of the change of the user interest. Instead using contents of the tweet inspected it. We were able to get consistency by reading the background that surrounded a target word. However, it is not interest itself of the user under the present conditions. The side as the specification of the process before tweet showing interest is stronger.

References

1. Chen, Y.: One consideration about an effect of Collective Intelligence and the company use of social media, pp. 241–266. Osaka Sangyo University
2. TOPSY, http://topsy.com/
3. Yuko, N., Osamu, K.: On a Differential Equation Moel of Booms. Transactions of the Operations Research, 83–105 (2004)

Part III

Design and Development Methods and Tools for Interactive Systems and Services

Unified Modeling Language:
The Teen Years and Growing Pains

John Erickson[1] and Keng Siau[2]

[1] Department of Marketing and Management,
College of Business Administration,
University of Nebraska at Omaha, Omaha, NE 68182, USA
johnerickson@unomaha.edu
[2] Department of Business & Information Technology,
Missouri University of Science and Technology, Rolla, MO 65409, USA
siauk@mst.edu

Abstract. Unified Modeling Language (UML) is adopted by the Object Management Group as a standardized general-purpose modeling language for object-oriented software engineering. Despite its status as a standard, UML is still in a development stage and many studies have highlighted its weaknesses and challenges - including those related to human factor issues. Further, UML has grown considerably more complex since its inception. This paper traces the history of Unified Modeling Language (UML) from its formation to its current state and discusses the current state of the UML language. The paper first introduces UML and its various diagrams, and discusses its characteristics and features. The paper then looks at UML's strengths, challenges, and possible future development. The human factor issues with using UML are discussed and elaborated. Potential research questions related to UML are also highlighted.

Keywords: Unified Modeling Language, Human Factors, Systems Analysis and Design, Object Orientation.

1 Object-Orientation and UML's Genesis

1.1 Introduction

The continuing proliferation and development of information systems has proceeded at a pace amazing to even those intimately involved in the creation of such systems. The number of large companies building, revising or re-engineering their information systems seems to be ever increasing. Fortune 500 companies currently engaged upon multi-hundred million dollar IS/IT projects include Union Pacific Railroad, ConAgra Foods, Walmart, eBay/PayPal, and Blue-Cross Blue Shield to name only a very few. Given the increasing use of Cloud-based services, there appears to be some moves toward modularization and standardization of software and systems. Even with much progress, it appears, however, that software engineering is not keeping pace with the advances in hardware and general technological capabilities.

S. Yamamoto (Ed.): HIMI/HCII 2013, Part I, LNCS 8016, pp. 295–304, 2013.
© Springer-Verlag Berlin Heidelberg 2013

While technological change continuously swirls around many businesses and organizations , systems development often still **adheres** to the general ADCT (Analyze, Design, Code, Test) rubric, and utilizes such specific methodologies as the Waterfall Method, the Spiral Method, the System Life Cycle (alternatively known as the System Development Lifecycle, or **SDLC**), Prototyping, Rapid Application Development (RAD), Joint Application Development (JAD), End-User development, Outsourcing in various forms, or 'simply' buying pre-designed software from vendors (e.g., SAP, J. D. Edwards, Oracle, and People Soft).

In the past, systems and software development methods did not require that developers adhere to a specific approach to building systems, and while this may have been beneficial in that it allowed developers the freedom to choose a method that they were most comfortable with and knowledgeable about, such open-ended approaches can affect and constrain the system in unexpected ways or even result in failure. For example, system development and implementation failure rates remain stubbornly high. Cost overruns and time overruns are still the norm, rather than the exception. Also, open-ended approaches sometimes result in maintenance issues as not all systems analysts are trained in all methods. . In the current development environment, a different approach to systems development, one that provides close integration between analysis, design, and coding, would appear to be necessary. Further, many of the information system project failures are the result of human issues and human factors. Thus, not only do we need to enhance systems analysis and design methods, but we also need to enhance them with the human factor issues in mind. In this paper, we explore the role of the Unified Modeling Language (UML) as a modeling language that enables such an approach.

The first section of the paper explores the concept of object-orientation, including object-oriented systems analysis and design, the idea of modeling and modeling languages, and the history of UML. The following section, Section 2, covers the basic UML constructs, and Section 3 examines UML from a practical or practitioner perspective, while Section 4 discusses the future of UML and the human factor issues that need to be studied in enhancing UML.

1.2   Object-Orientation

Over the past two to three decades, object-oriented programming languages have emerged as the approach that many developers prefer to use during the Coding part of the systems development life cycle. However, in most cases the Analysis and Design steps have continued to proceed in the traditional style. This has often created tension, since traditional analysis and design are process-oriented instead of being object-oriented.

Object-oriented systems analysis and design (OOSAD) methods were developed to close the gap between the different stages, the first methods appearing in the 1980s. By the early 1990s, a virtual explosion in the number of OOSAD approaches began to flood the new paradigmatic environment. Between 1989 and 1994 the number of OO development methods grew from around ten to more than fifty (Booch, Rumbaugh and Jacobson, 1999). Two of these modeling languages are of particular interest for the purposes of this paper, Booch and Jacobson's OOSE (Object-Oriented Software Engineering), and Rumbaugh's OMT (Object Modeling Technique). A partial listing of methods/languages is shown below:

Table 1. Examples of Object Oriented Method/Language

• Bailin	• Hood
• Berard	• Jacobson
• Booch	• Martin-Odell
• Coad-Yourdon	• Rumbaugh
• Colbert	• Schlaer-Mellor
• Embley	• Seidewitz
• Firesmith	• UML
• Gibson	• Wirfs-Brock

1.3   The Emergence of UML

Prominent developers of different object-oriented modeling approaches joined forces to create UML, which was originally based on the two distinct OO modeling languages mentioned above: Booch and Jacobson's OOSE (Object-Oriented Software Engineering), and Rumbaugh's OMT (Object Modeling Technique). Development began in 1994 and continued through 1996, culminating in the January 1997 release of UML version 1.0 (Booch, Rumbaugh and Jacobson, 1999). The Object Management Group (OMG) adopted UML 1.1 as a standard modeling language in November of 1997. Version 2.4.1 is the most current release.

2   Current UML Models and Extensibility Mechanisms

2.1   Modeling

UML, as its name implies, is really all about creating models of software systems. Models are an abstraction of reality, meaning that we cannot, and really do not care to model in total reality settings, simply because of the complexity that such models would entail. Without abstraction, models would consume far more resources than any benefit gained from their construction. For the purposes of this paper, a model constitutes a view into the system. UML originally proposed a set of nine distinct modeling techniques representing nine different models or views of the system. With the release of UML 2.0 in July, 2005, five additional diagramming techniques were incorporated into the language. The techniques can be separated into structural (static) and behavioral (dynamic) views of the system. UML 2.4.1, the latest version of the modeling language, includes additional diagram types for model management.

Structural Diagrams

Profile Diagrams, Class Diagrams, Object Diagrams, Component Diagrams, Deployment Diagrams, Composite Structure Diagrams, and Package Diagrams comprise the static models of UML. Static models represent snapshots of the system at a given point or points in time, and do not relate information about how the system achieved the condition or state that it is in at each snapshot.

Class diagrams represent the basis of the OO paradigm to many adherents and depict class models. Class diagrams specify the system from both an analysis and design perspective. They depict what the system can do – analysis, and provide a blueprint showing how the system will be built – design (Ambler, 2000). Class diagrams are self-describing, and include a listing of the attributes, behaviors, and responsibilities of the system classes. Properly detailed class diagrams can be directly translated into physical (program code) form. In addition, correctly developed class diagrams can guide the software engineering process, as well as provide detailed system documentation (Lago, 2000).

Object Models and Diagrams represent specific occurrences or instances of class diagrams, and as such are generally seen as more concrete than the more abstract class diagrams.

Component diagrams depict the different parts of the software that constitute a system. This would include the interfaces of and between the components as well as their interrelationships. Ambler (2000) and Booch, Rumbaugh and Jacobson, (1999) defined component diagrams as class diagrams at a more abstract level.

Deployment diagrams can also be seen as a special case of class diagrams. In this case, the diagram models how the run-time processing units are connected and work together. The primary difference between component and deployment diagrams is that component diagrams focus on software units, while deployment diagrams depict the hardware arrangement for the proposed system.

Profile Diagrams are structure diagrams that describe lightweight extension mechanisms to the UML by defining custom stereotypes, tagged values, and constraints. Profiles allow adaptation of the UML metamodel for different platforms and domains.

Composite Structure Diagrams depict the relationships and communications between the functional parts of a system. These diagrams depict high level and abstract views of the system being modeled.

Package Diagrams are essentially a subtype of Class or Object Diagrams. They are intended to depict or show a grouping of related UML elements. Package Diagrams make it easier to see dependencies among different parts of the system being modeled (Pilone and Pitman, 2005). As such, Package Diagrams represent a high level view of the systems being modeled and therefore a good possibility for conveying understanding to users and other interested parties.

Behavioral Diagrams

Use Case Diagrams, Activity Diagrams, State Diagrams are the primary types of Behavioral Diagrams. The set of four Interaction Diagrams form a sub-type of Behavioral Diagram: Sequence Diagrams, Communication Diagrams, Interaction

Overview Diagrams, and Timing Diagrams. In contrast to the static diagrams, the dynamic diagrams in UML are intended to depict the behavior of the system as it transitions between states, interacts with users or internal classes and objects, and moves through the various activities that it is designed to accomplish.

Use Case Diagrams. While class models and diagrams represent the basis of OO as previously discussed, use case models and diagrams portray the system from the perspective of an end-user, and represent tasks that the system and users must execute in performance of their jobs (Pooley and Stevens, 1999). Use case models and the resulting use case diagrams consist of actors (those persons or systems outside the system of interest that need to interact with the system under development), use cases, and relationships among the actors and use cases. Booch, Rumbaugh, and Jacobson (1999) proposed that developers begin the analysis process with use cases. By that, they mean that developers should begin the analysis process by interviewing end users, perusing the basic legacy system documentation, etc. and creating from those interviews and documents the use cases that drive the class model development as well as the other models of the system. Dobing and Parsons (2006) propose that Use Case Narratives, which are written descriptions of Use Cases, are also heavily employed by developers to aid in assembling and understanding Use Case Diagrams.

Activity diagrams model the flow of control through activities in a system and, as such, are really just flow charts. In addition, activity diagrams are special instances of statechart diagrams.

State diagrams model state machines. State machines model the transition between states within an object, and the signals or events that trigger or elicit the change in state from one value to another (Booch, Rumbaugh and Jacobson, 1999). For example, a change in air temperature triggers a thermostat to activate a heating or cooling system that regulates the temperature in a room or building. A rise in air temperature in this case would be sensed by the thermostat and would cause the cooling system to change states from inactive (or idle) to active, and begin the cooling process. Once the ideal temperature is reached, the thermostat would sense that and trigger a state change in the cooling system back to inactive.

Interaction Diagrams are intended to depict communications, such as messages and events between and among objects. UML 2.X substantially enhanced flow of control in Interaction Diagrams over UML 1.X. The old isomorphic Sequence and Collaboration Diagrams from UML 1.X have been supplemented by two new diagrams -- Interaction Overview Diagrams and Timing Diagrams. Collaboration Diagrams are known as Communication Diagrams in UML 2.X. The four interaction diagrams are briefly described below.

Sequence Diagrams portray and validate in detail the logical steps of use cases (Ambler, 2000). Sequence diagrams depict the time ordering of messages between objects in the system, and as such include lifelines for the objects involved in the sequence as well as the focus of control at points in time (Booch, Rumbaugh and Jacobson, 1999).

Interaction Overview Diagrams are a simplification of and a sub-type of Activity Diagrams. These diagrams can aid the user in understanding the flow of control as a system operates, but they suppress the details of the messages and information the messages pass among objects. These are high level diagrams that are not intended to convey the specifics or details of how a system interacts with other systems or subsystems.

Communication Diagrams stress or depict the items involved in the interactions as opposed to the sequencing and control flows. There is some level of isomorphism present between Communication and Sequence Diagrams because one can easily be converted to the other. However, the mapping is not one to one (a formal isomorphism). In other words, some details can be lost when converting from Sequence Diagrams to Communication Diagrams.

Timing Diagrams are most often used with real-time systems and attempt to convey the timing element related to the massages being passed throughout the system being modeled. Timing Diagrams show a lifeline and the events that occur temporally as the system works at run time. The details of temporal constraints included in messages are the elements highlighted in these diagrams.

2.2   Extensibility Mechanisms

UML is intended to be a fully expressive modeling language. As such, UML possesses a formal grammar, vocabulary, and syntax for expressing the necessary details of the system models through the nine diagramming techniques. Even though UML represents a complete and formal modeling development language, there is no realistic way that it can suffice for all models across all systems.

In order to help deal with the dual problems of the general nature of UML, and the necessity to make it also domain specific, UML 2.X was developed to create a modified version of the language that can extend the language so that it also covers specific domains, rather like SAP's "industry solutions" for customizing their ERP product to specific industries. Similarly, UML allows tool developers to create profiles that might be tailored to a specific type of system, real-time, for example. UML 2.x continues with the three Extensibility mechanisms from UML 1.x While UML provides for four commonly used mechanisms, Specifications, Adornments, Common Divisions, and Extensibility (Booch, Rumbaugh and Jacobson, 1999), we will concern ourselves only with Extensibility for the purposes of this exposition.

Stereotypes

In a basic sense, Stereotypes simply add new "words" to UML's vocabulary. Stereotypes are generally derivations from existing structures already found within UML, but yet are different enough to be specific to a particular context. Booch, Rumbaugh and Jacobson (1999) used the example of modeling exceptions in C++ and Java as classes, with special types of attributes and behaviors.

Tagged Values

Providing information regarding version numbers or releases is an example of tagged values in use (Booch, Rumbaugh and Jacobson, 1999). Tagged values can be added to any UML building block to provide clarity to developers and users during and after the development cycle.

Constraints

Constraints are simply that – constraints. UML allows developers to add constraints to systems that modify or extend rules to apply (or not apply) under conditions and triggers that might be exceptions to those rules.

3   The Current State of UML

3.1   UML's Teen Years: The Positives

The characteristics of UML described in the preceding discussion have helped it gain broad acceptance and support among the developer community. The widespread adoption and use of UML as a primary, modeling language for OO systems development efforts can be seen as at least indirect evidence of the usability of the language in analysis, design, and implementation tasks.

UML presents a standard way of modeling object-oriented systems that enhances systems development efforts, and future enhancements to UML will provide even greater standardization and interoperability. UML also provides a vital and much needed communication connection (Fowler, 2000) between users and designers by incorporating use case modeling and diagramming in its repertoire.

UML can be used with a variety of development methodologies, and is not shackled to only one approach. This can only broaden its appeal and overall usefulness to developers in the industry. In a nutshell, UML has provided some vital and much needed stability in the modeling arena, and the software development community as a whole can only benefit from that (Siau and Cao, 2001; Siau and Loo 2006; Siau and Tian 2009).

Selic, Ramakers, and Kobryn (2002) propose that as information systems become ever more complex, modeling software for constructing understandable representations of those systems will become correspondingly more important for developers in such complex and quickly changing environments. As such, UML is still positioned to provide modeling support for developers. The continuing push toward MDA (Model-Driven Architecture) is evidence that, if a developer wishes, executable models are ever closer and more practical.

3.2   UML's Teen Years: the Negatives

Use cases are more process than object-oriented. Thus, the use case-centric approach has been criticized because it takes a process-oriented rather than an object-oriented view of system. This is a point of controversy among researchers and developers alike. Dobing and Parsons (2000) go so far as to propose that since use cases, and resulting use case diagrams, are process-oriented, their role in object-oriented systems development should be questioned, and possibly removed from use in OO development methods for that very reason.

However, since nearly all businesses are process-oriented, or at least are seen that way by most end users, it might be desirable, even necessary, for developers to capture essential end-user requirements by means of their process-based descriptions of the tasks that they and the system must perform. Other proposals to extend UML include the one by Tan, Alter, and Siau (2011). They propose that service responsibility table be used to supplement UML in system analysis. Another proposal is by Siau and Tan (2006) to use cognitive mapping techniques to supplement UML.

In addition, UML has been criticized for being overly complex, too complex for mere mortals to understand or learn to use in a reasonable time (Siau and Cao 2001). Some research has been done with regard to complexity. Rossi and Brinkkemper's (1996) study established a set of metrics for measuring diagram complexity, while Siau and Cao (2001) apply the metrics to UML and other modeling techniques. Their results indicated that although none of the individual UML diagrams is more complex than those used in other techniques, UML as a whole is much more complex. Since UML 2.0 was released in 2005, the language reached new levels of complexity.

Siau, Erickson, and Lee (2005), extending the work of Siau and Cao (2001), argue that there is a different between theoretical and practical complexity. Siau and Cao (2001) study the theoretical complexity of UML. In practice, not all the constructs will be used and some constructs are more important than others. Therefore, the practical complexity of UML is not as great as that computed by Siau and Cao (2001).

However, Duddy (2002) takes a more pessimistic view of both current and future versions of UML. He believes that even though UML 2.X provides coverage for development tools and paradigms currently in use, there is no way that it can provide support for emerging application development approaches or tools, such as application servers, loosely coupled messaging, and Web services. To be fair, however, it is also somewhat unrealistic to expect any tool to be a panacea for whatever methodologies, approaches or paradigms capture the attention of developers at any given point in time.

Finally, with the appearance of aspect-oriented programming, it is entirely possible that the entire object-oriented approach could be supplanted with a new paradigm. If that were to happen, it might become problematic in that UML is constrained by its limited extensibility mechanisms. In other words, we must ask whether or not UML is robust enough to adapt, or be adapted to a radically new paradigm?

3.3   UML's Teen Years: Growing Pains and Acne

UML's complexity discussed above means one of two things: companies considering the use of UML will either have to provide extensive (that is, expensive) training if they plan to develop in house, or they will have to hire UML trained (that is, also expensive) consultants to carry out their systems development efforts. Either way, this indicates that UML-based systems development projects will probably not get any less expensive in the future. However, the same criticism could be leveled at most other modeling tools as well.

As evidenced by several research streams since UML 2.0 was released, many developers and projects make use of UML simply as a post hoc documentation tool (Dobing and Parsons, 2005, Erickson & Siau, 2008). This basically means that there is a dichotomous split between two different types of UML users, those who support

MDA and fully executable modeling, and those who use UML simply as a documentation tool. These behaviors beg the following question: if most systems developers do not use many of the features and capabilities of UML, is it worthwhile to maintain in the language those capabilities and features that are rarely used? Only research into the issue will be able to answer that question. For more information regarding this issue see Siau and Halpin (2001).

None of this should be surprising, since no modeling tool will be adopted by everyone. However, a critical point here is the middle group, those that use UML, but not in a formal fashion, may do so by changing the diagramming techniques as they feel necessary in the pursuit of their projects. Valid questions are, do they not fully use the capabilities of UML because the tools are too expensive, because fully using UML is too complex, or for any of a variety of other reasons?

While these questions and suppositions are based on anecdotal evidence, at least one highlights an issue with UML. Do developers feel that UML is too complex for them to use easily? If the development tool is extremely difficult to use, then it appears that perhaps more effort is expended toward understanding and using the tools than toward developing the system, which is the primary goal in the first place. If so, and this would need research, then does or will future versions of UML be improvements from a usage perspective?

The paper by Siau and Tian (2009) points out some of the human factor issues in UML graphical notations. Human factor studies seem necessary to evaluate the usability of many of the UML constructs and propose modifications to the existing UML constructs to make them more useable and user friendly.

4   Conclusions

Neither UML nor any other modeling language, development method, or methodology has proven to be a panacea for the Analysis, Design, and Implementation of information systems. As suggested by Brooks (1987), this is not surprising because the inherent, essential characteristics of software development make it a fundamentally complex activity. UML is not perfect but it integrates many important software engineering practices that are important enhancements to systems development, and it does so in a way that, if not clear to everyone, is at least enlightening to developers.

Finally, looking back at the past 40 years of systems development chaos and woes, it appears that UML can and should be seen, problems notwithstanding, as one of the most important innovations in systems development since the advent of the structured approaches.

References

1. Ambler, S.: How the UML Models Fit Together (2000),
   http://www.sdmagazine.com/articles/2000/003/003z/003z1.htmp?
   topic=uml
2. Booch, G., Rumbaugh, J., Jacobson, I.: The Unified Modeling Language User Guide. Addison-Wesley, MA (1999)

3. Brooks, F.: No Silver Bullet: Essence and Accidents of Software Engineering. IEEE Computer 20(4), 10–19 (1987)
4. Dobing, B., Parsons, J.: Understanding the Role of Use Cases in UML: A Review and Research Agenda. Journal of Database Management 11(4), 28–36 (2000)
5. Dobing, B., Parsons, B.: How UML is Used. Communications of the ACM 49(5), 109–113 (2006)
6. Duddy, K.: UML2 Must Enable a Family of Languages. Communications of the ACM 45(11), 73–75 (2002)
7. Erickson, J., Siau, K.: Theoretical and Practical Complexity of Modeling Methods. Communications of the ACM 50(8), 46–51 (2007)
8. Fowler, M.: Why Use the UML? (2000),
    `http://www.sdmagazine.com/articles/2000/003/003z/003z3.htmp?`
    `topic=uml`
9. Kobryn, C.: What to Expect from UML 2.0. SD Times (2002)
10. Lago, P.: Rendering Distributed Systems in UML. In: Siau, K., Halpin, T. (eds.) Unified Modeling Language: Systems Analysis, Design, and Development Issues. Idea Group Publishing, Hershey (2000)
11. Mellor, S.: Make Models Be Assets. Communications of the ACM 45(11), 76–78 (2002)
12. Miller, J.: What UML Should Be. Communications of the ACM 45(11), 67–69 (2002)
13. Pilone, D., Pitman, N.: UML 2.0 in a Nutshell. O'Reilly Media (2005)
14. Pooley, R., Stevens, P.: Using UML: Software Engineering with Objects and Components. Addison Wesley Longman Limited, Harlow (1999)
15. Rossi, M., Brinkkemper, S.: Complexity Metrics for Systems Development Methods and Techniques. Information Systems 21(2), 209–227 (1996)
16. Selic, B., Ramackers, G., Kobryn, C.: Evolution, Not Revolution. Communications of the ACM 45(11), 70–72 (2002)
17. Siau, K., Cao, Q.: Unified Modeling Language - A Complexity Analysis. Journal of Database Management 12(1), 26–34 (2001)
18. Siau, K., Erickson, J., Lee, L.: Theoretical versus Practical Complexity: The Case of UML. Journal of Database Management 16(3), 40–57 (2005)
19. Siau, K., Lee, L.: Are Use Case and Class Diagrams Complementary in Requirements Analysis? – An Experimental Study on Use Case and Class Diagrams in UML. Requirements Engineering 9(4), 229–237 (2004)
20. Siau, K., Loo, P.: Identifying Difficulties in Learning UML. Information Systems Management 23(3), 43–51 (2006)
21. Siau, K., Halpin, T.: Unified Modeling Language: Systems Analysis, Design, and Development Issues. Idea Group Publishing, Hershey (2001)
22. Siau, K., Tan, X.: Using Cognitive Mapping Techniques to Supplement UML and UP in Information Requirements Determination. Journal of Computer Information Systems 46(5), 59–66 (2006)
23. Siau, K., Tian, Y.: A Semiotics Analysis of UML Graphical Notations. Requirements Engineering 14(1), 15–26 (2009)
24. Sieber, T., Siau, K., Nah, F., Sieber, M.: SAP Implementation at the University of Nebraska. Journal of Information Technology Cases and Applications 2(1), 41–72 (2000)
25. Tan, X., Alter, S., Siau, K.: Using Service Responsibility Tables to Supplement UML in Analyzing e-Service Systems. Decision Support Systems 51(3), 350–360 (2011)
26. Zhao, L., Siau, K.: Component-Based Development Using UML. Communications of the AIS 9, 207–222 (2002)

Evaluation of System Engineers' Intellectual Productivity Focusing on Coding Procedures in Application Development Tools

Ryo Hirano, Yohei Nakamura, and Miwa Nakanishi

Keio University, Yokohama, Japan
ryohirano.dol@a5.keio.jp,
miwa_nakanishi@ae.keio.ac.jp

Abstract. In this study, we construct a method for evaluating thinking and judgment as intellectual productivity of system engineers, with a particular focus on a supporting system that the engineers engaged in software development. This method can be applied in two ways. The first application is an approach to evaluate the skill of system engineers. This method can not only evaluate the engineer's aptitude by scoring intellectual productivities but can also analyse tendencies related to the skill of system engineers by using proportions of each control processes and time-series graphs. The second application is an approach to improve the tools and manuals of the development environment. By comparing time-series graphs of the thinking process with operating logs, we can identify the specific point where system engineers have fallen into scrambled control processes so that we can specifically identify the problem in the corresponding instructions and manuals, which should result in improvements in development environment tools.

Keywords: Intellectual productivity, system engineers, application development tools

1 Introduction

Currently, from control systems for massive plants to the applications of portable information terminals, the occurrence of systems that operate using software is increasing explosively. Accuracy and speed are necessary in many software development cases. As a consequence, the burden on developers who are engaged in software development is also progressively increasing.

Research on the thinking and judgment of system operators, such as plant operators or stock traders, has largely not been focused on the thinking and judgment of system engineers. The characteristics of system engineers' behind-the-scenes work that does not directly involve users may contribute to the lack of research focused on these system engineers.

In case of software for business, system engineers generally code using development environment tools according to the characteristics of the hardware and operating

S. Yamamoto (Ed.): HIMI/HCII 2013, Part I, LNCS 8016, pp. 305–315, 2013.

systems by referring to the instructions from end users who use the software. Therefore, not only the quality of instructions but also the usability of the development
environment tools and its manuals significantly influence the performance of system
engineers.

Consequently, in this study, we construct a method for evaluating the thinking and
judgment as intellectual productivity of system engineers, with emphasis on supporting system that the engineers engaged in software development.

2   Experiment

First, we conducted an experiment to obtain operating logs to estimate the intellectual
productivity of system engineers by defining as data the operating logs recorded when
system engineers write code using development environment tools.

2.1   Task

We imposed the task of coding on the subjects in order to construct functions, as required by the instructions, using development environment tools for software development, which were installed on small business terminals. The subjects performed the
task on notebook PCs (Dell XPS L502X) while referring to printed instructions.
While coding, the subjects were allowed to refer to the manuals for the development
environment tool on a tablet PC (Apple iPad).

First, in order to adjust to the development environment tools, the subject performed a task for learning. The task for learning was a task in which the subject coded
the details of the software from the state in which the framework of the software (such
as the screen structure) was already completed in the development environment tool.
The subjects performed this task while referring to the manuals until the task was
completed. The subjects then performed practice tasks. They coded frameworks and
details from scratch on the development environment tool while referring to the
instructions on a tablet PC.

2.2   Measurement

While the subjects were performing the tasks, we recorded their operating logs. We
used software (ADGRec_120F) to capture the subjects' screens in order to record
their operations in a time series. In addition, we recorded the subjects' hand movements and facial directions using an overhead video camera. We analysed the animation captured by the screen-capturing software and output the results as operating-log
data. We output the operating logs by 65 fp (per 0.5 sec) because we recorded the
videos at 130 fp. An example of an operating log is shown in Table 1.

Table 1. Sample operating logs

Initiation frame	Termination frame	Initiation time	Termimation time	Btrate (kbps)	Frame size	E/F
0	64	00:00.0	00:00.5	5673.152	354	16.03
65	129	00:00.5	00:01.0	2098.528	131	16.02
130	194	00:01.0	00:01.5	5647.84	352	16.05
195	259	00:01.5	00:02.0	2810.88	175	16.06
260	324	00:02.0	00:02.5	6338.912	396	16.01
325	389	00:02.5	00:03.0	2810.88	175	16.06
390	454	00:03.0	00:03.5	5663.904	353	16.05
455	519	00:03.5	00:04.0	2832.224	177	16
520	584	00:04.0	00:04.5	5276.992	329	16.04
585	649	00:04.5	00:05.0	2464.096	154	16
650	714	00:05.0	00:05.5	7183.104	448	16.03
715	779	00:05.5	00:06.0	3068.448	191	16.07
780	844	00:06.0	00:06.5	6689.568	418	16
845	909	00:06.5	00:07.0	4254.016	265	16.05
910	974	00:07.0	00:07.5	6815.904	425	16.04
975	1039	00:07.5	00:08.0	3780.64	236	16.02
1040	1104	00:08.0	00:08.5	7353.152	459	16.02
1105	1169	00:08.5	00:09.0	4830.912	301	16.05
1170	1234	00:09.0	00:09.5	7850.144	490	16.02
1235	1299	00:09.5	00:10.0	3757.376	234	16.06
1300	1364	00:10.0	00:10.5	7313.376	457	16
1365	1429	00:10.5	00:11.0	5097.568	318	16.03
1430	1494	00:11.0	00:11.5	7568.544	473	16
1495	1559	00:11.5	00:12.0	3846.88	240	16.03
1560	1624	00:12.0	00:12.5	8541.184	533	16.02
1625	1689	00:12.5	00:13.0	4070.88	254	16.03
1690	1754	00:13.0	00:13.5	3524.48	220	16.02
1755	1819	00:13.5	00:14.0	7781.216	486	16.01
1820	1884	00:14.0	00:14.5	3495.712	218	16.04
1885	1949	00:14.5	00:15.0	6138.592	383	16.03

2.3 Participants

The subjects were five students who had elemental knowledge of coding but had no experience in using the development environment tool used in this experiment.

2.4 Ethics

We obtained informed consent of the individuals who agreed to participate in this experiment.

3 Analysis

3.1 Division into Elements and Classification of Operating Logs

We extracted the operations of the subjects from the operating logs. As a result, 45 types of operations were identified, and we found that coding was proceeded by a combination of these operations. We therefore classified the operations into eight groups, from A to H, according to the purpose of the operation.

Group A (Stopped State). In group-A operations, the subject did not move the pointer of the mouse and did not refer to instructions or manuals.

Group B (Moving of the Pointer of the Mouse). In group-B operations, the subject moved the pointer of the mouse.

Group C (Referring to Manuals or Instructions). In group-C operations, the subject referred to manuals or instructions.

Group D (Adding or Deleting Something). In group-D operations, the subject's purpose of operation was adding or deleting new screens, variables or files.

Group E (Choosing Menus). In group-E operations, the subject's purpose of operation was choosing various menus on the screen.

Group F (Editing Text). In group-F operations, the subject's purpose of operation was to edit the text of a name of an added screen, variable or file.

Group G (Moving Something on Screen). In group-G operations, the subject's purpose of operation was to move objects on the screen.

Group H (Configuring Properties of Software). In group-H operations, the subject's purpose of operation was to modify configurations involved with the behaviour of the software when the software was practically activated.

Table 2 shows an example of an operating log from Table 1 to which the eight types of classifications were applied.

Table 2. Eight types classification of a sample operating logs

Initiation frame	Termination fram	Initiation time	Termination time	Btrate (kbps)	Frame size	E/F	The name of operation	The number of operatic	The name of
0	64	00:00.0	00:00.5	5673.152	354	16.03	指示書参照		3.2 C
65	129	00:00.5	00:01.0	2098.528	131	16.02			3.2 C
130	194	00:01.0	00:01.5	5647.84	352	16.05			3.2 C
195	259	00:01.5	00:02.0	2810.88	175	16.06			3.2 C
260	324	00:02.0	00:02.5	6338.912	396	16.01		1	3.2 C
325	389	00:02.5	00:03.0	2810.88	175	16.06	指示書参照		3.2 C
390	454	00:03.0	00:03.5	5663.904	353	16.05	マウスの移動		2 B
455	519	00:03.5	00:04.0	2832.224	177	16			2 B
520	584	00:04.0	00:04.5	5276.992	329	16.04	マウスの移動		2 B
585	649	00:04.5	00:05.0	2464.096	154	16	新規画面作成		4.1 D
650	714	00:05.0	00:05.5	7183.104	448	16.03			4.1 D
715	779	00:05.5	00:06.0	3068.448	191	16.07			4.1 D
780	844	00:06.0	00:06.5	6689.568	418	16			4.1 D
845	909	00:06.5	00:07.0	4254.016	265	16.05	指示書参照		4.1 D
910	974	00:07.0	00:07.5	6815.904	425	16.04	指示書参照		3.2 C
975	1039	00:07.5	00:08.0	3780.64	236	16.02			3.2 C
1040	1104	00:08.0	00:08.5	7353.152	459	16.02	指示書参照		3.2 C
1105	1169	00:08.5	00:09.0	4830.912	301	16.05	マウスの移動		2 B
1170	1234	00:09.0	00:09.5	7850.144	490	16.02	マウスの移動		2 B
1235	1299	00:09.5	00:10.0	3757.376	234	16.06	新規画面作成		4.1 D
1300	1364	00:10.0	00:10.5	7313.376	457	16			4.1 D
1365	1429	00:10.5	00:11.0	5097.568	318	16.03	新規画面作成		4.1 D
1430	1494	00:11.0	00:11.5	7568.544	473	16	マウスの移動		2 B
1495	1559	00:11.5	00:12.0	3846.88	240	16.03	マウスの移動		2 B
1560	1624	00:12.0	00:12.5	8541.184	533	16.02	指示書参照		3.2 C
1625	1689	00:12.5	00:13.0	4070.88	254	16.03	新規画面作成		4.1 D
1690	1754	00:13.0	00:13.5	3524.48	220	16.02			4.1 D
1755	1819	00:13.5	00:14.0	7781.216	486	16.01	新規画面作成		4.1 D
1820	1884	00:14.0	00:14.5	3495.712	218	16.04	マウスの移動		2 B
1885	1949	00:14.5	00:15.0	6138.592	383	16.03	画面削除		4.5 D

3.2   Extraction of the Characteristic Sequences of Operations

Next, to read the subjects' process of thinking during the task, we focused on the patterns of sequences of the groups of operations. Hollnagel (E. Hollnagel, 1994) [1] has proposed a contextual control model (COCOM) that can divide workers' working situations into four phases depending on the degree of understanding. The four phases of situations that occurred during working were defined as follows:

1. Scrambled control mode. In the scrambled control mode, the choice of the next action is basically irrational or random, which is typically the case when situation assessment is deficient or paralysed and, accordingly, little or no correlation between the situation and the action is observed. The scrambled control mode includes the extreme situation of zero control.
2. Opportunistic control mode. In the opportunistic control mode, the salient features of the current context determine the next action. Planning or anticipation is limited, perhaps because the context is not clearly understood or because the available time is limited.

3. Tactical control mode. The tactical control mode corresponds to situations where performance more or less follows a known procedure or rule. Planning is of limited scope or range, and the needs taken into account may sometimes be ad hoc.
4. Strategic control mode. In the strategic control mode, the joint system has a wider time horizon and can look ahead to higher-level goals. The dominant features of this situation or the interface therefore have less influence on the choice of action.

According to the previous definitions, we divided the subjects' process of thinking into four phases:

1. Scrambled control process. In this control process, subjects are alternately referring to instructions and manuals, which means that the subjects do not understand what to do and that operations have no progress. The sequences of operations like this situation were categorized as scrambled control processes.
2. Opportunistic control process. In this control process, operations semantically unrelated to each other are being repeated, which means the subjects are operating in a haphazard manner. The sequences of operations like this situation were categorized as opportunistic control processes.
3. Tactical control process. In this control process, although operations semantically related to each other are being performed, operations are interrupted as the subjects refer to instructions or manuals, which means that, when the subjects' perspectives of what operations to perform are not clear, they are performing operations that they could understand one-by-one. The sequences of operations like this situation were categorized as tactical control processes.
4. Strategic control process. In this control process, subjects are correctly performing operations semantically related to each other without referring to instructions or manuals during operations, which means that the subjects' perspectives of what operations to perform are clear and the operations are being conducted. The sequences of operations like this situation were categorized as strategic control processes.

The specific patterns of the sequences of operations extracted for each of the four phases were as follows:

1. Sequences of operation groups that correspond to scrambled control processes

C→A. In this pattern, subjects fall into a stopped state despite having acquired information by referring to instructions or manuals.

A→B→A. In this pattern, subjects lose their focus and fall into a stopped state again, even though the subjects move the pointer of the mouse to perform some task after the stopped state.

C→B→A. In this pattern, subjects lose their purpose and fall into a stopped state; however, after acquiring information by referring to instructions or manuals, the subjects move the pointer of the mouse according to the acquired information.

B→A→B→A. In this pattern, subjects repeatedly move the pointer of the mouse and fall into a stopped state. The situation where operations of group D~H emerge after the movement of the pointer of the mouse has changed to a stopped state is not considered a scrambled control process because the subjects are judged to be thinking of the next operation during the transition from the movement of the mouse to the stopped state.

2. Sequences of operation groups that correspond to opportunistic control processes

B→E→B→E. In this pattern, subjects repeatedly move the pointer of the mouse and choose menus. This pattern is regarded as a situation where subjects are attempting to find clues to solutions by clicking somewhere without understanding what operations should be performed next.

B→A→E. In this pattern, subjects fall into a stopped state after moving the pointer of the mouse and choosing menus. In this pattern, subjects move the pointer of the mouse to perform a task but lose their purpose along the way and choose menus that appear to be related to the operation, or alternatively, the subjects move the pointer of the mouse to choose menus but lose their confidence along the way with respect to whether the choice is correct, and after having given the matter some thought, they finally choose a menu based on their estimation that the operation is correct.

3. Sequences of operation groups that correspond to tactical control processes

B→E, C→B→E, B→C→E. In these patterns, subjects choose menus after having moved the pointer of the mouse. This pattern is different from the pattern of B→A→E in opportunistic control processes in that a series of operations from moving the pointer of the mouse to choosing menus emerges only once, and then operations of group D~H are performed. The case where subjects refer to instructions or manuals before performing or while performing operations of group D~H is also included in these sequences.

B→G. In this pattern, subjects move objects after having moved the pointer of the mouse. In many cases, the text related to the objects is edited, which means the purpose of the operation has not yet been accomplished using this pattern.

B→D, B→D→B→D, C→B→D, B→C→D, C→A→B→D. In these patterns, the subjects change operations without editing variables or newly added files after having moved the pointer of the mouse, or the subjects repeatedly move the pointer of the mouse and add the necessary amount of variables. The case where the subjects refer to instructions or manuals before or while performing these operations is also included in these sequences.

4. Sequences of operation groups that correspond to strategic control processes

B→F, C→F, C→B→F, B→C→F. In these patterns, subjects edit the name of variables or files after having moved the pointer of the mouse, and they do so without falling into a stopped state. The case where subjects refer to instructions or manuals in order to obtain information before editing is also included in these sequences.

B→G→B→F, B→D→B→F. In these patterns, subjects successively add and edit objects or subjects edit objects after moving them. These patterns are characteristic sequences of operations that commonly emerged in subjects' operating logs.

B→H, C→H, C→B→H, B→C→H. In these patterns, subjects configure properties of software after moving the pointer of the mouse. The case where the subjects refer to instructions or manuals in order to obtain information before editing is also included in these sequences.

By searching for patterns of sequences of operation groups that correspond to the four previously described phases in the subjects' operating logs, we visualized changes in the subjects' thinking processes during the task. Table 3 provides an example of an operating log; strategic control processes are marked as green, tactical control processes as blue, opportunistic control processes as yellow and scrambled control processes as red.

Table 3. Example of a classified operating log

Initiation frame	Termination fram	Initiation time	Termination time	Btrate (kbps)	Frame size	E/F	The name of operation	The number of operation	The name of
37245	37309	04:46.5	04:47.0	3493.536	218	16.03	マウスの移動	2	B
37310	37374	04:47.0	04:47.5	7535.584	470	16.03		2	B
37375	37439	04:47.5	04:48.0	3475.36	217	16.02		2	B
37440	37504	04:48.0	04:48.5	7536.544	471	16	マウスの移動	2	B
37505	37569	04:48.5	04:49.0	4003.936	250	16.02	BHT画面切り替え	5.01	E
37570	37634	04:49.0	04:49.5	7002.208	437	16.02	マウスの移動	2	B
37635	37699	04:49.5	04:50.0	5118.656	319	16.05		2	B
37700	37764	04:50.0	04:50.5	8427.936	526	16.02	マウスの移動	2	B
37765	37829	04:50.5	04:51.0	4102.72	256	16.03	入力項目情報呼び出し	5.11	E
37830	37894	04:51.0	04:51.5	4681.248	292	16.03	マウスの移動	2	B
37895	37959	04:51.5	04:52.0	8992.352	562	16		2	B
37960	38024	04:52.0	04:52.5	3742.752	233	16.06		2	B
38025	38089	04:52.5	04:53.0	6853.12	428	16.01		2	B
38090	38154	04:53.0	04:53.5	3347.84	209	16.02		2	B
38155	38219	04:53.5	04:54.0	7263.68	453	16.02		2	B
38220	38284	04:54.0	04:54.5	3332.096	208	16.02		2	B
38285	38349	04:54.5	04:55.0	6827.744	426	16.03		2	B
38350	38414	04:55.0	04:55.5	3833.792	239	16.04	マウスの移動	2	B
38415	38479	04:55.5	04:56.0	6832.288	427	16	表示モード変更	8.17	H
38480	38544	04:56.0	04:56.5	3355.872	209	16.06		8.17	H
38545	38609	04:56.5	04:57.0	7072.576	442	16		8.17	H
38610	38674	04:57.0	04:57.5	3593.984	224	16.04		8.17	H
38675	38739	04:57.5	04:58.0	7506.24	469	16		8.17	H
38740	38804	04:58.0	04:58.5	3621.984	226	16.03		8.17	H
38805	38869	04:58.5	04:59.0	6306.624	394	16.01	表示モード変更	8.17	H
38870	38934	04:59.0	04:59.5	3477.12	217	16.02	マウスの移動	2	B
38935	38999	04:59.5	05:00.0	6685.792	417	16.03		2	B
39000	39064	05:00.0	05:00.5	3710.88	231	16.06		2	B
39065	39129	05:00.5	05:01.0	7608.672	475	16.02		2	B
39130	39194	05:01.0	05:01.5	3634.688	227	16.01		2	B
39195	39259	05:01.5	05:02.0	6689.344	418	16	マウスの移動	2	B

4   Results and Discussion

4.1   Evaluation of Intellectual Productivity in a Time Series

First, we paid attention to how thinking processes changed between the four phases while subjects were performing the task. Figures 1 and 2 represent changes in the thinking processes of subject A, who completed the task in the shortest time, and subject B, who required the longest amount of time to complete the task. The task

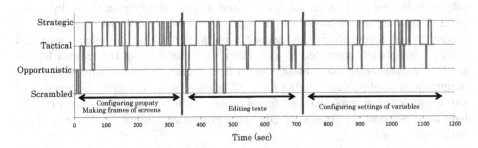

Fig. 1. Changes in subject A's thinking process

included three subtasks, and red lines on the graph indicate the initiation and the termination of the subtasks.

According to the changes in subject A's thinking process, changes between strategic and tactical control processes were frequently observed, and scrambled control processes were only observed when subject A started to perform the task and was configuring properties.

The operations in the first subtask mainly involved adding new screens and editing the names of objects. However, in addition to these operations, subject A was configuring the settings related to the screen's transitions that are normally an operation included in the second subtask, which means this subject had clear perspectives about the whole task. Although subject A exhibited scrambled control processes at the beginning of the task, the subject generally performed this subtask while changing thinking processes between strategic and tactical control processes.

The operations involved in the second subtask were mainly the addition of new objects onto the screen and the editing of text. In this subtask, subject A fell into scrambled control processes several times but immediately returned to strategic or tactical control processes.

In the third subtask, the subjects had to configure properties in detail, such as a setting for error control after adding variables or files. However, this subject A did not fall into a scrambled control process during this subtask and performed strategic control processes most of the time throughout this subtask.

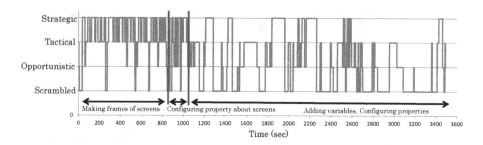

Fig. 2. Changes in subject B's thinking process

According to Fig. 2, which shows the changes in subject B's thinking process, this subject was more susceptible to falling into a scrambled control process than was subject A. During the first subtask, most of the subject's time was occupied by strategic and tactical control processes, although scrambled control processes were observed several times. During the second subtask, the subject discretely performed settings semantically unrelated to each other while configuring the settings for the screen's transitions. In this subtask, subject B frequently fell into a scrambled or opportunistic control process. During the third subtask, subject B again frequently fell into a scrambled or opportunistic control process, which means this subject did not have clear perspectives about configuring the properties. Ultimately, this subject did not complete the task.

When we compared the thinking processes between two typical subjects, we found that the thinking process of the subject with high task performance was mostly occupied by strategic or tactical control processes and that the subject tended to immediately recover from opportunistic or scrambled control processes to strategic control processes. In contrast, the thinking process of the subject with low task performance was found to frequently change between four phases of thinking processes; in addition, after this subject's thought process fell into a scrambled control process, the time required to return to a strategic control process was relatively long.

4.2   Qualitative Evaluation of Intellectual Productivity

We calculated the total time and proportion of the four phases (i.e. strategic, tactical, opportunistic and scrambled control processes) in order to qualitatively show the subjects' thinking processes during the task. Figures 3 and 4 show the results for subject A, whom we discussed in the preceding section.

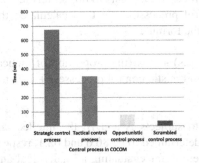

Fig. 3. Total time of each control process for subject A

Fig. 4. Proportion of each control process for subject A

The length of each control process in total time followed the order strategic control process > tactical control process > opportunistic control process > scrambled control process, and approximately 90 percent of the total time was spent in a strategic or tactical control process. On the basis of these results, subject A was performing the task with a clear perspective of the operations and rarely fell into a scrambled control process. Figures 5 and 6 show the results for subject B, whom we discussed in the preceding section.

The time spent in a scrambled control process was the longest and occupied approximately 40 percent of the total time. On the basis of these results, subject B faced numerous situations where he performed a task without understanding the operations necessary for completing the task.

We succeeded in quantitatively comparing the intellectual productivities of two subjects by calculating the proportion of their thinking processes during a task.

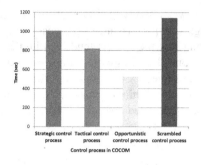

Fig. 5. Total time of each control process for subject B

Fig. 6. Proportion of each control process for subject B

Further, we attempted to score the intellectual productivities in order to directly evaluate both subjects' intellectual productivities. We assigned 4 points to strategic control processes, 3 points to tactical control processes, 2 points to opportunistic control processes and 1 point to scrambled control processes. We then calculated the intellectual productivity values on the basis of the formula:

4 × (the proportion of strategic control processes) + 3 × (the proportion of tactical control processes) + 2 × (the proportion of opportunistic control processes) + 1 × (the proportion of scrambled control processes).

When we applied this numerical formula to subjects A and B, the intellectual-productivity values for subjects A and B were determined to be 86.6 and 62.1, respectively. Thus, we succeeded in developing a method for evaluating an individual and tasks according to purpose by expressing the intellectual productivities using time-series graphs and the proportion of thinking processes using total points. s

5   Conclusions

In this study, we suggested a method for evaluating the thinking and judgment of system engineers who are engaged in software development; that is, a method for measuring their intellectual productivities. This method can express intellectual productivities based on operating logs by indexing different tasks. This method is therefore a simple method that can be applied to practical work.

This method can be applied in two ways. The first application is an approach to evaluate the skill of system engineers. This method can not only evaluate the aptitude by scoring engineers' intellectual productivities but can also analyse the tendencies of the skill of system engineers using the proportions of each control processes and time-series graphs. The results could be applied to effectively educate and train systems engineers. The second application is an approach to improve the tools and manuals of the development environment, i.e. the instructions. By comparing the time-series graphs of thinking processes with operating logs, we can find the point where system engineers fall into scrambled control processes so that we can precisely identify the correlation between the engineer's lack of productivity and the specific point in the instructions and manuals, which could lead to improvements in such documentation.

Reference

1. Hollnagel, E.: Human Reliability Analysis: Context and Control (Computers and People). Academic Press (1994)

Freiform: A SmartPen Based Approach for Creating Interactive Paper Prototypes for Collecting Data

Marcel Klomann and Jan-Torsten Milde

Fulda University of Applied Sciences, Computer Science Department
marcel.klomann@informatik.hs-fulda.de, milde@hs-fulda.de

Abstract. The creation of multi-modal data collection is a complex task for all empirically working scientific disciplines. Currently the data is collected using complex audio-video technology and is then manually processed, quite often in a computer supported way. In this project we developed a system allowing to easily create interactive paper prototypes for collecting data. The systems is based on smart pen technology, which allows the user to simply sketch out the form on paper by defining the field type and the field size. Once the sketch is available on paper, data collection can start. The system runs directly on the smart pen. Collected data will be stored in an XML-based, which can be further processed by external programs.

Keywords: interactive paper prototypes, electronic pen, data collection.

1 Introduction

The creation of multi-modal data collection is a complex task for all empirically working scientific disciplines (e.g. social sciences, psychology, linguistics or educational science). Currently the data is collected using complex audio-video technology and is then manually processed, quite often in a computer supported way. In order to collect the data, complex experimental setups have to be constructed, which are in many ways interfering with actual situation under investigation.

In this project we developed a system allowing to easily create interactive paper prototypes for collecting data. The systems is based on smart pen technology. A smart pen is an "electronic" pen that records it's movements and also creates an audio recording. The pen is equipped with a small text display and is able to play back sound files. The tracking of the pen's movement is realised by a micro pattern, which is printed onto the used paper, which is then analysed by a built in camera of the pen. As such, it becomes possible to store the collected data digitally, while having a paper transscript at same time. Applications for the smart pen, so called penlets, are written in java and are being uploaded onto the pen. A demonstration video of the running system can be found at the our media server[1].

---

[1] ``mms://mediasrv.hs-fulda.de/FBAI/public/MUC2012/
freiform_demo_1080.wmv"

S. Yamamoto (Ed.): HIMI/HCII 2013, Part I, LNCS 8016, pp. 316–321, 2013.

2   Defining Interactive Forms

The *Freiform* application allows to easily sketch out forms for collecting data on paper. Different types of input fields can be defined: text fields, number fields, counting fields, start and stop buttons, timing fields. The user is sketching out tool buttons for drawing the interface of the actual data collecting form.

Fig. 1. A number field containing 4 digits is interpreted as a single value

2.1   Sketching Out the User Interface

In doing so, he is not restricted in any ways, that is, any possible design can be sketched out. The process of creating the data collecting form is a two step process. First a couple of letters or symbols have to be written down. These symbols mark the tool buttons that will be later used to define the actual data collecting interface.

Fig. 2. Startup screen on the pen

The user interface of the Freiform system is maximally reduced, as the electronic pen is only equipped with a single line text display (see figure 2). Navigating through the pen's internal system menu is achieved by pointing the pen at a cursor cross printed onto the paper. Acoustic and visual feedback is given to the user. Starting the Freiform application requires a couple paper clicks.

Once the application is started, no further explicit navigation steps have to be initiated. Instead of providing a complex menu system, we have tried to model an optimal workflow, which will guide the user in an intuive way through the creation process and the data collecting process. Informal usability tests have shown, that users very easily adapted to the proposed interaction concept and were able to use the pen almost without any training.

During the first phase of form creation the user needs to set up the tool buttons for defining the data fields of the actual form. This step is nesseary, as we wanted the system to be as flexible and independent as possible. The user is completely free to use her own language and is able to design the interface using her prefered symbols. This approch allows to design minimal interfaces as well as interfaces with a more detailed design structure. It would have also been possible to print out the tool buttons onto the paper. We put down this approach, as we would to like to support the idea of *sketching out* functional interfaces in this research.

The only limitation to this idea is the design of the user interface on the pen itself. Here textual output had to used for communication, so we had to decide for a system language (currently English). The implementation restrictions make it hard to replace the interface language, as external ressource files are not provided by the smartpen API. Another approach would have been spoken language output through the built in speaker. Again, while this would have supported the workflow and could have lead to a more efficient form design process, yet we discarded this idea. The pen should be used in a non disturbing way, e.g. during an interview session in field work. Acoustic output would have interfered with these kind of delicate research situations.

In the example form we are using letters to mark down the tool buttons. The Freiform system instructs the user to write down the initial letter of an english term describing the tool category. When defining a *label* tool button, the user should write down a capital L (see figure 3).

Fig. 3. Defining a label tool button

Step by step the user has to mark down symbols for all tool buttons. Following the label tool button, the user is asked to define the *text* tool button. Again the inital letter should be used (see figure 4). This process is continued until all tool button are visible.

The user is not restricted to using letters for denoting the tool buttons. Any symbol could be used. In order to identify the end of sketching out a tool button symbol, we needed to define a timeout period. A symbol will be identified by continuously drawing strokes. Once the user stops drawing for more than a second, the strokes will be stored by the system and the user is requested to draw the next tool button. The timeout approach makes it possible to write down words and phrases as part of the user interface. As a result of this implementation, sketching out the tool buttons is very simple and very intuitive.

Fig. 4. Instructions for defining a text field

2.2 Sketching Out the Interactive Form

Once all tool buttons are defined (currently 6 tool buttons are available), the actual data collecting interface can be sketched out. The user clicks onto the tool button he likes to draw and then sketches out the data collecting field. This step is repeated until all fields of the form have been drawn.

In our example form three data fields have been defined: a text field, a number field and a counter field. In addition three labels have been written down, making it easier for the user to identify the semantics associated with a specific data field. These labels are optional.

In order to create a minimal form, only the outline of a data field has to be drawn. The graphical form of the drawing is ignored. Instead its bounding box is calculated. All user input, which is marked down inside this bounding box area will be associated with the data field. In the example an L shaped form is used for the data fields. This form is simple to draw, supports the user during the data collection step and the bounding box of the data field can be easily indentified (see figure 5).

Fig. 5. The final form consists of three labeled fields

More data fields can be added to the form. The system stays in the sketching mode until the user decides to start recording data. In order to get into record mode, the user has to activate the record tool button. It is also possible to return to sketching mode by activating the record button one more time (see figure 6).

Fig. 6. Once the sketch of the form is finished, data can be recorded

2.3   Collecting Data with Interactive Form

At this final step the interactive paper prototyp ist ready to be used. During data collection, the user writes down text into the text fields, sets marks into the counting fields or jots down numbers into the number fields. The pen is able to analyse the data, therefore digitizing it and stores it on the pen. Once the data collecting process is finished, all data can be transfered to a computer. The data is transfered as an XML file, which can easily be processed further by other applications.

In our example form, a counter field had been defined. As the name suggests, counter fields are used to store numerical data, where, in contrast to a number field, the data is stored grafically. The system analyses the user input and tries to identify separate strokes. The visual appearence of the stroke is not relevant. A standard way of marking down counts are simple lines. As can be seen in the figure 7, five strokes have been drawn by the user, four parallel strokes, with one final stroke overlapping all other. Overlapping strokes do not pose any major problems for the system.

Fig. 7. Five strokes insode the count field

Each data field is internally associated with a specific variable holding its current (interpreted) value. As we have put down five strokes inside the area of the counter field, the value amounts to five. Every time a change in value is detected, the current value will be prompted to the user (see figure 8). No acoustic feedback is given here.

The number field is is used to collect numerical data. Here the internal OCR system of the pen is processing the strokes and provides the appropiate digit to the Freifom system. The final field value will be calculated based on these digits

Fig. 8. Counter has value 5

(see figure 1). The text field works similar to the number field. The internal OCR of the pen tries to identify the letters and joins bigger units like words or phrases. Unfortuneatly, the OCR does not work as robust on letters as it does on digits. Even with block letters the recognition is error prone (see figure 9).

Fig. 9. OCR on text field is not really robust

3   Conclusions

The Freiform system allows to easily sketch out interactive paper prototypes. In order to design a data collecting form, the user is requested to draw a number of tool buttons, that will then be used to sketch out the actual data collecting form.

An important feature of the chosen approach is it's very low technological entry point. Writing down notes with a pen is a common scientific technique and is generally accepted. Defining the paper prototype is very simple and does not require a high level of computer skills.

Towards an Ontological Interpretation on the i* Modeling Language Extended with Security Concepts: A Bunge-Wand-Weber Model Perspective

Gen-Yih Liao, Po-Jui Liang, and Li-Ting Huang

Department of Information Management, Chang Gung University, Taiwan, R.O.C.
gyliao@acm.org, ricmailx@gmail.com, lthuang@mail.cgu.edu.tw

Abstract. Goal-oriented requirements engineering can facilitate the elicitation and representation of various types of requirements, including organizational and security requirements. This paper applies the Bunge-Wand-Weber ontological model to analyze and evaluate the security concepts in the extended i* modeling language that has been considered as one of representative methods concerning goal-oriented modeling languages. The findings revealed that among the seventeen terms analyzed, thirteen concepts can be directly mapped to ontological terms. The findings can help in future works develop modeling rules to assist security requirements engineering.

Keywords: i* modeling language, security requirement, Bunge-Wand-Weber ontological model, ontological analysis.

1 Introduction

Goal-oriented requirements engineering can facilitate the elicitation and representation of organizational requirements and security requirements [1, 2]. To specify goals and related concepts, many goal-oriented requirement languages (GRLs) have been proposed [2-5]. The modeling languages offer constructs to specify the agents involved in a modeled domain and the goals that the agents intend to achieve. Among the proposed GRLs, the i* language [5] is considered in this study due to the following rationales. Ongoing academic efforts have succeeded in giving birth to the ITU-I Recommendation Z.151 standard based on the i* language [6]. Furthermore, Elahi et al. enhance the expressiveness by extending the i* modeling language with the concepts of vulnerabilities, attacks, and countermeasures [7]. This integration enables an analyst to simultaneously express concepts with rich vocabulary regarding social characteristics, organizational information needs and security requirements in one modeling framework.

To understand the quality of the representations provided by a modeling language, Wand and Weber propose the Bunge-Wand-Weber (BWW) ontological model to analyze and evaluate conceptual modeling grammars [8, 9]. The BWW model has been applied to evaluate various modeling languages [10-15]. The evaluation results may provide some insights to improve the inspected languages. The effectiveness of ontological evaluations with the BWW model has been empirically validated in the study of Recker et al., which claims that the users of a conceptual modeling language

S. Yamamoto (Ed.): HIMI/HCII 2013, Part I, LNCS 8016, pp. 322–328, 2013.

can perceive ontological deficiencies and the deficiency perceptions of users should negatively be associated with usefulness and ease of use of the language grammars [16]. Accordingly, this study aims to examine the security concepts in the i* modeling framework based on the BWW ontological model. The examined language elements include all of the security elements proposed in [7].

This paper is organized as follows. Section 2 introduces the language elements to be analyzed. Section 3 briefly introduces the BWW ontological model. Section 4 describes the method conducted in the ontological analysis process. Section 5 describes the analysis results and Section 6 proposes some discussions on the results, followed by the conclusion in the last section.

2   Security Elements in the i* Modeling Language

Based on a belief that modeling intentional and social aspects are needed to address the diversity of software systems development, Yu proposed the i* modeling framework in his doctoral dissertation, attempting to reflect the social characteristics of complex software systems in the early phase of requirements engineering [5]. Recently, Elahi et al. incorporate security-related concepts into the i* modeling framework so that analysts can also specify the concepts of vulnerabilities, attacks, effects of vulnerabilities, and impacts of countermeasures [7]. Table 1 lists the seven security elements examined in this study.

Table 1. Security langue constructs and the definitions used in the ontological analysis

Construct	Definition
Malicious actor (attacker)	A specialization of actors that has malicious intentional elements inside its boundary
Malicious task	The necessary steps to fulfill a malicious goal via resource consumption
Malicious goal	A subtype of goals; also a supertype of malicious hard goals and malicious softgoals
Malicious hard goal	A subtype of hard goals that an analyst considers as malicious
Malicious softgoal	A subtype of softgoals that an analyst considers as malicious
Countermeasure	A protection mechanism employed to secure the system planned
Vulnerability	A weakness or a backdoor in IT systems
Vulnerability of resource	A state of a resource in which, while executing a task employing the resource, the system planned might be susceptible
Vulnerability of task	A condition caused by executing a task might render the system planned susceptible
Vulnerability effect	A relation between a vulnerability and a resource, a task, or a hard goal, indicating that the intentional element might be impacted once the vulnerability is exploited
Vulnerability effect on resources	A relation between a vulnerability and a resource, indicating that the resource might be impacted once the vulnerability is exploited
Vulnerability effect on tasks	A relation between a vulnerability and a task, indicating that the task might be impacted once the vulnerability is exploited

Table 1. (*continued*)

Vulnerability effect on hard goals	A relation between a vulnerability and a hard goal, indicating that the hard goal might be impacted once the vulnerability is exploited
Exploit link	A relation between a malicious task and vulnerabilities that it exploits
Exploit link with resource's vulnerability	A relation between a malicious task and a vulnerability of a resource that it exploits
Exploit link with task's vulnerability	A relation between a malicious task and a vulnerability of a task that it exploits
Impact of security countermeasures	A relation between a countermeasure and a malicious task, indicating the protection effect of the countermeasure against the malicious task

3   The Bunge-Wand-Weber Ontological Model

To evaluate the grammars of conceptual modeling languages, Wand and Weber propose a set of the ontological (real-world) constructs [8, 9] derived from Bunge's ontology [21, 22]. The ontological model, often referred to as the Bunge-Wand-Weber (BWW) model, provides a way to determine whether a conceptual modeling grammar contains all the necessary constructs needed to represent any phenomenon in the real world, and whether any grammatical construct can be unambiguously interpreted [8]. Thing and transformation, for example, are two primitive ontological constructs among the proposed constructs. A thing is the elementary unit in the BWW ontological model that argues that the real world is made of things. A transformation is a mapping from a domain comprising states to a co-domain comprising states [8, 9]. Readers are referred to their original publications [8] due to the space limitation.

The BWW model has been used in the literature to analyze existing conceptual modeling grammars. After applying the BWW model to examine the use case modeling grammar, Irwin and Turk suggested that the grammar should be considered as ontologically incomplete with regard to representing the system structure. Furthermore, construct overload exists. For example, an association in class diagrams can be mapped to a mutual property of two things, but an association in use case diagrams corresponds to a binding mutual property of an external entity and the system [12]. Green, et al. conducted an ontological analysis on four dominating interoperability standards and concluded that ebXML BPSS achieved the advantage over other standards in terms of ontological expressiveness. However, the findings also revealed that some fundamental BWW concepts (e.g., thing and system environment) remained unable to represent in all the standards examined [13].

4   The Method

Ontological analysis is often linked with the subjectivity issue [17]. To overcome the potential threat to the validity of the ontological analysis, this study employed the three-step methodology proposed in [17]. First, two authors separately read the language specification and mapped the examined language constructs to the BWW constructs. Next, the two authors who participated in the previous step met to discuss and defend their interpretations, which led to an agreed second draft version. Finally, the second draft version was inspected by a third author, who then independently reviewed and commented on the draft. This paper presents the results that have achieved consensus among all of the three authors.

5   Results

Our ontological analysis begins with identifying things (in BWW). Resources are defined in the i* language as physical or informational entities representing assets that are of value to actors and to attackers. Another characteristic of resources is that further decomposition on a resource can only derive resources. Since a thing (in BWW) is defined as an elementary unit in the modeled world, therefore, this study suggests mapping resources to things. Based on the same line of reasoning, an actor and an attacker are both considered as things (in BWW), because both can be defined as active entities planning and performing activities on resources (e.g., computer systems). This study assumes couplings (in BWW) exist not only between an attacker and the attacked resources but also between an actor and the resources.

The state space of a resource can be composed of secure (recovered) states, vulnerable states, and attacked states. Vulnerability of a resource is therefore treated as a lawful state space (in BWW), which is governed by a law (in BWW) that explains under what circumstances attacks can succeed. Similarly, vulnerability of a task refers to the vulnerable state in which the task is flawed and could be exploited by malicious actors. This study also considers vulnerability of a task as lawful state space (in BWW). Since vulnerability itself is a superclass of vulnerabilities of resources and vulnerabilities of tasks, it is interpreted also as lawful state space (in BWW).

Malicious tasks conducted by an attacker can cause state transitions from vulnerable states to attacked states and therefore are represented with transformations (in BWW). On the other hand, since *countermeasures* either can prevent computer systems from moving into vulnerable states or help attacked targets recover from attacked states, this study also considers countermeasures as transformations (in BWW).

Malicious goals are interpreted as intentional (mental) states that an attacker intends to achieve by conducting malicious tasks. According to the mindset theory of action phases, one undergoes four phases in pursuing goals: the predecisional action phase, the preactional phase, the actional phase, the postactional phase [23]. The theory argues that an individual sets goals in the preactional phase, creates plans to pursue goals in the preactional phase, strives for goals in the actional phase, and evaluates and learns from the overall goal pursuing process in the postactional phase. Please note that, for an attacker, the transition from the actional phase to the postactional phase depends on whether the malicious goals are achieved, which, in turn, is determined by the state of the attacked target. Accordingly, *malicious hard goals* and *softgoals* (and therefore malicious goals) are both interpreted as lawful state spaces (in BWW) governed by the laws that reflect the valuation of the attacker.

Vulnerability effects are interpreted as couplings (in BWW) between a vulnerability and the associated concepts. A *vulnerability effect* of a *resource* R1 on another resource R2 indicates a coupling (in BWW) between R1 and R2, which implies R1 operating in a vulnerable state might impact R2. Since tasks are seen as transformations on (resource) things, a *vulnerability effect on a task* can in effect be interpreted as a vulnerability effect on a resource. Furthermore, a *vulnerability effect of a resource R1 on a hard goal G* indicates there exists a coupling between R1 and the actor (interpreted as a thing in BWW as aforementioned) who sets the goal G. Accordingly, vulnerability effects can be interpreted as couplings (in BWW).

The term *"exploit links with resource' vulnerability"* refers to an association between malicious tasks and the vulnerability of exploited resources. Since vulnerability of resources and malicious tasks are both interpreted in the BWW model, the term "exploit links with resource's vulnerability" is treated a term that combine the meanings of two more primitive terms. This reasoning also applied to the term *"exploit links with task' vulnerability"* which therefore is interpreted in the same way. That is, all of the *exploit link* concepts in Table 2 are interpreted as no direct counterpart (in BWW).

Impact of security countermeasure indicates the semantic relation between malicious tasks and countermeasures. More precisely, the meaning of this term can be reasoned as follows: there exists a countermeasure that can move a (resource) thing from a vulnerable state caused by malicious tasks back to a secure state. Therefore, this term is considered as a term that can be combined from two primitive terms (i.e., malicious task and countermeasure) and has no direct counterpart in the BWW model.

Table 2 lists the ontological interpretation obtained through the analysis.

Table 2. Ontological interpretation on the security concepts in the extended i* language

Construct	Ontological Interpretation
Malicious actor (attacker)	Thing
Malicious task	Transformation (on resource)
Malicious goal	Lawful state space (of attacker)
Malicious hard goal	Lawful state space (of attacker)
Malicious softgoal	Lawful state space (of attacker)
Countermeasure	Transformation (on resource)
Vulnerability	Lawful state space (of resource)
Vulnerability of resource	Lawful state space (of resource)
Vulnerability of task	Lawful state space (of resource)
Vulnerability effect	Coupling
Vulnerability effect on resources	Coupling (between resources)
Vulnerability effect on tasks	Coupling (between resources)
Vulnerability effect on hard goals	Coupling (between resource and actor)
Exploit link	No direct counterpart
Exploit link with resource's vulnerability	No direct counterpart (the relation between malicious tasks and vulnerability of resources)
Exploit link with task's vulnerability	No direct counterpart (the relation between malicious tasks and vulnerability of tasks)
Impact of security countermeasures	No direct counterpart (Combined with malicious task and countermeasure)

6   Discussions

Thirteen terms in Table 2 can be directly map to ontological terms in the BWW model. This table also offers opportunities for further discussions. First, the distinction between hard goals and softgoals is not identified. Since the difference may lie with the goal evaluation process in which one determines whether a specific goal is achieved, future works are suggested to consider interpreting different types of goals as distinct lawful state spaces governed by particular state laws. Second, four occurrences of no direct counterparts were found in the analysis results. These terms add to the size of the vocabulary offered in the extended i* language, which may confuse the beginners learning the language. It would be interesting to examine whether this happens to the users of the extended i* language. Third, it seems difficult to express the distinction between malicious tasks by a malicious outsider and flawed tasks by an inadvertent insider, as long as tasks are modeled as transformations. More research efforts are suggested to undertake to analyze the ontological distinction between the scenarios associated with the two types of risks.

7   Conclusion and Future Works

This paper proposes the results obtained through an ontological analysis on the security concepts proposed in the extended i* language. To our knowledge, this is the first attempt to apply the BWW ontology to analyze security concepts in a conceptual modeling grammar. It is expected that the findings obtained in this study can help devise modeling rules for security requirements engineering. Since the i* modeling framework has been accepted as an international standard, it is expected that more analysis results may improve the design of the language. However, the results provided in this paper are still preliminary. We expect the suggestions proposed in the previous section can provide research objectives for future studies.

References

1. Al-Subaie, H.S.F., Maibaum, T.S.E.: Evaluating the effectiveness of a goal-oriented requirements engineering method. In: Proceedings of the Fourth International Workshop on Comparative Evaluation in Requirements Engineering 2006, pp. 8–19. IEEE (2006)
2. Mylopoulos, J., Chung, L., Yu, E.: From object-oriented to goal-oriented requirements analysis. Communications of the ACM 42(1), 31–37 (1999)
3. Kavakli, E.: Goal-oriented requirements engineering: A unifying framework. Requirements Engineering 6(4), 237–251 (2002)
4. Van Lamsweerde, A.: Goal-oriented requirements engineering: a guided tour. In: Proceedings of the Fifth IEEE International Symposium on Requirements Engineering 2001, pp. 249–262. IEEE (2001)
5. Yu, E.S.: Social Modeling and i*. In: Borgida, A.T., Chaudhri, V.K., Giorgini, P., Yu, E.S. (eds.) Conceptual Modeling: Foundations and Applications. LNCS, vol. 5600, pp. 99–121. Springer, Heidelberg (2009)

6. ITU, T.S.S.O.: Series Z: Languages and General Software Aspects for Telecommunication Systems. Formal Description Techniques (FDT) – User Requirements Notation (URN) - Language Definition (2011)
7. Elahi, G., Yu, E., Zannone, N.: A vulnerability-centric requirements engineering framework: analyzing security attacks, countermeasures, and requirements based on vulnerabilities. Requirements Engineering 15(1), 41–62 (2010)
8. Wand, Y., Weber, R.: On the ontological expressiveness of information systems analysis and design grammars. Information Systems Journal 3(4), 217–237 (1993)
9. Wand, Y., Weber, R.: On the deep structure of information systems. Information Systems Journal 5(3), 203–223 (1995)
10. Green, P., Rosemann, M.: Integrated process modeling: an ontological evaluation. Information Systems 25(2), 73–87 (2000)
11. Opdahl, A.L., Henderson-Sellers, B.: Ontological evaluation of the UML using the Bunge–Wand–Weber model. Software and Systems Modeling 1(1), 43–67 (2002)
12. Irwin, G., Turk, D.: An ontological analysis of use case modeling grammar. Journal of the Association for Information Systems 6(1), 1–36 (2005)
13. Green, P., et al.: Candidate interoperability standards: An ontological overlap analysis. Data & Knowledge Engineering 62(2), 274–291 (2007)
14. Zur Muehlen, M., Indulska, M.: Modeling languages for business processes and business rules: A representational analysis. Information Systems 35(4), 379–390 (2010)
15. Becker, J., et al.: Evaluating the Expressiveness of Domain Specific Modeling Languages Using the Bunge-Wand-Weber Ontology. In: Proceedings of the 43rd Hawaii International Conference on System Sciences. IEEE (2010)
16. Recker, J., et al.: Do ontological deficiencies in modeling grammars matter. MIS Quarterly 35(1), 57–79 (2011)
17. Rosemann, M., Green, P., Indulska, M.: A reference methodology for conducting ontological analyses. In: Atzeni, P., Chu, W., Lu, H., Zhou, S., Ling, T.-W. (eds.) ER 2004. LNCS, vol. 3288, pp. 110–121. Springer, Heidelberg (2004)
18. Bisht, P., Madhusudan, P., Venkatakrishnan, V.N.: CANDID: Dynamic candidate evaluations for automatic prevention of SQL injection attacks. ACM Trans. Inf. Syst. Secur. 13(2), 1–39 (2010)
19. den Braber, F., et al.: Model-based security analysis in seven steps—a guided tour to the coras method. BT Technology Journal 25, 101–117 (2007)
20. Tsipenyuk, K., Chess, B., McGraw, G.: Seven pernicious kingdoms: A taxonomy of software security errors. IEEE Security & Privacy 3, 81–84 (2005)
21. Bunge, M.: Treatise on Basic Philosophy. Ontology II: A World of Systems, vol. 4. Reidel Publishing Company, Holland (1979)
22. Bunge, M.: Treatise on Basic Philosophy. The Furniture of the World, vol. 3. Reidel Publishing Company, Holland (1977)
23. Gollwitzer, P.M.: Mindset theory of action phases. In: Van Lange, P.A.M., Kruglanski, A.W., Higgins, E.T. (eds.) Handbook of Theories of Social Psychology, vol. 1, pp. 526–546. Sage Publications Ltd. (2012)

Reconsidering the Notion of User Experience for Human-Centered Design

Hiroyuki Miki

Oki Electric Ind. Co., Ltd., R&D Center
1-16-8 Chuou, Warabi-shi, Saitama 335-8510, Japan
hmiki@cf.netyou.jp

Abstract. Recently, the word "User Experience (UX)" has been often used in usability-related areas such as web design and system design. Although it was defined in ISO 9241-210 and its importance has been growing, details of the notion and results of introduction of it have not been well clarified yet. After reviewing related research results, this paper firstly summarizes a historical transition from usability to UX by seeing transitions from ISO/IEC 9126-1 to ISO/IEC 25010 in the software quality international standard, and from ISO 13407 to ISO 9241-210 in the ergonomics international standard. Then details of the notion are discussed and a framework for UX is proposed.

Keywords: User Experience, Usability, ISO 9241, ISO 13407, ISO/IEC 25010, Guideline, American Customer Satisfaction Index, Customer Expectation Management, Theory of Consumption Value, Persona.

1 Introduction

Usability is a notion, for example, that addresses a degree of how easy one can use products, systems, or services. As products, systems, or services become complex and provide high-level functions to the user, designing and evaluation usability become more difficult. In addition, as business competitions go world wide and become fierce, conditions of successful products, systems, or services become more complex [3].

Norman considered this kind of changes and claimed that broader scope than usability should be considered [14]. He claimed that the user wants not only a good usability but also a high UX to be truly pleased with good products, systems, or services. To consider UX, one needs to consider user's good/ bad feelings and responses, namely results of relating products, systems, or services more than usability. It was the first time that UX was mentioned by an opinion leader of usability.

Since international standards provide common bases for international businesses, it was quite reasonable that the word UX was introduced in them under the changes described above. However, details of the notion and results of the introduction of it are not well clarified yet.

After reviewing related research results, this paper firstly reviews a historical transition from usability to UX by seeing transitions from ISO/IEC 9126-1 to ISO/IEC

S. Yamamoto (Ed.): HIMI/HCII 2013, Part I, LNCS 8016, pp. 329–337, 2013.

25010 in the software quality international standard, and from ISO 13407 to ISO 9241-210 in the ergonomics international standard. Then details of the notion are discussed and a framework for UX is proposed.

2   Background

Before the introduction and the discussion of UX in international standards, recent research results are briefly reviewed.

2.1   Various Definitions of UX

After the publishing of Norman's book in 1998, many definitions of UX have been proposed so far reflecting diversity of related areas and concepts. For example, 27 definitions are shown at "All About UX" web page (http://www.allaboutux.org/). The following are three definitions among them. Although contents of the definitions vary, they are quite broad in their meanings.

- UXPA
  Every aspect of the user's interaction with a product, service, or company that make up the user's perceptions of the whole. User experience design as a discipline is concerned with all the elements that together make up that interface, including layout, visual design, text, brand, sound, and interaction. UE works to coordinate these elements to allow for the best possible interaction by users.

- Microsoft
  An activity of encounter by a computer user with the auditory and visual presentation of a collection of computer programs. It is important to note that this includes only what the user perceives and not all that is presented.

- ISO 9241-210 [9]
  A person's perceptions and responses that result from the use or anticipated use of a product, system or service.

2.2   Time Span of UX: User Experience White Paper

User experience white paper [16] is a result from discussions among the invited experts of the Demarcating User Experience seminar in 2010. It goes beyond definition discussions, describes core concepts of UX, and clarifies different perspectives of UX. It addresses what are UX and what are not UX, time span of UX, factors affecting UX, and UX as a practice. In the description of UX as a practice, it refers to human-centered design (HC) [8, 9] and briefly explained what have to be done in HCD. Although it is a twelve page document, it briefly summarizes arguments at the time well. Fig.1 from the document shows time spans of UX, the terms to describe the kind of UX related to the spans, and the internal process taking place in the different time spans. While usability is on "during usage" only, UX covers all spans.

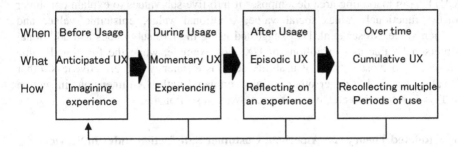

| When | Before Usage | During Usage | After Usage | Over time |
| How | Imagining experience | Experiencing | Reflecting on an experience | Recollecting multiple Periods of use |

Fig. 1. Time spans of UX, the terms to describe the kind of UX, and the internal process taking place. (This is created based on Fig.2 of the paper [16].)

2.3   Dimensions and Data Collection Methods for UX

Bargas-Avila and Hornbæk summarize dimensions and data collection methods for UX [2]. While the dimensions are more than usability dimensions, the data collection methods are similar to usability ones.

Table 1. UX dimensions and data collection methods for UX (created from Table 2, 3 of [2])

UX dimension	Generic UX, Affect/Emotion, Enjoyment/Fun, Aesthetic/Appeal, Hedonic Quality, Engagement/Flow, Motivation, Enchantment, Frustration, Other Constructs
Data collection method	Questionnaires, Interviews (semi-structured), User Observation (live), Videorecordings, Focus Groups, Interviews (open), Diaries, Probes, Collage or Drawings, Photographs, Body movements, Psychophysiological Measures, Other Methods

2.4   CHI SIG and Workshop Related to UX

Since 2008, a workshop on UX has been held at CHI conference every year. In the CHI'11 workshop, UX theories and theoretical frameworks were discussed. Based on the discussion, Obrist et al. [15] propose seven theory categories and nine disciplines. Severn theory categories are a) human/user, b) product/artifact, c) user/artifact/environment relations, d) social nature of UX, e) design focus, f) frameworks involving several themes from a) to e), and g) even broader frameworks related to human existence. Meanwhile, nine disciplines are psychology, sociology, marketing, philosophy, communication, education, art, anthropology, and design. Both the theory categories and the disciplines are quite broad.

2.5   Related Theory (1): Theory of Consumption Value in Marketing

Except for the case that UX simply represents an event, UX is subjective and is with some evaluation value like good or bad. About value, the theory of consumption value

(TCV) [17] in marketing area decomposes it into five sub values to explain consumer choices: functional value, social value, emotional value, epistemic value, and condition value. Moser et al. [12] suggested using the five sub values and additional interpersonal value as sub notions of UX. For example, while the functional value corresponds to most notions of usability such as efficiency and effectiveness, other sub values reasonably cover other notions compared with UX dimensions in section 2.3. TCV is referred to create an UX framework in section 4.3.

2.6   Related Theory (2): American Customer Satisfaction Index in Service Sciences

Satisfaction is related to UX in the sense that both represent some subjective feelings resulting from some perception and/or action. In Service Science area, American Customer Satisfaction Index is a popular method to treat satisfaction. It is used to compare different services such as hotel service, airline service, retail service, and so on. Starting from Customer Expectation, the index model shows causal relations of indices which are important to evaluate services. While Customer Expectation evaluates the customer's anticipation of the quality of products of services before an actual service, Perceived Quality and Perceived Value evaluate the quality during a service followed by Customer Complaints and Customer Royalty for the quality after a service. It should be noted that Perceived Value is a measure of quality relative to price paid. ACSI is used to create an UX framework in section 4.3.

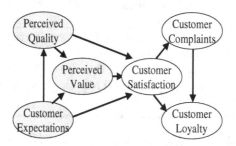

Fig. 2. American Customer Satisfaction Index (Arrows represent influence. This is created based on http://www.theacsi.org/index.php).

2.7   Practical Guidelines Related to UX

Apart from academic distinctions of conceptual categories, there are practical design guidelines to provide high UX. For example, Persona method and accompanied guidelines are very common in the usability community as a core method to provide high UX [4]. Other examples include iOS human interface guidelines [1] in which most descriptions are on usability except for those on mobile devices.

3   Usability and UX in International Standards

In the previous section, a wide range of related research results of UX are reviewed. International Standards, on the other hand, have the specific role to provide business organizations with technical standards. Currently, UX related standards are built mainly by the ergonomics committee (ISO/TC159) and the software committee (JTC1/SC7). In this section, fundamental standards related to UX are reviewed: ISO 9241-11:1998 [11], ISO/IEC 9126-1:2000 [6], ISO 9241-210:2010 [9], and ISO/IEC 25010:2011 [7].

3.1   ISO 9241-11:1998 and ISO/IEC 9126-1:2000

ISO 9241 part 10 - part17 are series of international standards on Ergonomic requirements for office work with visual display terminals (VDTs). In ISO 9241-11 (Guidance on Usability), the terminology "usability" was for the first time defined in international standards as the following.

- Usability in ISO 9241-11:1998 [10]:
  Extent to which a product can be used by specified users to achieve specified goals with effectiveness, efficiency and satisfaction in a specified context of use.

This definition which emphasizes effectiveness, efficiency and satisfaction was different from previous definitions which emphasized ease of operation. For example, before ISO 9241-11, Nielsen [13] defined usability as ease of operation in parallel with utility, and defined usefulness as composed of usability and utility. In short, the definition of ISO 9241-11 is almost same with Nielsen's definition of usefulness. In this sense, the definition of ISO 9241-11 is broader than previous definitions. This difference is often described as difference between "small usability" and "big usability": Namely, while Nielsen's definition is called as "small usability", the definition of ISO 9241-11 is called as "big usability". Since Norman called "small usability" as usability in a similar way with Nielsen, UX is conceptually closer to "big usability".

In software quality standards, on the other hand, ISO/IEC 9126-1 defines usability as "small usability" composed of understandability, learnability, operability, attractiveness, and usability compliance. It also defines "big usability" as "quality in use". Hence, ISO/IEC 9126-1 defines usability differently from ISO 9241-11. Although UX is conceptually close to usability of ISO 9241-11 and to "quality in use" of ISO/IEC 9126-1, differences among them were unclear.

3.2   ISO 9241-210:2010 and ISO/IEC 25010:2011

In 2010, ISO 13407 (Human-centred design processes for interactive systems) [8] was renewed and renumbered as ISO 9241-210 (Human-centred design for interactive systems) [9] in ergonomics standards. In ISO 9241-210, UX is for the first time defined in international standards as the following.

- User Experience in ISO 9241-210:2010 [9]:
  person's perceptions and responses resulting from the use and/or anticipated use of a product, system or service.

However, there are three other definitions described as notes in the document, which showed difficulties in defining it. In addition, there is no description about differences between usability and UX.

ISO/IEC 9126 series have also been under renewal to ISO/IEC 25000 series in software quality standards. ISO/IEC 9126-1 [6] was renewed to ISO/IEC 25010 [7] and the definition of usability was renewed. Unlike ISO 9241-210, the terminology UX is not used in ISO/IEC 25010. Instead, concepts of UX are included in the definition of satisfaction of usability definition; Satisfaction consists of not only usefulness but also trust, pleasure, and comfort.

4   Discussion

So far, related research results and related international standards to UX are reviewed. In this section, discussions are made on what are missing in the international standards to represent the notion of UX, and a framework on UX is newly proposed based on the discussions.

4.1   Different Kinds of Goals for UX

For a development of systems and services, clarifying user's goals with the systems and services is very important as emphasized in the international standards described in section three. "Goal" is defined in ISO 9241-11as "an intended outcome", which can be decomposed into sub-goals and accomplishing sub-goals result in accomplishment of an original goal.

When ISO 9241-11 is extended to cover not only usability but also UX, this definition of "goal" (intended goal) needs to be wider. Firstly, in addition to the intended goal, "expected" goal which can not be explicitly decomposed into sub-goals should be added to the notion of goal. Because, when it comes to service, it is often the case that what a customer thinks of for UX is expectation rather than the intended goal in the sense that expectation is so abstract to be decomposed into sub-goals [11]. Examples of the expected goal include "Be able to capture what she sees in 'her mind's eye' " [4].

Secondly, emotional goal should also be added since it is also difficult to be decomposed into sub-goals. Examples include "Feel like a 'real' photographer" [4].

Summaries are shown in Table 2. Three kinds of goals are added to the goal of ISO 9241-11. These different kinds of goals should be mentioned in ISO 9241-11 in the future.

Table 2. Four kinds of goals which should be covered by UX
("+" means addition to ISO 9241-11.)

	actional	emotional
Intended goal	ISO 9241-11	+
Expected goal	+	+

4.2 Different Kinds of Activities for Long Time Spans of UX

Fig.1 explained that time spans of UX are longer than that of usability, which is slightly mentioned in ISO 9241-210 [9].

When longer time spans are considered, two kinds of activities should be differentiated. First is a development activity that is based on existing usability activities and seeks for higher satisfaction than usability for UX. In this sense, this kind of activities could be called as for "Usability Experience" rather than for UX. Examples include activities conducted by Ease of Use Roundtable [18]. Their documents provide guidelines to solve basic usability issues considering wider time spans from Out of Box Experience to Maintenance and Serviceability. Another example is a Persona method which aims at high UX [4].

Second is not an extension of usability activity but an activity that various departments share some UX goal for a system or service and cooperate with each other for better UX throughout the product lifecycle. For this kind of activity, each department uses its own existing methods related to customer satisfaction and considers UX additionally.

These different kinds of activities and Fig.1 should be addressed in ISO 9241-210 in the future.

4.3 UX Framework

Since framework explains a notion by describing components and relationship among them, it is important to create a framework for a specific notion. Usability framework is explained in ISO 9241-11 as mentioned in section 3.1. In this section, considering discussions in section 4.1 and 4.2, UX framework is discussed and a new UX framework is proposed.

As a framework for UX in the international standard, it is preferable to satisfy the following conditions: 1) it fits together with existing standards, 2) it shows components of UX and relationship among them, 3) it encompasses notion of time spans explained in section 4.2, 4) it can differentiate goals explained in section 4.1, 5) it fits together with an well known existing framework to treat expectation.

Since ACSI of section 2.6 meets these conditions, it is adopted here as a base framework for further refinement. Fig.3 shows the result of refinement and proposes a new framework based on ISO 9241-11 and ACSI. Three major components and relationship among them are deployed similar to ISO 9241-11: goals, context of use, and measures. In the UX measure component, most components of ACSI are deployed. Since meanings of small components such as goals, perceived quality, and perceived value are changed from ISO 9241-11 and ACSI, they are explained in the following. First, considering section 4.1, "goals" are specified as composed of intended goals and expected goals.

Second, meaning of "perceived quality" is extended as composed of various qualities such as those mentioned in section 2.5. In ACSI, "perceived quality" was calculated as a total score of desired and undesired degrees against needs. As discussed in section 2, since quality measures of UX other than satisfaction and long term measures vary a lot, appropriate measures should be selected for a system and a service.

Third, meaning of "perceived value" is changed as relative quality against input compared with the relative quality against price in ACSI. Examples of "perceived value" include relative pleasure against stress in game, relative relief against anxiety in public machine usage, and so on. Although usability international standards do not treat a value as a measure, it should be added to consider UX.

Since ACSI has been widely applied to many services, the proposed framework can also be applied to many systems and services.

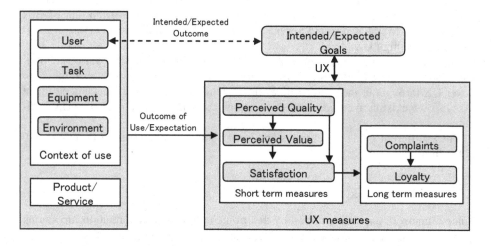

Fig. 3. Proposed UX framework based on ISO 9241-11 and ACSI

5   Concluding Remarks

After reviewing related research results, this paper firstly reviewed a historical transition from usability to UX by seeing transitions from ISO/IEC 9126-1 to ISO/IEC 25010 in the software quality international standard, and from ISO 13407 to ISO 9241-210 in the ergonomics international standard. Then details of the notion are discussed and a framework for UX is proposed.

Since UX is a complex notion [5], the proposed framework is expected to be applied and examined against real applications. Results of this paper are also expected to be considered in the creation of UX related international standards.

References

1. Apple: iOS human interface guidelines,
   http://developer.apple.com/library/ios/navigation/
2. Bargas-Avila, J.A., Hornbæk, K.: Old wine in new bottles or novel challenges: a critical analysis of empirical studies of user experience. In: Proc. CHI 2011, pp. 2689–2698. ACM, New York (2011)
3. Christensen, C.M.: The Innovator's Dilemma: The revolutionary book that will change the way you do business. Harvard Business School (1997)
4. Goodwin, K.: Designing for the digital age: how to create human-centered products and services. Wiley (2009)
5. Hartson, R., Pyla, P.S.: The UX Book: Process and Guidelines for Ensuring a Quality User Experience. Morgan Kaufmann (2012)
6. ISO/IEC 9126-1: Software engineering – Product quality – Part 1: Quality model. ISO/IEC (2001)
7. ISO/IEC 25010: Systems and software engineering – Systems and software Quality Requirements and Evaluation (SQuaRE) – System and software quality models. ISO/IEC (2011)
8. ISO 13407: Human-centred design processes for interactive systems. ISO (1999)
9. ISO 9241-210: Ergonomics of human-system interaction – Part 210: Human-centred design for interactive systems. ISO (2010)
10. ISO 9241-11: Ergonomic requirements for office work with visual display terminals (VDTs) – Part 11: Guidance on usability. ISO (1998)
11. Miki, H., Hosono, N., Yamamoto, S.: Transcending Human-centered Design by Service Sciences. In: Smith, M.J., Salvendy, G. (eds.) HCI International 2009, Part I. LNCS, vol. 5617, pp. 685–692. Springer, Heidelberg (2009)
12. Moser, C., Fuchsberger, V., Tscheligi, M.: A Value-based UX evaluation,
    http://di.ncl.ac.uk/uxtheory/files/2011/11/11_Moser.pdf
    (electronic version)
13. Nielsen, J.: Usability Engineering. Morgan Kaufmann (1994)
14. Norman, D.A.: Invisible Computer: Why good products can fail, the personal computer is so complex and information appliances are the solution. MIT, Cambridge (1998)
15. Obrist, M., et al.: In Search of Theoretical Foundations for UX Research and Practice. In: Proc. CHI 2012 Extended Abstracts, pp. 1979–1984. ACM, New York (2012)
16. Roto, V., et al.: User Experience White Paper,
    http://www.allaboutux.org/uxwhitepaper (electronic version)
17. Sheth, J.N., Newman, B.I., Gross, B.L.: Why we buy what we buy: a theory of consumption values. J. Business Research 22(2), 159–170 (1991)
18. Solenson, P.: Intel's Ease of Use/PC Quality Roundtables
    http://www.usabilityprofessionals.org/upa_publications/
    upa_voice/volumes/4/issue_1/intel_ease.htm (electronic version)

The Proposition of a Framework to Support the Design of Ecological Systems for the Web

Marcelo Morandini[1], Pedro Luiz Pizzigati Correa[2],
Tharsis Novaes[1], and Thiago Adriano Coleti[1]

[1] School of Arts, Sciences and Humanities, University of Sao Paulo, Brazil
[2] Engineering Politechnique School, University of Sao Paulo, Brazil
{m.morandini,pedro.correa,mntharsis,thiago.coleti}@usp.br

Abstract. Usability evaluation is one of the main steps in a product development life cycle and is responsible for providing a better level for its quality. Applying usability evaluation techniques is an important activity to achieve better definitions that can be used in the software development. Specifically, when is considered the development of interactive systems designed to support Ecological Simulation Environments, this process must be taken with prudence and rigor. So, their Human-Computer Interaction must be taken with efficacy, efficiency and user satisfaction. When the Ecological Simulation Environment is considered, this problem has a special feature that turns it into a special one: the information localization is one of the main important characteristic of its definition. These systems allow the manipulation, maintenance and visualization of geographic data as coordinated sets and the interest for their applications is increasing a lot in the last few years. Nowadays, we can consider the Web Ecological Simulation Environment as a reality, as in these web sites the geographic information and the simulation features for specific ecological environments are being disposed in different pages and their manipulation is being supported by the internet. On the other hand, some of these web sites are usually designed and implemented for specific users, such as the biological community and it makes them too specific for being used and analyzed by "regular and traditional" users that can be able to interact with them, since these sites may be available on the web. The Web mapping services and the ecological simulation systems are being accessed more regularly and most of them can be available through accessing web sites. These applications are based on the possibilities that the technology offers, such as spatial localization for specific interest places or addresses, calculation of simulation taxes and some distances between two addresses or places, among others. In this context, the internet is the better way users can interact with them. This does contribute a lot in the increase of the quantity and diversity of users, their features and restrictions. So, ecological simulation systems utilization is not always an activity that may be considered as trivial or easy. When performing the usability evaluations, we do not just aim to collect the evaluators answers for the questionnaires applied, but we also plan to ask to the evaluators to rank the level of importance for each one of the Ergonomic Criterion, since each question had, at least, one Ergonomic Criterion associated. So, based on these results, we may have conditions to create a framework for designing web sites for Ecological Simulation applications as we can be able to figure out which information is more relevant and, so, propose strategies for making them more usable.

S. Yamamoto (Ed.): HIMI/HCII 2013, Part I, LNCS 8016, pp. 338–346, 2013.
© Springer-Verlag Berlin Heidelberg 2013

1   Introduction

Ecological aspects concerning education, research and preservation are important issues discussed nowadays, mainly because past activities damaged many relevant ecological areas affecting the people lifestyle, increasing world temperature, thawing ice caps and many others undesirable impacts. The use of specific software to support ecological activities is a reality and the interest for this kind of environment is increasing a lot in the last few years. These tools could allow many specialists or novice users performing mapping, simulations, manipulations, maintenance and visualization of geographic areas using several interfaces resources in order to present a variety of information that may help users establishing strategies for conservation, public health, development and reconstructing ecological areas (Muñoz et al., 2009). Usually, these applications are based on the possibilities that the software could perform complex activities, for example advanced calculations, spatial localization and distance between two addresses or geographic points. The main and easier mechanism for users to access and perform their tasks using this type of application is through the Internet, i.e., software developed using a website approach.

There are web sites designed for specifics users such as the Biological Community that can be too specific for being used and analyzed by "regular and traditional" users and so, it is possible that they may not achieve their goals effectively and/or efficiently. Because of this, the Human-Computer Interaction (HCI) should be a concern to ecological systems development teams since this area of study can support the development of easy, full and acceptable ecological applications that can be used by all different skilled users, with different equipments, experiences and expectations.

The HCI process development involves some tasks such as analysis, prototyping, development and evaluation. It is aimed to help the development team producing interactive software with high levels of usability, i.e., applications that allow users to realize their task with effectiveness, efficiency and satisfaction (Cybis et al., 2010). The evaluation is one of the main steps in HCI development life cycle. Moreover, some guidelines are proposed to support all HCI development steps. For example, the Ergonomic Criteria proposed by Scapin & Bastien (Scapin et al., 2001) in order to help the designers and evaluators achieving a product with high level of usability and quality.

This paper aims to present a framework to support the development of Ecological Systems. For this reason, we are proposing the use of an Observation Method to evaluate and validate the software usability. This framework will consist, mainly, in the use of two evaluation approaches: (1) ErgoMonitor: Tool that collect data done directly from the user´s interaction and stored at the server log files; and (2) ErgoSV: this software supports usability evaluation using face and speech recognition (Coleti et al., 2012). Both of these tools are presented in further sections. These two applications when used together become a framework to be used during HCI design and evaluation phases to perform an iterative development.

We are proposing that the use of ErgoMonitor + ErgoSV can help to evaluate ecological systems usability identifying good features to be used as a guideline in developments of this sort of environment. The next section presents the Materials and

Methods used for ErgoMonitor and ErgoSV development and also presents how these environments can be used together for allowing Ecologycal Systems development team achieving their usability design and evaluation goals.

2   Material and Methods

This section presents the resources researched to make this framework that supports the HCI design and evaluation processes of Ecological Environments. Among the studied techniques, we are presenting aspects concerning the Usability Evaluation, and specifically both ErgoSV and ErgoMonitor tools.

2.1   Usability Evaluation

Evaluating is one of the main stages of the design development process and aim to certify if the interface is according with the specification and whether it allows users to perform their task with efficiency, effectiveness and satisfaction, i.e., with high levels of usability. The evaluation activities should be performed in all stages of usability engineering such as analysis, development and evaluation. So, specific techniques that are appropriated for each stage were developed, such as usability inspection and usability tests (Cybis et al., 2010).

Some HCI evaluation techniques are widely used to support usability tests such as filming, verbalization and the monitoring of users activities using log files. Log Files are registers that contain data about what a user has done during their visit on the website such as hour, IP address and electronic address accessed. The data can be processed by specific software and generate relevant information about website usability such as rate and metrics usability (Cybis et al., 2010; Morandini, 2003, Scapin et al, 2001).

The filming is performed using one or several cameras positioned near the user collecting images about face, hands, computer screen, environment and other resources according to evaluator needs and so recording the interaction. The images collected are used by evaluator to analyzing the interaction between user and software and can present exactly what moment a software error happened or when the test participant has difficult to perform any task usability (Cybis et al., 2010; Coleti et al., 2012). The Verbalization is a technique that the participant verbalizes their thought during or after performing the evaluation. This approach is based on the idea that the participant can verbalize what they are thinking about and so verbalizes you opinion about the software allowing evaluator and designer identify usability problems in the interaction design (Morandini, 2003; Coleti et al., 2012).

Monitoring the use by analyzing the log files, is a not-so-intrusive technique, i.e., the evaluation can be performed without boring the participants. This is extremely interesting for Ecological Systems supported by a web site since the users are can participate in the evaluations do not need to be in a specific place at any predefined time. Some tools were development and others have been developing in order to support usability evaluation based on observation method such as ErgoMonitor and ErgoSV. The next section presents details about these applications.

3   Theory / Calculation

This section presents the environments that should be used together to present a framework for helping the development of Ecological Systems based on the web: ErgoMonitor and ErgoSV. The joint utilization of these usability supporting tools may produce a complete guideline for the HCI design and/or evaluation processes and can be a meaningful tool for Ecological Environments development teams and even for their users.

3.1   ErgoMonitor

The ErgoMonitor is defined as a system able to be monitoring *real* interactions performed by *real* users in their *own working environment*. This defines the usability evaluations attention focus: the presence of usability problems without the total knowledgement about the use context involved (Brajnik, 2000).This project was inspired by a need that web site developers and managers deal regularly: continually assuring and improving the web site usability despite the constant updating of actions and informations (Scapin et al., 2001).

In the ErgoMonitor context, the possible tasks that could be performed by the users while interacting with the web site should be the ones considered as "objective" or "closed". These special tasks have a main feature: they present beggining and ending points (ie, urls) clearly well stated. So, the final url that could be accessed by an user while performing a task, and achieving success, must be an specific success-url. And so, for this same reason, an initial url, is probably the Homepage for most of the tasks that are supported by the web site. In this context, if the dilletantes users, that only wish to visit the web site and do not aim to conclude a task, are not considered.

The ErgoMonitor´s evaluator-operator must have an active participation in the environment configuration, since he/she should define a "service" parameter for the achievement of the server log files. Also, he/she should model the tasks and behaviours. This modelling is, basically, the presentation of a set of *urls* that are accessed while a task is being performed. So, the models needed include the success, cancels, desistances, help solicitations, error messages, and others.

3.2   ErgoSV

The ErgoSV Software is an application that is been developing based on observation techniques. The observation is used in usability evaluation in order to register images or sounds by user to create relevant quantitative and qualitative information about software usability (Cybis et al., 2010). To register these data the evaluator usually uses: (1) video cameras in order to film several relevant point of evaluation such as face, hands, keyboards and computers; (2)voice recorders in order to register what the participant/user say during the evaluation.

The face recognition is used in order to identify when the user has some reaction and express it by face. A default image is collected in initial and after test it is compared with other images collected during the test. The images are collected in an interval time stipulated by evaluator. After collected all images and the participant finish the test, the ErgoSV Software performs an image processing and two informations could be provided: The first one is the moment when the participant's face is different from the default image. The second is generated when the software don't recognize any face in image.

The speech recognition is performed in order to support verbalization method also known as Think Aloud. Ericsson and Simon proposed three ways to perform the Think Aloud (Verbalization): (1) the participant don't need to perform a hard mental load to transforming what he/she is seen to what they will pronounced, for example, whether the participant see a figure containing a number they can pronounce the number easily. (2) in this approach the participant needs to perform more mental load than the last one because he/she needs to transform what he is thinking about in a word to be pronounced; (3) the last approach of verbalization is more complex because the participant needs verbalizing about specific situations of things, moreover, the people could be required verbalizing something from past (Boren e Ramey, 2000). In ErgoSV the participant needs to transform a situation in a word that represents what he is thinking about the software.

To perform an usability evaluation using speech recognition the evaluator needs to choose words to the participant. Some words are initially established such as "good", "bad", "regular". After set the words, the usability test is started and so, when the participant pronounces one of the configurable words, the software performs the recognition, stored it in a database and after speech processing the application presents the word and the confidence (certain recognition rate).

Therefore, the ErgoSV Software is a tool based on observation techniques of usability evaluation that uses an approach improved from the traditional filming and verbalization. Also, this application collects data from voice and face emotion. This evaluation software can support the Ecological Software design in all stages of Usability Engineering. The next section presents an approach to support the analysis, development and evaluation of ecological systems.

4   The Ecological Software Design Development Process Framework

This section proposes an approach based on usability engineering and observation method to analyzing, developing and evaluating ecological websites so that the Human-Computer Interaction can be taken with efficacy, efficiency and user satisfaction.

The framework we are proposing in this work (the use of ErgoMonitor + ErgoSV) involves a series of activities focused on the usability evaluation, starting from analysis process and concluding on the final product evaluation performing, this way, an interactive development process that can allow the evaluator to collect meaningful data about software roles, user satisfaction and interface quality. This framework is strongly based on usability engineering phases: analysis, development and evaluation processes. The observation techniques are used in the development stages to support the evaluation of existing products, prototypes and final products.

The Interactive Process (Pressman, 2011) which this framework is based allows and guides the development team to repeat the activities with the final user several times in order to improve the concepts and user needs.

The Figure 1 presents the Ecological Software Design Development Process Framework and their activities.

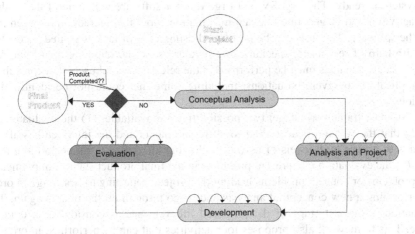

Fig. 1. Framework to Support the Design of Ecological Systems for the Web

The **Conceptual Analysis** is the first framework stage and did not have relevant changes compared to traditional usability engineering. In this stage, the designer should not be concerned about applications of technologies resources to be developed, but the main activities aim to present information about what the user needs in their applications, what problems to solve and what are the important data to be collected to help figuring out how should be the software developed. Mental models, notes, voice recorders and interviews can be used to support this stage (Cybis et al., 2011). Although both ErgoSV and ErgoMonitor are not used in this stage since that application is not the focus of this phase, the test participants chose is also realized in this stage. It should be interesting that a minimum of four or five testers should be selected to achieve a good result in this stage (Cybis et al., 2010; Pressman, 2011).

After performing the Conceptual Analysis, the designers must perform the **Analysis and Project Stage**. In this phase the designer must transform the user needs in interface (software) requirements and verify whether these requirements are in accordance to the concepts collected in previous stages. The number of tests that must be performed in order to support the phase activities can be defined by the development team and can vary according to requirements difficulties, participants´ skills and application tested.

The **Development Stage** aims to perform the development of the ecological websites and can be considered as one of the most important framework stages. In this stage, the development team must transform the user´ requirements, resources, features and standards established in previous phases into a final product, more exactly, a website for ecological activities. In this stage the use of observation methods supported by ErgoSV and ErgoMonitor must be considered by the development team to perform usability evaluation in prototypes and possible releases.

Finally, the **Evaluation Stage** is focused in evaluating the final product. The usability evaluation in final products must be performed by the same participants that realized the other tests and they must use the website completely as had done when the system is ready. The ErgoSV and ErgoMonitor software will support the evaluation activities and so generate relevant information about the interaction between user and the software. The tests can be performed using a list of task compiled by evaluator with help of real users, specialist and regular users, participating or not the previous test. All the tests must be performed in the releases by real users that can submit the application to several situations, including some that could not be identified in previous stages.

As the last framework stage, two possibilities are available: (1) the evaluator can certify that the website is according to all requirements and the interface has all the features to ensure high levels of usability allowing all skilled users performing their task; (2) the evaluation can present problems in the final product such as implementation problems or concept problems leading the project returning to first stage in order to performing a new conceptual analysis and so go through all the phases again. The evaluation is the last stage of the proposed lifecycle and is consider as a delicate phase. This framework also proposes four activities that can be performed in order to optimize the evaluation:

1. **Initial Stages:** The participants are orientated about the Ergonomic Criteria and how they can influence the interface utilization. Also, they are orientated to basically observe the interface according to the eight elementary criteria and the participants are informed that they can be taped and what words they will need to pronounce during the test and in which situations they should do that so.
2. **Configuration Stage** that consists making the configurations in the two applications that will support the evaluation using observation method: ErgoMonitor and ErgoSV. The evaluation software needs that the set of parameters should be defined. Among these parameters are the interval time to collect image faces, words to being pronounced and time to collect screen images. The ErgoSV contains some words predefined such as good, great, bad, regular, but other words can be configured.
3. In **Test performing** the participants perform the usability test and are being observed by ErgoSV and ErgoMonitor. The participants can be monitored by a evaluator in order to solve eventual problems or doubts. A list containing several tasks can be available to participants besides ask them to perform everyday task; and
4. **Test Analysis** is a stage on what the evaluators use the information generated by ErgoSV and ErgoMonitor in order to take decision about usability problems.

The next section presents the conclusions and expectations related to the use for this framework and the results that can be obtained with it.

5   Conclusions

HCI usability design and evaluation must be considered as very important in a product development life cycle and are responsible for providing a better level for its quality. Applying usability evaluation techniques is an activity to achieve better definitions that can be used in the software development (Cybis et al., 2010).

Specifically, when an Ecological Environment is considered, this problem has a special feature that turns it into a special one: the information localization is one of the main important part of its definition. Nowadays, we can consider the Web Ecological Simulation Environment as a reality, as in these web sites the geographic information and the simulation features for specific ecological environments are being disposed in different pages and their manipulation is being supported by the internet. On the other hand, some of these web sites are usually designed and implemented for specific users, such as the biological community and it makes them too specific for being used and analyzed by "regular and traditional" users that can be able to interact with them.

The Web mapping services and the ecological simulation systems are being accessed more regularly and most of them can be available through accessing web sites. But, ecological simulation systems utilization is not always an activity that may be considered as trivial or easy. One of the reasons for that is the great amount of users that may access them and so, due to their differences, achieving usability features for all these users is a challenge that the designers must deal with. And the framework we are proposing in this paper has the intention to be helpful for guiding designers and evaluators achieving their goals.

Therefore, it is really important that the mapping applications should be designed considering usability definitions, such as the Ergonomic Criteria (Cybis et al., 2010) that are strongly accepted and validated by the scientific community. Specifically, the use of questionnaires and checklists was considered as an important, low cost, fast and efficient approach. We plan to focus the use of this framework in the utilization of two initial different ecological web sites and in the using of the environments that can be accessed from them. These web sites (and environments) are:

- **OpenModeller** aims to provide a flexible, user friendly, cross-platform environment where the entire process of conducting a fundamental niche modeling experiment can be carried out. The project is currently being developed by the Centro de Referência em Informação Ambiental, Escola Politécnica da USP, and Instituto Nacional de Pesquisas Espaciais as an open-source initiative (http://openmodeller.sourceforge.net).
- **Knowledge Network for Biocomplexity:** The Knowledge Network for Biocomplexity (KNB) is a national network intended to facilitate ecological and environmental research on biocomplexity. The goal of KNB is to enable the efficient discovery, access, interpretation, integration, and analysis of complex ecological data from a highly distributed set of field stations, laboratories, research sites, and individual researchers (http://knb.ecoinformatics.org/index.jsp).

To conclude, it is important to say that this paper purpose is to have more environments being evaluated or designed using this framework. For this reason this paper was written and submitted: present the Ecological Environments Development Community a framework able to help their design and evaluation activities. When performing the usability evaluations, we do not just aim to collect the evaluators answers for the questionnaires applied, but we also plan to ask to the evaluators to rank the level of importance for each one of the Ergonomic Criterion (Cybis et al., 2010), since each question had, at least, one Ergonomic Criterion associated. So, based on these results, we may have conditions to create a framework for designing web sites for Ecological Simulation applications as we can be able to figure out which information is more relevant and, so, propose strategies for making them more usable.

Acknowledgment. Financial Supported by FAPESP

References

1. Cybis, W.A., Betiol, A.H., Faust, R.: Ergonomia e Usabilidade: conhecimentos, métodos e aplicações, 2nd edn. Novatec, São Paulo (2010)
2. Muñoz, M.E.S., et al.: openModeller: a generic approach to species' potential distribution modelling. GeoInformatica (2009), doi:10.1007/s10707-009-0090-7
3. Morandini, M.: Ergo-Monitor: Monitoramento da Usabilidade em Ambiente Web por Meio de Análise de Arquivos de Log. Tese (Doutorado) - Universidade Federal de Santa Catarina - Brasil (2003)
4. Coleti, T.A., et al.: The Proposition of ErgoSV: An Environment to Support Usability Evaluation Using Image Processing and Speech Recognition System. In: IADIS Interfaces and Human Computer Interaction 2012 (IHCI 2012) Conference, Lisbon, vol. 1, pp. 1–4 (2012)
5. Boren, M.T., Ramey, J.: Thinking aloud: Reconciling theory and practice. IEEE Transactions on Professional Communication, 261–278 (2000)
6. OpenModeller Project, http://openmodeller.sourceforge.net (accessed August, 2012)
7. Scapin, D., Leulier, C., Vanderbonckt, J., Mariage, C., Bastien, C., Palanque, P., Farenc, C., Bastilde, R.: Towards Automated Testing of Web Usability Guidelines. In: Tools for Working with Guidelines, pp. 293–304. Springer, London (2001)

Environment-Centered Approach to ICT Service Design

Takehiko Ohno, Momoko Nakatani, and Yurika Katagiri

NTT Service Evolutions Laboratories, Kanagawa, Japan
{ohno.takehiko,nakatani.momoko,katagiri.yurika}@lab.ntt.co.jp

Abstract. One of the key factors we should consinder in designing the new ICT services that provide high user experience is *environment*. In this paper, we show two example in which the use of ICT service strongly depends on the environment in which the service is provided. We then propose an environment-centered approach for desinging ICT services. Traditional user-centered approaches like the persona-scenario method focus on the user domain, but environmental factors are considered in little while designing servies. We found, however, that service use is diversed drastically in the different environments. We have started to examine the proposed approach for ICT service design. A preliminary finding is that we can focus on environmental factors, especially, the environmental difference at different times, which is not considered explicitly in the traditional user-centered approach.

Keywords: User experience design. user-centered design, ICT service design, environment-centered design, ethnography.

1   Introduction

Today's growing market for information-communication technology (ICT) service[1] for consumer users requires a new perspective far beyond the established concepts of functionality and performance, the traditional factors in service design. User experience (UX), the internal state of the user's mind during service use, has become a key concept in designing ICT services highly appreciated by the users [4]. User experience explores how a user feels about using a service, i.e., the experiential, affective, meaningful and valuable aspects of service use [11]. However, even though the importance of UX has been discussed in the field of human-computer interaction (HCI) [2,3,4] and marketing research [9,10], it is still not unclear what factors should be addressed when designing ICT service that provide good experience.

Our goal is to establish the service design process of ICT service that provides high user experience. In the last decade, a variety of ICT services and technologies used to implement the services has been emerged and diffused. For designing ICT services, those factors must be under the consideration carefully and definitely. For home use, various products including PC, smartphone, featurephone, tablet, game console, digital television, DVD recorder (DVR) and Blue-Ray Disk recorder (BDR)

---

[1]   In this article, the word "service" refers to services, products and systems.

S. Yamamoto (Ed.): HIMI/HCII 2013, Part I, LNCS 8016, pp. 347–356, 2013.

are available in commercial. Those products are connected on the broadband network, where various network technologies including fixed-line (e.g. ADSL and FTTH), wireless (e.g. WiFi) and also mobile network (e.g. LTE and WiMax) are supplied. Because ICT service has become popular in everyday life, diversified users from children to elderly persons now use ICT services. The service design process must deal in those factors in the unified perspective.

In this paper, we propose the environment-centered approach for designing ICT services that provide high user experience. In the approach, we focus on the environments that contain both users and services, and from the depiction of the environments, service specifications are derived. Because environment sometimes changes drastically when the context is changed, different environments in the different contexts are described.

In the rest of the paper, we first overview the concept of environment-centered approach for ICT service design, and then we show two example in which the use of ICT services strongly depends on the environment. Next, we denote the detail of the proposed approach and discuss the strength and limitations. Finally, conclusion and future works are described.

2   Three Factors That Affect User Experience

As Hassenzahl noted in his article, UX is a consequence of the characteristics of the designed system, a user's internal state, and the context or environment within which the interaction occurs [4]. Here, as illustrated in Figure 1, we employ those three factors to understand what type of the elements we should consider for designing services. The first factor is "system", the characteristics of the designed system consisting of the performance side [7] including usability, functionality, complexity, pragmatic, and also the emotional side [8] including aesthetic and hedonic.

The second factor is "user", a user's internal state which is not limited to user's temporal aspects like expectation, needs, motivation, goal, mood, but also user's psychological characteristics and social rules. User's characteristics have been considered little for understanding UX, but in our research, it is sometimes the major factor for determining experience. For example, Nakatani figured out that absence of self-efficacy for ICT affects the inactive use of ICT service [5]. Another example is that implicit belief about one's ability, such as whether one's intelligence is fixed or malleable influences her/his experience [12]. For considering user's internal state, it is also important to focus on his/her social rules because interactions between users and services highly depend on the social rules. For example, Japanese high-school students prefer online chatting service on the smartphone, and would like to touch the smartphone for communication at any time. However, in our interview, we found that they often hide smartphone while talking with their friends because they think that touching smartphone during talking with their friends is a very bad manner. On the other hand, they think it is not a bad manner to use the smartphone while talking with their parents.

The last factor is "environment", the context or environment within which the interaction occurs contains organizational and social setting, meaningfulness of the activity, voluntariness, and physical environment. Here, physical environment represents places, artifacts, and also the arrangement of the room in the house. Even though Hassenzahl did not mention the physical environment as the major factor for considering context and environment, we believe it is necessary to include it because it often determines the usage pattern of the ICT services. For example, various ICT services and other artifacts are located in the same place, and the arrangement of them affects ICT service use. In addition, in the mobile services, they are used in the different places in the different manner.

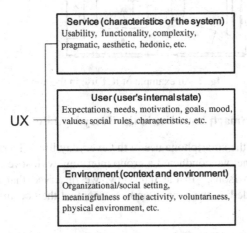

Fig. 1. Three factors that affect user experience

2.1   Example 1: ICT Service Use in the Home

Here, we show two examples in which the use of ICT services strongly depends on the environment. The first example is the use of ICT services in the home. Figure 2 illustrates a floor map of a family's home created from our field study. They were living in an apartment, and the family consisted of husband, wife, and two elementary school children. In the family, we found that the husband used iPad mainly while sitting at the table in the living room. In the position, it is possible to watch the TV while interacting with the iPad. On the other hand, PC was placed in the children's room locating next to the living room. The PC was used mainly by the wife, and she could not watch the TV while interacting with the PC. In our field study, we found that in various families, PCs were sometimes located near the printer and their position was determined if there was enough space to put the PC and the printer. Therefore, it is not convenient to use them while doing something else like watching TV. This phenomenon may reduce the frequency of PC use. iPad is different. There are little locational constraints to use the iPad. In the example illustrated in Figure 2, iPad was stored under the very narrow space of the counter, and the husband could pick it up while sitting at the table. For designing ICT services in the home, it is very important to consider accessibility to the service. If it requires more effort to use the service than competitive services, it is difficult to get the major position in the family.

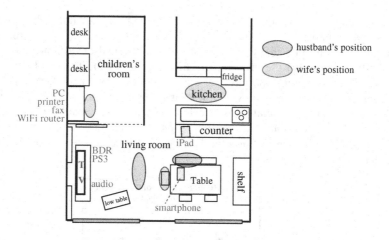

Fig. 2. An example of ICT use in the home

2.2   Example 2: Smartphone Use in the Everyday Life

Another example is the smartphone use in the everyday life. To understand everyday use of the smartphone, we conducted a group interview with seven university students and nine business persons. In the interview, we observed that their use of smartphone highly depended on the context and environment they occurred.

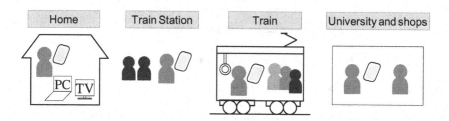

Fig. 3. An example of smartphone use in the everyday life

Figure 3 illustrates an example of smartphone use in their everyday life. Here, four different contexts, in the home, at the train station, on the train, and in the university and shops are described. In the interview, they reported that they used ICT services with different manners in the different contexts. In the home, there were different artifacts including PC and smartphone. All of them had both smartphone and PC, but their environment was different between users. They preferred the PC because it had large screen. However, they sometimes used the smartphone instead of the PC. It was because it took much time to start using PC. Some users kept their PC in the sleep mode, so it required short time (e.g. within 10 seconds) to start the PC, but they still thought that the smartphone was better because it was possible to use it with no burden time to wait. When they thought they required large screen, e.g. browsing the Web sites with multiple windows or reading PDF documents, they switched to the PC.

While riding on the train, their ICT service use was sometimes restricted due to the network condition. Some of them could not use the online services because network condition was not good on the train, so a contents prefetch service was preferred. Another example is the train condition. If they sat on the train, they could use the social network services (SNS) and the email but while standing on the crowded train, some of them hesitated to use them because the smartphone screen might be glanced by other persons.

In the university and the shops, the use of smartphone highly depends on whether they stayed with their friends or not. With their friends, they did not use the smartphone frequently, but if they had a time to become alone, i.e. in the toilet, they often checked SNS and email quickly.

For designing mobile services, it is necessary to consider how they use services in the different contexts and environments, and design the service to fit into the contexts. Especially, it is necessary to determine which context will be the major one, and the service should be designed to be used comfortably in the context.

3   From User-Centered Design to Environment-Centered Design

The traditional user-centered design focuses on the user, and considers how the user interacts with the services. Figure 4(a) illustrates the interaction between the user and the service. For example, the persona-scenario method creates 'persona', a description of a fictitious user based on field data as well as statistical data for understanding interaction pattern, user needs and user values [1,6]. Traditional user-centered design assumes implicitly that there is only one user and she/he interacts with one service. It is because when the user-centered design was proposed in the end of '80s, most computers were large, and the user interacted with only one computer at the same time. It was difficult to consider mobile and ubiquitous services in the real-world. However, as described in Section 1, interaction between users and services is changed drastically in the last quarter of the century, and various interaction patterns are available today. Different services are supplied in the different artifacts, and users interact with different services simultaneously. In addition, two or more users sometimes interact with the one service. For example, the smart TV in the home can be shared by two or more users. For understanding interaction in the real-world, as illustrated in Figure 4(b), it is necessary to focus on the environment that contains both users and services. Based on the basic idea, we propose the environment-centered design where users and services existing in the environment are described simultaneously, and the service specification is derived from the description.

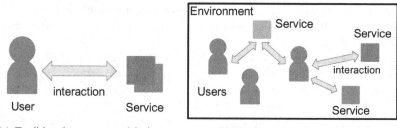

(a). Traditional user-centered design   (b). Environment-centered design

Fig. 4. From user-centered design to environment-centered design

In the environment-centered design, the fundamental process is to describe the environments in the different contexts at first, and then depict people and interaction pattern of the services available in the environment. Next, from the environmental description, service restrictions and opportunities are derived. By describing more environments in the different contexts, more service restrictions and opportunities can be derived. Those service restrictions and opportunities derived from the contexts become strong clue to determine the service scenario and specifications for designing new services.

In the rest of the section, the detail of the design process is described. Figure 5 illustrates the overview of the proposed method. In Step (1), the 'real' data is collected from field study and interview. For describing environment, it is highly important to use the real data. It is because when the service developers describe those factors just from their imagination, they might be different from the real-world. In addition, the detail of the environment description will be lacked. In addition, it is very difficult to describe the user's internal state like their expectation, needs and social rules. The idea to create the description from the real data is taken from the persona-scenario method. However, the importance of using the real data is more essential because service restrictions and opportunities are derived from the contextual difference between different environments. If it is not possible to describe the prominent features that are unique in the context, it is difficult to extract the interesting and valuable restrictions and opportunities. Deep understanding of user's internal state is also required in this approach. In addition, it is also necessary to select the target user group for collecting data because context might be absolutely different if you focus on the different user group instead of the target group. Therefore, it is necessary to determine the target user group before collecting the real data. If it is not possible to define the target user group when collecting the data, it is better to choose users from the different user groups, and by comparing environmental difference, target user group can be selected. In the interview, it is better to ask everyday life from the morning to the night. In general, one-day life consists of different contexts, e.g. meal time, commute time, working time, housekeeping, and so on. Therefore, by understanding the contexts in one-day life, it will become easy to understand the environment and service use for the each context.

In Step (2), contexts are determined from the collected data. It is not necessary to select all contexts appeared in the interview. However, it is necessary to select several important contexts that will be valuable in designing the new ICT services.

If there are unique environments and artifacts, prominent use style, and interesting values and experiences in some context, the context should be selected.

In Step (3), environment, people, and usage of existing ICT services are described in the each context. Like creating persona in the persona-scenario method, real data taken from different users are filtered and merged for creating fictitious environment. In the environment description, it is necessary to retain interesting, valuable and distinctive features found in the real data. People are not limited to the user of the service, but also other persons who may affect the user's ICT service use. For example, in the commute time, users sometimes get on the crowded train where bunch of people are jammed every day. As mentioned before, some of them hesitate to user SNS in such environment. In this case, it is necessary to describe that the train is jammed with people and the user does not use SNS in the environment. While describing services, it is not necessary to mention the new service designing here, but taken from the interview and field study, write down what type of the existing services they used and how they interacted with the services in the each context. It is important because in our observation, the way to use the service highly depends on the context and the environment. Therefore, it is possible to estimate how to use the new service in the same context and environment. For example, in our interview, some people used weather forecast service on the smartphone in the busy morning, and rushed to get the latest forecast in the very short time. In the context, services must be designed as simple as possible, and required to get the answer quickly with a few or no operations.

In Step (4), write down the service restrictions and opportunities driven from the each context. For example, from the context 'busy morning', it is possible to describe that 'service must be simple and requires no operation' as the restriction, and if the existing services are not simple, 'more simple than existing services and an user can obtain information just by glancing at or without looking at the screen' will become the opportunity for the new service. In case of 'crowded train', privacy problem will become a restriction if the service is designed for young users.

Finally, in Step (5), service scenario and specifications are derived from the service restrictions and opportunities. For emerging new services, existing design process like the persona-scenario method can be applied in the step.

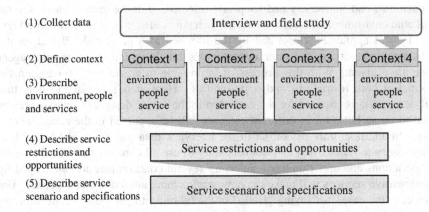

Fig. 5. Five steps of the environment-centered approach to design ICT services

4   Case Study: Designing Voice Agent System on Smartphone

Here, we show a case study that highlights the strength of the environment-centered approach. The goal in this case study is to design a new voice agent system on the smartphone for young people.

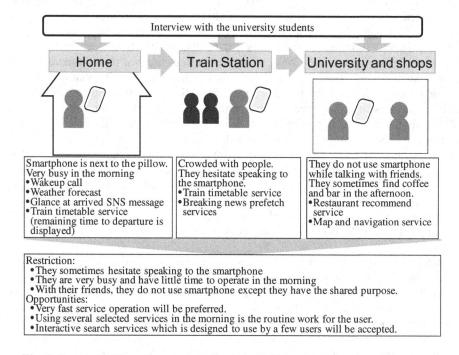

Fig. 6. Overview of the voice agent service design in the environment-centered approach

Figure 6 illustrates the overview of the voice agent service design in the environment-centered approach. In the example, three different contexts consist of 'home', 'train station', and 'university and shop' are selected. For the each context, several remarkable environmental features and user behaviors are derived from the interview data. Typical applications operated by the user are also presented. Based on the results, three restrictions and three opportunities for designing the new voice agent service are derived. With this process, it is possible to create the service scenario that satisfies both restrictions and opportunities. Here, it is necessary to note that detail description is required for the each step in the actual design. Contexts are not limited to three, but a lot of different contexts will be appeared in the actual service design. In addition, only the subset of the interview data was described here. It is also necessary to remark that it is not necessary to use all contexts for describing service restrictions and opportunities. Selecting several contexts that are not scoped by the competitive services will make the new service more attractive and superior. For example, in the case, just saying "Hello" in the morning to get the constant information required every morning will be preferred for the users.

5   Discussion

The strength of the proposed design approach is that it is possible to deal with the environment, the users and the services in the different context simultaneously. On the other hand, because the proposed design approach is based on the interview and field study, there are several limitations. The first limitation is the clarity of the target service at the beginning. If there are no conditions and restrictions in the new service, it might be difficult to conduct interview and field study for acquiring valuable data. Therefore, the approach may be difficult to use in the very early stage of the service design. However, in our case, there is rare case that there are no conceptual ideas in designing new ICT services.

The second limitation is the difficulty to innovate the completely novel service which is not available now. It is because we cannot estimate their usage pattern of the novel service from the existing social rules. In general, when a novel service is emerged, social rules are formed gradually in the long period, and it is difficult to estimate the rule before the service appearance in the society. We should examine how those two limitations will actually affect in the service design process in our future works.

6   Conclusion and Future Works

In the paper, we propose the environment-centered approach for ICT service design. We have started examining the proposed approach for ICT service design and confirmed the strength of the approach. However, we need a lot more case studies to determine what factors in the each step are the most important and how to derive them from the field study and interview data. For applying this approach to various services, we are planning to make the design process more explicit and easy to use for service designers and developers for designing high UX services.

References

1. Cooper, A., Reimann, R., Cronin, D.: About Face 3: The Essentials of Interaction Design. Wiley Publishing (2007)
2. Fallman, D.: Design-oriented Human-Computer Interaction. In: Proc. of the 2003 Annual Conference on Human Factors in Computing Systems (CHI 2003), pp. 225–232. ACM Press (2003)
3. Fallman, D.: The New Good: Exploring the Potential of Philosophy of Technology to Contribute to Human-Computer Interaction. In: Proc. of the 2011 Annual Conference on Human Factors in Computing Systems (CHI 2011), pp. 1051–1060. ACM Press (2011)
4. Hassenzahl, M., Tractinsky, N.: User Experience - A Research Agenda. Behaviour & Information Technology 25(2), 91–97 (2006)
5. Nakatani, M., Ohno, T., Nakane, A., Komatsubara, A., Hashimoto, S.: How to Motivate People to Use Internet at Home: Understanding the Psychology of Non-Active Users. In: Proc. on APCHI 2012, pp. 259–268. ACM Press (2012)
6. Nielsen, L.: Personas - User Focused Design. Springer (2013)

7. Norman, D.: The Psychology of Everyday Things. Basic Books (1988)
8. Norman, D.: Emotional Design: Why We Love (or Hate) Everyday Things. Basic Books (2005)
9. Pine II, J., Gilmore, J.H.: The Experience Economy: Work is Theater & Every Business a Stage. Harvard Business Scholl Press (1999)
10. Schmitt, B.H.: Customer Experience Management. John Wiley & Sons (2003)
11. Vermeeren, A.P., Law, E.L., Roto, V., Obrist, M., Hoonhout, J., Väänänen-Vainio-Mattila, K.: User Experience Evaluation Methods: Current State and Development Needs. In: Proc. of NordiCHI 2010, pp. 521–530. ACM Press (2010)
12. Yamauchi, T., Ohno, T., Nakatani, M., Kato, Y., Markman, A.: Psychology of User Experience in a Collaborative Video-Conference System. In: Proc. of CSCW 2012, pp. 187–196. ACM Press (2012)

Overview of Global User Interfaces for Localization

Clara Peters[1], Mazhar Sajjad[2], Myungkwon Hwang[3], Jinhyung Kim[3],
Sa-Kwang Song[3], Do-Heon Jeong[3,*], Seungwoo Lee[3], and Hanmin Jung[3]

[1] Dept. of International Information Management, University of Hildesheim, Germany
petersc@uni-hildesheim.de
[2] University of Science and Technology (UST), Korea
ms@kisti.re.kr
[3] Dept. of Computer Intelligence Research,
Korea Institute of Science and Technology Information (KISTI), Daejeon, Korea
{mgh,jinhyung,esmallj,heon,swlee,jhm}@kisti.re.kr

Abstract. In today world user interfaces must meet the demands of an international environment. User Interface (UI) based on the user preferences and targeting a specific group of people can improve the usability, it fulfilled market demand and reduced the service cost. It is very difficult and costly process to localize a user interface before internationalize it. This paper highlights both the verbal and the visual part of the interface that can play a very important role while creating a user interface that aims at being adapted to local user groups. This paper gives an overview of cultural differences such as different color associations, divergent meaning of metaphors as well as different standards concerning typography. The goal of the work is to emphasize the usability of localized user interfaces and guarantee the comfortable and intuitive use for local users.

Keywords: localization, globalization, internationalization.

1 Introduction

Against the background of the proceeding globalization, the user interfaces of computer–based products and services need to operate in a global environment. Within this paper, the term globalization refers to the establishment of products and services for a worldwide consumption/use [1].

First of all, it is to be questioned why a global user interface (UI) is necessary. The answer is simple: a globalised UI increases the probability of users all over the world to find the UI more appealing and as a result get more engaged with the product or service and use it more efficiently. Simply, globalised UI can help to improve usability. Furthermore, users from different cultures are used to different standards of UI and therefore might be dissatisfied or frustrated when not being able to intuitively understand the UI of a product or service [1].

A basic example to demonstrate the importance of globalised UI concern different date formats used across the world. Most of the European countries use the

---

* Corresponding author.

S. Yamamoto (Ed.): HIMI/HCII 2013, Part I, LNCS 8016, pp. 357–364, 2013.

date format DD/MM/YYYY, whereas many Asian countries like Japan use YYYY/MM/DD. The format MM/DD/YYYY is unique to the United States. Within different countries and cultures, slashes, dashes or periods might be used as separators. Sometimes leading zeroes are used, in other cases they might be left out If a native Japanese speaker is reading a US English web page from a web site in Germany that contains the date 03/04/02 how do they interpret it? [2], there are different approaches to global user interface solutions: rather universal and general approaches or localized and individual approaches [1].

This paper first gives an overview of user interfaces. Both localization and internationalization are dealt with and the benefits of global UI are addressed. Further the paper highlight the guidelines for UI developers to design their interface with the consideration of the multicultural backgrounds of their users in order to aim at a globally enhanced usability.

2   Background Work

International firms try to create global UI in order to adapt to the international environment with a solution that is not or minimal to be changed for different user groups and represents one solution for the majority of the worldwide users. The concept of user interface for all, it means that the development of one interface that appeals to the broadest range of users and is in accord with their abilities, skills, requirements and preferences [3].

However, for certain markets localized versions are necessary in order to achieve positive feedback from certain users. Localization refers to the process of customizing a UI to a specific market or culture. One part of this customization is the translation of the content. Yet, localization efforts go far beyond the mere translation and creation of a superficial local appearance. Localized UIs are developed for a specific group of users, which can mean a country, a culture, a region or broadly speaking even a corporate culture [1].

Often enough one product or service is first designed for one particular culture, before localization efforts for other cultures are made. Once the attempt was made to localize one UI for several cultures, it became evident that certain preparations could be done in advance to simplify multiple localization efforts and avoid the step of re-engineering. Internationalization refers to exactly that, the separation of localizable data from the primary functionality when preparing code. This means that localizable items are externalized and the code is becomes language-independent. Hence, the necessity for re-design in later stages becomes redundant, as the translation into different languages is already prepared during the development stage of the product or service. Sometimes internationalization is also referred to as localization enablement, because it aims at making the localization and translation easier [4, 5].

3   User Interface Localization: Pros and Cons

The main goal of a globalized UI is to have only one version for all users over the world, which would be in English. However, this might cause a lower satisfaction among users as the interests of the broadest range of users might highly differ from those of many individuals. Research shows that web-site visitors stay twice as long on local language sites [1]. A product or service will rarely achieve global acceptance with a one-size-fits-all concept.

A localized UI causes higher initial development costs as content has to be adjusted to different cultures and translated into different languages. However these higher costs go along with more satisfied users and an expanded target market [6]. As a localized user interface leads to an increased comprehension among the users, customer–service costs might be decreased and in the end localization efforts might be a profitable investment [1].

When a user interface is adapted to familial structures and preferences of the user, it becomes more usable. The international Standards Organization (ISO) defines the word usable as effective, efficient and satisfying [1]. Therefore, from the user's perspective, localization can lead to an effective, efficient and satisfying user interface.

4   Globalizing User Interfaces

Internationalization is an important preparation to enable localization for several cultures. But what needs to be considered when internationalizing a user interface? They can serve as a general approach to start addressing concerns that need to be considered within the global user interface design process.

When trying to internationalize a user interfaces and thereby enable localizations, the visual and verbal are the two areas of concern that need to be considered. The visual includes issues like images, icons, symbols, colors and the layout whereas the verbal includes wording, text, typography and translation.

4.1   Verbal Aspects of the User Interface

The difficult task of verbally adjusting an interface to local user groups is probably the most important step of localization. The verbal part of the UI can be internationalized and enabled for localization efficiently; e.g. how to go about the translation process and which cultural typography differences need to be considered.

Usually an interface that aims at being globalised is first written in English. One basic rule to follow is to use simple English, because it is generally easier and cheaper to translate. This can be achieved by using a restricted vocabulary as well as a restricted sentence structure. Most suitable is the noun-verb-object structure. Another benefit of simple English is that non-native English speakers are more likely to understand and a translation might not even be necessary, as non-natives might be able to apply their English knowledge to access the content of the interface [7].

Generally, acronyms and abbreviations should be avoided, as they are difficult to translate. Translated acronyms might not be concise or could have a negative connotation. Additionally it is advisable to not string together three or more nouns. After the translation process, the relationship between those nouns is more likely to become confusing or cloudy. To solve this problem, prepositions can be used to clarify the relationships between nouns [7].

The cultural context and local idioms must be kept in mind when writing content for the user interface. Words might have different meanings or obtain a new meaning after the translation process. If the cultural context is not considered, embarrassing or dangerous faux-pas can be a negative consequence. Numerous brand blunders can be used as an example for an insufficient consideration of the cultural context. Pepsi, for example, introduced their slogan, come alive! You're the Pepsi generation, to the Chinese market. However, translated into Chinese the slogan read, Pepsi brings your ancestors back from the grave [1, 4].

When a word cannot be translated, it is best to keep the original term. Some words simply do not exist in other languages. Looking at linguistic evolution foreign words are often adapted when they do not exist in a language. Schadenfreude, for example, is a German word that describes malicious joy or pleasure from another's misfortune. This word has been adapted to the English language, as no English term existed to describe this meaning and hence a mere translation would not assure to deliver the same content meaning [1, 7].

Furthermore it is recommendable to keep additional screen space for translation. Generally in English the same information can be carried across with a lot less words than needed in other languages. The word fuse for example, can be translated as Absicherung in German, almost three times as many letters. Therefore expansion room for translation should be allowed [1, 7].

4.2   Verbal Part of the User Interface – Translation

Language and country are related, but there are several reasons why they cannot be equated. First of all, many countries share the same language; there are roughly 70 English-speaking countries worldwide. However, these countries obviously do not all share the same culture. Secondly, some countries are officially bilingual, for example Canada or India. This means that the designer of global user interfaces must consider both the language and the country and its cultural background as a potential determinant of language rendering and translation [4].

How to proceed when the user interface is meant to be globally used and therefore to be translated into most languages in the world? Generally the language world is divided into three parts: Europe, the Middle East and the Far East, reported how Microsoft Inc. goes on with their translation [1]. They begin with a translation into German for Europe, Arabic for the Middle East and Japanese for the Far East. According to Microsoft with these three languages many problems that arise in that language group can be solved and the translation into similar languages is simplified. Once the text has been translated into German, problems such as gender, expansion and accent have already been addressed for other European languages. After a translation into Arabic the issue of bidirectional and cursive letters will have already been solved. Thirdly, written Japanese is one of the most difficult Asian languages. With this translation the issue of double-byte will already be solved [7].

4.3   Verbal Part of the User Interface – Typography

Among different languages various kind of character-encoding schemes are used. ASCII (American Standard Code for Information Interchange) is generally used for English. Different schemes are used for European and for Asian languages [1].

It is necessary to adhere to local formats, such as date, time, money measurements, addresses, telephone numbers and temperature formats. Localization is needed, in order to provide a comfortable environment for the user and avoid misunderstandings. The Table.1 below shows exemplary portrays the differences among different countries [1, 7]. If the developer already uses separable variables for date and time in the code, instead of using fixed dates, and leaves enough space in the UI for any possible date and time representation, the correct date format can be inserted when the UI is localized without having to change the layout design [4].

ISO furthermore has established some standards concerning the typography like The 24 hour clock, the Gregorian calendar and the date format YYYY/MM/DD.

Table 1. Exemplary Typography Differences

Format/Type	United States	Europe	South Asia, Gulf Countries	Korea
Numeric Numbers	1,753.77 (e.g.$1753 and 77 cents)	1 754,77 or 1.754,77	1'754,77	1,755.77
Data and Time	MM/DD/ YYYY, hh:mm:ss a.m/p.m (12 Hour)	DD/MM/ YYYY, hh:mm:ss (24 Hour)	DD/MM/ YYYY, hh:mm:ss a.m/p.m (12 hour)	YYYY/MM/ DD, hh:mm:ss (24 Hour)
Temperature	Fahrenheit	Celsius (or Kelvin)	Celsius	Celsius
Calendar	Gregorian Calendar	Gregorian Calendar	Gregorian Calendar, Islamic Calendar	Gregorian Calendar

4.4   Visual Part of the Interface

Images and Symbols are the visible language of a culture, just like the verbal counterpart, very strongly among different cultures, and can cause problems when not carefully selected. Therefore it is important to adhere to local norms as there are variations in the meaning of symbols, objects and gestures. The following section highlight the visual component of the user interface focusing on images, symbols, layout, and orientation as well as the use of color.

It is beneficial to use internationally recognized objects, when possible. An example is to use an envelope-image to indicate mail instead of using a mailbox symbol, because different looking mailboxes exist in the world with a huge variety of color and shape. There are internationally accepted symbols that have been developed by trade or standards organizations like ISO. Before designing a customized symbol, it should be checked whether the needed symbol has already been created and is internationally acknowledged which would make the design redundant. When no culture-free or internationally recognized icon is available, different icons for different cultures must be implemented in order to not confuse the user [4, 7].

It is advisable to be cautious when using images that have potential to be sensitive or incorrect in certain culture, to make sure that no user feels uncomfortable, offended or even insulted. Sensitive subjects include pictures of animals and people. Showing a country's flag to indicate the according language, might not always be clear, because some countries are bilingual, which means that a flag cannot be directly associated with the language. Furthermore the display of maps, which include controversial regional or national borders, should be avoided. Caution is also appropriate when using the x or the check mark. Those do not universally have the same meaning. In some areas the x in a check box means that the option is not applicable, in others it means that the option is selected [1, 4].

Another important thing to consider concerning graphics is not to present text directly within the graphic. If text and graphics are not overlaid, the graphic does not need to be redone when the UI is localized/ translated. This will simplify the localization process [4].

4.5   Layout and Orientation of the User Interface

Sometimes it is necessary to give directions on how graphical, non-text elements should be read. Therefore it is necessary to check that the arrangement of these is not inconsistent with the language reading direction.

Furthermore appropriate printing formats and sizes should be used. In the US a standard office letterhead size is 8.5 x 11 inches whereas in Europe it is 210 mm x 297 mm [1].

Generally perceptual guidelines concerning good color usage should be followed. No more than five colors should be used (as a minimum there needs to be one background and one foreground color) in order to not burden the user with having to recall more in their short-term memory. In principle warm colors should be used for advancing elements and cold colors for receding elements [1].

Important aspects to color usage in globalized user interfaces are different color associations among different cultures. The color red is a good example to portray how different cultural color associations can be. Red means happiness in China, whilst in the United States it is a signal for danger or a warning signal to indicate to stop. Red stands for creativity and life in India, but symbolizes death in Egypt and aristocracy in France [7].

Table 2. Some Cultural Associations [1]

Country Name	Red	Yellow	Green	Blue	White
China	Happiness	Birth Wealth Power	Ming Dynasty Heavens Clouds	Heavens Clouds	Death Purity
Egypt	Death	Happiness Prosperity	Fertility Strength	Virtue Faith	Joy
France	Aristocracy	Temporary	Criminality	Truth Freedom Peace	Neutrality
India	Life Creativity	Success	Prosperity Fertility	National Sports	Death Purity
Japan	Anger Danger	Grace Nobility	Future Youth Energy	Villainy	Death
United States	Danger Stop	Cowardice Caution	Safety Go	Masculinity	Purity

5   Conclusion

Nowadays, considering the proceeding globalization, user interfaces have to meet the demands of international environment to be internationally successful. The paper emphasis the needs of localizing the user interface of a product or service. Adapting the UI to the preferences and knowledge of a specific group of users goes along with more satisfied users and an expanded target market. Furthermore localization enhances comprehension among user groups and helps to increase usability, which in later stages might spare service costs.

As mentioned before, localization efforts of a user interface are very often done after a UI of a product or service is adapted and finished for one culture. It is a complex and costly process to localize a user interface that is not internationalized, which means that culture and content is separated whilst the UI is created. Therefore it is recommendable to regard internationalization as a necessary step to enable localization in the design process.

The given overview concerning both the verbal and the visual part of the interface can be considered when creating a user interface that aims at being adapted to local user groups. They consider cultural differences such as different color associations, divergent meaning of metaphors as well as different standards concerning typography. Recommendations have been given about which strategies will simplify the localization of one UI for many different cultures such as the avoidance of certain topics and symbols or the order of translating content.

These guidelines cover basic things to consider when attempting to internationalize and localize a user interface but obviously do not cover all possible challenges that a developer is confronted with when dealing with many different cultures. To assure the usability of localized user interfaces and guarantee the comfortable and intuitive use for local users other approaches need to be considered as well. A possible step would be to conduct user tastings in order to receive the feedback of real users.

References

1. Marcus, A.: Global/Intercultural User Interface Design. In: Sears, A., Jacko, J.A. (eds.) The Human–Computer Interaction Handbook. Fundamentals, Evolving Technologies and Emerging Applications, pp. 355–379. Lawrence Erlbaum Associates, New York (2008)
2. Honomichl, L., Ishida, R.: W3C Internationalization. Date formats (2010), http://www.w3.org/International/questions/qa-date-format (retrieved November 19, 2012)
3. Stephanidis, C. (ed.): User interfaces for all. Lawrence Erlbaum Associates, New York (2000)
4. Aykin, N. (ed.): Usability and Internationalization of Information Technology. Lawrence Erlbaum Associates, New Jersey (2005)
5. Cadieux, P., Esselink, B.: GILT: Globalization, Internationalization, Localization, Translation (2012), http://www.localization.org/globalizationinsider/2002/03/gilt_globalizat.html (retrieved November 14, 2012)
6. Schmitz, K.-D., Wahle, K.: Softwarelokalisierung. Stauffenburg-Verlag, Tübingen (2000)
7. Galitz, W.: The Essential Guide to User Interface Design. Principles and Techniques, 3rd edn. Wiley Publishing, Indianapolis (2007)

Quantifying the Impact of Standards When Hosting Robotic Simulations in the Cloud

Sekou L. Remy

School of Computing,
Clemson University
Clemson SC
sremy@clemson.edu

Abstract. Cloud computing has the ability to transform simulation by providing access to computation remotely. The transformations are not without cost however. The physics-based simulations required in robotics are sensitive to timing, and given the complexity of the operating environments, there are many reasons for a roboticist to be concerned.

In this work we explore the impact of the cloud, web, and networking standards on the control of a simulated robot. Our results show that, on average, there is a noticeable impact on performance, but this impact is not statistically significant in five of the six considered scenarios. These results provide support for efforts that seek to use the cloud to support meaningful simulations. Our results are not globally applicable to robotics simulation. When using cloud-hosted simulations, roboticists yield fine tuned control of the environment, and as such there are some simulations are simply not viable candidates for this treatment.

1 Introduction

Realistic computer based simulation has been an effective tool – in both academia [1,2] and industry [3,4] – to explore content that is difficult to recreate in the physical world (safety, distance), challenging to understand because of scale, or even impossible to occur under easily reproducible conditions. Simulation technology benefits from advances in computing and information technology, but only if these advances can be incorporated in effective and timely ways.

Cloud computing is a "model for enabling ubiquitous, convenient, on-demand network access to a shared pool of configurable computing resources" [5]. It is one example of technology that has the potential to impact simulation, especially in scenarios where the simulations are computationally intensive or data intensive. It also bears promise for simulations that are difficult to manage, or administer. Cloud computing is just one (set) of a host of standards or pseudo-standards that impact the way that simulation is developed and deployed. These standards are often developed in different communities and as such, it is not uncommon that multiple efforts to accomplish the same aim exist. It is critical that developers try the tools (and standards) that are developed in other communities, and comprehensive understanding of these tools is the doorway to such cross-community participation.

S. Yamamoto (Ed.): HIMI/HCII 2013, Part I, LNCS 8016, pp. 365–374, 2013.
© Springer-Verlag Berlin Heidelberg 2013

Cloud computing, while an example of exactly such a standard, also provides a means for this participation to occur. It can do so by providing shared access and management of tools, algorithms and data (more broadly, resources). In this work we consider an application of cloud computing to share open-source simulation environments. These simulation environments are built upon several standards (and pseudo-standards) themselves. Our aim is to identify these standards, so as to promote their use, and to also study how two sets of standards, (cloud computing and web standards) can impact the use of the overall simulation that they facilitate.

In robotic simulation, time has a higher priority than in typical computing scenarios. Sharing much in common with controls [6], timing variability and latency both impact the operation of simulations (and physical robots too), but are often invisible properties. Since many of the standards that we consider in this work add a layer of abstraction and time overhead, the impact of time must have some effect, and it is our aim to begin the process of quantifying how significant this impact is for the many combinations of possible configurations.

2   Background

The Defense Advanced Research Projects Agency (DARPA) Virtual Robotics Challenge (VRC) is an exciting competition slated to occur June 10 – 24, 2013. In support of this challenge, the agency has funded the creation of a "cloud-based, real-time, operator-interactive virtual test bed that uses physics-based models of inertia, actuation, contact and environment dynamics". More simply stated, DARPA has funded the development of cloud-hosted robotic simulation environment. This type of simulation is an avenue to increased access to meaningful interaction with robotics, and has the promise to stimulate the robotics industry worldwide.

This cloud-hosted simulation leverages Infrastructure as a Service (IaaS) to provision a virtual machine on which well vetted open source simulation can be hosted. IaaS in essence provides virtualization of operating systems and the infrastructure to run them on, including both networking and storage. Currently there are scores of IaaS providers, and in many ways this cloud model is one of the most readily understood "cloud standards". While there are differences in the configuration processes, and in payment options, all of the provided offerings enable the same basic premise: remote access to an operating system. The value proposition of IaaS is interesting beyond defense related research. The prospects of scale, on-demand flexibility, managed hosting, are only but a few of the reasons that this approach is also quite relevant to education and training.

Cloud computing is just one of the developments in Internet and Computing Technologies that are exciting for robotic simulation. The falling costs of memory, increasing clock cycles, the advent of manycore machines, and the mash-up of all of these in modern graphics processing units (GPUs) have all been good things for simulation. They have helped to make high quality, feature rich and photo realistic, real-time physics-based simulations possible.

The process of hosting and accessing remote simulations in cloud infrastructures is not without challenges. For instance, cloud technologies are inherently networked and as such, their use is subject to the overhead and uncertainty associated with several formal and informal standards. Examples of these standards include TCP [7] and HTTP [8] which are networking protocols, HTML [9] and ECMAscript [10] which enable content to be rendered and processed on remote clients, and URI [11] and XMLHttpRequest [12] which facilitate the transfer of data over the network. In addition to these formal standards, there is a powerful set of informal standards (or pseudo-standards) that exist in the web ecosystem. These resources, like web servers, web browsers and URL libraries like CURL, support defined standards and serve as powerful cross platform pathways to enable modern software development.

In our context, these are the core standards with which we are concerned. These standards provide tremendous flexibility in development and delivery of these simulations, but many in the controls community are wary about the impact that they have on the dynamics of the overall simulation and control of the robot.

For well over a decade, the networked controls community has developed approaches to control systems in the presence of delay and jitter associated with network use in the control systems [6]. The remote simulation of physical systems, especially when the simulation is performed on a cloud-hosted virtual machine has the potential to amplify the challenges faced thus far, hence the reticence displayed by the community is not without just cause. These challenges can be detrimental to the usability of the cloud-hosted simulation, and can result in inconsistencies in applications like the DARPA VRC.

3   Methodology

The scope of our investigation is focused on the impact that the suite of relevant standards can have on remote simulation. We do not seek to address the concerns of the merits of simulating a robot; instead we are concerned with the potential benefits (or drawbacks) on performance when these simulations are moved to the cloud. To that end, we begin by exploring a configuration similar to that devised for the DARPA Challenge. It involves the use of the Robot Operating System (ROS) infrastructure [13], coupled with a third party simulation environment. ROS is a high-quality open source "meta operating system" that provides the core infrastructure for message/services and abstractions of other useful robotic resources.

We initially intended to study the use of Gazebo [14] with ROS (as used in the Challenge), but it was observed that the simulation environment crashed randomly in the cloud infrastructure (See Fig. 1). The simulation environment did not demonstrate this instability in hardware, and for this reason we chose to replace Gazebo with the Stage simulator [15] and limit the control to the two dimensions permitted by this third party tool.

It is our aim to quantify the impact of the use of standards on performance of a robotic simulation, and to uncover whether that impact has a significant effect

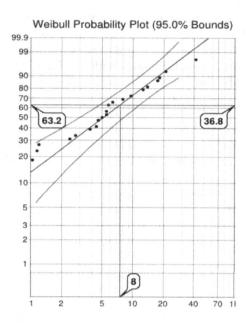

Fig. 1. Distribution of time to failure for this cloud-hosted Gazebo simulation

on the performance of a mobile robot during a navigation task. Time is at the root of the impact of these standards. The effect of time with web standards is associated with delay while with IaaS (cloud computing), it is directly linked to the approximation of time that comes from hardware virtualization. To explore these properties we use the following seven scenarios depicted in Fig. 2.

For each of the scenarios, the client issues velocity commands to the simulated robot over a duration of 200 minutes. The values for the X and Y components of the velocity are derived from (1) and (2). In these equations t is time in nanoseconds. The commands are issued every 1.05 seconds (as measured by the client process). The client is limited by the OS capabilities, in addition to the limitation of the clock that the OS is accessing.

$$v_x = .3 * cos(0.2 * t) \tag{1}$$

$$v_y = .2 * (1.5 * cos(0.3 * t) + .5 * cos(-0.1 * t)) \tag{2}$$

The simulation environment is updated at 10Hz. The simulation does not include any obstacles, so the motion of the robot is only influenced by the velocity commands issued by the client controller. There is a 0.2 second timeout applied to account for potential for disrupted communication between the controller and the simulation environment. All of these timing constraints are subject to the operating environment on the simulation computer.

The webserver used to provide access to the simulation makes use of webpy framework (webpy.org). This server is implemented as a ROS package, and provides an API to convert velocity commands in the form of a query-encoded string

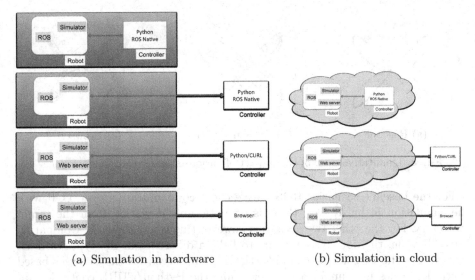

(a) Simulation in hardware   (b) Simulation in cloud

Fig. 2. The seven scenarios where the robotic simulation was run on a hardware platform as well as in a cloud-hosted virtual machine (provisioned through IaaS). The scenarios also feature different combinations of web standards that are relevant in the delivery of remote simulation to end-users.

to Twist messages [16], which are then published to ROS. Twist messages are a ROS standard message type in ROS that defines the linear and angular component of velocity. This web server also hosts the HTML page that is downloaded and "run" by the browser on the client machine to run a controller in-browser. Any scenario that uses the web server to communicate with the robot also makes use of the Hypertext Transfer Protocol (HTTP) communication protocol. In this work HTTP uses TCP to actually facilitate the communication over the network.

The baseline for comparison will be the hardware-based simulation that uses a ROS-native controller. This baseline, and in fact, any scenario that features a ROS-native controller, directly uses TCP for network communication (and there is no additional communication overhead).

4 Results

In this work successfully capture the impact of the use of web and cloud standards on performance of a navigation task. In this section we first take a qualitative view, and then proceed to the quantitative assessment of the impact.

Figure 3, shows the trajectories of the robot under the baseline scenario, as well as when the hardware simulation is controlled with Python and a web browser over the network. These trajectories capture the robot's motion through nine cycles of the "butterfly" pattern. These three figures each capture the same number of samples of the trajectory of the robot. From these plots it can be seen that there are different types of errors evident in performance.

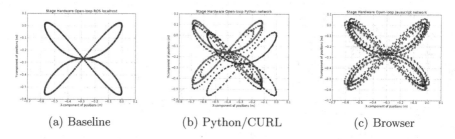

(a) Baseline   (b) Python/CURL   (c) Browser

Fig. 3. Qualitative view of the impact of various standards on performance

For the baseline scenario (ROS native client communicating over TCP with the simulation in hardware), there is no noticeable deviation from the target trajectory. For the other two scenarios however this is not the case. Comparing Figs. 3b & 3c, the data also appears to belie a difference in the types of deviations from the target. For example, the error observed for the Browser based controller varies in a uniform manner, while the Python/CURL controller appears to perform more consistently, except for jolts that move the robot from the expected position.

It should be clear from the data that the use of different standards (browser, URI, etc.) has visibly different effects on the observed movement of the robot. This is as we expected as the use of different standards is coupled with varying impact on time. Since time is modeled as fixed increments, when it varies, this changes the actual position of the robot in space, and thus this deviation is quite evident.

Focusing on the X-component of the robot's position, this qualitative assessment can be readily quantified. We recall that the X-component target velocity for the robot is defined as a pure sinusoid (1). The derivative of a pure sinusoid is another pure sinusoid of the same frequency but with a different phase. This means that it is possible to determine the intended position of the robot at the time that the position was actually sampled. The timing on the simulation machine influences the sampling time, so only approximations of the desired 10Hz update cycle are actually obtained.

To quantify the performance in the presence of different standards, error is measured. This error is defined as the difference between the target position and the actual position over a fixed interval (see Fig. 4). Using this formulation, the performance can be quantified and compared. For the following data, the positions were partitioned into 120 contiguous windows and the errors calculated. Each window (of length 550 samples) approximated the completion of one cycle of the "butterfly" pattern.

Because networking is required to access simulation in the cloud, it is noteworthy that while there is an impact of the use of the network, that impact is not statistically significant (See Fig. 5a). Moreover, the effect of the network appears to be a large contributing factor to negative effects on performance

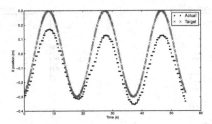

Fig. 4. Example of the difference between target and actual position during velocity based control of the simulated robot

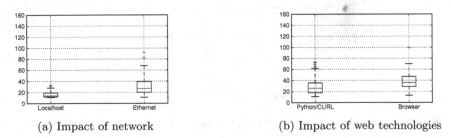

(a) Impact of network   (b) Impact of web technologies

Fig. 5. Impact of web/network standards on velocity control of the simulated robot on a hardware platform

since when the web technologies are applied (Fig. 5b), there is no significant additional impact on performance with this metric. Fig. 5b also allows us to observe the impact of browser technologies on performance. The browser, using the same URI/HTTP access to the webserver, on average performs worse than the Python/CURL client. The takeaway from the results so far is that for remotely accessed simulations, the browser and the URI encoded access of the webserver both have a noticeable impact (on average), but this impact does not result in a statistically significant degradation of performance for the considered this task.

We next shift focus slightly to the impact of the final standard, the use of cloud virtualization as a substitute for hardware. To explore this impact we consider two types of cloud usage: one with no external network traffic and another with traffic initiated from a browser based client. As seen in Fig. 6, performance in both of these scenarios is impacted by the use of the cloud virtualization infrastructure. Fig. 6a shows this impact without concern for an intranetwork connection between client and robot simulation. This data suggest that the distributions of the error (a measure of performance) are again not statistically significant. The same pattern is seen when comparing the impact of virtualization on the browser-mediated control (Fig 6b). So again, the use of the standard (in this case cloud virtualization) has an impact, but not one that is statistically significant.

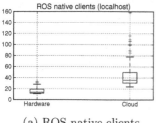
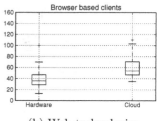

(a) ROS native clients   (b) Web technologies

Fig. 6. Impact of cloud virtualization (IaaS) on velocity control of the robot

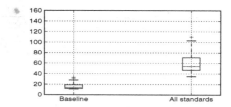

Fig. 7. Comparison of the use of all the considered standards and the baseline

These results effectively quantify the impact of the use of standards on performance of a robotic simulation. They also show that in five of the six scenarios, the impact of the use of standards has no significant effect on the performance of a mobile robot during a navigation task. By this metric, the only case where the difference is significant is when comparing the use of all of the standards to the use of none of the standards (Fig. 7).

5 Summary and Future Work

In this work we have applied several standards and pseudo-standards that can be used to amplify the potential of robotics simulation, and we have quantified how the performance of the open-loop control systems were impacted. Our results show that, as expected, on average the use of (web and cloud) standards does impact performance. There are indeed differences between running the robotic simulation in a cloud virtualization and running the same simulation in hardware. Some of these differences are well understood because of experiences gained from the networked controls community, but the effects of all of these new combinations of component/technologies are at present not well characterized.

Moreover, our results also confirm our hypothesis that the impact is not statistically significant in five of the six considered cases when compared to a baseline simulation. This baseline simulation used communication that bypassed the network interface hardware. With the metrics considered in this work, the differences in performance for any scenario that used the network interface were not significant. The implications are good for the use of cloud-hosted robotic simulation and motivate future work in the following directions.

First, since the browser has been shown to be a viable interface for remote access of the simulation, this means that it provides a path for human studies testing with remote subjects teleoperating mobile robots. Browsers like Chrome now have gamepad APIs and speech to text built-in so such resources reduce the burden on the client side code needed for studies. Of specific interest with user studies is exploring the impact of these standards on human performance of teleoperation tasks. Also, we would be interested in the potential variations due to network conditions, and the impact on performance.

The second area of interest includes increasing the operating frequencies by two orders of magnitude. Studies performed at such frequencies with cloud-hosted simulations over the network will help to quantify the impact of the use of these standards in cases where more autonomy is needed. For example, the PUMA robotic arm [17], a device often used when learning kinematics and controls, operates at 100Hz. If our results were not favorable, this could have provided a critical nail in the coffin as open-loop control at low frequencies provide the best opportunity to experience the negative impacts on performance.

References

1. Gourdeau, R.: Object-oriented programming for robotic manipulator simulation. IEEE Robotics Automation Magazine 4(3), 21–29 (1997)
2. Corke, P.I.: Robotics, Vision & Control: Fundamental Algorithms in Matlab. Springer (2011)
3. Ma, O., Buhariwala, K., Roger, N., MacLean, J., Carr, R.: MSDF – A generic development and simulation facility for flexible, complex robotic systems. Robotica 15, 49–62 (1997)
4. Lerner, M.A., Ayalew, M., Peine, W.J., Sundaram, C.P.: Does training on a virtual reality robotic simulator improve performance on the da Vinci surgical system? J. Endourol. 24(3), 467–472 (2010)
5. Mell, P., Gance, T.: The NIST Definition of Cloud Computing (September 2011)
6. Lin, H., Zhai, G., Antsaklis, P.: Robust stability and disturbance attenuation analysis of a class of networked control systems. In: 42nd IEEE Conference on Decision and Control, vol. 2, pp. 1182–1187 (December 2003)
7. Postel, J. (ed.): Information Sciences Institute: RFC 793 (1981), http://www.ietf.org/rfc/rfc793.txt
8. Fielding, R., Gettys, J., Mogul, J., Frystyk, H., Masinter, L., Leach, P., Berners-Lee, T.: Hypertext transfer protocol – http/1.1 (1999)
9. Raggett, D., Le Hors, A., Jacobs, I.: HTML 4.0 specification. World Wide Web Consortium, Recommendation REC-html40-19980424 (April 1998)
10. International, E.: Ecma-262 ecmascript language specification 5.1. JavaScript Specification, 1–245 (June 2011)
11. Berners-Lee, T., Fielding, R., Masinter, L.: Uniform Resource Identifiers (URI): Generic Syntax, RFC3986 (2005)
12. van Kesteren, A. (ed.): Information Sciences Institute: XMLHttpRequest Living Standard (February 2013), http://xhr.spec.whatwg.org

13. Quigley, M., Conley, K., Gerkey, B.P., Faust, J., Foote, T., Leibs, J., Wheeler, R., Ng, A.Y.: ROS: An Open-Source Robot Operating System. In: ICRA Workshop on Open Source Software (2009)
14. Koenig, N., Howard, A.: Design and use paradigms for gazebo, an open-source multi-robot simulator. In: IEEE/RSJ International Conference on Intelligent Robots and Systems, pp. 2149–2154 (2004)
15. Vaughan, R.: Massively multi-robot simulation in stage. Swarm Intelligence 2(2), 189–208 (2008)
16. Foote, T. (ed.): ROS: geometry_msgs/Twist Message (February 2013), http://www.ros.org/doc/api/geometry_msgs/html/msg/Twist.html
17. Hayati, S., Lee, T., Tso, K., Backes, P., Lloyd, J.: A unified teleoperated-autonomous dual-arm robotic system. IEEE Control Systems 11(2), 3–8 (1991)

Survey and Expert Evaluation for e-Banking

Basil Soufi

Hamdan Bin Mohammed e-University,
P.O. Box 71400, Dubai, UAE
basil.soufi@gmail.com

Abstract. A variety of factors impact customer take-up of and satisfaction with e-commerce platforms. Aspects of functionality, usability, security and customer service are considered key determinants of perceived service quality. The study examines e-banking platforms in the United Arab Emirates using survey and expert evaluation. The evaluation has identified the platforms that were considered better overall and highlighted areas for improvement. The paper reflects on the usefulness of the methods employed in the evaluation and outlines issues for future work.

Keywords: Evaluating e-commerce, e-banking case study, survey and expert evaluations.

1   Introduction

Online banking or e-banking has seen rapid development and take-up recently. It offers customers potential benefits of convenience, cost savings, accessibility and flexibility. Yet barriers to take-up still exist and can be related to a variety of factors. Based on the technology acceptance model (Davis, 1989) and more recent research on trust in electronic commerce (e.g. Casalo et al, 2006; Schlosser et al, 2006), Soufi and Maguire (2010) have developed an evaluation framework for e-Banking platforms. According to this framework, there are 4 key determinants of trust and perceived service quality. These are:

- Functionality
- Usability
- Security and Privacy
- Customer Service

Functionality refers to the functions or capabilities provided on the online banking system. When evaluating an interactive system, the evaluation of functionality should be given high priority as it concerns the ability and success of the system in meeting the goals of the user. The e-banking platform should help the provider accomplish their business goals by helping users accomplish *their personal missions*.

The usability of an e-business platform can also have an appreciable impact on the ability of customers to achieve their goals and do business. Good usability leads to

S. Yamamoto (Ed.): HIMI/HCII 2013, Part I, LNCS 8016, pp. 375–382, 2013.

improved customer satisfaction, higher conversion rates and returning customers (Rhodes, 2000; UsabilityNet, 2003).   Conversely, bad usability leads to frustrated customers and loss of business.

Privacy and security controls form an important part of the recommendations of the Basel Committee's 'Risk Management Principles for Electronic Banking' (Basel Committee, 2001). Privacy refers to the protection of personal information. Security technologies ensure the integrity, confidentiality, authentication and non-recognition of relationships (Casalo et al, 2007). Privacy can therefore be described as a set of legal requirements and good practices with regards to the handling of personal information whereas security refers to the technical guarantees that ensure that these legal requirements and good practices will be met effectively. Perceived security refers to perception of security regarding the means of payment and the mechanism for storing and transmission of information.

Customer service is related to a number of factors including customer care, responsiveness and user support.   In a very competitive environment, customer service is an important differentiator and contributes to the perception of service quality and trust. For a more detailed review of the theoretical foundations relating to the framework and an exploration of the relationships between the various factors see Liao and Cheung (2008); Yap (2010), Jayawardhena (2004) and Bauer et al (2004).

2   A Case Study Evaluation of e-Banking

2.1   e-Banking in the UAE and Elsewhere

The UAE is one of the countries that make up the Gulf Cooperation Council or 'GCC'. According to the World Bank, the UAE had an estimated population of 7.89 million and a per capita gross national income of 40,760 USD in 2011 (World Bank, 2011). The UAE is one of the fastest developing countries with a very high human development index ranking. The UAE was ranked 30 in the world according to the United Nations Human Development Report, 2011). The UAE is served by a number of local (e.g. Emirates National Bank of Dubai, First Gulf Bank, Union National Bank, Abu Dhabi Commercial Bank, RAK Bank etc.) and foreign banks (e.g. Citibank, HSBC, Standard Chartered). According to the UAE Central Bank's report of registered banking institutes, 23 locally incorporated banks and 28 foreign banks operate in the UAE as of 31st October 2010. This makes for a highly competitive market where banks strive to improve customer service and innovate in their product and service offering.

Although e-Banking has grown steadily, several factors have impeded the take-up of e-banking transactions.   Lack of trust is an important factor that affects e-commerce as purchasing and transacting over the Internet requires consumer trust (Schlosser et al, 2006).   Other usability problems that e-banking sites still suffer from are difficult navigation and the need to remember more codes to access an account such as a user code, password, or answering security questions (Nielsen, 2001).

These can affect users across different cultures. Another factor is the apparent reluctance to do banking online for certain cultures (Williams & Richardson, 2005; Guru et al, 1999).

e-Banking practices and customer satisfaction have been the subject of several research studies. Studies of e-Banking in China (Laforet and Li, 2005), Estonia (Eriksson et al., 2005), Iran (Sadeghi and Hanzaee, 2010), Malaysia (Guru et al, 1999; Wei and Nair, 2006), Taiwan (Wang et al., 2003), Turkey (Sayar and Wolfe, 2007) and USA (Southard and Siau, 2004) are some examples. The technology acceptance model (Davis, 1989) and the quality dimension of Servqual (Parasuraman, 1985) are considered as conceptual foundations to many of these studies as they provide empirical evidence for the 'perceived usefulness' and 'perceived ease of use' attributes.

2.2   Study Methods and Findings

The evaluation methods to be used in this study must be capable of collecting data for the four key aspects described above. Where it comes to usability, two of the most popular usability evaluation techniques are user testing and heuristic evaluation. Studies that compare the efficiency and effectiveness of the 2 methods suggest that the two methods address different usability problems and are complementary (Tan et al., 2009; Batra & Bishu, 2007). Because the evaluations considered here are multi-faceted and involve 4 dimensions, the evaluation method needs to capture customer perceptions of e-banking functionality, usability, security and customer service. Both interviews and surveys can have the required breadth and flexibility. Surveys have the advantage of reaching a larger group and the capability of being administered online. Surveys were therefore selected as the core data collection method in this study. In order to provide a different perspective and the scope for the corroboration of findings, the study included expert evaluation of three of the key determinants; functionality, usability and security. The study focused on some of the largest and most recognized locally incorporated banks. Four banks were selected for this purpose and these are referred to as Banks 1 to 4.

Survey Evaluation. This method involves administering a set of questions to a large sample of users. Surveys can help determine information on customers, work practice and attitudes. Surveys are normally composed of a mix of 'closed' questions with fixed responses and 'open' questions, where the respondent is free to answer as they wish. Surveys are useful for obtaining qualitative data from users about existing tasks or the current system. If well designed, surveys have the main benefits of being quick and relatively inexpensive to administer. Results can be subjected to statistical analysis to provide quantitative data. This 'hard' data can supplement the more subjective, qualitative information such as unstructured opinions. However survey design is not straightforward and it may be hard to follow up on interesting comments as it requires maintaining contact with the respondents.

A web based survey containing 25 closed questions was created. These included four introductory questions about the respondent's age, profession, use of the Internet, and experience with e-banking. There were 21 questions relating to functionality, usability, security and privacy, and customer service i.e. the 4 key determinants of service quality. Respondents rated their e-banking service on a standard 1-5 scale. The survey also included 4 open questions at the end. Sixty two respondents took part in the survey.

The results of the survey are summarized in Figure 1. This shows the average of the responses of survey participants. Figure 1 shows that for functionality Bank 2 received the highest score whilst Bank 4 received the lowest. Bank 2 received the highest usability score and Bank 1 the lowest. Banks 1, 2 received a higher score for security than Banks 3, 4. Bank 2 received the highest customer service score whilst Bank 1 the lowest. Overall, the scores for usability and security are higher than those for functionality and customer service. This indicates that these factors have been given more attention by the banks considered and that there is more scope for improvement in aspects of functionality and customer service. There was more disparity in the scores for functionality and security indicating that customer perceptions of these factors varied considerably.

It is noted that Bank 2 received the highest score in every aspect of the survey evaluation and was the preferred bank overall. It may be that Bank 2 is superior in every aspect or it may simply be a reflection of customer preference. Bank 1 was ranked second. Banks 3 and 4 were ranked third and fourth in close succession.

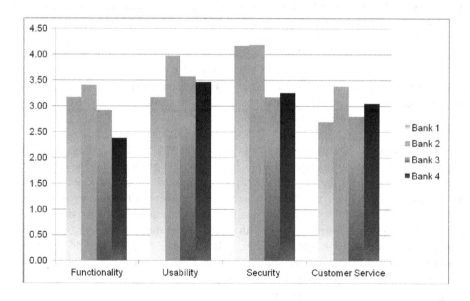

Fig. 1. Survey evaluation summary findings

Expert Evaluation. This method involves analysts evaluating the system with reference to established guidelines or principles, noting down their observations and often ranking them in order of severity. The analysts are usually experts in human factors or HCI, but others, with less experience have also been shown to report valid problems. The method provides quick and relatively cheap feedback to designers and the results can generate good ideas for improving the user interface. If experts are available, carrying out a heuristic evaluation (categorizing the feedback according to design rules) is beneficial before actual users are brought in to help with further testing, as well as when an existing system is in use (Nielsen and Mack, 1994).

In this study, expert evaluation focused on three of the four determinants, namely functionality, usability, and security. Two experts performed a set of 10 tasks on all four e-banking platforms and recorded their observations. Each of the two experts is considered a 'double' expert. The first expert had extensive knowledge of e-banking functionality and security. The second expert had extensive knowledge of e-banking functionality and usability. The tasks used included a mix of informational, administrative and transactional tasks. The tasks are considered representative of what customers typically do through e-Banking. The evaluation utilized checklists and evaluator's expertise.

It has been found that all banks supported the first 5 tasks. These deal with everyday transactions such as check balance, validate payment, request statements, make a transfer etc. Task 6 involved making a bill payment to the national telecommunication company Etisalat. Although this was supported, the usability of this facility varied between the banks. This concerns the ability of the user to receive feedback and providing them with the opportunity to verify details which varied between the banks. Three tasks were either not supported or could only be carried out in a limited way. These are 'opening new bank accounts online', 'standing order facility', and 'Government fee payment'.

Usability was generally found to be quite good with 3 out 4 platforms having clear layout and simple navigation. One of the banks had a cluttered interface and confusing navigation (Bank 3).

Where it comes to security and privacy, the banks evaluated varied considerably. Although all platforms use high security SSL encryption methods and provide confirmation of transactions through SMS and e-mail, the login protocol is one area that requires some attention both in terms of security and usability. Only one of the 4 banks features strong authentication of the user identity through the use of a security token generator. This provided a means of enhancing security while maintaining usability. The login protocol for Bank 3 is considered poor as it features minimal security. Bank 4 does not use strong authentication but requires multiple passwords that need activation by telephone contact. This has resulted in a cumbersome login process.

A summary of the key findings from the expert evaluation is given in Table 1. Overall, Banks 1, 2 were evaluated as better than Banks 3 and 4. As noted above, experts identified both usability and security issues to be addressed by Bank 3 which was considered most in need of improvement.

Table 1. Expert evaluation key findings

		Bank 1	Bank 2	Bank 3	Bank 4
Functionality	**Support for opening new bank account online**	Limited	No	Yes	No
	Standing Order Facility	No	No	Limited	No
	Government Fee Payment	No	No	Limited	No
Usability	**Layout and Navigation**	Clear layout easy navigation	Simple and intuitive	Cluttered I/F Confusing Navigation	Simple
	Etisalat Bill Payment - Integration	Good	Limited	Limited	Good
Security	**Login Protocol**	Adequate	Good	Poor	Cumbersome
	Privacy Policy	No	No	Yes	Yes

3   Discussion and Conclusions

The results from the evaluations were useful in obtaining ranking scores for the e-banking platforms and identifying areas of improvement. All platforms offered basic e-banking functions but differed for advanced features. Experts identified specific usability and security improvements for certain banks. Usability issues of layout and navigation as well as the usability and integration of certain types of bill payment were highlighted. Security and privacy, as evaluated by the survey, were different across the banks. Experts identified different practices in the areas of login protocol and privacy policy leading to recommended enhancements in these areas.

It can be seen that there was good agreement between the survey and expert evaluations in terms of overall findings. However, experts were more specific in their assessments of the different aspects of the platforms. For example, although Bank 2 received the highest survey score for each of the 4 aspects, the expert evaluation showed that it did not offer the best functionality.

Further work is required to extend expert evaluation to include the relationship between banks and their customers. This may be achieved by developing scenarios involving various types of problem resolution through multiple channels over a longer time frame. Customer service - the fourth determinant of trust and service quality – was excluded from expert evaluation in this study. By comparison, all four determinants were included in the survey evaluation.

A criticism that is often leveled at both survey and expert evaluations is that they are subjective and results are influenced by the opinions of survey participants and the expert reviewers. It is interesting to consider the interaction between the four determinants of service quality in survey evaluation. When survey participants preferred one of the e-banking platforms for one determinant e.g. security, there was a tendency for this preference to be exhibited for the other determinants. The two methods were different in that expert evaluation was less susceptible to such interaction. It can therefore be argued that of the two methods used in this study, expert evaluation showed less subjectivity and was more specific than survey evaluation.

The use of the two methods is considered a success as it has highlighted specific areas for the banks to attend to and the findings from the two methods were generally in agreement. Future work should focus on the issues that have been identified and enable security enhancements to be achieved without compromising usability.

References

1. Basel Committee on Banking Supervision: Risk Management Principles for Electronic Banking. Bank for International Settlements (2001)
2. Batra, S., Bishu, R.R.: Web usability and evaluation: Issues and concerns. In: Aykin, N. (ed.) HCII 2007, Part I. LNCS, vol. 4559, pp. 243–249. Springer, Heidelberg (2007)
3. Bauer, H.H., Hammerschmidt, M., Falk, T.: Measuring the quality of e-banking portals. International Journal of Bank Marketing 23(2), 153–175 (2005)
4. Casalo, L.V., Flavian, C., Guinaliu, M.: The role of security, privacy, usability and reputation in the development of online banking. Online Information Review 31(5), 583–603 (2007)
5. Davis, F.D.: Perceived usefulness, perceived ease of use, and user acceptance of information technology. MIS Quarterly 13(3), 319–340 (1989)
6. Eriksson, K., Kerem, K., Nilsson, D.: Customer acceptance of Internet banking in Estonia. Int. J. of Bank Marketing 23(2), 200–216 (2005)
7. Guru, B.K., et al.: Electronic Banking in Malaysia: A Note on Evolution of Services and Consumer Reactions (1999),
   http://www.arraydev.com/commerce/JIBC/0103_01.htm
   (accessed February 22, 2013)
8. Jayawardhena, C.: Measurement of service quality in Internet Banking: The Development of an Instrument. Journal of Marketing Management 20, 185–207 (2004)
9. Laforet, S., Li, X.: Consumers' attitudes towards online and mobile banking in China. Int. J. of Bank Marketing 23(5), 362–380 (2005)
10. Liao, Z., Cheung, M.T.: Measuring Consumer Satisfaction in Internet Banking: A Core Framework. Communications of the ACM 51(4), 47–51 (2008)
11. Nielsen, J.: Did Poor Usability Kill E-Commerce? (2001),
    http://www.useit.com/alertbox/20010819.html
    (accessed February 22, 2013)
12. Nielsen, J., Mack, R.L. (eds.): Usability inspection methods. Wiley, Chichester (1994)
13. Parasuraman, A.Z., et al.: A Conceptual Model of Service Quality and its Implications for Future Research. Journal of Marketing 49(4), 41–50 (1985)

14. Rhodes, J.S.: Usability can save your company (2000),
    http://webword.com/moving/savecompany.html
    (accessed February 22, 2013)
15. Sadeghi, T., Hanzaee, K.H.: Customer satisfaction factors (CSFs) with online banking
    services in an Islamic Country. Journal of Islamic Marketing 1(3), 249–267 (2010)
16. Sayar, C., Wolfe, S.: Internet banking market performance: Turkey versus the UK. Int.
    Journal of Bank Marketing 25(3), 122–141 (2007)
17. Schlosser, A.E., et al.: Converting web site visitors into buyers: How web site investment
    increases consumer trusting beliefs and online purchase intentions. Journal of
    Marketing 70, 133–148 (2006)
18. Soufi, B., Maguire, M.: Personal Internet banking – a UAE case study. In: Kommers, P.,
    Isaias, P. (eds.) Proceedings of IADIS e-Society 2010, pp. 315–321 (2010)
19. Southard, P.B., Siau, K.: A Survey of Online E-Banking Retail Initiatives.
    Communications of the ACM 47(10), 99–102 (2004)
20. Tan, W., Liu, D., Bishu, R.: Web evaluation: Heuristic evaluation vs. user testing. Int. J. of
    Industrial Ergonomics 39(4), 621–627
21. UAE Central Bank,
    http://www.centralbank.ae/en/index.php?option=com_content&vi
    ew=article&id=117&Itemid=97 (accessed February 22, 2013)
22. United Nations Development Programme: Human Development Report - HDI Rankings
    (2011), http://hdr.undp.org/en/statistics/ (accessed February 22, 2013)
23. UsabilityNet: The business case for usability (2003),
    http://www.usabilitynet.org/management/c_business.htm
    (accessed February 22, 2013)
24. Wang, Y.Y.M., Lin, H., Tang, T.I.: Determinants of user acceptance of Internet banking:
    an empirical study. Int. J. of Service Industry Management 14(5), 501–519 (2003)
25. Wei, K.K., Nair, M.: The effects of customer service management on business
    performance in Malaysian banking industry: an empirical analysis. Asia Pacific Journal of
    Marketing and Logistics 18(2), 111–128 (2006)
26. Williams, K., Richardson, N.: Online Banking: Are You Ready? Black Enterprise 35(12),
    93–99 (2005), http://www.blackenterprise.com/mag/online-banking-
    are-you-ready/ (accessed February 22, 2013)
27. World Bank: Data (2011), http://data.worldbank.org/country/united-
    arab-emirates (accessed February 22, 2013)
28. Yap, K.B.: Offline and online banking – where to draw the line when building trust in e-
    banking? International Journal of Bank Marketing 28(1), 27–46 (2010)

Framework for Quantitatively Evaluating the Quality Requirements of Software System

Yuki Terawaki

Research Center for Computing and Multimedia Studies,
Hosei University, 3-7-2 Kajinocho, Koganei, Tokyo 184-8584, Japan
yuki.terawaki.dc@k.hosei.ac.jp

Abstract. Quality requirements (QR) are a description which indicates how well the software's behavior is to be executed. It is widely recognized that quality requirements are vital for the success of software systems. Therefore, to define the quality requirements and to check the quality attributes carefully is necessary for bringing good- quality software and ensuring quality of the service. This paper proposes a framework that measures the quality attributes in the requirements document such as SRS. The effectiveness of this framework was briefly described, we discuss approach was to enrich the representative quality corpora.

Keywords: Requirements Engineering, Quality Requirements, Non-Functional Requirements, text-mining.

1 Introduction

Quality requirements (QR) are a description which indicates how well the software's behavior is to be executed. It is widely recognized that quality requirements are vital for the success of software systems. So, it is necessary to check the quality requirements carefully to bring good-quality software for the user and to ensure the quality of service. However, in the requirements acquisition phase, functional requirements are highly focused, quality requirements are not necessarily sufficiently defined [1]. Despite the importance of QR, it is generally acknowledged that QR are difficult to capture and specify. Several studies [2] [3] [4] [5] have identified challenges of QR as: difficult to gather, often poorly understood, general stated informally in a non-quantifiable manner, where should QR document, and difficulties to get attention for QR.

To define quality requirements adequately and sufficiently, we must know how much QR are stated in the software requirements specifications (SRS). It will make a good base to explore ways for eliciting, representing and implementing QR. For that purpose, this paper proposes a framework to identify where in a SRS quality requirements are stated and which characteristics class each requirement belongs to. The proposed framework can analyze QR found in an SRS in terms of their volume, balance and structure. This framework can analyze the SRS written in natural language,

S. Yamamoto (Ed.): HIMI/HCII 2013, Part I, LNCS 8016, pp. 383–392, 2013.

Japanese [icons ref]. Today, it's a fact that SRS are mostly written in natural language. In this framework, natural language processing techniques, particularly the text similarity detecting methods, are employed to measure the degree of quality factors in each requirement sentence.

The paper is organized as follows. In section 2, the background and related work are presented. In section 3, the proposed framework and the implementation of tool are described. Section 4 introduces case studies briefly. Section 5 presents the discussion. In section 6 conclusion and future works are provided.

2   The Previous Practice in Industry and Academic

Today, though software development requires quick delivery, it is not unusual for development documents (such as SRS or Request for Proposal: RFP) to be over several hundred pages long. As the scale of the SRS gets bigger, the structure of the SRS becomes complicated. At present, despite of the increasing number of documents which should be inspected, shortening of development time is desired. To respond these demands of the present age, some templates of reader-friendly SRS have been proposed. These templates are often recommended to write Functional Requirements and QR separately. For example, FR and QR are to be described in separate chapters in IEEE Std. 830-1998 [6]. Wiegers's book [1] introduces another template adapted from the IEEE 830, which also separates FR and NFR. Lauesen [7] said the SRS written in industry were inspired by the IEEE830 guidelines, but when it came to the specific requirements, they were bewildering because IEEE 830 suggested no guidance. Moreover, Lauesen's book introduces SRS of good example. These SRS are not similar to IEEE 830 structure, and it is more instructive to grasp how QR's are distributed over the document and how they are mixed with FR or not. Particularly, visualization of the distribution is helpful.

The following researches are developing the tool which detects the defect of requirements. William M. Wilson et al proposed the Automated Requirements Measurement (ARM) [8].   The Quality Analyzer for Requirements Specifications (QuARS) was proposed by A. Fantechi et al [9]. These researches aim at pointing out the inaccuracy of the requirement specification document written by natural language. The advantage of this research over these researches is as follows. This research provides stronger support function for quality requirements. This framework gives the evaluation criterion of quality requirements (development documents) to the author of RS. The author of RS can focus on improving the quality requirements.

Moreover, the following researches are related to specification, classification, and measurement of QR. Grimshaw and Draper [10] found that QR are often overlooked and there is a lack of consensus about quality requirements. Johansson et al. found that reliability was identified by a multitude of stakeholders to be the most important QR[10]. Our research objective is to investigate an SRS, what kind of QR are actually written, how they are distributed over quality characteristics as categorized in the ISO/IEC 25010 standard. There are already some works that attempt to discern and classify QR in SRS. H. Kaiya et al. [12] calls the distribution of requirements sentences across QR characteristics as 'spectrum'. In Kaiya's research, the policy of distinguishing QR from FR is not clear, so, it is required to classify requirements quality characteristics by hand. That implies making up the spectrum they needs keyword-to-quality matrix. The matrix is constructed for each system by a human, although there is a possibility of reusing the existing one if the application domain is the same. Svensson et al. [13] analyzed how quality requirements are specified and which types of requirements exist in a requirements specification from industry by manual work.   By contrast, in our approach, a text mining technique is used to filter out QR statements from SRS, classifying them into the ISO/IEC 25010 quality characteristic categories at same time. So, the original of our approach is to identify where in a SRS quality requirements are stated and which characteristics class each requirement belongs to. We can identify how each QR characteristic scatters over the document, i.e. how much in column and in what way.

3   Proposed Framework

3.1   Our Approach

When we manage QR, We can apply a sentence of requirements to each characteristic of the software quality attributes of ISO/IEC 25010 and can check the requirements for quality. However, it is difficult to evaluate correspondence with attribute and requirements for a general reason. This is because some quality requirements overlap two or more quality attributes. Also, when identifying attributes and requirements, human judgment may change over time. Thus, it is difficult to review every quality requirements in terms of coherent thinking. However, if the quality attributes can be quantitatively measured, then they could potentially help the author of SRS decide if a revision is needed. Additionally, almost all development documents are described in natural language. If the quality requirements needed are written to the document created to the upper process, quality can be measured at the time of the acceptance inspection. However, it is difficult to review every quality attributes in terms of time. These problems bring deterioration in the quality of development document and play a role in the failure of the project. So, text-mining technique is employed.

The Requirements Process includes 4 processes. There are requirements elicitation, evaluation, specification (documentation) and quality assurance. This process is iteration on successive increments according to a spiral model [14]. In the spiral process, when requirements document will become elaborate, the error of requirements may be made. In spiral process, the revised document (SRS) can check without spending hours using text-mining technique. The quality attributes contained in SRS are showed quantitatively because the text mining analyzes where quality attributes are contained, and how much.   The rate of documentation of quality attribute can be showed using the output of text mining. Thus, the quality requirements are checked by coherent thinking. Therefore, the workload for verification of SRS will be decreased.

3.2   Overview of Framework

We propose a framework for mining QR in SRS. This framework can be use to improve the quality of SRS through the requirements definition process. As criteria for evaluating the quality requirement, the quality model of ISO/IEC25010 [15] is used. The proposed framework can specify the statement related to quality attribute of ISO/IEC 25010. The framework is conceptually composed of two parts. One is the QR mining mechanism and the other is its usage in the RE process. Figure 1 shows the conceptual diagram of this framework.

The QR mining mechanism analyzes the similarities of the quality content of a given piece of requirements text between the similarity with a corpus of typical requirements sentences that state the target quality characteristic such as Performance Efficiency (PE), Compatibility (Co), Usability (U), Security (Se), etc. A detailed discussion of the calculation method of similarity can be found in [19].

In Kaiya et al.'s work [12], keywords are used to link requirements with quality attributes. In comparison our approach is not keyword-based but based on text similarity metrics using an associative search engine. It is more suitable to our purpose than a keyword-based approach, because it is not affected strongly by a particular choice of keywords.

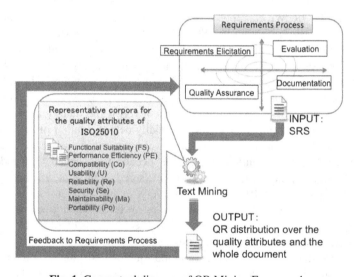

Fig. 1. Conceptual diagram of QR Mining Framework

Regarding the usage in the RE process, the output of tool can contribute to different phases of the RE process cycle. For example:

- Documentation phase: As unfinished requirements documents can be analyzed in this framework, findings obtained from QR mining can be used to give a feedback when writing an SRS. The authors of SRS can find the redundant description and the overlapping statements more effectively and quickly by using the output of tool.

- Quality Assurance phase: Probably, the most natural usage of QR mining is in the phase of evaluation. When the SRS is completed and passed to a quality assurance team for reviewing, the output of the QR mining will be informative in analyzing and improving the SRS. And in inspection process [20] the output of the QR mining helps inspectors examine the work product to identify possible defects.

3.3   Tool

We developed a tool *QRMiner* that supports the proposed framework. This tool was developed as a CUI application by using Java programming language and shell scripts. The Japanese morphological analyzer Sen [16] is employed for morphological analysis. The Japanese WordNet [18] is used to add Synonyms and extracted through a method that first acquires a lower level of the word group against the original words and then acquires the sum of the sets of each upper level word group. For the Quality-to-term matrix file creation and search operations, GETA associative engine is employed [21]. GETA, an acronym for "Generic Engine for Transposable Association", is an efficient tool that accepts a group of queries in text and returns highly related documents from the designated repository in their relevance order. It is open to public use. Such as mkw command, a part of GETA commands are provided only as the C library, so we developed an execute format to wrap the I/O for the connection by using the Java program and standard I/O. A detailed discussion of the tool can be found in [22], [19], [23].

4   Case Studies

This case study presents the results of analysis of SRS that collected from the public sector of universities and governments. After an early analysis of the SRS, a paper [19] was presented at conference. This paper extends our previous report on findings with more description of the SRS and account of idea of future works.

4.1   Overview

Total of nine SRS's are analyzed, which are consists of two groups; six are systems for universities and three are for governments. The nine SRS was analyzed by QRMiner and manually by the three experts. Moreover, to evaluate the usefulness of QRMiner quantitatively, we calculated the precision and recall between the results by QRMiner and those decided by the human experts for all the SRS. Precision and recall in total are 0.60 and 0.62, which is not so bad, the evaluation of the tool in terms of precision and recall was satisfactory. The followings are findings of the previous study [19].

QR structure: The QRMiner can show the structure of SRS. As noted before chapter of this paper, a well-structured SRS, where QR and FR are written in separate chapters. When they are mixed apparently randomly, the SRS commonly have got the following problems.

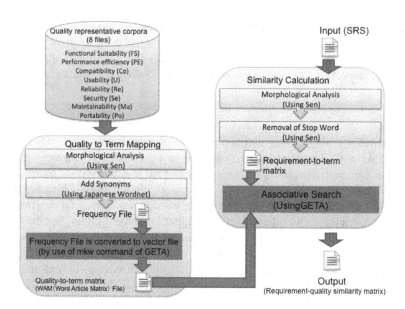

Fig. 2. Structure of QRMiner

Redundancy: The QRMiner output detects the same quality requirements in the early part and also in the later part of the document. Inspecting those parts manually, it was suggested that they are rather redundant and had better be merged in one place.

- Overloading: The QRMiner detects that some sentences are found to have multiple QR overloaded within. By inspection, it was suggested to divide the sentence to enhance the readability.

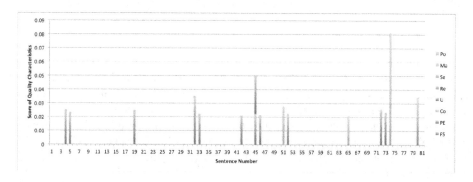

Fig. 3. Distriburion of quality characteristics over the whole document

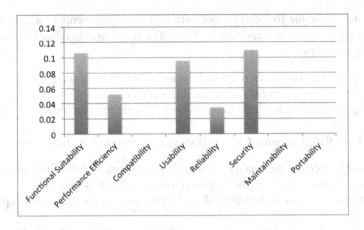

Fig. 4. Result of QRMiner

4.2   Difference between University and Government Systems

As regarding the evaluation of precision and recall, there is no particular difference found between the university systems and the government systems. However, the SRS that we used have distinct characteristics of " Request for Proposal (RFP)". The SRS that the public sector wrote have some features.

1. The requestor does not have much technical knowledge. The requestor often gets a suggestion from competitor several times, and then the requestor perfects the SRS through the suggestion.
2. The requirements are not only for software but integrated with those for hardware and includes rules for administration of system.
3. The upper limit budget is determined but usually hidden to the tenders. A proposal with cost estimation under the budget limit and with high values will obtain the contract.

5   Discussion

This research concentrates on analyzing QR. The proposed framework in terms of precision and recall is satisfactory. However, such as SRS for procurement, when the SRS that mentioned chapter 4.2 are treated, it is required to have a point of view.

5.1   Aspect of Procurement

The software requirements specifications are often referred to as the information system procurement specifications or specification requirements for information system procurement at universities or government agencies. This means requirements specifications are made on the essential basis. When you aim to accomplish quality improvement on requirements specification made in universities or government agencies, it is desirable to focus on not only system requirements characteristics but also analyzing requirements comprehensively. The requirements related to system are specifically as follows;

— Handling of Precondition or reference for software /system structure
— Service agreement among software providers and contractors
— Handling of indeterminate requirements before completing an order

5.2   System Requirements Categorization and Service Level Agreement

It is required to increase the quality representative corpora to accumulate sentences, to deal with problems above with the proposed framework in this study.

ISO/IEC25030 [24] and ISO20000-2 are helpful to increase the quality representative corpora.

This tool registers corpus sentences according to ISO/IEC25010. ISO/IEC25010 is an international standard stated in system and software product quality requirements and evaluation (SQuaRE) series. The SQuaRE series consist of some standards. For example, ISO/IEC25030 describes that a system consists of number of interacting elements and they can be defined and categorized in different ways. And it defines classes of requirements. ISO/IEC 25010 deal with the gray part (Σφάλμα! Το αρχείο προέλευσης της αναφοράς δεν βρέθηκε.) of classes for requirements. It is efficient to accumulate corpus sentences according to ISO/IEC25030 to manage any requirements connected to Precaution for operation, system running, and maintenance conditions.

ISO/IEC2000-2 is a standard guideline for concluding Service Level Agreement. There are 20 items listed. When you accumulate corpus sentences connected to support system and scope of work, for example, emergency contact during any trouble occurrence, job commission to system engineers who is continuously presence.

System requirements		Software requirements	Software product requirements	Inherent property requirements	Functional requirements		
					Software quality requirements	Quality in use requiremens	
						External quality requiremens	
						Internal quality requirements	
				Assigned property requirements	Managerial requirements including for example requirements for price, delivery date, product future, and product supplier		
			Software development requirements	Development process requirements			
				Development organisation requirements			
		Other system requirements	Include for example requirements for computer hardware, data, mechanical parts, and human business processes				

Fig. 5. System requiremens categorisation (ISO/IEC 25030)

Lately, in Japan, the basic guideline for procurement of information systems and handling of government procurement of information systems were established. There exists the improvement we found with this case, and assistance with this framework that correspond with the government basic guideline. Therefore, this framework can make a contribution to improve the quality of requirement specification by enhancing corpus sentences with using ISO/IEC25030 and ISO/IEC2000-2.

6   Conclusion and Future Work

We propose a QR mining framework and developed a tool QRMiner that supports the framework. The effectiveness of this framework was briefly described, we discuss approach was to enrich the representative quality corpora. We will prepare representative corpora by hand using ISO/IEC25030 and ISO/IEC2000-2. Another different approach is the use of a learning mechanism. However, in our first attempt will be to collect more documents and to extend the scope of target system types. In near future, we may find a better way of a learning mechanism.

References

1. Wiegers, K.E.: Software Requirements. Microsft Press (2003)
2. Chung, L., Nixon, B.A., Yu, E., Mylopoulos, J.: Non-Functional Requirements in Software Engineering. Kluwer Academic Publishers (2000)
3. Berntsson Svensson, R., Gorschek, T., Regnell, B., Torkar, R., Shahrokni, A., Feldt, R.: Quality Requirements in Industrial Practice – an extended interview study at eleven companies. IEEE Transaction on Software Engineering (2011) (in print)
4. Borg, A., Yong, A., Carlshamre, P., Sandahl, K.: The Bad Conscience of Requirements Engineering: An Investigation in Real-world Treatment of Non-functional Requirements. In: Third Conference on Software Engineering Research and Practice in Sweden (SERPS 2003), Lund, Sweden (2003)
5. Chung, L., do Prado Leite, J.C.S.: On Non-Functional Requirements in software engineering. In: Borgida, A.T., Chaudhri, V.K., Giorgini, P., Yu, E.S. (eds.) Conceptual Modeling: Foundations and Applications. LNCS, vol. 5600, pp. 363–379. Springer, Heidelberg (2009)
6. IEEE, Recommended practice for software requirements specifications, IEEE, Tech. Rep., IEEE Std830-1998 (1998)
7. Lauesen, S.: Software Requirements styles and Techniques. Addison-Wesley (2002)
8. Wilson, W.M., et al.: Automated Analysis of Requirement Specifications. In: Proceedings of the International Conference on Software Engineering ICSE 1997, pp. 161–171 (1997)
9. Fantechi, A., et al.: Application of Linguistic Techniques for Use Case Analysis. In: Proceedings of the IEEE Joint International Conference on Requirements Engineering, pp. 157–164 (2002)
10. Grimshaw, D., Drapper, G.W.: Non-functional requirements analysis: Deficiencies in structured methods. Information and Software Technology 43, 629–634 (2001)
11. Johansson, E., Wesslen, A., Bratthall, L., Host, M.: The importance of quality requirements in software platform development –a survey. In: Proceedings of the 34th Annual Hawaii International Conference on System Sciences (2001)

12. Kaiya, H., Sato, T., Osada, A., Kitazawa, N., Kaijiri, K.: Toward quality requirements analysis based on domain specific quality spectrum. In: SAC 2008 Proceedings of the 2008 ACM Symposium on Applied Computing (2008)
13. Olsson, T., Sevenssion, R.B., Regnell, B.: Non-functional requirements metrics in practice – an empirical document analysis. In: Workshop on Measuring Requirements for Project and Product Success (2007) (a full version is to appear in the Information and Software Technology)
14. Kotonya, G., Sommerville, I.: Requirements Engineering: Processes and Techniques. John Wiley & Sons Ltd. (1997)
15. ISO/IEC, ISO/IEC 25010 Systems and software engineering- Systems and software Quality Requirements and Evaluation (SQuaRE) -System and software quality models (2011)
16. Sen (December 2010), http://ultimania.org/sen/
17. GETA (December 2010), http://geta.ex.nii.ac.jp/e/index.html
18. 日本語 WordNet (December 2010),
    http://nlpwww.nict.go.jp/wn-ja/index.en.html
19. Terawaki, Y., Tamai, T.: A Framework for Mining Quality Requirements in Software Requirements Specifications. In: The International Symposium on Requirements Engineering (RE) (submitted)
20. Fagan, M.: Design and Code Inspections to Reduce Errors in Program Development. IBM Systems Journal 15(3), 182–211 (1976)
21. Takano, A.: Association computation for information access. In: Grieser, G., Tanaka, Y., Yamamoto, A. (eds.) DS 2003. LNCS (LNAI), vol. 2843, pp. 33–44. Springer, Heidelberg (2003)
22. Terawaki, Y.: Supporting of Requirements Elicitation for Ensuring Services of Information Systems Used for Education. In: Smith, M.J., Salvendy, G. (eds.) HCII 2011, Part I. LNCS, vol. 6771, pp. 58–65. Springer, Heidelberg (2011)
23. Terawaki, Y., Tamai, T.: A practical approach to Quality Requirements Handling in Software Systems Development. In: The Eighth International Conference on Systems, ICONS 2013, pp. 160–163 (2013)
24. ISO/IEC, ISO/IEC 25030 Software engineering – Software product Quality Requirements and Evaluation (SQuaRE) – Quality requirements, 1 edn. (2007)

Effective Practice of HCD by Usability Modeling and Standardization

Hideo Zempo

Software & Service Design Division, FUJITSU DESIGN LIMITED
1812-10, Shimonumabe, Nakahara-ku, Kawasaki, 211-8588, Japan
zempo@jp.fujitsu.com

Abstract. Human-centered design (HCD) is one possible approach to enhancing usability, and it is important to take the HCD method to the development process. However, there is a realistic problem with insufficient resource such as manpower and time for the HCD method. Then, in order to practice HCD and to use know-how concerning the usability available more easily, the template defined of nine basic screens based on current findings was made. As a result, system engineers and developers came to be able to develop systems with a certain level of usability by using the templates, and that leads to the efficiency of the systems development and the improvement of the design quality.

Keywords: Human-centered design, usability, screen template, system development.

1 Challenges for HCD Application in System Development

High usability, an established requirement for general consumer software applications, is also becoming an important requirement in business system applications for B2B use these days. In developing business systems, the tendency has been to give priority to functionality over user-friendliness, since system users and scope of use are largely limited. However, problems have arisen from little consideration for usability, such as human errors and additional development cost requirements for reworking. As a result, the importance of system development from the user's standpoint is now widely recognized even in the B2B context, as exemplified by the "Electronic Government Usability Guidelines"[1] issued by the Cabinet Office of Japan in 2009 regarding electronic administrative application systems. Human-centered design (HCD) is one possible approach to enhancing usability, but it must be applied to the entire process of development.

FUJITSU has a standard process called SDEM (Solution-oriented system Development Engineering Methodology) for system development mainly involving SI construction. As in general development processes, SDEM describes, comprehensively and systematically, such required work steps as planning, design, development, testing, operation and maintenance, as well as results expected from these steps, mainly to avoid omissions and ensure efficient project operation. HCD was integrated into SDEM in 2007.

S. Yamamoto (Ed.): HIMI/HCII 2013, Part I, LNCS 8016, pp. 393–399, 2013.

In SDEM, specific steps of usability improvement are summarized as follows: (1) integrate usability into information system strategy, (2) clarify usability requirements, (3) understand current status of use and record user and environmental attributes in requirement definition phase, (4) design and develop usability in development phase, (5) evaluate usability, (6) introduce and operate system and perform support activities in operational testing phase, (7) plan and implement HCD throughout entire development process .

It would be ideal to practice HCD as an integral part of a standard system development process, as in SDEM. In actual development, however, realistic challenges such as limited budget and insufficient expert resources often hinder HCD application, though its importance is well understood (still poorly understood, in some cases). As well, design departments charged with supporting development projects may have sufficient know-how for HCD process implementation, but lack the resources and time needed to handle the actual numbers of products and projects.

The most effective way to overcome these challenges in the long run is to get system engineers and developers working in the field to acquire knowledge and know-how relating to usability. Some organizations have already put educational programs in place to this effect. On the other hand, many extremely busy workplaces simply cannot afford to dedicate extra time, energy and labor to such an endeavor. For them, one immediately effective solution would be to convert usability-related know-how into tools. While this is difficult to do at the upper reaches of the HCD process, in the phases of (4) usability design and development and (5) usability evaluation, it is possible for system engineers and developers to secure, without the involvement of designers or HCD specialists, a certain level of usability by using standardized models such as a screen template or checklist. Furthermore, the use of standardized models can improve efficiency in system development.

To illustrate how a template for usability improvement can positively impact system development efficiency and design quality, this paper presents the FUJITSU GUI Design Platform, which we developed at FUJITSU DESIGN, along with the background to the creation of a template and its characteristics.

2   How Usability Models Can Be Standardized

2.1   Viewpoint of Usability Modeling and Standardization

FUJITSU's accumulated experience in usability evaluation, usability improvement design and so on, mainly concerning business system applications, enabled us to identify their common traits. This in turn led us to conclude that, in terms of user tasks as expressed on the display screen, most systems have a similar screen composition, which can be broken down into simple and typical screens and screen transitions.

Since user interface characteristics are in question, business systems discussed here are those linked with a database and mainly executed on a web browser, and not clerical software, whose principle purpose is document production, or creative software, such as Visual Studio and Photoshop. Clerical software, mainly for document production, involves creating a text with or without images on a blank screen; therefore, only one task window is mainly used, necessitating few other screens or screen transitions. On the other hand, business systems mainly consists of adding new data to the database or editing registered data; screen types and transitions are required in accordance with functions, and are suited to standardization.

From the standpoint of software quality, the screen types and transitions that interest us here are system user interfaces, which influence the quality of use, that is, internal and external software quality. Focusing on usability at this level enables the formulation of models as concrete screens [2].

It is also effective to standardize UI at the component level, and there are cases in which standardized UI patterns are converted into tools [3]. However, screens, which are composed of combinations of component-level patterns, are more important as a unit that can determine the quality of use. This is why we conducted screen-level standardization.

2.2   Defining Nine Basic Screens and Incorporating Them in a Template

A typical operational flow of tasks that a user performs proceeds chronologically as follows (Figure 1): The user first logs in to use the system (1. log-in screen). In most cases, this is followed by transition to the screen on which an item can be selected from a menu (2. menu screen). The user then selects a task (function) to perform. If the system involves interaction with a database, following menu item selection, in most cases, the data retrieval function is proposed at the top of each function (3. data retrieval screen). The user then executes a search, and a list of data to be processed appears (4. retrieval result list screen). In some cases, the data retrieval function and list of results appear on the same screen (5. retrieval and result list screen). The user selects an item from the list to edit, update, delete or otherwise process (6. input screen). The user can also create new data on the same screen. Following new input or data update, the user confirms the content of the task (7. confirmation screen) and completes the operation.

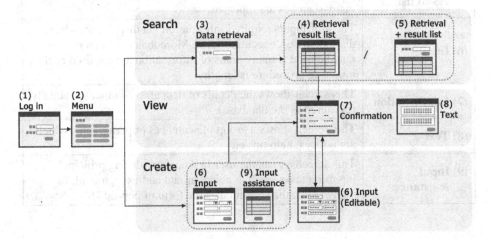

Fig. 1. A typical operational flow with nine basic screens

The above can be considered the most simplified typical sequence of screen types and transitions. A point to note regarding usability in processing is whether or not the sequence incorporates the two options of creating new data and editing already existing data, and whether this is done in an easy-to-follow manner. In terms of user intention, an important point for ensuring usability is the general division of tasks into three types: search, create and view, which respectively correspond to the functions of data retrieval, new input and confirmation. The fundamental key to usability improvement of a business system is to arrange screen types and transitions that take into account these points, together with functions offered.

To create a template of screens, we identified nine basic screens for a web-based business system application, that is, the seven screens described above, plus two additional screens: a text screen (8) that offers sample textual descriptions on the web browser, and an input assistance screen (9) that serves as an auxiliary screen for inputting date and other information items (Table1).

Table 1. Nine basic screens and their functions

Screen type	Function
(1) Log in	User inputs user ID and password via this screen, to log in to the system.
(2) Menu	This screen shows a menu summarizing functions, as the entry to the task.
(3) Data retrieval	The user inputs data retrieval conditions via this screen to execute a search.
(4) Retrieval result list	This screen shows a list of retrieval results. The user selects an item or items from the list and proceeds to the next task (confirmation or input).
(5) Retrieval + result list	The user inputs data retrieval conditions and views retrieval results via this same screen. This screen type is used when many searches are repeated.
(6) Input	The user inputs required information via this screen, which displays a task execution form. More than one screen (page) may be used if many items of information are required or the inputting procedure is lengthy.
(7) Confirmation	This screen shows the details of data already input (or already registered in the database).
(8) Text	This screen shows a group of sentences or paragraphs, which are notices, help tips etc.
(9) Input assistance	This screen assists the user in data entry during principal inputting tasks, such as calendar and address retrieval. In many cases, the screen takes the form of pop-up UI.

2.3   Providing Tools Readily Usable in the Field

With the nine basic screens, we created a template (Figure 2). In this process, in accordance with screen layout principles, we optimized and standardized header and footer placements for area division and role definition, and did same for the arrangement of controls and buttons that realize respective screen functions. We also prepared about 50 themes from which color scheme and other design particulars can be selected to accommodate various use settings. We gave sufficient consideration to ensuring accessibility by, for example, optimizing character visibility. In addition, we produced the template in HTML and CSS versions that conform to the widely applied web standards, enabling simple and efficient customization.

As a tool to complement the template, we prepared guidelines describing usability features on each screen. These features, which are incorporated into the screens in various aspects, range from such basic features as proximity of log-in ID and password input fields and log-in button on the menu screen, and clear indication of required items on the input screens, to more complex features such as buttons on the list screens by which an item is selected from a list of functions ("edit," "delete" etc.) for execution (that is, whether to provide both selection and execution buttons for each item on the list, or a selection button for each item and only one execution button). The usability features are summarized in a checklist at the end of the guidelines to serve as a quality assurance tool for verifying usability as part of application design and development.

The template thus created enables system engineers and developers to design and develop screens from the template according to the purpose of use. In this process, they can ensure a certain level of usability by limiting customization of screen layout, color adjustment etc. to the necessary minimum, while referring to the guidelines. They can also expect development efficiency to improve, since the template eliminates the need to create screens from scratch.

Fig. 2. Template sample

3   Actual Use and Effects

At FUJITSU DESIGN, in 2007 we created the intranet site FUJITSU GUI Design Platform from which FUJITSU Group personnel can download the template and other tools. The template was initially provided in HTML; versions such as ASP.NET and others corresponding to FUJITSU's development platform have been gradually added, in consideration of needs in and requests from the development field.

From the intranet site, developers typically download templates they need, together with accompanying guidelines. Currently, some 2,000 templates are downloaded per year for a wide range of purposes, from small in-house application development projects to business transactions with customers.

User feedback collected via questionnaire surveys and interviews points to the advantages of the tools, as summarized below:

- General advantages:

  - Members can share a color scheme and layout at the project outset, making it possible to proceed without deviation from the project orientation.
  - Less time is needed to arrive at well-balanced character and color arrangements.
  - The concreteness of lifelike simulated screens makes proposals more effective.
  - The idea of a web screen template is unique and excellent as a tool.

- Advantages relating to design and usability:

  - System developers need not be concerned about design.
  - Screens that are attractive in terms of character design and color scheme can be easily created.
  - Functions such as button placement unification enhance usability.

Although the template was initially conceived for use in developing actual systems, we soon learned that it was also used in the pre-development proposal phase, since it is useful in producing mockups that can be included in proposal documents as visual aids, or in presentations as demonstration samples. Such mockups are highly effective in rendering concrete images of systems proposed to customers. The template has come to be effectively used in this manner because it has an aesthetically attractive appearance perfected by designers, in addition to its primary function of screen standardization.

We also conducted a comparative study regarding screen production efficiency, in which the template enabled HTML/CSS beginners to create mock screens in about 40% fewer man-hours than when they did not use the template. This is a significant reduction in man-hours, even considering that template use generally improves efficiency, as compared to creation from scratch.

In view of the above, it can be said that template use is effective in enhancing system development efficiency and usability quality, as well as in communicating concepts in proposal and other early stages of system development. This indicates that HCD-based development, which actively incorporates the user's perspective, is an important element not only in actual manufacturing, but also in acquiring superiority in SI business.

4   Summary and Future Work

This paper has presented an example of HCD application to SI development, specifically in usability modeling and standardization that can be carried out in the design and evaluation phases-- that is, the latter part of the development process.

Other companies have conducted similar projects, identifying similar challenges in practicing HCD and proposing possible solutions. Some projects take a more research-oriented approach to examining screen design patterns in each of the system development phases, dealing with the characteristics and systems of screen design patterns. There are also similar reports on the effectiveness of screen design patterns in external design and on needs in the field in the planning and proposal-preparing phases [4].

In the future, it will be necessary to further advance our template development in response to new technologies and devices, aiming at, for example, tie-up with proto-typing tools, templates for HTML5-based mounting and licensing-out of templates with new screen patterns compatible with smart devices. Moreover, when category classification in the style of the grade chart used in the Non-Functional Requirements Grades Usage Guide [5] become possible, and corresponding screen patterns and screen transition patterns are identified and sorted out, screen design modeling can be automated in a way adaptable to upper reaches of the system development process, rendering the template more effective and more widely adopted by those in the development field.

References

1. Cabinet Office of Japan: Electronic Government Usability Guidelines (2009) (in Japanese),
   http://www.kantei.go.jp/jp/singi/it2/guide/
   index_before090916.html
2. Nagano, Y., Utamura, S., Zempo, H.: Usability Requirements in Information System Development. In: The Proceedings of the 53rd Annual Conference of the Japan Ergonomics Society, p. 176 (2012) (in Japanese)
3. Sociomedia, Inc.'s: UI design patterns,
   https://www.sociomedia.co.jp/category/uidesignpatterns
   (in Japanese)
4. Okubo, R., Noda, H., Tanikawa, Y., Fukuzumi, S.: Development of Design Pattern for HI Design. NEC Giho 64(2) (2011) (in Japanese)
5. Software Engineering Center, Information-technology Promotion Agency. Non-Functional Requirement Grade Usage Guide, Japan (2010) (in Japanese),
   http://sec.ipa.go.jp/reports/20100416.html

Quality of Service Ontology Languages for Web Services Discovery: An Overview and Limitations

Furkh Zeshan[1], Radziah Mohamad[1], and Mohammad Nazir Ahmad[2]

[1] Department of Software Engineering, Faculty of Computing,
Universiti Teknologi Malaysia (UTM), 81310 Skudai, Johor, Malaysia
`farrukh05@hotmail.com, radziahm@utm.my`
[2] Department of Information Systems, Faculty of Computing,
Universiti Teknologi Malaysia (UTM), 81310 Skudai, Johor, Malaysia
`mnazir@utm.my`

Abstract. Web services discovery, ranking and selection based on QoS parameters is remained a hot topic for research since the start of the semantic web. Quality of service (QoS) plays an important role to resolve the issue of best service among the functional similar services. Semantic web relies on the ontologies for providing metadata schema and the vocabulary of concepts used in semantic annotation; resulting improved accuracy of web search. This is why; the success of semantic web depends on the proliferation of ontologies. Depending on the nature of the application, different companies may use different ontology languages and QoS models for web services selection which lead to the issue of heterogeneity. In this paper we have presented ontology evaluation criteria that if satisfied, can solve the problem of heterogeneity and interoperability. Moreover, ontology developers may also use these criteria to evaluate their developed ontology for the refinements. We have evaluated different ontologies in-order to know their strengths and limitations along with the new research directions.

Keywords: Web Services, Semantic Web, Semantic Web Services, QoS, Ontology.

1   Introduction

Service Oriented Computing relies on services for the development of dynamic, flexible, distributed and cost effective application. Service Oriented Architecture (SOA) is a style of design that guides at all steps of creating and using services throughout their lifecycle [1]. Service Oriented Architecture (SOA) enables different applications to exchange data and participate in different processes regardless the complexity of the applications.

Semantic Web services with machine readable interface promises to enable the web services to be selected dynamically at run time to achieve the business goals within and across the organizational boundaries [3]. To find out the most relevant service among functionally similar that meet the requirements of users is the key issue in the web service discovery [4, 5]; however there is a need to define a set of well

S. Yamamoto (Ed.): HIMI/HCII 2013, Part I, LNCS 8016, pp. 400–407, 2013.

defined Quality of Services (QoS) criteria and user preferences [6]. Typically QoS resolves the issue of best service among the functional similar services by ranking and selection based on non-functional requirements. Hence QoS can be used as main factor for ranking the web services.

Efficiently locating the web service registries and the efficiently retrieval of services with QoS from registries (UDDI) is one of the major challenge for web services [9]. This problem is becoming worst with the ever increasing of web services in the UDDI; the reason behind this problem is that the current web service technology is lack of semantic support. Researchers are trying to add semantics to web services to facilitate the web services discovery, ranking and selection process easy and call it as Semantic Web Services [9]. Ontologies are the proposed solution of heterogeneity among web services [7] and present the human knowledge as a critical component among the web services [8].

In this paper we have presented criteria that if satisfied, can solve the problem of heterogeneity and interoperability. We have evaluated different ontologies [15, 16, 18, 19, 20, 21, 22, 27] on these criteria to know, which one is the best ontology that can be used efficiently for web services discovery while addressing its limitations.

The remaining paper is organized as; Section 2 presents state-of-the-art; Section 3 comparative evaluation, while Section 4 discusses the findings and finally Section 5 summarize the paper.

2   State-of-the-Art

In this section the review of different QoS ontologies have been presented.

DAML-QoS [15]; It consists over three layers; profile layer, property definition layer and metrics layer. QoS property definition layer is used for elaborating the domain and range constraints of the property; QoS profile layer is used for QoS requirements matchmaking, while the metric layer is used for measuring the QoS properties. DAML-QoS is the enhanced form of DAML-S for QoS support. This ontology has a number of drawbacks; QoS ontology vocabulary is missing, concrete definition for QoS properties are also missing. For measuring the QoS information the scale and type of metric is not presented. The metric model is also not rich enough, approach is not perfect, and the use of OWL for imposing QoS values is also incorrect.

QoSOnt [16]; ontology has three layers; base, attribute and the domain specific layers. Base layer consists on the generic concepts and the unit ontology. Attribute layer defines the particular metric of the QoS attribute. Dependability and the performance ontology are defined by a common set of QoS attributes introduced in [2]. The domain specific layer is used for defining the specific type of system, for example, web services or network system. This layer provides the QoS connection concepts in lower layer with OWL-S service profiles. QoSOnt is similar with [18, 19], but it does not support QoS profile and the QoS relationships. Conversion mechanism does not support units for mapping the different QoS properties; the usage aspect of the ontology is also poor.

OWL-Q [18]; is an upper level ontology that extends OWL-S [14] specification for describing QoS of Web services. It consists of six facets; In Connecting Facet,

QoS attribute refers to service elements like preconditions, input, effects, parameters etc. It provides the high level concepts for defining QoS advertisements and demands. The Basic Facet is associated with several QoS offers or with only one QoS request. In this facet, QoS specification is used for the actual description of web services in-terms of validity period of the offer, cost of the service, associated currency with cost and security etc. QoS Metric Facet represents the upper ontology containing formal definitions of QoS metric model. It also represents the relationships between two metrics which may be independent and related. Function, Measurement Directive and Schedule Facets describe all the important properties and concepts for the definition of the metric function, while the Function and Schedule facets are used for computing and measuring the metrics. Unit Facet describes the unit of a QoS metric. A Unit is divided into BaseUnits, MultipleOfUnits and DerivedUnits but most of the time base units are used for measurements. Although OWL-Q ontology provides a detailed specification for modeling QoS information but it has weak support for the usage of the ontologies, for example QoS priority, quality level, QoS mandatory. It also does not include concrete definitions of common QoS properties.

onQoS [19]; ontology was developed for specifying the QoS requirements by service consumers and by the service providers for advertising. It gives a clear description for a set of QoS properties. It is composed of three layers: upper, middle and lower. The onQoS upper ontology describes the QoS ontological language and answers the QoS information. Middle ontology refines the concepts of the upper ontology. Qos parameters, scales and metrics are defined in middle layer; this layer also gives the clear specification for metrics and the value types. In low level ontology domain specific properties, constraints and the QoS information are defined. But this ontology is quiet on specifying the QoS relationships, quality level, QoS priority, dynamism etc.

QoS-MO [20]; has different quality levels for the requesters according to his demands, and can represent the interdependent QoS requirements between providers and requesters. This is an upper level ontology based on OWL-S and consists of three levels. First layer is for defining the general characteristics; QoS group related characteristics, for measurements and mapping the characteristics of the service. In second layer three types of constraints are defined, these constraints must be obeyed; service provider can specify the constraints for the service requester to follow in-order to make the service quality better. In third layer different QoS levels for different QoS usage models are defined. But this ontology has very weak support for metric transformation, units, value types and QoS priority.

QoSHOnt [21]; author has presented QoS ontology for semantic service discovery, which provides a unified semantic model for users to advertising and querying the web services. Due to its context, service providers can describe different QoS specification for different circumstances. QoSHOnt consists of three parts, top level ontology is based on general requirements and it is independent to any application domain, middle level ontology is used to integrate quality features defined in the top ontology, while low level ontology is constructed for domain specific requirements. Author also has extended this ontology for contexts, by which service providers can describe different QoS specifications for different circumstances. The algorithm presented in this ontology has been used for matching and ranking the web services.

OSQS [22]; author has proposed ontology consisting of six components. OSQS is the extension of OWL-S for QoS. In this proposed ontology author has tried to integrate the quality standards like ISO/IEC 9126-1 and ISO/IEC 13236 [12, 13]. For web service discovery they also have extended the SPARQL query language for searching the web services according to the quality criteria but the quality properties are not used in query as other properties. Results of queries are produced without considering relationships that can be establish between quality properties. The extended SPARQL solve the problem to much extent. User discovers the services with required functionalities and then further classify on non-functional requirements. It does not provide the unit conversion facility as well as the metric is also not rich enough.

3   Comparative Evaluation

The defined criteria for ontologies evaluation are quite limited defined over the general requirements (questions defined above) and obviously not sufficient to fulfill all of the requirements of different applications. We have organized the criteria into three groups; Model related, Process related and runtime related criteria. We have compared different ontologies on these criteria, in-order to know the best approach that meets the maximum requirements. The short introduction of the criteria is given below.

3.1   Model Related Criteria

Short introduction of model related criteria is given below.

Relationship: Relationship defines that how the qualities are related to each other [18].

Metric: Metric defines that how the values can be assigned to the QoS property [18].

Modularity: This requirement allows for adapting QoS ontology for different domains and applications.

3.2   Process Related Criteria

Short introduction of process related criteria is given below.

Comparison: This property is an important factor for evaluating QoS metrics and their values. A QoS property can have one of five comparative effects: negative, positive, close, exact, and none.

Prioritization: In prioritization the requester defines that which qualities may be given more weight over others [24, 25].

Grouping: This feature allows for grouping several QoS properties which share similar characteristics or impacts in order to facilitate the evaluation and computing of the whole QoS ranking value of a Web service.

3.3   Runtime Related Criteria

Short introduction of runtime related criteria is given below.

Scalability: it defines whether the service capacity (ability to process more transactions in the defined period) can be increased as per requester requirements [10, 11, 23].

Dynamicity: Dynamicity defines the nature of the property. Dynamic properties are needed to be updated frequently while the static properties are updated once [24, 25, 26].

Interoperability: Means, that any two systems will drive the same inference from the same information, which is very difficult. It also deals with the compatibility of service with the standards [11, 23].

4   Discussion

In Table 1, we have analyzed different QoS ontologies to know their strengths and limitations. We have concluded that none of the existing ontologies cover all over the aspects of defined criteria; and still, there are many open issues for research.

Most of the ontologies support the model related criteria, less of the process related and least in runtime related criteria. So, the runtime related aspects should be considered seriously for building an affective ontology. However, the phases (model and process) cover the maximum criteria aspects, but ontology support for runtime stage is still very small. Most of the ontologies described in the literature provide guideline for ontology development but still there is no agreement for best practices for ontology development.

Table 1. Web service composition approaches

Properties / Ontologies		Model Related			Process Related			Run-Time Related		
		Relationship	Metric	Modularity	Comparison	Prioritization	Grouping	Dynamicity	Scalability	Interoperability
DAML-QoS	[15]		√							
QoSOnt	[16]			√						
OWL-Q	[18]	√	√	√				√		√
onQoS	[19]		√	√		√				
QoS-MO	[20]		√							
QoSHOnt	[21]				√			√		
OSQS	[22]	√		√		√				
OWL-SQ	[27]									

The results show (Table 1) that OWL-Q is the best ontology language among the rest as it fulfills the most of the parameters of the defined criteria. Despite of the recent efforts there is still a lot to do in enhancing the description of quality aspects of services. Some of our proposed research areas are as under.

- Most of the ontologies described in the literature provide guideline for ontology development but still there is no agreement for best practices for ontology development.
- The number of best practices that must be followed by designers and developers is still very small, while there is no technical standard for ontology development.
- Fine-grained ontology development guidelines are needed to develop. In case of conflicting viewpoints fine-grained ontology can specify more accurately the vocabulary meanings.

Ontology support for runtime stage is very small. So, the runtime related aspects should be considered seriously for building an affective ontology.

5   Summary

Web services discovery, ranking and selection based on QoS parameters is remained a hot topic for research since the start of the semantic web. In this paper we have pointed out some problems associated with the current ontology models for effective discovery, ranking and selection of services based on QoS. In this paper we have presented criteria that if satisfied, can resolve these issues. We have evaluated different ontologies on these criteria to know, which one is the best ontology that can be used efficiently for web services discovery while addressing its limitations. We also have proposed the new research directions in this paper.

Acknowledgement. We would like to thank Software Engineering Research Group (SERG) of Universiti Teknologi Malaysia for providing the facilities and support for the research.

References

1. Newcomer, E., Lomow, G.: Understanding SOA with Web Services, ch. 1. Addison Wesley Professional (December 2004)
2. Laprie, J.C., Randell, B., Landwehr, C.: Basic Concepts and Taxonomy of Dependable and Secure Computing. IEEE Transactions on Dependable & Secure Computing 1(1), 11–33 (2004)
3. Cabral, L., Domingue, J., Motta, E., Payne, T.R., Hakimpour, F.: Approaches to semantic Web services: An overview and comparisons. In: Bussler, C.J., Davies, J., Fensel, D., Studer, R. (eds.) ESWS 2004. LNCS, vol. 3053, pp. 225–239. Springer, Heidelberg (2004)
4. Hu, J., Guo, C., Wang, H., Zou, P.: Quality driven Web services selection. In: Proceedings of the 2005 IEEE International Conference on e-Business Engineering, ICEBE 2005, Beijing, China, pp. 681–688 (2005)

5. Seo, Y.J., Jeong, H.Y., Song, Y.J.: Best Web service selection based on the decision making between QoS criteria of service. In: Yang, L.T., Zhou, X.-s., Zhao, W., Wu, Z., Zhu, Y., Lin, M. (eds.) ICESS 2005. LNCS, vol. 3820, pp. 408–419. Springer, Heidelberg (2005)
6. Serhani, M.A., Dssouli, R., Hafid, A., Sahraoui, H.: A QoS broker based architecture for efficient web services selection. In: IEEE International Conference on Web Services, ICWS 2005, Florida, USA, pp. 113–120 (2005)
7. Chhabra, M., Lu, H.: Towards agent based web service. In: 6th IEEE/ACIS International Conference on Computer and Information Science (lCIS 2007), pp. 93–99 (July 2007)
8. Benatallah, B., Hacid, M.S., Leger, A., Rey, C., Toumani, F.: On automating Web services discovery, pp. 84–96. Springer (February 2004)
9. Wang, H., Zhang, Y., Sunderraman, R.: Extensible soft semantic web services agent. Soft Comput. 10, 1021–1029 (2005)
10. Giallonardo, E., Zimeo, E.: More Semantics inQoS Matching. In: Proc. of the IEEE Intl. Conf. on Service Oriented Computing and Applications, pp. 163–171. IEEE Computer Society, Los Alamitos (2007)
11. Yao, S.J., Chen, C.X., Dang, L.M., Liu, W.: Design of QoS ontology about dynamic web service selection. Computer Engineering and Design 29(6), 1500–1548 (2008)
12. ISO/IEC91 26-1, Quality characteristics and guidelines for their use. International Organization for Standardization I International Electrotechnical Commission. Tech. Rep. (2001)
13. ISOIIEC1 3236, Quality of service: Framework. International Organization for Standardization I International Electrotechnical Commission. Tech. Rep. (1999)
14. Ankolekar, A.: OWL-S: Semantic Markup for Web Services (2003),
    http://www.daml.org/services/owl-s/1.0/
15. Zhou, C., Chia, L.T., Lee, B.S.: DAML-QoS Ontology for Web Services. In: Proceedings of the IEEE International Conference on Web Services, ICWS 2004 (2004)
16. Dobson, G., Lock, R., Sommerville, I.: QoSOnt: a QoS Ontology for Service-Centric Systems. In: Proceedings of the 2005 31st EUROMICRO Conference on Software Engineering and Advanced Applications (EUROMICRO-SEAA 2005) (2005)
17. Li, S., Zhou, J.: The WSMO-QoS Semantic Web Service Discovery Framework. IEEE (2009)
18. Kritikos, K., Plexousakis, D.: Semantic QoS Metric Matching. In: Proc. of European Conf. on Web Services, pp. 265–274. IEEE Computer (2006)
19. Giallonardo, E., Zimeo, E.: More Semantics in QoS Matching. In: Proc. of IEEE Intl. Conf. on Service Oriented Computing and Applications, pp. 163–171. IEEE Computer (2007)
20. Tondello, G.F., Siqueira, F.: The QoS-MO Ontology for Semantic QoS Modeling. In: SAC 2008, March 16-20 (2008)
21. Yu, C., Junyi, S., Yang, Y., Zhizhong, L.: A QoS Ontology for Semantic Service Discovery. In: 2009 International Conference on Networking and Digital Society (2009)
22. Jean, S., Losaviot, F., Matteot, A., Levy, N.: An Extension of OWL-S with Quality Standards. 978-1-4244-4840 2010 IEEE
23. Garcia, D.Z.G., Toledo, D., Felgar, M.B.: Semantic-enriched QoS Policies for Web Service Interactions. In: ACM International Conference Proceeding Series - Proceedings of the 12th Brazilian Symposium on Multimedia and the Web - WebMedia, vol. 192, pp. 35–44 (2006)
24. Papaioannou, I.V., Tsesmetzis, D.T., Roussaki, I.G., Anagnostou, M.E.: A QoSOntology Language for Web-Services. In: Proceedings of the 20th International Conference on Advanced Information Networking and Applications, pp. 101–106 (2006)

25. Tran, V.X.: WS-QoSOnto: A QoS Ontology for Web Services. In: IEEE International Symposium on Service-Oriented System Engineering, pp. 233–238 (2008)
26. Papaioannou, I.V., Tsesmetzis, D.T., Roussaki, I.G., Anagnostou, M.E.: A QoS Ontology Language for Web Services. In: Proc. of 20th Intl. Conf. on Advanced Information Networking and Applications, pp. 18–25. IEEE Computer (2006)
27. Guo, G., Yu, F., Chen, Z., Xie, D.: A Method for Semantic Web Service Selection Based on QoS Ontology. Journal of Computers 6(2) (February 2011)

Part IV

Personalized Information and Interaction

Placebooks: Participation, Community, Design, and Ubiquitous Data Aggregation 'In the Wild'

Alan Chamberlain[1], Andy Crabtree[1], Mark Davies[1], Kevin Glover[1],
Stuart Reeves[1], Peter Tolmie[1], and Matt Jones[2]

[1] University of Nottingham,
Jubilee Campus, Wollaton Road, Nottingham
{Alan.Chamberlain,Andy.Crabtree,Mark.Davies,Kevin.Glover,
Stuart.Reeves,Peter.Tolmie}@nottingham.ac.uk
[2] Swansea University,
Singleton Park, Swansea
{matt.jones}@swansea.ac.uk

Abstract. This paper outlines and describes the development of a multi-media data aggregation system called Placebooks. Placebooks was developed as a ubiquitous toolkit aimed at allowing people in rural areas to create and share digital books that contained a variety of media, such as: maps; text; videos; audio and images. Placebooks consists of two parts: 1) a web-based editor and viewer, and 2) an Android app that allows the user to download and view books. In particular, the app allows the user to cache content, thereby negating the need for 3G networks in rural areas where there is little-to-no 3G coverage. Both the web-based tools and the app were produced in the English and Welsh languages. The system was developed through working with local communities using participatory approaches: working 'in the wild'. Placebooks is currently being used by a Welsh Assembly Government project called the People's Collection of Wales/ Casgliad y Werin.

Keywords: collaborative work, Community computing, Electronic publishing, Participatory design, Quality of life and lifestyle.

1 Introduction

In this paper we outline the development of an application called Placebooks. Within this short paper we give an overview of the Placebooks system before progressing to consider the approaches that we have used in regard developing and designing this ubiquitous multimedia data aggregation system 'in the wild'. This brief introduction opens the paper, but is complimented by an overview of the system following on from the introduction. The core focus of this research related to the development of IT systems 'in the wild', this paper introduces the system that was developed and gives a brief insight into the approaches that developed as part of the design and development of the system in a rural context.

S. Yamamoto (Ed.): HIMI/HCII 2013, Part I, LNCS 8016, pp. 411–420, 2013.

2   Placebooks

Placebooks is the product of a research project having a brief to explore the development of up-to-date digital solutions that would enable people to map rural spaces in a similar way to that in which Alfred Wainwright mapped the Lake District – i.e., through the use of various media and personalised accounts of place. The result is a ubiquitous computing toolkit that allows people to create, publish and share digital books about the places they visit and inhabit – see *www.placebooks.org*. The system allows users to embed various types of digital content including video, audio, photos, web pages, maps, routes and sensor data alongside text to create personal digital books about places. The system is currently bilingual using both Welsh and English.

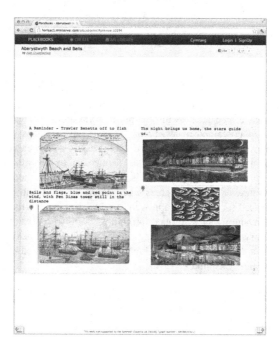

Fig. 1. A user's Placebooks about Aberystwyth

A user's books are organised and stored in their own Placebooks library. Each Placebook can be shared within a group or global network. A user can browse for public Placebooks from an archive and add elements of other people's Placebooks to their own. They may also add content from other online sources and services to their Placebook and they may specify access rights and privileges to allow other users to add content to a Placebook. A mobile app enables users to access Placebooks 'in the wild' for viewing and navigation, and they can search for nearby Placebooks based on their current location.

Placebooks is predicated on a collaborative model that exploits a map-based user-interface to filter an archive of Placebooks on the basis of the activities they represent (e.g., cycling, bird watching, walking, etc.), local knowledge they articulate (e.g., local history, flora and fauna, archaeology, etc.), and services they provide (e.g., places to eat, places to stay, places to buy goods, etc.). The system has 4 key parts:

— A web browser-based interface for authoring and viewing Placebooks.
— A mechanism for linking external data sources to Placebooks.
— A mobile application for viewing Placebooks.
— A server-side infrastructure for managing Placebook construction and use.

2.1   Web Interface

The initial design for a Placebook was based on a tri-fold leaflet metaphor. This is a single A4 size canvas, which is made up of 6 panels (3 on the front, 3 on the back). However, this was re-designed into the book-like editor that can be seen below in Fig. 2. Although initially the leaflet editor was developed, stakeholders involved in the co-design process started to suggest that it might be more appropriate to move to a book-based metaphor that one could flick though and share. Other stakeholders were asked about the metaphor change and the design was developed. In this respect we can see how engaging the stakeholders in the design process lead directly to changes within the system.

The web interface first requires individuals to create their own user account in order to make a Placebook. Once an individual is signed up, they can access the Placebooks editor. The editor enables users to create and manipulate Placebooks via a simple GUI. A 'palette' metaphor provides access to digital media items that can be 'dragged and dropped' on to the visual book canvas. Digital media can be added from the user's computer, from online sources, and third party service providers. Each book has the option of including 25k Ordnance Survey (OS) OpenSpace maps. Every item in a Placebook can be represented as a geo-point on a map. When users have finished creating a Placebook, they can 'publish' it to share with others.

2.1.1 Publishing

Once a user starts to use the editor to make their Placebook, the system will auto-save the book. However this version of the book is not seen publicly until the user decides to publish the book. Once the book is published it is then available to all users of the system and can be downloaded by the mobile part of the system. If we look at Figure 3 it shows the editor's library view, unpublished books are all blue and published books appear with the orange marker on their cover.

Editing rights can also be shared. A user can invite other users to co-create a book if the original author wishes. This means in practice that a book can have many co-authors that may be working on creating the content for one book.

Once the book is published it can also be shared (as a published item) through Facebook and Google+.

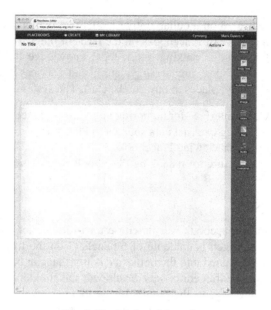

Fig. 2. The book web interface

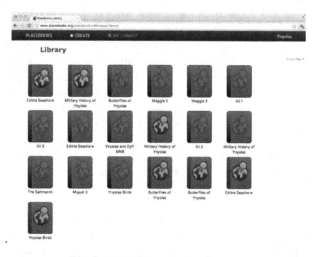

Fig. 3. The Editor – library view

2.2   Linking External Data Sources

We currently support two third party service providers:

– *EveryTrail*, a popular mobile phone application that enables people to record GPS trails and geo-tag content, including photos and videos.
– *People's Collection Wales* (PCW), an online archive for creating and sharing geo-tagged content.

The linking component allows Placebook users to synchronise their EveryTrail and PCW data with the editing palette to add content to books they are creating. The PCW data currently includes routes and geo-tagged images.

2.3   Mobile Application

The mobile application enables users to take their Placebooks 'offline' and into areas without data connectivity. Placebooks are represented in a 'bookshelf' GUI, from which users can select and download books to the mobile device. These downloaded Placebooks are then available for viewing within the application, which adapts the content to the device they are displayed on. Currently an Android app is available for download at Google Play (search for Placebooks). An iPad app is currently in development. Figure 4. gives an example of the way that the Placebook is rendered onto an Android phone. The first picture illustrates and example of the user's library, while the second shows and example of the content that is presented to the user.

Users can search for nearby Placebooks relative to their current position and download these books to their bookshelf. Placebooks can also be searched by 'type' (e.g., surfing, walking, eating out, etc.), allowing users to quickly find the Placebooks that interest them.

Map items in a Placebook are stored as map tile images. When a Placebook gets downloaded to a mobile device, the map image tiles get cached on the phone to enable them to be used in areas without data connectivity. If the mobile device has GPS enabled, then a You-Are-Here (YAH) marker will be appear on the map and update its position in relation to the user's movement.

Different types of geo-tagged media are represented on the map by using small, touchable icons to match the data type they represent (e.g., video, images, audio).

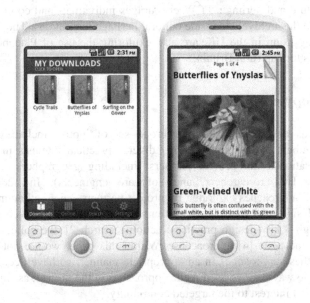

Fig. 4. The Placebooks mobile app

2.3.1 Mobile Maps

Many smart phone apps that use maps rely on mobile 3G services to update the map tiles, so as users move from one place to another the map tiles are updated, they are not stored locally. By delivering mapping services in this way, the user needs to have a connection to the map server, yet within many rural areas in the UK there is little to no 3G-coverage, meaning that many mobile apps relying on map-based services are of little to no use. In order to remedy this we developed a method to cache map tiles locally on the mobile device to allow the user to access map tiles without the need of a data connection to a map server, whilst in-field.

2.4   Server-Side Infrastructure

The server-side, cloud-based infrastructure offers a variety of services for the web interface, mobile application and linking of external data sources. It provides the system's media data types (e.g., video, audio, maps etc.). It also provides database persistence capabilities for storing and retrieving these data types as they are converted from external data sources, authored, retrieved, and so on. It provides the 'bookshelf' and packaging service that translates a user's Placebooks collection into a format that the mobile application component may interpret. It can also provide the account structure. It offers a publishing mechanism, which copies a given Placebook into a new instance that is accessible to other account holders as well as non-account holders. It provides textual and locative search services.

Placebooks is a free-to-use service that has been taken up by the People's Collection Wales (PCW) to support its core business activities. PCW is an innovative bilingual digital platform that aims to collect, interpret and display the history of Wales, its culture and heritage. PCW encourages individuals and community groups to contribute to the archive, alongside cultural heritage institutions. The Ramblers, the largest walking group in the UK, are also exploring the use of Placebooks, in their ongoing efforts to map rural Britain.

3   Development Practices

Placebooks was developed through a broad set of inputs, including input from individual members of the public having diverse practical interests in rural places, public organisations, and project partners (including geographers, cartographers, ethnographers, HCI researchers, and software engineers). In addition to the methodological approaches exploited by project partners – e.g., ethnographic studies [1], concept design, and mockups – systems development was driven in significant respects through 3 key design practices: action research 2], the collective resources approach [3], and agile [4] approaches. Within this paper we are not able to fully expand upon these approaches in an appropriate manner, so have decided to briefly expand upon the way that we used Agile approaches in the project, as we feel that this would be of most interest to the targeted community.

3.1   Collective Resources Approach

CRA is a Participatory Design (PD) approach to design that explicitly privileges the views of the worker. In using the term "worker", CRA refers to the community that is worked with (often through the medium of workforce unions and their plans) in order to affect a beneficial change for the good of the workforce, and in so doing prevent the workers being exploited in the workplace by the capitalist system that creates conflict within the workplace arena. The CRA aims to engage the workers in the design process through the workers not only being the object of study, but also through them co-operatively working with PD-based designers. In order to accomplish this, both the design team and workers take part in workshops, feedback sessions, prototyping, demos and so on. This method of co-design is seen as having a democratising effect that mitigates the inherent conflict (seen by CRA designers) existing in relation to the workers' struggle for workplace democratisation in the capitalist system. In terms of practice it could be said that CRA extends upon AR by taking a left leaning approach, but still retains 'design by doing' [5] as a core practice. *For a fuller discussion of PD methods see Voss et al (2007, Chapter 2), and Muller et al (1993) [6], for a PD taxonomy overview.*

Although we have borrowed certain elements from CRA in our approach to design, we were not involved in using these methods to enable the democratisation of the workplace through design as we earlier stated. However, when we further examine the literature relating to the CRA it can be seen from the list below [5] that we have been engaged in activities that are CRA-based. The list below shows the elements of the CRA that we have used within our engagement.

- design by doing;
- using languages that are familiar to the participants;
- design as mutual learning;
- participation in design as enjoyable;
- design as situated.

Key to our approach was enabling the community to directly respond to the research, input into the design and evaluate the system as we went along (co-operative evaluation). In this regard we were doing research with the user, for the user, and with the users - having their interests at heart. By taking this design approach and working with a range of stakeholders (with diverse and overlapping) interests, it is important to emphasize a degree of flexibility when responding to their situated interests and needs. These may not necessarily be the designers' interests but those of the stakeholders', and to plot a path between the varying interests that stakeholders may have.

In using this approach we were able to initially develop a concept, working with stakeholders in the wild, rather than bringing them to labs.

Actively being in the community and working with people showing them paper prototypes, discussing ideas and feeding back to the development team. What worked, what didn't, what was understood and what wasn't and what they themselves could see as working for them.

This work with stakeholders in the community informed and added to our initial mix of ideas based around a project brief, that was originally shaped around interests in 'interpretation' from the Countryside Council for Wales and geographic interests in 'vernacular' maps and user-generated content from the Ordnance Survey. We also carried out ethnographic studies of the work-practices involved in visiting places.

As the system has developed the Peoples Collection Wales, a national peoples' archive have decided to use the Placebooks system and test it in its beta format in order to add it to their toolset (as part of the collection). This interest has enabled us to work with them and has also allowed them to think about the design of their own system and what the best way may be for the public to use tools to provide content to their national archive. This continued interest has also led to shaping the continued development of Placebooks and interest from their international partners and UK partners (the Ramblers) as a platform that they could use.

3.1.1 Limitations of Collective Resources Approach

Although CRA has influenced the way that we have been working, collectively, both as a team and with the communities, we did not use CRA as initially intended [3]. What in fact enabled the community to engage in design was action and reflection upon the activity they were engaged in. By giving the community a highly developed prototype, as previously stated, they were able to use the prototype and use the experiences gained from interacting with the prototype as a platform from which they could engage with the design process. We did not treat our engagement with the communities as having any sort of political agenda or as using a methodology for "democratic innovation" [7].

Indeed this would have been difficult to do if we had intended to work with them as a group, a majority of the engagement happened at an individual/family level. Meetings often occurred in the domestic context of the person using the system. As people lead busy, and sometimes complicated lives, it was appropriate to meet people in a place and time that they stipulated and not attempt to corral people in workshops, design studios and labs (this also fitted in with the, in the wild ethos of the project). Although this took more time, it became apparent that once people had invited us into their home, they were more comfortable with our presence. This also gave the in-situ researchers a more intimate understanding of the people they were dealing with. When working with the organisational members, who worked in the wildlife centre, they were often there as a group, and that is how we worked with them. In that context, people came and went, as required by their work schedules.

It is important to stress that within this approach we also took note of the expertise within the research team, that was made up of researchers (ethnographers, HCI researchers, software engineers) with multiple competences allowing us to pull on a range of knowledge and expertise, and it was this weaving together through using a collective competence and collective problem solving that related heavily to the ethos of CRA.

This allowed us to collectively pool the resources of both the community and the research team in order to design and develop appropriately. This collective problem solving approach meant that, unlike other general models of systems development, [8] we did not end up with an isolated division of labour. That is to say, that sometimes researchers whose expertise was programming would come to work in the field, in order to get first-hand experience of the research environment, ethnographers would sit-in on technical discussions and all of the team would actively engage in design. We found that it was important to have people coming and engaging with the community and doing fieldwork because they were able to get directly involved. Without this direct involvement the researcher is at a disadvantage: they are at a distance from the phenomena that they want to understand.

4   Conclusion

Within this paper we have given a brief overview of the system and discussed some of the issues that we have encountered whilst developing the Placebooks system, we have also expanded upon the CRA approach that we employed to accomplish this. Although this is a short paper, we hope that this overview will act as an introduction, prove useful to the community, and in particular to those people that are developing systems for use in rural areas unlike many pervasive technologies that have focused upon urban settings (8,9). With an ever-growing archive of Placebooks it will be possible to further understand the users' motivations for creating content, the types of content that they create and how the system's use develops at a future point in time.

Acknowledgments. This work was supported by the Research Councils UK Bridging the Rural Divide (RCUK) [grant number EP/I001816/1] and Scaling the Rural Enterprise [grant number EPSRC EP/J000604/1].

References

1. Crabtree, A., Rouncefield, M., Tolmie, P.: Doing Design Ethnography. Springer (2012)
2. Hayes, G.R.: The Relationship of Action Research to Human-Computer Interaction. ACM Transactions on Computer-Human Interaction 18(3) (July 2011)
3. Ehn, P., Kyng, M.: The Collective Resource Approach to Systems Design. In: Bjerknes, G., Ehn, P., Kyng, M. (eds.) Computers and Democracy - A Scandinavian Challenge, pp. 17–58. Avebury, Aldershot (1987)
4. Beck, K., et al.: Manifesto for Agile Software Development. Agile Alliance (2001), http://agilemanifesto.org/ (retrieved September 6, 2012)
5. Voss, Hartswood, Ho, Procter, Slack, Rouncefield, Buescher (eds.): Configuring user-designer relations: Interdisciplinary perspectives. Springer (2007)
6. Muller, M.J., Wildman, D.M., White, E.A.: Taxonomy of PD Practices: A Brief Practitioner's Guide. Special Issue on Participatory Design, Communications of the ACM, 36(4) (June 1993); Muller, M., Kuhn, S. (eds.)

7. Yndigegn, S.L., et al.: Mobilizing for community building and everyday innovation. In: 2011 CHI Workshop. ACM (2001)
8. Chamberlain, A., et al.: Locating Experience: touring a pervasive performance. Personal Ubiquitous Computing Journal 15(7) (2011)
9. Chamberlain, A., et al.: Them and Us: an indoor pervasive gaming experience. Entertainment Computing Journal 4, 1–9 (2013)

A Study of Different Consumer Groups' Preferences of Time Display on Watches

Wen-Chih Chang and Wei-Ting Chen

Industrial and Commercial Design Department,
National Taiwan University of Science and Technology,
Taipei, Taiwan
{wchang,M9810119}@mail.ntust.edu.tw

Abstract. Nowadays, through creative time displays, designers increase the value and novelty of watches for consumers in order to increase their purchase intention. Moreover, the diversity of consumer demands to watches has created many niche markets. This study raises the questions of whether designers' different time display techniques for specific consumer groups be identified by the target groups, and what are the differences between the different groups' preferences for time displays on watches. A questionnaire survey was conducted. The findings are: a. Different groups of consumers have different preferences of time displays on watches. b. There is high correlation between consumers' preference and purchase intention regarding time displays on watches. c. There is significant correlation between cognition of time display attributes (readability, playfulness, and innovation) and preference. Among the three attributes, readability influences preference the most. Thus, regarding time displays on watches for different consumer groups, there should be different designs.

Keywords: Watch time display, Consumers preference, Consumer group.

1 Introduction

Nowadays, the demand for watches is highly prevalent; however, with the convenience and advancements of technology, the simple time functions of watches are replaced by various kinds of technological products, thus, changing the use of watches from the single function of precision time to symbolic implication. Watches now represent their owner's identity and personal style (Coat, 2003). Current watch markets can be divided into 2 categories, luxury watch designs made from expensive metals and worn as jewelry, and low-price watches that are easily changed with fashion trends (Tseng and Tseng, 1996). In intensely competitive low-price markets, the functions and materials of watches are restricted by sale prices and production costs, thus, the appearance of watches becomes the key to the design of the products on the market. In recent years, design techniques and surface materials are diverse. The time display of watches is one of the important techniques for designers to convey their design language. Through creative time displays, designers increase the value and

S. Yamamoto (Ed.): HIMI/HCII 2013, Part I, LNCS 8016, pp. 421–430, 2013.
© Springer-Verlag Berlin Heidelberg 2013

novelty of products for consumers in order to increase their purchase intention. More-over, the diversity of consumer demands has created many niche markets. New brands and sales channels continue to expand, and enterprises tend to divide consum-ers into different consumer groups, according to market segmentation, and establish marketing and design strategies according to consumer groups' characteristics in or-der to satisfy consumers' needs more precisely and win the market shares (McCarthy, 1981; Kotler, 1994). This study raises the questions of whether designers' different time display techniques for specific consumer groups be identified by the target groups, and what are the differences between the different groups' preferences for time displays on watches. These issues are worthy of further study. Differences of gender and age can be the criteria for watch designers. In addition, regarding the differences of consumers for design and non-design backgrounds, designers should not focus on their own preferences when designing time displays on watches, while neglecting the consumers' preferences.

2   Research Method

This study included three stages. First, the researcher collected, classified, and record-ed images of watch samples available on the market; in the second stage, a consumer questionnaire was designed; and in the third stage, a questionnaire survey was con-ducted in order to identify different groups' preferences for time displays of watches.

2.1   Questionnaire Sample Selection and Image Production

The functions of watches on the market are varied. In addition to time displays, there are time zone displays, dates, and time counters. In order to balance the directions of research, according to time display of watches currently on the market, this study divided them according to indicator hands, numbers, electronics, and various combi-nations. This study limited the samples to watches with indicator hands that are cur-rently available on the market. Time display has the basic functions of hours and minutes; however, the types of movements and displays are unlimited. First, through catalogues, magazines, and the internet, the researcher collected pictures of watches available on the market, and selected pictures of front angles, with 86 samples col-lected. By the focus group research method, samples were selected. The focus group of this study was the graduate students of the Department of Industrial and Commer-cial Design, National Taiwan University of Science and Technology, including 2 males and 4 females. By group discussion, the samples were clustered according to similarity of pictures into 12 clusters. In each cluster, the researcher selected one rep-resentative as the sample. In order to avoid subjects' confusion with the appearance and modeling of products and errors in research findings, the researcher eliminated the factors of appearance and modeling, including color, materials, quality, brand names, etc. Thus, the subjects judged preference according to the time display of the watches. However, for some specific samples, since the appearance was significantly associated with time design techniques, the appearance factor was retained. Processing of samples is as shown in Figure 1.

Fig. 1. Final Samples for the questionnaire

2.2   Questionnaire Design

In order to obtain the latest market situation, this study did not set exclusion criteria. Investigation data included only basic information, such as gender, age, and design background. In addition to consumers' preference and purchase intentions, the questionnaire included the attributes of time display of watches, "readability", "playfulness", and "innovation". Scoring was based on a Likert 7 point scale, ranging from 1 (strongly disagree) to 7 (strongly agree). The subjects completed the questionnaire according to subjective feelings regarding the time display of watches.

2.3   Questionnaire Survey

The questionnaires were distributed by the internet and convenience sampling areas located on roadsides. There were totally 298 subjects, with 295 valid questionnaires. Descriptive statistics was conducted by SPSS. Frequency distribution is as shown in Table 1.

Table 1. Frequency distribution of subjects

Variables	Levels	Numbers	%
age	below 20 years old	60	20.3
	aged 21-40	190	64.4
	above 41 years old	45	15.3
gender	Male	191	64.7
	Female	104	35.3
Design background	Yes	20	6.7
	No	275	93.3

3   Results and Analysis

The results regarding the subjects' views of time display attributes, namely, readability, playfulness, innovation, preference, and purchase intention are organized in Table 2.

Table 2. The result of five dimensions measurement

	Readability	Playfulness	Innovation	Preference	Purchase intention
Sample1	3.08	4.53	4.65	3.18	2.87
Sample 2	2.44	4.29	4.72	2.85	2.52
Sample 3	4.22	4.37	4.22	3.81	3.35
Sample 4	4.55	4.22	4.07	4.03	3.75
Sample 5	3.64	3.78	3.89	3.38	3.03
Sample 6	5.93	3.54	3.12	4.81	4.49
Sample 7	4.86	5.32	5.35	4.71	4.31
Sample 8	2.32	3.97	4.59	2.67	2.52
Sample 9	2.49	4.07	4.57	2.73	2.47
Sample 10	4.57	4.52	4.59	3.82	3.52
Sample 11	4.23	4.28	4.34	3.82	3.51
Sample 12	4.77	4.01	3.85	3.84	3.53

3.1   Analysis on Preference of Consumers of Different Genders for Time Displays on Watches

Consumers' preferences for time displays on watches, in terms of gender, were analyzed by the t test of mean difference. The results are shown in Table 3. As seen, male and female consumers' preferences for Sample 1, 5, and 10 are significantly different.

Table 3. Analysis on preference of consumers of different genders

	Male		Female			
Sample	Mean	SD	Mean	SD	t	P-Value
Sample 1	3.32	1.55	2.90	1.39	2.306	**0.022***
Sample 2	2.83	1.60	2.90	1.57	-0.396	0.693
Sample 3	3.80	1.47	3.84	1.42	-0.230	0.818
Sample 4	4.14	1.37	3.84	1.39	1.814	0.071
Sample 5	3.51	1.58	3.14	1.38	1.972	**0.050***
Sample 6	4.77	1.33	4.88	1.34	-0.708	0.480
Sample 7	4.80	1.55	4.56	1.69	1.221	0.223
Sample 8	2.72	1.56	2.60	1.52	0.643	0.521
Sample 9	2.82	1.48	2.58	1.51	1.319	0.188
Sample 10	3.96	1.34	3.57	1.48	2.268	**0.024***
Sample 11	3.94	1.44	3.60	1.56	1.884	0.061
Sample 12	3.92	1.38	3.70	1.47	1.277	0.203

"*" Represents reaching significance level of 0.05.

Regarding time display attributes of readability, playfulness, and innovation, male consumers suggested that the time display of Sample 1 is simple, unique, and creative; whereas, the time display of Sample 1 appeared dull to female consumers, and the time is not easily identified. Male consumers suggested that the time display of Sample 5 is industrial, clear, and simple. However, for female consumers, the number fonts are too small, and the time is not easily identified. Thus, their preferences are different. Male consumers' cognition of readability, playfulness, and innovation of Sample 10 is higher than those of female consumers, indicating positive preferences. This study found that male consumers prefer simple designs of hour and minute hands; whereas, female consumers prefer more clear and specific time information.

3.2   Analysis on Preference of Consumers of Different Ages for Time Displays on Watches

Regarding the preferences of consumers of different ages for time displays on watches, One-way ANOVA, was conducted, and the results are shown in Table 4. As seen, consumers of different ages have significantly different cognitive outcomes regarding Sample 1, Sample 2, Sample 6, Sample 7, and Sample 12.

Table 4. One-way ANOVA of ages difference

Sample	Group 1 below 20 years old	Group 2 aged 21-40	Group 3 above 41 years old	F	P-Value	Scheffe
Sample 1	3.65	2.99	3.31	4.627	**0.011***	G1> G2, G1 ≒ G3, G2 ≒ G3
Sample 2	3.38	2.72	2.73	4.280	**0.015***	G1>G2, G1>G3, G2 ≒ G3
Sample 3	4.07	3.72	3.84	1.310	0.271	--
Sample 4	4.05	4.11	3.69	1.700	0.184	--
Sample 5	3.72	3.32	3.20	1.969	0.141	--
Sample 6	4.37	4.82	5.36	7.418	**0.001***	G3>G1, G2 ≒ G1, G2 ≒ G3
Sample 7	4.98	4.79	4.00	5.738	**0.004***	G1>G3, G2>G3, G1 ≒ G2
Sample 8	2.82	2.69	2.40	0.982	0.376	--
Sample 9	3.05	2.68	2.51	1.962	0.142	--
Sample 10	3.80	3.86	3.71	0.209	0.812	--
Sample 11	3.88	3.82	3.73	0.129	0.879	--
Sample 12	3.75	3.73	4.44	4.927	**0.008***	G3>G2, G3>G1, G1 ≒ G2

"*" Represents reaching significance level of 0.05.   In Scheffe test, "--" represents no significant difference.

Scheffe test found that consumers below 20 years old have higher evaluations for the time display of Sample 1, in comparison to consumer groups aged 21-40. According to the investigation results of time display attributes of readability, playfulness, and innovation, consumers below 20 years old suggest that the time display of Sample 1 is simple and has high quality. For consumer groups aged 21-40, the time display of Sample 1 is dull, and thus, their preference is low. Regarding the preference for Sample 2, in comparison to the other two groups, consumers below 20 years old have a higher preference. For consumers below 20 years old, the time display of Sample 2 is unique, simple, and interesting. For the other two groups of above 21 years old, Sample 2 is disordered, and thus, their evaluation is low. Regarding the preference for Sample 6, groups above 41 years old are different from those below 20 years old. Groups above 41 years old find it is easy to read the time display of Sample 6, which matches their personal needs. For consumers below 20 years old, Sample 6 is similar to traditional watches and the appearance is not unique, thus, preference is low. Regarding the preference for Sample 7, the groups' cognitive results are significantly different. Groups above 41 years old have less preference for Sample 7, in comparison to the other groups, as they feel that Sample 7 is not easily read, and regard it an inconvenient utility. For the other two groups, the time display of Sample 7 is simple, easy to read, and unique, thus, the groups are different. Regarding the preference for Sample 12, consumers above 41 years old like it the most, as the movements of the hour and minute hands are the same as traditional watches and easy to read. Thus, in comparison to the other two groups, they prefer Sample 12. For groups below 21 years old and aged 21-40, the preference for the time display of Sample 12 is similar to traditional watches. They do not understand the numbers on surface of the watch, which influences their reading, thus, their preference is low. Generally speaking, the group below 20 years old prefers new and interesting designs, and their preference is higher than the other two groups. Groups aged 21-40 and above 41 years old value the convenience of easily reading the time on a watch. However, according to the preference results of the two groups, those aged 21-40 prefer innovative designs, in comparison to consumers above 41 years old.

3.3   Analysis on Preference of Designers and Consumers for Time Displays on Watches

Regarding the preference results of designers and consumers for time displays on watches, t test of mean difference was conducted, and the results are shown in Table 5. As seen, designers' and consumers' preferences for Sample 1, Sample 2, and Sample 11 are significantly different.

Table 5. Analysis on preference of designers and consumers

Sample	Designers		Consumers		t value	P-value
	Mean	SD	Mean	SD		
Sample 1	4.6	0.99	3.36	1.01	3.596	0.001*
Sample 2	3.75	1.01	2.9	1.56	2.145	0.037*
Sample 3	4.0	1.21	4.2	1.37	-0.528	0.6
Sample 4	4.2	1.71	4.06	1.17	0.328	0.744
Sample 5	3.05	1.63	3.53	1.47	-1.084	0.284
Sample 6	4.7	1.45	5.03	1.24	-0.867	0.39
Sample 7	4.7	1.80	4.6	1.68	0.66	0.947
Sample 8	2.9	1.97	2.43	1.31	1.009	0.318
Sample 9	3.0	1.91	2.6	4.56	0.887	0.380
Sample 10	3.1	1.33	3.6	1.56	-1.171	0.247
Sample 11	2.55	1.27	3.53	1.01	-3.036	0.004*
Sample 12	3.85	1.59	4.0	1.51	-0.336	0.738

"*" Represents reaching significance level of 0.05.

According to the investigation results of time display attributes, readability, play-fulness, and innovation, designers suggest that the time display of Sample 1 is simple, easy to read, and the appearance is fashionable. For consumers, it is not easy to read Sample 1 and the style is too simple, thus, preference is low. Regarding the cognitive results of preference for Sample 2, designers and consumers are significantly different. Designers suggest that the time display is the same as traditional displays; however, the design of the hour and minute hands are creative, thus, the evaluation is high. Regarding preference for Sample 11, consumers highly prefer Sample 11, suggest it is creative to divide night and day as black and white, and it is easier to read the time. Designer evaluation of Sample 11 is lower, they suggest the time display is not creative, and the numbers on the watch surface are too numerous and disordered. Generally speaking designers highly prefer creative time displays, whereas consumers prefer designs with easy reading of time.

3.4   Correlation Analysis between Preference and Purchase Intentions

Regression analysis is conducted by means of preference and purchase intentions of time displays on watches. According to analytical results regarding cognition of preference for time displays on watches, the F value of variance significance test is 1073.42 and the P value of significance testing is 0.000, which is below the significance level 0.05. Thus, the overall explained variance of the regression model of preferences and purchase intentions is significant. There is significant correlation between preference and purchase intention. It can explain 99.1%of the variance and the correlation coefficient is 0.995. Thus, preference and purchase intentions are highly related. Results of regression analysis are as shown in Table 6.

Table 6. Results of regression analysisof purchase intentions

Predicting Variables	B	S.E.	Beta(β)	T
Intercept	0.158	0.108	--	1.464
Purchase intention	1.047	0.032	0.995	32.763***
R^2=0.991,Adjusted R^2=0.990, F=1073.42***				

"***" Represents reaching significance level of 0.001.

3.5   Correlation Analysis Between Readability, Playfulness, Innovation, and Preference

Regression analysis is conducted by means of investigation of preference, readability, playfulness, and innovation of time displays on watches. According to analytical results, the F value of variance significance testing is 62.542, and the P value of significance testing is 0.000, which is below the significance level of 0.05. Therefore, the overall explained variance of the regression model regarding readability, playfulness, innovation, and preference is significant. The regression coefficient of readability is 0.624, playfulness is 0.166, and innovation is 0.122, which explains95.9%of the variance. Thus, there is a significant correlation between cognition of time display attributes and preference. Among the three attributes, readability influences preference the most. Regression analysis results of time display attributes and preferences are organized, as shown in Table 7.

Table 7. Results of regression analysis of purchase intentions

Predicting Variables	B	S.E.	Beta(β)	T
Intercept	-0.044	0.617	--	-0.072
Readability	0.624	0.121	1.006	5.138*
Playfulness	0.166	0.501	0.106	0.332
Innovation	0.122	0.457	0.097	0.267

R^2=0.959, Adjusted R^2=0.944, F=62.542*

"*" Represents reaching significance level of 0.05.

4　Conclusions

Based on the above investigation results and analysis, the conclusions are shown, as follows.

1. Male and female consumers have different preferences for time displays on watches. Male consumers prefer simple hour and minute hands, creative time displays, and their purchase intentions are higher. Female consumers prefer samples with more clear time information. Time displays of unique design with difficult reading will negatively influence female consumers' purchase intentions.
2. Consumers with different ages have different preferences for time displays on watches. Groups below 20 years old prefer new and interesting designs, and their preferences and purchase intentions are higher than the other two groups. Groups aged 21-40 and above 41 years old pay attention to the convenience of reading the time on watches. However, according to preference results of the two groups, groups aged 21-40 prefer creative designs, in comparison to consumer groups aged above 41.
3. Designers and consumers have different preferences regarding time displays of watches. Designers highly prefer creative time displays and have higher purchase intentions. Consumers prefer designs that are easily and clearly read.
4. There is high correlation between consumers' "preference" and "purchase intention" regarding time displays on watches.
5. There is significant correlation between cognition of time display attributes and preference. Among the three attributes, readability influences preference the most.

Based on the above, different groups of consumers have different preferences of time displays on watches. Thus, regarding time displays on watches for different consumer groups, there should be different designs. The research findings of the preferences for different consumer groups can serve as references for designs of time displays on watches in order to satisfy different consumers' needs.

References

1. Tseng, S.H., Tseng, C.H.: Project Study on Watches. IEK System Energy Department of Industrial Technology Research Institute of Taiwan, R.O.C (1996)
2. Coates, D.: Watches Tell More than Time. McGraw-Hill, New York (2003)
3. Kotler, P.: Marketing Management: Analysis, Planning, Implementation, and Control. Prentice Hall, New Jersey (1994)
4. McCarthy, J.E.: Basic Marketing: A managerial Approach. Homewood, Richard D. Irwin Inc., Illinois (1981)

Evaluation of Superimposed Self-character Based on the Detection of Talkers' Face Angles in Video Communication

Yutaka Ishii and Tomio Watanabe

Faculty of Computer Science and System Engineering,
Okayama Prefectural University, Japan
{ishii,watanabe}@cse.oka-pu.ac.jp

Abstract. We build upon an embodied video chat system, called E-VChat, in which an avatar is superimposed on the other talker's video images to improve the mutual interaction in remote communications. A previous version of this system used a headset-type motion capture device. In this paper, we propose an advanced E-VChat system that uses image processing to sense the talker's head motion without wearing sensors. Moreover, we confirm the effectiveness of the superimposed avatar for face-to-face communication in an experiment.

Keywords: Multimodal interaction, Human Interface.

1 Introduction

The effectiveness of modern video-based teleconference systems is confirmed by their widespread commercial use [1], [2], [3], [4]. Video images help individuals to directly observe nonverbal information, such as nodding, gestures, and facial expressions. As such, video is considered to be a very useful communication media. However, remote talkers have difficulty interacting because they do not share the same communication space; hence, they rely only on a video image. Some telecommunication systems have been developed using computer generated (CG) characters in cyber-space, or avatars, which allow remote talkers to communicate through a common virtual space [5], [6], [7]. Recently, new devices and methods have been proposed for movement of the avatars. Takahashi et al. suggested a head motion detection method that uses an active appearance model (AAM) that is sensitive to eye blinks [8]. A virtual communication system for human interaction, called "VirtualActor," uses a human avatar that represents the upper body motion of the talker [9]. This system experimentally demonstrated the effectiveness of communication through avatar embodiment.

A more effective remote communication system can be developed by allowing talkers to observe each other's nonverbal information, such as facial expressions. To take advantage of both avatars and video images, we developed an embodied video communication system in which VirtualActor is superimposed on each partner's video image in a virtual face-to-face scene [10]. Moreover, we developed a headset motion-capture device that uses an acceleration sensor and gyro sensor to track the talker's head movements directly. The device allows an avatar to mimic the talker's

S. Yamamoto (Ed.): HIMI/HCII 2013, Part I, LNCS 8016, pp. 431–438, 2013.

motion and automatically move in response to the on-off pattern of the talker's voice. The combined system was implemented in a prototype communication system called "Enhanced-VideoChat (E-VChat)" [11].

In this paper, we propose an advanced E-VChat system that uses image processing to track the talker's head motion and facial angles, thereby avoiding the need for a wearing sensor and expanding the practicality of the system. The effectiveness of the new system is confirmed experimentally.

2   Concept of E-VChat System

Figure 1 shows the E-VChat system concept. Talkers communicate using the video image of the other. In the E-VChat system, a voice-driven substitute character is superimposed on a video image of the partner. The character's motions are automatically generated based on the talker's voice and head motions as measured by a motion capture device.

Figure 2 depicts how a talker's gaze line is dependent on camera position. In general, the web camera is placed on the periphery of the monitor, and the talker casts his/her eyes outside of the monitor. By including an embodied avatar on the talker's screen, each talker can observe a virtual face-to-face interaction between the self-avatar and an image of the other talker.

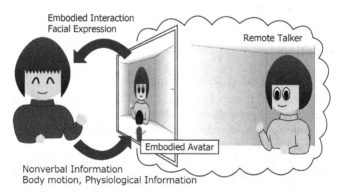

Fig. 1. Concept of the E-VChat System

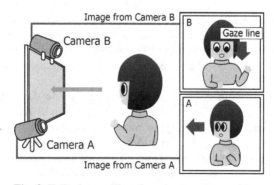

Fig. 2. Talker's gaze lines based on camera positions

This system is unique in that the talker's avatar is only visible to the talker. On the screen, the talker observes the avatar overlaid on the other talker's image, but the other talker is unaware of the avatar. We expect to extend this effect for all communication between remote talkers.

3   System Configuration

Talkers using the original E-VChat systems were required to wear a headset device or magnetic sensors to track the talker's motion. Our simple device using an acceleration sensor and gyro sensor also had problems for the practical or universal use, and the magnetic sensors for detecting talker's motions had some problems, such as a sense of restraint owing to the sensor cables and the sensors' lack of port-ability. To address this issue, the advanced E-VChat system uses image processing to track the talker's head motion. A description of the image processing algorithm is provided here.

3.1   Character Motions Generated Automatically on the Basis of Speech Input

An avatar motion generation method that is based on the talker's voice has already been developed [12]. Nonverbal actions that express a talker's intention are important in serious situations such as negotiations, counseling, and agreements. The avatar's head motion, which plays an important role in communication, synchronizes with the talker's motion to facilitate communication.

The Moving-Average (MA) model, which times nodding on the basis of a talker's voice data, is used to auto-generate avatar motions for the "listener" [12]. The MA model estimates nodding timing from a speech on-off pattern, using a hierarchy model consisting of a macro stage and a micro stage. When $Mu(i)$ exceeds a threshold value, the nodding value, $M(i)$, is estimated as the weighted sum of the binary speech signal, $V(i)$. Avatar body movements are introduced when speech input timing exceeds a body threshold. The body threshold is set lower than that of the nodding prediction of the MA model, which is expressed as the weighted sum of the binary speech signal to nodding.

$$M_u(i) = \sum_{j=1}^{J} a(j)R(i-j) + u(i) \tag{1}$$

$$R(i) = \frac{T(i)}{T(i) + S(i)} \tag{2}$$

$a(j)$: linear prediction coefficient
$T(i)$: talkspurt duration in the i-th duration unit
$S(i)$: silence duration in the i-th duration unit
$u(i)$: noise

$$M(i) = \sum_{k=1}^{K} b(j)V(i - j) + w(i) \tag{3}$$

$b(j)$: linear prediction coefficient
$V(i)$: voice
$w(i)$: noise

The MA model of the "speaker" allows the avatar's head and body motions to be linked to the on-off pattern of speech.

3.2   Character Motions Measured by a Headset Motion-Capture Device

More effective communication would be supported by not only the auto-generated motions based on the voice input as described in the previous section but also talkers' own measured motions for their intentions by a motion-capture device (Kinect for Windows L6M-00005). The talker's head motions are detected based on three-axis angles and three-dimensional positions. The positions are measured using a depth sensor. The face angle detection range is shown in Figure 3. The avatar's motions are represented based on measured head motions.

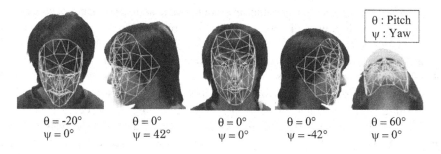

θ : Pitch
ψ : Yaw

$\theta = -20°$ $\theta = 0°$ $\theta = 0°$ $\theta = 0°$ $\theta = 60°$
$\psi = 0°$ $\psi = 42°$ $\psi = 0°$ $\psi = -42°$ $\psi = 0°$

Fig. 3. Detection range of the face angle

4   Communication Experiment

4.1   Experimental Setup

A communication experiment was conducted in three modes: mode A used only head-motion, mode B used auto-generated motion based on speech input, and mode C used both head motion and auto-generated motion. A population of 12 pairs of subjects was evaluated. The talkers in each pair were familiar with one another and were observed using the system in unrestrained conversations. Subjects could select from seven different types of avatar, such as human, robot, or animal. An example of a communication scene using the E-VChat is shown in Figure 4. The experimental setup is shown in Figure 5.

Fig. 4. Communication scene using the E-VChat

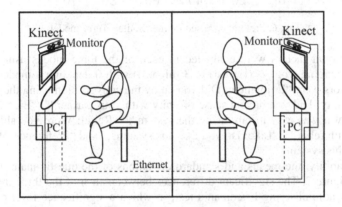

Fig. 5. Experimental setup

4.2 Result of Sensory Evaluation

The results of the paired comparisons of the three modes, in terms of talker prefe-rence, are shown in Table 1. Figure 6 shows the Table 1 data calculated using the Bradley-Terry model given in Equation (4). Mode C, which used both head motion and auto-generated motion, received the most positive talker feedback.

Table 1. Result of pair comparison in the communication experiment

	A	B	C	Total
A		11	3	14
B	13		1	14
C	21	23		44

$$P_{ij} = \frac{\pi_i}{(\pi_i + \pi_j)} \qquad (4)$$

$$\sum_i \pi_i = const. (= 100)$$

(π_i: intensity of i, P_{ij}: probability of judgment that i is better than j.)

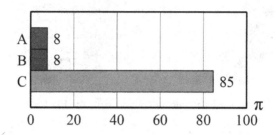

Fig. 6. Preference based on the Bradley-Terry model

Six additional factors were evaluated in each of the three modes using a seven-point scale ranging from -3 (lowest) to 3 (highest) with 0 denoting a moderate score. The six factors were "Enjoyment: Did you enjoy the conversation using the system?," "Sense of unity: Did you have a sense of unity with your partner?," "Ease of talking: Did you feel it was easy to talk using the system?," "Relief: Were you able to communicate with relief?," "Like: Do you like this system?," and "Preference: Would you like to use this system?"

For readability, the means and standard deviations of the questionnaire results are shown in Figure 7. The significant differences between each of the three modes were obtained by administering Friedman's test, in which a significance level of 1% was obtained for all factors. Significant differences were also obtained by administering the Wilcoxon's rank sum test for multiple comparisons. A significance level of 1% was obtained for all factors between Modes A and B and for the "Sense of unity,"

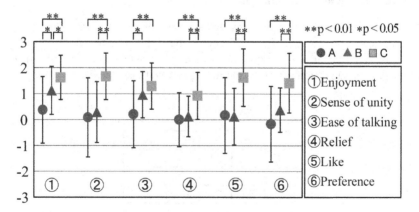

Fig. 7. Seven points bipolar rating

"Relief," "Like," and "Preference" factors when comparing Modes B and C. A significance level of 5% was obtained between Modes B and C for the "Enjoyment" factor. Mode C was positively evaluated as the paired comparison.

5   Conclusion

In this paper, we described an advanced E-VChat system that allows talkers to smoothly communicate using nonverbal information via a self-avatar that is displayed alongside video images. The avatar motions are based on image processing. The effectiveness of self-avatar using talker's head motion and auto-generated motion based on the speech input was confirmed in a communication experiment that evaluated 12 pairs of subjects in three separate communication modes: one mode in which only head-motion was used, another mode in which motion was auto-generated based on speech input, and a final mode that used both head-motion and auto-generated motion based on speech input.

References

1. Sellen, A.J.: Speech Patterns In Video-Mediated Conversations. In: Proc. of CHI 1992, pp. 49–59. ACM (1992)
2. Buxton, W.A.S.: Living in Augmented Reality: Ubiquitous Media and Reactive Environments. In: Finn, E.K., et al. (eds.) Video-Mediated Communication. Computers, Cognition, and Work, pp. 363–384 (1997)
3. Ishii, R., Ozawa, S., Mukouchi, T., Matsuura, N.: MoPaCo: Pseudo 3D Video Communication System. In: Salvendy, G., Smith, M.J. (eds.) HCII 2011, Part II. LNCS, vol. 6772, pp. 131–140. Springer, Heidelberg (2011)
4. Kim, K., Bolton, J., Girouard, A., Cooperstock, J., Vertegaal, R.: TeleHuman: Effects of 3D Perspective on Gaze and Pose Estimation with a Life-size Cylindrical Telepresence Pod. In: Proc. of CHI 2012, pp. 2531–2540 (2012)
5. Cassel, J., et al.: An Architecture for Embodied Conversational Characters. In: Proc. of WECC 1998, pp. 21–29 (1998)
6. Yahoo! Inc., Yahoo! Avatar, http://avatars.yahoo.com/
7. Linden Lab, Second Life, http://secondlife.com/
8. Takahashi, K., Mitsukura, Y.: Eye Blink Detection Using Monocular System and its Applications. In: Proc. of 21st IEEE International Symposium on Robot and Human Interactive Communication (RO-MAN 2012), pp. 743–747 (2012)
9. Ishii, Y., Watanabe, T.: An Embodied Avatar Mediated Communication System with VirtualActor for Human Interaction Analysis. In: Proc. of the 16th IEEE International Workshop on Robot and Human Interactive Communication (RO-MAN 2007), pp. 37–42 (2007)
10. Ishii, Y., Watanabe, T.: An Embodied Video Communication System in which Own VirtualActor is Superimposed for Virtual Face-to-face Scene. In: Proc. of the 13th IEEE International Workshop on Robot and Human Interactive Communication (RO-MAN 2004), pp. 461–466 (2004)

11. Ishii, Y., Watanabe, T.: A Video Communication System in Which a Speech-driven Embodied Entrainment Character Working with Head Motion is Superimposed for a Virtual Face-to-face Scene. In: Proc. of 21st IEEE International Symposium on Robot and Human Interactive Communication (RO-MAN 2012), pp. 191–196 (2012)
12. Watanabe, T., Okubo, M., Nakashige, M., Danbara, R.: InterActor: Speech-Driven Embodied Interactive Actor. International Journal of Human-Computer Interaction 17(1), 43–60 (2004)

Modeling of Music Recommendation Methods to Promote the User's Singing Motivation – For Next-Generation Japanese Karaoke Systems

Satoshi Isogai[*] and Miwa Nakanishi

Keio University, Yokohama, Japan
isogaisatoshi@a3.keio.jp, miwa_nakanishi@ae.keio.ac.jp

Abstract. This study attempted to build a model that recommends music choices to encourage karaoke-system users to sing by using data about the music preferences and inner characteristics of each user. First, we conducted an auditory experiment in two phases. Additionally, we analysed the acoustics and lyrics of music pieces. Using these data, we built a map of the music based on user impressions, and used this map to reveal the relationship between the user's most favourite music piece and the music piece that a user was highly motivated to sing. Thus, we were able to establish a basic model of the system that recommends the music piece a user would be highly motivated to sing.

Keywords: music recommendation, singing motivation, karaoke system.

1 Introduction

Recently, with the spread of the Internet, it is possible to compile the characteristics of users and the characteristics of the goods and services in a large database. The providers of goods and services want to find a method of associating the users' characteristics with the characteristics of their offerings. For example, in a typical shopping site, the system recommends goods for each user based on the user's age, gender and purchase history data. Many recommendation methods have been developed with a focus on recommending 'as similar as possible' products and services. However, the purpose of the recommendation system is to increase the motivation of the user to purchase goods and services. Presenting 'as similar as possible' products and services as recommendations do not necessarily correspond to this goal.

In psychological theory, users' motivation for products or services is categorised as a type of intrinsic motivation. Hunt [1] discussed the psychological theory that intrinsic motivation is evoked when human beings perceive an adequate gap between their own characteristics and those of an object, from the viewpoints of emotion, cognition, and ability. This theory is interesting in the study of the recommendation method that motivates users to make a purchase.

---

[*] Corresponding author.

S. Yamamoto (Ed.): HIMI/HCII 2013, Part I, LNCS 8016, pp. 439–448, 2013.

This study attempts to develop a recommendation model that applies psychological theory to engineering. In particular, this study aims to build a model that compares the characteristics of music selections to the characteristics of each user in order to make recommendations that would motivate the user to sing a selection.

2   Experiments

2.1   Experiment 1

The participants were 20 students (10 males and 10 females whose average age was 22 years) who had singing experience using a karaoke machine. After asking them to listen to several music pieces, we asked them to answer 36 questions, including questions on their impression of, experience with and singing motivation for each music piece. The music piece choices consisted of 80 tracks from four genres. For each genre, there were 20 tracks of Japanese popular music sung by a male (J-Pop male), Japanese popular music sung by a female (J-Pop female), music pieces sung in a foreign language (non-Japanese) and music pieces closely tied with movies or anime films.

In addition, we asked participants to use a free scale from 0 to 6 in order to assess 26 adjectives, such as 'novelty' or 'quiet', when answering questions about their impressions of the music pieces, with 0 meaning 'strongly disagree' and 6 meaning 'strongly agree'. They also used a free scale from 0 to 6 to indicate how motivated they would be to sing a music piece (singing motivation) and to listen to a music piece (listening motivation). They used a multiple-choice method to answer questions on how know they were about each music piece and their impression of the listening experience.

2.2   Experiment 2

A different set of students (10 males and 10 females whose average age was 22 years) participated in a similar experiment. In this case, the participants listened to 55 music pieces. Of the 55 music pieces, 51 were commonly known and 4 were each participant's favourite music pieces and music pieces which he or she tended to sing when using a karaoke machine. These preferences were determined during preliminary research study.

The music pieces were edited to be approximately 50 s long, usually ending at the climax of the second verse. Participants listened to each music piece three times. The order of the music pieces was randomised across participants. To help participants separate their impression of one music piece from the next, a 5 s long mechanical sound was inserted between each music piece. Participants listened to the music with headphones that included a noise-cancelling function, and they entered their answers on a computer. We explained the content of the experiment and obtained the informed consent of the individuals who agreed to participate in this experiment.

3   Appointing the Impression Map of Music

If it is possible to map the impressions of music, it seems that it is possible to capture the impressions of listeners for different features of the music. Therefore, instead of mapping listeners' impressions of the acoustic aspects of the music, we mapped their impressions of the emotional aspects.

3.1   Method

We created an impression map of the music for each experiment and compared the two. Thus, we confirmed the universality of using an impression map. The map was made using the average rating score for each adjective, analyzing the principal components of each experiment.

3.2   Results

For both results, we adopted the second principal component as a guide to establish the 70% cumulative contribution ratio. The loadings of both Experiment1 and Experiment 2 are very similar. The first principal component can be interpreted as indicating 'energetic', because the parameters 'flashy' and 'dynamic' make a positive contribution and the parameter 'quiet' makes a negative contribution. The second principal component can be interpreted as indicating 'familiar', because the parameters 'healthy' and 'flesh' make a positive contribution and the parameters 'alien' and 'stubborn' make a negative contribution. For this reason, impressions of the music for each user can be explained by the spatial relationship formed by the two axes of 'energetic' and 'familiarity'. This can be considered universal irrespective of the type of music and the participant.

4   Establishment of Impression Map Mapping Based on the Features of Music

When considering building a real system, in order to know the position in space of each music piece impression, it is not practical to ask the user to rate all music pieces as described above. Therefore, we built a model that positions any music on an impression map based on 'energetic' and 'familiarity'. We built the model using the data from Experiment 2 and we verified the model using the data from Experiment 1.

4.1   Quantitative Estimation of 'energetic'

From past studies [2, 3], it can be said that the use of acoustic feature to estimate the impression of music is effective. This study attempts to build a model of estimating 'energetic' using acoustic features.

4.1.1   Method
From the results of the second experiment, we obtained the principal component 'score of energetic' and built a model that had 'score of energetic' as its objective

variable and acoustic features as its explanatory variable. In particular, we used five acoustic features: MFCC-13 [4], the spectral centroid, spectral roll off, brightness [5] and chroma vector [6]. We used these features to generate 80 variables in a size 16 vector-quantisation codebook. We adopted six explanatory variables. There is a high correlation with 'scores of energetic'.

The model was built from six variables that are high correlation coefficients combined of 80 variables and 'scores of energetic'. The estimate parameters were derived using the least-square method.

$$E = -0.43 \times \sqrt{x1} - 0.19 \times x2 - 0.37 \times \log(x3) + 1.08 \times \log(x4) - 0.52 \times \sqrt{x5} + 1.60 \times \log(x6) + 2.65 \quad (1)$$

E: Scores of energetic

There was a high correlation between the 'scores of energetic' that were derived by analysing music features from Experiment 2 and the 'scores of energetic' that were derived by analysing the principal components as clarified in Section 3 (R^2=0.82).

4.1.2   Verification

The correlation is very high between the 'scores of energetic' and the 'scores of energetic' (R2=0.66). Therefore, Equation 1 is accurate as a model to estimate the 'energetic' music characteristics for each music piece. In other words, using Equation 1, we can estimate the 'energetic' characteristics of any piece of music without listening to it.

4.2   Quantitative Estimation of 'familiar'

Other than acoustic features, there are lyrics and degrees of recognition of music that can be obtained as data. By using these facts, we could build a model that substantively estimates 'familiar'.

4.2.1   Method

From the results of the second experiment, the second principal component of 'score of familiar' was obtained and a model was built that used 'score of familiar' as its objective variable and a degree of recognition of music as well as its lyric features as its explanatory variables. We used 0 for 'nothing' responses and 1 for high-awareness responses. When 70% or more of the responses was 1, then the level of awareness was set at 1 and when 70% or less of the responses was 1, then the level of awareness was set at 0.

On the other hand, after the lyrics were divided into words, they were analysed by focusing on the adjectives. This analysis used 'Hevner's adjective circle' [7]. Using this method, we divided the lyrics into eight groups of 66 words representing the feelings suitable to represent the music. Collecting about 50–70 synonyms for each group, we created a list of related words. Each group was counted up when a word in the lyrics matched the word list for each music piece. In addition, the total number of the counted words for each group was divided by the total number of the counted words for all groups (Table 1).

Table 1. Classification results of eight groups of adjectives (The upper row is the number; the lower row is the percentage)

	Group of related words1	Group of related words2	Group of related words3	Group of related words4	Group of related words5	Group of related words6	Group of related words7	Group of related words8	sum
music1	0	1	1	0	0	4	1	3	10
music1 (percent)	0	0.1	0.1	0	0	0.4	0.1	0.3	1

The model was built from 'awareness' and the percentage of each group 1–7. The estimate parameters were derived using the least-square method.

$$F = -2.23 \times x1 - 1.95 \times x2 + 0.04 \times x3 + 0.37 \times x4 + 0.23 \times x5 + 0.23 \times x6 - 0.70 \times x7 + 0.84 \times x8 - 0.07 \quad (2)$$

F: Scores of familiar

The correlation is very high between 'scores of familiar', which was derived by analysing lyrics and awareness from Experiment 2, and 'scores of familiar', which was derived by analysing the principal components from Section 3(R^2=0.61).

4.2.2 Verification
We verified the accuracy of the model using 40 music pieces from Experiment 1, not including foreign language music pieces. When we applied these 40 music pieces to Equation 2, the coefficient of determination was 0.53. Therefore, Equation 2 is accurate as a model to estimate the 'familiar' characteristics of music by using lyrics and the awareness for each music piece. In other words, we can estimate the 'familiar' characteristics of any piece of music without listening to it by using Equation 2.

5   Trend Analysis of the User's Music Preference

To build a system that recommend music pieces that karaoke users would be highly motivated to sing based on each users' most favourite music piece, this study attempts to vectorise the positional relationship to a music piece that a user is highly motivated to sing from the user's most favourite music piece on the impression map that we built in Section 3.

5.1   Common Map and Each User's Map

The impression map built in Section 3 represents the average of all participants' music impressions, that is, a common user's map. On the other hand, each user's impression of a music piece can vary based on the user's characteristics (e.g. preference of music and movies or other hobbies). Therefore, instead of using a common map, we will examine in each user's map the positional relationship between the user's most favourite music piece and the music piece that the user is highly motivated to sing. Each user's map is made from the rating scores of each user by multiplying the loadings of experiment.

5.2   Trend Analysis

We defined a piece of music that has a singing motivation score above 5 as the music piece that a user is highly motivated to sing. We defined music pieces that are sung well during karaoke as the user's most favourite music pieces. We examined the positional relationship between the two.

Based on where users' most favourite music pieces appear on the map, the trend was divided to show on a separate map of each participant the relationship between the different relative positions of the users' most favourite music pieces and the music pieces that they were highly motivated to sing. Figure 1 shows that groups 1, 2 and 3 define the user's favourite music piece as 'familiar', 'energetic', and 'lethargic', respectively. Unfamiliar music pieces were excluded, because there are very few cases in which an unfamiliar music piece is the user's most favourite music piece.

Next, we used the following process to examine the positional relationship to the music piece that a user is highly motivated to sing from the user's most favourite music piece (Figure 2). At first, for each participant, we used the vectorisation of the relationship between user's most favourite music piece and the music piece that a user was highly motivated to sing in order to obtain the distance and orientation. After dividing the distance by one and the orientation into increments of $\pi/6$, we found out in which area a music piece that a user was highly motivated to sing was placed when seen from the viewpoint of the user's most favourite music piece.

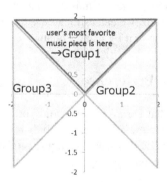

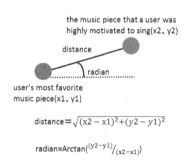

Fig. 1. Grouping of participants by the position of their most favourite music pieces

Fig. 2. Relationship of the position of the music piece that a user was highly motivated to sing when compared with the user's most favourite music piece

Figures 3, 4 and 5 show the probability of the presence of a music piece that a user is highly motivated to sing when the user's most favourite music piece is placed in the centre. In group 1 (Figure 3), a music piece that a user is highly motivated to sing tends to be placed in the unfamiliar area, which is slightly lower when viewed from the user's most favourite music piece. In group 2 (Figure 4), a music piece that a user is highly motivated to sing tends to be placed in the upper left area (inferior to 'energetic' but more than 'familiar') when viewed from the user's most favourite music piece. In group 3 (Figure 5), a music piece that a user is highly motivated to sing tends to be placed in the lower right area (inferior to 'familiar' but more than 'energetic') when viewed from the user's most favourite music piece.

Thus, we built a model to estimate the location of a music piece that a user is highly motivated to sing in order to make a recommendation.

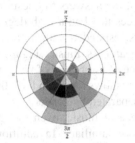 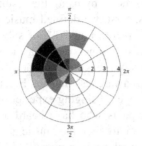 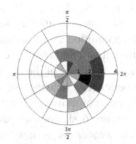

Fig. 3. Probability that there is a music piece that the user is highly motivated to sing (group 1)

Fig. 4. Probability that there is a music piece that a user is highly motivated to sing (group 2)

Fig. 5. Probability that there is a music piece that a user is highly motivated to sing (group 3)

6 Establishing a Personalised Music Mapping Method Based on the User's Profile

We attempted to construct a model to convert a common map to an individualized map for each user by using the users' profile to estimate positions without asking the users to listen to music. We built a model using the data from Experiment 2. We verified the model using the data from Experiment 1.

6.1 Analysis of the Relevance between a Personalised Music Map and a User's Profile

The correlation between the 'energetic' scores of all participants obtained from the experiment and the 'energetic' scores derived using Equation 1 in Section 4 is very high(R^2=0.69). The correlation between the 'familiar' scores of all participants obtained from the experiment and the 'familiar' scores derived using Equation 2 in Section 4 is relatively low (R^2=0.36). The results show that 'familiar' is a more sensitive index to individuality than 'energetic'.

Next, we focused on the analysis of the personality of the scores of 'familiar'. We focused on the mere exposure effect [8], which is well-known in the field of psychology in analyzing. The effect is that both the degree of courtesy and impressions of the target increase with repeated contact. According to this theory, a person feels that the music they have heard personally on several occasions is 'familiar'. With this in mind, we analysed for each user the relationship between the variability of 'familiar', 'degree of singing experience' and 'degree of viewing experience'. For each music piece, we defined it as '+' if the position on each user's map moved positively from the common position to the 'familiar' one, and defined it as '−' if the position moved negatively. We examined the trend of the direction of movement, the degree of singing experience and the degree of viewing experience. In addition, we determined 'awareness' by using the results of the answers to questions on awareness of music pieces. First, we defined music pieces that had a high degree of recognition as those music pieces that 70% of subjects responded with a choice other than 'nothing'. We defined other music as low-awareness music. Figure 6 shows the trend of the direction of movement by each degree of awareness of viewing experience. Focusing on high-awareness music, Figure 7 shows the trend of the direction of movement by the level of singing experience, separated by gender.

Figure 6 shows that participants who have heard a piece of music, even though their awareness is low, tended to feel the music as more familiar'. In addition, participants who have never heard a music piece that has a high 'awareness' and for which a lot of people feel 'familiar', have a tendency to feel the music piece as 'unfamiliar'. As seen in Figure 7, male subjects tend to feel music pieces that they recently sang during a karaoke session as more 'familiar'.

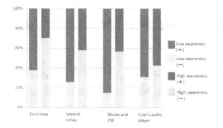

Fig. 6. Moving direction of the degree of viewing experience by awareness

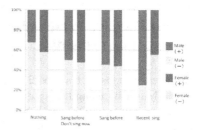

Fig. 7. Moving direction of the degree of singing experience by gender

When we analysed the results in more detail, we found that among the music pieces that have a low 'awareness' and especially the music pieces that have a negative value on the 'scores of familiar' on the common map, 'friendliness' on each user's map moves positively by a higher degree of viewing experience (average 0.4). In addition, among the music pieces that have a high 'awareness', especially the music pieces that have a value under −0.5 for 'scores of familiar' on the common map, 'friendliness' on each user's map moves negatively by a lower degree of viewing experience (average −0.5). Furthermore, only among male participants, the music pieces that have a value under 0.5 for 'scores of familiar' on the common map, 'friendliness' on each user's map moves positively by a higher degree of singing experience (average 0.6).

6.2   Modeling the Conversion from the Common Map to Each User's Map

Table 2 shows the rules to convert from the common map to each user's map, established by the above analysis.

Table 2. Movement pattern by acoustic feature and user characteristic

	Music characteristic	User characteristic	Pattern
Rule1	Lower awareness "Score of familiar" is under 0	Contained in the playback device	0.4
Rule2	Lower awareness "Score of familiar" is under 0	heard repeated to movies and CM	0.65
Rule3	Higher awareness "Score of familiar" is under −0.5	listened for the first time	−0.5
Rule4	"Score of familiar" is under −0.5	Male participant Recently sang	0.6

The correlation coefficient between 'score of familiar' on the common map and 'score of familiar' on each user's map was 0.562 in Experiment 1 and 0.604 in Experiment 2. When we applied the above rule to convert from the common map to each user's map, the correlation coefficient was 0.574 in Experiment 1 and 0.626 in the Experiment 2. In this way, the impression of personal "familiarity" for each user could be estimated more accurately. Using this method, we can also estimate the position of any piece of music on each user's map without the process of listening.

7   Conclusion

This study attempted to develop a method of recommending music on the basis of user's singing motivation with the aim of applying the method to next-generation karaoke services.

First, to locate music at the emotional side, we built an impression of space. As a result, we found 'energetic' and 'familiar' as the two axes that made up the impression of space. Next, in the impression map, we examined the relationship of the position between the music piece for which users are highly motivated to sing and the most favourite music piece of each user.

When considering the application of the method to a real system, we built a model that can find the position in space of each music piece impression based on acoustic features, lyrics and user awareness. Furthermore, to build a system with high accuracy, we established a method to reconstruct the spatial impression of each user using the user's profile.

After constructing the above results, we proposed a method of recommending music that is expected to highly motivate the user to sing by using the music characteristics and the user characteristics as data.

References

1. Hunt, J.M.V.: Motivation inherent in information processing and action. In: Harvey, O.J. (ed.) Motivation and Social Interaction, Cognitive Determinants, pp. 35–94. Ronald, New York (1963)
2. Kim, Y.E., et al.: Music Emotion Recognition: A State of the Art Review. In: ISMIR 2010, pp. 255–266 (2010)
3. Nishikawa, et al.: Design and Evaluation of a Musical Mood Trajectory Estimation Method Using Lyrics and Acoustic Features. IPSJ-SIGMUS 2011-MUS 91(7), 1–8 (2011)
4. Nishimura, et al.: Noise-robust speech recognition using band-dependent weighted likelihood IPSJ SIG 2003(124), pp. 19-24 (2003)
5. Juslin, P.N.: Cue utilization in communication of emotion in music performance: relating performance to perception. Journal of Experimental Psychology: Human Perception and Performance 26(6), 1707–1813 (2000)
6. Bartsch, M.A., et al.: To Catch a Chorus: Using Chroma-based Representations for Audio Thumbnailing. In: WASPAA 2001, pp. 15–18 (2001)
7. Hevner, K.: Experimental studies of the elements of expression in music. Amer. J. Psychol. 48, 246–268 (1936)
8. Zajonc, R.: Attitudinal effects of mere exposure. Journal of Personality and Social Psychology 9(2 Pt. 2), 1–27 (1968)

Analysis of Purchasing Behavior Focusing on the Passage of Time at a Group Buying Site of Coupon

Takuto Kobayashi[1], Toshikazu Yamaguchi[1], and Yumi Asahi[2]

[1] Department of Engineering Management Science, Tokyo University of Science, Tokyo, Japan
{t.kobayashi,yamaguchi}@ms.kagu.tus.ac.jp
[2] Management of Business Development, Shizuoka University, Shizuoka, Japan
tyasahi@ipc.shizuoka.ac.jp

Abstract. In late years, the spread of Internet advances. The diffusion rate of the Internet in 2011 became 79.1%, and the Internet made generalization. With the spread of Internet, marketing technique called the flash marketing came up. As delegate of flash marketing, Group buying sites of coupon are receiving attention in Japan. But people relating to its business think that the sales are having peaked. In this study, we assume that behaviors of users using Group buying sites of coupon change by the time elapsed. By analyzing the change of their behavior, we understand the change of behavior to lead to the continued buying. As a final objective, we hope that we can give help that the sales are having peaked.

Keywords: Group buying site, Coupon, the Internet, Sequence analysis, RFM analysis, Cluster analysis.

1 Introduction

The business of a Group buying site of coupon was born in 2008 at USA. In two years, its month's sales reached 3 million [3]. In its site, user can buy sale items within the limited time. If a sale item doesn't buy a certain number, its sale is disabled. By this way, sellers can know the number of customers in advance. This can lead to expense reduction. As a result of this reduction, seller can sell goods at cheap prices. And its market was expanded in Japan. But because of reduction of user, sales growth has peaked in 2012. It is difficult for site operator to increase the number of ongoing users [5]. We focus on the change of purchase behavior. By this analysis, we discover the patterns of behavior. And we propose methods for encouraging the ongoing purchasing behavior.

2 Data

Data of joint Association Study Group of Management Science was used. This data contains sale data, user attribute data and site view data, product data of a Group buying site of coupon. Data was collected from June 30th 2011 to July 1st 2012. In this study, we analyzed by 2,963 users attribute data, 19,723 products data, 16,925

S. Yamamoto (Ed.): HIMI/HCII 2013, Part I, LNCS 8016, pp. 449–455, 2013.

purchase data and 281,967 site view data. User attribute data contains user ID, age, sex and site registration. Product data contains Product ID, price and product category. Purchase data contains the date of purchase and purchased product ID. Site view data contains the date of view, buy flags and viewed product ID. In this study, we focused on the purchase behavior of since a user started using the site. Therefore, target users are the person who registered the site from June 30th 2011 to July 1st 2012.

3   Analysis

There are three flows in this analysis. First, we divide the data into five by using the number of days from the date of first purchase. Second, we characterize purchase behavior of users each period. Third, we discover patterns of change of purchase behavior.

3.1   Data Partitioning

We divide the data into five by using the number of days from the date of first purchase. Table 1 shows the definition for each term. Table 2 shows the number of people belonging to each term. From table 2, you know the number of people belong to each term is nearly equal. We set the boundary values for term as much as possible is to reduce the variation of the number of people belonging each term.

Table 1. Contents of each term

	content
term1	From site registration to date of first purchase
term2	1~37 days from date of first purchase
term3	38~100 days from date of first purchase
term4	101~200 days from date of first purchase
term5	Over 201 days from date of first purchase

Table 2. The number of people who belong to each term

content	number of people
From site registration to date of first purchase	1017
1~37 days from date of first purchase	498
38~100 days from date of first purchase	483
101~200 days from date of first purchase	481
Over 201 days from date of first purchase	484

3.2   Characterization of the Purchasing Behavior

To classify users based on their purchase behavior, we introduce RFM analysis. RFM analysis is one of the customer classifications. RFM is a "Recently", "Frequency" and

"Monetary" initial was taken. And by ranking each indicator, users are classified. In this study, we evaluate the users' purchase behavior in five indicators based on RFM analysis concept. Using RFM analysis, it is possible to reduce the impact of outliers of each indicator. Table 3 shows five indicators and the boundary values for 5-star

Table 3. The boundary values of 5-star rating

term	rank	Average amount(yen)	Number of purchasing	Number of view	View priod(day)	Purchasing piriod(day)
term1	1	~100	1	~2	~0	–
	2	101~1100	2	3~4	1	–
	3	1101~2000	3	5~7	2~7	–
	4	2001~4000	4	8~14	8~24	–
	5	4001~	5~	15~	25~	–
term2	1	~99	0	~2	~0	Not purchasing
	2	100~1400	1	3~6	1~12	0
	3	1401~3000	2	7~15	13~25	1~12
	4	3001~8000	3~4	16~40	26~32	13~22
	5	8001~	5~	41~	33~	23~
term3	1	~99	0	~2	~0	Not purchasing
	2	100~1300	1	3~7	1~23	0
	3	1301~4000	2	8~20	24~44	1~20
	4	4001~12000	3~4	21~57	45~57	21~40
	5	12000~	5~	58~	58~	41~
term4	1	0	0	~2	~0	Not purchasing
	2	100~2500	1	3~8	1~28	0
	3	2501~6000	2~3	9~26	29~64	1~32
	4	6001~15000	4~7	27~80	65~91	33~69
	5	15001~	8~	81~	92~	70~
term5	1	~99	0	~2	0	Not purchasing
	2	100~2600	1	3~9	1~30	0
	3	2601~7500	2~3	10~30	31~75	1~39
	4	7501~19500	4~7	31~100	76~120	40~85
	5	19501~	8~	101~	121~	86~

Table 4. The number of users having each rank of indicator

term	rank	Average amount(yen)	Number of purchasing	Number of view	View priod(day)	Purchasing piriod(day)
term1	1	1038	2479	732	1779	
	2	489	419	591	382	
	3	502	46	537	257	
	4	478	14	570	269	
	5	456	5	533	276	
term2	1	917	889	464	581	889
	2	343	694	433	427	761
	3	325	274	439	418	205
	4	338	218	453	415	194
	5	337	185	471	419	211
term3	1	674	610	382	435	610
	2	274	470	344	335	518
	3	269	236	334	339	217
	4	288	212	341	355	202
	5	259	236	363	300	217
term4	1	460	400	238	278	400
	2	201	289	247	246	321
	3	202	255	255	250	180
	4	203	186	263	254	185
	5	195	131	258	233	175
term5	1	252	187	131	115	187
	2	105	152	130	132	165
	3	105	134	134	127	106
	4	108	96	140	153	105
	5	101	102	136	144	108

rating. Table 4 shows the number of users having each rank of indicator. From table 4, we set the boundary values for rank as much as possible is to reduce the variation of the number of people having each rank. In term1, the data is obtained only from the date of first purchase. Therefore purchasing period data does not exist.

Next, we perform a cluster analysis by using the ranked value which was gotten 5-star rating. As a result of a cluster analysis, four clusters were created. Figure 1 show the average value of each rank of each cluster.

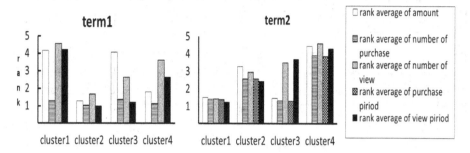

Fig. 1. The average value of each rank of each cluster

From figure 1, we characterized each cluster.

In term 1, cluster 1 was named "seeking information". These people trend to fully browse items. Cluster 2 was named "campaign". These people like a campaign. Cluster 3 named "purpose". These people trend to buy item they bought at the beginning. Cluster 4 named "carefully". These people trend to fully browse items. But they rarely buy item.

In term 2, cluster 1was named "breakaway". These people trend to stop using site. Cluster 2 was named "normal". These people don't have an unusual feature. Cluster 3 was named "views". These people trend to watch the site considerably. But they rarely buy item. Cluster 4 was named "heavy". These people trend to watch the site considerably. And they trend to buy an item too.

3.3   Discovery of Patterns of Purchasing Behavior

To discover the patterns of buying behavior of users, we introduce a sequence analysis. A sequence analysis is the analysis method discovering the patterns of results considering the time series. As the indicators for the patterns that were discovered there is lift value. The pattern whose lift value is greater than 1 is a valid pattern. Figure 2 shows the patterns whose lift value is greater than 1.

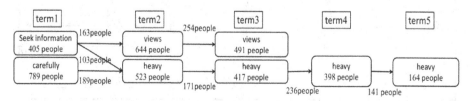

Fig. 2. The patterns whose lift value is greater than 1

From figure 2, the numbers in the frameworks represent the number of people belonging to each cluster. And the numbers on the arrows represent the number of people during the transition. From these results, people belonging to "heavy" in tern 1 trend to belong to "heavy" in other term too. After all, we thought that it is important to change to "heavy" in term 2. Therefore, we investigate the changes of purchase behavior from term 1 to term 2.

3.4   Change of Purchase Behavior from Term 1 to Term 2

We investigate the changes in each cluster of term 2 from each cluster of term 1. And we propose a method encouraging the ongoing purchase.

About cluster "seek information"
Figure 3 shows the change from cluster "seek information" to each cluster in tem 2. From figure 3, people who belong to "seek information" transition in the order of "views" "heavy" "breakaway" "normal".

People belong to "seek information" often use the money. So we propose the strategy that specialized content.

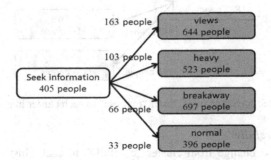

Fig. 3. A change from cluster "seek information" to each cluster in tem 2

About cluster "campaign"
Figure 4 shows the change from cluster "campaign" to each cluster in tem 2. From figure 4, people who belong to "campaign" transition in the order of "breakaway" "normal" "views" "heavy".

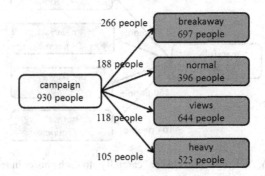

Fig. 4. A change from cluster "campaign" to each cluster in tem 2

People belong to "campaign" trend to prefer cheaper items or campaign items. So we propose the campaign that target to people who continued to use the site for certain days.

About cluster "purpose"

Figure 5 shows the change from cluster "purpose" to each cluster in tem 2. From figure 5, people who belong to "purpose" transition in the order of "breakaway" "views" "heavy" "normal".

People belong to "purpose" trend to breakaway because they achieve objective at the beginning of the purchasing. So we propose the strategy that is pushing the items related first purchase.

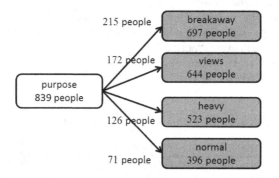

Fig. 5. A change from cluster "purpose" to each cluster in tem 2

About cluster "carefully"

Figure 6 shows the change from cluster "carefully" to each cluster in tem 2. From figure 6, people who belong to "seek information" transition in the order of "views" "heavy" "breakaway" "normal".

People belong to "carefully" are not aggressive to spend money. So we propose the strategy that specialized lowest price items.

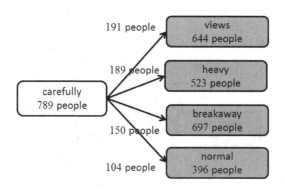

Fig. 6. A change from cluster "carefully" to each cluster in tem 2

4   Conclusion

The purposes of this study are to propose methods for encouraging the ongoing purchasing behavior at a Group buying site of coupon. By analyzing the change of purchase behavior, we lead to methods for encouraging the ongoing purchasing behavior.

First, we divided the data into five by using the number of days from the date of first purchase. As a result, all users were classified: people who use the site longer, people who use the site shorter and so on. And each period, users' data were stored.

Next, we characterized purchase behavior of users each period. We used RFM analysis and Cluster analysis. We evaluated their purchase behavior by RFM analysis. Then we characterized their purchase behavior by Cluster analysis. As a result of Cluster analysis, their purchase behavior was divided into four each period.

Last, we discovered patterns of change of purchase behavior by Sequence analysis. As a result of Sequence analysis, we figured out changing trends of purchase behavior.

Based on the results of this analysis, we propose methods for encouraging the ongoing purchasing behavior. Analysis using this study will provide new type findings. Until now, there were few studies which focus on changes of user behavior. And there were few studies about a Group buying site of coupon. Using novelty of theme and analysis, this study said new type of research. With the popularization of the internet service, it will be important for site operator to catch the change of users' behavior at all time. We hope this study becomes a vanguard to help understanding users' behavior.

As future challenge, analyzing every product genre, we clarify the difference of change by product genre.

Acknowledgment. We would like to thank to professor Yamaguchi, T. (Department of Management Science, Faculty of Engineering, Tokyo university of Science) for his support on our experiment.

References

1. Hiroshi, E.: Zirei Bunnseki De-tabunseki Ma-kethinngu (The case analysis Database Marketing). Chuo Keizai Sya (1997)
2. Group Buying Site of Coupon.jp, World Wide Web:
   http://couponsite.jp/ (retrieved December 7, 2012)
3. Nikkei trend net, World Wide Web:
   http://trendy.nikkeibp.co.jp/article/column/20110225/1034627/ (retrieved December 30, 2012)
4. Hidero, N.: Kurasuta Bunnseki To Sono Ouyo (The Cluster analysis and application). Nishida Hiderouen (1988)
5. Ponpare, World Wide Web: http://ponpare.jp/doc/about.html (retrieved December 7, 2012)
6. The Challenge and future of Group Buying Site of Coupon, World Wide Web:
   http://www.asahi-kasei.co.jp/arc/topics/pdf/topics017.pdf (retrieved December 31, 2012)

Research on Website Usage Behavior through Information Search Perspective: A Comparison of Experiential and Goal-Directed Behaviors

Juihsiang Lee[1] and Manlai You[2]

[1] Department of Digital Multimedia Design,
China University of Technology,
Taiwan R.O.C.
[2] Department of Industrial Design,
National Yunlin University of Science and Technology,
Taiwan R.O.C.
{Juihsiang Lee, leockmail}@gmail.com

Abstract. Along with the rapid growth of the Internet, online information search has become a prevalent Internet activity. However, little research has addressed the factors and website features that influence website information search behavior. Prior studies investigate factors that affect consumer preferences in online shopping websites. And, seldom distinguish between pre-purchase and post-purchase experiences and tend to focus on post-purchase assessment only. Therefore, this study aimed at the Internet users' searching behavior, and further probed into users' willingness of continuous websites use. But when purchasing tourism products, Information search is even more important than information search before buying manufactured goods. Tourism products and services are seldom routine purchases (Swarbrooke & Horner, 1999). Choices of tourism products usually involve considerable emotional significance and perceived and actual risk for the individual(Xie, Bao, & Morais, 2006). Based on the prior literatures (Lee, 2005; Lin & Chen, 2009) a model was proposed and empirically tested to gain a better understanding on Internet users' search behavior. The results showed that Internet user's willingness to revisit was mainly influenced by his/her involvement and satisfaction toward the website, and these two factors were affected by website information quality, website interactivity, and hedonic value. Also, the research model was moderated by goal-directed and experiential behavior.

Keywords: On-line Shopping Website, Information Search Behavior, Interactivity.

1 Introductory

The growth of interactive media, especially the Internet, inspires an examination of the impact of marketing communication using new media (Klein, 1998). Even though many practitioners and researchers suggest that interactivity is a boon for marketing

S. Yamamoto (Ed.): HIMI/HCII 2013, Part I, LNCS 8016, pp. 456–464, 2013.
© Springer-Verlag Berlin Heidelberg 2013

communication (e.g., Chen et al., 2005; Wu, 2005), some find negative consequences of interactivity (e.g. Bezjian-Avery et al., 1998; Bucy and Chen-Chao, 2007; Sundar and Kim, 2005; Kim, Spielmann, & McMillan, 2012).

Besides, the internet has influenced human lives in numerous ways over the past years, having become a mainstream information resource that people turn to for information and communication. To better understand information searching behavior and information retrieval interaction, researchers have emphasized the importance of the difference of searching behavior.

Information search is a stage of the decision making process in which consumers actively collect and utilize information from internal and/or external sources to make better purchase decisions.

Human factors and individual differences were recognized as a key aspect for understanding user search behaviors (Egan, 1988; Nielsen, 1993). Novak, Hoffman & Duhachek (2003) pointed out, one fruitful focus of research on online consumer experience has been on two distinct categories of consumption behavior—goal directed and experiential consumption behavior. Drawing distinctions between these behaviors for the Web may be particularly important because the experiential process is, for many individuals, as or even more important than the final instrumental result. However, the general and broad nature of flow measurement to date has precluded a precise investigation of flow during goal-directed versus experiential activities(Novak, Hoffman & Duhachek, 2003).

2   Literature Review

2.1   Internet Users' Searching Behavior

Information search has been one of the most enduring issues in consumer behavior research (Beatty & Smith, 1987). For marketing departments, it is crucial to understand the determinants of information search behavior for designing effective marketing communication.

Previous research on information search behavior has identified a number of factors affecting this construct, such as, the nature of decision making (Fodness & Murray, 1999), residency (Pennington-Gray & Vogt 2003), family life cycle (Fodness, 1992), socio-economic status (Fodness & Murray 1999), involvement (Cai et al,. 2004), travel expenditures (Snepenger et al., 1990) , prior knowledge (Kerstetter & Cho, 2004), and search cost (Gursoy & McCleary, 2004).

When purchasing tourism products, information search is even more important than information search before buying manufactured goods. Tourism products and services are seldom routine purchases (Swarbrooke & Horner, 1999). Choices of tourism products usually involve considerable emotional significance and perceived and actual risk for the individual(Xie et al., 2006).

Pan and Fesenmaier (2003, 2006) first consider internet-based tourism information search from the perspective of the search process. Based on the mental model which emphasizes information search behavior from the cognitive information retrieval perspective and the knowledge structure of information searchers, their major research findings are that tourists' vacation planning online follows a hierarchical structure of episodes, and the information searchers use information hubs containing many links to other related Websites to facilitate the navigation process.

Currently, social media not only constitute a significant portion of results for online tourism information search, but also demonstrate their increasingly important role as an information source (Xiang & Gretzel, 2010).

2.2   Goal-Directed and Experiential Behavior

In marketing, the distinction between goal-directed and experiential behavior has long been formally noted. Indeed, it underlies the entire purchase/consumption process, beginning with the consumer constructs of extrinsic versus intrinsic motivation (Bloch& Richins, 1983; Celsi & Olson, 1988; Davis, Bagozzi, & Warshaw, 1992) and situational versus enduring involvement (Bloch, Sherrell, & Ridgway, 1986; Richins & Root-Shaffer, 1988; Wolfinbarger& Gilly, 2001).

Drawing these distinctions between goal-directed and experiential behavior is particularly important in online environments, because the experiential process is, for many individuals, as or even more important than the final instrumental result (Hoffman & Novak, 1996).

Table 1. Distinctions Between Goal-Directed and Experiential Behavior

Goal-Directed	Experiential
Extrinsic motivation	Intrinsic motivation
Instrumental orientation	Ritualized orientation
Situational involvement	Enduring involvement
Utilitarian benefits/value	Hedonic benefits/value
Directed (prepurchase) search	Nondirected (ongoing) search; browsing
Goal-directed choice	Navigational choice
Cognitive	Affective
Work	Fun
Planned purchases; repurchasing	Compulsive shopping; impulse buys

Source: (Novak et al., 2003)

2.3   Website Interactivity

Effective communication with customers is the key to successful business. One of the most important factors for effective communication is known as interactivity(Yoo, Lee, & Park, 2010) . Interactivity is central to Internet marketing communication.

On the Internet, consumers no longer interact with salespeople or have a direct physical experience of a store and its products. Instead, their experience is mediated through the web, using a graphical display without any face-to-face interaction with the e-vendor. Therefore, understanding users' communication behavior in these emerging Computer Mediated Environments is important.

Although there have been many studies on interactivity under various contexts and disciplines, researchers still have mixed views on the concept of interactivity (Yadav and Varadarajan, 2005).

Zeithaml et al. (2002) distinguish communication with people via a computer from interacting with the website through a computer. They defined interactivity as "the extent to which website users can (1) communicate with the people behind the website, (2) interactively search for information, and (3) conduct transactions through the website." (Yoo et al., 2010)

Previous research by Lee (2005) has particular relevance to the current work. Lee identified (1) user control, (2) responsiveness, (3) personalization, and (4) connectedness as important components to interactivity in a mobile commerce setting. User control refers to the user's ability to control the information display and content. Responsiveness refers to the site as being able to respond to user queries. Personalization concerns the mobile Internet site that enables the purchase of products and services that are tailored to the user and unique desires. Finally, perceived connectedness refers to whether customers share experiences regarding products or services offered with other visitors to the mobile site. We adopt these three components: user control, responsiveness, connectedness, to fit on the website environment.

2.4 Website Quality

The World Wide Web is a very complex information technology network currently consisting of several hundred million web pages and over a hundred million users. Each day, users search websites in order to find the most convenient, relevant, and up-to-date information they need.

On the web, users typically forage for information by navigating from page to page, along web links. The content of pages associated with these links is usually presented to the user by some snippets of text or graphic. Based on the above-mentioned, quality management concepts and models, I propose to identify values and criteria enabling a website surfer/user to evaluate and select websites and pages.

As companies have become more effective in their use of websites, they have become more complex. For some organizations, they serve as repositories of information for various stakeholders and the public. For others, websites also offer transaction capabilities, providing an additional mechanism from which to serve customers.

Studies examining website quality have found the construct to be multidimensional, Zhang and von Dran compiled an extensive list of 42-scale items grouped a priori into eleven dimensions: (1) information content, (2) cognitive outcomes, (3) enjoyment, (4) privacy, (5) user empowerment, (6) visual appearance, (7) technical support, (8) navigation, (9) organization of information, (10) credibility, (11) impartiality.

2.5 Website Satisfaction

Since websites serve as an important point of contact for most companies, assessing their effectiveness or quality of the website is important as a way to understand whether the company is providing the type and quality of information and interaction to satisfy website users. This is especially true for companies selling goods and services on their websites. Customers must be satisfied with their experience with the website or they will not return.

Satisfaction is a post-consumption evaluation based on the comparison between the expected value in the pre-consumption stage and the perceived post-consumption value after the purchase or after the use of services or products (Oliver, 1981; Ravald and Gronroos, 1996).

2.6   Involvement Theory

Research on advertising and on consumer behavior is paying an increasing amount of attention to the 'involvement' construct. Cognitive Dimension researcher proposed that psychological functions affected by involvement. These functions relate to the cognitive notion of information processing (e.g. Krugman, 1965; Houston & Rothchild, 1977).

Some other researchers claim that involvement is mainly a state of activation or arousal, and therefore motivational factors are more important (e.g. Mitchell, 1979; Cohen, 1983). They argued involvement is a state of arousal caused by some 'antecedents' and revealed by some 'consequences'. There are different kinds of antecedents: personal (needs, values, aims, etc. of the subject), situational (e.g. the time left to make a decision on the product to purchase), and stimulus-related antecedents (the physical features of a product, the content of the advertisement, etc.) (García, Olea, Ponsoda, & Scott, 1996) .

Exploring the notion of searching behavior in internet, the factors of user involvement must be concerned.

3   Method

3.1   Hypotheses Formulation

Based on the above literature review, the following hypotheses are formulated:

H1: Greater website involvement will correspond in greater willingness to use.

H2: Greater website satisfaction will correspond in greater willingness to use.

H3: Greater website interactivity will result in greater involvement of website.

H3a: Goal-directed users' perceived website user control will result in greater involvement of website.

H3b: Goal-directed users' perceived website responsive will result in greater involvement of website.

H3c: Goal-directed users' perceived website connectedness will result in greater involvement of website.

H3d: Experiential users' perceived greater website user control will result in greater involvement of website.

H3e: Experiential users' perceived greater website responsive will result in greater involvement of website.

H3f: Experiential users' perceived greater website connectedness will result in greater involvement of website.

H4: Greater website interactivity will result in greater satisfaction of website.

H4a: Goal-directed users' perceived greater user control will result in greater satisfaction of website.

H4b: Goal-directed users' perceived website responsive will result in greater satisfaction of website.

H4c: Goal-directed users' perceived website connectedness will result in greater satisfaction of website.

H4d: Experiential users' perceived greater website user control will result in greater satisfaction of website.

H4e: Experiential users' perceived greater website responsive will result in greater satisfaction of website.

H4f: Experiential users' perceived greater website connectedness will result in greater satisfaction of website.

H5: Greater website quality will result in greater involvement of website.

H6: Greater website quality will result in greater satisfaction of website.

3.2   Method

To test the hypothesis, an plot test was conducted with 52 undergraduate students from a large vocational university in Taiwan. 23% were male and 77% were female.

To analyze the relationship among these variables and examine the fitness of the conceptualized framework, this study conducts Structural Equation Modeling (SEM) and uses online tourism websites as the research sample. The operational definition of each variable is tailored to fit the characteristics of online tourism websites and shown in the table 2. The questionnaire is designed in Likert 7 point scale and adjusted according to the advices of 3 experts on e-commerce including 1 manager engaging in e-commerce business for years and 2 academic professors devoting in this field. Participants are asked to fill in the questionnaire and indicate their current situation for each variable item (1=strong disagreement and 7=strong agreement). The higher score the respondents indicated, the more they agree with these questions. 1 means that the subject disagrees highly with the questions while 7 signifies high agreement.

Table 2. Measurement scales

Items	Mean	SD	α
Searching behavior			
Do you have fix habit to searching tourism information online?			
If you want to purchase tourism product, which website will visit to acquire information?			
Please write down the website address where you often to visit it.			
How often do you visit the website?			
Fix: one day one time, 2~3 times a week, 1 time a week			
No fix time			
Website Quality Dimension			
I felt that I getting information from the website was useful.			
I felt that I getting information from the website was complete.			
I felt that I getting information from the website was clear.			
When I clicked on the links for the website, I felt I was getting instantaneous information			
I felt that I getting information from the website was easy to understand.			
I felt that I getting information from the website was correct.			
Website Interactivity Dimension			
Customers share experiences about the product or service with other customers of this website (**connectedness**).			
Customers of this website benefit from the community visiting the website (**connectedness**).			
Customers share a common bond with other members of the customer community visiting the website (**connectedness**).			
Customers share experiences about the product or service with other customers of this website (**connectedness**).			
The information shown when I interacted with the site was relevant (**responsiveness**).			
The information shown when I interacted with the site was appropriate (**responsiveness**).			
The information shown when I interacted with the site met my expectations (**responsiveness**).			
I was in control over the information display format, condition when using this website (**user control**).			
I was in control over the content of this website that I wanted to see (**user control**).			
Website Satisfaction			
Overall this online searching experience was satisfying			
Overall this online searching experience was pleasant			
Overall I liked this online searching experience			
Website Involvement			
I felt that the website information is important to me.			
I felt that the website is closely to my live.			

References

1. Cai, L., Feng, R., Breiter, D.: Tourist purchase decision involvement and information preferences. Journal of Vacation Marketing 10(2), 138–148 (2004)
2. Chen, S.Y., Macredie, R.: Web-based interaction: A review of three important human factors. International Journal of Information Management 30 (2010)
3. Cohen, J.B.: Involvement and you: 1000 great ideas. Advances in Consumer Research 10, 325–328 (1983)
4. Egan, D.E.: Individual differences in human–computer interaction. In: Helander, M.G., Landauer, T.K., Prabhu, P.V. (eds.) Handbook of Human-Computer Interaction. Elsevier, Amsterdam (1988)
5. Fodness, D.: The impact of family life cycle on vacation decision-making process. Journal of Travel Research 31, 8–13 (1992)
6. Fodness, D., Murray, B.: A model of tourist information search behavior. Journal of Travel Research 37, 220–230 (1999)
7. García, C., Olea, J., Ponsoda, V., Scott, D.: Measuring Involvement from Its Consequences. Psicothema 8(2) (1996)
8. Gursoy, D., McCleary, K.W.: An integrative model of tourists' information search behavior. Annals of Tourism Research 31, 353–373 (2004)
9. Houston, M.J., Rothschild, M.L.: A paradigm for research on consumer involvement. Working Paper 11-77-46, University of Wisconsin-Madison (1977)
10. Kerstetter, D., Cho, M.: Prior knowledge, credibility and information search. Annals of Tourism Research 31, 961–985 (2004)
11. Kim, J., Spielmann, N., McMillan, S.J.: Experience effects on interactivity: Functions, processes, and perceptions. Journal of Business Research 65 (2012)
12. Kim, S., Stoel, L.: Apparel retailers:website quality dimensions and satisfaction. Journal of Retailing and Consumer Services 11 (2004)
13. Krugman, H.E.: The impact of television advertising: Learning without involvement. Public Opinion Quarterly 29, 349–356 (1965)
14. Lee, T.: The impact of perceptions of interactivity on customer trust and transaction intentions in mobile commerce. Journal of Electronic Commerce Research 6(3), 165–180 (2005)
15. Lee, Y., Kozar, K.A.: Investigating the effect of website quality on e-business success: An analytic hierarchy process (AHP) approach. Decision Support Systems 42 (2006)
16. Lin, J.C.C., Chen, W.Y.: Research on website usage behavior through information search perspective: A comparison of experiential and goal-directed behaviors. Journal of Information Management 16(4) (2009)
17. Mitchell, A.A.: Involvement: A potentially important mediator of consumer behavior. Advances in Consumer Research 6, 191–196 (1979)
18. Nielsen, J.: Usability engineering. Morgan Kaufmann, San Francisco (1993)
19. Novak, T.P., Hoffman, D.L., Duhachek, A.: The Influence of Goal-Directed and Experiential Activities on Online Flow Experiences. Journal of Consumer Psychology 13(1&2) (2003)
20. Pan, B., Fesenmaier, D.R.: Travel information search on the Internet: a preliminary analysis. In: Frew, A.J., Hitz, M., O'Connor, P. (eds.) Information and Communication Technologies in Tourism 2003: Proceedings of the International Conference on Information Technology and Tourism, pp. 242–251. Springer, New York (2003)
21. Pan, B., Fesenmaier, D.R.: Online information search: vacation planning process. Annals of Tourism Research 33, 809–832 (2006)

22. Pennington-Gray, L., Vogt, C.: Examining welcome center visitors' travel and information behaviors: Does location of centers or residency matter? Journal of Travel Research 41, 272–280 (2003)
23. Snepenger, D., Meged, K., Snelling, M., Worrall, K.: Information search strategies by destinationnaïve tourists. Journal of Travel Research 29, 13–16 (1990)
24. van Noort, G., Voorveld, H.A.M., van Reijmersdal, E.A.: Interactivity in Brand Web Sites: Cognitive, Affective, and Behavioral Responses Explained by Consumers' Online Flow Experience. Journal of Interactive Marketing 26 (2012)
25. Xiang, Z., Gretzel, U.: Role of social media in online travel information search. Tourism Management 31, 179–188 (2010)
26. Xie, H., Bao, J., Morais, D.B.: Exploring Gender Differences in Information Search among Domestic Vistors to Yellow Mountain and Guilin, PRC. Paper presented at the Proceedings of the 2006 Northeastern Recreation Research Symposium (2006)
27. Yoo, W.S., Lee, Y., Park, J.: The role of interactivity in e-tailing: Creating value and increasing satisfaction. Journal of Retailing and Consumer Services 17 (2010)

Semantically Structured VDL-Based Iconic Tags System

Xiaoyue Ma and Jean-Pierre Cahier

UTT (Université de Technologie de Troyes) ICD/Tech-CICO Lab,
BP 2060, 10010 Troyes, France
{xiaoyue.ma,cahier}@utt.fr

Abstract. Iconic tags system based on Visual Distinctive Language has been developed and assessed improving tagging effectiveness by considering tagging quality and tagging speed. This amelioration benefits from semiotic interpretation of tag meaning and graphical code of tag structure. To make in-depth research about this special iconic tags system, we study tags arrangement in this paper and hypothesized that semantically arranged iconic tags would imply better tagging results. A supplementary experiment was taken place by comparison between randomly and semantically arrangement method, which has validated our hypothesis.

Keywords: tags system, icon, visual distinctive language, tags cloud, semantic relations, knowledge organization system.

1   Introduction

Knowledge Organization System (KOS) [1] is a general term referring to, among other things, the tools that present the organized interpretation of knowledge structures. The notion of tags system mentioned in this paper is a cluster of tags to centralize used tags and suggest potential tags from experts and users. The representation of tag structure is as important as that of each single tag in a tag system. On one hand, an explicit tag structure facilitates to find and find again an appropriate tag in a large group of tags. On the other hand, tag structure offers a possible link between documents tagged by these tags. This connection of documents through tags is useful especially when documents are dispersedly represented without clear categorization. The structure of tags enhances the implicit network of tagged targets which provides easier managing and searching in KOS.

VDL-based iconic tags [2] have been validated improving the effectiveness of tag system (defined as integration of tagging quality and tagging speed). These special tags are represented under iconic form and graphical code of VDL (Visual Distinctive Language) where pre-icons visualize the tag structure. The experiment having been done proved that VDL-based iconic tags system was the most efficient compared to textual tag system and iconic tags system without explicit structure mainly due to its visual tag structure. Users in this group easily identified semantic relations of tags structured by Hypertopic [3] knowledge model which was helpful for tagging process.

S. Yamamoto (Ed.): HIMI/HCII 2013, Part I, LNCS 8016, pp. 465–474, 2013.

After validating the format of iconic tags, we have to think of how to display them together. To display a cluster of recommended tags has a strong connection with the arrangement of tags in tags system. When a small group of tags is involved, the displayer of tags system can be considered as tags cloud. The only difference is that the purpose of tags cloud is to search required information while tags in tags system serve for centralizing and providing used tags for further tagging. However, the common goal of two is to provide an interface of tags presentation to find and find again a tag accurately and quickly. This issue is associated with how to efficiently arrange tags together which has been largely studied in textual tags cloud. As mentioned before, VDL-based iconic tags, as a newly developed tag form, performed better than textual tags in tagging process. It needs to continue making deeper study on the arrangement of these special tags, the results of which will be also useful for large scale of tags system. For example, if it is proved that semantically structured iconic tags show a more efficient tagging process than other arrangement in tags cloud cases, recommended tags in one category have to be sorted under the same menu when more VDL-based icons are involved.

In the next section, we will look back onto existing studies on semantic relations of tags and semantically structured tags cloud. This review of former studies makes it clearer on what is missed and what has to be improved in our iconic tags system. Then in the third part, a "tagging on computer" experiment will be presented to validate our hypothesis on the semantically arranged VDL-based iconic tags. Finally, we discuss the result from analysis and possible future directions.

2   Background

In spite of the vocabulary problem existing [4], there has been accumulating evidence suggesting that emergent structures do exist in social tagging system [5] [6]. Despite the diverse backgrounds and information goals of multiple users, co-occurring tags exhibited hierarchical structures that mirrored shared structures that were "anarchically negotiated" by the users.

Halvey and Keane [7] investigated the effects of different tags clouds and list arrangements comparing the performance for searching specific items. They found that respondents were able to more easily and quickly find tags in alphabetical orders (both in lists and clouds). Rivadeneira et al. [8] compared the recognition of single tags in alphabetical, sequential–frequency (most important tag at the left-upper side), spatially packed (arranged with Feinberg's algorithm) and list-frequency layouts (most important tag at the beginning of a vertical list of tags). Results did not show any significant disparity in recognition of tags. However, respondents could better recognize the overall categories presented when confronted with the vertical list of tags ordered by frequency. Hearst and Rosner [9] discuss the organization of tag clouds. One important disadvantage of tag cloud layouts they mention is that items with similar meaning may lie far apart, and so meaningful associates may be missed.

The following studies stared to focus on the semantic relation within tags and try to represent this in textual tags cloud. Hasan-Montero and Herrero-Solana [10] claimed that the alphabetical arrangements neither facilitate visual scanning nor infer semantic relation between tags. They developed a k-means algorithm to group semantic similar tags into different clusters and calculate tag similarity by means of relative co-occurrence between tags. Similar work can be found in [11]. Likewise, Fujimura et al. use the cosine similarity of tag feature vectors (terms and their weight generated from a set of tagged documents) to measure tag similarity. Based on this similarity they calculate a tag layout, where distance between tags represents semantic relatedness. Another very similar approach is proposed by [12].

An empirical evaluation of semantically structured tag clouds [13] has manifested that topically layouts (semantically structured tags clouds) can improve search performance for specific search tasks compared to random arrangements, but they still perform worse than alphabetic layouts. Considering that we used very simple clustering and arrangement algorithms we expect further advancement on semantic arrangements with more elaborate procedures. Semantic layouts should only be used when the quality of the arrangement can be assured. Test participants also commented that it was difficult to identify clusters and relations beyond single lines.

The former test allowed us to draw lessons on how the code affects visual tagging, either in the aspect of the recognition tag or the aspect of habituation of categorization. In addition, in this study, we propose to produce a more in-depth research of VDL-based icon system taking a small group of tags that act as tags cloud. More precisely, we propose to develop a supplementary experiment of the first one to get more complete view on how to construct a better VDL-based iconic tags system.

3   Experiment

To complete the implement of VDL-based iconic tag system, we proposed to carry out a second computerized experiment, in which another factor of tag system was tested: arrangement. This experiment was taken place into two sessions of iconic tags: iconic tags without explicit structure and VDL-based iconic tags. For each session, further comparison was realized between randomly presented tags and semantically presented tags. The same protocol and evaluation method of previous experiment [2] were applied in this one that we continued to focus on the effectiveness of tagging process under these four patterns of tags system. We assume that VDL-based iconic tags and arranged by categories will improve tagging efficacy compared to other patterns. What has to be mentioned is that all the iconic tags in this experiment were not subtitled because of the former argument that subtitle text could influence the outcome of tagging.

3.1   Participants Material (Electronic Documentation on the Web)

48 French speaking students in University of Technology of Troyes have participated in this experiment. They were divided into four groups corresponding to four types of tested tag systems: group A for iconic tags without explicit structure and presented randomly (12 persons); group B for iconic tags without explicit structure and

presented by categories (12 persons); group C for VDL-based iconic tags and presented randomly (12 persons); group D for VDL-based iconic tags and presented by categories (12 persons). They were 26 male and 22 female with computer science as their master major.

Table 1. Four groups and their corresponding displayer of tag system

	Randomly	Semantically (by categories)
Iconic tag system without explicit structure (Session 1)		
	Group A, Type 1	Group B, Type 2
VDL-based iconic tag system (Session 2)		
	Group C, Type 3	Group D, Type 4

The material for this experiment conducted entirely on the web included 24 items under the topics on Sustainable Development (the same documents in the first experiment); four displayers of tags system with the same symbols for corresponding tags (see Table 1), a pre-questionnaire and a post-questionnaire.

3.2   Procedure

This experiment kept the same architecture as that of last one which was composed of three parts: pre-questionnaire, tagging test and post-questionnaire.

All the participants logged in the system with their e-mail address and assigned password. The system produced automatically for each of them a group code in order (A1, B1, C1, D1, A2, B2, C2, D2 ...). The letter of this code corresponded to the type of tags system they used. In purpose to get the level of prior knowledge in the field of Sustainable Development, each participant firstly completed a pre-questionnaire of 10 questions: five of them concerned academic knowledge test in the field while others about personal understanding and conscious of Sustainable Development.

Once participant finished pre-questionnaire, they started tagging test which was conceptually the same with former one: tagging an item using the tags on displayer of tag system. Brief instruction appeared first told them what to do and how to do in this part. If they need help, there was a "Help" button in the upper right corner of screen to display the entire contents of instruction.

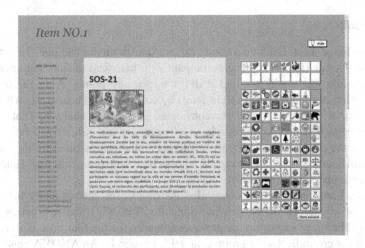

Fig. 1. Interface of tagging test system (example of item 1 for group B)

A double left click of the icon on the displayer allowed submitting an icon into empty box of tags selection zone (choose an iconic tag) while a double left click on the icon in the selection zone was to return it to the former location on the displayer, as well a simple right click on the icons made corresponding text of the icon visible. Participant could confirm his tagging choices of an item and continue to the next one by clicking the button "next item". Once a tagged item has been confirmed, it could not be modified. Similarly, an untagged item could not be slit up to the next one. When participants click on "finish the tagging" button on the 24th item, they arrived to the last part of the test: post-questionnaire. The post-questionnaire was designed in purpose to test the recognition of tag structure using four different types of iconic tags systems. Participants should browse these icons (the type of displayer remained that they used before), identify their structure by symbolic interpretation and graphical regularity, and then write down one of the categories of icons. They did the same operation of click as before to hand up and repeal an icon. However, they could not get help by consultation of text of icons but only by the symbol of icons. They were as well asked to propose a name for this category to see whether they get better understanding of tag meaning. This test considered the relevance of visual representation of tag structure, which was essential in tags system. In the end of experiment participants commented on the activity, leaving a few lines of text. They were encouraged to notice core benefit of the system and difficulty they met, also making suggestions to improve it.

24 items to be tagged remained the same with the previous experiment presented through a title, a photo and a short description. There were three parts for each tagging page (see Fig.1): task list to track well (left), presentation of item (center), 16 squares of tags selection zone (upper right) and displayer of tags system (bottom right). The type of tags on the displayer should match the group code (from A to D) of participants.

3.3   Results

Pior Knowledge Test. Each question in the pre-questionnaire had one correct answer from three options (a, b or c). The participant who managed to find that answer won one point while that could not find it did not earn any points. After the test, there would be a list of points earned (10 in total) by each person. Participants whose point was above or within 6 to 2 were not considered in the final analysis. That is to say, they are excluded from the average level of prior domain, which will influence the outcome of the experiment. Individual difference also was implied by the frequency of click on button "Help". Participant who asked more frequent for "Help" could show a worse understanding of test.

Levene's homocedasticity test revealed no significant heterogeneity between the variances on the score in the pre-questionnaire (P=0.572) and instruction reading (P=0.812). The mean scores on the pre-questionnaire for the four groups were 8.5 for group A, 8 for group B, 8.4 for group C and 9 for group D. An ANOVA conducted on the subjects' performances in the pre-questionnaire revealed no significant difference (F<1).

As far as the instruction reading was concerned, the mean times were 2 for group A, 1.7 for group B, 1.7 for group C and 2.2 for group D. The performances of the subjects revealed also no significant difference (F<1). The two results manifested there was no significant individual difference on prior knowledge test which could influence latter tagging test.

Tagging Process. The method to analyze the quality of tagging remained the same as the previous experiment [2] using expert matrix and Rx[1] criterion. All the RXs in one group were considered as a one-dimensional table to perform an ANOVA analysis among groups. It was assumed that the group working with VDL-based iconic tags and presented by categories would result in better performance compared to others.

---

[1] Variable predefined to analyze tagging effectiveness among four groups. Details can be seen in previous paper [2].

Tagging result was integration between tagging quality and tagging speed. The test noted the time when a participant started and ended an item. It was meaningful to record average tagging duration per item for each participant and we considered it in tagging result. The final statistical element needing to be compared was Rx/tagging duration of each participant. It represented tagging quality in per unit time.

Levens's homocedasticity test indicated significant heterogeneity between the variances on the tagging process: Rx/tagging time, $P<0.05$. Consequently, these performances were analyzed using a nonparametric Kruskal-Wallis test. This latter test implied a significant effect of the semantically structured VDL-based icons on subjects' tagging performances, $N=40$, $P<0.05$. A more thorough analysis using a Mann-Whitney test indicated a significant difference between group D (M=342.1) and group C (M=238.2), Mann-Whitney U=32, P= 0.04. Similarly, the performances of group D were significantly better than group B (M=215.2), Mann-Whitney U = 5, P <0.05. As what has been proved before, group A (M= 154.4) was significantly poorer than group C. Mann-Whitney U = 15, $P<0.05$. In contrast, the performances obtained for group A and B did not differ significantly for the tagging process, Mann-Whitney U = 32, P=0.173.

Post-questionnaire. The critical prediction of structure identification on tags was to compare the categories proposed by participants with predefined VDL categories (seven categories of topics and three categories of attributes names - the same as before). Participants who were in complete correspondence with one of these categories will get 2 points. Those whose category was partially correspondent were scored 1 point. No points were awarded to participants who mixed more than one proposed category.

After checking that the homocedasticity of the variances was not respected ($P<0.05$), Kruskal-Wallis test revealed a significant difference among four groups, H=40, $P<0.05$. More precisely, group D (M=12.4) performed significantly better than group B (M=1.6), Mann-Whitney U=8, P=0.001 and group C (M=3.2) Mann-Whitney U=12, P=0.004. As what has been manifested in the former experiment, Rx of group C was significantly higher than that of group A (M=0.6), Mann-Whitney U=26.5, P=0.037. In contrast, group B did no obvious improvement compared to group A, Mann-Whitney U=44, P=0.465.

3.4   Discussion

The present results are partially in accordance with out predictions. Semantically structured VDL-based iconic tags system manifested a better effectiveness on tagging process (tagging quality in per tagging time) than other three types of tags system.

As what has been proved in textual tags cloud, semantically structured tag clusters leads to a quicker and more accurate localizing of specific tag. Compared between tags system of type 3 and type 4, semantically structured tags displayed the lays of tag clusters even clear with visual signals, such as different colour, different shapes. The participants in group D said as soon as they got the displayer of tags system, they found clear categories represented by icons in several graphical base in common.

In contrast, those in group C, although they had identified the visual structure of tags finally, it took much more time than semantically structured group to catch this implied information. The significantly better performance on structure identification in post-questionnaire validated also what was hypothesized here. The semantically arranged VDL-based icons indeed influenced the visualization of tag structure compared with randomly arranged group.

The advantage of semantically structured VDL-based icons was demonstrated also in tagged documents. Users are likely to tag associated document with the same tags or at least, the tags in one category. For example, if they tagged a document talking about the environment with a green tag, this tag or its neighbour is supposed to be used again for another environment-concerned document. In the case of randomly arranged VDL-based iconic tags system, users know that there are still other choices of green tags in this displayer. However, finding again these green tags takes time and it risks omitting some of tags if they were not used before. Otherwise semantically structured VDL-based iconic tags system keeps all the green tags together. Once one member in a category has been found, all other element in this category appear one by one. Taking use of this, it not only saves time to localize a tag, but also increases the tagging quality because all the alternatives listed together, with the same structure information implied by visual code, influence users' choosing accuracy and confidence.

However in session 1, semantically structured iconic tags without explicit structure did not revealed significant better performance on tagging process compare with randomly arranged group. Neither did what has been done in the post-questionnaire. Testers in group A and B did almost the same score in the identification of tag structure. This can be illustrated that the semantically structured arrangement did not bring supplementary effect. As declared in previous investigation on semantically structured tags cloud [13], the semantic arrangement must good enough otherwise users will not be able to distinguish it from random layouts and semantic layouts therefore should only be used when the quality of the arrangement can be assured. Iconic tags without explicit structure did offer graphical interpretation of tags, yet they did not provide visual information on tag structure – semantic relations within them. Consequently, users used semantically structured icons totally like what they did with randomly arranged icons, which was previously verified poorer than randomly arranged VDL-based icons [2] on tagging process.

How to define a solid and clear semantic structure or said semantic layout among a group of tags is a crucial topic to discuss. On one hand, if the tags are in text or in icons without explicit structure, they have to be in so high accordance with daily comprehension using less ambiguous words that users are easy to realize the tags cluster. On the other hand, if most of the tags may be sorted into several layers, it has to add complementary information for specifying the structure of them, like VDL and pre-icons. Meanwhile, this information saves users' time on identifying semantic layer from a large scale of tags because of a more precise and intuitional tag structure. What's more, testers in group C did better than those in group B which also leads to an interesting argument. It is assumed that in a tags system the representation of single tag and their structure is more essential than the way to arrange tags.

Comparing between group B and group C, one was changed arrangement to semantically structured way from group A while the other one was altered the icon representation by adding pre-icon of VDL to original icons in group A. The statistical results implied significant improvement between A and C [2] but not between A and B. For no visual structure tag system, even though tags are semantically structured, it did not ameliorate tagging process. However reconstructing iconic tags with visual code allow the tagging efficiency enhancing. In a result, reforming a tags system needs firstly making better representation on tag and tag structure, and then implementing the arrangement.

4   Conclusion

The experiment presented in this paper have validated again the VDL-based icon tags system was more effective than icon system without explicit structure with the advantage of pre-icons. What's more, it demonstrated that semantically structured VDL-based icon system improved significantly the tagging process considering tagging quality and tagging speed. In other words, iconic tags with common pre-icons needs to be arrange together in an interface, which is in accordance with previous observation in textual tags cloud. Results drawn from this experiment allows getting a more complete assessment of VDL-based icon tag system and also lead to a theoretical standard of visual tag system we want to construct.

References

1. Hodge, G.: Systems of Knowledge Organization for Digital Libraries. Beyond Traditional Authority Files. The Council on Library and Information Resources, Washington DC (2000)
2. Ma, X., Cahier, J.P.: Visual Distinctive Language: using a Hypertopic-based Iconic Tagging System for Knowledge Sharing. In: IEEE WETICE 2012, pp. 456–461 (2012)
3. Zhou, C., Lejeune, C.H., Bénel, A.: Towards a standard protocol for community driven organizations of knowledge. In: Proc. ISPE CE 2006, pp. 338–349. IOS Press (2006)
4. Ames, M., Naaman, M.: Why we tag: the motivations for annotation in mobile and online media. In: Proceedings of the SIGCHI Conference on Human Factors in Computing Systems, CHI 2007 (2007)
5. Golder, S.A., Huberman, B.A.: Usage patterns of collaborative tagging systems. J. of Information Science 32(2) (2006)
6. Cattuto, C., Loreto, V., Pietronero, L.: Semiotic dynamics and collborative tagging. Proc. Nat. Acad. Sci. 104, 1461–1464 (2007)
7. Halvey, M.J., Keane, M.T.: An assessment of tag representation techniaues. In: Proc. WWW 2007, pp. 1313–1314. ACM Press (2007)
8. Rivadeneira, A.W., Gruen, D.M., Muller, M.J., Millen, D.R.: Getting our head in the clouds: toward evaluation studies of tagclouds. In: Proc. CHI 2007, pp. 995–998. ACM Press (2007)
9. Hearst, M.A., Rosner, D.: Tag Clouds: Data Analysis Tool or Social Signaller? In: Proc. HICSS 2008 (2008)

10. Hassan-Montero, Y., Herrero-Solana, V.: Improving tagclouds as visual information retrieval interfaces. In: Proc. InfoSciT (2006)
11. Provost, J.: Improved document summarization and tag clouds via singular value decomposition. Master thesis, Wueen's University, Kingston, Canada (September 2008)
12. Berlocher, I., Lee, K., Kim, K.: TopicRank: bringing insight to users. In: Proc. SIGIR 2008, pp. 703–704. ACM Press (2008)
13. Schrammel, J., Leitner, M., Tscheligi, M.: Semantically structured tag clouds: an empirical evaluation of clustered presentation approaches. In: Proceedings of CHI 2009, Boston, MA, USA, April 4-9, pp. 2037–2040 (2009)

A Model of Living Organisms to Integrate Multiple Relationship Network Descriptions

Tetsuya Maeshiro

School of Library and Information Science,
and Research Center for Knowledge Communities,
University of Tsukuba

Abstract. We present a description of a living organism that integrates multiple relationship networks, where each network represents a different facet of the target phenomena. The lifestyle illness and diabetes related phenomena are described using the proposed model. The relationship network model denotes a representation model where the focused phenomena or element is represented as a node, and nodes are connected if the represented phenomena or elements are somehow related. Each relationship network is a hypernetwork model, whose representation power is stronger than conventional models. Different viewpoints can be selected from a single model, thus the user can grasp the represented phenomena according to his needs.

1 Introduction

A useful model to represent a living organism is the relationship network. Basically, one has to elucidate the elements that interest and connect the elements that have some kind of relationships that one intends to describe.

A living organism has multiple facets, but a single facet is focused to describe or study a given aspect of an organism. For instance, a simple multicellular organism, *C. elegans*, can be described by various viewpoints. The locomotion mechanism consists of sensors that detect ambient conditions and internal control that activates muscles. Control signals are represented as relationships among elements. The feeding mechanism is a more complex phenomena that includes the locomotion mechanism, where sensors that detect nutrient presence control the locomotion, and digestive mechanism is also included in description. Another example is development. The cell lineage is at higher description level, where cells are connected according to the relationships among mother and daughter cells in time sequence. At lower description level, the cell division mechanism based on gene regulation is also represented as a relationship network, where genes that regulate other genes are connected. Furthermore, the cell division is described in two different detail levels, where the lower level describes the general cell division mechanism in *C. elegans*, and the higher level describes the mechanism of cell fate and cell type determination mechanism based on the cell position and time lineage, i.e., the development control mechanism. In other words, at least two

S. Yamamoto (Ed.): HIMI/HCII 2013, Part I, LNCS 8016, pp. 475–483, 2013.

levels of phenomena are described in any function of a living organism: cellular level phenomena and molecular level phenomena.

High throughput experiment techniques are main methods used in today's biological experiments, which generate a large amount of data in a single experiment. With the advance of these techniques, the amount of generated data from a single experiment has been rapidly increasing. Another trend is the increase in the variety of high throughput experiment types used in a research project to complement other experimental data, which further increases the amount of generated data. Moreover, deployment of different experiments to study the target organism or phenomena allow understanding of multiple aspects to analyze living organisms.

For instance, analysis of the behavior control mechanism of *C. elegans* requires a behavior model on individual organism model, locomotion control model on organism model that involves sensor input and muscle control. It implies that the use of a single aspect is insufficient for research. Furthermore, integration of results from different viewpoints' experimental results is a prerequisite for the research, thus a simple set of unrelated multiple representations is powerless. The true power of multiple aspect analysis is not just providing different viewpoints that fulfill the lack of information by single facet, but in offering the relationships among different viewpoints that help researchers interprete better the experimental results. Therefore, a knowledge representation corresponding to each experiment method and generated data is valuable to analyze and interprete experimental data. Our approach is to represent the related knowledge of a single experiment based on relationship network of concepts. Each experiment elucidates different aspect of the analyzed living organism, so the corresponding knowledge representation offers different viewpoint. Integrated analysis that collects different experimental results corresponds to knowledge representation that integrates descriptions of different viewpoints. In our opinion, description of relationships among viewpoints is also important to study living organisms, thus integrated representation is fundamental.

Constantly increased size of generated data requires methods to extract unique features and increased computational power. This is a quantitative aspect. However, qualitative aspect is becoming increasingly important, which is to use the knowledge inherent in generated data and background concepts related to these data. The knowledge is crucial to interprete experimental data, and if the knowledge can be "hard-coded" into the analytical system, it will improve the analysis efficiency. Furthermore, the same data is sometimes referred by different viewpoints, where different meanings are assigned to the data.

Another closely related research direction is the large scale simulation of living organisms. The simulation precision is increasing, and recently a whole simulation of a very simple unicellular organism was successful [9]. We are also conducting high speed large scale simulations using specialized hardware system [11]. With the advance of computer hardware technology, simulations of larger scales are becoming real, which generates huge amount of data. This situation is similar to the advance of high throughput experiments. Additional problem of computer simulation is the necessity to relate simulation models with actual phenomena observed in living organisms.

Gene level phenomena is insufficient to understand the organism behavior. This is especially valid when disease and its mechanism is involved. A holistic representation of the target organism is also necessary, besides the detailed representation of its parts and relationships among parts. This direction is partly similar to the Oriental Medicine. Furthermore, phenomena of internal organ level is important in Medicine. The condition of an organ and the status of functional relationship among organs are focused in medical treatments. Gene level condition and regulation status is rarely considered or monitored, because of difficulty of practical instrumentation techniques and the lack of clear causality mechanism between gene level and organ and/or organism level phenomena.

2   Representation of Multiple Relationship Networks

When describing or representing a living organism using the relationship network model, multi-hierarchy relationship networks are possible depending on the objective and viewpoint. The relationship network model denotes a representation model where the focused phenomena or element is represented as a node, and nodes are connected if the represented phenomena or elements are somehow related. We use the hypernetwork model[13], whose representation power is stronger than conventional models such as semantic network or ER-model that are based on graph theory.

A single living organism can be represented as a relationship network describing gene regulation, another network describing protein reactions and functions, and a network representing functional relationships among organs. These networks are enumerated in increasing hierarchical level. A group of organisms is also possible, and when different species are considered, predation relationship network can be described, for instance. Individual relationship networks exemplified above grasps a single facet among multiple viewpoints, but all these relationship networks should be integrated to understand completely and capture the entire picture of the living organism.

This paper proposes a model to integrate multiple relationship networks, where each network represents a different facet of a living organism. Following assumptions are employed: (1) The target living organism can be described using various viewpoints, belonging to different hierarchical level based on the granularity that a node represents. (2) The principles that drive the phenomenon on relationship network is fundamentally different from those driving the relationship network above or below the referred network's hierarchical level. Therefore, the phenomena are usually different, and they are the results of different principles. (3) The phenomena observed in a relationship network cannot be directly described using the elements and relationships that exists in the relationship network of immediately lower hierarchical level. Conventionally denoted as emergence, the mechanism has never been successfully described. We agree that the relationship and interactions among elements cause emergent behavior on a immediatly higher level network. However, the relationship between the emergent phenomena and functions in lower hierarchical level cannot be described.

We present the integrated representation model of lifestyle illness and diabetes related phenomena observed in *Mus musculus* and Human, and discuss the validity of the proposed model.

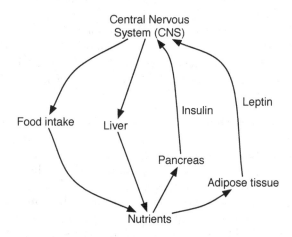

Fig. 1. Internal organ level relationship network of energy balance. Compiled from [8,6].

Fig. 1 is the energy balancing mechanism that is commonly described. The Central Nervous System (CNS) in the Figure represents a group of insuline and leptin receptor neurons and neurons that emit energy intake signals to organs. In the case of *C. elegans* and *M. musculus*the signal from CNS may cause directly the food intake behavior. In the case of Human, however, food intake mechanism involves more factors, particularly the decision making process.

Figures 2 and 3 are more detailed description generated from the definition of the term *insulin*, describing phenomena and concepts related to insulin, the central concept in these figures. Figure 4 is another representation of signal transduction pathway related to insulin, emphasizing the substances involved in processing, which describes from a different viewpoint.

When a person feels hungry, caused by a signal from CNS, in normal situation he does not grasp the first food that comes insight. Depending on the time of the day, the food is a meal (breakfast, lunch or dinner) or a light snack. If it is a meal, he may cook himself or go to a restaurant. He may go alone, with family, friends or with some group of people depending on the occasion. The choice of the restaurant is another decision making process, which involves the type of food (japanese, italian, french ...). Once at the restaurant, he should choose a food from the menu, to select a single plate or a set or *a la carte*. If he goes

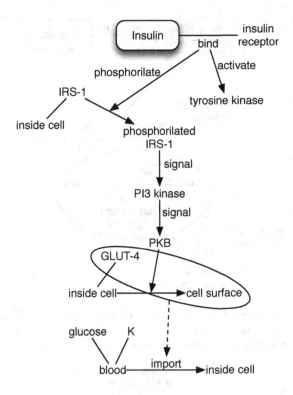

Fig. 2. Molecular level description of insulin

to a restaurant accompanied, food choice is influenced from other people of the group. These and other decision makings are driven by principles fundamentally different from the mechanism of Fig. 1.

Another fact that supports our assumption is the spread of fatness (obesity) influenced by person-to-person contact manner [1]. The similarity and closeness among people are strong factors, and generates groups of people consisting of similar BMI. There is a clear social influence that has been quantified [1]. The fatness seems to spread in human society, at least in US society, following the social network. It is similar to infectious diseases, but without the "fatness carrier" that corresponds to pathogens. A significant correlation of social relationship on fatness suggests that food intake is also controlled by other people's daily behavior and habits. However, the control pathway from the recognition of other people's actions to the stimulation of food intake is unclear yet. Although unclear, it is evidently different from the genetic level pathway that involves gene regulation. Then the fatness mechanism on social level is clearly different from the internal organ level mechanism (Fig.1), where the hunger is detected by the brain through the insulin and leptin levels in blood, and the release of aternative nutrients and food intake action is activated.

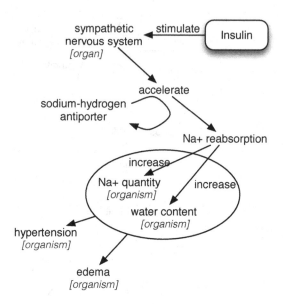

Fig. 3. Molecular level description of insulin. To be integrated to Figure 2. "[Organ]" and "[Organism]" denotes the hierarchy that the element belongs. For instance, "hypertension" is a symptom of an entire organism.

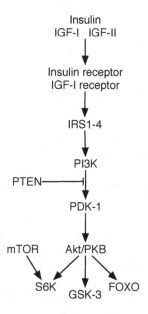

Fig. 4. Insulin signal transduction network in Mammals. Arrowed lines denote positive regulation, and barred lines denote repression.

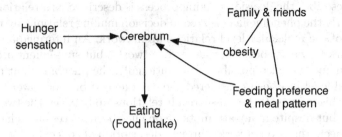

Fig. 5. Decision level relationship network of meal pattern

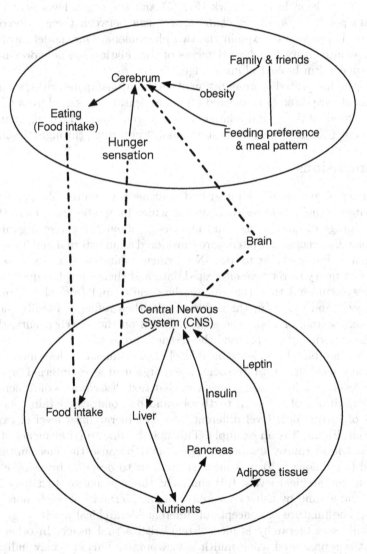

Fig. 6. Integrated representation of relationship networks

Fig. 5 describes the decision making process is described as a relationship network. Clearly the phenomena observed in decision making relationship network is the result of the molecular level relationship network. An intermediate relationship network may exist between these two networks, but subsequent propagation of the phenomena is also possible. Conventionally, the phenomena at the higher hierarchical level has been considered the emergence from the lower level interactions. If this is correct, the cause–result relationship between the two networks is possible, but despite many attempts no one has been successful. The proposed model connects the two networks through description of concepts that relate the two networks.

Since the decision level network (Fig. 5) and the organ level network (Fig. 1) are independent, no direct connection exists between them. Moreover, no description is possible to explain the two phenomena. Our model incorporates an intermediate entity to relate elements of the relationship networks based on concepts defined in biological knowledge.

Fig. 6 is an integrated representation of two relationship networks, where identical elements are directly connected ("hunger sensation"–signal from CNS, and "eating"–"food intake"), and related elements are connected through superordinate concept ("Central nervous system" and "cerebrum" through "brain").

3   Conclusions

The primary objective of the integrated multinetwork representation presented in this paper is the hybrid research system which integrates the human thinking and the storage of known facts and knowledge about the target organism and phenomena. Conventional systems are considered as an external and independent from humans. For instance, to use DNA sequence databases, a user (researcher) formulates a query to retrieve interested data and then input the query into the database system, and then the user receives the output from the system. The user analyzes and evaluates the search result, then refine or modify the query for the next search, or abort the search. Based on the search results, the user design the experiments to proceed the research project.

Classification based on hierarchical level of phenomena or described elements is commonly used, for instance social level, organism level, internal organ level and gene level. It is interesting, however, that text descriptions of a hierarchical level or definitions of terms in textbooks and dictionaries contain concepts or elements of hierarchical level different from the hierarchical level of explained phenomena. Figure 3 is an example. This may be due to (i) elements of higher hierarchical level (more abstract level) is used because the mechanism to be described is unknown; (ii) it is more convenient to describe by using elements of different hierarchical levels; (iii) similarly, the explanation text may become easier to understand by using concepts of higher hierarchical level, more general concepts. The mixture of concepts of different hierarchical levels suggests that the usefulness of hierarchy is inconsistent with actual usage. In other words, a concept is represented using multiple viewpoints. This fact may indicate the usefulness of the proposed multiple relationship network description model.

References

1. Christakis, N.A., Fowler, J.H.: The Spread of Obesity in a Large Social Network over 32 Years. N. Engl. J. Med. 357, 370–379 (2007)
2. Cone, R.D.: Anatomy and regulation of the central melanocortin system. Nat. Neurosci. 8, 571–578 (2005)
3. Jordan, S.D., Konner, A.C., Bruning, J.C.: Sensing the fuels: glucose and lipid signaling in the CNS controlling energy homeostasis. Cell. Mol. Life Sci. 67, 3255–3273 (2010)
4. Porte Jr., D., Baskin, D.G., Schwartz, M.W.: Insulin Signaling in the Central Nervous System: A Critical Role in Metabolic Homeostasis and Disease From C. elegans to Humans. Diabetes 54, 1264–1276 (2005)
5. Sainsbury, A., Cooney, G.J., Herzog, H.: Hypothalamic regulation of energy homeostasis. Best Pract. Res. Clin. Endocrinol. Metab. 16, 623–637 (2002)
6. Badmin, M.K., Flier, J.S.: The Gut and Energy Balance: Visceral Allies in the Obesity Wars. Science 307, 1909–1914 (2005)
7. Demuro, G., Obici, S.: Central Nervous System and Control of Endogenous Glucose Production. Curr. Diab. Rep. 6, 188–193 (2006)
8. Lam, T.K., Schwartz, G.J., Rossetti, L.: Hypothalamic sensing of fatty acids. Nat. Neurosci. 8, 579–584 (2005)
9. Karr, J.R., et al.: A Whole-Cell Computational Model Predicts Phenotype from Genotype. Cell 150, 389–401 (2012)
10. Okano, Nakayama, Ito, Maeshiro: Estimation of gene regulatory network related to worm embryo. In: Japan Molecular Biology Society 33rd Symposium, vol. 4P, p. 1255 (2011)
11. Maeshiro, T., Hemmi, H., Shimohara, K.: Ultra-fast Genome wide Simulation of Biological Signal Transduction Networks - Starpack. In: Frontiers of Computational Science, pp. 177–180. Springer (2007)
12. Schierenberg, E.: Embryological variation during nematode development. WormBook (2006)
13. Maeshiro, T., Maeshiro, M., Shimohara, K., Nakayama, S.-i.: Hypernetwork model to represent similarity details applied to musical instrument performance. In: Jacko, J.A. (ed.) Human-Computer Interaction, Part I, HCII 2009. LNCS, vol. 5610, pp. 866–873. Springer, Heidelberg (2009)

Similar or Not Similar:
This Is a Parameter Question

Andrey Araujo Masiero, Flavio Tonidandel, and Plinio Thomaz Aquino Junior

FEI University Center
Av. Humberto A. Castelo Branco, 3972
09859-901 - S. Bernardo Campo - SP - Brasil
{amasiero,flaviot,plinio.aquino}@fei.edu.br ·

Abstract. There is much information of users to be analyzed to develop a personalized project. To perform an analysis, it is necessary to create clusters in order to identify features to be explored by the project designer. In general, a classical clustering algorithm called K-Means is used to group users features. However, K-Means reveals some problems during the cluster process. In fact, K-Means does not guarantee to find Quality-Preserved Sets (QPS) and its randomness let the entire process unpredictable and unstable. In order to avoid these problems, a novel algorithm called Q-SIM (Quality Similarity Clustering) is presented in this paper. The Q-SIM algorithm has the objective to keep a similarity degree among all elements inside the cluster and guarantee QPS for all sets. During the tests, Q-SIM demonstrates that it is better than k-means and it is more appropriate to solve the problem for user modeling presented in this paper.

Keywords: Q-SIM, Clustering, User Modeling, Personas.

1 Introduction

The users' diversity has been growing up while the time passes [1]. The analysis of diversity in a group of users is a complex work and it usually requires unnecessary extra time of the specialist. It is important to identify a likeness between the groups to help the specialist to keep his focus on the most relevant characteristics.

It is important to determine which users are similar to each other, in order to minimize the number of profiles. To reach this understanding, Jung [9] defined a term called *Personas* to represent unique profiles. He identified that a person assumes different behaviors depending on the current scenario or on collective conventions. *Personas* was popularized by Cooper [4], defining it as hypothetical archetypes of users. This technique also could be defined as a descriptive model of users, which represents a group of real users and their features [2].

In previous research [11], a methodology to support the process to automatically create *Personas* by using clustering algorithms was proposed. The algorithm used in that case was the classical clustering method called K-Means [8]. There are several weak points on the use of K-Means for the propose to create

S. Yamamoto (Ed.): HIMI/HCII 2013, Part I, LNCS 8016, pp. 484–493, 2013.
© Springer-Verlag Berlin Heidelberg 2013

Personas. First of all, the parameter used in K-Means is the number of groups that will be created (a k number). This parameter can turn the process imprecise due to the specialist not always knows the number of groups the data contains. In this case, the specialist needs to analyze the data and identify how many groups exist before using the algorithm, which demands an unnecessary extra time of the specialist. Another problem in K-Means is its randomness of possible results what turns the entire process unpredictable and unstable since the final clusters sets could vary according to the centroid initialization.

We look for a Quality-Preserved Sets (QPS) to define *Personas*. A QPS is a concept where a set of objects guarantees a minimum value of similarity among all objects, i.e., if the minimum value is 0.8, any element of a QPS has at least 0.8 of similarity to all others elements. QPS is important to find high quality *Personas*. If we consider *Personas* as a fictitious character that represents a group of real users [1], a group with similar elements (users) that regards a certain similarity among them is needed in order to guarantee a definition of more representative *Personas*. K-Means doesn't guarantee this similarity among all elements in a group since it depends on the pre-defined number k and the clustering process only cares about the similarity of the elements to the k centroids randomly distributed, which does not guarantee the QPS for the clusters.

In order to guarantee better representative *Personas*, this paper proposes a novel clustering algorithm called Q-SIM (Quality Similarity Clustering), which creates clusters based on the degree of similarity to preserve QPS concept. Q-SIM inverts the K-Means process and instead of require a k number of clusters, it requires a parameter Q of quality and it finds the appropriate number of clusters that guarantee the QPS for all groups based on the parameter Q indicated. The Q value is a similarity threshold that varies from 0 to 1. The Q-SIM algorithm also needs a similarity metric equation to calculate similarities between elements, like K-Means uses the Euclidean distance, for instance.

This paper is organized as following, section 2 presents the problem with *k*-means which motivate this research. Section 3 details the Q-SIM algorithm. Section 4 discusses the results of comparison between Q-SIM and *k*-means. Beyond that is presented the result of the application of Q-SIM into a project of Research and Statistic based on Digital Collection of Patient Medical Record in Center User Telemedicine (PEAP-PMPT, in portuguese) which *Personas* are created by the use of the Q-SIM algorithm. And the last two section (5 and 5) present the conclusion of work and acknowledgments that supports this research.

2   Clustering for User Modeling

During the process to create *Personas* by using K-Means clustering algorithm, a designer must decide how to overcome the problem to establish the number of cluster for input. Some works execute *k*-means algorithm many times with different number of cluster and compare the results. The comparison of results involves all project team and stakeholders which demand much time [1][11].

Another work involving *k*-means and *Personas* are presented by Weber and Jaimes [13], which use the algorithm to create an segmentation between the information search by the user. With this information, they create *Personas* to head the marketing advertisement. For defining the number of cluster, authors tried different number of cluster. The range 8 to 20 was tried and the centroids and the clusters were compared in order to determine if its necessary to merge or not some cluster to reach a low number of cluster. All these works does not guarantee to preserve the QPS for the found groups.

This problem present by k-means motivated the research of this paper and the creation of an algorithm called Q-SIM that can find the number of cluster based on the similarity value determined by the specialist and preserving QPS. The quality of a set is determined by a proximity on its elements. The proximity of elements can be calculated by a similarity metric that must be well defined.

There are many similarities' calculus. This decision depends on the project and the best way to represent database information for determining patterns into it [6]. One example is the Euclidean distance, useful for numerical data that can be represented by data points into a physical space.

Any categorical data, e.g. textual data, can be used by the euclidean distance if there is any method to convert categorical data into numeric codes. There are methods that is more related to categorical data. An example is the method presented by Dutta et al.[6].

These methods can also be combined for the calculation of similarity between objects composed by two or more variables with different types. For this kind of similarity, it is used a combination of local similarity (for each variable contained into object) and global similarity. Local similarity uses the equation 1.

$$sim(X_i, Y_i) = 1 - \left(\frac{|X_i - Y_i|}{(\max - \min)} \right) \tag{1}$$

Global similarity calculus are based on local similarity. The equation 2 define the global similarity.

$$Sim(X, Y) = \frac{\sum W_i \cdot sim(X_i, Y_i)}{\sum W_i} \tag{2}$$

Where Wi is a weight for each variable i of the object.

The result of this step is a similarity matrix between all objects. The similarity is a good calculation of the proximity of elements and it is a parameter to guarantee the QPS for the clustring process. Q-Sim uses similarity as the core parameter to find the clusters, as presented in the next section.

3   Q-SIM Algorithm

The Q-SIM (Quality Similarity Clustering) algorithm aims to automatically detect the number of suitable clusters in order to preserve the quality among all elements in a set. Q-Sim algorithm comprises 3 distinct phases: (I) Preparation of data; (II) Selection of sets; (III) Refinement of the clusters.

For the first phase, Q-SIM algorithm tries to determine groups of elements by manipulating data into sets. In this phase, Q-SIM uses the similarity matrix among objects to determine what it calls Related Sets. An object's Related Set is a set of all objects that has at least Q similarity value from the target object o. The formal definition, adapted from [12], is:

Definition 1. *(Related Set) A Related Set of object target o, denoted by RS(o), is an object's set formed by following formula:*

$$RS(o \in \mathcal{O}) = \forall p \in \mathcal{O}/similarity(o, p) \leq Q$$

Where $\mathcal{O}$ is the object's set of the domain and Q is similarity value, between 0 and 1. Notice that o is part of its own Related Set since $similarity(o, o) = 1$. Although all objects into a Related Set are similar to object target o, there is no guarantee that an object p is similar to object q, when $p, q \in RS(o)$. Considering that Q-SIM looks for a QPS cluster, it must find a subset of $RS(o)$, which reaches a minimum Q value among all elements. This subset is called *Reduced Related Set*, defined as following.

Definition 2. *(Reduced Related Set) A Reduced Related Set of object target o, denoted by RRS(o), is a group of objects formed by following formula:*

$$RRS(o) = \{\{c_1 \dots c_n\} \in RS(o)/similarity(c_i, c_j) \geq Q, 1 \leq i \leq n, 1 \leq j \leq n\}$$

Notice that it is possible to exist many subsets $RRS(o) \in RS(o)$. However, the best RRS is the one that contains a biggest number of objects from original RS. Nevertheless, to choose objects from a certain group to maximize the number of objects inside RRS is hard to calculate and claim an algorithm with a high computational time. Considering that each element p of $RS(o)$ has its own $RS(p)$, any intersection between $RS(o)$ and $RS(p)$ will create a group of elements, called $RS'(o)$ that has similarity at least Q for o and for p.

As a solution to approximate the best RRS, Q-SIM uses a greedy algorithm which first locates the element $p \in RS(o)$ that maximizes the intersection $RS'(o) = RS(o) \cap RS(p)$. The process repeats recursively for the elements within $RS'(o)$, until any intersection becomes empty. The object o and chosen p values recursively obtained form the $RRS(o)$ set from the original $RS(o)$. Notice that all elements within $RRS(o)$ maintain the QPS concept based on Q value.

Q-SIM determines a RRS set for all elements of $\mathcal{O}$. Obviously, it exists a lot of intersection between all RRSs since each object has its own RRS and it belongs to another RRS from many different objects. The union of all RRSs creates the domain set of all existing objects $\mathcal{O}$.

Next phase, called Selection of Sets, is characterized to find the smallest number of subsets $RRS \in \mathcal{O}$ which comprises all objects of $\mathcal{O}$. A set of RRSs that cover all $\mathcal{O}$ objects is called $\mathcal{C}$. The problem to determine the smallest $\mathcal{C}$ is known as set-cover problem and it is proven to be NP-Complete [7]. An approximate solution used by Q-SIM is also a greedy algorithm that picks the RRS set that covers the greatest numbers of elements not covered by sets $RRS \in \mathcal{C}$. It is a good approximate algorithm for the set-cover problem and it provides a good solution near to the optimal one.

Not only the greatest number of elements is essential to choose a RRS to compose the set $\mathcal{C}$, but also a metric that show how close the elements are among them in RRS. Q-SIM uses a density function that takes into consideration the size of the RRS and the proximity of its elements. The density function definition is presented as following.

Definition 3. *(Density Function) The density of $RRS(o)$ is calculated by following formula:*

$$density(RRS(o)) = \frac{size(RRS(o))}{\dfrac{\sigma(RRS(o))}{\mu(RRS(o))}}$$

Where $\sigma(RRS(o))$ is the standard deviation of the object's similarities into $RRS(o)$ and $\mu(RRS(o))$ is the average of the object's similarities into $RRS(o)$. If $\sigma(RRS(o))/\mu(RRS(o)) = 0$, the density becomes $size(RRS(o))$.

With density values(definition 3) of all $RRS \in \mathcal{O}$, Q-SIM selects the RRS which has the biggest density value to be part of set $\mathcal{C}$. During this process of selection, all elements in $\mathcal{C}$ are not considered for the next selection and so on. In fact, after a selection of a RRS to compose $\mathcal{C}$, the density function is calculated again for all $RRS \in \mathcal{O}$ excluding any element already chosen and part of $\mathcal{C}$.

When a $RRS \in \mathcal{O}$ is choose by the density function, Q-SIM verifies if the objects into the RRS can be included into another existing group in $\mathcal{C}$. To do that, it is necessary to validate the Q value among all elements of both groups. If all objects in RRS can be included in a existing group, no new group is created in $\mathcal{C}$. However, if only one single object remains in the RRS, the entireRRS set becomes a new group of elements in $\mathcal{C}$ and none of its objects are inserted into another group. Since there are common elements among this new group formed by RRS and others groups in $\mathcal{C}$ and each group must be independent of others, i.e, two groups $\mathcal{A}$ and $\mathcal{B}$ are independents if $\mathcal{A} \cap \mathcal{B} = \emptyset$, Q-SIM must perform an algorithm to solve any intersections in $\mathcal{C}$ caused by the insertion of a new RRS.

A separation of groups to solve intersections problems is based on the centroids (definition 4) of involved groups. It is important the perception that each RRS is related with an object o which was responsible for the RRS formation but it is not the best representation of its group.

Definition 4. *(Centroid) Given a set of characteristics $\{c_1 \ldots c_m\}$ belongs to an object o and a group of n objects denoted by $\mathcal{A}$, where $o \in \mathcal{A}$. The centroid of $\mathcal{A}$ contains a set of characteristics $\{k_1 \ldots k_m\}$. It is defined as following:*

$$\forall o \in \mathcal{A}, \forall k \;\exists\; Centroide(\mathcal{A}), k_i = \sum_{j=1}^{n} \frac{o_j(k_i)}{n}, 1 \leq i \leq m$$

The process to create independent groups is presented in figure 1, where: (I) Groups with intersection are identified; (II) Their centroids are calculated; (III) Objects' similarities inside the intersection are compared with groups' centroids; (IV) The object is allocated into the group that the centroid is more similar.

The phase Selection of Sets ends when all elements of $\mathcal{O}$ are also in $\mathcal{C}$. The groups formed in $\mathcal{C}$ are the first tentative to form clusters. However, these

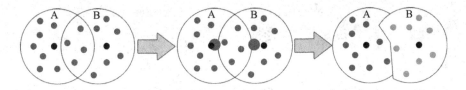

Fig. 1. Result of the process to create independent groups between the groups A and B. Red points represent the centroids calculated for each group

clusters can be optimized, what takes the Q-SIM to the 3rd and final phase: The Refinement of the clusters.

The Q-SIM performs two processes with the objective to minimize the number of groups formed and to smooth the boundaries of each one. Both processes are greedy algorithms that obtain a sub-optimal solution at most.

The first process is responsible to smooth groups' boundaries. For this process, Q-SIM compares all objects $o_i \in C$ with the centroids of each existing group. If the object is more similar to another centroid than the centroid of its group, the object can be reallocated to the new group if the QPS based on Q value is not violated.

The second process is to join two or more existing groups. Q-SIM verifies if all objects of one group keep the Q value among all object of the second group. If this condition is true, these two groups are joined and becomes one.

Thus, the Q-SIM process is complete and it is possible to generate a number of groups with Q value, keeping the QPS concept. To create *Personas*, the information produced by Q-SIM is analyzed and inputted into *Personas* description. The next section presents the results obtained with Q-SIM based on data collected in PEAD-PMPT project system.

4   Results and Discussions

Before using Q-SIM to create *Personas*, it is necessary to validate its clustering processing. To validate the Q-SIM we use two database which contains data from 2-D space points, normally used in this kind of validation [10]. The results present by Q-SIM are compared with a classic algorithm of clustering k-means [8]. After analyze the results of both algorithms through the obtained graphics of clustering process, three clustering metrics are applied into results and it is discussed during this section. The three metrics used in this paper are: (I) data variance [10]; (II) Dunn's index [3]; and (III) Davies-Bouldin's index [5].

The two database used in validation process are presented in figure 2. These databases presented in figure 2, represent the most common information for clusters. The first database demonstrates a sparse data which has four solid groups. The second one is a database which is common for user information data. These 2-D databases can represent information from user of a real project.

To make the tests and compare the results betweens k-means and Q-SIM, we need to establish a pattern for analyzing the cluster result. K-means has a

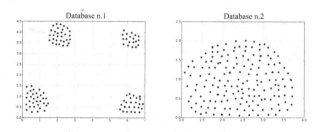

Fig. 2. Validation Databases

random process to generate the clusters, and needs to be informed how many cluster the specialist wants. The k number is a problem for some projects, mainly when the specialist wants to guarantee a degree of similarity between the user profiles and he doesn't know the exactly number of cluster into database.

For comparison reasons, we use the number of cluster found by Q-SIM,when Q value is set to 0.6, as the input k of k-means algorithm. Due to k-means randomness, we execute it 10 times and considered on the best(+) and the worst(-) results to be compared with the result of Q-SIM. The figure 3 presents the results of both algorithms for database n.1.

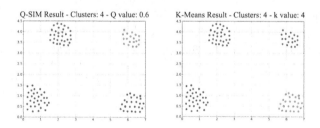

Fig. 3. Results of Q-SIM and k-means for the database n.1

Q-SIM found 4 clusters into database n.1, as expected, using the Q value 0.6 which represents 60% of similarity between cluster's elements at least. K-means also separated the database in 4 clusters, but this scenario is just possible if the specialist knows the number of clusters existing into database.

Further analysis can be made based on the indexes presented in the beginning of this section. These indexes measure the similarity between cluster's elements and how dissimilar the elements in different groups are. Figure 4 introduces the indexes result for the database n.1, for both algorithms.

Q-SIM and k-means present the same results in all indexes. The variance index measures the similarity between all elements of the cluster. The best result for variance is determined by the value closer to zero. In this case, both algorithms reach the value of 0.0014 which means very similar clusters. The other two

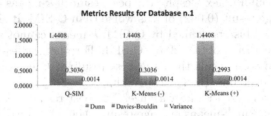

Fig. 4. Results' Metrics of Q-SIM and k-means for the database n.1

indexes measure how similar are the elements inside a cluster and how different they are to the others. The best Dunn's index is the one with higher value and the best Davies-Bouldin's index is the lower one. For these two indexes, Q-SIM and k-means reach also the same value but the best result of k-means reach a value 0.0043 better than Q-SIM. However, the average of both algorithms is the same for database n.1.

Continuing with the test, figure 5 presents the result for the database n.2.

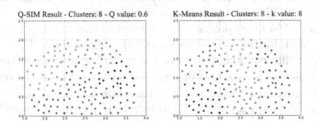

Fig. 5. Results of Q-SIM and k-means for the database n.2

The clusters found by k-means are similar to the Q-SIM clusters. However, the randomness of k-means can find bigger clusters than Q-SIM which may prejudice the similarity of the elements inside the clusters. To verify this situation we can analyze the indexes obtained for database n.2, present in figure 6.

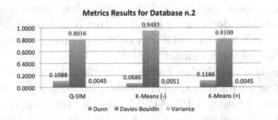

Fig. 6. Results' Metrics of Q-SIM and k-means for the database n.2

Analyzing the Dunn index, despite the best result of k-means are better than Q-SIM, the average result (0.092) of it is worse than Q-SIM. It shows that even with a number k of clusters defined by Q-SIM, k-means cannot always improve the quality of the result obtained by Q-SIM. For the Davies-Bouldin index, Q-SIM reaches a better result than the best result of k-means. In this index, k-means does not overcome the Q-SIM results.

The last index analyzed is the variance. The best result of k-means is quite better than Q-SIM, but k-means average result (0.0048) is a worst choice in the final analysis. After all, only Q-SIM guarantees the QPS concept in all groups.

When the information about the problems of k-means presented in section 2 is joined with the results obtained along this section, we can conclude that Q-SIM reach better results than k-means. The Q-SIM algorithm reach these result without the knowledge of specialist about how many groups exist into database and guarantees a degree of similarity among the elements of a cluster.

With these results, the Q-SIM algorithm is applied into the PEAP-PMPT project to find *Personas* based on characteristics of skills and behavior during the use of the system. The database of user information contains the following variables: (I) Time to fill text components; (II) Typing Speed; (III) Use of backspace; (IV) Number of Errors to fill a form; (V) Two or more errors in the same form; and (VI) Double click in link component.

Information of 154 users profile was collected during the experiment. We executed Q-SIM with for different Q value, 0.2, 0.4, 0.6 and 0.8. For each Q value Q-SIM find one different number of cluster, 1, 3, 3 and 5, respectively. In this case, we select the result with Q value equals 0.8 that obtained the best distribution of the user profiles into the clusters. Based on the knowledge extracted for the cluster, the *Personas* are created and help to improve the system's interface.

5   Conclusion

Based on the results, Q-SIM is the best option when compared with k-means. For the specialist to find well defined *Personas*, choosing the parameter Q is more appropriate to find groups with similar elements inside than choosing the k parameter. The similarity among elements in a group is very important in user modeling, because how much similar are the user profile that leads to the models, more closer of the real users they are. Furthermore, it is possible that the specialist vary the Q value from Q-SIM and verifies how many clusters are found during the increase and decrease of Q value. But it is important to remember that Q-SIM always will keep the similarity between elements of cluster, according with the solicitation of the specialist.

Q-SIM is not only an algorithm for user modeling, but it also can be applied into other kind of problems that need clusters for knowledge extraction. It can be used into recommend system or PICAPS [1]. Beyond these application, as future work, we want to map another variables that generate knowledge about the user and automatic improve the interface and shortcuts for the user navigation. And one more work that we are working on is the *Personas* evolution in order to identify the life time of each one and how positive is that for the projects.

Acknowledgment. To CNPq Scholarship 383677/2011-4 and PEAP-PMPT project, ref. 1465/10, In- stitutional Process number 01.10.0765.00, MCT/ FINEP/SAUDE TELESAUDE E TELEMEDICINA No - 1/2010 and FAPESP funding process number 2013/07837- 3.

References

1. Aquino Jr., P.T., Filgueiras, L.V.L.: A expressao da diversidade de usuarios no projeto de interacao com padroes e personas. In: Proceedings of the VIII Brazilian Symposium on Human Factors in Computing Systems, IHC 2008, pp. 1–10. Brazilian Computer Society, Porto Alegre (2008)
2. Aquino Jr., P.T., Filgueiras, L.V.L.: User modeling with personas. In: Proceedings of the 2005 Latin American Conference on Human-computer Interaction, CLIHC 2005, pp. 277–282. ACM, New York (2005)
3. Bezdek, J., Pal, N.: Cluster validation with generalized dunn's indices. In: Proceedings of the Second New Zealand International Two-Stream Conference on Artificial Neural Networks and Expert Systems, pp. 190–193 (November 1995)
4. Cooper, A.: The Inmates Are Running the Asylum. Macmillan Publishing Co. Inc., Indianapolis (1999)
5. Davies, D.L., Bouldin, D.W.: A cluster separation measure. IEEE Trans. Pattern Anal. Mach. Intell. 1(2), 224–227 (1979)
6. Dutta, M., Mahanta, A.K., Pujari, A.K.: Qrock: A quick version of the rock algorithm for clustering of categorical data. Pattern Recogn. Lett. 26(15), 2364 (2005)
7. Garey, M.R., Johnson, D.S.: Computers and Intractability; A Guide to the Theory of NP-Completeness. W. H. Freeman & Co., New York (1990)
8. Jain, A.K.: Data clustering: 50 years beyond k-means. Pattern Recogn. Lett. 31(8), 651–666 (2010)
9. Jung, C.: The archetypes and the collective unconscious (1991)
10. Legany, C., Juhasz, S., Babos, A.: Cluster validity measurement techniques. In: Proceedings of the 5th WSEAS International Conference on Artificial Intelligence, Knowledge Engineering and Data Bases, AIKED 2006, pp. 388–393. World Scientific and Engineering Academy and Society, Stevens Point (2006)
11. Masiero, A.A., Leite, M.G., Filgueiras, L.V.L., Aquino Jr., P.T.: Multidirectional knowledge extraction process for creating behavioral personas. In: Proceedings of the 10th Brazilian Symposium on on Human Factors in Computing Systems and the 5th Latin American Conference on Human-Computer Interaction, IHC+CLIHC 2011, pp. 91–99. Brazilian Computer Society, Porto Alegre (2011)
12. Smyth, B., McKenna, E.: Competence guided incremental footprint-based retrieval. Knowledge-Based Systems 14, 155–161 (2001)
13. Weber, I., Jaimes, A.: Who uses web search for what: and how. In: Proceedings of the Fourth ACM International Conference on Web Search and Data Mining, WSDM 2011, pp. 15–24. ACM, New York (2011)

Generalized Algorithm for Obtaining a Family of Evaluating Attributes' Sets Representing Customer's Preference

Takuya Mogawa, Fumiaki Saitoh, and Syohei Ishizu

Aoyama Gakuin University 5-10-1 Fuchinobe, Sagamihara City, 252-5258, Japan
c5612132@aoyama.jp,
{saitoh,ishizu}@ise.aoyama.ac.jp

Abstract. Product developments become complex and diversified. Many products appear which have a variety of features for adapting a customer's preference. A single evaluating attributes' set don't perform to evaluate these products. Because products which straddle multiple market segments are evaluated by customer's preferences which switch with the usage. Therefore it is necessary to evaluate products by a family of evaluating attributes' sets (hereinafter referred to as "FEAS") which corresponds to the customer's preferences. Mogawa [1] proposed an algorithm which guarantees to obtain FEAS under the conditions that Customer's Preference Grid (hereinafter referred to as " *CPG* ")is reflexive. It is not until the algorithm limited relations of customer's preference that this allows to obtain FEAS. Our main aim is to provide a generalized algorithm for obtaining FEAS. Where, we present the conditions under FEAS existing and we extract the required relations of evaluating attribute for obtaining FEAS. We propose an algorithm for obtaining FEAS by defining propositions and an extraction procedure.

Keywords: customer's preference, attribute's set, a family of evaluating attribute's sets, Data-mining, Rough Set.

1 Introduction

There is a current trend toward diversification of customer demand according to customer lifestyle, resulting in the development of products with a variety of features for application to multiple market segments. Products are normally evaluated within individual market segments according to evaluating attributes' set. Evaluation occurs within a single market segment according to a given a set of evaluating attributes. However, evaluation of products that straddle multiple market segments cannot be performed according to a single evaluating attributes' set. Because the products have multiple usage and a single evaluating attributes' set can't represent customer's preference exhaustively that is considered to use the products with multiple usage.

"Rough evaluation structures" have been proposed by Ishizu [2] as a method for understanding such FEAS for obtaining customer's preference. This study showed

S. Yamamoto (Ed.): HIMI/HCII 2013, Part I, LNCS 8016, pp. 494–504, 2013.

that use of concepts from an approximation of rough set theory can be used to determine FEAS by composing classes which are named similarity classes of preferences. While that study guarantees the existence FEAS in cases where there are sufficient evaluating attributes to represent customer's preference and CPG is reflexive, it does not clarify to get FEAS when CPG is not reflexive. Additionally, it is true that the more practically we want to represent customer's preference, the less reflexive CPG is.

Representing FEAS taking into practical customer's preference is extremely important. Algorithm for representing FEAS should be more than dealing with reflexive CPG. One of main aims of this paper is to propose a generalized algorithm which is able to be applied practical customers' thought when customers select products that straddle multiple market segments. We move onto introduce basic concept of obtaining FEAS.

2   Concepts of Constructing FAES

Mogawa [1] proposed an algorithm for obtaining FEAS by defining added relations and required attributes. This algorithm defined relations among CPG and evaluating attributes for obtaining FEAS because customer's preference is required for organizing the product which a customer desires and customer's preference is based on relations among evaluating attributes. Proposed algorithms [1,2] simply account for customer's preference which are limited by CPG whose diagonal elements are filled, in other words CPG is reflexive. CPG is defined as the following.

$$CPG \subset U \times U \tag{1}$$

CPG is composed by questionnaire from a pairwise comparison method which defined by Ishizu [4].

Proposed algorithms were made in based on Rough Set Theory [6] which treats indiscernibility of datum. Rough Set Theory was proposed by Zdzisław Pawlak. He proposed how to extraction decision rules by using information system. Characters of rough set theory can search database which consists of incomplete information. Human's decision-making is not always logical. So recently rough set theory is widely used in the field of *Kansei* engineering which handle human's preference.

The previous study [2] explained definitions and concepts of the algorithm for obtaining FAES. A system is named an information system when they apply rough set theory to data analyses and diagnoses.

A total ordered information system in the algorithm [2] is defined as the following 5-tuples.

$$< U, Q, V, f, \{ T_q \mid q \in Q \} > \tag{2}$$

Where U is a finite set of objects such as a set of products. Q is a finite set of attributes, $V = \{ V_q \mid q \in Q \}$ is a finite set of all attributes' values where V_q is a finite set of values of attribute q and $f : U \times Q \rightarrow V$ is called information function such that $f(x,q) \in V_q$ for every $q \in Q$ and $x \in U$. $\{ T_q \mid q \in Q \}$ is a set of total orders which is defined by an attribute q. Ishizu [4] assumes V_q is a totally ordered set for each $q \in Q$ and denotes total order on V_q as $T_q \subset V_q \times V_q$. They use the notation UT_q which is the ordered relation on U against the thing that T_q is the ordered relation on V_q.

$$UT_q = \{ (x,y) \in U \times U \mid (f(x,q), f(y,q)) \in T_q \} \tag{3}$$

Since T_q is a total order, UT_q is a pre-total order, where a pre-total order is a binary relation that satisfies reflexivity, transitivity and comparability. For any $q \in Q$ and $(x,y) \in U \times U$, $S(x, y)_p$ denotes the following similarity class of a preference pair (x,y).

$$
\begin{aligned}
S(x, y)_p &= \cap \{ UT_q \mid q \in P, (x,y) \in UT_q \} \\
&= \{ (v.w) \mid \forall q \in Q : (x,y) \in UT_q \rightarrow (v.w) \in UT_q \}
\end{aligned}
\tag{4}
$$

It is easy to show that if $(v.w) \in S(x, y)_p$ for any $q \in P$ and for any $(x,y) \in UT_q$, then $(v.w) \in UT_q$. This means if for any $q \in P$, x is preferable to y, then v is preferable to w. $(v.w) \in S(x, y)_P$ can be regarded that a preference pair $(v.w)$ is similar and consistent with the preference pair (x,y) with regard to P. Note that $S(x, y)_p$ may not be equivalence class.

In some cases, customer's preference is not consistent, and previous studies do not assume the customer's preference is total order or partial order. In the following discussion, they do not assume that CPG is consistent, and they only assume the preference's relation is reflexive. Then, they defined accuracy of approximation for treating inconsistency. They followed a definition of upper and lower approximation and accuracy of approximation based on Rough Set Theory. For any $CPG \subset U \times U$ and $P \subset Q$. Upper and lower approximations are defined as follows.

P- Upper approximation $P^*(CPG)$ of CPG

$$P^*(CPG) = \cup \{ S(x, y)_P \mid (x,y) \in CPG \} \tag{5}$$

P- Lower approximation $P_*(CPG)$ of CPG

$$P_*(CPG) = \cup \{ S(x, y)_P \mid S(x,y) \subset CPG \} \tag{6}$$

From the definition, it is easy to show that $P_*(CPG) \subset CPG \subset P^*(CPG)$.

For every $CPG \subset U \times U$, accuracy of approximation of CPG by P is defined as the following.

$$\alpha_P(CPG) = card(P_*(CPG))/card(P^*(CPG)) \tag{7}$$

$card(X)$ means a cardinality of a set X.

They showed how to construct FEAS. Let $< U, Q, V, f, \{ T_q \mid q \in Q \} >$ be a total ordered information system, and CPG be customer's preference grid on U. The family of subsets $\{ I_1, \ldots, I_n \}$ of Q is called FEAS of CPG, if the following condition is satisfied.

$$CPG = \cup \{ \cap \{ UT_q \mid q \in I_i \} \mid i = 1, ..., n \} \tag{8}$$

When accuracy of approximation $\alpha_P(CPG)$ is 1, (8) indicates that a family of subsets $\{ I_1, ..., I_n \}$ becomes FEAS and CPG can be represented by $\{ I_1, ..., I_n \}$. Therefor $\alpha_P(CPG)= 1$ if and only if CPG can be represented by FEAS as a family of subsets $\{ I_1, ..., I_n \}$.

In order to identify the attributes as FEAS for evaluating objects, we usually gather all attributes which relate to customer's preference grid CPG. They usually try to use all gathered attributes to explain CPG, where they suppose $CPG = \cup \{ \cap \{ UT_q \mid q \in I_i \} \mid i = 1, ..., n \}$.

We refer to $< U, Q, V, f, \{ T_q \mid q \in Q \} >$ as a total information system and use the concept of accuracy of approximation, defined by Pawlak [3] as an index showing whether FEAS can be obtained or not. In other words, the accuracy of approximation indicates how closely the evaluation attribute sets represent the customer preference relation. An accuracy of approximation of 1 ensures that a FEAS which completely represents the customer preference relation can be obtained.

Proposition 1
Let U be any set of objects and CPG be customer's preference grid on U. Then $\alpha_P(P_*(CPG))= 1$, and $\alpha_P(P^*(CPG))= 1$.

Proposition 1 shows that accuracies of upper and lower approximations are 1.

From the following discussion, Previously proposed algorithms allowed to obtain customer's preference as FEAS under the condition that CPG's diagonal elements are filled. In other words, CPG is reflexive.

We insist repeatedly that representing FEAS taking into practical customer's preference is importance. It is easy to think customer's preference which doesn't include CPG's diagonal elements. For instance, when customers want evaluate products by order of "prefer" excluding equal or when customers want the product with the a particular attribute's value like brand. These measurement among products are usual things and CPG's diagonal elements are not filled all at least in these situations.

We regard it as problem that previous algorithm did not represent sufficiently customer's measurement among products obtaining FEAS. It is necessary to integrate conceivable measurement among products into the previous algorithm and make the algorithm to be generalization.

More concretely we say, algorithm for representing FEAS should be more than dealing with reflexive CPG. This study proposes a generalized algorithm which is able to be applied practical customers' thought when customers select products that straddle multiple market segments.

Next chapter, we clarify the conditions under FEAS existing and we extract the required relations of evaluating attributes for obtaining FEAS.

Table 1. Relations among evaluating attributes

Condition of *CPG*	Required kind of evaluating attribute to represent *CPG*	Required sufficient relations of the attributes to represent *CPG*
CGP is total ordered relation	single evaluating attributes	total ordered relation
CGP is partial ordered relation	a set of evaluating attributes	total ordered relation
CGP's diagonal elements are filled	a family of evaluating attributes' sets	total ordered relation
CGP's diagonal elements are void	a family of evaluating attributes' sets	total ordered relation proper total order relation
CGP's diagonal elements are arbitrary	a family of evaluating attributes' sets	total ordered relation proper total order relation equivalent subset's relation

3   Concepts of Generalized Algorithm for Obtaining FAES

Table 1 summarizes relations among evaluating attributes. If CGP is total ordered relation, we simply apply single evaluating attributes to it. If CGP is partial ordered relation, it has to think on Multi-Attribute Decision-Making (MADM) proposed by Keeney [7] and it need a set of evaluating attributes.

Next we move when CPG's diagonal elements are filled. As you know it is the previous situation. In the case that CPG is reflexive, an existence of FEAS is assured by the following proposition.

Proposition 2

Let CPG be reflexive Then, there exists a total ordered information system $<U, Q, V, f, \{ R_q \mid q \in Q \} >$ in which the accuracy of approximation is 1.

Where a total ordered information system indicates that $\{ R_q \mid q \in Q \}$ is a total ordered relation;

$$\{ R_q \mid q \in Q \} = \{ T_q \mid q \in Q \} \tag{9}$$

$\{ T_q \mid q \in Q \}$ is a total ordered relation. This proposition is presented by the form that a family of subsets $\{ I_1, \dots, I_n \}$ is obtained when CPG is reflexive [2].

Next we move when CPG's diagonal elements are void. For representing an existence of FEAS we propose new information system which is defined by the following proposition.

Proposition 3

Let CPG' diagonal elements be void. Then, there exists a proper total ordered information system $< U, Q, V, f, \{ R_q \mid q \in Q \} >$ in which the accuracy of approximation is 1.

Where a proper total ordered information system indicates that $\{ R_q \mid q \in Q \}$ includes a proper total ordered relation, this is defined by

$$\{ R_q \mid q \in Q \} = \{ T_q \mid q \in Q \} \cup \left\{ ((T_q)^{-1})^c \mid q \in Q \right\} \tag{10}$$

$((T_q)^{-1})^c$ is a proper total order relation. Proper is derived from proper subset. This relation means the relation that equivalence relations have been removed from total ordered relation. This relation supports "prefer" of customer's preference.

This proposition assures that a family of subsets $\{I_1, \ldots, I_n\}$ is obtained when CPG's diagonal elements are void.

Finally, we move when CPG's diagonal elements are arbitrary. In other words, there is no limitation on CPG's diagonal elements. For representing an existence of FEAS we propose new information system which is defined by the following proposition.

Proposition 4

Let CPG be customer's preference grid on U. Then, there exists an extended total ordered information system $< U, Q, V, f, \{R_q \mid q \in Q\} >$ in which the accuracy of approximation is 1.

Where an extended total ordered information system indicates that $\{R_q \mid q \in Q\}$ includes an equivalent subset's relation, this is defined by

$$\{R_q \mid q \in Q\}$$
$$= \{T_q \mid q \in Q\} \cup \{((T_q)^{-1})^c \mid q \in Q\} \cup \{T_q' \mid q \in Q\} \tag{11}$$

T_q' is an equivalent subset's relation, when $T_q' = U' \times U'$ and $U' = [x]_{T_q \cap ((T_q)^{-1})^c}$, for any $q \in Q$ and $x \in U$.

From the following discussion, these are 3 information systems; a total ordered information system, a proper total ordered information system and an extended total ordered information system. A total ordered and a proper total ordered information systems are subsets of an extended total ordered information system. Because an extended total ordered information system does not let CPG' diagonal elements to any limitation.

Our main aim in this paper is to provide a generalized algorithm for obtaining FEAS. Here, we present the conditions under which FEAS exist and we extract the required relations of evaluating attribute for obtaining FEAS. We summarize the followings and propose definitions for obtaining FEAS after that.

An extended total ordered information system in the generalized algorithm is defined as the following 5-tuples.

In order to obtain FEAS, we define the following entities.

$$< U, Q, V, f, \{R_q \mid q \in Q\} > \tag{12}$$

Where $U, Q, V, f: U \times Q \to V$ are the same as information system defined in chapter 2. R_q defined in Definition (11) is a set of relations on q. R_q loads customer's preference grid on U by using a total ordered relation T_q, a proper total order relation $((T_q)^{-1})^c$ and a equivalent subset's relation T_q'. We define UR_q as follows.

$$UR_q = \{(x, y) \in U \times U \mid (f(x, q), f(y, q)) \in R_q\} \tag{13}$$

$S(x, y)_p$ denotes the following similarity class of a preference pair (x, y).

$$S(x, y)_p = \cap \{UR_q \mid q \in P, (x,y) \in UR_q\} \tag{14}$$
$$= \{(v.w) \mid \forall q \in Q : (x,y) \in UR_q \rightarrow (v.w) \in UR_q\}$$

Where $(v.w), S(x, y)_P, q$ and Q are the same definitions as the formers. Upper and lower approximations are the same too.

Proposition 4 shows that $\alpha_P(CPG) = 1$ if and only if CPG can be represented by FEAS as a family of subsets $\{I_1, ..., I_n\}$. Note that

$$CPG = \cup \{\cap \{UR_q \mid q \in I_i\} \mid i = 1, ..., n\} \tag{15}$$

means the following condition,

$$(x,y) \in CPG \leftrightarrow \exists I \in \{I_1, I_2, ..., I_i\} : \forall q \in I : (x,y) \in UR_q \tag{16}$$

Proposition 5

Let $(v.w) \notin CPG$, $\alpha_P(CPG) \neq 1$, $(v.w) \in S(x,y)_P$, $(x,y) \in CPG$. Then there be attribute $h \in P$, such that $(x,y) \in UR_h$ and $(v.w) \notin UR_h$. Let all of attribute h's set be H. If $P' = (P \cup H)$, Then $\alpha_{P'}(CPG) = 1$.

Proposition 5 proves that accuracy of approximation converges at 1. Even if accuracy of approximation is not 1, accuracy of approximation is converged by addition attributes which let accuracy of approximation to increase.

From Propositions 1 and 4, it is easy to show that for any CPG, $\alpha_P(P_*(CPG)) = 1$, and $\alpha_P(P^*(CPG)) = 1$. And then there exist FEAS as a family of subsets $\{I_1, I_2, ..., I_i\}$.

4 Calculation According to the Algorithm

In this chapter, we show a simple example according to the algorithm in Figure 1. These relations are shown at Table 2.

We construct CPG from pairwise comparison at first step. In a questionnaire of pairwise comparison, we ask him/her the following preference in number of combinations from all object pairs.

Both are preferred to each other,	mark "=".
One is preferred to the other,	mark ">"or"<".
One is preferred and equal to the other,	mark "≥"or"≤".
Both are not comparable each other,	not any mark.

Let $U = \{a, b, c, d\}$, then there are 6 combinations of pairs. We get Table 3 as a result of pairwise comparison and show relations among U in Figure 2. CPG is constructed as Figure 3. In the Figures from 3 to 6, mark "×" is at row X and column Y means that the object X is preferred to the object Y.

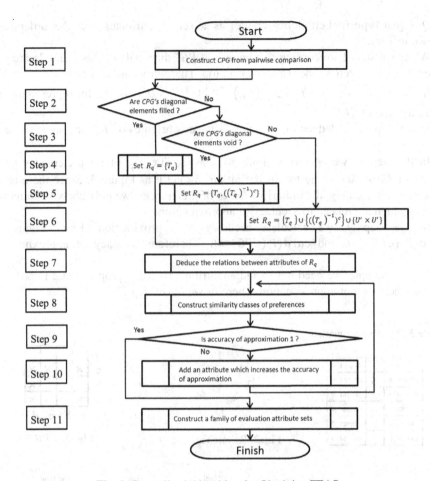

Fig. 1. Generalized Algorithm for Obtaining FEAS

Table 2. Relation between Step to Definitions and Propositions

		Content	Definition	Proposition
Step,	1	Construct CPG from pairwise comparison	(1), (12)	–
Step,	2	Are CPG's diagonal elements filled ?	–	–
Step,	3	Are CPG's diagonal elements void ?	–	–
Step,	4	Set $R_q = \{T_q\}$	(9)	2
Step,	5	Set $R_q = \{T_q\} \cup \{((T_q)^{-1})^c\}$	(10)	3
Step,	6	Set $R_q = \{T_q\} \cup \{((T_q)^{-1})^c\} \cup \{U' \times U'\}$	(11)	4
Step,	7	Deduce the relations between attributes of R_q	(13)	–
Step,	8	Construct similarity classes of preferences	(14)	–
Step,	9	Is calculate Accuracy of approximation 1 ?	(5),(6),(7)	1
Step,	10	Add an attribute which increases the accuracy of approximation	–	5
Step,	11	Construct a family of evaluating attributes' sets	(15),(16)	1,4

$Q = \{\text{car type}, \text{fuel efficiency}, \text{space}\}$ is a set of attributes and the orders are shown in Table 4.

We move step 2. According to Figure 3, CPG' diagonals of this example are not filled. We move step 3. These are not void too. Therefor we move step 6.

In the step 6, We set $\{T_q\} \cup \{((T_q)^{-1})^c\} \cup \{U' \times U'\}$ as R_q for representing an arbitrary type of CPG .

In the step 7, we deduce the relations between attributes of R_q and show these at Figure 4.

In the step 8, we construct similarity classes $S(x,y)_p$ of all preferences pairs (x,y) in CPG. According to this definition, we get it as Figure 5. Since there is no space for representing all similarity classes of preferences, we only show 6 similarity classes which are related to accuracy of approximation.

In the step 9, we calculate accuracy of approximation. From Figure 6, $card(P^*(CPG))$=6 and $card(P_*(CPG))$=6. Therefore accuracy of approximation is 1.

In this example, we need not to add an attribute by using proposition 2 in order to increase accuracy of approximation. Therefor we move step 11.

Table 3. Pairwise comparison

object a		object b
object a	≤	object c
object a	>	object d
object b		object c
object b	>	object d
object c	>	object d

Fig. 2. Relation among U

Fig. 3. CPG

Table 4. Attribute's orders

	car type	fuel effi-ciency	space
object a	0 (Hi–brid)	1	3
object b	1 (Gas)	3	1
object c	0 (Hi–brid)	2	2
object d	1 (Gas)	4	4

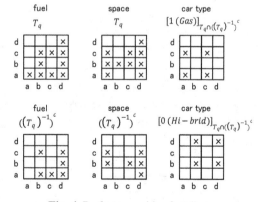

Fig. 4. Preference grids of attributes

At final step, we construct FEAS. (a, a) on CPG is construct by $S(a, a)_p$ and $S(a, a)_p$ consists of $\{Hi\text{-}brid(U' \times U'), \text{fuel efficiency}(T_q), \text{space}(T_q)\}$. It regards I_1. We construct remaining 5 preferences on CPG; the same shall apply hereinafter. After we calculate these and consolidate these into Table 5. Table 5 indicates on which a set of attributes all pair of preference are based.

According to the generalized algorithm for obtaining FEAS, we get FEAS of customer's preference which does not show that CPG is reflexive

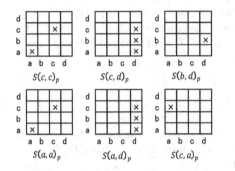

P-Upper approximation   P-Lower approximation

Fig. 5. $S(x, y)_p$ related to accuracy of approximation

Fig. 6. Accuracy of approximations

Table 5. Relaions among prefernce pairs and attributes' set of FEAS

Pair No	Prefernce pair	FEAS' No	Attributes' set of FEAS
1	$(a, a), (c, c)$	I_1	$\{Hi\text{-}brid(U' \times U'), \text{fuel efficiency}(T_q), \text{space}(T_q)\}$
2	(a, d)	I_2	$\left\{\text{fuel efficiency}\left(((T_q)^{-1})^c\right), \text{space}\left(((T_q)^{-1})^c\right)\right\}$
3	$(b, d), (c, a), (c, d)$	I_3	$\left\{Hi\text{-}brid(U' \times U'), \text{space}\left(((T_q)^{-1})^c\right)\right\}$

5   Conclusion

It is important to pursue FEAS which represents diversified relations of customer's preferences. It was shown that there was FEAS which represents reflexive relations of customer's preferences. Even if relations of customer's preferences are not shown as reflexive, we propose the method which represents FEAS in this paper. We clarify the conditions under FEAS existing and we extract the required relations of evaluating attributes for obtaining FEAS. Consequently, we propose the generalized algorithm which allows obtaining FEAS without limited status of CPG's diagonal elements. Obtaining customer's preference as FEAS means to understand features or functions on which customers focus. In the former example, these are preference of Hi-brid and space and if car type is gas, fuel efficiency and space are needed. It was shown that a customer had multi attributes' set and switched these properly by how to use.

The diversification of the consumers' demand changed a marketing method. Target of current marketing is not a set of customers who have some stable information but individual. Where, some stable information means like address, sex and what not. In actually, advertisements are changed by personal queries in Google. Other way, recommended products change by a personal purchasehistory in the Amazon. More and more companies will investigate large quantity information of individual consumer.

Applying our proposed Algorithm, we may say that we can do product development or recommendation with high accuracy. Because we clear the customer's thought which we were not able to express so far. The information helps to supply products which customer desire.

References

1. Mogawa, T., Saitoh, F., Ishizu, S.: Algorithm for a Family of Evaluation Attributes Sets Representing Customer Preference Relation. In: Proceedings of Asia Network Quality Congress 2012 (ANQ 2012), vol. 10, p. 86 (2012)
2. Ghehmann, A., Nagai, Y., Yoshida, O., Ishizu, S.: Rough evaluation structure: Application of rough set theory to generate simple rules for inconsistent preference relation. Kansei Engineering International Journal 10(1), 1–9 (2010)
3. Ghehmann, A., Ishizu, S.: Minimal Evaluation Structure for Inconsistent Multi-attributes Decision-Making – Selection and Addtion Method of Evaluation Attributes. Journal of the Japan Society for Management Information 14(1), 85–95 (2005)
4. Ishizu, S., Gehrmann, A.: Rough preference: extended concept of rough se theory. In: ISQFD 2006, Tokyo (2006)
5. Pawlak, Z., Slowinski, R.: Rough set approach to multi-attribute decision analysis. European Journal of Operations Research 72, 443–459 (1994)
6. Saaty, T.L.: Decision Making for Leaders: The Analytic Hierarchy Process for Decisions in a Complex World, vol. 2. Rws Pubns. (1999/2000)
7. Keeney, R.L., Raiffa, H.: Decision with multiple objectives, preferences and value tradeoffs. John Wiley & Sons Inc. (1976)

TAGZILLA: Tag-Based File Storage and Retrieval

Vikram Nair, Vijayanand Banahatti, and Niranjan Pedanekar

Systems Research Lab, Tata Research Development & Design Centre,
Tata Consultancy Services, 54 B Hadapsar Industrial Estate, Pune 411013, India
{vikram.nair,vijayanand.banahatti,n.pedanekar}@tcs.com

Abstract. Users have to rely on memory for storing or retrieving data in Hierarchical Folder Organization (HFO) such as the Microsoft Windows Explorer for managing their information. We propose 20 Interface Design Objectives (IDOs) for Personal Information Management (PIM) interfaces. We find IDOs of HFO that need the most improvement using a qualitative survey of 66 users on importance and satisfaction scales. We present an alternate tag-based interface called TAGZILLA based on the concept of the 'Stream of Consciousness'. TAGZILLA provides users with an interface to create tags for storing files and retrieve files based on tags. It also suggests tags during storage and retrieval. We report an increase in satisfaction for all IDOs using a return survey with 20 participants who used TAGZILLA. We also present a preliminary quantitative experimental comparison of TAGZILLA with the Windows Explorer interface for the IDOs needing most improvement.

Keywords: Microsoft Windows Explorer, Personal Information Management, Tagging, Human Computer Interfaces, Hierarchical Folder Organization.

1 Introduction

A vast majority of users use the tree-based Hierarchical Folder Organization (HFO) such as the Microsoft Windows Explorer to organize information on computers. This would seem natural in the last century when users were used to physically filing paper documents in folders. But even in today's connected world with a much wider variety of information, 56-68% of file retrieval is still done using folder navigation despite advances in technologies such as desktop search [1].

Information can belong to multiple folders as humans naturally associate information with multiple concepts. But HFO has conditioned users to think of information in terms of hierarchies and not in terms of correlation with other concepts. They have made users think of 'where' to look rather than 'what' to look for [2].

Search using location is perhaps natural when information is limited. Let us consider the real world task of storing and retrieving a blue shirt. One would simply have to find a good place to store it, and then remember the location where the shirt was kept in order to retrieve it. The problem is that this works for a limited number of shirts, but would be taxing when the number of shirts and storage locations increase.

S. Yamamoto (Ed.): HIMI/HCII 2013, Part I, LNCS 8016, pp. 505–514, 2013.

Furthermore, a user could describe a blue shirt uniquely by a stream of concepts that appears in her mind such as 'worn at graduation' or 'gifted on Valentine's Day' in order to differentiate it from or associate it with other shirts or things. But, the HFO forces the user to take a decision for storing the shirt – whether to choose the 'Blue' folder inside the 'Shirts' folder OR to make a new folder called 'Graduation' inside it OR to choose the 'Graduation stuff' folder, even if all are valid storage places. At the time of retrieval of the blue shirt, the user would either have to recall where exactly the shirt was kept or would have to explore several possible paths using partial recall and even brute force.

This need for relying on memory of a path rather than how the user recognizes the object is a major drawback of the HFO. Bloehdorn and Völkel [3] summarize the deficiencies of the HFO as: need to know exact file location, inability to represent orthogonal information as folders, dependence on order of directories, absence of query refinement and lack of navigation aids. Given such limitations, we believe that there is a need to find alternative interfaces which depend on remembering associations rather than recalling its exact location and traversal path.

In this paper, we present TAGZILLA, a tag-based approach to Personal Information Management (PIM) that we have built to complement the way humans think. Our specific contributions are:

1. We present the TAGZILLA interface, which is based on the concept of the 'Stream of Consciousness'.
2. We define 20 specific interface design objectives for a PIM interface.
3. We find the objectives which need improvement in an HFO interface, specifically Microsoft Windows Explorer, using an importance-satisfaction survey of users.
4. We report an increase in user satisfaction for these objectives in a return survey of users test driving TAGZILLA.
5. We present quantitative results from preliminary experiments comparing TAGZILLA with a traditional HFO, viz. the Microsoft Windows Explorer.

2 What Needs to Improve in PIM Interfaces

Voit et al. [4] suggest broad requirements for PIM interfaces such as compatibility with current user habits, minimal interference and support for multiple contexts under which user plans to retrieve files. Before we set out designing a new interface, we wanted to get a better understanding of which specific PIM functionality needed improvement for a traditional HFO. We divided the PIM functionality in two broad categories, viz. 'store' and 'retrieve'. 'Store' had further subcategories, viz. create file, categorize / group files, copy file and delete file. 'Retrieve' also had further subcategories, viz. search file, find related / similar files, compare files, view file contents, and filter / sort files. Based on user operations normally carried out in each of the above subcategories, we came up with 20 Interface Design Objectives (IDOs), e.g. 'reduce navigation path to find a file', 'reduce time required to find a file', 'increase likelihood of finding related files'.

We followed the Importance-Satisfaction (I-S) model [5] for identifying the functionality needing improvement. An I-S model finds the product or service attributes which need the most improvement by rating each attribute in terms of its perceived importance and the perceived level of satisfaction with it [5-7]. The 'to-be-improved' attributes lie in the high importance and low satisfaction quadrant of an importance-satisfaction graph. We conducted an I-S survey on 66 users consisting of scientists, administrative staff, IT professionals and students. They rated the 20 IDOs on their importance and satisfaction with an HFO interface, viz. Microsoft Windows Explorer. Both scales were 5-point Likert scales ('not at all important' to 'extremely important' and 'not at all satisfactory' to 'extremely satisfactory').

We found the most important 'to-be-improved' IDOs in the high importance and low satisfaction region, viz. 1. Reduce navigation path to find desired location, 2. Reduce time required to find a file, 3. Increase likelihood of finding the most appropriate file, 4. Reduce time required to find related or similar files, and 5. Make PIM operations more natural. The survey results are shown in Fig. 3 in comparison with a return survey using the TAGZILLA interface (See Section 5).

3   The Key Idea Behind TAGZILLA

Consider the shirt scenario that we mentioned in Section 1. Now imagine a hypothetical assistant. You tell him the things that come to your mind when you see the shirt. For example, you tell him that 'it was bought at Acme' and 'worn at graduation'. In addition, the assistant himself notices obvious things about the shirt such as color and brand. While retrieving the shirt, you may recall 'the Acme shirt' and tell the assistant about it. If there are two shirts from Acme, the assistant narrows down your quest by suggesting 'graduation' for this shirt, and 'Valentine's day' for another one. If you just remember 'blue', the assistant suggests further options which might include 'graduation'. This helps you quickly find the shirt by remembering things that come to your mind when you think of that shirt.

We present a PIM interface called TAGZILLA that simulates the above process. It relies on capturing the concepts that come to user's mind on seeing a file while storing, and on thinking of a file while retrieving. The Concise Oxford English Dictionary defines a similar concept as the 'Stream of Consciousness' (SOC) as *"a person's thoughts and conscious reactions to events, perceived as a continuous flow"* [8]. In our context, we define it as *"a series of concepts that come to a user's mind one after the other on seeing or thinking of an object"*. We use this definition as a basis for our interface design. We capture the SOC as a series of tags as tagging is emerging as a promising alternative to HFOs [9].

In TAGZILLA, the user utilizes her SOC to create tags for a file she encounters. At the time of retrieval, the user remembers a file by tags associated with it and is able to generate the SOC, albeit not in the same order or number. TAGZILLA provides help during storage and retrieval by suggesting tags of files associated with the tag typed in, and narrowing down the search space.

4   User Interface Design

We developed the prototype of TAGZILLA as a web interface that opens in a browser on Windows XP and 7 machines. A Windows service monitors addition of a new file or changes to a file. Before we describe the interface flow, we define the types of tagging that TAGZILLA provides:

Automated Tags: A set of pre-defined tags are automatically assigned to a file based on parameters such as extension, type and date. These are extracted from the ID3 metadata associated with the file. If a file 'Vijay.jpeg' is introduced to TAGZILLA, it automatically tags it with the tags such as 'Pictures', 'jpeg' and '23/01/2012' based on the ID3 metadata.

Personalized Tags: When a user uses her SOC for a file, she comes up with unique tags that might help her identify the file in future. Also, TAGZILLA suggests questions such as 'Who gave the file(s)?', 'On what occasion?', 'Where will you use it?' to aid the user's SOC. For the example mentioned above, let us assume that Vijay is wearing a blue shirt in the picture 'Vijay.jpeg' at the time of his graduation. The above questions might prompt him to create personalized tags such as 'Me', 'Blue Shirt' and 'Graduation'. He could also add other tags such as 'happy' that come to his mind on seeing this picture.

Tag Suggestions: TAGZILLA also aids the SOC by providing tag suggestions during file storage and retrieval. It does so by finding files with the tag given by the user, and suggesting the tags associated with these files as 'related tags'. The related tags are extracted using their proximity in the tag file graph and other factors such as most recent usage and file extensions. For the example mentioned in Fig. 1, if the user thinks of the tag 'ACME', TAGZILLA aids the SOC by suggesting 'Development', 'Testing', and 'Research' based on the tag file graph.

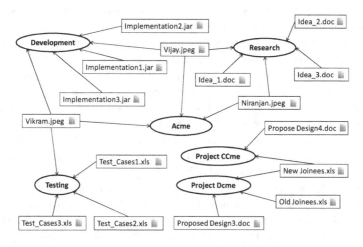

Fig. 1. An example of a tag-file graph in TAGZILLA

The TAGZILLA interface consists of two screens: one for storing (or tagging) files, and one for retrieval. The interface flow is as follows:

4.1 File Storage

1. When a file(s) is copied or created into the file system or in a central folder, a Microsoft Windows service registers a change in the file system.
2. At this point, TAGZILLA creates automatic tags for the file(s).
3. TAGZILLA interface prompts the user to create personalized tags. It also provides an autocomplete feature to quickly recreate existing tags.
4. TAGZILLA also gives tag suggestions aiding the user's SOC.
5. Personalized tag(s) created by the user, selected from suggestions, and automated tags created by TAGZILLA are stored against the file in the TAGZILLA database.
6. User can also assign tags to untagged files listed under the 'Untagged files'.

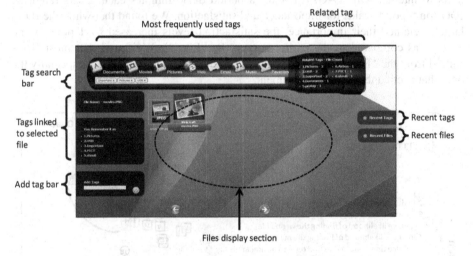

Fig. 2. File Retrieval Page

4.2 File Retrieval

1. At the time of retrieval, the user uses the retrieval screen shown in Fig. 2.
2. The frequently used tags are provided at the top for quicker retrieval.
3. The user enters a tag that comes to her mind about a file(s) she wants to retrieve in the search bar. An autocomplete feature is provided if the tag already exists to avoid minor variations in tags such as 'Shirt' and 'Shirts'.
4. TAGZILLA displays thumbnails of all the files tagged with this tag in the display section below the search bar.
5. Based on the current tag, TAGZILLA suggests further tags as 'related tags' on the right hand of the search bar to aid user's SOC.
6. As the user adds another tag in the search bar, the search results in the display section are updated by showing the files also having this tag.

7. A tag in the search bar can be deleted by clicking a cross provided on the tag. The search results are updated accordingly.
8. On hovering over the file thumbnail, one can see the tags associated with the file on the left hand side of the display section. One can also add a new tag to a file using the 'Add tag' box on the bottom left.
9. The 'Recent tags' and 'Recent files' shortcuts on the right hand side allow quick access to recent activity.
10. The file can be launched by double clicking the thumbnail within the browser.

5   Results and Discussion

In order to evaluate the effectiveness of TAGZILLA, we first conducted an I-S survey-based evaluation similar to the one mentioned in section 2. We allowed 20 users to interact with TAGZILLA for a period of 30 minutes each. Users rated the IDOs on 5-point scales for importance and satisfaction. We found that while the IDOs largely retained their importance, the satisfaction levels increased by 1 point on an average as compared to the earlier survey (See Fig. 3). We found that most IDOs shifted from the 'To-be-improved' quadrant to the 'Excellent' quadrant, especially the ones that needed the most improvement.

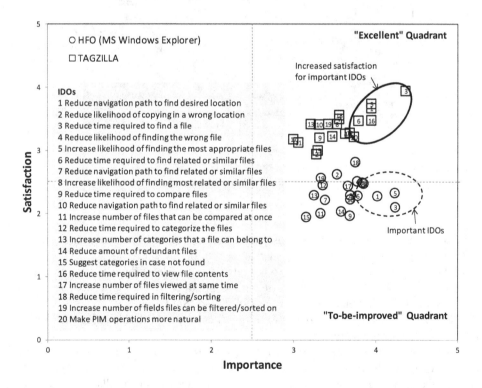

Fig. 3. I-S survey results for HFO and TAGZILLA interfaces

We then conducted a preliminary controlled experiment on 18 test subjects to compare TAGZILLA to the Windows Explorer interface. The test subjects were given 30 files along with their descriptions. Group A consisted of 9 test subjects. Each subject was asked to form a directory structure to store these files. Group B consisted of 9 test subjects. Each subject was asked to create tags for each file. After a week, the test subjects were asked to retrieve files for 10 practical scenarios (e.g. 'My home interior decoration plan need to be shared with my wife', 'Need to apply for home loan, so need the latest soft copy of my pay slip', 'I need to refer some old project architectures document as reference'). Group A used the Microsoft Windows Explorer for this task, while Group B used TAGZILLA. We recorded the screen activity as each test subject performed the given tasks. We then analyzed the recordings, and measured the number of clicks and the time required to complete each task. We present a discussion on the results for each important IDO:

1. **Reduction in navigation path to find desired location:** For TAGZILLA, we counted a text entry, a tag deletion and a tag selection as a click. We found that the number of clicks required for retrieving files reduced by an average of 26% with TAGZILLA. We attribute the larger number of clicks to the brute force directory traversal behavior shown by the HFO users, where a user selects a folder, browses content and repeats the process if the file is not found [10].

2. **Reduction in time required to find a file:** We found that the time required to retrieve a file increased by an average of 27% with TAGZILLA. We attribute this to the inclination of TAGZILLA subjects to start typing in the first 'tag-like' term in the task description rather than understanding its context as we normally do in case of Windows Explorer. We believe that this behavior will reduce with training and prolonged real-life use of the interface. Also, as number of files and tags increase, the suggestions in TAGZILLA will be able to provide more SOC help to users.

3. **Increase in likelihood of finding the most appropriate files:** We found that relevant files were not found in 3 cases by HFO users. All TAGZILLA users were able to find relevant files eventually. We attribute this to the reluctance of some HFO users to traverse all directories using brute force. Instead, the TAGZILLA users found it easier to try out multiple tags in case they chose the wrong tags.

4. **Reduction in time required to find related or similar files:** We did not have specific test cases to evaluate this IDO and will take it up in the next phase.

5. **Make PIM operations more natural:** We did not have measurable data on this IDO, though the I-S survey reports an increase of an average of 0.73 points.

We did not separately measure the storage times for HFO and TAGZILLA. But we found that qualitatively, storage for TAGZILLA was much quicker as the users had to use their SOC rather than think about where a file would go in an HFO.

We made an interesting observation with the correlation between the number of clicks and the time it took to retrieve a file (See Fig. 4). The median number of clicks for HFO was 4, while that for TAGZILLA was 3. We considered two groups X (<=3 clicks) and Y (>3 clicks). For group X, we found that the average time per click was 6.24 second for HFO and 5.47 second for TAGZILLA. For group Y, the same metric was for 3.09 second for HFO and 6.57 second for TAGZILLA. We explain this by some HFO users using brute force directory traversal when they cannot find a file. Since they are experienced in using the HFO interface, they do it efficiently. But when a user is able to find a file quickly, the TAGZILLA interface is more or as efficient as HFO. We believe that the brute force traversal is not practical with a larger number of folders and deeper trees. We also believe that as the number of files increase, the associations among files also increase enabling TAGZILLA to suggest related tags more often further increasing the efficiency of retrieval.

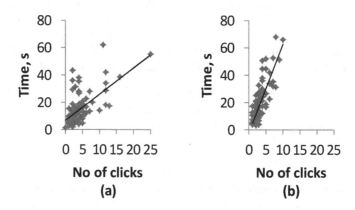

Fig. 4. Correlation between number of clicks and time of retrieval for (a) HFO and (b) TAGZILLA interfaces

6   Related Work

Researchers have proposed a variety of approaches to overcome deficiencies of HFOs: predictive systems such as FolderPredictor [11] which uses machine learning algorithms to predict folders a user might want to access, 'Stuff I've seen' [12] which indexes information from multiple sources that a user has 'seen' before; semantic systems such as the work by Faubel and Kuschel [2] which expands the metadata about a file into a folder path; and tagging-based solutions such as TagFS [3] and tagstore [9].

As tagging is a key concept in TAGZILLA, we discuss some of the tagging approaches developed to overcome the limitations of HFO.

Bloehdorn and Völkel [3] present TagFS that converts a folder structure into tags and adds semantic data such as name, user and a tag label. This makes the retrieval independent of the order of the folder structure. Unlike in TAGZILLA, TagFS does not provide tag suggestions and does not automatically tag files with their metadata.

The most relevant study to our work is the one by Voit et al. [9]. They present a comprehensive study using their tagging framework 'tagstore'. Tagstore allows user to tag files and expands the tags into trees called 'TagTrees'. So, a tagged file can be found under each permutation of trees created using its tags. Users use these HFO structures to locate their files. In doing so, they increase the likelihood of coming across a directory named after a tag, which houses symbolic links for other tags as well the file. A main differences between TAGZILLA and tagstore are that the former does not require the user to depend on HFO and it provides additional tags as suggestions based on their proximity in the tag graph.

In the same paper, Voit et al. present an experimental study comparing Microsoft Windows Explorer and tagstore. They report no noticeable difference in retrieval times between tagstore and HFO, while we report an increase of 27% in retrieval using TAGZILLA. This could be attributed to the users using a more familiar HFO for retrieval in case of tagstore. The same study also reports a decrease in number of clicks (27%) similar to that reported for TAGZILLA (26%). These two comparisons are interesting given that TAGZILLA did not use a familiar HFO for retrieval, had a larger time interval (1 week as opposed to 15 minutes) between storage and retrieval tasks, and did not have any test subjects familiar with tag-based interfaces. The same study also finds that 'fast' users performed well in tagging. While we second that, we report in our study that the users of HFOs who spent their time in brute force directory navigation were doing it 'fast', but not efficiently.

7   Conclusion and Outlook

We developed TAGZILLA, a tag-based PIM interface, as an alternative to HFO. The main contribution of TAGZILLA is that it provides a means to capture a user's SOC during file storage and retrieval as tags. It uses association among tags to suggest tags to the user and aid her SOC. Our other contribution is definition of 20 IDOs for PIM interfaces and determination of PIM functionality that needs to be improved in a traditional HFO using a user survey. We observed a 1 point increase on a 5-point satisfaction scale for users who took a test drive on TAGZILLA. We conducted a preliminary controlled experiment to compare the performance of TAGZILLA with a traditional HFO such as Microsoft Windows Explorer. We found that the number of clicks required for file retrieval reduced by an average of 26% with TAGZILLA, while the time required increased by an average of 27%. We found that TAGZILLA was comparable to HFO in retrieving files when files could be found in less number of clicks.

We propose to conduct more experiments in a realistic setting where users use TAGZILLA as an alternative PIM for longer periods of time. We also plan to improve tag suggestions with semantic association using WordNet and Wikipedia. We also plan to include the 'hard-won understanding of information' by users [13] using a tag-file visualization in the interface.

Acknowledgments. We would like to thank the associates of TRDDC for participating in user surveys, Yahya Poonawala and Natasha Shah for help in conducting surveys, and Maitreya Natu for review and useful comments. We also thank Sachin Lodha and Prof. Harrick Vin for their support in this activity.

References

1. Bergman, O., et al.: Improved search engines and navigation preference in personal information management. ACM Transactions on Information Systems (TOIS) 26(4), 20 (2008)
2. Faubel, S., Kuschel, C.: Towards Semantic File System Interfaces. In: Proceedings of the Poster and Demonstration Session at the 7th International Semantic Web Conference, ISWC 2008, vol. 401 (2008)
3. Bloehdorn, S., et al.: TagFS -tag semantics for hierarchical file systems. In: Proceedings of the 6th International Conference on Knowledge Management, I-KNOW 2006 (2006)
4. Voit, K., Andrews, K., Slany, W.: Why personal information management (PIM) technologies are not widespread. In: ASIS&T 2009 Workshop on Personal Information Management, PIM 2009 (2009), http://pimworkshop.org/2009/papers/voit-pim2009.PDF.2009
5. Yang, C.-C.: Establishment and applications of the integrated model of service quality measurement. Managing Service Quality 13(4), 310–324 (2003)
6. Matzler, K., Hinterhuber, H.H.: How to make product development projects more successful by integrating Kano's model of customer satisfaction into quality function deployment. Hinterhuber 18(1), 25–38 (1998)
7. Ulwick, A.W.: Turn customer input into innovation. Harvard Business Review 80(1), 91 (2002)
8. Soanes, C., Stevenson, A. (eds.): Dictionary, Oxford English. Concise Oxford English Dictionary. Oxford University Press, Oxford (2006) (revised)
9. Voit, K., Andrews, K., Slany, W.: Tagging might not be slower than filing in folders. In: Proceedings of the 2012 ACM Annual Conference Extended Abstracts on Human Factors in Computing Systems Extended Abstracts. ACM (2012)
10. Barreau, D., Nardi, B.A.: Finding and reminding: file organization from the desktop. ACM SigChi. Bulletin 27(3), 39–43 (1995)
11. Bao, X., Dieterich, T.G.: FolderPredictor: Reducing the cost of reaching the right folder. ACM Transactions on Intelligent Systems and Technology (TIST) 2(1), 8 (2011)
12. Dumais, S., et al.: Stuff I've seen: a system for personal information retrieval and re-use. In: Proceedings of the 26th Annual International ACM SIGIR Conference on Research and Development in Information Retrieval. ACM (2003)
13. Jones, W., et al.: Don't take my folders away!: organizing personal information to get things done. In: CHI 2005 Extended Abstracts on Human Factors in Computing Systems. ACM (2005)

Proposal of Avatar Generating Method
by Composition of the Portraits Made by Friends

Masashi Okubo and Satoshi Nobuta

Doshisha University,
1-3 Miyakodani, Tatara, Kyotanabe,
Kyoto,610-0321, Japan
mokubo@mail.doshisha.ac.jp,
dum0136@mail4.doshisha.ac.jp

Abstract. Recently, the Remote communication through the Internet has been performed actively. And as a remote communication tool, the uses of graphic avatars are especially popular in Japan. However, in many cases, the avatar used on the communication is not mirrored to a user who creates the avatar himself using the application software provided for the remote communication support system. Therefore, the remote friends cannot imagine the appearance of the user from his/her avatar at all. In this research, we will propose a method of creating an avatar. The method shows that the avatar is constructed by merging some portraits, which are created by user's friends. We have developed the prototype systems for creating a portrait and an avatar composed of some portraits. This paper describes methods and systems of creating a portrait and an avatar. We performed some experiments to evaluate the usability of the proposed system and the quality of an avatar created on the proposed system. As an experimental result, it is revealed that the avatar, which is created on the proposed system, tends to be preferred by the user and friends.

Keywords: Avatar, Portrait, Avatar communication.

1   Introduction

Recently, the Remote communication through the Internet has been performed instead of Face-to-face communication. We can use various kinds of communication support applications, and choose one of them depending on the situation and the relationship between us and our remote speakers. From this viewpoint, the avatar chat is one of the superior applications as an anonymous communication tool [1], [2].

Generally, it is said that there are two types of user's recognition of an avatar. The first is that the user uses an avatar for expressing himself. In this type, the user creates the avatar based on his physical appearance. The other type is that the user uses an avatar for his ideal image.

There are various kinds of methods of creating an avatar. Generally, the user uses his/her preferred picture in the communication system, such as chat, SNS, and video

S. Yamamoto (Ed.): HIMI/HCII 2013, Part I, LNCS 8016, pp. 515–523, 2013.

game, where the avatar creating system is pre-installed. However, in this case, while the avatar is preferred by the user, it may be difficult for his/her friends to imagine the user's appearance.

There are some researches and applications for creating an avatar. One is that the system provides various kinds of facial parts, and the user chooses one of them to put it on the face as a base [3]. The other one is that the system creates an avatar from the user's portrait [4]. The avatar created by the first method may be preferred by the user; however friends may not be able to imagine the user. In the case of second method, there are some possibilities that the user does not prefer the automatically-created avatar; however this avatar makes it easier for the friends to imagine the user. One of the important things is that the user can prefer the graphic avatar as his/her own avatar, and that avatar also can make it easier for the friends to imagine the physical appearance of the user.

Therefore, we propose a new method and system for creating an avatar, which are that some friends create some portraits of a target person, and the system creates an avatar by calculating the average of the portraits. The graphic avatar created by our proposed method has high possibility to be preferred by the user, and makes it easier for the friends to imagine the target person.

In this research, we propose the avatar creating system which consists of two sub-systems, the portrait making support system and the avatar constructing system. This paper describes the idea and outline of the proposed system and the sensory evaluation for the system efficiency. In this paper, the image created by friends is called 'portrait' and the image constructed by the proposed method is called 'avatar".

2   Proposed System

The proposed system has been developed on the Android Tablet PC. It is because the tablet PC allows users to intuitively create a portrait by the touch panel operation. The proposed system consists of two sub-systems, the portrait making support system and the avatar constructing system. Some friends of a target person create his/her portrait on the portrait making support system, and the avatar constructing system creates an avatar of the target person based on the average of all his portraits.

2.1   Portrait Making Support System

A Nigaoe Channel, the pre-installed application on the Nintendo Wii, allows users to create different types of avatars by combining a variety of facial parts [3]. The portrait making support system uses the same method as Nigaoe Channel. Figure 1 shows the screen shot example on the portrait making system.

The portrait consists of nine facial parts; contour, hair, eyes, eyebrows, nose, mouth, ears, facial hair and glasses. By combining these features, the user can create a portrait. The portrait can be adjusted by enlarging, reducing, tilting, and moving each facial part to be similar to the target person.

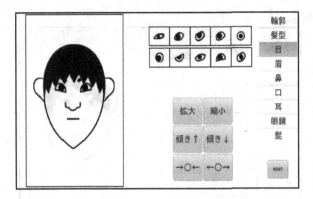

Fig. 1. Screen shot example on the portrait making system

2.2   Avatar Constructing System

The avatar constructing system uses the portraits, which are created on the portrait making support system, and the property data of each facial part used for the avatar.

Each facial part is defined by multiple feature points and their relative coordinates, which are stored in the property data. The number of points is, for example, the mouth has 24 points and the eye has 29 points. The avatar construction on the proposed system is based on the average of positions, sizes, and shapes for each facial part, which is obtained from the portrait. To decide the position and size of each facial part, the system makes an average of the positions in the upper-left corner, and the width and height of the whole facial part. The system decides the shape of each facial part by obtaining the average of each coordinate on the corresponding feature points of the selected part in the property data. For example, in the case of mouth part, loading the coordinates on each feature point of the mouth from all portraits, the system obtains the average coordinate on each feature point, and connects it to the neighbor points. The system connects every point in the same way to configure the facial part, and combines the facial parts by deciding the position and size as described above to create the avatar.

However, only when a large number of portraits with facial hair or glasses exist, the system configures the facial hair or the glasses. The facial hair is configured in the same way as the mouth. For the glasses, most commonly-used one is selected in an avatar.

Figure 2 shows the screen shot example on the avatar constructing system.

3   System Evaluation

3.1   Satisfaction and Similarities of Constructed Avatar

3.1.1   Experimental Object
The sensory evaluation of the satisfaction and similarities of the constructed avatar by the subjects as the portrait creators was investigated to evaluate the portrait making support system and the avatar constructing system.

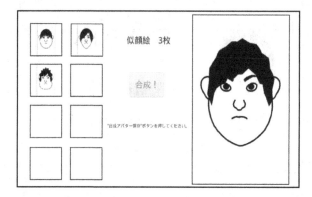

Fig. 2. Screen shot example on the avatar constructing system

3.1.2   Procedures

In this experiment, the subjects were to form a group of four or five people. All subjects create a portrait through looking at a photograph using the portrait making support system. This experiment used the photograph of a famous actor. The avatar constructing system created an avatar by merging all portraits they created. After that, each subject ranked all the portraits and the avatar in order of similarity without knowing which one was the avatar constructed on the avatar constructing system. Next, the experimenter let the subjects know which one was the avatar, and then the subjects declared the degrees of satisfaction and similarities between the target model and the constructed avatar. The subjects are 22 students in their 20s.

Figure 3 shows the experimental scene. And Figure 4 shows the example of portraits created by some subjects (left), and the avatar (right).

Fig. 3. Experimental scenes

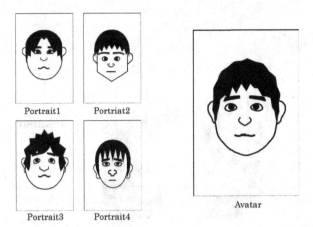

Fig. 4. Example of the portraits created by the subjects (left) and the avatar (right)

3.1.3   Experimental Results and Discussion

Figure 5 shows the graph indicating the ranking place of the avatar when the subjects ranked all portraits and avatar in order of similarity. The figure shows that five of subjects picked the avatar as 1st place, and eleven of them picked it as a 2nd. In this graph, there is a tendency for many of subjects to think that the avatar is more similar to the target person than the portraits they created.

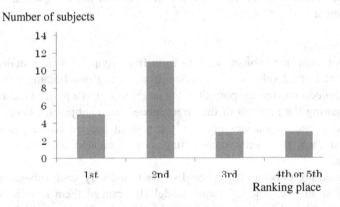

Fig. 5. Ranking histogram place of the avatar among all portraits and avatar

Figure 6 shows the graph indicating the average degrees of satisfaction and similarities between the portrait or the avatar and the target person. In this figure, there is no significant difference between the satisfaction and similarities of the portrait and those of the avatar.

As a result of this experiment, it is found, whereas the constructed avatar tends to be more similar to the target person than each portrait, the satisfaction and similarities are not significantly different between the portrait and the avatar.

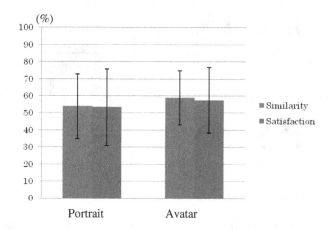

Fig. 6. Average degrees of satisfaction and similarities

3.2   Satisfaction and Similarities for Constructed Avatar from Portraits Created by Friends

3.2.1 Experimental Object

The sensory evaluation of the satisfaction and similarities of the constructed avatar by the target person and his/her friends, who creates his/her portraits, was investigated in this experiment.

3.2.2 Procedures

In this experiment, the subjects were to form five groups of 4 or 5 students in their 20s, for a total of 22 subjects. One person from each group became a target model, and other subjects created the portrait of the target model as a portrait creator.

After creating the portraits of the target model, each subject declared the degrees of satisfaction and similarities between the portrait created himself and the target model. And then, the avatar constructing system created the avatar by merging all portraits.

Viewing all portraits and the avatar displayed randomly, each subject ranked them in order of similarity. And the target model also ranked them in order of ones he wants to use. After that, the experimenter let the subjects know which one was the avatar. And then the subjects declared the degrees of satisfaction and similarities between the avatar and the target model, and the target model also declared the degree of fondness for his avatar.

Figure 7 shows the example of a target model (left), his portraits created by the portrait creators (center), and the avatar constructed by merging the portraits on the avatar constructing system (right).

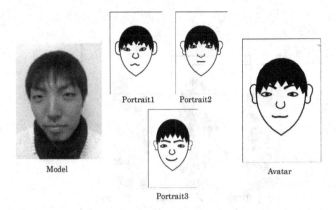

Fig. 7. Example of target model (left), portraits (center) and avatar (right)

3.2.3 Experimental Results and Considerations

Figure 8 shows the graph indicating the ranking place of the avatar when the target model and portrait creators ranked all portraits and avatar in order of similarity.

From this figure, it is obvious that both of them think the avatar constructed on the proposed system is more similar to the target model than the portraits. This shows the effectiveness of the proposed method

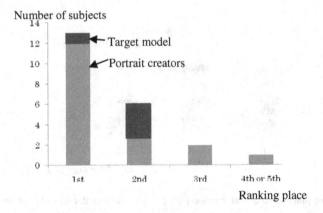

Fig. 8. Ranking place of the avatar among all portraits and avatar

Figure 9 shows the graph indicating the average degrees of satisfaction and similarities between the portrait or the avatar and the target model, which are declared by the target model and portrait creators. There is a significant difference of 10% between the satisfaction and similarities of the portrait and those of the avatar, which are declared by the portrait creators. From these results, the satisfaction and similarities of the avatar constructed on the proposed system tend to be higher than those of the portraits created by the creators.

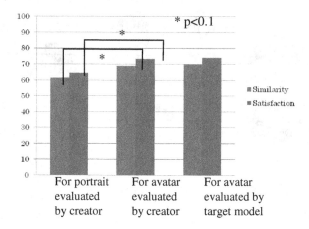

Fig. 9. Average degree of similarity and satisfaction

Figure 10 shows the graph indicating the ranking place of the avatar when the target model ranked all portraits and avatar in order of ones he wants to use.

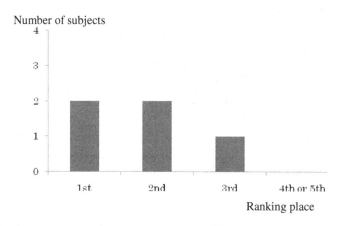

Fig. 10. Ranking place of the avatar among all portraits and avatar in order of ones the target model wants to use

Furthermore, Table 1 shows the degree of fondness for the avatar by the target model of each group.

Table 1. Degree of fondness for the avatar by the target model

Group #	1	2	3	4	5	average
Fondness (%)	50	80	80	90	70	74

From Figure 9, the degrees of satisfaction and similarities between the avatar and the target model declared by the target model (right bars) are the same as those by the portrait creator (center bars). In Figure 10, there is a tendency that the target model wants to use the avatar better than any other portraits. And from Table 1, the fondness for the avatar is different depending on each target model, however, the average degree of fondness means the avatar is highly evaluated by the target model. From these results, there is a high possibility that the avatar can make it easier for the friends of a target model to imagine him, and also tends to be preferred by the target model.

4   Conclusions

In this paper, we propose the method of constructing an avatar by merging the user portraits which are created by friends. The proposed system consists of two subsystems, the portrait making support system and the avatar constructing system. The portrait making support system helps friends of a target model to easily create the portrait, and the avatar constructing system creates an avatar of the target person using the average of all portraits which are created on the portrait making support system. We demonstrated the effectiveness of these proposed systems by performing two experiments. In these experiments, some friends created the portraits of a target model on the portrait making support system, and the avatar was constructed on the avatar constructing system. The results of these experiments show that the avatar tends to be preferred to the portraits, and to give the satisfaction to both the target persons and friends.

We are planning to introduce the face color function into the system, and also emphasize the functionality of the avatar.

References

1. Nishikawa, H., et al.: Consideration of the avatar effect in an online community. Ritsumeikan Business Journal 4, 17–36 (2010)
2. Ogaki, T., Itou, J., Munemori, J.: Analysis on the Relationships between Visual Entertainment Factor and Chat Communication, Research report of Information Processing Society of Japan, 2010-DPS-145(17), 1–8 (2010)
3. Nintendo ®,
   http://www.nintendo.co.jp/wii/staff/
   mii-channel/articles/index.html
4. Heike, M., Kawasaki, H., Tanaka, T., Fujita, K.: Study on Deformation Rule of Personalized-Avatar for Producing Sense of Affinity. Journal of Human Interface Society 13(3), 243–254 (2011)

Usability Compliance Audit
for Technology Intelligence Services

Nadine Pietras[1], Mazhar Sajjad[2], Myunggwon Hwang[3], Jinhyung Kim[3],
Sa-Kwang Song[3], Do-Heon Jeong[3,*], Seungwoo Lee[3], and Hanmin Jung[3]

[1] Dept. of Applied Linguistics and Language Technologie,
University of Hildesheim, Germany
pietras@uni-hildesheim.de
[2] University of Science and Technology (UST), Korea
ms@kisti.re.kr
[3] Dept. of Computer Intelligence Research
Korea Institute of Science and Technology Information (KISTI),
Daejeon, Korea
{mgh,jinhyung,esmallj,heon,swlee,jhm}@kisti.re.kr

Abstract. Usability has become a central aspect of the success of applications in the mobile environment. However most usability engineering theories are rather cost intensive and involve the work of usability experts. This paper presents an approach for a "discount usability" check in the means of a usability compliance audit. Being composed of various international usability guidelines, policies and legislation as well as specific development tools for the iOS and Android platform, we have created an audit of 189 general usability recommendations as well as 39 statements focusing on usability issues within the tablet environment. The audit model has been tested at the example of the technology intelligence service application InSciTe (Intelligence in Science and Technology), designed by KISTI (Korea Institute of Science and Technology Information). The results of the audit, conducted by researchers within the development team, show first insights into areas of usability compliance as well as areas in need for improvement. Although the model has a limited scope and needs further development, it can be seen as a starting point to employ usability testing means within the development lifecycle of tablet application projects.

Keywords: Discount usability, auditing, usability compliance audit.

1   Introduction

Usability has become an increasingly important aspect within the HCI research field. There exists a variety of theories and methodologies to test and ensure the usability compliance of different kinds of applications. However as the definition and scope of usability as well as standard measures to evaluate interfaces and to detect errors

---

* Corresponding author.

S. Yamamoto (Ed.): HIMI/HCII 2013, Part I, LNCS 8016, pp. 524–533, 2013.

incorporate diverse fields of research, there is no such thing as a perfect approach. Throughout the last years, a variety of methodologies has evolved to primarily conduct usability testing as a means of exposing usability issues of mobile applications. As these methods however are cost and time intensive and require the involvement of specialists in the field of mobile HCI as well as facilities and testing equipments, there is the need for a "discount" usability evaluation method to discover issues and give first insights into areas of improvement.

This paper discusses the possibility of focusing on usability inspection methodologies by setting up a usability compliance audit that can be carried out with limited resources and without the need of specialists trained in the field of HCI. The goal is to outline a methodology for easy usability measurement that can assure a basis for understanding usability metrics, which promote usability measurement practices and can be carried out by researchers without background in usability engineering, serving as a guidance and foundation for communicating with software developers. The research has been conducted as a model for the tablet application InSciTe Adaptive, an intelligent system in KISTI.

After an introduction to literature sources, section 3 will outline the scope of the test as well as its realization and results, before sections 4 and 5 will focus on results and discussion of the model. The last chapter will give a conclusion as well as giving suggestions for further research to broaden the field of in-house "discount" usability techniques.

2   Literature Review

The proposed methodology has been set up by combining a variety of international guidelines, legislation standards and policies within the usability field of HCI. To cover the additional specifications of applications in the mobile and thus tablet environment, the list has been complemented with propositions of the main mobile environments.

The WCAG 2.0 is an authoritative principle of the W3C with strategies, instructions and implementation means for usable and accessible web interfaces. The four principles perceivable, operable, understandable, and robust follow 61 success criteria and techniques to test the interface against its conformance [1].

Other recommendations of the W3C, specifically referring to mobile devices, are the Mobile Web Best Practices and Mobile Web Application Best Practices. These practices address the specific usage environment of mobile applications, its delivery context as well as "How to do" sections, and groups its statements into application data, security and privacy, user awareness and control, conservative use of resources, user experience, and handling variations in the delivery context [2][3].

A further source of guidance and standards is the International Organization for Standardization. Within the Ergonomics of Human System Interaction, the ISO 9241-11

Guidance on Usability standard defines usability in terms of efficiency, effectiveness, and user satisfaction. It lays out principles of how to achieve these goals within the development lifecycle by describing the application options [4].

2.1   Policies and Legislations

Jakob Nielsen and the Nielsen Norman Group have published a set of 113 Design Guidelines for Homepage Usability resulting the many years of work in the usability engineering field and conducting an immense variety of research. The guidelines serve as requests and are grouped into 24 categories, such as Content Writing, Graphic Design, Search, Dates and Times, and Gathering Customer Data [5]. The Quality in Use Integrates Measurement Model (QUIM) approaches usability evaluation standards by portraying a consolidated and hierarchical model of usability measurement. It covers 10 factors which are as follows: efficiency, effectiveness, productivity, satisfaction, learnability, safety, trustfulness, accessibility, universality, and usefulness. The model calls to be a basis under which other methodologies can derive [6].

Usability issues are furthermore addressed as national requirements for ensuring the accessibility of web content within different countries all over the world. The proposed methodology has included aspects of the American and German law to eliminate barriers in information technology. The new Section 508 Standards Guide of the US Rehabilitation Act addresses legal and technical compliance of information technology of federal agencies to eliminate usage barriers for disabled users. The subchapter Software Applications and Operating Systems focuses on the accessibility of software [7].

The German equivalent, the regulation for accessible information technology, Barrierefreie Informationstechnik Verordnung (BITV 2.0) follows the WCAG 2.0 by setting two priorities to follow the four principles. Public authorities are intended to follow the attachment with guidelines to implement the standards [8].

2.2   Mobile Environment Specifications

The iOS Human Interface Guidelines give recommendations and implementation examples for developers and are divided into Platform Characteristics, Human Interface Principles, App Design Strategies, User Experience Guidelines and iOS Technology Usage, and UI Element Usage Guidelines. The recommendations are precise and specific; however they do not give design implementation in code [9].

The Android Developers Design recommendations provide a framework for building an application according to the Android experience to be consistent and enjoyable to use. The recommendations are split up into Style, Patterns, and Building Blocks and are to ensure to learn about Android principles and resources to implement good design decisions to enhance the user's experience [10].

3   Methodology Framework

The proposed model for "discount usability evaluation" is a summary of the works listed in section 2. The model is set up as a review questionnaire which can easily be checked by selecting one of the following choices: Applies, Does not apply and N/A. The audit consists of 228 statements, whereof 189 are general usability and accessibility statements and 39 statements refer to specific requirements for tablet applications within the iOS or Android platform. There are a total of 17 categories with each category of statements varying between 4 and 25 questions. The difference is based according to the scope and importance of each category.

3.1   Preparation and Realization

The audit has been transported to a free online survey platform to enable easy sharing, data collection and analysis means. The used platform is Obsurvey (www.obsurvey.com), which gives the option to set up a questionnaire without limitation in the amount of questions and portrays a variety of functionalities for data preparation and exporting. The audit furthermore collects different results from those researchers testing the application on an Apple iPad, and those testing on the Android Platform. The following figure (Fig.1) gives an example of the layout.

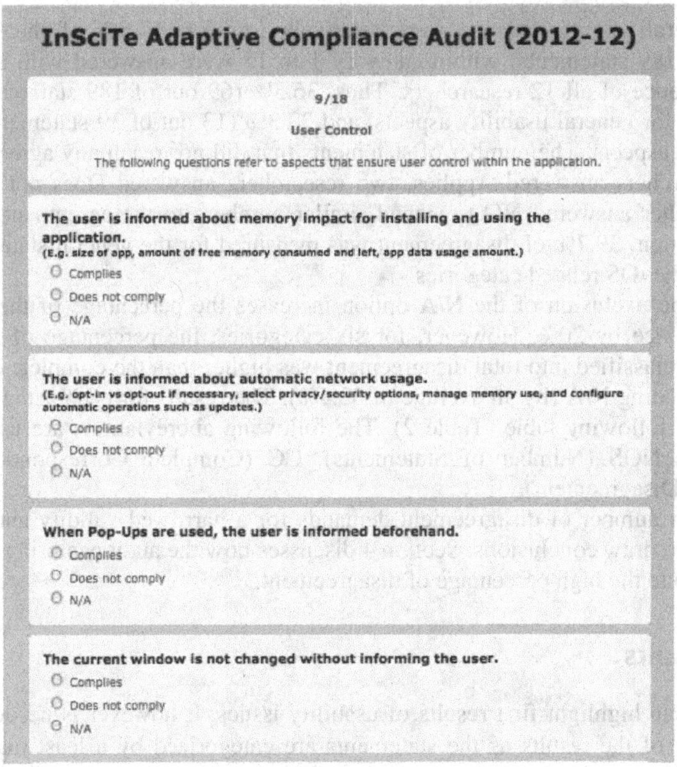

InSciTe Adaptive Compliance Audit (2012-12)

9/18

User Control

The following questions refer to aspects that ensure user control within the application.

The user is informed about memory impact for installing and using the application.
(E.g. size of app, amount of free memory consumed and left, app data usage amount.)
○ Complies
○ Does not comply
○ N/A

The user is informed about automatic network usage.
(E.g. opt-in vs opt-out if necessary, select privacy/security options, manage memory use, and configure automatic operations such as updates.)
○ Complies
○ Does not comply
○ N/A

When Pop-Ups are used, the user is informed beforehand.
○ Complies
○ Does not comply
○ N/A

The current window is not changed without informing the user.
○ Complies
○ Does not comply
○ N/A

Fig. 1. Survey Questionnaire Sample

3.2   Data Collection

The model has been tested by 12 researchers within the InSciTe Adaptive Service Team at KISTI. As no statement was mandatory to answer in order to distinguish which statements of the audit posed difficulties to the researcher, the following table (Table 1) lists the number of participants replying to the questions in total.

Table 1. Statement Answers in Total

# of Answers per Question	Amount of Questions Answered (in %)	# of Questions in Total
12	65.4	149
10	28.9	66
8	4.8	11
6	0.9	1

All researchers tested the application on an iOS Tablet. Some researchers made use of the comment option after each category. The comments can be categorized into general feedback about the layout of the audit, questions about the wording of the statements, questions about the statements' meaning, and feedback about the Obsurvey interface.

The overall correspondence were relatively low i.e. 17.5% of the statements (33 out of 189 statements) within category 1 to 15 were answered with a complete correspondence of all 12 researchers. Thus, 36.5% (69 out of 189 statements) could be attained for general usability aspects, and 33.3% (13 out of 39 statements) for the iOS related aspects. The number of statements that did not reach any agreement (e.g. three researchers answered Applies, two researchers answered Does not apply and one researcher answered N/A) reached similar numbers to the agreement excluding the N/A option. 29.7% of disagreement was measured for the general statements and 20.5% for the iOS related categories.

Hence the exclusion of the N/A option increases the percentage of the complete correspondence by 20%. However, for six categories, the percentage of statements that can be classified into total disagreement was higher than the complete correspondence, excluding N/A (by an average of 32.4%). The results for each category can be seen in the following table (Table 2). The following abbreviations are used for the field titles: NOS (Number of Statements), CC (Complete Correspondence), CD (Complete Disagreement).

The high number of disagreement demands for a narrowed validity and scope of the results to draw conclusions. Section 4 discusses how the audit can bring about first results despite the high percentage of disagreement.

4   Results

The audit can highlight first results of usability issues. It however is needed to limit the validity of the results as the statements are categorized by a least majority. By totaling the answers of each researcher, each statement is classified by the answer

Table 2. Overall Results Divided into Categories

Category	NOS	CC	CC (in %)	CC excluding N/A	CC excluding N/A (in %)	CD	CD (in %)
Layout	25	5	20	5	20	12	48
Navigation	13	2	15.4	3	23.1	5	38.5
Visual Design	21	0	0	2	9.5	12	57.1
Accessibility	14	0	0	4	28.6	3	21.4
Content Language	14	1	7.1	3	21.4	8	57.1
Task Orientation	7	1	14.3	1	14.3	4	57.1
Application Behavior	5	2	40	3	60	1	20
Personalization	4	0	0	2	50	0	0
User Control	17	4	23.5	9	52.9	3	17.7
User Input	6	2	33.3	2	33.3	1	16.7
Search	21	3	14.3	8	38.1	7	33.3
Forms and Data Entry	19	8	42.1	16	84.2	0	0
Help, System Feedback and Error Messages	11	1	9.1	4	36.4	0	0
Internationalization	6	3	50	5	83.3	0	0
Trust, Credibility and Identity	6	1	16.7	2	33.3	2	33.3
iOS Guidelines	21	1	4.8	6	28.6	4	19.1
Multitasking with iOS	4	0	0	0	0	1	25
iOS Gestures	14	2	14.3	7	50	3	21.4

option that has been selected the most. Statements that did not reach a least majority are not able to be added to the results and thus are excluded. In a second step, the classification is then considered in a greater context for every single category to group these into areas that need to be checked with ratings that are very low (the majority of statements is classified as Does not apply); areas that should be double checked with ratings classifying the category as *N/A* or those which cannot be classified; and areas that show first results for a compliance of usability standards and guidelines and thus can give confidence to the research team. The classification scheme is as follows.

- Highly complies (100% to 80% Complies for a section).
- Complies (79% - 60% Complies for a section).
- Partly complies (<60% Complies, but majority of answer options for a section).
- N/A (majority of answer options for section is N/A).
- No classification (there is no majority as two answer options are almost identical).
- Does not comply (the majority of answer options for a section is Does not comply).

The audit results show that the majority of the categories was positively classified: two categories were classified as being highly compliant with 80% and 100%; two categories were classified as compliant and four categories got at least partly compliant results, their positive classification outnumbering the other options by a minimum. Three categories were classified as being not applicable to the application. Their results for N/A were chosen more often than other answer options. However these categories should be double-checked to ensure that their validity is true.

Four categories could not be classified, as the least majority of the answer options was too similar to draw conclusions and two categories need to be evaluated in detail, as the major answer option was Does not comply. The following table (Table 3) shows the distribution within each category and the classification selection.

5   Discussion

The results as stated in section 4 can draw first conclusions and feedback for areas of usability improvement. Although the process of the auditing itself needs to be advanced and the number of researchers was limited, the methodology can be seen as a starting point to further develop "discount" usability methods. The audit helps to give quick and easily obtainable results for further usability testing.

Hence, the statements with negative grading should be extracted and overlooked by the research team. Some recommendations might be easy to change, whereas other recommendations will demand an expert to be involved for the correction process. For example, the statement "The double tap gesture enables zooming in or out of the touched area of the screen." might be easily checked and corrected by someone within the research team who is familiar with iOS Gesture activation and thus can ensure a better compliance of the application to tablet platform standards.

The example statement "Constructive advice to fix an error is provided within an error message." on the other side is less easy to adapt, as constructive advice might be something subjective, being differently perceived by users. Furthermore sources of

Table 3. Final Classification Scheme

Category	Classified	Complies (in %)	Not comply (in %)	N/A (in %)	No least majority (in %)
Layout	Complies	68	24	0	8
Navigation	Partly Complies	54	23	8	15
Visual Design	Complies	62	19	5	14
Access	Partly Complies	57	21	14	8
Content Language	Partly Complies	57	14	0	29
Task Orientation	Complies	72	14	0	14
Application Behavior	Highly Complies	80	0	0	20
Personalization	N/A	0	25	75	0
User Control	No classification	35	24	24	17
User Input	Highly complies	100	0	0	0
Search	No classification	38	34	14	14
Forms and Data Entry	N/A	0	0	100	0
Help, System Feedback and Error Messages	Does not comply	18	27	9	46
Internationalization	N/A	17	0	83	0
Trust, Credibility and Identity	Partly Complies	52	16	16	16
iOS Guidelines	No classification	38	24	5	33
Multitasking with iOS	No classification	25	0	25	50
iOS Gestures	Does not comply	29	64	0	7

error need to be identified beforehand, creating a complex correction process. Thus, subjective and rather vague statements that were negatively classified should be discussed within the research team to set up a grading and correction frame. Obsurvey has proved to be an easy to use open source tool with a variety of options for the creation and data collection process. However there are some limitations and the audit process itself still has room for improvement to be optimized and to ensure a greater scope of validity of the results.

6   Conclusion and Future Work

This paper presented a model for "discount usability" which enables quick and easy first insights of application's usability issues from within the research team. A usability compliance audit for a tablet application has been constructed using the examples of different international guidelines, policies, and legislations, as well as specific mobile platform guidelines. The wording of the statements emulates the W3C guidelines and additionally gives short descriptions or examples to enable non-usability experts to classify the statements.

The collected results of 12 researchers can draw feedback for first areas of usability improvement needs, as well as reassuring areas that already partly comply with usability guidelines. However, the results can only be seen with limited scope and validity as there is room for improvement of the process of the completion as well as the wording, platform and audit itself.

Furthermore there needs to be additional research in order to evaluate the validity of the answers as some statements might demand to be answered by usability experts. The results show that, with a minimum effort, first insights into usability compliance can be collected and should then be further evaluated through the help of e.g. Usability Testing or involving usability experts. Usability compliance audits can serve as a starting point for usability discussion within the research team and be guidance for status checks. If implemented throughout the whole project process, results can be compared to indicate areas that need to be focused on and give first answers for project communication as well as to stakeholders or other third parties involved.

References

1. WCAG, World Wide Web Consortium. Web Content Accessibility Guidelines (WCAG) Overview (2011), http://www.w3.org/WAI/intro/wcag.php
2. W3C Mobile Web Best Practices 1.0. Basic Guidelines, http://www.w3.org/TR/mobile-bp/
3. W3C Mobile Web Application Best Practices. Recommendations, https://www.w3.org/TR/mwabp/
4. ISO 9241-11:1998. Ergonomic requirements for office work with visual display terminals (VDTs) - Part 11: Guidance on usability
5. Group, N.N.: Nielsen Norman Group. 113 Design Guidelines for Homepage Usability, http://www.nngroup.com/articles/113-design-guidelines-homepageusability/

6. Seffah, A., Donyaee, M., Kline, R.B., Padda, H.K.: Usability measurement and metrics: A consolidated model. Software Qual. J. 14, 159–178 (2006)
7. US Rehabilitation Act. Section 508 Standards,
   https://www.section508.gov/index.cfm?fuseAction=stdsdoc
8. BITV, Barrierefreie Informationstechnik Verordnung (2011),
   http://www.gesetze-im-internet.de/bitv_2_0/
9. iOS Human Interface Guidelines. iOS Developer Library,
   https://developer.appleapple.com/library/ios/#documentation/
   UserExperience/Conceptual/MobileHIG
10. Andoid Design. Developers Tools,
   http://developer.android.com/design/index.html

Factor Models for Promoting Flow by Game Players' Skill Level

Mamiko Sakata[1], Tsubasa Yamashita[2], and Masashi Okubo[2]

[1] Department of Culture and Information Science, Doshisha University,
1-3 Tatara Miyakodani, Kyotanabe City, 6100394, Japan
[2] Department of Information Systems Design, Doshisha University,
1-3 Tatara Miyakodani, Kyotanabe City, 6100394, Japan
{msakata,mokubo}@mail.doshisha.ac.jp

Abstract. In this study, to investigate the influence of game types and opponent's ability on the player's state of mind and performance, we developed a simple numerical calculation game system. Using this system, we performed some experiments under controlled situations. All subjects solved the calculations at a similar rate, except when factoring for the players' recognition of the cooperator or competitor' skill level. However, the subjects' performance and emotions are different depending on the situation, which suggests that the video game system has an effect on the player's emotional state.

Keywords: Flow, Video Game, Competitive Type, Cooperative Type, Factor Model.

1 Introduction

Recently, network games, such as social games, have become popular because of the diffusion of the Internet into homes and onto hand-held devices. Further, popularity has grown   not only for competitive-type games in which the player brings down an opponent, but also for cooperative-type games in which the player obtains a goal by cooperating with online partners. In this study, we will investigate the influence of the difference between competitive and cooperative-type games as well as the opponent's effect on the primary player's state of mind and performance.

The concept of "Flow" is widely acknowledged in sociology. As mentioned previously, Flow is advocated by the social psychologist Csikszentmihalyi [1] and is the state in which a game player is fully immersed in a feeling of energized focus. A person can feel Flow when he recognizes his skill level is just enough to accomplish the task, which may also be adjusted by changes in the challenge level as the player gains experience. We think that video game players can feel Flow easily because they can increase their skill level by simply playing the game, and the game system can raise the game level based on the player's ability automatically. In this paper, we also wish to discuss the possibility of the game system itself inducing Flow on the player's state of mind.

S. Yamamoto (Ed.): HIMI/HCII 2013, Part I, LNCS 8016, pp. 534–544, 2013.

Until now, a great variety of game systems have been developed with success in the video game market. Some researchers in this field have focused on motivating workers by using video games and enhancing the elements of entertainment and game design that have this effect [2]. Other research has investigated the influence of a player's skill and his competitor's behavior on the player from the viewpoint of brain activity by using fNIRS [3]. Still, other research studies of game systems based on the Flow theory have been performed using commercial games [4]. This study will also examine game systems and human-computer interactions based on the Flow theory.

In this paper, our goal is to propose a game system which induces Flow and to experimentally measure this experience based on the influencing factors of game type (cooperative vs. competitive) and opponent's ability (lower/equal/higher). Moreover, we tried to develop factor models for promoting Flow based on game players' skill level. Eventually, we think that the knowledge gained from this research can be utilized in various kinds of computers and machine interfaces.

2   What is Flow

Fig. 1 shows the model of the Flow state, which is advocated by Csikszentmihalyi. When the task challenge level, which means the difficulty of the task, is higher than the operator's skill, he/she probably feels 'Anxiety' and/or 'Stress'. Conversely, in cases where the challenge level is lower than the operator's skill, he/she will feel 'Relief' and/or 'Boredom'. In cases where the operator recognizes the challenge level is just right for his/her skill, he/she will feel 'Flow'. Additionally, when both levels are high and well balanced, then the player will feel it more strongly.

In this study, the challenge level, as a component of Flow in games, sports and the like, is thought to be replaced by skill level (Fig.2). Thus, the change in the skill level of the opponent is likely to trigger Flow.

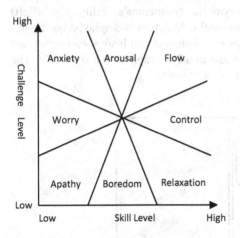

Fig. 1. Model of the Flow state [5]

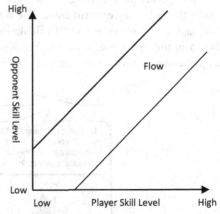

Fig. 2. Proposed Model of Flow state

3   Influence of Relationship between Player and Opponent on the Player's Performance and Emotion

3.1   Experimental Method

To investigate the influence of the relationship between the player and his/her opponent on the player's performance and emotions, we performed some sensory evaluations under various conditions. For that purpose, a simple calculation game was produced. Using this system, the subjects solve a numerical calculation under controlled conditions; the opponent is a competitor or a cooperator, and the opponent's skill level is either high, even or low. After the game, we make the subjects respond to a questionnaire. Our subjects are 15 male and female students in their twenties.

We used calculation problems for our game tasks for the following three reasons: 1. To maximize the influence of having/not having game experience: 2. Easy quantification of the players' skill levels; and 3. Easy setting of the skill level of the opponent.

3.2   Experiment I (Competitive Type Game)

In the first part of our experiment, the subject is asked to go into a room and sit on the chair in front of the PC shown in Fig. 3. Next, he is asked to solve some two-digit numerical calculations on the computer display, just for practice. The subject is then told that there is an competitor seated in the next room and that the game victory or loss is determined by the number of correct answers given by each player when the combined number of calculations solved by the two players reaches 50.

In fact, the competitor is a computer and the competitor's skill is adjusted based on the subject's skill, which is measured in the practice session. The skill of the competitor (computer) is set to high ability, equal ability or low ability. It means the competitor's calculating speed is twice, the same as or half of the subject's calculating speed. In the experiment, the subject does not know the competitor's ability. Fig. 4(left) shows the G.U.I. of experiment I. The numerical calculation is displayed on the left side, and the numbers of solved calculations of the subject and his/her competitor are shown in the lower region in number form and in a bar graph on the right side. The subject competes with three competitors, in a random order.

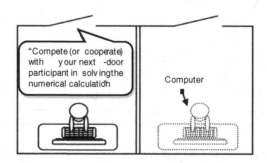

Fig. 3. Experimental Setup

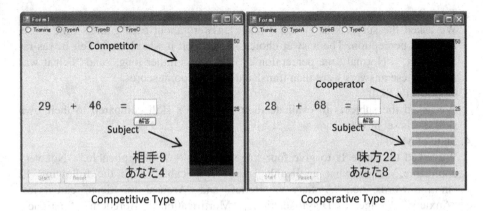

Competitive Type   Cooperative Type

Fig. 4. G.U.I. of Experimental System

3.3 Experiment II (Cooperative Type Game)

Experiment II is almost the same as I. However, unlike Experiment I, the subject is told to solve the calculation problems until 50 correct answers are reached, by working with "one cooperator." Fig. 4(right) shows the G.U.I. of experiment II. The numbers of calculations solved by the subject and the cooperator are shown in the lower region in number form and in a bar graph on the right side.

3.4 Questionnaire

After each trial, we asked the subjects to answer a set of questions listed on a questionnaire.

1. Immersion in the Game
   Based on the Csikszentmihalyi Flow theory, we asked the subjects to give five-stage answers about the seven states of mind which constitute Flow, which are listed below. The answers are: "I can't agree," "I cannot fully agree," "Neither", "I agree a little" and "I totally agree."

   · I was always aware of the purpose during the game.
   · I was able to concentrate on the game.
   · I was able to immerse myself in the game.
   · I felt that I controlled the game.
   · The game's difficulty and skill level were well-balanced.
   · I felt significance and value in the game.
   · I felt fulfilled.

   The answers were translated into 1-5 point scores. By adding the score for each state of mind, we obtained the "flow score", which is an indication of the player's immersion in the game.

2. Time Perception

We asked the subjects to give five-stage answers about each game's time lapse, i.e., time perception. The answer choices were "Felt it was short," "Felt it was rather short," "Normal time perception", "Felt it was rather long," and "Felt it was long." These answers were then translated into 1-5 point scores.

3. Opponent's Skill

We asked the subjects to evaluate their opponent's skill compared to their own skill levels set at 100.

4. State of Mind

We asked the subjects to give four-stage answers – "Not applicable," "Not very applicable," "Somewhat applicable," and "Applicable" – to the following 12 emotion words, i.e., "Anxiety vs. Relief" and "Arousal vs. Sleep" categories: "Anxiety", "Anger", "Dissatisfaction", "Mortification", "Boredom", "Fatigue", "Relaxation", "Composure", "Satisfaction", "Pleasure", "Surprise", "Excitement", "Impatience", "Volition", "Apathy", and "Relief" during the game.

4   Experimental Result

4.1   Game Type, Opponent's Skill Level and Flow

In order to examine if the "flow score" (absorption into the game) varies with the type of game (competitive vs. cooperative) and the opponent's skill level (high/equal/ low), we conducted a type (2) ×level (3) analysis of variance. Fig. 5 shows the average flow score at different skill levels. As a result, we found the main effect of the "game type" at the 10% significance level and the main effect of the "op-

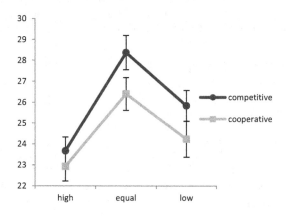

Fig. 5. Average of Flow Score

ponent's skill level" at the 5% significance level. We did not find any interactions. In other words, there was greater immersion in the game with the "competitive" type game than with the "cooperative" type game. It was shown that there was greater Flow when the opponent's skill level changed from "equal" to "low", and then again from "low" to "high".

We can say that it has been statistically proven that the game type (competitive vs. cooperative) and the opponent's skill level (high/low/equal) affect the game player's state of mind even in solving the same tasks, i.e., doing calculations.

Table 1. Frequency of Emotion Words

	Competitive			Cooperative		
	high	equal	low	high	equal	low
Anxiety	27	24	13	22	13	13
Anger	11	4	3	6	1	2
Displeasure	16	5	5	7	1	5
Mortification	10	1	4	5	1	7
Boredom	6	3	10	6	3	11
Fatigue	14	10	16	13	13	17
Relaxation	3	10	18	11	17	20
Composure	0	10	14	13	16	13
Satisfaction	3	21	21	6	23	14
Satisfaction	2	18	17	6	10	12
Surprise	21	9	5	15	5	3
Excitement	22	25	12	11	15	10
Impatience	29	26	12	23	17	13
Volition	21	28	13	17	22	16
Apathy	17	2	0	6	1	3
Relief	0	8	20	9	14	17

4.2   Emotions for Game Types and Skill Levels

As shown under Section 3.4 above, we asked the subjects to evaluate the 16 emotion words by using four-stage answers, i.e., "Not applicable," "Not very applicable," "Somewhat applicable" and "Applicable." Score 0 was assigned to the first two answers, and score 1, to the last two answers. The subjects' emotions were numerically processed this way and listed in Table 1.

The shadows indicate the top five emotion words that were selected most frequently for each game. (Six emotion words are shadowed when selection frequency was the same.) The frequently selected emotion words for each skill level are shown as a flow model in Fig.6. It was found that the emotions felt by the subjects differed with

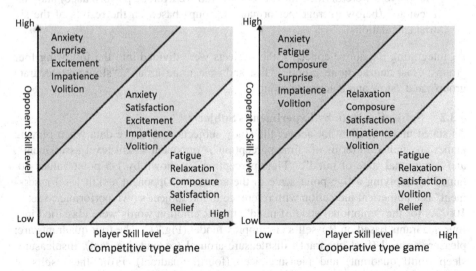

Fig. 6. Flow Model for Competitive and Cooperative Games

different skill levels. For example, if the subject's skill level is "equal" with his/her opponent, they felt "Excitement" and "Anxiety" in a competitive game. They felt more "Relaxation" and "Composure" playing a cooperative game. Even though the tasks performed by the subjects were exactly the same, it is interesting to note that their "state of mind" caused different emotions, depending on whether they were "competing" or "cooperating" with their opponents.

4.3   Game Player's Individual Traits and Flow

In 4.1, we examined how the game type and the opponent's skill level affected the game player's state of mind as a general trend seen among all of our experiment subjects. The player's individual traits, however, are also considered to affect his/her emotions, which are aroused by the game or the feeling of immersion in the game. In this section, we build a quantitative model to show "how the factors affecting the feel of immersion vary with each game player's individual traits. In this study, we also build a model that will allow us to foresee the sense of immersion by different groups, after grouping the subjects by their skill levels."

4.3.1   Player's Individual Traits (Skill Level)

In this study, each player's attributes, i.e., skill level, are obtained objectively using the following indices:

— Calculation speed

 The average time taken to answer one problem is the player's "calculation speed." Each player completes six trial calculations, so an average speed was obtained from these results. The subjects showing an above-average speed belong to the "fast" group; those below the average speed, to the "slow" group.

— Accuracy

 The players were divided into "accurate" (above average performance) and "inaccurate" (below average performance) groups based on the results of the six trial calculations.

By integrating the above concepts, the subjects were divided into the following four groups: "fast and accurate group", "fast and inaccurate group", "slow and accurate group", and "slow and inaccurate group".

4.3.2   Subjective Data by Experiment's Subjects

As stated under Section 3.4 above, the study subjects' subjective data when playing games are gained in terms of "time perception", "opponent's skill level assessment", and "emotional state of mind". "Time perception" is shown by 1-5 point values obtained by applying a five-point scale to the answers. "Opponent's skill level assessment" is a numerical indication with reference to the subject's own performance set to 100. As for the "emotional state of mind", the 12 emotion words were classified into four quadrants based on Russell's circumplex model (Fig.7). The four quadrants are: pleasure-arousal (first quadrant), displeasure-arousal (second quadrant), displeasure-sleep (third quadrant) and pleasure-sleep (fourth quadrant). From the results of four-point scale answers, we calculated the number of emotion words which the subjects felt were "Somewhat applicable" and "Applicable". This value is defined as "emotional state of mind."

4.3.3 Factor Models for Bringing Out Flow

We then tried to obtain a multivariate regression model to show what emotional state leads to Flow. We conducted a multivariate regressional analysis using the flow score as a dependent variable, the six subjective data shown in the previous section, i.e., "time perception", "opponent's skill level assessment", and "emotional state of mind (first~fourth quadrants)", as independent variables, and using a forced entry method. Table 2 shows standardized coefficient and adjusted R^2. Fig. 8 shows the proportion of the standard coefficients.

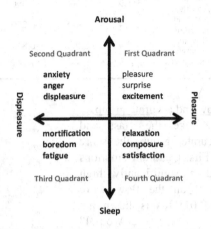

Fig. 7. Emotional Classification based on Russell's Circumplex Model

Fast and accurate group
The effect of the emotional scores in the First Quadrant was significantly high on the flow score ($p<0.05$). When the subject is in the "Pleasure-Arousal" state, the emotions such as "pleasure," "surprise" and "excitement" may be the contributing factors that trigger Flow. The contribution rate was particularly low compared with the other groups. This is not a fitting model.

Fast and inaccurate group
The emotional state had no effect, but "time perception" and "opponent's skill level" had a significantly high effect on the flow score ($p<0.01$). This group perceives time to be moving quickly and is likely to feel Flow when the opponent's skill level is lower than the subject's. The model showed the best fitting out of the four groups.

Table 2. Result of Multiple Regression Analysis

	1st quadrant	2nd quadrant	3rd quadrant	4th quadrant	time perception	opponent's skill level	adjusted R^2
Fast and accurate	0.265*	0.188	-0.175	0.131	-0.043	-0.253	0.098
Fast and inaccurate	0.227	-0.152	-0.023	0.193	-0.551**	-0.557**	0.577
Slow and accurate	0.774**	-0.300	-0.247	-0.075	0.361	-0.200	0.411
Slow and inaccurate	-0.139	0.576	-0.746**	0.274	0.051	-0.313	0.459

* $p<0.05$, ** $p<0.01$.

Table 3. List of Coefficients by Multiple Regression Analysis

	constant	1st quadrant	2nd quadrant	3rd quadrant	4th quadrant	time perception	opponent's skill level
Fast and accurate	23.029	0.600	0.396	-0.408	0.241	-0.200	-0.029
Fast and inaccurate	32.504	0.458	-0.270	-0.052	0.376	-2.432	-0.050
Slow and accurate	19.369	2.020	-0.841	-0.661	-0.181	1.725	-0.027
Slow and inaccurate	25.567	-0.284	1.404	-1.424	0.504	0.231	-0.032

Slow and accurate group

Just like the 'fast and accurate' group, the score of First Quadrant emotions had a significantly high effect on the flow score (p<0.01). It was shown that the "Pleasure-Arousal" state, in other words, emotions like "pleasure," "surprise" and "excitement", is a contributing factor for triggering Flow. This model's overall contribution rate was higher than the "fast and accurate" group. These emotions, therefore, were found to strongly affect Flow.

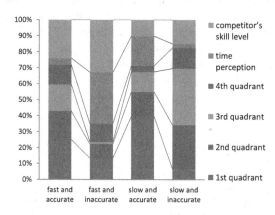

Fig. 8. The proportion of Standardizing Coefficients

Slow and inaccurate group

Different from the other groups, only the emotions in the Third Quadrant had a significantly high effect on the flow score (p<0.01). The negative standardization coefficient shows that the "Displeasure-Sleep" state, or feeling the emotions of "mortification," "boredom" and "fatigue", does not lead to Flow. Conversely, Flow is easier to feel when such emotions are not being felt. This model's fitting was moderate.

Table 3 lists the coefficients of independent variables obtained by multiple regression analysis and the constants. We predicted the flow score for individual players in each group, using these figures. The predicted and actual flow scores are plotted on the horizontal axis and vertical axis, respectively (Fig. 9).

From the above results, we found that the emotional state leading to Flow differed with the player's skill level. It was also shown that the player's immersion in the game can be predicted to some degree by looking at his/her emotional state.

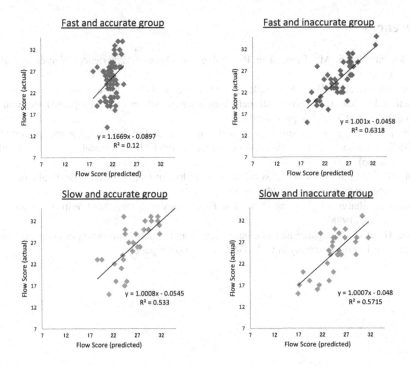

Fig. 9. Predicted and Actual Flow Scores by Multiple Regression Analysis

5 Conclusion

In this study, we developed a simple numerical calculation game system in order to investigate the influence of game types and opponent's ability on the player's state of mind and performance. Using this system, we performed some experiments under controlled situations. All of our subjects solved the calculations at a similar rate, except when factoring for the players' recognition of the cooperator or opponents' skill level. However, the subjects' performance and emotions are different depending on the situation, which suggests that the video game system has an effect on the player's emotional state.

The experiments in this study were performed under a controlled video game situation. One cannot deny that some people wonder if there are game elements in such simple tasks as "solving calculation problems." However, even when doing simple and monotonous work, people would be able to enjoy work by finding game elements in their jobs. On the other hand, some people would be stressed out if they couldn't find any game elements in their jobs. This study, therefore, has great significance in that it has empirically shown that the state of mind about games, the emotional status during a game and the factors that lead to Flow change with the players' characteristics.

References

1. Csikszentmihalyi, M.: Flow: The Psychology of Optimal Experience. Harper and Row, New York (1990)
2. Kuramoto, I., et al.: Weekend Battle: an Entertainment System for Improving Workers' Motivation. In: Proc. of 2nd International Conference on Advances in Computer Entertainment Technology (ACE 2005), pp. 43–50 (2005)
3. Tamakoshi, S., et al.: A study in the entertainment of fighting video game measured by fNIRS: a comparison vs. human and vs. computer, IPSJ SIG Technical Report EC-3 (2006) (in Japanese)
4. Takatalo, J., et al.: Presence, Involvement, and Flow in Digital Games. In: Evaluating User Experience in Games, pp. 23–46. Springer
5. Csikszentmihalyi, M.: Finding Flow: The Psychology of Engagement With Everyday Life. Basic Books (1998)
6. Suto, H., et al.: Designing and estimating action and structure including enjoyment. Journal of Human Interface Society 7(4), 541–546 (2005) (in Japanese)

Social Experiment on Advisory Recommender System for Energy-Saving

Hiroki Shigeyoshi[1], Ken'iti Tamano[1], Ryosuke Saga[1], Hiroshi Tsuji[1], Shuki Inoue[2], and Tsuyoshi Ueno[3]

[1] Osaka Prefecture University, 1-1, Gakuen-cho, Naka-ku, Sakai-shi, Osaka, Japan
`shigeyoshi@mis.cs.osakafu-u.ac.jp`, `tama@a7m3.jp`,
`{saga,tsuji}@cs.osakafu-u.ac.jp`
[2] Energy Use R&D Center, The Kansai Electric Power Co., Inc., 3-11-20 Nakoji,
Amagasaki-shi, Hyogo, Japan
`Inoue.shuuki@d4.kepco.co.jp`
[3] Central Research Institute of Electric Power Industry,
2-11-1, Iwadokita, Komae-shi, Tokyo, Japan
`ueno@criepi.denken.or.jp`

Abstract. This paper describes a social experiment on an advisory recommender system for home energy-saving, called KNOTES. Based on the user's value sense and the effectiveness of the advice, KNOTES aims to recommend highly effective advices over the user's own preferences. In addition, KNOTES uses an advice reference history to avoid the repetition of redundant advice. For the social experiment, forty-seven subjects used KNOTES for about two months. Introducing four metrics for comparing KNOTES with a random recommender, this paper verifies that KNOTES could recommend the advices which are desirable from the view of energy-saving and could avoid the repetition of redundant advices. The remaining issue has been prediction of the users' preferences according to their value sense.

Keywords: recommender system, home-energy-saving, man-machine interaction, knowledge management.

1 Introduction

Various recommender systems have been proposed to help users effectively select contents that interest them from a potentially overwhelming set of choices [1]. The traditional systems have usually dealt with business products such as books and music, focusing on users' preferences that show what they are most likely to accept. Meanwhile, they are not designed for a recommendation of advices that change and improve our lifestyle, such as energy saving, weight control, and smoking stoppage. In such cases, effective recommendations are not always based on the user's preferences as the best results cannot be achieved when they choose only the advice that they like. Not all preferred advice is effective for all users. Thus, it is desirable that the systems focus on not only user's preference but also the effectiveness of advice.

S. Yamamoto (Ed.): HIMI/HCII 2013, Part I, LNCS 8016, pp. 545–554, 2013.

For evaluating such advisory recommender systems, it is necessary to collect log data by social experiments. Based on the advice execution history from the log data, the effect of advice can be verified. It is also necessary to simultaneously define the evaluation metrics by considering the system characteristics [2].

This paper describes an advisory recommender systems and its social experiment. The system is named KNOTES (KNOwledge & Transaction based domestic Energy saving support System), which we developed in the previous study [3]. This system specializes in energy saving and aims to select effective advices that are in user's interest. The experiment includes forty seven subjects who used KNOTES for about two months. Analyzing the log data, KNOTES was evaluated with the proposed evaluation metrics.

In chapter 2, this paper will introduce the traditional recommender systems and requirements for advisory recommender systems. In chapter 3, this paper will show overview of an advisory recommender system for energy-saving and its recommendation algorithm. In chapter 4, this paper will describe the social experiment, which verifies whether the purposes of the system are accomplished. In chapter 5, this paper will conclude and suggest the future issues.

2   Recommender Systems

2.1   Overview of Related Systems

By offering useful information, recommender systems support users in various decision-making processes, such as what books to buy, what music to listen or what online news to read [4]. There are two major traditional recommendation methods. One is content-based filtering, which chooses content that is similar to the user's current interests. The other is collaborative filtering, which chooses content based on the interests of similar users. Both methods attempt to predict users' interest in an item by focusing on their preferences.

Accuracy metrics are widely used as an evaluation tool for systems based on such methods by expressing how precisely the system can predict the user's preference. These are arguably the most important metrics, because there is marginal use of recommendations for content that does not interest the user [5].

In recent attempts to improve the user's satisfaction for the systems, other metrics have attracted attention [2], [6], focusing on novelty, serendipity [7], and diversity [6]. However, when these systems tried to simultaneously improve several metrics, a trade-off problem occurred [4]. In particular, accuracy decreased as the system put a higher priority on novelty, thus, it is essential to improve several metrics while maintaining accuracy.

In addition, it was also pointed out that the performance of the system changes according to the number of users and the number of items [8].Therefore, it is necessary to select recommendation methods that are most appropriate to the purpose of the system and data size [2].

2.2   Requirements for Advisory Recommender Systems

In this section, we consider the case in where a recommender system provides advice which changes and improves our life-style, such as energy-saving, weight control and smoking stoppage. It was reported that energy saving, such as time restricting the use of an air-conditioner, reduces comfort [9]. Such advice is often disliked by a user because of the mental workload. If the system makes recommendations only according to the user's preferences, some effective advices might not be suggested, thus, it is necessary to consider not only user's preference but also the effectiveness of advice. The advisory recommender system should suggest advice which is acceptable for a user and yet desirable for energy-saving.

It is suggested that users dislike getting the same advice. This problem prevents the users from repeatedly using the system. Thus, it is desirable to avoid repeating advice which a user has already followed and advice and overly repetitive advice.

The most important requirement is that the system prompts users to act on the advice given, because the essence of recommender systems is to support users in decision-making processes. Implementing this requirement imposes a change of consciousness to the user, thus, it also seems to be the most difficult issue. Encapsulating the above discussion, there are three requirements on advisory recommender systems:

- To recommend highly effective advice in the user's interest,
- To avoid the repetition of redundant advice,
- To prompt user to execute the given advice.

3   Advisory Recommender System on Energy-Saving

3.1   System Structure

To implement these requirements, we developed an advisory recommender system named KNOTES [3]. This system deals with energy-saving advice. An overview of the system is shown in Figure 1. First, users input their profile data including value sense and appliances owned by them. Next, they are required to input their monthly energy consumption about electricity, gas, and kerosene. Based on the data, KNOTES gives advice to users and records its recommendation logs. If the user follows the advice given in recommendations, the execution logs record it. The user can simultaneously evaluate the advice on a scale of 1–5 on how easy it felt to comply and how likely he would be to recommend it to others. Users can repeatedly receive different recommendations.

To reflect the user's preferences in recommendations, KNOTES collects data about user value sense using questionnaires, allowing the system to predict which advice will be favorable. The value sense and the effectiveness in advice data are used to recommend highly effective advice that remains in the user's interest. An advice reference history, including recommendation logs and execution logs, is used to avoid the repetition of redundant advice.

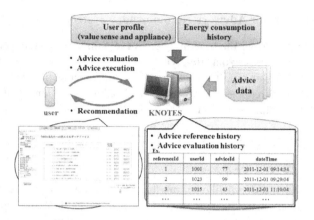

Fig. 1. Advisory recommendation from KNOTES

3.2   Advice Features

Advice in KNOTES has attributes such as those shown in Table 1. The advice data is based on data that was introduced in the report [10]. *"Energy-saving"*, *"CO₂ reduction"*, and *"Cost saving"* show the prospective amounts saved when the advice is executed once. *"Maximum number of available times"* shows the number of times that the advice is ideally executed in one year, thereby avoiding the repetition of advice to avoid user resistance. *"Difficulty level"* and *"Recommended-level"* are dynamic scores of 1–5 that are updated to be a mean value by advice evaluations. *"Easiness"* is the combination of *"Maximum number of available times"* and *"Difficulty level"*. *"Energy type"* shows the energy target of the advice: electricity, gas, and kerosene. If the energy target is not recognized, *"no data"* is inputted. *"Season"* shows when the advice should be executed.

Table 1. Example of advice data

| Suggestion | Appliance | Energy saving [MJ/time] | CO₂ reduction [g/time] | Cost saving [yen/time] | Easiness | | Recommended level (unrecommend:1, recommend:5) | Energy type | Season |
					Maximum number of available times [times/year]	Difficulty level (easy:1, difficult:5)			
Use a saving water shower	Water heater	2,549.00	130,772.00	7,257.00	1	5.0	3.0	No data	Whole year
Reduce the cooling time	Electric fan	0.22	10.53	0.53	112	3.0	3.0	Electricity	Summer
Reduce the heating time	Electric stove	3.47	162.08	8.08	169	3.0	3.0	Electricity	Winter
...	...	...	...	...	...	...	...	...	...

3.3   Algorithm for Recommendation

KNOTES calculates the scores to select advice from all advices user by user. According the score, advices in top n (n is 10 in social experiment of chapter 4) are selected to become recommendations. The algorithm is divided into the following five steps.

I. Based on user value sense and the effectiveness of advice, the system scores each advice.

First, based on user value sense given in user profile, KNOTES calculates the weight v_i of each attribute i (i is in the range 1–5): "*Energy saving*", "*CO_2 reduction*", "*Cost saving*", "*Easiness*", and "*Recommended-level*". These weights express how important the user considers the five attributes. Then, the system calculates the score p_j of advice j (j is in the range of $1 - N$ (N is a 104 in the social experiment of chapter 4)) with the weight v_i and the attribute data a_{ij} using formula (1). The total of the weights is normalized as one. The maximum data in each attribute is normalized as one for calculation.

$$p_j^1 = \Sigma_i \, a_{ij} \, v_i \qquad (1)$$

In this calculation, "*Easiness*" has two attributes, "*Maximum number of available times*" and "*Difficulty level*", which are reversal values. Thus, they are subtracted from each maximum data before normalization. The normalized "*Difficulty level*" is multiplied by the normalized "*Maximum number of available times*", and the value is used as "*Easiness*". In this step, a score of the advice that matches user value sense and have high effects will be raised.

II. Considering user energy consumption volume, each score is revised.

Based on the ratio of the energy consumption in the last month c_1 and that in the same month of the previous year c_0, each score is revised by the following formula (2).

$$p_j^2 = (c_1/c_0)p_j^1 \qquad (2)$$

III. Recognizing user's own appliances and season, the system chooses available advices.

The advice about unowned appliances and off-season advice is not available.

$$\begin{cases} \text{owned appliance} & p_j^3 = p_j^2 \\ \text{not owned appliance} & p_j^3 = 0 \end{cases} \qquad (3)$$

$$\begin{cases} \text{on season} & p_j^4 = p_j^3 \\ \text{off season} & p_j^4 = 0 \end{cases} \qquad (4)$$

IV. Referring to advice reference histories, each score is revised.

Using formula (5), advice seldom executed has a greater chance of being recommended. In addition, the system can avoid the repetition of the same advice over the available time. For advice j, m_j is the maximum number of available time, and x_j is the number of executed times.

$$p_j^5 = (m_j - x_j)p_j^4/m_j \qquad (5)$$

The system can avoid repeating the same advice. k is a decay constant from 0 to 1 (k is 0.95 in the social experiment of chapter 4). d_j is the number of recommended times on advice j. With this calculation, the score p_j decreases as d_j increases.

$$p_j^6 = k^{d_j} p_j^5 \tag{6}$$

V.   At random, a score of the advice is raised.

To promote energy saving, it is desirable to inform users of every available advice. Thus, the system tries to recommend even low effect advice at least once a year. With the following formula (7), the system chooses one advice and raises its score at random with the 25% probability.

$$p_j^7 = p_j^6 + \{0, 1, 2, 3, 4, 5\} \tag{7}$$

4   Social Experiment

4.1   Overview of Experiment

A social experiment was conducted to verify the three requirements for advisory recommender systems in chapter 2. This section describes the data collection and the evaluation metrics according to the requirements.

Data Collection. First, we distributed the manual and questionnaires to forty seven subjects to collect the users' data. The questionnaires included questions about appliances owned by users, value sense, among others. They also included questions about the monthly amounts of energy consumption and bills for electricity, gas, kerosene from September 2009 to August 2011. This energy consumption data was used for recommendation algorithm in formula (2). Every subject answered these questionnaires by October 21, 2011.

Next, each subject used KNOTES online from December 1, 2011 to February 8, 2012, and its action logs were simultaneously recorded in the system. In this experiment, 10 suggestions were recommended from a total of 104 pieces of advice at once. Moreover, each subject was prescribed to input the monthly amounts of energy consumption into the system. Thus, it was expected that every subject would use the system once a week during experiment.

To collect user ratings for each advice, we performed our investigation from February 1, 2012 to February 8, 2012. Each subject answered a question about user rating (want to execute: 5, not: 1) on a web site. The rating data was transformed into a binary scale by converting every rating of 4 or 5 to "*like*", and those of 1–3 to "*dislike*".

Evaluation Metrics. To verify the three requirements, this subsection proposes four evaluation metrics: accuracy, excess, achievement and accumulation recall. Then, a random recommender system is introduced for a comparative evaluation with KNOTES.

- To recommend highly effective advice in the user's interest

It is necessary to identify effective advices. Thus, all advice is divided into two equal groups, "*high effect*" and "*low effect*", according to the sum of attributes in the advice data: "*Energy saving*", "*CO₂ reduction*" and "*Cost saving*". The proportion of "*like*" and "*high effect*" advices in all of the recommended advices is calculated to verify this requirement.

Accuracy is defined as confirmation that the system can reflect the user's preferences. The mean absolute error and mean square error have been used widely as accuracy metrics [11]. However, the metrics have been useful only when the system predicts user rating of each suggestion. Therefore, the metrics are not useful for KNOTES. Here accuracy is defined as a mean of user ratings in recommended advices.

$$\text{Accuracy} = \text{Mean of user ratings in recommended advices} \qquad (8)$$

- To avoid the repetition of redundant advice

Excess is defined as the sum of ratios of the number of excess times to the maximum number of available times on each advice, as shown in formula (9). If the user executes the advice more than the ideal times, the user may not efficiently save energy. Excess becomes better as the value gets closer to zero. For advice j for user u, E_u is the set of available advice, m_j is a maximum number of available times and x_j^u is a number of executed times.

$$\text{Excess} = 100 \frac{1}{|E_u|} \sum_{j \in E_u} \frac{max\left(m_j, x_j^u\right) - m_j}{m_j} \qquad (9)$$

- To prompt user to execute the given advice

For the verification of this requirement, achievement and accumulation recall are defined. Achievement is defined as the sum of ratios of the number of executed times to the maximum number of available times of each advice. For the user, it is desirable to execute all available advices according to the maximum number of available time on each advice.

$$\text{Achievement} = 100 \frac{1}{|E_u|} \sum_{j \in E_u} \frac{min\left(m_j, x_j^u\right)}{m_j} \qquad (10)$$

Accumulation recall is defined as the ratio of the sum of the number of executed times to the sum of the maximum number of available times on each "*like*" advice. T_u is the set of "*like*" available advice for user u.

$$\text{Accumulation recall} = 100 \frac{\sum_{j \in T_u} min\left(m_j, x_j^u\right)}{\sum_{j \in T_u} m_j} \qquad (11)$$

To comparatively evaluate KNOTES, a random recommender system is used. Recognizing user's own appliances and season, the random recommender also chooses available advices, as shown in formulas (3) and (4). Then, the system selects 10 suggestions at random from the available advices.

For three metrics, excess, achievement and accumulation recall, it is necessary to calculate the number of executed times x_j^μ. This number is calculated using the advice execution ratio in the social experiment.

4.2   Results

Experimental Results

As a result of the social experiment, twenty seven subjects were regarded as valid data. The average subject used the system six times during experiments, as shown in Table 2. This table shows the top and bottom three users in descending order by the number of times the system was used. The execution ratio varied user by user and showed marginal correlation with the number of times the system was used.

Table 2. Results of social experiment on KNOTES (top and bottom three users)

User id	Number of use times	Types of available advice	Types of like-advice	Total number of recommended advice (Types)	Total number of executed advice (Types)	Execution ratio
1003	16	65	12	160 (45)	11 (9)	6.9%
1001	15	74	17	150 (44)	53 (16)	35.3%
1024	13	79	30	130 (44)	77 (18)	59.2%
...	...	...	...	...	...	...
1048	2	79	37	20 (14)	12 (8)	60.0%
1014	1	63	25	10 (10)	0 (0)	0.0%
1034	1	74	20	10 (10)	0 (0)	0.0%
mean	6.3	74.4	30.4	62.6 (23.1)	18.3 (7.7)	26.5%

Evaluation Results. The proportions of "*like*" and "*high effect*" advice in all recommended advice are shown in Table 3, along with the values of the t-test in each proportion. The "*like*" and "*high effect*" advices were likely to be recommended in KNOTES more than when using the random recommender. Effective advice was given high priority compared with interesting advices in KNOTES, because the proportions of "*high effect*" and "*dislike*" advice were better than those of "*low effect*" and "*like*" advices.

The results for four metrics are shown in Table 4. From t-value, the differences between KNOTES and the random recommender were not proven for the following metrics: accuracy, achievement and accumulation recall. The excess metrics was better than the random recommender, and the difference between the systems was also proven. The value of excess in KNOTES was zero, therefore, it was verified that the system could avoid the repetition of redundant advice. However, the accuracy of KNOTES was not better than that of the random recommender.

Table 3. Proportions in recommended advice

	high effect		low effect	
	like	dislike	like	dislike
KNOTES	31.87%	43.64%	6.95%	17.54%
Random	20.93%	23.57%	20.02%	35.49%
t-value	4.61	11.07	−8.69	−11.01

Table 4. Results for four metrics

	Accuracy	Excess [%]	Achievement [%]	Accumulation recall [%]
KNOTES	2.41	0	2.54	0.11
Random	2.51	0.85	2.36	0.07
t-value	-0.99	-2.84	0.89	1.86

4.3   Discussion

In results, the number of times KNOTES was used was fewer than expected, and the execution ratio was not good, possibly because the interface of KNOTES was difficult to use. Moreover, users hesitated to execute an advice because of the mental workload required. In an advisory recommender system, it is important that the system prompts users to execute advice in a user-friendly way.

Conversely, it is conceivable that the advisory recommender system should store several small advices for recommendation. Some energy-saving methods have not only a significant effect but correspondingly significant drawbacks. By collecting many small advices, it will become easier to reflect the life rhythm and demand of the user in making recommendation. It will also become easier to recommend advices at more opportune times for the user.

KNOTES was likely to recommend "*like*" and "*high effect*" advices more than the random recommender, as shown in Table 3. This is because the system focuses on not only user's preference but also the effectiveness of advice in first step of recommendation algorithm. However, at the same step, the system failed to predict user's preferences by using user value sense. It resulted in a decline in accuracy, as shown in Table 4.

To precisely predict user's preferences, it is desirable to investigate the tendency of the user from log data. Analyzing what advice is more readily accepted by a user is regarded as a future issue. This social experiment provided useful data for such an analysis. Moreover, it is considered as a remedy to combine the traditional method focusing user's preferences with KNOTES.

5   Conclusions

An advisory recommender system that provides advice in the domain of energy saving, weight control and smoking stoppage is required. Unlike the traditional recommender systems, the system needs to focus on not only user's preference but also the effectiveness of advice. Moreover, the system should be user-friendly by the avoidance of the repetition of redundant advice. To implement the requirements, this paper has described an interactive system, named KNOTES, and its social experiments. The social experiment was conducted with forty seven subjects for about two months. To verify the requirements, the evaluation metrics have been defined: accuracy, excess, achievement and accumulation recall.

It has verified that KNOTES recommended the *"high effect"* advices and avoided the repetition of redundant advice. Meanwhile, it has not verified that the system recommend *"like"* advices, because of inaccuracy in the prediction of users' preferences based on their value sense. Improving the accuracy of the recommendations is one of remaining issues by applying the traditional method to KNOTES.

References

1. Resnick, P., Varian, H.R.: Recommender Systems. Communications of the ACM 40(3), 56–58 (1997)
2. Herlocker, J., Konstan, J., Terveen, L., Riedl, J.: Evaluating Collaborative Filtering Recommender System. ACM Transactions on Information Systems 22(1), 5–53 (2004)
3. Shigeyoshi, H., Inoue, S., Tamano, K., Aoki, S., Tsuji, H., Ueno, T.: Knowledge and Transaction Based Domestic Energy Saving Support System. In: König, A., Dengel, A., Hinkelmann, K., Kise, K., Howlett, R.J., Jain, L.C. (eds.) KES 2011, Part IV. LNCS, vol. 6884, pp. 242–251. Springer, Heidelberg (2011)
4. Ricci, F., Rokach, L., Shapira, B., Kantor, P.B.: Recommender Systems Handbook (2010)
5. Swearingen, K., Sinha, R.: Beyond Algorithms: An HCI Perspective on Recommender Systems. In: ACM SIGIR Workshop on Recommender Systems, New Orleans, Louisiana, vol. 13, pp. 393–408 (2001)
6. Ziegler, C., McNee, S.M., Konstan, J.A., Lausen, G.: Improving Recommendation Lists Through Topic Diversification. In: 14th International Conference on World Wide Web, Chiba, Japan, pp. 22–32 (2005)
7. Sawar, B., Karypis, G., Konstan, J., Riedl, J.: Item-based Collaborative Filtering Recommendation Algorithms. In: 10th International Conference on World Wide Web, Hong Kong, China, pp. 285–295 (2001)
8. Ben Schafer, J., Konstan, J.A., Riedl, J.: E-commerce Recommendation Applications. Data Mining and Knowledge Discovery 5, 115–153 (2001)
9. Fanger, P.O.: Thermal Comfort. Danish Technical Press, Copenhagen (1970)
10. Ueno, T., Nakano, Y.: An Approach for Ranking Energy-Saving Activities in Residential Buildings -Characteristics of the Model-, CRIEPI Report: R06006, Japan (2007); Breese, J., Herlocker, J., Kadie, C.: Empirical Analysis of Predictive Algorithms for Collaborative Filtering. In: 14th Conference on Uncertainty in Artificial Intelligence, Madison, Wisconsin, USA, pp.43–52 (1998)

Modeling a Human's Learning Processes to Support Continuous Learning on Human Computer Interaction

Kouki Takemori[1], Tomohiro Yamaguchi[1], Kazuki Sasaji[1], and Keiki Takadama[2]

[1] Nara National College of Technology
Nara, Japan
{Takemori,yamaguch,sasaji}@info.nara-k.ac.jp
[2] The University of Electro-Communications
Tokyo, Japan
keiki@inf.uec.ac.jp

Abstract. This paper presents the way to design the continuous learning support system for a human to achieve continuous learning. The objective of this research is to make a prototype system based on a learning process model to guide a human to achieve continuous learning. The main problem is how to keep supplying new goals to a learner for achieving continuous learning. To encourage the sense of continuous awareness toward goal discovery, we propose an idea to provide a human learner with invisible goals. This paper formalizes the continuous learning by a simple maze model with invisible goals and designs the maze sweeping task which involves multiple solutions and goals.

Keywords: continuous learning, invisible goals, maze sweeping task.

1 Introduction

Since 1980s, computer systems have been used in many different ways to assist in human learning. Computer-based systems have been applied in the field of human learning for three different purposes [1]: (1) to replicate human behavior, (2) to model human behavior, or (3) to augment human behavior. Described above, the position of our research is based on the second class toward the third class. However, there is a basic problem that these previous methods commonly depend on observable behaviors or activities. On the other hand, a learning process of a human has a major difficulty in observing since it is a mental process. So it is necessary to add a new twist to observe the learning process of a human.

In the field of management in business, psychological research on human motivation comes to the frontline. While, there is a great need to facilitate continuous improvement and innovation in business processes since an organization is to be successful in today's rapidly changing environment. And so, a learning process model to achieve continuous improvement has been proposed, it is defined as a process that results in changed behavior [2]. There are three elements for this process to be effective: the hows, whys, and whats of learning. The "hows" of learning is a technique to

S. Yamamoto (Ed.): HIMI/HCII 2013, Part I, LNCS 8016, pp. 555–564, 2013.

help the learning process. The "whys" of learning creates an environment and a task which provides meaning. The "whats" of learning enables a focus on goals or tasks. Learning process is consists of several learning-stages. Table 1 shows the stages of learning process [2]. This paper focuses on the learning-stages of awareness, understanding and commitment as shown in table 1.

Table 1. The Learning-stages of Learning process

Learning-stage	Meaning	The role of leadership
6 Reflection	"What/How have we learned?"	
5 Enactment	"I want to try this"	Allow risk taking
4 Commitment	"I want to know about this"	Remove barriers
3 Understanding	"I need to know about this"	Develop shared vision "whys"
2 Awareness	"I ought to know about this"	Develop shared vision "whats"
1 Ignorance	"I do not know and do not care"	Question

The main problem is how to keep supplying new goals to a learner for achieving continuous learning. To solve this problem, we propose an idea to provide a human learner with invisible goals to encourage the sense of continuous awareness toward goal discovery. Figure 1 shows modeling a learning process by invisible stimulus. Invisible stimulus means that it has no impact on sensory perception before action, but the response of the action differs from the past. Thus a human learner who encounters an invisible barrier becomes the state of being aware of something different. Awareness that results in change behavior is one of the shallow understandings, called *single-loop learning* that consists of normal level learning with fixed goal. In figure 1, the blocks with broken line mean that they are not given explicitly to a learner. The learner is expected to aware them, goals, barriers and rule of the learning task by understanding the maze sweeping learning task.

An invisible goal provides the learner with unforeseen success of goal discovery. It is expected to enhance the need for discovering unknown goals, then it results in a goal commitment of the learner. Commitment that results in goal discovery is one of the deep understanding, called *double-loop learning* that consists of two kinds of learning level: normal level (change behavior) and meta level (goal discovery). This paper focuses on goal discovery for continuous learning by invisible goals. For modeling the major learning-stages of a learning process as shown in figure 1, this paper formalizes the continuous learning by a simple maze model with invisible goals and designs the maze sweeping task which involves multiple solutions and goals.

For designing a learning environment, there are two points as follows:

(i) easy to monitor a learning process.
    For a learner, self-monitoring the learning processes assists the awareness to improve them. For the system, observing the learner's learning processes enables to evaluate the effect of the learning support system.

(ii) capture the essential features of continuous learning.
To evaluate a discovery learning task by the experiment with subjects within minutes, it is important to be easy to pass on meaning of the experimental task to a human learner.

Next, we describe the concept for designing the "whats" of learning in a maze model. For designing the maze sweeping task to encourage the process of continuous learning for a human learner, there are two points as follows:

(i) to drive single-loop continuous learning, the maze sweeping task is requested to collect all optimal solutions for each goal.
(ii) to drive double-loop continuous learning, the goal aspects of invisible and multiple goals are designed.

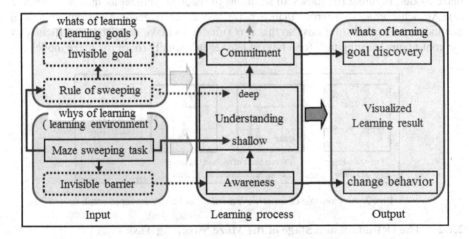

Fig. 1. Modeling a learning process by invisible stimulus

2 Designing the Continuous Learning by a Maze Model

First we describe designing the "whys" of learning to create a learning environment as a grid maze model, second, designing the "whats" of learning as the maze sweeping task is illustrated. For detail, please refer [3].

2.1 A Learning Environment by a Maze Model with Invisible Goals

As a learning environment, a maze model is defined by five elements, state set, transitions, action set, a maze task with its solution, and invisible goals. An invisible goal is defined as the undiscovered goal state of a maze sweeping task. In a 2D grid maze model, S is the start state of the maze, and G is the goal state of the maze.

2.2   The Maze Sweeping Task That Involves Multiple Goals

2.2.1   The Definition of an Achievement of the Maze Sweeping Task

To begin with, we describe a *maze sweeping task* with a fixed goal. It is defined as to find (shortest) paths from S to G which visits all states only at once in the maze model. Note that S is the fixed position. The *continuous learning task* is defined as to collect all solutions [4] of the task. The optimality of a maze task is defined as the minimum length of a path from S to G. An *achievement* is defined as the single-loop continuous learning of a maze sweeping with a fixed goal. Inputs of the learning are a maze environment and two kinds of states, a start state S and a goal state G in it. Note that a goal state G maybe a dummy goal. The *single-loop learning goal* is to find all optimal maze sweeping paths from S to G in a given maze.

Figure 2 shows an illustrated example of an achievement of 3x3 maze sweeping task. Figure 2 (a) shows an initial situation of an example an achievement of 3x3 maze model. Figure 2 (b) shows all solutions of the achievement as shown in figure 2 (a). An achievement is harder than a maze task since it needs a systematic search method to collect all solutions. So that it is suitable to make an adequate difficulty of the continuous learning task for a human learner in a small size of the maze model.

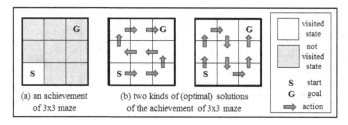

Fig. 2. An example of an achievement of 3x3 maze sweeping task

2.2.2   The Definition of a Stage of the Maze Sweeping Task

Next, we introduce a maze sweeping task that involves multiple goals. A maze sweeping task with multiple goals is defined as to find the paths from S which visits all states only at once in the maze model, note that G is the last state in the path.

A *stage* is defined as the double-loop continuous learning of a maze sweeping with multiple achievements. Inputs of the learning are a maze environment and a start state S. Note that a goal state G is normally invisible. The *double-loop learning goal* is to find all achievements in the given maze by discovering corresponding invisible goal state for each achievement. Figure 3 shows an illustrated example of the stage of 3x3 maze sweeping task invisible goals condition. Figure 3 (a) shows an initial situation of the stage of 3x3 maze invisible goals condition. There are three kinds of goals in a stage of the maze model as follows:

(i)   visible goal
      This type of goal is displayed for a learner as shown in figure 3
(ii) *invisible goal*
      This type of goal is not displayed for a learner in the beginning. After all solutions of the corresponding invisible goal are found, it is displayed as a discovered goal DG as shown in figure 3 (b).

(iii) dummy goal
> This type of goal is not displayed for a learner in the beginning just like an invisible goal, and it has no solution associated with the dummy goal. A dummy achievement is defined as an achievement which has no solution.

In this stage of 3x3 maze, there are four invisible goal states displayed as DG within eight states as shown in figure 3 (b), and other states are dummy goal states of this stage.

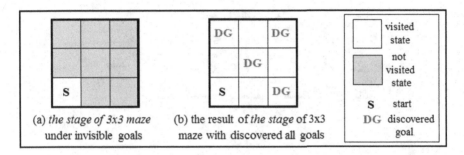

(a) *the stage of 3x3 maze* under invisible goals	(b) the result of *the stage* of 3x3 maze with discovered all goals	

Fig. 3. An illustrated example of the stage of 3x3 maze sweeping task

3 The Layout Design of Mazes for the Continuous Learning Task

3.1 Overview of the Continuous Learning Support System

Our system consists of three layers, top-layer, maze-layer and achievement-layer. The main function of top-layer for a learner is to select a stage associated with the maze-layer to proceed continuous learning according to the difficulty. The main function of maze-layer for the learner is to discover all achievements to learn.

(i) top-layer
> Figure 4 shows the overview of the top-layer of the system for a learner. A user can operate to start or exit the experiment, select the current maze (current stage) to challenge, and can verify the state of progress of continuous learning by the display of several measurements described below at section 4.1.

(ii) maze-layer
> In this layer, the user can select an achievement to challenge by clicking one of states in the current maze displayed in the center of the maze-layer window. If he/she find all solutions in the achievement, the goal state in the achievement is displayed as DG as shown in figure 3 (b), then it becomes to non-selective.

(iii) achievement-layer

In this layer, the user can challenge the maze sweeping task of the achievement selected at the maze-layer. If the user finds a solution of the achievement, it is registered, then the system goes back to the maze-layer. If he/she visits G without finding a solution, the small window appears to notice failure, then he/she can restart this achievement.

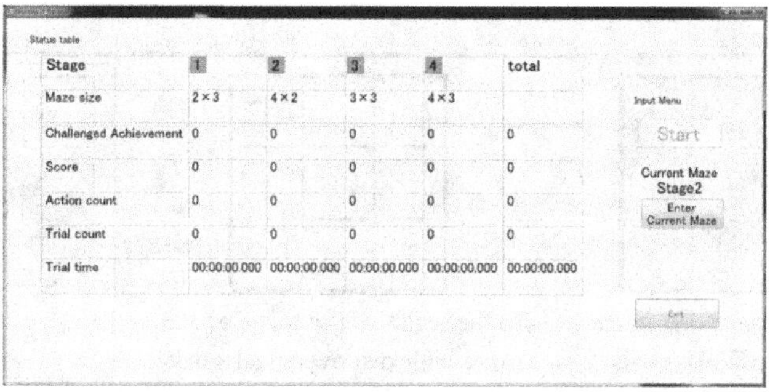

Fig. 4. Graphical User Interface for a learner - top-layer of the system

3.2   The Layout Design of Mazes on the Thinking Level Space

Now we coordinate the layout design of mazes on the thinking level space for designing the continuous learning task. Figure 5 shows the layout design of mazes for the continuous learning task. It is composed of four stages.

stage 1:   visible goals under unique solution.
It consists of 2 x 3 maze model with three visible goals and two dummy goals. Each goal is linked with an achievement of the 2 x 3 maze with a fixed goal. The solution of each achievement with a visible goal is unique, on the other hand, each dummy achievement with a dummy goal has no solution.

stage 2:   invisible goals under unique solution
It consists of 4 x 2 maze model with four invisible goals and three dummy goals. Note that for a learner, showing of both goal and dummy goal is the same until the learner finds a solution on an achievement with an invisible goal. The solution of each achievement with an invisible goal is unique, on the other hand, a dummy achievement has no solution.

stage 3:   *invisible goals* under multiple solutions
It consists of 3 x 3 maze model with four invisible goals as shown in figure 3 (b) and four dummy goals. Each achievement with an invisible goal has two solutions, on the other hand, a dummy achievement has no solution. In stage 3, there are total eight solutions.

stage 4: *invisible goals* under many solutions

It consists of 4 x 3 maze model with six invisible goals and five dummy goals. In this stage, there are total seventeen solutions much more than the number of solutions in stage 3. Within six goals, three goals have four solutions each, another two goals have two solutions each, and the rest of a goal has one solution.

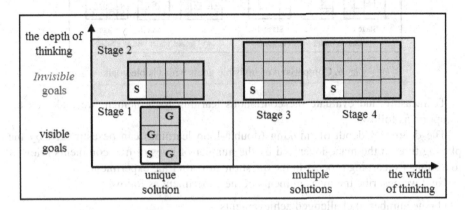

Fig. 5. The layout design of mazes for the continuous learning task

4   Experiment

4.1   Experimental Setup

To examine the effects our continuous learning support system, we perform the experiment in which total of twelve subjects are divided into two groups for comparative conditions. There are two objectives. First one is "dose our system support the continuous learning for a human?" Second question is "does the condition of invisible goals work so well to assist the continuous learning for a human?" Then, we describe the experimental task and the instruction for subjects, comparative conditions, assumptions and measurements, and the hypothesis. The experimental task explained to the subjects is to collect solutions of the maze sweeping task as many as possible as we described at section 2.2. To examine the degree to work through the continuous learning for the maze sweeping task, we prepare four stages as we described at section 3.2.

All subjects are instructed as follows:

(i)   Stage 1 is the practice maze to get used to the maze sweeping task.
(ii) Stage 2 and 3 are the real part, collect solutions as many as possible.
(iii) Stage 4 is a bonus maze, if you want to continue this experiment, you can challenge this stage as long as you can.

Figure 6 shows the experimental condition whether goals of each maze are invisible or not. Note that Stage 1 is the common condition that all goals are visible.   Figure 6

(a) shows the condition of mazes invisible goals condition. In this condition, all goals in the maze are invisible. Figure 6 (b) shows the condition of mazes visible goals condition. In this condition, all goals in the maze are visible.

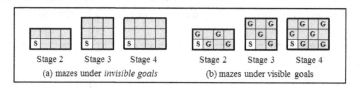

Fig. 6. Comparison of invisible goals with visible goals

To measure and evaluate the continuous learning for a human, we make an assumption as follows:

The degree of depth of thinking (double-loop learning) can be estimated by the playing time in the maze-layer and by the number of lines of free comments relevant to a subject's learning process in the questionnaire after the experiment.

Next we describe the measurements of the experiment as follows:

(1) the number of challenged achievements
(2) the number of collected solutions (displayed as Score in figure 4)
(3) the number of actions of the challenged achievements
(4) the number of trials of the challenged achievements
(5) the playing time in the achievement-layer
(6) the playing time in the maze-layer
(7) the number of lines of free comments relevant to a subject's learning process in the questionnaire after the experiment

First four measurements are counted on each stage as shown in figure 4. Fifth measurement is to estimate the degree of shallow understanding (single-loop learning), The last two measurements are to estimate the degree of depth of thinking (double-loop learning). Note that these measurements except (7) include the play data in dummy achievements.

Then we make a hypothesis as follows:

The condition of invisible goals encourages the deep thinking in the maze layer, and it results in the longer continuous learning than the condition of visible goals.

4.2   Experimental Results

4.2.1   Dose Our System Support the Continuous Learning for a Human?

This section evaluates the effectiveness of our continuous learning support system. All twelve subjects performed the bonus stage 4, and each four subjects of both conditions collected all 17 solutions of stage 4. The data of table 2 and table 3 is the averaged value of six subjects for each condition, and (data) is the standard deviation of six subjects for each condition. Table 2 shows the experimental result of the total results of stage 1, 2, 3 and 4. The seven measurements are described at section 4.1. As shown in table 2 (2), about 87 percent solutions (28 solutions among total 32 solutions) are collected in both conditions. Therefore, these results suggest that our continuous learning support system is effective for both conditions.

4.2.2   Does the Condition of Invisible Goals Work So Well to Assist the Continuous Learning for a Human?

This section evaluates the effectiveness of the condition of invisible goals compared to the condition of visible goals. In table 2, there is no significant difference in first five measurements (1), (2), (3), (4) and (5) between both conditions. However, the last two measurements (6) and (7) which are relevant to the degree of depth of thinking (double-loop learning) seems to be different. Analyzing the ratio of (6) divided by (5) the playing time in the achievement-layer, 4 out of 6 subjects are over 4 times invisible goals condition, relative to 1 out of 6 subjects is over 4 times visible goals condition.

Next, we analyze the measurements in stage 4 to evaluate the degree of continuous learning in straightforward way. Table 3 shows the experimental result of stage 4. The six measurements are same as table 2. In table 3, there is no significant difference in first four measurements (1), (2), (3), and (4) between both conditions. However, the last two measurements (5) and (6) the playing time in the maze-layer, both of the results invisible goals condition are longer than the results visible goals condition. The reason is that most subjects tend to find correct path at the maze-layer before select a goal state associated with the achievement in order to avoid failure at the achievement-layer. Therefore, these results suggest that the invisible goals condition is more effective to assist deep thinking of the maze sweeping task than the visible goals condition.

Table 2. The experimental result: total results of stage 1, 2, 3 and 4

measurements	(1) [times]	(2) [times]	(3) [times]	(4) [times]	(5) [sec]	(6) [sec]	(7) [lines]
Invisible goals conditions	17.6 (3.67)	28.0 (6.33)	341 (63.0)	39.8 (6.11)	270 (240)	1080 (1230)	9.00 (4.00)
Visible goals conditions	18.0 (1.27)	27.8 (7.06)	340 (114)	42.0 (9.19)	245 (140)	527 (250)	4.50 (4.04)

Table 3. The experimental result of stage 4

measurements	(1) [times]	(2) [times]	(3) [times]	(4) [times]	(5) [sec]	(6) [sec]
Invisible goals conditions	6.50 (2.95)	14.0 (5.62)	214 (67.9)	21.3 (6.74)	201 (243)	648 (1045)
Visible goals conditions	6.00 (0.63)	14.0 (5.29)	219 (112)	21.7 (10.4)	112 (65.0)	199 (172)

5   Discussions

The objective of the depth of thinking is to find learning goals to achieve toward continuous learning. It is defined by the condition of goals, that is whether goal states are visible (for single-loop learning) or invisible (for double-loop learning). The case of invisible goals is deeper level of thinking than the case of visible goals. A learner thinks by shallow understanding (single-loop learning) under visible goals condition since the goal states are given and known. On the other hand, under invisible goals condition, the learner thinks by deep understanding (double-loop learning) since the goal states must be discovered.

Then we discuss the awareness of learning objectives by a learner. Minimum requirements for double-loop learning are to find all goal states of a given maze sweeping task. However, the objective of "whys" of learning is to understand the rule of maze sweeping deeply. (For example, the regularity of the positions of DG in figure 3 (b).) Since "Reflection" is a sort of an interpretation of learning results by the learner, it is essential to aware various reflections (interpretation of learning results) in order to discover various learning goals for continuous learning.

6   Conclusions

We described the way to design the continuous learning support system based on a learning process model to guide a human to achieve continuous learning. Experimental results suggest that the invisible goals are more effective to assist deep understanding in a learning process than the visible goals. As one of the future works, we are planning to quantitate degree of difficulty of continuous learning as the complexity of maze model and action sequences of a learner, to keep maintaining the flow state of the human learner according to the learner's skill up.

Acknowledgement. The authors would like to thank Prof. Habib and Prof. Shimohara for offering a good opportunity to present this research. We also thank the reviewer for important comments. This work was supported by JSPS KAKENHI (Grant-in-Aid for Scientific Research (C)) Grant Number 23500197.

References

1. Sklar, E., Richards, D.: Agent-based systems for human learners. The Knowledge Engineering Review 25(02), 111–135 (2010)
2. Buckler, B.: A learning process model to achieve continuous improvement. The Learning Organization 3(3), 31–39 (1996)
3. Yamaguchi, T., Takemori, K., Takadama, K.: Modeling a human's learning processes toward continuous learning support system. In: Habib, M.K., Paulo Davim, J. (eds.) Mechatronics Engineering. Wiley-ISTE (to be appeared June 2013)
4. Yamaguchi, T., Nishimura, T., Sato, K.: How to recommend preferable solutions of a user in interactive reinforcement learning? In: Mellouk, A. (ed.) Advances in Reinforcement Learning, pp. 137–156. InTech Open Access Publisher (2011)

Part V

Cognitive and Emotional Aspects of Interacting with Information

On the Reading Performance of Text Layout, Switch Position, Topic of Text, and Luminance Contrast for Chinese E-books Interface Design

Wen-Te Chang[1,*], Ling-Hung Shih[2], Zunhwa Chiang[3], and Kuo-Chen Huang[1]

[1] Department of Product Design, Ming Chuan University
[2] Department of Visual Design, National Taiwan Normal University
[3] Department of Industrial Design, Ming Chi University
{kuochen,mimi,ccchuang}@mail.mcu.edu.tw,
redart@ntnu.edu.tw,
zchiang@mail.mcut.edu.tw

Abstract. This study investigated the effects of four independent variables—text layout, switch position, topic of text, and luminance contrast of Chinese E-books—on reading time and reading accuracy. Forty-eight college students, 26 females and 22 males aged 18–23 years, were recruited for the experiment. The present study demonstrated that a down-to-up text direction with a switch located to the right was the best layout for Chinese E-books in terms of reading time and accuracy. Moreover, the present study also addressed the effects of interactions between text direction and luminance contrast on level of visual fatigue and between text direction and topic of text, between switch position and topic of text, and between text direction and switch position on reading time. The results of this study should contribute to research related to the impact of touch-pad or interface designs on reading, luminance contrast, interface layout, satisfaction, and reading comprehension.

Keywords: Text layout, Switch position, Topic, Luminance contrast, E-book.

1 Introduction

Since ancient times, paper books (Conventional paper Books/ C-books) have been the main tools for reading and acquiring knowledge and information. However, 'E-books," digital readable works that can be implemented on smart phones, notebooks, and other mobile digital visual devices, were introduced recently and have experienced tremendous growth in total sales, becoming more popular than C-books (Peek, 2005). E-books are superior to C-books from diverse perspectives, including those that emphasize storage, transfer, delivery, and accessibility; these devices can also save time and add value as a collective online reference that acts as a dynamic and cost-effective information assistant for all professions. Moreover, the rapid

---

* Corresponding author.

S. Yamamoto (Ed.): HIMI/HCII 2013, Part I, LNCS 8016, pp. 567–575, 2013.

progress of related technology and applications has led to a new reading behavior based on digital interactive interface, which is gradually transforming the traditional behavior associated with C-books. Using iPhones and iPads as examples (Apple Inc., 2012), touch-pads have emerged as a ubiquitous medium with which most people become familiar while using cell phones or E-books. Previous studies have indicated that information about the relationships between touch-pad or interface design and reading interaction, luminance contrast, interface layout, satisfaction, and reading comprehension is urgently needed (Wu, Lee, & Lin, 2007; Kang, Wang, & Lin, 2009).

We hypothesized that significant main and interaction effects would be found between reading speed, and accuracy of understanding, on the one hand, and document layout, switch position, and luminance contrast, on the other. Therefore, we investigated the effects of four independent variables—text layout, switch position, topic of text, and luminance contrast—on reading time, and reading accuracy. The results have implications for design issues related to layout, switch position, topic of text, and luminance contrast; they can also be applied to attempts to design and evaluate user interfaces for the small portable devices serving as Chinese E-books.

2   Methods

2.1   Participants

A total of 48 college students, 26 females and 22 males, between 18 and 23 years of age ($SD = 1.87$) were recruited for the experiment. All participants were college students from the Design School of Ming Chuan University, Taiwan and spoke Chinese as their first language. All participants reported 16/20 or better corrected visual acuity; their color vision was tested by the experimenters using the Ishihara color test plates. None of the participants had color deficiencies. The participants received a reward of 150 New Taiwan dollars/hr for their participation.

2.2   Stimulus Materials and Design

The present study tested four independent variables: text direction, switch position, topic of text, and luminance contrast. There were four different text directions: up-to-down (Fig. 1a), down-to-up (Fig. 1b), left-to-right (Fig. 1c), and right-to-left (Fig. 1d). Three switch positions were used: top (Fig. 2a), right (Fig. 2b), and bottom (Fig. 2c). Twelve of level-3 texts chosen from among Taiwan's junior high school textbooks and a selection of leisure-time reading materials were used for the reading test. Each text contained 1,370–1,400 Chinese regular characters (kǎi shūin) in 14-point type presented on two pages, which necessitated page-turning operations. Three levels of luminance contrast, 1:3, 1:5, and 1:7, were used for the tests. A reading test was designed for each text to test reading accuracy.

Text direction and switch position were within-subjects variables, whereas topic of text and luminance contrast were between-subjects variables. In total, 12 stimuli (four directions × three switch positions) were randomly assigned and presented to each participant by a computer program.

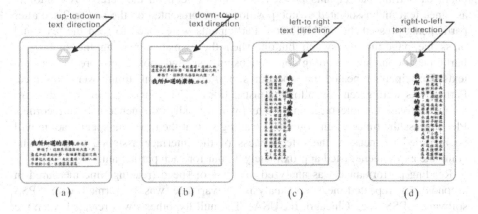

Fig. 1. The four text directions with the top switch position

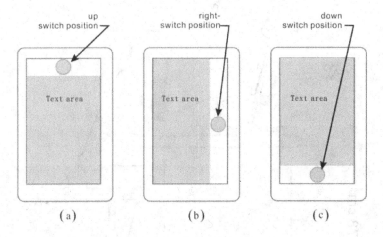

Fig. 2. The three switch-position interface layouts

2.3   Procedure

Layouts of stimuli were created with Adobe Reader (version X) and were displayed on a 7-in color E-book (MID VIA256, by VIA Technologies, Inc.) with the Android 2.2 operating system. The screen resolution was 800 × 600, with a refresh rate of 75 Hz. The monitor was placed on a table 73 cm in height, and the display was tilted to 75°. A head-and-chin rest was used to maintain a constant viewing distance of 50 cm (Fig. 3). All participants were tested individually in a quiet experimental room in which the light level was approximately 300 lux.

At the beginning of the experiment, participants spent 1 min reading on-screen instructions to familiarize themselves with the experimental procedure. Before exposure to the experimental items, participants engaged in three practice trials. To begin each trial, participants pressed the START icon on the screen. A randomly assigned text and associated switch position were presented on the screen 2 sec after participants pressed the START icon. Participants were asked to read the texts and press the page-turning switch button when they finished reading the first page. Participants completed reading comprehension tests and took 2-min breaks between texts. Participants repeated the procedures until all 12 formal stimuli were presented. Participants were given the following instructions: "Use your finger to press the start icon to activate the interface, and the test will formally commence and be recorded. Please press the timer when you finish reading so that the time you spent reading will be recorded to measure the effectiveness of the interface assigned to you." The complete experiment lasted approximately 2 hour for each participant.

Reading performance was analyzed in terms of speed (reading time measured in seconds). A repeated-measures analysis of variance was performed with SPSS software (SPSS, Inc., Chicago, IL, USA). The null hypothesis was rejected when the p-value was equal to or less than 0.05.

Fig. 3. Seated participant and display

3   Results

3.1   Reading Time

We found a main effect of text directions on reading time (F3, 126 = 41.94, p <.001). Multiple comparisons using the least-significant-difference (LSD) method showed that significantly less time was spent reading text in the down-to-up direction than in the up-to-down, left-to-right, or right-to-left direction. Less time was spent reading text in the up-to-down than the left-to-right and right-to-left directions. However, we found no difference between the latter two conditions.

Analysis of variance showed that switch position significantly affected reading time (F2, 84 = 10.23, p < .001). Switch position was compared in the same manner as was text direction. Significantly less time was spent reading when the right and bottom switch positions were used than when the top position was used; however, no difference between the former two conditions was found. Additionally, the main effect for topic of text on reading time was significant (F1, 42 = 4.76, p < .05). The reading time for textbooks was less than that for leisure-time materials, indicating that the difficulty of a text has a significant effect on reading time. No significant effect was associated with luminance contrast (F2, 42 = 2.78, p = .07).

The results showed three two-way interaction effects. The first was a significant effect of the interaction between text direction and topic of text (F3, 126 = 20.37, p < .001) on reading time. The simple effect of text direction (up-to-down vs. down-to-up vs. right-to-left vs. left-to-right) on reading time was significant for both the textbook (156.9 vs. 162.8 vs. 183.9 vs. 178.5; F3, 69 = 9.97, p < .001) and leisure-time materials (210.4 vs. 150.8 vs. 216.5 vs. 219.9; F3, 69 = 45.06, p < .001).

The second significant interaction effect was that between switch position and topic of text on reading time (F2, 84 = 16.81, p < .001.11). The simple effect of switch position on reading time was significant for textbooks (194.2 vs. 148.3 vs. 169.2; F2, 46 = 41.68, p < .001); however, the simple effect of switch position on reading time was not significant for leisure-time reading material (197.2 vs. 203.2 vs. 197.8; F2, 46 = 0.42, p = .66).

A third interaction effect was that between text direction and switch position on reading time (F6, 252 = 10.72, p < .001). Under the up-to-down text condition, subjects recorded longer times for switches at the top (M = 208.1), intermediate times for switches at the bottom (M = 178.9), and the shortest amounts of time for switches on the right (M = 164.0) (F2, 94 = 19.06, p < .001). Under the down-to-up condition, shorter times were observed for switches on the right (M = 141.2), intermediate times were observed for bottom switches (M = 150.5), and longer times were recorded for switches at the top (M = 178.6) (F2, 94 = 19.32, p < .001). However, under the right-to-left and left-to-right conditions, no differences in reading times were found among three switch positions, F2, 94 = 0.68, p = .51; F2, 94 = 0.63, p = .53, respectively.

3.2 Accuracy

The effect of text direction on accuracy was significant (F3, 126 = 5.58, p < .05). Multiple comparisons using the LSD method indicated that participants' reading comprehension was significantly less accurate under the right-to-left than under the up-to-down, down-to-up, and left-to-right conditions. However, no difference among the three latter conditions was found.

We also found an effect of switch position on accuracy (F2, 84 = 8.09, p<.05). LSD comparisons revealed that greater accuracy was achieved with the bottom switch position than with the top and right positions; however, no difference between the latter two conditions was found. The main effect of topic of text on accuracy was also significant (F1, 42 = 25.68, p < .001), indicating that the accuracy for the leisure-time reading material was significantly greater than that for the textbook. However, no effect of luminance contrast on accuracy was found (F2, 42 = 2.47, p =.10).

Three significant two-way interactions were also found. The first involved the effect of the interaction between text direction and topic of text (F3, 126 = 7.22, p < .001) on accuracy. The simple effect of text direction (up-to-down vs. down-to-up vs. right-to-left vs. left-to-right) on accuracy was significant for leisure-time reading material (84.0 vs. 83.3 vs. 66.7 vs. 90.1; F3, 69 = 10.25, p < .001) but not for textbooks (72.9 vs. 68.8 vs. 70.8 vs. 68.1; F3, 69 = 0.76, p = .52).

The second significant interaction effect was that between switch position (top vs. right vs. bottom) and topic of text on accuracy (F2, 84 = 6.68, p < .05). The simple effect of switch position on accuracy was significant for textbooks (79.2 vs. 71.9 vs. 59.4; F2, 46 = 9.76, p < .001) but not for leisure-time reading material (84.4 vs. 77.1 vs. 82.3; F2, 46 = 2.96, p = .06).

A third significant interaction effect was that between text direction and switch position on accuracy (F = 6,252 = 29.16, p < .0015). The simple effect of switch position (up vs. right vs. down) on accuracy was significant for the down-to-up (62.5 vs. 94.8 vs. 70.8; F2,94 = 19.11, p < .001), right-to-left   (88.5 vs. 38.5 vs. 79.17; F2,94 = 40.42, p < .001), and left-to-right   (98.6 vs. 81.3 vs. 58.3; F2, 94 = 24.36, p < .001) positions, but it was not significant for the up-to-down direction (77.1 vs. 83.3 vs. 75.0; F2, 94 = 1.04, p = .36).

4   Discussion

4.1   Interaction between Text Direction and Topic of Text

The data reflected significant main effects of text direction and topic of text on reading time and accuracy as well as a significant effect of the interaction between these two independent variables on both dependent variables. The split-data analysis further revealed that, with one exception, more time was spent reading leisure-time materials than reading textbooks. The exception was text presented in a down-to-up direction, which may indicate that a vertically arranged down-to-up text layout effectively reduces reading time, thereby eliminating the effect of topic of text. This outcome is similar to that of a previous study (Hall, Sabey, & McClellan, 2005), which reported that readers were not as familiar with the content of leisure-time reading materials as they were with the content of textbooks, leading to the need to devote more time to reading the former. The significant interaction involving topic of text complicates the issues that remain unresolved in this domain of research and suggests that tests of the design of the layout of Chinese script should consider the interaction between text direction and topic of text.

For the accuracy rate analysis, as simple effect of split-data analysis indicated, leisure-time reading material are significantly higher than textbook except on the left-to-right text direction, because horizontal, left-to-right, text direction compensate the effect of text type with the lowest accuracy percentage. The outcomes discussed above contradict those reported by a previous study (Hwang et al., 1988), which found no significant effects of vertical vs. horizontal text direction and suggested that the vertical, down-to-up text direction may compensate for the effect of topic of text by improving reading efficiency, whereas the horizontal, left-to-right text direction may decrease accuracy.

4.2   Interaction between Switch Position and Topic of Text

The main effects of switch position and topic of text on reading performance were statistically significant, and the two-way interactions involving these factors were also significant. The split-data analysis further revealed that leisure-time material took longer to read than did textbook material and that a right switch position strengthened this effect; thus, less time was needed for textbooks, whereas more time was needed for leisure-time material.

For the accuracy rate analysis, as split-data analysis indicated, leisure-time reading materials are significantly higher than textbook especially on the bottom switch position. A previous study (Vogel & Baudisch, 2007) suggested that touch errors would also have an effect on reading comprehension. The aforementioned results further clarify the relative advantages of various E-book interface switch designs by revealing the effect of the interaction between reading time and accuracy, which not examined by previous study. Moreover, these findings suggest that a switch position on the right would reinforce the effect of text type in Chinese E-books, and a bottom switch would decrease reading accuracy.

4.3   Interaction between Text Direction and Switch Position

The data analysis revealed that text direction and switch position had significant main effects on reading performance and that the two-way interactions between these variables were also significant. The split-data analysis of simple effects showed that up-to-down text took more time to read than did down-to-up text, but no significant difference involving switch position or left-to-right vs. right-to-left text directions was found. However, text presented in a down-to-up text direction with a right switch required less reading time than did other combinations of text layout and switch positions (141 sec.).

The split-data analysis of simple effects indicated that the highest levels of accuracy were associated with the left-to-right text direction with the switch position at the top (98.6%) and the down-to-up direction with the switch position on the right (94.8%). The lowest levels of accuracy were associated with the right-to-left text direction with the right switch position (38.5%) and the left-to-right text direction with the bottom switch position (58.3%).

In summary, the interaction between text direction and switch position indicated that down-to-up text with a right switch position was the best combination for Chinese E-books, as this combination was associated with the best reading performances as measured by reading time (141 sec.) and accuracy (94.8 %) in the present study. This result is similar to of a previous study (Parhi et al., 2006), which concluded that touch errors consumed more time during reading due to the interaction between screen information and switch buttons. A previous study pointed out that English readers tend to favor left or right switch positions due to the horizontal direction of the text (Park, & Han, 2010), but demonstrated not true for the Chinese E-book settings in the present study (Inhoff, & Liu, 1998; Rayner, 1998). Our experiment showed that the effect of text direction disappeared under the horizontal, right-to-left, and left-to-right conditions, leading to more time spent reading. Note that the present study did not test different screen sizes, background directions, or background colors of E-books. Future research should focus on related interactive and interface-design issues.

5   Conclusion

In conclusion, this study clearly points to the importance of the related issues of text direction, switch position, topic of text, and luminance contrast for the design of Chinese E-books in terms reading performance as reflected in reading time and accuracy.

With respect to interface-design issues related to Chinese E-books, the present study demonstrated that, contrary to results of most studies on English E-books, down-to-up text with a right switch position was the best arrangement in terms of reading time and accuracy. The results of this study should contribute to research on issues related to the relationships of touch-pad and interface designs with reading interaction, luminance contrast, interface layout, satisfaction, and reading comprehension.

Acknowledgement. The authors thank Yi-Ling Lo for her assistance with this study. Financial support of this research by National Science Council under the grant NSC 101-2628-H-130-002-MY2 is gratefully acknowledged.

References

1. Hall, A.D., Cunningham, J.B., Roache, R.P., Cox, J.W.: Factors affecting performance using touch entry systems: tactile recognition fields and system accuracy. Journal of Applied Psychology 73, 711–720 (1988)
2. Inhoff, A.W., Liu, W.: The perceptual span and oculomotor activity during the reading of Chinese sentences. Journal of Experimental Psychology: Human Perception and Performance 24, 20–34 (1998)
3. Apple Inc. (retrieved date March, 2012), http://www.apple.com/ipad/
4. Vogel, D., Baudisch, P.: Shift: A technique for operating pen-based interfaces using touch. In: ACM CHI Conference on Human factors in Computing Systems, pp. 657–666 (2007)
5. Wu, H.C., Lee, C.L., Lin, C.T.: Ergonomic evaluation of three popular Chinese E-book displays for prolonged reading. International Journal of Industrial Ergonomics 37, 761–770 (2007)

6. Rayner, K.: Eye movements in reading and information processing: 20 years of research. Psychological Bulletin 124, 372–422 (1998)
7. Peek, R.: The e-books radix. Information Today 22, 17–18 (2005)
8. Hwang, S.L., Wang, M.Y., Her, C.C.: An experimental study of Chinese information displays on VDTs. Human Factors 30, 461–471 (1988)
9. Park, Y.S., Han, S.H.: Touch key design for one-handed thumb interaction with a mobile phone: Effects of touch key size and touch key location. International Journal of Industrial Ergonomics 40, 68–76 (2010)
10. Kang, Y.Y., Wang, M.J.J., Lin, R.: Usability evaluation of E-books. Displays 30, 49–52 (2009)

Search Results Pages and Competition for Attention Theory: An Exploratory Eye-Tracking Study

Soussan Djamasbi, Adrienne Hall-Phillips, and Ruijiao (Rachel) Yang

User Experience & Decision Making Research Laboratory,
Worcester Polytechnic Institute, USA
{djamasbi,ahphillips,rachel.yang}@wpi.edu

Abstract. The World Wide Web plays a central role in many aspects of our modern life. In particular, using search engines to access information about products and services has become an integral part of our day-to-day activities. In this study we look at users' viewing behavior on search engine results pages (SERPs) through the lens of competition for attention theory. While this theory has been used for examining consumer behavior on e-commerce websites, little work has been done to test this theory for viewing behavior on SERPs. We use eye tracking data to analyze viewing behavior. The results show that viewing behavior can have an impact on a user experience and effective search, providing theoretical direction for studying the viewing behavior of SERPs.

Keywords: Eye Tracking, Search Engine Result Pages (SERPs), Viewing Behavior, Fixation, Competition for Attention.

1 Introduction

Visual search can be grouped into two categories: 1) goal-directed search involving decisions about where to find desired information and 2) exploratory search involving decisions about how to visually explore an environment [8]. Goal-directed search models assert that salience and/or relevance of stimuli drive a person's search behavior, while exploratory search models suggest that search behavior is influenced by competition among stimuli that attracts a person's attention. Information search behavior is often a combination of both types of visual search activities [6]. In fact, exploratory search behavior can often provide a more complete understanding of goal-directed search behavior, and thus, even in situations where users are looking for specific information, it is important to consider the effect of exploratory search, in addition to goal-directed search, on their behavior [8]. When searching for information online, a goal-directed search or an exploratory search involves the use of several types of objects in the visual field, including text, photos, moving objects, and varying instances of color. We know from previous studies (i.e. [1, 3]) that the size and proximity to the point of focus of an object can affect visual acuity, giving way to a type of competition for the user's attention.

In this study we examine the influence of exploratory search behavior on users' reaction to search engine result pages (SERPs). Therefore, we examine users' viewing

S. Yamamoto (Ed.): HIMI/HCII 2013, Part I, LNCS 8016, pp. 576–583, 2013.

behavior through the lens of competition for attention theory. According to this theory items in our visual field compete for our attention. Naturally, those items in the visual field that face less competition are likely to receive a greater deal of attention compared to those that face higher levels of competition in one's field of vision. While the competition for attention theory was used to examine users' reactions to shopping tasks on e-commerce web sites[7] little work has been done to examine users' viewing behavior on SERPs using this theory. Thus, in this study we examine whether competition for attention theory can help predict users' viewing behavior on SERPs.

To test users' reactions to SERPs from the competition for attention point of view, we conducted an exploratory eye tracking study. First, using the competition for attention theory, we determined a score for each area that contains information on the SERPs used in our study. These scores represented the level of competition faced by their corresponding areas. Next, we determined the amount of attention received by each area by examining the number of users who viewed these areas as well as the amount of time the areas were fixated upon by users. In this study, we examine viewing behavior during the time period between the appearance of the search results on the screen to the time users take their first action, that is, either scrolling or clicking on a link. Competition for attention theory pertains to a set of objects that are present in one's visual field. To examine competition for attention among a set of objects on the screen, it was necessary to select a time period where all of the items in the set were present in users' visual field.

2   Background

According to the competition for attention theory [8], each item on a page competes for user attention. The amount of competition experienced by each item can be represented as a numerical value or a competition for attention (CFA) score, which is determined by the size and the distance of surrounding objects. The higher the CFA value for an item, the higher the competition the item experiences. Using simple objects on PowerPoint slides, Janiszewski [8] has shown that items with lower CFA scores receive longer fixations. This is because items with lower CFA scores have fewer items around them to compete with them for attention [8].

This theory has also been used in the context of web pages. Hong et al. [7] used this theory to examine the impact of information layout of retail websites on user performance of a shopping task. They posited that competition for attention is higher when items are arranged in a list format. This finding has important implications for SERPs because search results are typically displayed in a list format. While the predictions of competition for attention theory can have a significant impact on the viewing behavior of SERPs, little work has been done to examine SERPs using this point of view. For this reason, we conduct an exploratory eye tracking study to examine users' viewing behavior on a SERP.

3   Methods

To collect users' eye movements, we used the Tobii X120 eye tracker, with a sampling rate of 120Hz. The eye tracker was placed in front of a 24-inch monitor with a resolution of 1920 x 1200.

3.1   Task

The task required users to carry out a web-based search using Google on a desktop computer. Participants were told to look for a snack place in Boston that they would like to visit with their friends. They were instructed to enter a specific phrase in the search box, namely, "best snack in Boston." The participants used the actual real-time Google search engine website to perform the task. Hence, the returned search results were not altered in any way. This allowed for an organic user-experience environment.

3.2   Participants

Data from a total of 11 participants was used in this study. Participants were from a pool of undergraduate students in a major university in the Northeast. They ranged in age from 18 – 24 and they self-reported to be "expert" users of Google search engine. Participants also self-reported to use Google search engine on a daily or hourly basis.

3.3   Measurements

Competition for Attention Score. As in prior research (i.e. [8]), for each area of the page that contained information, a CFA score was calculated. On SERPs used in our study, there were five main areas that contained information: 1) the area located on top of the screen, 2) the area where the search box was located, 3) the area where the links were located, 4) the area where search results were located, and 5) and the sign in area (Figure 1). To account for the use of organic searches; CFA scores were calculated for each of the areas on each page viewed by the participants.

Shift in Attention Score. When users are engaged in a goal-directed search their attention would shift more easily when it is easy for them to identify the next area to attend [8]. This situation can be represented by the shift of attention (SA) score, which is determined for each item by calculating the ratio of strongest to second strongest non-focal CFA of the item [8]. We calculated the shift of attention (SA) score for each item on the SERPs.

Attention. We used fixation to measure users' attention to an area of interest (AOI). While a user's field of vision typically consists of an array of objects one can attend to only one of the objects at a given moment [2, 5]. A user's eyes scan the visual field with rapid and continuous movements to collect information, which can happen during the period of time that one fixates on an item or holds a steady gaze on that item [9-11]. In addition, reading text requires steady gazes that are about 60 ms long [10]and SERPs are mainly comprised of text, therefore for this study we examined fixations that were 60 ms or longer. As in prior studies (e.g., [3]) we used fixation duration on and the proportion of viewers of the AOIs as measures of attention. Additionally, we calculated a new metric, fixation score, by multiplying viewer's rate and fixation duration. This new metric allows us to determine a composite score for an AOI by combining two important indicators of attention.

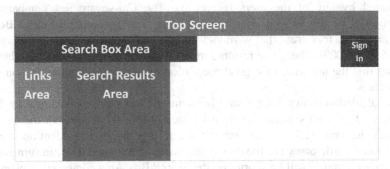

Fig. 1. Areas with information on the SERPs used in the study

4   Results

We calculated the CFA scores for the areas that contained information on the SERPs used in our study (Figure 1). Since organic search results were used in this study, a CFA score for each of the five areas of interest was calculated, for each page viewed, and for each user. The one-way ANOVA test showed that the average CFA scores for the five areas of interest were significantly different ($F(4,50)$= 215295, p=0.000) (see Table 1 for descriptive statistics).

Table 1. Descriptive Statistics for CFA scores for each AOI: Mean (SD)

Top Screen	Search Box	Links Area	Sign In Area	Search Results
2.10 (0.01)	2.59 (0.01)	2.39 (0.01)	2.88 (0.01)	0.71 (0.00)

Figure 2 displays the ranking based on the calculated CFA scores for each of the five areas of interest. As shown in the Figure 2, the Search Results Area faces the lowest level of competition, then the Top Screen, the Links Area, then the Search Box Area, and finally the Sign In Area. Because the Search Results Area had a much lower CFA score compared to other areas, we ran another ANOVA without the Search Results Area. The results showed that the CFA scores for Top Screen, Search Box Area, Links Area, and Sign In Area were also significantly different ($F(3,40)$=26310, p=0.000).

While users' attention during search on SERPs is naturally directed toward the search results, it is likely that their attention is also diverted to other areas on the page that compete for their attention. To test this possibility we looked at number of people who viewed the five areas outlined in Figure 2. Note that the following results refer to viewing behavior right after the search results were displayed on the screen. As expected, our analysis showed that 100% of users viewed the Search Results area as the task required them to do so. However, users also visited the Search Box Area, the Link Area, and the Top Screen Area. These areas were visited by 55%, 18%, and 18% of users respectively. The Sign In area, which had the highest CFA score, was not visited by any of the users (Figure 3). The Chi-square test comparing the proportion of people viewing the Search Results, Top Screen, and Search Box and Links areas (the four areas that were viewed by users) was significantly different ($X^2 = 19.95$, p = 0.000). The above results support the competition for attention theory by showing that the attention of a good proportion of users was diverted to non-search results areas.

Our calculation shows that the shift in attention (SA) scores was largest for Search Box Area (1.21) and smallest for Sign In Area (1.08); for the rest of the areas this ratio was the same (1.11). These ratios indicate that the shift in attention would be easiest when participants are looking at the Search Box Area. This, in turn suggests that fixation duration will be shorter on the Search Box Area compared to other areas [8]. Contrary to our expectation, The Search Box Area did not receive the least amount of fixation compare to other areas of interest (Figure 2). An ANOVA comparing fixation duration between the above mentioned areas showed that these areas did not differ significantly in regard to amount of fixation they received ($F(3,40)=2.35$, p=0.09). These results suggest that differences in SA scores among Search Box, Top Screen, Links, and Sign In areas may have not been large enough to facilitate an easier shift of attention from the Search Box Area to the other areas.

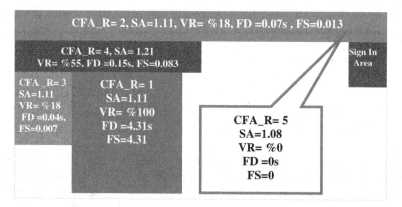

Fig. 2. Statistics for areas of interest. CFA_R: CFA ranking, SA: shift in attention, VR: viewer's rate, FD: fixation duration, FS: fixation score

Next, we looked at viewing behavior in the Search Results Area only. Just as before, we calculated the CFA scores for each entry in the Search Results area. The one-way ANOVA showed that the average CFA scores for entries 1 to 9 were significantly different ($F(8,81)$=461, p=0.000). The CFA scores for entries 2 to 6 were quite similar, indicating that these entries face similar amounts of competition. Entries 1 and 7 also had similar CFA values. Entry 9 had the lowest CFA value. We also calculated the SA ratios for each entry. Our calculation shows that the ratios for all entries had the same value (1.00) except entry 4 which had a slightly higher value (1.01).

For exploratory search behavior, according to competition for attention theory, the above CFA scores indicate that middle entries are likely to receive the smallest amount of attention. For goal-directed search behavior, SA scores suggest that middle entries, particularly Entry 4 should receive shorter fixations than others because these locations facilitate an easier shift to other locations.

The analysis of fixation duration showed that the amount of fixations on the 9 entries was significantly different ($F(8,81)$=5.38, p=0.000), with the top two entries receiving the most fixation. As shown in Table2, fixation duration was minimal below the fifth entry. Therefore, these results do not support the predictions of competition for attention theory. A Chi-square test showed that the proportion of people that viewed the entries was significantly different (X^2 = 47.20, p = 0.000). Most users looked at the top 4 entries, with the second entry having the most viewers. Fixation scores also reflect that the top 4 entries received the most attention.

Table 2. Statistics for Search Results

AOI	CFA mean (SD)	CFA Rank	%viewers	Fixation Duration(s)	Fixation Score
Entry 1	11.16 (0.50)	3	82%	1.39	1.140
Entry 2	12.31 (0.25)	6	91%	1.15	1.047
Entry 3	12.66 (0.14)	8	64%	0.66	0.422
Entry 4	12.70 (0.14)	9	73%	0.75	0.548
Entry 5	12.53 (0.12)	7	27%	0.42	0.113
Entry 6	12.16 (0.11)	5	9%	0.01	0.001
Entry 7	11.54 (0.10)	4	9%	0.04	0.004
Entry 8	10.49 (0.09)	2	9%	0.01	0.001
Entry 9	8.19 (0.08)	1	9%	0.02	0.002

5   Discussion

We conducted an exploratory study to test whether competition for attention theory can explain users' viewing behavior on SERPs. This theory has been used to examine search behavior for shopping tasks on e-commerce websites [7]; however, to our knowledge this theory has not been used to study search behavior for SERPs. Our analysis supported the predictions of the theory at the page level, showing that despite the goal-directed nature of the task used in our study, some of the users' attention was diverted to non-focal areas on the page. Within the Search Results Area however, competition for attention had little effect on how the entries were viewed. Users exhibited a top-to-bottom pattern of viewing; paying the most attention to the top two entries.

These results have important implications for theory and practice. From a theoretical point of view, the results show that the competition for attention theory can be extended to SERPs at the page level. That is, even in highly goal-directed search tasks, such as the one used in our study, attention can be diverted to non-focal areas. However, the viewing behavior within the Search Results Area was not explained by the amount of competition faced by the individual entries. One possible explanation is that the entries of the search results were displayed in a simple textual list format. According to the theory of visual hierarchy [5], this type of top-down display of information creates a clear hierarchy favoring the top entries by signaling that these entries are more important than others.

From a practical point of view, the results show that even in goal-directed searches attention can be diverted to non-focal areas. This is good news for advertisers, providing support for placing advertisements in non-traditional spaces (i.e. banners at the top or on the right-hand side). The diverted attention of a user also maintains the potential for motivating a user to click on an ad for revenue generation. For designers, the results suggest that making the non-focal areas of the page less salient may help users utilize the search results more effectively.

6   Limitations and Future Research

As with any experiment our study is limited to its setting. Nevertheless, the laboratory environment allowed us to capture users' eye movements. As customary in eye tracking studies, we had a small sample size [4] . Future studies are needed to replicate our non-significant results with a larger sample size. The participants in our study were drawn from a pool of college students. Previous studies suggest that generation may have an impact on how we view web pages [2]. Thus, future studies including other generations are needed to increase the confidence in generalizability of our results.

7   Contribution

Our results show that despite the goal-directed nature of search on SERPs, users' fixation can be diverted to non-focal areas of the page. This viewing behavior can potentially have an impact on effective search and thus user experience of SERPs. Our study provides a theoretical direction for studying the viewing behavior of SERPs, which can assist with improving the design of such pages.

References

1. Anstis, S.: Letter: A chart demonstrating variations in acuity with retinal position. Vision Research 14, 589 (1974)
2. Djamasbi, S., Siegel, M., Skorinko, J., Tullis, T.: Online viewing and aesthetic preferences of generation y and the baby boom generation: Testing user web site experience through eye tracking. International Journal of Electronic Commerce 15, 121–158 (2011)
3. Djamasbi, S., Siegel, M., Tullis, T.: Faces and viewing behavior: An exploratory investigation. AIS Transactions on Human-Computer Interaction 4, 190–211 (2012)
4. Djamasbi, S., Siegel, M., Tullis, T.: Visual hierarchy and viewing behavior: An eye tracking study. In: Jacko, J.A. (ed.) Human-Computer Interaction, Part I, HCII 2011. LNCS, vol. 6761, pp. 331–340. Springer, Heidelberg (2011)
5. Faraday, P.: Visually critiquing web pages. In: Proceedings of the 6th Conference on Human Factors the Web, pp. 1–12 (2000)
6. Groner, R., Walder, F., Groner, M.: Looking at faces: Local and global aspects of scanpaths. Advances in Psychology 22, 523–533 (1984)
7. Hong, W., Thong, J.Y., Tam, K.Y.: The effects of information format and shopping task on consumers' online shopping behavior: A cognitive fit perspective. Journal of Management Information Systems 21, 149–184 (2005)
8. Janiszewski, C.: The influence of display characteristics on visual exploratory search behavior. Journal of Consumer Research 25, 290–301 (1998)
9. Pan, B., Hembrooke, H.A., Gay, G.K., Granka, L.A., Feusner, M.K., Newman, J.K.: The determinants of web page viewing behavior: An eye-tracking study. In: Symposium on Eye Tracking Research & Applications, pp. 147–154 (2004)
10. Rayner, K., Smith, T.J., Malcolm, G.L., Henderson, J.M.: Eye movements and visual encoding during scene perception. Psychological Science 20, 6–10 (2009)
11. Vertegaal, R., Ding, Y.: Explaining effects of eye gaze on mediated group conversations: Amount or synchronization? In: Proceedings of the 2002 ACM Conference on Computer Supported Cooperative Work, pp. 41–48. ACM (2002)

Assessing Mental Workload of In-Vehicle Information Systems by Using Physiological Metrics

Susumu Enokida[1], Kentaro Kotani[2], Satoshi Suzuki[2], Takafumi Asao[2], Takahiro Ishikawa[3], and Kenji Ishida[3]

[1] Graduate School of Science and Engineering, Kansai University
3-3-35 Yamate-cho, Suita, Osaka 564-8680, Japan
[2] Faculty of Engineering Science, Kansai University
3-3-35 Yamate-cho, Suita, Osaka 564-8680, Japan
[3] Research Laboratories, DENSO CORPORATION
500-1 Komenoki-cho Minamiyama, Nisshin, Aichi 470-0111, Japan
k238046@kansai-u.ac.jp

Abstract. Use of physiological indices including ECGs and EMGs was investigated for estimation of drivers' mental workload induced by using in-vehicle information system (IVIS). The subject performed multiple simultaneous task paradigm consisted of driving using driving simulator, use of car navigation system and stimulus detection task paradigm. The results indicated that muscular loads obtained by EMGs tended to show higher activity in coherent with the level of mental workload and high correlation coefficient between muscular loads. The performance associated with stimulus detection task revealed the potential use of EMG signals as an index for evaluating mental workload.

Keywords: human engineering, bioinstrumentation/driving, physiological measurement, Electromyography.

1 Introduction

Recent advances in in-vehicle information systems (IVIS) have enabled drivers to drive more safely and more conveniently. On the other hand, these systems may decrease drivers' attention to driving or cause driver distraction. Therefore a method for assessing drivers' mental workload when they operate IVIS while driving is needed. The assessment method should be efficient, low cost, and easy to use.

Subjective, behavioral, and physiological indices can assess the mental workload for a certain working condition [1]. Many studies using subjective indices for assessing mental workload have been introduced. NASA-TLX is one of the main evaluation methods [2]. In addition, various behavioral indices have been used for assessing mental workload. In recent years, studies using a multimodal stimulus detection task (MSDT) with the use of the sensory modalities of multiple visual, tactile, and auditory mutually compremental modalities have been developed [3] [4]. This MSDT has been reviewed for standardization as the distraction test for IVIS [5]. As studies using physiological indices for assessing mental workload, event related potentials (ERPs),

S. Yamamoto (Ed.): HIMI/HCII 2013, Part I, LNCS 8016, pp. 584–593, 2013.

electrocardiograms (ECGs), and blood pressure have been extensively investigated [6] [7] [8]. These studies using physiological indices for assessing mental workload reported its potential for detecting influences to a human body by mental strain, however, there have been no clear evidences to establish the level of mental workload by physiological indices, and thus no successful intervention to assess changes of mental workload quantitatively with using physiological indices was available. This study aims to develop an algorithm for the quantitative assessment for mental workload with using physiological indices. In this paper, physiological index reacted by changes of operating IVIS was discussed. In addition, relationship between physiological indices reacted to mental workload and subjective index (NASA-TLX), and a behavioral index (MSDT) were validated. Especially in this paper, identification of physiological indices reacted by mental workload, was empirically conducted. Possibility for assessing mental workload for operating IVIS, using these physiological indices is discussed as well.

2   Experiment

2.1   Participants

Nineteen males participated in the experiment with payment. They were right-handed licensed drivers (average age: 21.7 with a standard deviation of 0.57; average driving experience: 2.79 years with a standard deviation of 1.28). This study was carried out after authorization by the Depart-

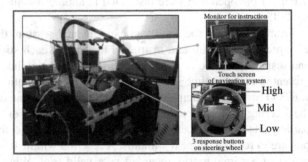

Fig. 1. Experimental Apparatus

ment of Psychology and Behavioral Sciences Research Ethics Committee of the Graduate School of Human Sciences, Osaka University, with due ethical considerations such as the acquisition of participants' informed consent.

2.2   Experimental Tasks and Instructions

The participants performed three tasks at the same time: operating a driving simulator (DS), operating visually-manually a touch panel IVIS, and MSDT. The participants were instructed to perform these tasks in the priority order of DS operation, IVIS operation, and MSDT. The experimental apparatus is shown in Figure 1.

The participants were instructed to operate the DS and follow, without coasting, a leading vehicle running at 80 to 85 km/h in the center lane of a continuously S-curved expressway with three lanes in each direction, while keeping a safe distance from the vehicle in front.

From the start to the end of an experimental session, the participants repeatedly received IVIS operation instructions, operated the IVIS, and suspended the IVIS operations for approximately five seconds. Four IVIS operations were used in the experiment:

(1) Control: The participants didn't operate IVIS. No image transition and no touch control were required.
(2) Map Scroll: The participants scrolled a map image twice in the direction of an arrow instructed in the monitor. Two image transitions and three touch controls were required.
(3) Radio Station Selection: The participants sequentially selected two radio stations instructed in the monitor. Five image transitions and six touch controls were required.
(4) Telephone Number Input: The participants entered a telephone number instructed in the monitor to set a destination. Five image transitions and fourteen touch controls were required.

In the IVIS operation task, the start time was instructed by recorded voice, while the details of the operation were instructed in another monitor located on the rear side of the IVIS screen.

From the start to the end of an experimental session, the participants were repeatedly presented stimuli and instructed to react to each stimulus by pressing a button, and suspend the task. A visual stimulus, a tactile stimulus or an auditory stimulus was presented one at a time in random order. The presentation duration of each stimulus was 300 ms. The participants were required to press one of three buttons mounted on the steering wheel immediately when they perceived one of the above stimuli. The participants were instructed to suspend the task for 2000 to 4000 ms randomly, and to prepare to receive the next stimulus. A reaction within 100 to 2000 ms after the application of a stimulus was regarded as a valid trial. When no reaction was observed within 2000ms, the trial was regarded as a detection error. The experimental session ended at the moment the participants made 60 valid responses for visual stimuli, 50 for tactile stimuli, and 50 for auditory stimuli.

2.3   Experimental Protocol

First we examined (1) DS operation (single task, 3 min), (2) MSDT (single task, 3 min), (3) DS operation plus map scroll on IVIS (dual task, 3 min), (4) DS operation plus radio station selection on IVIS (dual task, 3 min), (5) DS operation plus telephone number input on IVIS (dual task, 3 min) which were not analyzed in this study.

Then we examined the following four conditions to analyze the performance of MSDT in this study: (6) DS operation plus MSDT (dual task, 12 min; CONTROL), (7) DS operation, map scroll on IVIS plus MSDT (triple task, 12 min; MAP), (8) DS operation, radio station selection on IVIS plus MSDT (triple task, 12 min; RADIO), (9) DS operation, telephone number input on IVIS plus MSDT (triple task, 12 min;

TEL). The order of the three levels (7) through (9) was counterbalanced between eighteen of the participants, while the above levels were assigned in a totally randomized manner to the remaining one participant.

During the experiment, the vehicle behavior signals calculated from the DS and participant's biological signals (ECG, EMG, pulse waves, respiration, brain waves, and EOG) were also recorded. After completion of the experiment at each condition, participants rated their subjective workload using the NASA-TLX. However, this paper does not describe the results of the above bioinstrumentation and subjective workload ratings.

The experiment took two days to practice and complete the conditions for each participant.

2.4   Bioinstrumentation

Biological signals measured at the experiment include ECGs, erectromyograms (EMGs), pulse waves, thoracic respiration, electroencephalograms (EEGs), and electrooculograms (EOGs). ECGs were obtained by using CM5 instruction. EMGs were obtained by active electrodes (NM-512G, Nihon Kohden) affixed to the top of the trapezius muscle on the right shoulder. Pulse wave by the finger-prove (TL/201T, Nihon Kohden) was placed at the second finger of the left foot. Thoracic respiration was obtained by using a belt-shaped sensor (TR-512G, Nihon Kohden) rolled around the abdominal region. In addition, these signals were recorded by using multi-telemeter (WEB-9000, Nihon Kohden) and basic medical system software (QP-110H, Nihon Kohden) as 500 [Hz] of sampling frequency. The rib abdomen was used as a body ground for EMGs and ECGs.

In addition, EEG signals (F3, F4, C3, C4, O1, O2: unipolar induction, reference electrode was placed on the left earlobe A1) and Vertical EOG signals were recorded by a silver plate electrode (NE-116A, Kohden) for EEG, amplified by biological monitor (BIOTOP 6R12, NEC) with 1000 [Hz] of sampling frequency.

2.5   Data Analysis

In this paper, physiological indices for analysis were ECGs (R-R Interval, %HF, LF/HF, where, HF as High Frequency, LF as Low Frequency), EMGs (Root Mean Square: RMS), EEGs (Background Activity, β/α), pulse wave, and respiratory rates [1/s]. Trends of changes of the above physical indices were validated corresponding to the changes of mental workload by the difficulty of the tasks set on the experiment. Analysis of variance was conducted among participants as dependent variable with each of physiological indices, and independent variable as task condition. All physiological indices were normalized between the tasks on each participant to exclude influence of the individual differences. In this paper, results of EMGs were shown.

Previous research attempting to evaluate the ease of driving by instability of vehicle reported that EMGs at masseter was raised by the stress while driving with sense of anxiety [9], and EMGs were included correspondingly to the change of the level of strain by the difference of riding comfortability while driving [10]. Results of above studies showed the possibility that mental workload such as a mental stress and mental strain can be evaluated by using a change of EMGs. Therefore, in this study, it was verified whether mental workload such as mental strain while operating IVIS in particular can be evaluated by using EMGs.

Analysis of EMGs started with calculation of RMS values from raw EMG data obtained by the experiment. RMS was obtained such that a total of 100 data points, separated into half, that is, before and after the onset, were averaged into a single plot. Because participants having low averages of RMS values at all times of all tasks were considered not actively performed using the trapezius muscle for steering, these participants' muscle activities were less sensitive to the changes in mental workload. Therefore, we set a threshold value as 50% of the average RMS of all tasks on all participants, and participants that had average RMS lower than these thresholds were excluded from analysis, yielding EMG data for eight of participants were not analyzed farther. On the other hand, mental workload such as a mental strain while operating IVIS corresponded to the motions induced by perception, judgment, and manipulation of participants, hence, because factors causing mental workload to the participants could be identified by EMGs grouped by a unit of single motion, we performed data processing as follows. In this paper, we assumed three factors that influence EMGs recorded from participants, (1) presence or absence of influences from mental workload by operating IVIS, (2) differences of sensitivity to the mental workload by differences of motions of the left hand while operating IVIS, and (3) presence or absence of effects on the sensitivity as the evaluation index for EMGs by steering positions griped by the right hand. Therefore, we identified motions of participants by visual inspection with using videotaped data on the experiment, for the purpose to examine above three conditions to be the factors for affecting EMG data. We analyzed data in terms of the following three methods to clarify the relationship between muscle activity and the details of pattern of motions while operating IVIS.

(1) Comparison of EMGs while steering by the right hand when IVIS was operated, with steering with both hands before/after IVIS was operated.

Driving operations by participants were divided into "steering by the right hand when IVIS was operated, " that is, participants steered and operated IVIS in the same time, and "steering with both hands before/after IVIS was operated" that is, participants steers by their both hands without operating IVIS. We obtained muscular loads as EMGs for these two steering performances and compared for each task. If muscular loads on operating IVIS are sensitive to the differences of task conditions, differences of mental workload such as a mental strain and time pressure by operating IVIS can be evaluated by using EMGs. In addition, it is conceivable that changes in EMGs while steering with both hands can be an index to reflect general mental workload during the task.

Moreover, correlations between muscle activity while operating IVIS and, behavioral indices (miss rates for MSDT) and subjective indices (WWL scores by NASA-TLX) were evaluated as well.

(2) Comparison of muscular loads among three types of motions by the left arm on steering while the right hand for IVIS operation.

We hypothesized that the left hand motion played an important role for reflecting mental workload more sensitively, by verifying changes in EMG signals during operating IVIS. Therefore, after instructions were given to start operating IVIS, EMGs for each action were recorded. The actions can be classified into three; 'the action when participant moved his left hand to IVIS from steering wheel', 'the action when participant stayed his left hand on IVIS', and 'the action when participant returned his left hand to steering wheel from IVIS'.

(3) Differences in sensitivity of the EMGs by the location of the right hand on the steering wheel.

Differences in the location of the right hand would be considered as a potential factor for biasing EMG signals. At the time of the experiment, participants were able to steer any locations on the steering wheel. However, post-hoc observation for participants driving videos and their associated EMG signals, revealed that difference of grip positions on the steering wheel were varied by postures during operating IVIS, hence the variety of postures may affect muscular loads for the upper right trapezius, which demonstrate characteristic responses to maintain postures of the upper limb. Therefore, whether or not changes in EMGs by differences of the right hand's grip positions on steering wheel was validated. At the time of steering in the experiment, it was instructed that grip positions were set to either upper, middle, or lower position on steering wheel as shown in figure 1. Accordingly, by calculating and comparing RMS-values of each grip position and on each task for each participant, we decided to examine difference of sensitivity of EMG as classified by the grip position as an index for the mental workload.

EMGs of each detailed motion for operating IVIS by obtaining results through the analysis (1) and (2), were averaged on the basis of operations and motions, and were used for evaluating mental workload. RMS values for EMGs normalized by each participant were obtained and their statistical analysis was conducted.

On the other hand, for the analysis (3), different data comparison was conducted because participants were instructed to change the grip position freely on the steering wheel throughout the experiment. Hence, there were many participants who change the grip positions several times within one task trial. Thus, average values of muscular loads by each grip position were compared among grip positions despite the differences in participants and tasks. These RMS values were standardized for each participant.

3   Results

(1) Comparison of EMG while steering by the right hand when IVIS was operated, with steering with both hands before/after IVIS was operated.

Figure 2 shows the relationship between tasks and the muscular loads of the upper trapezius when the participants perform driving steered by the right hand with IVIS operation. Because hypothesis of sphericity for muscle activities of the upper trapezius while driving by the right hand with IVIS operation was not rejected (p=0.76), correction of degrees of freedom was not applied. As showing in figure 2, muscular loads at the tasks with IVIS operation and the right hand-steering were significantly higher than those at the CONTROL condition (F (3, 30) =10.44, p<0.05). Figure 3 shows the relationship between task and muscle activities of the right upper trapezius at the time from the end of operating IVIS, that is, period while driving with both hands, to the beginning of the next instruction for operating IVIS. Again, hypothesis of sphericity was not rejected (p=0.78), and correction of degrees of freedom was not taken into account. While steering by both hands before/after operating IVIS, there was no significant difference of muscular loads between tasks (F (3, 30) =0.70, n.s.).

Positive correlation was found between behavioral indices (miss rates on MSDT) and muscular loads (RMS-values) while operating IVIS (r=0.68, t (44) = 5.97, p<0.01). In addition, positive correlation was found between subjective indices (WWL-point obtained by NASA-TLX) and muscular loads (RMS-values) while operating IVIS (r=0.65, t (40) = 5.27, p<0.01). Note that number of participants obtained for correlation between subjective indices and EMGs became 10 because omission of filling out NASA-TLX by one of participants was found after the experiment.

(2) Comparison of muscular loads among three types of motions by the left arm on steering while IVIS was operated by the right hand.

Figures 4, 5, and 6 show trends of muscular loads among tasks by differences of motions of the left arm while operating IVIS (figure 4: the left hand moves to IVIS, figure 5: the left hand stayed on IVIS, figure 6: the left hand returns from IVIS). Participants performed driving by using one hand when they operate IVIS, thus tasks targeted for comparison were following three tasks, that is, MAP, RADIO, and TEL. In addition, because hypothesis of sphericity for two conditions were not rejected (move to IVIS: p=0.50, stay at IVIS: p=0.33), correction of degrees of freedom was not applied. On the other hand, because hypothesis of sphericity for EMGs when participants returned their hand to steering wheel from IVIS was rejected (p=0.034), correction of degrees of freedom was applied using the Greenhouse-Geisser's method. As shown in figure 4, there were no significant differences in EMGs among different IVIS operations when participants moved their left hand to IVIS (F (2, 20) =0.98, n.s.). In addition, figure 5 shows that there were no significant EMG differences among different IVIS operations when participants stayed their left hand on IVIS (F (2, 20) =1.83, n.s.). When the participants returned their hand to the steer, there were marginally significant EMG differences among different IVIS operation (F (1.31, 13.09) =3.35, p<0.10), shown in figure 6. Among them, EMGs on TEL task were significantly higher than those in MAP task (p<0.05).)

(3) Differences in sensitivity of the EMGs by the location of the right hand on the steering wheel.

Figure 7 shows the tendency of average EMGs on each grip location for steering by the right hand, summarized as a ground average. Figure 7 shows that EMGs when participants gripped high position of steering wheel was higher than those when participants gripped low position of steering wheel.

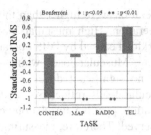

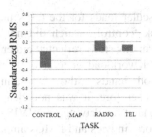

Fig. 2. Relationship between task and standardized RMS of right trapezius muscle when car navigation system was handled

Fig. 3. Relationship between task and standardized RMS of right trapezius muscle before/after car navigation system was handled

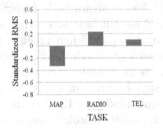

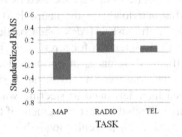

Fig. 4. Comparison of standardized RMS of right trapezius muscle between tasks while participant's left hand was moved to car navigation system

Fig. 5. Comparison of standardized RMS of right trapezius muscle between tasks while participant's left hand stayed on car navigation system

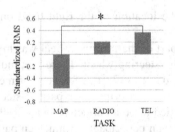

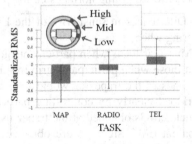

Fig. 6. Comparison of standardized RMS of right trapezius muscle between tasks while participant's left hand was returning to car navigation system

Fig. 7. Differences in standardized RMS by grip positions

4   Discussion

(1) Comparison of EMGs while steering by the right hand when IVIS was operated, with steering with both hands before/after IVIS was operated.

Muscular loads for the tasks including IVIS operation were higher than those for the task 'control', which did not require IVIS operation. High muscular loads observed in this study reflected either high mental workload caused by IVIS operation or physical workload generated by right-hand steering. Muscular loads while driving with both hands without operating IVIS showed no significant difference among tasks. Therefore, it was not clear that these muscular loads reflect overall mental workload at the driving with IVIS operation. In addition, positive correlation between behavioral indices and EMGs among tasks was observed. Therefore, measuring EMG signals while operating IVIS by performing MSDT is one of the potential methods for evaluating mental workload.

(2) Comparison of muscular loads among three types of motions by the left arm on steering while IVIS was operated by the right hand.

Muscular loads on the tasks 'RADIO' and 'TEL' were significantly higher than those on the task 'MAP', when participants returned his left hand to steering wheel from IVIS. Intention for a return to steering from operating IVIS may relate to these significant differences of muscular loads. Because participants felt these anxiety and stress and deserved to avoid such situation as soon as possible, they would have moved their left hand to steering wheel faster to steer by his both hands. Muscular strain generated by fast movement of the left hand would influence EMGs of the right trapezius. High muscular loads by the masseter, supposedly muscle strain, reflected stress and anxiety, reported by the previous study [9]. Thus, increasing tendency for muscular loads found in this experiment may reflect mental stress and anxiety as well. In addition, this anxiety may be caused by the mental stress during transition from normal steering to IVIS operation back and forth. Future study includes additional verification required for confirming participants' intention to move their left hand quickly for returning normal steering position.

(3) Differences in sensitivity of the EMGs by the location of the right hand on the steering wheel.

Muscular loads when participants grip upper part of the steering wheel was higher than those when participants grip lower part of the steering wheel. Therefore, muscular loads of the trapezius would be a potential index to reflect differences of mental workload clearly by controlling participants' posture to grip upper part of steering wheel. EMGs obtained at the trapezius was clarified to be an effective index, only if apparent EMG signals were obtained, that is, eleven participants of nineteen participants in this paper. Therefore, it is important to set configuration of environment for detecting clear muscle activities of the right trapezius by controlling the grip position on the steering wheel. In addition, it would be necessary to determine the appropriate indices by comparing EMGs of the other muscles as well. EMGs when participant returned his left hand to steering wheel from IVIS especially changed the level of mental workload by operating IVIS from the above results (1) (2) and (3). Therefore, our results clearly opened up the possibility that EMGs were a valid index for evaluating mental workload.

5   Conclusion

In this paper, we validated physiological indices which reflected levels of mental workload, that is, the effect induced by differences in the IVIS operation. EMGs reflected levels of mental workload and they showed correlation with subjective and behavioral indices. It was still marginal to infer that, possibility of using EMGs for evaluating mental workload could be demonstrated. We must identify the environment and the kind of muscle locations which reflect levels of mental workload more sensitively, and validate sensitivities of these muscles hereafter.

Acknowledgement. This study was conducted in collaboration with Osaka University. We would like to express our gratitude to collaborators, Kazumitsu Shinohara, Hiroshi Naito, and Shuhei Yoshida.

References

1. Haga, S.: Indices for assessing mental workload. Theory and measurement for mental workload, pp. 19–22 (2001)
2. Haga, S., Mizugami, N.: Japanese version of NASA Task Load Index: Sensitivity of its workload score to difficulty of three different laboratory tasks. Ergonomics 32(2), 71–79 (1996)
3. Shinohara, K., Shimada, A., Kimura, T., Ohsuga, M., Wakamatsu, M.: Assessing driver's cognitive load by stimulus detection task when a driver operates an in-vehicle information devise. In: (2012 JSAE Spring Convention) Proceedings, No. 81-12, pp. 13–18 (2012)
4. Merat, N., Jamson, H.A.: The effect of stimulus modality on signal detection: Implications for assessing the safety of in-vehicle technology. Human Factors 50, 145–158 (2008)
5. Visual-Manual NHTSA Driver Distraction Guidelines for In-Vehicle Electronic Devices, from the U.S. Federal Register,
   http://www.gpo.gov/fdsys/pkg/FR-2012-02-24/pdf/2012-4017.pdf
   (accessed July 31,2012)
6. Jin, H., Shimomura, Y., Iwanaga, K., Katsuura, T., Sugiura, K., Mochizuki, M.: Evaluation of the mental workload during a visual search task with working memory by various physiological indices. Journal of Physiological Anthroporogy 10(4), 33–40 (2005)
7. Ohsuga, M., Boutani, H., Shimada, A., Shinohara, K., Kimura, T., Wakamatsu, M.: Assessing driver's cognitive load by physiological indices. In: (2012 JSAE Spring Convention) Proceedings, No. 81-12, pp. 19–24 (2012)
8. Kamakura, Y., Ohsuga, M., Hashimoto, W., Lucian, G., Sato, H.: Evaluation of driver's cognitive load caused by presented information using P3 latency in eye-fixation related potential. Transactions of Society of Automotive Engineers of Japan 40(5) (2009)
9. Kuramori, A., Koguchi, N., Kamijo, M., Sadoyama, T., Shimizu, Y.: Evaluation method for vehicle handling and stability focusing on muscle tension of driver. Journal of Japan Society of Kansei Engineering 6(2), 87–92 (2006)
10. Zheng, R., Yamabe, S., Nakano, K., Aki, M., Nakamura, H., Suda, Y.: Evaluation of driver physiological nurden during automatic platooning using physiological index: development of energy-saving ITS technologies. In: (2010 JSAE Spring Convention) Proceedings, No. 7-10, pp. 29–32 (2010)

Evaluation of Somatosensory Evoked Responses When Multiple Tactile Information Was Given to the Palm: A MEG Study

Akihito Jinnai[1], Asuka Otsuka[2], Seiji Nakagawa[2], Kentaro Kotani[3], Takafumi Asao[3], and Satoshi Suzuki[3]

[1] Graduate School of Science and Engineering,
Kansai University 3-3-35 Yamate-cho, Suita, Osaka 564-8680, Japan
[2] Health Research Institute, National Institute of Advanced Industrial Science and Technology
(AIST) 1-8-31 Midorigaoka, Ikeda, Osaka 563-8577, Japan
[3] Faculty of Engineering Science, Kansai University,
3-3-35 Yamate-cho, Suita, Osaka 564-8680, Japan
k066748@kansai-u.ac.jp

Abstract. In this study, as a part of comprehensive approach to develop an interface for tactile information delivery, we aimed at capturing the relationship between neuronal and perceptual sensitivity characteristics of in human hand as indexed by neuromagnetic and psychometric responses.

Airpuff stimuli were presented to multiple locations on the ventral side of subjects' palm, which somatosensory evoked responses were observed.

As a result, it was observed that the latency and amplitude of the evoked responses in the primary somatosensory area (SI) was not related to the location on the palm. Although mechanoreceptors in the palm area distributed densely at both the center of the palm and the proximal part of the proximal phalanges, no effects on location were found by the amplitude of the evoked responses at SI area. These results suggested that amplitude of the evoked responses at SI did not depend on the distribution of the mechanoreceptors.

Keywords: Magnetoencephalography, Tactile, Airpuff stimuli, Somatosensory evoked responses, Primary somatosensory area.

1 Introduction

People who visually handicapped obtain information about outside world by using braille. It was reported that only 10.6% of handicapped people can use brailles [1]. Hence, tactile display became common as an information presentation device for the visually disabled. Mizugami et al.[2] reported that it was possible to recognize simple characters by a tactile display with at most 9 actuators, used for character presentation. However, National Institute of Vocational Rehabilitation reported that size of characters proportional to the tactile display and individual differences were key issues for obtaining high identification rates [3]. Thus, there have been demands to improve the identification rates for various users. When people perceived the tactile

S. Yamamoto (Ed.): HIMI/HCII 2013, Part I, LNCS 8016, pp. 594–603, 2013.

stimuli, four types mechanoreceptors with different characteristics detect the stimuli. Sakai, et al.[4] reported that it was important to present information by considering the distribution patterns of cutaneous mechanoreceptors for improving character identification rates. We used magnetoencephalography (MEG) to capture the dynamic changes of information processing in the brain. There have been several studies which evaluated activity of somatosensory areas by using MEGs when tactile stimulation was delivered. Forss, et al. compared MEG responses when electric stimuli were presented to the median nerve and airpuff stimuli were presented to the hairy skin at the dorsum of the proximal phalanx of the middle finger. This study showed that the mean dipole moments for the earliest responses were significantly smaller when airpuff stimuli were given than those when electric stimuli were given [6]. Hashimoto, et al. reported that the amplitude and the latency of the first component of the evoked responses for different areas to the body to clarify distal-proximal relathionship did not change significantly [7]. Thus, many of these studies focused on somatosensory evoked responses when tactile stimuli were presented to the fingertip. On the other hand, there was been little number of reports which investigated the activity of somatosensory areas when tactile stimuli were presented to the palm. Because tactile display is mainly for presenting tactile stimuli to the palm, it is important to evaluate the activity of the somatosensory area by the differences in stimulated locations on the palm. Anatomically, Johansson reported that mechanoreceptors in the palm area distributed densely at both the center of the palm and the proximal part of the proximal phalanges [8]. Mizugami, et al.[9] collected subjective responses when tactile stimuli were presented at various areas of the palm and concluded that the center of the palm had less sensitive than the other part of the palm. In other words, sensitivity of the center of the palm was low, in spite that mechanoreceptors distributed densely at the center of the palm. Hence it is possible to obtain the inference about the mechanism of sensory perception, if there is a relationship between the amount of perception given by tactile stimuli and the amplitude of somatosensory evoked responses. In addition to the distribution patterns of the mechanoreceptors, innervation areas to convey tactile information are different by the locations of the palm. Such differences may appear as the latency of the first component of evoked magnetic responses. In this study, total of 16 locations on the palm were designed to present tactile stimuli, for examining the effect due to the density difference for mechanoreceptors and innervation areas. The aim of experiment is to evaluate the influence about amplitude, latency, and activated location for somatosensory evoked responses when tactile stimuli were presented at the different location of the palm.

2   Method

2.1   Subjects

A total of 6 healthy college students (age range: 20-22 years; right-handed) participated in the experiments. An informed consent was obtained from each subject after the purpose and procedures of the experiment were fully explained.

2.2   Tactile Stimuli Presentation Device

Tactile stimulus presentation device used in the experiment was an air compressor through precision regulator, followed by an electro-pneumatic regulator, and solenoid valve for ejecting air-jet from the nozzle (Fig.1).

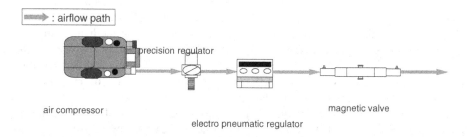

Fig. 1. Airpuff stimuli presentation device

2.3   Presentation of Airpuff as Tactile Stimuli

Airpuff stimuli are medium which spreads stimulus to the areas nearby. The objective of the experiment is to evaluate the effects associated with somatosensory evoked responses when stimulated locations were different. Therefore, it is important to control the diffusion of the airpuff stimuli minimum to establish accurate evaluation for the location difference given by the tactile stimuli. Thus, we made a device whose structure can suppress the stimuli around the skin for minimizing skin deformation over the broad area by the air (Fig.2).

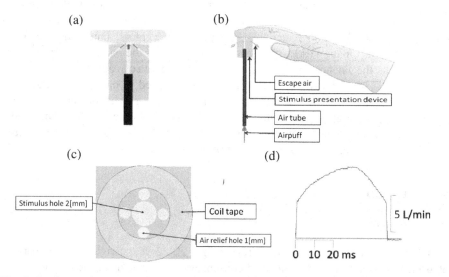

Fig. 2. Device made for the study and the dynamic characteristics of air flow (a), lateral side view (b) schematic, (c) top view, (d) air flow volume given by the new device

2.4   Stimulation Design

By providing the stimulated locations across the palm, the influence of the difference in the stimulated locations of the palm was evaluated. Stimulated locations were divided into two groups, one was aimed for clarifying distal-proximal relationship and the other was for medial-lateral relationship (Fig.3-(b, c)).

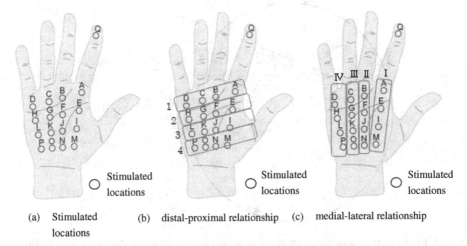

(a)   Stimulated   (b)   distal-proximal relationship   (c)   medial-lateral relationship
       locations

Fig. 3. Stimulated locations and groups

The airpuff was used to stimulate one location of the palm 100 times repeatedly. As parameters of the airpuff stimulus, the flow volume was set to 20 [L / min], duration was set to 40 [ms], and inter-stimulus interval was set to 3200 [ms]. The experiment was completed in approximately 120 minutes.

2.5   Signal Analysis

The signals recorded by MEG were filtered (High pass filter 0.3Hz: Low pass filter 50Hz). Averaging of 100 trials between -1000 ms and 1800 ms of the offset was performed. Baseline was set to the average amplitude between -100 and 0 ms of MEG signals. Root mean square (RMS) values obtained for evaluating the latency and the amplitude of MEG signals at the somatosensory area. Algebraically RMS was calculated as follows:

$$B_{RMS} = (\textstyle\sum B_i^2/n)^{1/2} \quad (B_i: \text{Signal of each sensor, n: Number of sensors})$$

By using the moving equivalent current dipole (ECD) estimation, the localized source for each condition was estimated (Goodness of fit>75%, Confidence Volume<100mm³). Fixed ECD estimation, used in the previous study [10], was applied to estimate time changes in the intensity of the ECD and the peak latency and the amplitude were obtained temporal changes of the amplitude of the dipole moment were estimated, and the peak latency and amplitude of the ECD were identified.

3   Results

Fig.4 illustrated a typical example for averaged MEG waveforms obtained at whole scalp area when airpuff stimuli were presented.

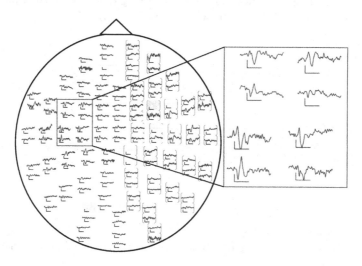

Fig. 4. Evoked MEG waveforms (Subject B, stimulated location A) Vertical axis: Amplitude [fT/cm], Horizontal axis: Time [ms] (from -100[ms] to 500[ms]), close-up wave forms sharply illustrated peaks appeared in the left hemisphere after airpuff stimulus presentation

Characteristic peak signals were found in the channels at the left-hemisphere. RMS analysis was conducted to the channels located at the left hemisphere.

Fig.5 illustrates a RMS-processed waveform.

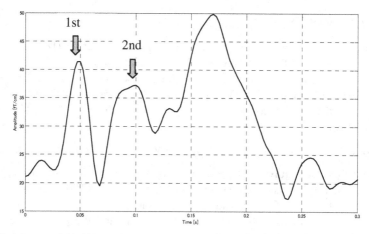

Fig. 5. Waveforms of the left hemisphere as represented by RMS data (Subject B, stimulated location A)

Three peaks were apparent from the RMS waveform. ECD estimation to each peak revealed that the first response was estimated in SI area (6 subjects in 6 subjects) and the second response was estimated in the contralateral secondary somatosensory area (SIIc, 3 subjects in 6 subjects). Fig.6 shows the MRI images, superimposed with ECD activated locations.

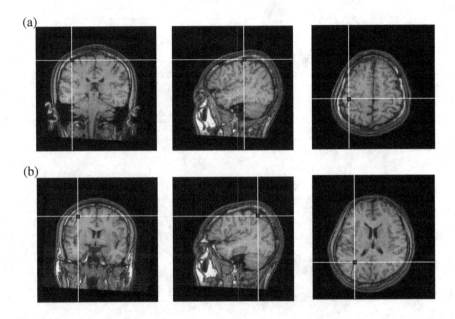

Fig. 6. Source localization for the first component superimpose a with MRI images((a) Subject A, location A, (b) Subject B, location A)

Source localization was estimated to the SI area in which all subjects found peak activities. When evaluating the activity of the SI for each position where the stimuli were presented, a fixed ECD estimation method was used to obtain accurate sources for identifying exact activated locations. Fig.7 shows temporal transition of MEG activities overlapped for all conditions at SI.

Peaks apparently exist at 50 ms after the stimulus onset. This trend was apparent for all subjects. The peak time and the amplitude were extracted from data, and the average latency and amplitude in each stimulated location were estimated. Table 1 summarizes the latency and amplitude of the first component by subjects. Table 2 shows the average latency and amplitude of the first component by distal-proximal relationship. Table 3 shows the average latency and amplitude of the first component by medial-lateral relationship.

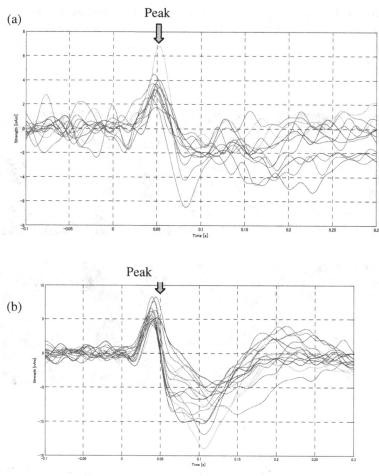

Fig. 7. Temporal transition about MEG activity which focuses on SI for each stimulated location.((a) Subject B, (b) Subject E)

Latency showed large variability between subjects, whereas the amplitude of the activity had small variability between subjects. Analysis of variable (ANOVA) revealed that there were no significant differences on distal-proximal and medial-lateral relationships.

4   Discussion

Peak strength of evoked responses at SI

There were no significant differences in the amplitude of evoked responses at SI by the distal-proximal and the medial-lateral relationships as well as the differences of stimulated locations. It was possibly because the amplitude of evoked responses at SI

Table 1. Latency and amplitude of the first component by subjects

	latency [ms]	strength [nAm]
A	50.8 ± 15.3	6.1 ± 2.7
B	53.2 ± 18.6	5.1 ± 3.6
C	55.6 ± 19.2	5.2 ± 3.1
D	54.4 ± 15.7	4.8 ± 1.2
E	54.8 ± 12.3	5.4 ± 2.4
F	54.8 ± 13.9	6.9 ± 3.1
G	60.4 ± 22.9	5.1 ± 1.7
H	56.4 ± 16.4	5.3 ± 1.4
I	56.0 ± 15.4	5.3 ± 2.6
J	60.4 ± 16.5	5.8 ± 2.6
K	54.8 ± 17.7	5.3 ± 2.5
L	56.8 ± 17.4	4.5 ± 1.4
M	57.9 ± 17.7	3.8 ± 1.2
N	59.4 ± 18.8	5.9 ± 1.1
O	61.3 ± 20.7	5.3 ± 1.3
P	58.4 ± 19.9	4.6 ± 1.2

Table 2. The average latency and amplitude of the first component by distal-proximal relationship

		latency [ms]	strength [nAm]
distal	1	53.5 ± 16.2	5.3 ± 2.7
↑	2	56.6 ± 15.9	5.7 ± 2.2
↓	3	57.0 ± 15.7	5.2 ± 2.2
proximal	4	59.2 ± 17.7	4.9 ± 1.4

Table 3. The average latency and amplitude of the first component by medial-lateral relationship

		latency [ms]	strength [nAm]
medial	I	54.7 ± 14.3	5.2 ± 2.3
↑	II	56.8 ± 16.1	5.9 ± 2.7
↓	III	57.9 ± 18.9	5.2 ± 2.1
lateral	IV	56.4 ± 16.1	4.8 ± 1.3

reflects the physical quantity of the stimulation. Fujiwara, et al. reported that perceived physical intensity and amplitude of SII were increased whereas there were no differences in the amplitudes of evoked responses in SI when the subjects concentrated on the stimuli [11]. The previous study which investigated the relationship between psychophysical characteristics of the stimulus intensity and somatosensory evoked potentials reported that early responses at SI were correlated with physical intensity of the stimulus, and late responses were correlated with perceptual intensity associated with the stimuli [12]. Mechanoreceptors in the palm area distribute densely at both the center of the palm and proximal part of the proximal phalanges [8], and the amplitude of evoked responses at SI did not change if the stimulated locations were changed. Goodness of fit for the ECDs obtained at SI in this study was set to more than 75% and the criteria for confidence volume was as low as 100mm3, which were more than the criteria used in the previous studies[6]. According to the results, it was suggested that the amplitude of evoked responses at SI did not depend on distribution of mechanoreceptors. Thus, it might be suggested that the differences of stimulated locations did not affect the amplitude of evoked responses observed at SI.

5   Conclusion

When airpuff stimuli were presented to each stimulated location on the palm, neuromagnetic activities were observed at the SI area for all subjects. Goodness of fit for
the ECDs obtained at SI in this study was set to more than 75% and the criteria for
confidence volume was as low as 100mm^3, which were more than the criteria used in
the previous studies[6]. Although mechanoreceptors in the palm distribute densely at
both the center of the palm and the proximal part of the proximal phalanges, no effects on location were found by the amplitude of the evoked responses at SI area. This
result suggests that differences in location of the stimulus presentation did not affect
the amplitude at SI. In the future, it will be necessary to evaluate latency and amplitude of evoked responses and estimated dipole locations observed at SII on each stimulated location to validate whether difference of the stimulated locations affect the
MEG signals. Previous study reported that amplitudes of evoked responses at SII
correlated with perceptual intensity associated with stimulus intensity [13]. Also,
perceptual intensity for the stimulus intensity may vary with the location on the palm
[9]. Therefore, psychological intensity of the MEG signal evoked by stimulus intensity should be further evaluated and the relationship between the amplitudes of evoked
responses at SII and perceptual intensity reflected on the stimulus intensity should be
examined.

Acknowledgement. This study was supported by JSPS KAKENIHI (24370103,
24657182) in part.

References

1. Ministry of Health, Labour and Welfare: Field survey of the disabled children (2001)
2. Mizukami, Y., Sawada, H.: A Tactile device using Shape-memory Alloys for the Information Transmission by Higher-level Perception. Transactions of Information Processing
   Society of Japan (2007)
3. Study of communication support equipment to support the employment of people with disabilities overlapping visual and auditory. National Institute of Vocational Rehabilitation
   Report, No. 46 (2002)
4. Sakai, T., Tazaki, M., Ito, T.: An Evaluation of an Optimum Stimulus Presentation Method
   Considering Tactile Sensation on Passive 6-Finger Braile. The Journal of the Institute of
   Electronics, Information and Communication Engineers. D, Information System J90-D(3),
   742–753 (2007)
5. Yamaguchi, H.: Mystery of cutaneous sensation. In: KODANSHA, pp. 26–28 (2006)
6. Forss, N., Salmelin, R., Hari, R.: Comparison of somatosensory evoked fields to airpuff
   and electric stimuli. Electroencephalography and Clinical Neurophysiology 92, 510–517
   (1994)
7. Hashimoto, I., Mashiko, T., Kimura, T., Imada, T.: Are there discrete distal-proximal representations of the index finger and palm in the human somatosensory cortex? A neuromagnetic study. Clinical Neurophysiology 110, 430–437 (1999)

8. Johansson, R.S., Vallbo, A.B.: Tactile sensitivity in the human hand: relative and absolute densities of four types of mechanoreceptive units in glabrous skin. J. Physiol. 286, 283–300 (1979)
9. Mizukami, Y., Uchida, K., Sawada, H.: Presentation of rubbing sensation by a tactile display. The Institute of Electronics, Information and Communication Engineers Technical Report 108(84), 67–72 (2006)
10. Roβ, B., Borgmann, C., Draganova, R.: A high-precision magnetoencephalographic study of human auditory steady-state responses to amplitude-modulated tones. Acoustical Society of America 108(2), 679–691 (2000)
11. Fujiwara, N., Imai, M., Nagamine, T., Mima, T., Oga, T., Takeshitaa, K., Tomaa, K., Shibasakia, H.: Second somatosensory area (SII) plays a significant role in selective somatosensory attention. Cognitive Brain Reseach 14, 389–397 (2002)
12. Hashimoto, I., Yoshikawa, K., Sasaki, M.: Somatosensory evoked potential correlates of psychophysical magnitude estimations for tactile air-puff stimulation in man. Experimental Brain Research 73, 459–469 (1988)

The Right Level of Complexity in a Banner Ad: Roles of Construal Level and Fluency

Chih-Tung Kao and Man-Ying Wang[*]

Department of Psychology, Soochow University, Taipei, Taiwan
athena1011@gmail.com,
mywang@scu.edu.tw

Abstract. The current study examined the emotional consequences involved in processing different levels of information complexity in a banner ad as well as the role of construal level [15] in the process. The entropy measure of information theory was used as a metric of complexity. This measure showed high correlation with subjective ratings of complexity. Complexity manipulation adopting this measure found reliable effects on subjective complexity across two experiments. On the other hand, construal level, manipulated or measured, interacted with complexity in determining banner preference. Participants preferred medium complexity banners over low or high complexity ones when the construal level was low. Complexity did not affect banner preference when the construal level was high (Experiments 1 and 2). The inverted U-shaped function of complexity on preference was interpreted in terms of the composite effect of perceptual and conceptual fluency that varied in opposite directions as complexity increased (Experiment 3). Research and practical implications of these findings were also discussed.

Keywords: Information complexity, construal level, fluency, preference, banner ads.

1   Introduction

What is the optimal amount of information to be placed in a banner ad? This decision is usually ill-guided in many e-commerce contexts that could be, in part, attributed to the lack of understanding on how psychological processing is affected by information complexity. The current study examined the emotional consequences involved in processing different amount of visual information in a banner ad as well as attempted to supply a theoretically founded understanding of the underlying process.

Previous studies frequently found an inverted U-shaped function of stimulus complexity on cognitive performance for stimuli ranging from natural objects to random visual patterns [1], [2], [3]. The inverted U-shaped function also applied to evaluative responses so that stimuli of moderate level of complexity were preferred over stimuli with less or greater complexity [4]. Reber, Schwarz, and Winkielman (2004) explained the inverted U-shaped function in terms of processing fluency (i.e., ease of

---

[*] Corresponding author.

S. Yamamoto (Ed.): HIMI/HCII 2013, Part I, LNCS 8016, pp. 604–613, 2013.

processing) and attribution. Although high fluency is associated with low-complexity stimuli, this fluency is likely attributed to the simplicity of the stimuli and not liking. In a similar vein, the disfluent processing of high-complexity stimuli was attributed to their complexity. Only for stimuli of intermediate complexity can intermediate level of fluency be misattributed to liking.

For banner ads or webpages, the effect of visual complexity was not very consistent. Although some studies did show the inverted U-shaped effects of visual complexity [6], [7], other studies found a decrease in evaluation and performance as visual complexity increased [8], [9]. One possible reason for the inconsistencies is related to the differences in complexity metrics used. The inverted U-shaped effects were found in studies using complexity measures reflecting the number and the type of information sources (i.e., text, image etc.) [10] or subjective complexity [6] while strict deteriorating effects of complexity were found for measures using JPEG file sizes [8], [9]. Differences in the evaluative responses requested by different studies could be another possible reason.

The current study again examined the effect of complexity of banner ads using a measure derived from the information theory [12]. The information entropy measure 'H = log2 N' was used to quantify the information contained in a banner ad, where N represents the number of information sources (details of computation are listed in the method section). It was expected that banners of intermediate information complexity would be preferred over low- or high-complexity banners.

In addition to banner complexity, the role of construal level (CL) [13] in banner evaluation was also examined. Construal level refers to how individuals represent external world in terms of mental distance [14], [15]. Consumers of low CL focus on the detailed process(es) and the manners by which behavioral outcomes result from (i.e., concrete thinkers). In contrast, high CL consumers focus on the outcomes of an action and think holistically (i.e., abstract thinkers) [16], [14], [15]. Previous research showed that low CL consumers in general relied on processing fluency for preference judgments while high CL consumers determined their preference using specific information contents [13]. The current study thus expected the increase in complexity to decrease processing fluency as well as preference for low CL participants. High CL participants were not affected by fluency or information complexity.

Three experiments were conducted using woman's apparel as the theme of banners. Experiments 1 manipulated CL using an imagination task. In Experiment 2, the effect of CL was evaluated using individual differences in scores on the Behavior Identification Form (BIF) [17]. Experiment 3 examined if the inverted U-shaped effect of complexity is related to the fluctuation of conceptual and perceptual fluency whose direction of change was the opposite with the increasing complexity.

2   Experiment 1

2.1   Method

Participants. Participants were forty-one undergraduate students (aged between 19 and 25) attending the experiment to fulfill partial course requirement. Considering the nature of the banner ads (i.e., women's apparel), all participants were females.

Design and Materials. The experiment was a construal level (2) x banner complexity (3) within-subject design.

Thirty banner ads were collected from the internet. The information entropy measure H (bits) was used to compute information complexity for each banner. That is,

$$H = \log_2 N \tag{1}$$

N represents the number of information sources. Four types of information could be exhibited in banner ads of women's apparel. First, product images: product(s) on the model, details of the product, the product by itself, the product in different colors etc. Second, text descriptions: appearance, function, name, price of the product and the name, time period and details of marketing campaign etc. Third, navigation buttons: arrows, posture, text instruction etc. Fourth, brand information: brand names, logos, slogans etc. An item in each information category counted as one separate piece of information and N equals the total number of items. The calculation showed that H ranges from 1 to 5.1 bits of information for the thirty banners collected (see Table 1 for examples).

Table 1. Examples of banner ads and the computation of H

Information complexity	Examples	
	Computation of H	Banner image
Low (H ≤ 2 bits)	1(product image) + 2(product text descriptions) + 1(brand information) = 4 $H = \log_2 4 = 2$ bits	
Medium (H = 2.3 ~ 3.2 bits)	1(product image) + 6(product text descriptions) = 7 $H = \log_2 7 = 2.8$ bits	
High (H > 3.3 bits)	5(product image) + 8(product text descriptions) = 13 $H = \log_2 13 = 3.7$ bits	

A pretest was performed on a separate group of thirty participants who rated each banner ad for its attractiveness and subjective complexity. The entropy measure H manifested a high correlation with the subjective complexity measure ($r = 0.85$). After deleting six banners with extreme attractiveness ratings, the rest twenty-four banners were divided into three complexity groups (see Table 1 for the range of H of the three complexity groups). The twenty-four banner ads were divided in halves so that half was associated with high-construal level manipulation and the other half with low-construal level. BIF items were also divided in halves to be used in the manipulation checks in the high and low CL conditions respectively. The versions of banner and BIF items were counterbalanced.

Procedure. The high CL manipulation was devised in order to focus participants' processing on the "why" question and think abstractly for distant future events while the low CL manipulation focused participants on the "how" question and think concretely for recent events [13] [14]. They were provided with pictures of apparel items for an undergraduate female student May. In the low CL condition, participants were asked to imagine that May was going to wear these clothing for some occasions next week. They should help May list, in as much details as possible, ways of mixing and matching them to create different looks. In the high CL condition, participants imagined that May was to wear these clothing next year. They were asked to list possible occasions in which May would like to wear these clothes and to suggest possible styles of the looks that could be created from these apparel items.

Participants were tested in small groups of two to eight persons. Each banner ad was presented on the screen for five seconds of viewing time after which participants made rating responses. Both the high and the low CL imagination tasks were followed by the administration of the BIF and the presentation of banner ads. Participants rated the subjective complexity and preference for each banner ad. The order of construal level manipulation was counterbalanced across participants so that half of the participants received high-CL manipulation first while the other half received low-CL manipulation first.

2.2   Result

The manipulation check of CL manipulation was not significant. However, separate examination of the two versions of BIF (that was each constituted by half of the BIF items) showed that the manipulation check was significant for one, $F(1,39) = 4.04$, $p < .05$, but not the other, $p > .10$.

The CL (2) x complexity (3) ANOVA on the subjective complexity rating found only one significant effect - complexity, $F (1.5, 57.9) = 194.85 \cdot p < .001$, high (M = 3.76) > medium (M=2.48) > low (M=1.76) (see Fig. 1).

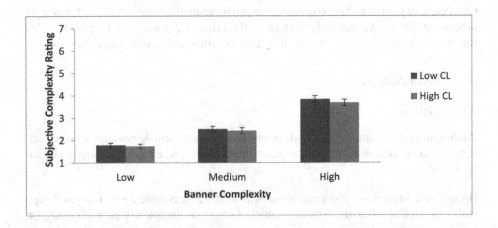

Fig. 1. The effect of construal level and information complexity on the subjective complexity rating of banner ads (Experiment 1)

The analysis of preference rating found significant complexity effect F (1.8, 70.8) = 3.40 , p = .04, as well as significant CL x complexity interaction, F (1.7, 66.4) = 5.02 , p = .01 (see Fig. 2). In the low CL condition, mean preference rating of medium complexity banners was higher than that of low and high complexity banners (p = .02; p = .001) while there was no difference between low and high complexity banners (p = .09). The preference ratings of the three complexity groups did not differ from another in the high CL condition.

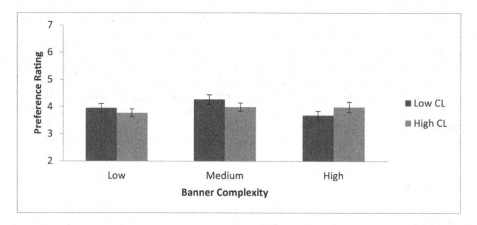

Fig. 2. The effect of construal level and information complexity on the preference rating of banner ads (Experiment 1)

The information complexity manipulation indeed resulted in changes in experienced (subjective) complexity for banner ads. Construal level interacted with information complexity to affect banner preference. Information complexity affected preference only in the low construal condition when they relied on the fluency of processing for preference judgment [13]. Experiment 2 attempted to replicate this finding using individual differences in BIF as the construal level manipulation.

3   Experiment 2

3.1   Method

Participants. Participants were forty-four undergraduate female students who participated in the experiment for course credit or received a small gift to compensate for their time.

Design and Materials. The experiment was a CL (2) x complexity (3) mixed design with construal level as the between-subject factor and complexity as within-subject. The banner ads used in this experiment are similar to those in Experiment 1.

Procedure. Participants were tested in small groups. They filled out the BIF after which they rated the subjective complexity and preference ratings for each banner.

3.2   Result

Participants who scored higher than the 25th or lower than the 75th percentile of BIF scores were included in the analysis (the cutoffs were $P_{25}=11$ and $P_{75}=16$). The CL x complexity ANOVA on subjective complexity replicated findings of Experiment 1 that the only significant effect was that of complexity, $F(1.59, 39.7) = 140.26$, $p < .001$, high ($M = 3.53$) > medium ($M = 2.32$) > low ($M = 1.63$). The analysis of preference ratings showed that the effect of complexity as well as the interaction between complexity and construal level failed to reach significance,   complexity: F (1.6, 38.6) = 3.28 ‚ $p = .06$; complexity x CL: F(1.6, 38.6) = 1.35 ‚ $p = .27$. Nevertheless, planned comparison found the results had indeed replicated findings of Experiment 1. For low CL participants, medium > high ($p = .002$) and medium < low ($p = .049$), low = high ($p = .387$). Preference ratings did not differ across complexity groups for high CL participants (see Fig. 3).

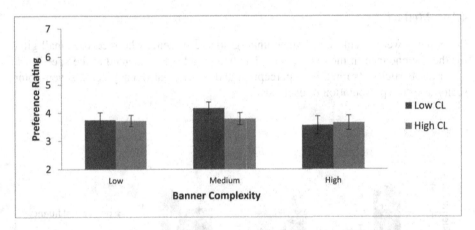

Fig. 3. Effects of construal level and information complexity on the preference ratings of banner ads (Experiment 2)

Preference rating was also regressed over the entropy measure of complexity for banner ads using a quadratic model. The regression ($y = -0.16 x^2 + 0.9 x + 2.85$) accounted for 18% of total variance for low CL participant. The negative quadratic parameter ($p < .05$) and the positive linear parameter ($p = .07$) resulted from the inverted U-shaped function of information complexity. For high CL participants, the regression accounted for only 2% of total variance   ($y = 0.05 x^2 + 0.05 x + 3.59$).

The result of Experiment 2 replicated and extended findings of Experiment 1. That is, the effect of complexity on preference rating was inverted U-shaped and the effect was restricted to low CL participants. CL exerted similar effects on banner preference both when it was manipulated and when it was measured to reveal individual differences. The effect of information complexity was restricted to low CL participants the finding of which was explained in terms of the reliance on processing fluency for preference judgments in low but not high CL participants. As to the inverted

U-shaped function of banner complexity, the Reber et al. (2004)'s fluency and attribution account was unclear in when and why fluency was misattributed to liking. Alternatively, the increase in information complexity may have resulted in opposite changes in perceptual and conceptual fluency. The ease of perceptual processing, i.e., perceptual fluency, may indeed decrease with the increase in information complexity. However, increasing information could also benefit the conceptual processing or the comprehension of the banner ad by increasing information redundancy and the efficiency in the retrieval of conceptual representation. The inverted U-shaped effect was more likely due to the conjunctive effect of perceptual and conceptual fluency that changed in opposite directions as information complexity increased. Experiment 3 thus asked participants to rate the perceptual and conceptual fluency of each ad in order to provide support for this latter interpretation.

4   Experiment 3

4.1   Method

Participants were twenty-one female undergraduate students who received small gifts for their attendance in the experiment. The banner ad was presented at the speed of 5 s. per ad. Participants rated both perceptual and conceptual fluency using seven-point scales after the presentation of each ad.

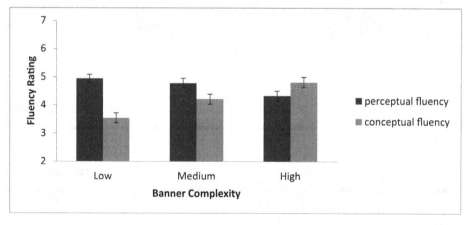

Fig. 4. The effect of fluency type and information complexity on fluency rating (Experiment 3)

4.2   Result

Fluency ratings were submitted to fluency type (2) x complexity (3) ANOVA. There was a significant interaction between complexity and fluency type, $F_{(2,40)} = 13.20$, $p < .001$. For perceptual fluency, high < medium and high < low complexity (both $ps < .0001$), medium = low complexity ($p = .22$). For conceptual fluency, high > medium > low complexity (all $ps < .001$) (see Fig. 4).

These results showed that ratings of perceptual fluency decreased and those of conceptual fluency increased with the increase in information complexity. The increase in information complexity exerted opposite effects on perceptual and conceptual fluency. The inverted U-shaped effect of complexity on preference may result from these opposite effects of complexity on perceptual and conceptual fluency.

5   Discussion

Two major findings of the current study are: (1) Information complexity affected viewer's preference for the banner when the processing was of low construal level. Information complexity did not affect ad preference when the construal level was high. (2) The complexity effect was exhibited by an inverted U-shaped function that was interpreted by conjunctive effects of perceptual and conceptual fluency.

The modulating effect of construal level suggested a reason for previous inconsistent findings on the effect of complexity. The lack of control of this (and possibly other) modulating factor across different studies may have, at least in part, contributed to the inconsistencies. The practical implication for the CL effect concerns the type of user tasks associated with CL. Banner complexity did exert an effect on preference when the viewer was engaged in low construal level processing or concrete thinking but not when the viewer processed at high CL. Users in a directed purchase mode conducted planned and immediate purchase. The nature of this processing mode appeared to be associated with low construal level. These users pay more visits to and spent more time on product detail pages [20]. The possible association with low CL processing for users viewing these pages suggests that information complexity would be an important design consideration for banner ads presented at the product detail page. When ads were presented at pages where viewers' construal levels are likely to be varied (such as product listing pages, the land page, recommendation page etc.), adopting an intermediate level of information complexity (i.e., about two or three bits) in banner design would be an optimal choice that could maximize the preference for the banner ad regardless of construal level.

One caveat should be mentioned that is related to the relationship between information complexity and perceptual/conceptual fluency. Experiment 3 showed that perceptual fluency increased while conceptual fluency decreased with the increase in information complexity. Since high fluency is associated with liking [20], [21], the composite effect of perceptual and conceptual fluency resulted in the inverted U-shaped function of complexity. As such, it is possible that experienced fluency (perceptual and conceptual) and (thus) the nature of complexity-fluency relationship are affected by other design factors in the ad and task goals [22], resulting in different complexity-preference relations.

Overall, the current attempt to use the information entropy measure as the metric of complexity in banner ads was fruitful in terms of revealing the nature of relationships between banner complexity and preference. These findings helps guide the consideration of the amount of information to be placed in a banner ad.

References

1. Zusne, L.: Visual Perception of Form. Academic Press, N. Y. (1970)
2. Michels, K.M., Zusne, L.: Metrics of visual form. Psychological Bulletin 63, 74–86 (1965)
3. Wang, M.Y., Huang, J.T.: The effect of global diagnosticity and complexity on object recognition. Chinese Journal of Psychology 44, 189–210 (2002)
4. Berlyne, D.E.: Aesthetics and psychobiology. Appleton-Century-Crofts, New York (1971)
5. Reber, R., Schwarz, N., Winkielman, P.: Processing fluency and aesthetic pleasure: Is beauty in the perceiver's processing experience? Personality and Social Psychology Review 8(4), 364–382 (2004)
6. Geissler, G.L., Zinkhan, G.M., Watson, R.T.: The Influence of Home Page Complexity on Consumer Attention, Attitudes, and Purchase Intent. Journal of Advertising 35(2), 69–80 (2006)
7. Huhmann, B.A.: Visual complexity in banner ads: The role of color, photography, and animation. Visual Communication Quarterly 10(3), 10–17 (2003)
8. Pieters, R., Wedel, M., Batra, R.: The stopping power of advertising: Measures and effects of visual complexity. Journal of Marketing 74, 48–60 (2010)
9. Tuch, A.N., Bargas-Avila, J.A., Opwis, K., Wilhelm, F.H.: Visual complexity of websites: Effects on users' experience, physiology, performance, and memory. International Journal of Human-Computer Studies 67(9), 703–715 (2009), doi: http://dx.doi.org/10.1016/j.ijhcs.2009.04.002
10. Huhmann, B.A.: Visual complexity in banner ads: The role of color, photography, and animation. Visual Communication Quarterly 10(3), 10–17 (2003)
11. Reber, R., Schwarz, N., Winkielman, P.: Processing fluency and aesthetic pleasure: Is beauty in the perceiver's processing experience? Personality and Social Psychology Review 8(4), 364–382 (2004)
12. Shannon, C.E.: A Mathematical Theory of Communication. Bell System Technical Journal 27(3), 379–423, 27(4), 623–656 (1948)
13. Tsai, C., Thomas, M.J.: When do feelings of fluency matter? How abstract and concrete thinking influence fluency effects. Psychological Science 22(3), 348–354 (2011)
14. Trope, Y., Liberman, N.: Temporal construal. Psychological Review 110, 403–421 (2003)
15. Trope, Y., Liberman, N.: Construal-level theory of psychological distance. Psychological Review 117, 440–463 (2010)
16. Shanks, D.R., Darby, R.J.: Feature- and rule-based generalization inhuman associative learning. Journal of Experimental Psychology: Animal Behavior Processes 24, 405–415 (1998)
17. Vallacher, R.R., Wegner, D.M.: Levels of Personal Agency: Individual Variation in. Action Identification. Journal of Personality and Social Psychology 57(4), 660–671 (1989)
18. W.D., Tellegen, A.: Toward a consensual structure of mood. . Psychological Bulletin 98, 219–235 (1985)
19. Roets, A., Van Hiel, A.: Item selection and validation of a brief, 15-item version of the need for closure scale. Personality and Individual Differences 50(1), 90–94 (2011), doi:10.1016/j.paid.2010.09.004
20. Moe, W.W.: Buying, searching, or browsing: Differentiating between online shoppers using in-store navigational clickstream. Journal of Consumer Psychology 13, 29–40 (2003)

21. Reber, R., Winkielman, P., Schwarz, N.: Effects of perceptual fluency on affective judgments. Psychological Science 9(1), 45–48 (1998)
22. Winkielman, P., Cacioppo, J.T.: Mind at ease puts a smile on the face: Psychophysiological evidence that processing facilitation elicits positive affect. Journal of Personality & Social Psychology 81, 989–1000 (2001)
23. Pieters, R., Wedel, M.: Goal control of attention to advertising: The Yarbus implication. Journal of Consumer Research 34(2), 224–233 (2007)

Physiological Responses and *Kansei* Evaluation on Awareness

Keiko Kasamatsu[1,*], Hiroaki Kiso[2], Misako Yamagishi[3],
Hideo Jingu[4], and Shini'chi Fukuzumi[5]

[1] Department of Industrial Art, Graduate School of System Design,
Tokyo Metropolitan University, Tokyo, Japan
kasamatu@sd.tmu.ac.jp
[2] Information and Media Processing Laboratories, NEC Corp., Nara, Japan
h-kiso@ah.jp.nec.com
[3] Department of Clinical and Experimental Neuroimaging,
Center for Development of Advanced Medicine for Dementia,
National Center for Geriatrics and Gerontology,
Aichi, Japan
yamagisi@ncgg.go.jp
[4] Research Laboratories for Affective Design Engineering,
Kanazawa Institute of Technology, Ishikawa, Japan
jinguh@neptune.kanazawa-it.ac.jp
[5] Knowledge Discovery Research Laboratories,
NEC Corp., Kanagawa, Japan
s-fukuzumi@aj.jp.nec.com

Abstract. For tasks in which the steps to achieve a goal are not specified, a user adopts the trial and error method to achieve the goal. If the system is able to induce "awareness" to user, the goal can be achieved in an effective manner. We aim to elucidate the mechanism of "awareness" in order to develop a system that incorporates induction of "awareness".

In this study, we examined the changes in the physiological indices of autonomic nervous activity before and after the occurrence of "awareness". We selected three types of tasks, namely, a jigsaw puzzle, a slide puzzle, and target shooting for which "awareness" was represented by the following items: "can see the end in sight", "I think I may do it", and "grasp the techniques". *Kansei* evaluation was performed for each task.

Keywords: Physiological response, *Kansei*, Affectiveness, Awareness.

1 Introduction

Some sort of "awareness" occurs in the process of achieving the tasks. For example, when performing a task in situations where there are no manual handling procedures and steps. The user repeats trial and error on the task which is not clear steps for the

---

[*] Corresponding author.

S. Yamamoto (Ed.): HIMI/HCII 2013, Part I, LNCS 8016, pp. 614–619, 2013.
© Springer-Verlag Berlin Heidelberg 2013

goal. Then, the user explore the steps that can reach the goal, the user will reach the goal. If the system is able to induce "awareness" to user, the goal can be achieved in an effective manner. We aim to elucidate the mechanism of "awareness" in order to develop a system that incorporates induction of "awareness".

There are several studies using physiological indices to measure the awareness. Paynter et al.[1] investigated possible non-conscious learning mechanisms by giving subjects three runs of task while recording ERPs. ERP showed clear evidence of information about the correctness of a move well before subjects were making progress on the task behaviorally, let alone being able to consciously determine if a move was correct or not. Furthermore, McIntosh et al.[2] obtained evidence for neural system interactions related to awareness and performance in a positron emission tomography(PET) regional cerebral blood flow study of sensory associative learning. Meanwhile, Schraw and Dennison[3] were constructed a 52-item inventory to measure adults' metacognitive awareness. They developed a 53-item self-report instrument that includes multiple items within each of the eight component processes subsumed under knowledge and regulation of cognition.

These studies revealed that the awareness could be measured by PET and ERP. However, it is difficult to measure awareness using these physiological indices when users were used the system in their life. In this study, we examined the changes in the physiological indices of autonomic nervous activity before and after the occurrence of "awareness".

2   Methods

2.1   Participants

Thirty participants (15 men, 15 women; 21~25 years old) participated in the study. Each participant performed the same task thrice. Physiological indices were measured during the experiment. *Kansei* evaluation of performance was conducted after the completion of each task.

2.2   Experimental Tasks

We selected three types of tasks, namely, a jigsaw puzzle, a slide puzzle, and target shooting for which "awareness" was represented by the following items: "can see the end in sight" , "I think I may do it" , and "grasp the techniques". The three tasks were performed on a personal computer, and each task had three patterns.

The jigsaw puzzle (Fig.1) consisted of 50 pieces to make three pictures (a tree, shell, and beach). These pictures were shown for 10 seconds before the task; the participants were not shown the picture while they were solving the jigsaw puzzle. The point at which the participant's operation became faster after he/she had seen daylight was considered the "change point"; this point indicated the occurrence of "awareness".

The slide puzzle (Fig.2) had three levels (low, middle, and high) and was performed from the low level to the high level. The participants said the time point when they thought they might do it as the occurrence of "awareness". This time point was recorded.

The target shooting task (Fig.3) consisted of six arrows on a set. If participants ran out these arrows before reaching a reference point, the task come to an end. The task was performed thrice. The participants said the time point when they felt to grasp the techniques as the occurrence of "awareness", and this time point was recorded.

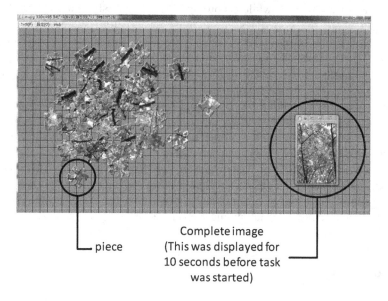

piece

Complete image
(This was displayed for
10 seconds before task
was started)

Fig. 1. Jigsaw puzzle sample

red block

EXIT
for red block

Fig. 2. Slide puzzle sample

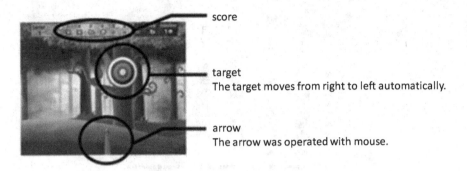

score

target
The target moves from right to left automatically.

arrow
The arrow was operated with mouse.

Fig. 3. Target shooting task sample

2.3 Physiological Indices

The physiological indices consisted of the electrocardiogram (ECG), blood volume pulse (BVP), change of salivary amylase activity, and number of eye blinks. ECG, BVP and eye blinks were measured during the rest for a minute and the experiment. Salivary amylase was measured before and after the experiment. The values of physiological indices were considered as 100% at rest.

2.4 Evaluation Items

The 31 items related to "awareness" were selected for the *Kansei* evaluation. In addition, three items, namely, "can see the end in sight", "I think I may do it", and "grasp the techniques" were added as items representing "awareness". Participants were evaluated for each item on a seven-point scale using the semantic differential method.

3   Results and Discussion

Data for the physiological indices measured 10 seconds before and after "awareness" (remark or change point), or before and after task were examined.

The R-R interval on the ECG and the amplitude of BVP tended to be lower after "awareness" than before "awareness". The number of eye blinks and the change of salivary amylase activity before and after task were not significantly different.

The R-R interval is influenced by the sympathetic-parasympathetic activity. The R-R interval significantly reduced after the slide puzzle and target shooting tasks but not after the jigsaw puzzle task (Fig.4). It was difficult to appear psychological changes in the jigsaw puzzle task. This was because it acquired "awareness" not based on the participant' remark but based on action data.

The amplitude of BVP is influences by the sympathetic-parasympathetic activity. The amplitude of BVP significantly reduced after the slide puzzle task but not after the target shooting task and jigsaw puzzle (Fig.5).

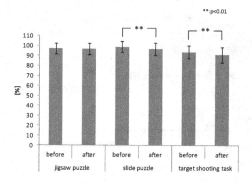

Fig. 4. The result of before and after awareness on R-R Interval

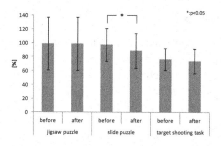

Fig. 5. The result of before and after awareness on BVP

Next, the *Kansei* evaluations of "can see the end in sight", "I think I may do it", and "grasp the techniques" were examined on each task. The score of "can see the end in sight" on jigsaw puzzle was 6.4, and the score of "I think I may do it" was 6.3, the score of "grasp the techniques" was 5.3. In the other words, the score in the items related to the sense of accomplishment at the time of clearing was high. The score of "I think I may do it" on slide puzzle was 6.3, the score of "can see the end in sight" was 5.6, and the score of "grasp the techniques" was 4.7. The items of other high score were "pleasant" and "delightful" and so on. The score of "I think I may do it" and "grasp the techniques" on target shooting task was 5.2, and the score of "can see the end in sight" was 5.1. In addition, the items for which the scores were higher than average in the target shooting task were related with a feeling of satisfaction, such as "delightful", "satisfaction", and "refreshing".

As described in 2.2, we selected three types of tasks, namely, a jigsaw puzzle as "can see the end in sight", a slide puzzle as "I think I may do it", and target shooting task as "grasp the techniques". This results were confirmed that the score of "I think I may do it" for slide puzzle was high and the scores of "can see the end in sight" and "I think I may do it" for jigsaw puzzle were high. Therefore, the induction of awareness was confirmed for selected tasks. It is necessary to examine for the other task in the future.

4   Conclusions

This study aimed to investigate the occurrence of "awareness" with a focus on the role of the autonomic nervous activity in the underlying physiological response. The results showed significant differences in the R-R interval and amplitude of BVP before and after the occurrence of "awareness". This indicates that occurrence of "awareness" could possibly be detected by measuring the autonomic nervous activity. Furthermore, our results for *Kansei* evaluation suggest that the action of the mind tended to vary depending on the type of "awareness".

References

1. Paynter, C.A., Kotovsky, K., Reder, L.M.: Problem-Solving Without Awareness: An ERP Investigation. Neuropsychologia 48(10), 3137–3144 (2010)
2. McIntosh, A.R., Rajah, M.N., Lobaugh, N.J.: Interactions of Prefrontal Cortex in Relation to Awareness in Sensory Learning. Science 284(5419), 1531–1533 (1999)
3. Schraw, G., Dennison, R.S.: Assessing Metacognitive Awareness. Contemporary Educational Psychology 19(4), 460–475 (1994)

Analysis of Spatiotemporal Memory Using Air-Jets as Tactile Stimuli for Development of Noncontact Tactile Displays

Kentaro Kotani, Nobuki Kido, Satoshi Suzuki, and Takafumi Asao

Abstract. The effects of delay and distance of a pair of tactile stimuli on the memory of the two locations were analyzed. Tactile stimuli were induced at the palm with seven levels of interstimulus distances and seven levels of interstimulus intervals. The results showed that the smallest two-point differential threshold was when the delay time was around 0.5–2.0 s. The fundamental characteristics associated with spatiotemporal tactile memory that were obtained in the present study can lead to the design of a noncontact tactile display.

1 Introduction

Many studies have recently focused on the development of tactile displays, which have the potential to effectively present information to users in situations where other sensory modalities cannot be used [1]. Various types of stimulus modalities have been proposed for the tactile display; these have been discussed as a key issue for effectively presenting stimuli [2][3][4]. Most studies have used vibrotactile and electrocutaneous stimuli, where pins and electrodes are directly attached to the surface of the human body to generate stimuli. However, this type of tactile display is plagued by unstable stimulus presentation owing to poor contact between the skin and actuators and discomfort with prolonged dwell times [2]. In this study, we used air-jet stimuli to develop a noncontact tactile display that avoids such problems induced by physical contact between the body and display.

For developing such a display, it was important to clarify the information transmission characteristics of the noncontact tactile display because the stimulus transmission medium was air jets, which have significantly different physical properties compared to stimuli using mechanical pins and electrodes.

To clarify the characteristics of tactile perception, Murray et al. [5] investigated the tactile differential threshold at 12 body sites by using an aesthesiometer. They evaluated not only the conventional two-point differential threshold, where two stimuli are given at the same time, but also obtained the differential threshold for the delayed stimulus condition, where the second stimulus is given after a certain delay. In their results, they obtained a two-point threshold of 7.8 mm at the palm with simultaneous stimulus presentation, whereas the threshold dropped to 2.5 mm when a 1.0-s delay was given for the second stimulus presentation. When the second stimulus was delayed by 8.0 s, the threshold was reduced to 5.0 mm. They reasoned that the change in thresholds was because lateral inhibition was generated for simultaneous stimulus presentation and suppressed when there was a delay between two stimuli.

S. Yamamoto (Ed.): HIMI/HCII 2013, Part I, LNCS 8016, pp. 620–627, 2013.

Our tactile display that uses air-jet stimuli has a structure consisting of a matrix of 1.0-mm-diameter nozzles; hence, the tactile perception characteristics may differ from the experimental results reported by Murray et al. in terms of fluid-based stimulation and stimulation size. The aim of the present study was to investigate the spatiotemporal characteristics of tactile perception induced by an air-jet-based tactile display. In particular, the effects of stimulus delay and different palm areas on the change in tactile differential thresholds were empirically identified.

2 Methods

2.1 Tactile Display Using Air-Jet Stimuli

Figure 1 shows the schematic diagram of the apparatus. The air-jet stimuli are presented by means of a 12 × 12 air-jet array controlled by a precision pressure regulator. The pressure level and airflow duration are controlled by an electro-pneumatic regulator (CKD EVD-1900-P08 SN), and the location selector used for determining the location to generate stimuli is controlled by an electromagnetic valve (KOGANEI 025E1-2).

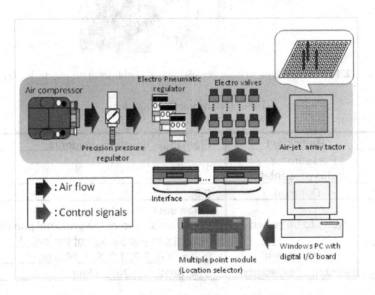

Fig. 1. Structure of the tactile display used in this study

2.2 Participants and Experimental Procedure

Eight male participants volunteered for this study. All were university students and reported normal tactile perception. The sets in the experiment took two days to complete. As shown in Figure 2, each participant placed the palm of his non-dominant hand on top of the tactile display surface. The location of the hand was then marked and fixed throughout the experiment. Each participant wore earplugs and headphones to completely eliminate the airflow noise generated from the tactile display. In each trial, two tactile stimuli with a certain interstimulus interval (ISI) were presented to the participant. The participant responded as to whether the two stimuli were presented at the same location. Each set consisted of 49 trials with seven levels of delay time and seven levels of interstimulus distance. Nine sets of three replicates and three palm locations (proximal area of the proximal phalanx and distal and middle parts of the palm) were tested. Short breaks were given to the subjects between sets. The experimental conditions are summarized in Table 1.

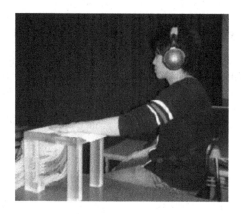

Fig. 2. Posture of the participant perceiving the stimuli from the tactile display

Table 1. Experimental conditions

Participant	Eight male university students
Pressure for stimulus presentation	100kPa
Duration	0.5s
Areas to be tested	Three sections at the palm area (The proximal area of the proximal phalanx, the distal and middle part of the palm)
Time interval	0, 0.5, 1.0, 2.0, 4.0, 8.0, 16.0 [s]
Interstimulus distance	0, 4, 8, 12, 16, 20, 24 [mm]

2.3   Data Analysis

The percentage of correct answers was calculated for each condition, and the differential threshold for the condition was extrapolated as the distance such that the percentage of correct answers would be 50%. The following formula was used to determine the differential threshold:

$$d_{\text{threshold}} = d_L + \left\{ \frac{50 - E(d_H)}{E(d_H) - E(d_L)} \right\} \times (d_H - d_L)$$

where $d_{\text{threshold}}$: estimated differential threshold [mm]

d_L: minimum interstimulus distance, which was set to 4 mm

d_H: minimum interstimulus distance at which the percentage of correct responses significantly changed [mm]

$E(d)$: percentage of correct responses at the interstimulus distance d [%]

Figure 3 shows the relationship between the differential threshold and percentage of correct responses.

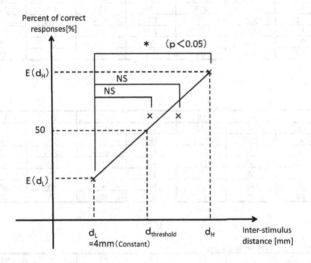

Fig. 3. Relationship between the differential threshold and percentage of correct responses

3   Results

Table 2 shows the percentage of correct responses by interstimulus distance and ISI. As shown in the table, the percentage of incorrect responses was low when the interstimulus distance was 4–8 mm for all sections of the tested hand sites. The percentage of correct responses significantly decreased as the applied stimulus locations approached the middle of the palm from the proximal part of the proximal phalanx ($p < 0.01$). Figure 4 shows the relationship between the interstimulus distance and percentage of correct responses. The percentage of correct responses gradually increased as the interstimulus distance became wider. A 100% correct response rate was obtained when an interstimulus distance of more than 20 mm was given. Table 3 summarizes the estimated tactile differential thresholds by section and ISI. The estimated tactile differential threshold was about 9.0 mm for the simultaneous stimulus presentation.

The threshold fluctuated between 7.4 and 8.3 mm for the delayed stimulus presentation. For all tested hand sites, the smallest threshold was obtained when an ISI of 0.5 s was given. When stimuli were presented simultaneously, the differential threshold was significantly higher than the thresholds for the delayed stimuli.

Table 2. Percentage of correct responses by the interstimulus distance and ISI

(a)

		Time interval [s]						
		0.0	0.5	1.0	2.0	4.0	8.0	16.0
	0	–	17%	4%	4%	0%	8%	33%
	4	75%	67%	83%	83%	75%	79%	67%
Interstimulus	8	63%	42%	38%	38%	42%	38%	58%
distance	12	25%	4%	13%	25%	21%	13%	13%
[mm]	16	0%	8%	13%	4%	8%	13%	8%
	20	4%	4%	0%	8%	0%	0%	4%
	24	0%	0%	0%	0%	4%	0%	0%

(b)

		Time interval [s]						
		0.0	0.5	1.0	2.0	4.0	8.0	16.0
	0	–	0%	8%	13%	4%	21%	17%
	4	79%	83%	96%	83%	83%	71%	67%
Interstimulus	8	71%	54%	46%	63%	50%	42%	42%
distance	12	29%	21%	4%	8%	21%	8%	29%
[mm]	16	4%	4%	8%	4%	4%	13%	4%
	20	4%	0%	0%	4%	0%	0%	8%
	24	0%	0%	0%	0%	4%	0%	4%

(c)

		Time interval [s]						
		0.0	0.5	1.0	2.0	4.0	8.0	16.0
	0	–	4%	0%	4%	8%	25%	29%
	4	92%	92%	75%	79%	79%	67%	71%
Interstimulus	8	75%	50%	54%	71%	46%	46%	50%
distance	12	25%	8%	42%	25%	33%	46%	29%
[mm]	16	17%	17%	21%	21%	4%	21%	8%
	20	0%	0%	0%	0%	4%	0%	0%
	24	4%	0%	4%	0%	13%	0%	8%

Table 3. Estimated tactile differential thresholds by different hand sites and ISIs

Time	0.0s	0.5s	1.0s	2.0s	4.0s	8.0s	16.0s	
Proximal phalanges	8.0	6.2	7.7	6.9	7.7	7.5	6.5	
Distal palm	8.6	8.2	8.0	7.5	8.2	6.7	7.6	
Middle palm	11.3	8.0	9.5	8.3	9.1	8.5	8.0	
Average	9.3	7.5	8.4	7.6	8.3	7.5	7.4	[mm]

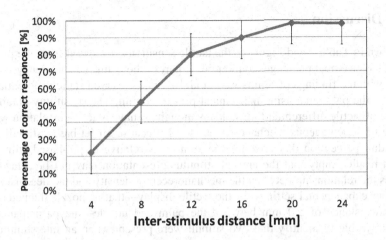

Fig. 4. Relationship between the interstimulus distance and percentage of correct responses

Figure 5 shows the relationship between the delay time and differential thresholds at different hand sites. There was a significant difference in differential thresholds among the hand sites. The differential threshold was shortest at the proximal part of the proximal phalanges followed by the distal part of the palm and middle part of the palm.

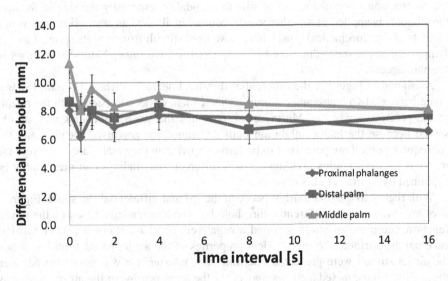

Fig. 5. Relationship between the delayed time and differential thresholds at different hand sites

4   Discussion

As shown in Table 2 and Figure 5, the tactile sensitivity decreased from the proximal part of the proximal phalanges to the middle part of the palm. This tendency was consistent with the findings of Shimawaki et al. [6], who observed static differential thresholds at the palm area using mechanical pins as stimuli. The sensitivity obtained by the size of tactile differential thresholds is thought to have a good correlation with the density of subcutaneous mechanoreceptors [6]. Because air-jet-based stimuli give a rather dull perception that covers large skin areas relative to pin-based stimuli, the present results imply that the area of stimulus presentation may not be a factor that violates the relationship between the mechanoreceptor density and tactile sensitivity.

At our experimental settings for the tactile display—that is, nozzle diameter of 1.0 mm and distance of 5.0 mm between the palm and nozzle—the participants were apparently able to identify that two stimuli were present when an interstimulus distance of at least 20 mm was given. However, the interstimulus distance should be easily adjustable by changing the distance between the nozzle and palm because the nozzle–palm distance affects the size of the area being presented with the stimuli owing to the dynamic properties of fluids.

Murray et al. [5] examined two-point differential thresholds by using an aethesiometer. A comparison of their study with the present results showed that the differential threshold in the present study was 1.5 mm wider for simultaneous stimulus presentation and 2.5–5.0 mm wider for delayed stimulus presentation. The results of the comparison imply the effect of stimulus modality, especially the size of the area the stimulus is applied to. In other words, Murray et al. used an aesthesiometer, which consists of fine mechanical pins, whereas we used stimuli from air-jets sprayed from a 1-mm-diameter nozzle; this may have appeared to give rather blurred sensations to the participants.

As shown in Figure 5, the differential threshold decreased when a certain ISI was given between two consecutive stimuli. This tendency was consistent with the results of the previous study [5]. Murray et al. reasoned that such tendencies may be observed because the lateral inhibition built up around the perceived location and the subsequent stimuli are perceived to be further apart than they really are. Although the medium for the stimulus presentation was different, our findings can presumably be explained by Murray et al.'s reasoning.

With regard to the relationship between the ISI and differential threshold, Figure 5 does not show that the differential threshold became less sensitive based on the power function; the previous study reported a negatively accelerated curve [5]. The difference can be attributed to the physical properties of the air-jet-based stimulus. When the air-jet stimuli were presented intermittently, interference was generated between the airflows; thus, mixed airflows may cover the areas nearby, or the air pressure may cover not only the area being stimulated but also induce pressure indirectly to adjacent areas, which lowers or masks the tactile sensitivity of the area.

5   Conclusion

In this study, two-point differential thresholds were investigated on human palms to obtain characteristics for the development of a noncontact tactile display. The following results were found. The tactile differential threshold was approximately 9 mm and became more sensitive when the presentation of subsequent stimuli was delayed. The most sensitive value was 7.5 mm when a 0.5-s ISI was given. The differential threshold was blurred after 0.5 s of the ISI, which differed from the previous study where a power function for forgetting the rate of tactile sensation was observed. In this study, the memory characteristics for a tactile display using air-jet stimuli was obtained. Further study is needed, especially on the clarification of the relationship between the pressure level and spatiotemporal memory characteristics, for the design of a noncontact tactile display that can transmit information effectively.

Acknowledgment. This study was partly supported by JSPS KAKENHI (24370103, 24657182).

References

1. Gallace, A., Tan, H.Z., Spence, C.: Tactile change detection. In: Proceeding of the First Joint Eurohaptics Conference (2005)
2. Evesa, D.A., Novak, M.M.: Extraction of vector information using a novel tactile display. Displays 18(3), 169–181 (1998)
3. Rahal, L., Cha, J., El Saddik, A.: Continuous tactile perception for vibrotactile displays. In: IEEE International Workshop on Robotic and Sensors Environments, pp. 86–91 (2009)
4. Iwamoto, T., Akaho, D., Shinoda, H.: High resolution tactile display using acoustic radiation pressure. In: SICE Annual Conference in Sapporo, pp. 1239–1244 (2004)
5. Murray, D.J., Ward, R., Hockley, W.E.: Tactile short-term memory in relation to the two-point threshold. Quarterly Journal of Experimental Psychology 27, 303–312 (1975)
6. Simawaki, S., Sakai, N., Suzuki, A.: Measurement of tactile sensation on human hand by static and moving two-point discrimination tests. Journal of the Japan Society of Mechanical Engineers 71(704), 210–214 (2005)

Understanding the Impact Congruent Images and News Articles Have on Mood and Attitude

Eleanor T. Loiacono and Miaokun Lin

Worcester Polytechnic Institute, Worcester, MA USA
{eloiacon,mlin}@wpi.edu

Abstract. As more people turn online to get their news, the significance of on-line advertisements becomes even more important to companies seeking to enhance their bottom line. This paper is part of a larger project looking into how the congruency of online news articles and advertisements affect user's moods and attitudes towards both the ad and news article. Preliminary results indicate that congruency does impact user's moods and attitudes.

Keywords: Mood induction, online advertisement, Web, Internet.

1 Introduction

As the predominance of print media declines and online activities soar, the need to investigate and understand the significance of online advertisements becomes even more important to companies. Advertisers want to enhance their bottom lines while businesses hope to get their message out to potential consumers thereby increasing their revenues. This movement towards online advertisements was made clear by the significant increase in digital spending over the past several years. In fact, online advertising has grown to almost $40 million and has surpassed that spent on print media (eMarketer 2012). This trend is projected to continue.

More and more people are looking to online news outlets to keep current on daily happenings. These sites attract a wide range of visitors. In fact, the top 25 news sites pulled in an average of 342 million unique visitors in 2011 (a 17% increase from 2010) (Mitchell and Rosenstiel 2012). Four out of ten Americans interviewed acknowledge receiving a majority of their news from the Internet (Center 2011).

Out of this phenomenon arises the question, how can advertisements placed on online news outlets be more effective in influencing potential customers?

2 Literature Review

A key influencer of decision making in general (Isen and Labroo 2003, Isen 2008), and consumer behavior in particular (Morrison, Gan et al. 2011, Swinyard 1993), is mood. Mood refers to an individual's mild, enduring, and objectless affective state (Lazarus 1991, Fredrickson 2003, Isen 2003). Previous affective literature reveals that factors such as music (Fulberg 2003), aroma (Chebat and Dube 2000), and images (Mathur and Chattopadhyay 1991) can impact a consumer's mood which in turn affects his or her attitude and subsequent behavior.

S. Yamamoto (Ed.): HIMI/HCII 2013, Part I, LNCS 8016, pp. 628–634, 2013.
© Springer-Verlag Berlin Heidelberg 2013

Specifically, research into advertisements has shown that induced moods can impact users' attitudes towards an ad. For example, viewers watching a happy program are more apt to have a positive attitude towards a commercial than the same ad presented within a sad show (Goldberg and Gorn 1987). These finding were supported using the mood congruency theory (Isen 1984) which states that people in a positive mood are more likely to recall information that is positive since it is congruent with their current mood. When studied in isolation, positive television ads induced a more positive attitude towards the ad than did those that were negative in nature (Russell 1979, Brown, Homer et al. 1998).

Within online ad research, multiple studies have investigated the annoyance of online ads. Not only are the multiple types of online ads, such as "pop-up," "floating," or "overlay", annoying (Segal 2006), they have resulted in a decline in click-through and attention to the ad (Yaveroglu and Donthu 2008). The response has been to focus on the impact ad-context congruency has on ad recognition. One such study found that depending on the task of the online user (information seeking or simply surfing), ad-context congruency does matter (Zanjani, Diamond et al. 2011). Information seekers are better able to recall an ad within an e-magazine when it is congruent with the context. This task is similar to a person seeking the latest news.

This preliminary study investigates the impact that congruent positive online images and news articles have on users' moods and their attitude towards the image and story.

H^1: Web users exposed to a (congruent) positive image and news article will have a positive influence on their mood compared to those who are exposed to a non-congruent image or news article combination.

H^2: Web users exposed to a (congruent) positive image and news article will have a better attitude towards the story and image compared to those who are exposed to a non-congruent image or news article combination.

3   Methodology

In order to examine the impact of congruent images and news articles on one's mood, a series of t-tests and a two-way ANOVA method was employed to compare the four treatment groups. One group will receive a positive news article with a positive image. A second will be exposed to a positive article with neutral image, while the third will review a neutral story with a positive image. Finally, the last group will receive both a neutral news article and image (see Table 1).

The news articles and images included in the study were selected from previously tested and validated research to determined their type (i.e., positive or neutral in nature). The two images were taken from the International Affective Picture System

Table 1. Image and News Article Mood Type

		Image	
		Positive	Neutral
Article	Positive	n=53	n=49
	Neutral	n=55	n=51

(IAPS) (Bradley and Lang 2007), one representing a positive mood evoking image and the other a neutral one. The positive image contains three puppies next to each other. The neutral image is of several baskets lined up. The positive puppy picture has a valence measure of 8.34 (out of a scale from 1 through 10, 10 being the most positive) indicating a strong positive mood evocation. The image of the baskets had a moderate or neutral valence score of 4.99.

The two articles (one positive and one neutral in tone) were taken from a previous study looking at online mood induction (Loiacono, Taylor et al. 2005). The positive news article conveyed the story of a young woman who helped a drought devastated town in Kenya. It received a score of 6.94 (out of a 1 to 7scale, 7 being the most positive). The neutral story was selected had a score of 4.5 and discussed Sprints create in-store solutions for customers. The stories were of similar length. The positive story was 312 words in length and the neutral story 297 words.

3.1   Participants

A sample size of 208 users has been collected. Such a sample size allows for the detection of significant differences with medium effect size and a 95% power level. Participants were recruited from a national online market research firm located in the United States. They are all adult online web users, over in age 18. Additional demographic information, such as gender, level of education, experience using the Internet, and Web usage was collected and appears in Table 2. All subjects will be asked to review and sign a consent form, approved by the Internal Review Board. The incentive to participate is the regular incentive provided by the marketing firm—points towards gift cards or prizes. All subjects received a similar reward.

Table 2. Demographic Information

	Average
Gender	72.6% females
Age	47.79 years
Education Level	10.1% Graduate degree 21.2% Bachelor degree 13% Associate degree 32.2% Some college, but no degree 22.6% High school or equivalent degree 1% Less than high school degree
Internet Experience	89.4% More than 7 years 8.2% 5 to 7 years 1.9% 3 to 4 years .5% 1 to 2 years
Web Usage	97.1% daily 2.4% once a week .5% once every two weeks

3.2   Measures

Mood. Consistent with previous research, mood data was collected using the Positive and Negative Affect Schedule (PANAS) (Watson, Clark et al. 1992) mood scale. It contains 20 items, wherein 10 items measure positive mood and 10 negative mood. The measure has been shown to have high internal reliability as well as discriminant and convergent validity.

Attitude towards News Article and Image. In addition to gathering mood information, data on the subjects' attitudes towards the news article and image were also collected. For example, was it worth remembering, amusing or meaningful to you were some of the questions asked. This paper uses the item, "worth remembering," to determine subjects' attitudes towards the news article and the image.

Task. After accessing the survey site, subjects were briefed on the study and asked to accept the terms of the consent form before proceeding. Those who declined to participate were thanked and taken out of the survey site. Those who agreed to participate were asked to answer some demographic information, such as gender, age, education level, and years of Internet and Web usage. They were then asked how they felt at this moment. Several words describing different feelings and emotions were presented and they were asked to rate each on a scale of 1 (very slightly tor not at all) to 7 (extremely) based on how they feel "at the present moment" (Watson, Clark et al. 1992).

Next, the subjects were taken (randomly) to one of the four news article/image combinations. They were asked to read the article. Once they finish reading the article and click on the next button, they were asked to record their current mood similar to how they did prior to reading the article and seeing the image.

They were then asked to describe or summarize in 4 to 5 words the news article and image they saw. This information allowed for the confirmation that the subjects actually read the article and saw the image. It also provided additional information on how well they were able to recall the article and image.

After completing the survey, the subjects were thanked and taken to an exit site. The total survey time was approximated to take 20 minutes to complete.

4   Preliminary Results

Out of the 208 subjects, 57 were men. The average age of participants was approximately 47.56 years with a range of 18 to 81. Most (76%) had at least some college education. In terms of Internet experience and usage, 89.4% had over 7 years of Internet experience and approximately 97.1% use the Web on a daily basis.

Initial analysis of the data reveals partial support for H^1. Congruency does impact a user's mood, but only if the congruency is positive. Through the use of paired sample t-tests, analysis was conducted on the positive and negative moods of subjects receiving each of the four treatment groups. For those receiving a congruent positive image and news article, there was no significant change in their positive mood (t-value = -.221, p = .826), however, there was a decrease in their negative mood (t-value = 2.902, p = .005). Similarly, those who received a non-congruent (neutral) image and (positive) news article, did not have a significant change in their positive mood (t-value = -.672, p = .505), but there was a drop in their negative mood (t-value = 3.050, p = .004). It appears that the impact of the story on individuals' moods was more powerful than that of the image. Regardless of the image (positive or neutral), the positive mood of the participants stayed the same. A follow-up analysis, comparing the post-treatment moods of both groups receiving the positive news article, revealed no significant difference in mood (positive t-test = -.257, p = .798; negative t-test = -.304, p = .762). This suggests that the news story's mood induction may have a strong influence on a person's negative mood regardless of the image type (positive or negative) that is placed near it.

As expected, the exposure to a non-congruent (neutral) story and (positive) news article did not have any significant impact on subjects' positive (t-value = .937, p = .353) or negative (t-value = 1.534, p = .131) moods. Interestingly, a comparison of the pre and post-treatment moods of those receiving a congruent (neutral) image and news article, revealed that the positive mood actually decreased (t-value = 2.317, p = .025), while their negative mood (t-value = 1.809, p = .076) did not. Table 3 shows changes in moods for each group.

This is interesting because it indicates that mood congruency may have different affects depending on the type of mood influencer (news story or image). When both image and news articles are positive, mood is affected in a more positive manner (negative mood decreases). However when both image and news story are neutral, users may have an overall negative mood response. Further analysis is warranted in this area to see if the resulting change in mood is due to annoyance of image and news article topics being unrelated. In this study the neutral news story discussed Sprint services, while the neutral image was an unrelated picture of baskets. This is an area that will be investigated in future research.

Table 3. Preliminary Results based on Mood

		Image	
		Positive	**Neutral**
Article	**Positive**	$P_b = P_a$ $N_b \searrow N_a$	$P_b = P_a$ $N_b \searrow N_a$
	Neutral	$P_b = P_a$ $N_b = N_a$	$P_b \searrow P_a$ $N_b = N_a$

P_b = Positive mood before treatment, P_a = Positive mood after treatment.
N_b = Negative mood before treatment, N_a = Negative mood after treatment.

Further analysis looking into H^2 revealed that congruency does not appear to impact attitude. News articles do impact a user's attitude towards the image, but not vice-versa. In particular one variable, "worth remembering" captured how users' felt about the image or story they saw. An Analysis of Variance on the current sample revealed that the type (positive or neutral) of an news article has an influence on a user's attitude towards the news story (F-test = 17.421, p = .000) and the image (F-test = 6.487, p = .012), however, the type of image only impacts one's attitude towards the image (F-test = 7.236, p = .008), but not his or her attitude towards the news article (F-test = .567, p = .452). There does not appear to be any interaction effect between image and news story, which indicates that congruency may not play as significant a role as hypothesized. Thus, H^2 is not supported.

5   Discussion and Future Research

These results are interesting because they suggest that when looking at news articles, the combination of images and story presented can impact a visitor's mood and subsequent attitude. The type of news story can impact the attitude one has towards the image that is near it. This is similar to the findings related to television viewers watching a happy program who were more apt to have a positive attitude towards a commercial than the same ad presented within a sad show (Goldberg and Gorn 1987). Thus, advertisers may want to consider the news stories they are presented near. Additionally, the congruency of the image to the text can influence a visitor's mood and may be helpful to advertisers, since people in a positive mood are likely to have a more positive attitude towards an ad.

There is much more work to be done. As mentioned earlier, this is the first step in much larger project. Future research should (and we plan to) look at the impact of negative mood inducing news article and image. This will allow for a fuller picture of how mood evoking articles and images together impact a visitor's mood. It may be that negative text and images have a stronger or different impact on mood, especially when there is congruency between them.

References

1. Bradley, M.M., Lang, P.J.: Affective Norms for English Text (ANET): Affective ratings of text and instruction manual. University of Florida, Gainesville (2007)
2. Brown, S.P., et al.: A Meta-Analysis of Relationships Between Ad-Evoked Feelings and Advertising Responses. Journal of Marketing Research 35, 114–126 (1998)
3. Center, P.R.: Internet Gains on Television as Public's Main News Source (2011), http://pewresearch.org/pubs/1844/poll-main-source-national-international-news-internet-television-newspapers (retrieved December 1, 2012)
4. Chebat, J., Dube, L.: Evolution and challenges facing retail atmospherics: the apprentice sorcerer is dying. Journal of Business Research 49(2), 89–90 (2000)
5. eMarketer. US Digital Ad Spending to Top $37 Billion in 2012 as Market Consolodates (2012)
6. Fredrickson, B.L.: Positive Emotions and Upward Spirals in Organizations. In: Cameron, K.S., Dutton, J.E., Quinn, R.E. (eds.) Positive Organizational Scholarship, pp. 163–175. Berret-Koehler Publishers, Inc., San Francisco (2003)

7. Fulberg, P.: Using sonic branding in the retail environment: an easy and effective way to create consumer brand loyalty while enhancing the in-store experience. Journal of Consumer Behavior 3(2), 193–198 (2003)

8. Goldberg, M.E., Gorn, G.J.: Happy and Sad TV Programs: How They Affect Reactions to Commercials. Journal of Consumer Research 14, 387–403 (1987)

9. Isen, A.M.: Towards Understanding the Role of Affect in Cognition. In: Wyer, R.S., Srull, T.K. (eds.) Handbook of Social Cognition, vol. 3, pp. 179–236. Erlbaum, Hillsdale (1984)

10. Isen, A.M.: Positive Affect as a Source of Human Strength. In: Aspinwall, L., Staudinger, U.M. (eds.) A Psychology of Human Strengths, pp. 179–195. American Psychological Associations, Washington, DC (2003)

11. Isen, A.M.: Some Ways in Which Positive Affect Influences Decision Making and Problem Solving. In: Lewis, M., Haviland-Jones, J.M., Barrett, L.F. (eds.) Handbook of Emotions, 3rd edn. Guilford Press, New York (2008)

12. Isen, A.M., Labroo, A.A.: Some Ways in Which Positive Affect Facilitates Decision Making and Judgment. In: Schneider, L.S., Shanteau, J. (eds.) Emerging Perspectives on Judgment and Decision Research, pp. 365–393. Cambridge University Press, Cambridge (2003)

13. Lazarus, R.S.: Emotion and Adaptation. Oxford University Press, New York (1991)

14. Loiacono, E., et al.: Online Mood Induction. In: Americas Conference on Information Systems, Omaha, NE (2005)

15. Mathur, M., Chattopadhyay, A.: The Impact of Moods Generated by Television Programs on Responses to Advertising. Psychology & Marketing 8(1), 59–77 (1991)

16. Mitchell, A., Rosenstiel, T.: The State of the News Media 2012. Pew Research Center's Project for Excellence in Journalism (2012)

17. Morrison, M., et al.: In-store music and aroma influences on shopper behavior and satisfaction. Journal of Business Research 64, 558–564 (2011)

18. Russell, J.A.: Affective Space is Bipolar. Journal of Personality and Social Psychology 37, 345–356 (1979)

19. Segal, D.: Annoying Floating Ads Are This Guy's Fault. Washington Post (2006)

20. Swinyard, W.: The effects of mood, involvement and quality of store experience onshopping experience. Journal of Consumer Research 20(2), 271–281 (1993)

21. Watson, D., et al.: Affect, Personality, and Social Activity. Journal of Personality and Social Psychology 63(6), 1011–1025 (1992)

22. Yaveroglu, I., Donthu, N.: Advertising Repetition and Placement Issues in On-Line Environments. Journal of Advertising 37(2), 31–44 (2008)

23. Zanjani, S.H.A., et al.: Does Ad–Context Congruity Help Surfers and information SeeKers Remember Ads in Cluttered e-magazines? Journal of Advertising 40(4), 67–83 (2011)

Eyes Don't Lie: Understanding Users' First Impressions on Websites Using Eye Tracking

Hong Sheng, Nicholas S. Lockwood, and Sirjana Dahal

Missouri University of Science and Technology, MO, USA
{Hsheng,lockwoodn}@mst.edu, dahalsirjana@gmail.com

Abstract. Websites are prevalent these days. Web users make instantaneous judgments regarding a website based on their first impressions and usually decide either to stay on the website or bypass it during their initial interaction with the website. Hence, understanding users' first impression is important for both practitioners and researchers. This research examines users' first impression of websites using an eye tracker. Eye tracking can provide fixation points where users focus their attention on a stimulus. The eye tracking results indicate that users take at least 2.66 seconds to scan the website before they fixate their eyes on an element of the website. Our analysis also shows that first fixation duration lasted for 180 milliseconds. This indicates that after allocating attention to a specific area on a website, the eyes stopped to focus for 180 milliseconds during which the brain processed the visual information received from the eyes to organize the information and form an impression of the website.

Keywords: First impression, Websites, Eye Tracking, Attention.

1 Introduction

Websites are pervasive and commonplace these days, so they need to create a favorable first impression on users during initial exposure (Thomson, 2006). Web users make instantaneous judgments regarding a website based on their first impressions and usually decide either to stay on the website or bypass it within the first couple of minutes (Thilmany, 2003).

First impressions are powerful and often have a long-term effect on users' perceptions and attitudes towards a website. Therefore, it is critical for the designers, web developers, and organizations to understand how users form their first impressions of websites. In this study, we use an eye tracker to track and analyze users' interactions with various websites during their initial exposures, which shed light on the time needed to form first impressions as well as the processes involved in selecting and organizing relevant information to form first impressions.

2 Literature Review

First impressions have been studied in various contexts such as psychology, medicine, usability, marketing, etc. (Lingaard et al., 2006). In marketing, first impression is

S. Yamamoto (Ed.): HIMI/HCII 2013, Part I, LNCS 8016, pp. 635–641, 2013.
© Springer-Verlag Berlin Heidelberg 2013

defined as a quick evaluation made by the customer during the first few minutes of an encounter with a product/object (De Groot, 2006). Consumers' impressions usually remain stable (Mitchell and Corr, 1998) and have long-term effects, sometimes referred to as the 'halo effect'.

In examining a person's perception of another, Hamilton et al. (1980) define impression as a perceiver's cognitive representation of another person. They focused their inquiry on the cognitive processes involved in the development of that cognitive representation from the stimulus information available to the perceiver (Hamilton et al., 1980). Willis and Todorov (2006) further concluded that a minimal exposure time of 100 milliseconds is sufficient for a person to make a specific trait inference of others, such as attractiveness, trustworthiness, likeability, competence, and aggressiveness, based on facial appearance.

In the decision-making literature, first impression is referred as a cognitive confirmation bias (Lingaard et al., 2006). Confirmation bias occurs when participants who have formed positive first impressions may ignore negative issues and errors that they encounter later. Likewise, participants find it hard to accept the positive information when negative first impressions have been formed. Lindgaard et al. (2006) conducted a study to determine the exposure time required for the participants to form first impressions and concluded that users take 50 milliseconds to make a decision on whether they like or dislike what they see.

According to Hamilton et al. (1980), forming an impression is an active process in which the perceiver organizes the information available about a target to develop a coherent representation of that target. Fiske and Neuberg (1990) proposed a continuum model of impression formation in which attention to and interpretation of information underlies the impression formation process. Attention is a selective process that allows us to prioritize and focus on certain areas or aspects of a visual stimulus while ignoring others (Canasco, 2011). Perceivers allocate attention to the target if the target is of at least minimal interest (Fiske and Neuberg, 1990). Once this information is processed, it is organized into a cognitive representation which leads to impression.

3 Research Methodology

This research is an exploratory examination of users' first impressions of websites. An eye tracker was used in collecting users' eye movements during the exposure of the websites, which provided insights into users' impression formation process.

Twenty students from a mid-sized Midwestern university participated in this study. The participants all had normal vision with no color blindness. Among the 20 participants, 15 were male and 5 were female, with ages ranging from 19-36. They all had substantial Internet experience.

In this study, twenty-five websites from the top five tiers of university ranking of the Unites States that offer Law as a graduate or undergraduate degree were selected. These websites vary in levels of visual appeal and design features. Compared to other public websites, these websites receive less public exposure and traffic, which is appropriate for understanding users' first impressions.

The study was conducted in the laboratory setting with each session lasting for approximately 60 minutes. Upon arrival at the lab, the participants were briefed about the experiment and eye tracking equipment. They were then asked to sign a consent form. Before the start of the experiment, each individual participant's eyes were calibrated using the eye tracker. A short questionnaire was also provided to collect the participant's demographic information. The stimulus was then presented on the eye tracking monitor to collect data on the participant's eye movements and fixation points. The twenty-five websites were displayed in random order. The participants were asked to view each website until they have formed their first impressions on the website and then move on to the next website. No time constraint was imposed. After viewing each website, the participants were then asked to rate each website based on their first impressions. An qualitative interview was conducted at the end of each session.

A Tobii 1750 eye tracker system was used to capture participants' eye movements and fixation points. The Tobii 1750 eye tracker—which functions without the need for glasses, lenses, or headgear—can gather eye tracking data without intruding and interfering with participants' performance on assigned tasks.

4   Results and Discussion

4.1   Time to First Fixation

Human eyes are constantly moving until they stop and focus on a point. When the eyes stop to focus, it is called a fixation (Technology, 2011). The length of the stops, when the eyes fixate, varies from about 100 to 600 milliseconds depending on what the eyes are looking at. During this stop, the brain starts to process the visual information received from the eyes (Rayner, 1998). Fixations are important because they locate the foveal vision. Users cannot interpret what they have seen until they pay attention to it or fixate their eyes on it (Wedel and Pieters, 2007). Hence, the length of fixation is an indication of information processing and cognitive activities.

Time to first fixation is the time in seconds from when the stimulus was shown until the start of the first fixation within a page. In this study, time to first fixation was extracted from the eye tracker by considering each website as an area of interest (AOI). The descriptive statistics shows a mean of 2.66 seconds, which means that it took an average of 2.66 seconds for the participants to allocate their attention to the webpages.

4.2   First Fixation Duration

First fixation duration is the duration of the first fixation on an image regardless of whether it is the only fixation or the first of multiple fixations on an image (Technology 2011). First fixation duration was extracted from the eye tracker for all twenty-five websites. Average duration of the first fixation is 180 milliseconds.

Our analysis shows that first fixation duration lasted for 180 milliseconds. This indicates that after allocating attention to a specific area on a webpage, users' eyes stopped to focus for 180 milliseconds on the area. During this time, the brain processed the visual information received from the eyes to organize the information and form a cognitive representation of the website. This suggests that at least 180 milliseconds are needed in order for a user to form a first impression of a website, contrary to prior findings that first impression only takes 50 milliseconds to form (Lindgaard et al., 2006).

Table 1. Impression Rating Dimensions

Item	Negative Anchor	Positive Anchor
1	Boring	Interesting
2	Irritating	Charming
3	Pale	Vibrant
4	Complex	Simple
5	Inconsistent	Consistent
6	Awkward	Straightforward
7	Cluttered	Clear
8	Unreliable	Reliable
9	Unattractive	Attractive
10	Unappealing	Appealing
11	Brief	Lasting
12	Emotionless	Soulful
13	Unpleasant	Pleasant
14	Insignificant	Significant
15	Pacifying	Exciting
16	Abominable	Likable
17	Poor	Rich
18	Conservative	Progressive
19	Dull	Witty

4.3 Impression Perceptions

Participants were asked to rate their impressions of each website along the nineteen semantic differential dimensions shown in Table 1. The items were coded on a -3 to +3 scale and aggregated to obtain a single overall measure of first impression valence. Thus negative scores indicated unfavorable impressions and positive scores indicated favorable impressions. Sixteen of the stimulus websites were found to elicit favorable impressions on average and nine were found to elicit unfavorable impressions.

4.4 Total Fixation Duration

An independent samples t-test was conducted to compare the mean total fixation duration of participants between the favorable and unfavorable websites. Based on the results shown in Table 2, we see that there is a significant difference between the two groups (p=0.026). The mean values shown in Table 3 indicate that participants spend more time on favorable websites than unfavorable websites.

Table 2. Comparison of Total Fixation Duration between Favorable and Unfavorable Websites

	t-test for Equality of Means						
				Mean	Std. Error	95% Confidence Interval of the Difference	
	t	df	Sig.	Difference	Difference	Lower	Upper
Total Fixation Duration	2.380	23	.026	2.20681	.92736	.28841	4.12520

Table 3. Mean Values of Total Fixation Duration

	Websites	N	Mean	Std. Dev.
Total Fixation	Favorable	16	19.991	1.924
Duration	Unfavorable	9	17.784	2.701

4.5   Qualitative Data Analysis

The qualitative analysis identified various issues with the website design and also revealed a number of ways in which the website design can be improved to affect first impressions. The responses from participants were analyzed, coded, and categorized with reference to design factors identified by various researchers (Fitneva et al., 2010; Cyr et al., 2006; Rayner, 1998; Zhang, 2000). The participants were shown the gaze plots and asked questions regarding the pattern of their fixation. They were also asked to provide recommendations on the design of the website. The responses were coded and categorized as below:

Colors. The first design factor identified by participants was use of color. Pacifying and relaxing use of colors such as light green, light blue, and yellow were preferred and the use of colors such as bright red, dark blue, and black were not preferred by the participants. Participants recommended the main color and background color to be pleasant and attractive and the contrast of the text color should be such that it is easier to read. One of the participants stated, *"The use of three colors like blue, red and white reminds me of an airline website rather than website of a university."* Another participant stated, *"The use of background color as light blue and text color as white makes it harder to read the text."*

Images. Another design factor identified by participants was the use of images. Participants suggested that use of meaningless and irrelevant pictures by some of the websites led to negative impression on those websites. Participants recommended that the main image has to be professional and related to the university. The website should not be cluttered with too many images either. One of the participants stated, *"Too many images have made the website cluttered. They could have used a flash player for all the images and animated them."* Another participant stated, *"Big image on the home page gives me good impression."*

Navigation. One of the most common design factors identified by the participants was navigation. Navigation can further be classified into navigation on the main menu, left navigation, right navigation, top navigation, and bottom navigation. A majority of the participants suggested that the main menu be located on the top or left of the website drew more attention to the website since they know where to navigate the website. Too many navigation links on the bottom and right of the website led to confusion and negative impressions toward the website. One of the participants stated, *"Menus on menus does not look attractive. The sub menus should be hidden within the main menus."*

Text. Another design factor identified by the participants was text, which includes font size and style. Use of irregular text size and fonts were an issue to a few participants. Most of the participants suggested that the font type and size used on the websites be clear and readable. Some of the websites that used too much text on an image or unreadable text due to bad contrast of the color with the background led to negative impression of the users towards the website.

Position. Sequential position of images and text on the website were identified as other design factors that led to the formation of impressions towards that website. Participants suggested that use of a large and meaningful image on the area where eyes hit the website leads to the formation of a positive impression. Websites that are cluttered with too many images, links, and text do not capture attention toward the website. One of the participants stated, *"This website is complete pain to navigate because of the weird position of images and texts. It looks like an advertisement of a product rather than a website of a university."*

Space. Proper use of white space is also important. One problem identified on the unfavorable websites was the improper use of white space. Participants recommended that the websites need to make good use of white space by providing the right content. The websites with too much white space are repulsive since they provide very little content.

5   Conclusion

This study examined initial impression formation of twenty-five different university law school websites. Participants were asked to view each website with no exposure time limitation and their eye movements were tracked during the interaction.

The eye tracking results indicate that users take at least 2.66 seconds to scan the website before they fixate their eyes on an element of the website. Our analysis also shows that first fixation duration lasted for 180 milliseconds, which indicates the time needed for the brain to process the visual information received. In addition, the total fixation time was greater for websites that received generally favorable impressions than for websites that received generally unfavorable impressions.

A follow-up qualitative analysis highlights key website features that participants noticed when forming their first impressions. Positive impressions were formed when websites made use of relaxing colors, relevant and professional images, simple navigation, readable text, well-positioned elements, and proper use of white space.

References

1. Hamilton, D., Katz, L., Leirer, V.: Cognitive representation of personality impressions: Organizational processes in first impression formation. Journal of Personality and Social Psychology 39(6), 1050–1063 (1980)
2. Lindgaard, G., Fernandes, G., Dudek, C., Brown, J.: Attention web designers: You have 50 milliseconds to make a good first impression! Behaviour & Information Technology 25(2), 115–126 (2006)
3. Thomson, A.: Does your website attract or detract? Risk Management 53, 50 (2006)
4. Thilmany, J.: Web search measure website appeal in seconds. Mechanical Engineering 125, 10–14 (2003)
5. De Groot, N.: Importance of first impressions. American Book Publishing, Salt Lake City (2006)
6. Mitchell, M., Corr, J.: The first five minutes: How to make a great first impression in any business situation. Wiley (1998)
7. Willis, J., Todorov, A.: First impressions: Making up your mind after a 100-ms exposure to a face. Psychological Science 17(7), 592–598 (2006)
8. Fiske, S., Neuberg, S.: A continuum model of impression formation: From category-based to individuating processes as a function of information, motivation, and attention. Advances in Experimental Social Psychology 23, 1–74 (1990)
9. Technolog. Eye tracking as a tool in package and shelf testing, http://www.tobii.com/Global/Analysis/Training/WhitePapers/ Tobii_EyeTracking_in_Package_and_Shelf_Testing_WhitePaper.pdf (accessed on: October 25, 2011)
10. Rayner, K.: Eye movements in reading and information processing: 20 years of research. Psychological Bulletin 124(3), 372 (1998)
11. Wedel, M., Pieters, R.: Informativeness of eye movements for visual marketing: Six cornerstones. In: Visual Marketing: From Attention to Action, pp. 43–71 (2007)

Cognitive Analysis of Driver's Behavior with Seamless Display of Back-Monitor and Side-View Mirror

Naoyuki Susuki, Kenta Takiguchi, Makoto Oka, and Hirohiko Mori

Tokyo City University, 1-28-1, Tamadutumi, setagaya, Tokyo, Japan
{g1281815,moka,hmori}@tcu.ac.jp,
takiguchi@ims.tcu.ac.jp

Abstract. The accidents during reverse operation of vehicle are one of the traffic accidents often occur. To solve this problem, back-monitor system becomes very popular to provide blind spot information of car for drivers. The back-monitor system assists driver to get visual information of the rear of the car. This camera's view is usually displayed on the car navigation monitor in the dash board panel and drivers must watch many independent viewers, such as mirrors, monitors, and outside, while switching. This separating information and position must cause the difficulties to imagine the images of the wide area of the rear of the cars. In this paper, we proposed a display manner for display method of the back-monitor system which allows objects to not increase more. We conducted the experiment to investigate whether the distance that line of sight has been moved affects the parking and to consider the display method (Seamless, Overlap, and Discrete) of the rear vision before proposing our system. The results showed that overlap picture had good results as the distance between the monitors close. We proposed the rear view system that combines back-monitor system and side-view mirror. The part that reflects body of the car of side-view mirror displayed rear vision that overlaps vision of side-view mirror. We conducted the experiment to evaluate whether this system allows to drivers to park their car safety and precisely using our system. And we compared this proposed system to the traditional back-monitor system. The results showed that it is possible to exactly grasp the situation around the driver by our system. In particular, it is effective for the recognition of the right rear.

Keywords: Service applications, back-monitor system, side mirror, ITS, parking.

1 Introduction

Though the time for the reverse operation is very short in whole of driving a car reverse operation is dangerous and the accidents often occur during it because there are many blind spots. To solve this problem, a variety of systems to provide blind spot information of car for drivers have been developed [1]. A driver can obtain the rear views by the mirrors and through the windows directly when they go back into parking area. The back-monitor system assists driver to get visual information of the

S. Yamamoto (Ed.): HIMI/HCII 2013, Part I, LNCS 8016, pp. 642–649, 2013.

rear of the car. This camera's view is usually displayed on the car navigation monitor in the dash board panel. Driver must watch many independent viewers, such as mirrors, monitors, and outside, switching their views and attentions and imagining situation around. This separated information and position must cause the difficulties to imagine the images of the wide area of the rear of the cars. As the results of adding a back-monitor system to the traditional viewers, drivers must increase the loads.

2   Related Work

Shirahata proposed new back-monitor system that is composed of the side mirror and the monitor [2]. As the result, proposed system was effective for accurate parking. He think it is probably due to a lack of eye movement but he has not been confirmed it. we think that a seamless display of the wide area of rear views makes driver to grasp the state backward of the cars easily.

3   Inquest of Display Method

To investigate some requirements to understand driver's rear view image, we conducted an experiment in advance to the development of the system. As we assume that less driver's eye movements and a seamless display of the wide area of rear views makes him/her to grasp the state backward of the cars easily, we conducted an experiment to investigate their effects.

Fig. 1. The picture reflected on the display is divided into three

3.1   Experiment

Supposing the situation where a driver grasp the state backward to try to change lanes in driving the middle lane of the three lanes, we displayed the three pictures which the whole rear view of the three lanes are divided into on the three monitors. The monitor size was 7 inch because the monitor size is almost the same as side mirror (Fig. 1). We changed the distance among the monitors to investigate effect of the eye movements, and displayed the pictures in three different ways to consider the display method of the rear vision. The distances between the monitors are 0cm, 10cm, and 20cm.

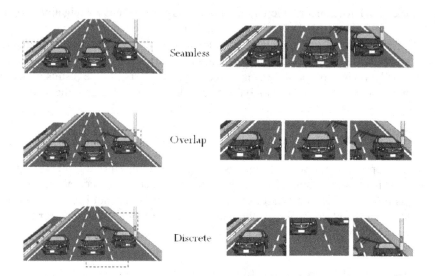

Fig. 2. The pictures in three different ways

The pictures in three different conditions are Seamless, Overlapped, and Discrete (Fig. 2). In the seamless condition, the pictures are just divided into three. In the overlapped condition, pictures are done in the way to some area the neighbors are overlapped. In the discrete condition, the pictures are done in the way that the border parts between the neighbors lack.

3.2   Method

The experiment was done by the following steps:

1. The pictures are presented to the subjects.
2. The pictures are disappeared when he/she grasp the position of the cars backward.
3. We asked him/her to explain the state backward

These steps were repeated in each condition of the combination between the monitor distance conditions and the display manner conditions.

3.3   Results and Discussions

There were some differences among the display manner conditions. Table 1 indicates correct rates the car position backward. There is a significant difference between the discrete condition and the other conditions.

Table 1 also indicates that it took more time significantly to condition. These results mean that the lacks of the views prevent drivers to grasp the state backward.

Comparing the conditions between the seamless and the overlapped, though the both results of the overlapped condition in the both factor are better, there were no significant differences.

The factor of the monitor distance also gives the effects on the results. Table 2 indicates there were significant differences between 20 cm and the others. The 20cm condition also took more time significantly comparing to the other distances. This means that long eye movements among the rear viewers, including not only the monitors but also mirrors, gives ill effects to grasp the rear state.

Table 3 indicates the interactions between two conditions. This table shows there were no interactions between two conditions.

According to the results, we decided to employ the overlapped display manner of the rear vision in our proposed back-monitor system described in the next section because the results are slightly better than the seamless display one.

Table 1. The results for each type of image

The type of image	Seamless	Overlap	Discrete
Percentage of correct	0.74	0.79	0.51
Time(s)	6.74	7.01	7.88

Table 2. The results for each distance

Distance	0cm	10cm	20cm
Percentage of correct	0.73	0.71	0.71
Time(s)	7.00	6.99	7.27

Table 3. The results of percentage of correct and recognition time

		0cm	10cm	20cm
	Seamless	0.78	0.70	0.75
Percentage of correct	Overlap	0.80	0.80	0.75
	Discrete	0.50	0.50	0.54
	Seamless	6.68	6.85	6.68
Time(s)	Overlap	6.73	7.06	7.25
	Discrete	8.21	7.08	8.35

4   The Proposed System

We proposed a rear view system that the views obtained by the back-monitor camera are superimposed side-view mirror (Fig. 3). The reason we choose these viewers is that we want to make drivers' eye movements between the side-view mirror and the back-monitors because the traditional back-monitor is mounted located far from the side mirrors and drivers are required the long-distant eye movements which prevents

Fig. 3. Proposed system

drivers from grasping the rear state as we described above. The images obtained from the back-monitor camera are superimposed on the area where the body of the car reflects in the side view mirror and to overlap each other around the border parts.

5   Evalution of Proposed System

We conducted experiments to evaluate whether this proposed system allows to drivers to park their car safety and precisely using our system. We mounted our system only on the right side-mirror. To compare to the traditional back-monitor system, we also conducted the experiment with it.

5.1   Method

The subjects are asked to back into the parking slot with our system and with the traditional back-monitor system (Fig4). The subjects were tried twice in each condition. They started to park form right ahead of parking slot. The subjects could cut the wheel any number of times. And each trial completed in the subjects' decision. When the car hit any pylons, the trial was over. We measured the number of hitting the brake, the number of cutting the wheel, the distance from the rear of the right tire and the rear corner of the parking slot, the obliqueness of the car to parking slot, and the parking time. We also utilized an eye mark recorder to monitor the subject's eye movement and their gazed objects.

5.2   Results and Discussion

Results of the Number of Failures and the Number of Cutting Wheel. Table 4 shows the results of failures and cutting the wheel. Number of failures show proposed

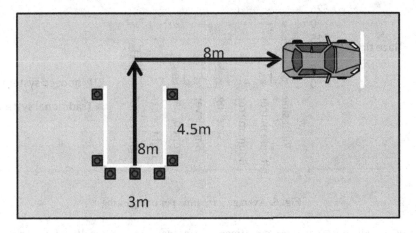

Fig. 4. Enviroment of experiment

Table 4. The results of failures and cutting the wheel

	Proposed system	Traditional system
Number of failures:Total	3	9
Number of cutting the wheel:Total	27	34

Table 5. The results of parking position and parking time

	Proposed system	Traditional system
Distance from the rear of the right tire and the rear corner of the parking slot (cm):Average	101.33	102.48
Obliqueness of the car to parking slot(cm):Average	11.64	9.11
Parking time(s):Average	58.80	59.61

system can grasp situation around than traditional system, because result of proposed system was three times better than traditional system.

Results of Parking Position and Parking Time. Table 5 shows the results of parking position and parking time. Results of the distance from the rear of the right tire and the rear corner of the parking slot, and the obliqueness of the car to parking slot show proposed system can   park exactly as same as traditional system. Result of the parking time shows similar in traditional system and proposed system. Therefore, acceptability of proposed system for driver is same compared with traditional system.

Results of the Subject's Eye Movement and Their Gazing Objects. Proposed system is composed of the back-monitor in the right side mirror. back-monitor is nothing on dashboard of car   in proposed system. we sum results of right side mirror and back-monitor in traditional system, and we treat result of sum as same way as results of right side mirror in proposed system (Fig. 5)(Fig. 6)(Fig. 7).

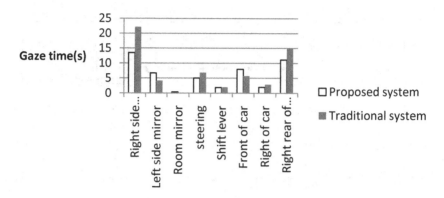

Fig. 5. Average gaze time per one parking

Fig 5 indicates there are significant differences in the results of the right side mirror and the right rear. Proposed system is effective for right rear of the car, because gaze time of the right side mirror and the right rear is shorter than traditional system.

We think because it is possible to grasp exactly the right rear in the proposed system, number of failures in proposed system in table 4 is less than traditional system.

Gaze time may mean being able to grasp surrounding situation. When the gaze time is short, subjects grasp situation around of car. When the gaze time is long, subjects doesn't grasp situation around of car. Fig 6 indicates gaze time of traditional system is longer than proposed system only right side mirror and right of car. Therefore, subjects using the proposed system can look the situation around of the car than traditional system. Fig 6 and Fig 7 indicates there are significant differences in

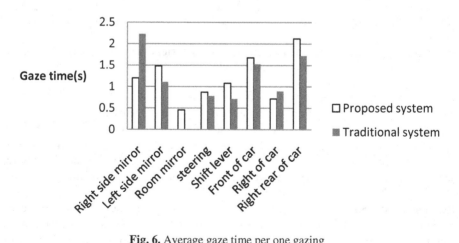

Fig. 6. Average gaze time per one gazing

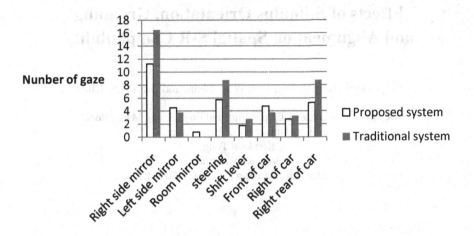

Fig. 7. Average number of gaze per one parking

the results of the right side mirror and the right rear. Therefore, subjects grasp the situation of the right rear by the number of gaze is less and the gaze time is short in proposed system.

6   Conclusion and Future Work

The present study, we have suggested that the proposed system is effective to grasp situation around than traditional system. Results of the number of failures suggested that proposed system can grasp the situation around than traditional system because result of proposed system was three times better than traditional system. Results of the gaze time and the number of gaze suggested that proposed system is valid to grasp right rear of car. As the reason, subjects grasp the situation of the right rear by the number of gaze is less and the gaze time is short in proposed system. Subjects usually look right rear in traditional system. Therefore, subjects using the proposed system can look the situation around of the car than traditional system.

We were able to record the eye movement is the only two people, we must monitor subject's eye movement more. We used pylons in experiment, but we consider to need moving objects. Angle of view of the web camera is narrower than traditional system, we would need to use the wide angle camera.

References

1. Shimizu, H., Yanagisawa, H.: Bird's-eye view Parking Support System. Dennso Technical Review 11(1) (2006)
2. Kenji, S., Masahiro, S., Takashi, J., Hirohiko, M.: Making Blind Spots Visible:A Mixed Reality Approach for ITS. In: SICE Annual Conference 2005 in Okayama. CD-ROM Proceedings (2005)

Effects of Stimulus Orientation, Grouping and Alignment on Spatial S-R Compatibility

Steve Ngai Hung Tsang, Ken W.L. Chan, and Alan H.S. Chan

Department of Systems Engineering and Engineering Management
City University of Hong Kong
Kowloon Tong
Hong Kong, China
nhtsang2@gapps.cityu.edu.hk

Abstract. Effects of stimulus orientation, grouping, and alignment on spatial compatibility were investigated in this study. With eight possible stimulus locations mapped to two response keys, the parallel orientation was found to be responded to faster than the orthogonal orientation. As to the grouping effect, responses for the split stimulus array were superior to that for the continuous one, which seems to be the result of better reference frames and clearer distinction between visual signals. Comparing the single relative position (Left-Right-Left-Right/Up-Down-Up-Down) alignment to the double one (Left-Left-Right-Right/Up-Up-Down-Down), no significant difference in RT was noted, but the single relative position alignment was less prone to error responses than the double one. The effect of stimulus grouping and alignment interacted significantly that the single relative position alignment with split grouping was responded to much faster than that with continuous grouping. Also, the significant interaction effect of orientation and S-R compatibility showed that the up-left and down-right stimulus-response mappings were better than the mappings the other way round.

Keywords: Spatial Compatibility, Human-Computer Interfaces, Horizontal and Orthogonal displays.

1   Introduction

Around 60 years ago, Fitts and his colleagues introduced the concept of spatial stimulus-response compatibility (SRC), showing that some spatial arrangements for displays and controls are better than others for good human performance [1, 2]. When the spatial relation between stimuli and responses is direct and natural, it is described as compatible, while when the relation is indirect and unnatural, it is described as incompatible [3, 4]. Spatially compatible S-R mappings were always responded to faster than incompatible S-R pairings [4] - [9] as a result of lower coding demands and higher rates of information transfer, and as well more attentional resources are available for attending to the target [10, 11].

S. Yamamoto (Ed.): HIMI/HCII 2013, Part I, LNCS 8016, pp. 650–659, 2013.
© Springer-Verlag Berlin Heidelberg 2013

Aircraft cockpits, nuclear plant control rooms, interactive driving simulation and interfaces for industrial equipment always involve a lot of displays and controls interacting with human operators [12] - [15]. Because of the limited and confined work space, the number of control keys need to be reduced to a minimum and they may need to be closely spaced; the human operators have to monitor several displays or signals at the same time and produce timely responses to the stimuli. In many situations, the stimulus sets are placed in close proximity and located in parallel or orthogonally to the response sets [4, 16], making the display-control mappings far from simple. Therefore, it is of utmost importance to understand the effects of variations in stimulus presentation in terms of orientation, grouping and alignment on response preference as well as spatial compatibility in order to enhance the overall human-machine system performance.

In the past, spatial S-R correspondence was always regarded as an underlying requirement for the existence of spatial compatibility effects, and thereby such effects existed only when the stimulus and response sets shared the same spatial dimensions. However, Bauer and Miller [17] demonstrated that when the stimulus and response sets are oriented orthogonally, e.g. the vertical (up-down) stimulus (response) mapped to the horizontal (right-left) response (stimulus), significant orthogonal S-R compatibility effects with up-right/down-left mapping were found. This up-right/down-left advantage was then explained by salient features coding principle [18] that the codes for right and up (or above) are more salient than those for left and down, such that the up-right/down-left mapping can benefit from the correspondence of relative salience of the positions (or correspondence of asymmetric stimulus and response codes), resulting in faster translation of stimuli to responses.

Apart from stimulus-response orientation, another factor needs to be considered was the grouping effect of the stimuli. Several studies have shown that stimuli are coded relative to multiple frames of reference [19] - [21]. In this experiment, different from previous studies with precue showing the hemispace/size of the stimulus before stimulus presentation [4, 19], eight prefixed existing outline boxes were displayed in the experiment and the stimulus could occur in any of the eight possible locations. The boxes on each side were further grouped either into two (split field) or four (continuous field) for testing, forming different frames of reference. As most, if not all, of previous studies concerning the effects of reference frames were tested with precuing, it is then believed that the results of this experiment can provide further evidence on whether stimulus coding with multiple reference frames depends upon the precuing effect. It was expected that when stimuli were grouped into two, the relative right-left (up-down) position of the stimulus was salient, leading to significant response advantages. However, when the stimuli were grouped into four, the right-left (up-down) reference cue was minimized, resulting in relatively worse response performance compared with the split field condition.

As to the effect of alignment, two types of stimulus alignments – single relative position (Left-Right-Left-Right/Up-Down-Up-Down (LRLR/UDUD)) and double relative position (Left-Left-Right-Right/Up-Up-Down-Down (LLRR/UUDD)) – were investigated in the experiment. The LRLR/UDUD condition was similar to any previous studies in which the left (up) and right (down) directions can provide relative position of the stimulus for spatial coding. However, for the LLRR/UUDD condition, the stimulus coding rendered by the relative left (up) and right (down) difference was minimized or even eliminated and the result of which might be a lengthening in translation time for mapping the stimulus-response relationship. The experimental layouts of different combinations of stimulus orientation, grouping, alignment and S-R compatibility are shown in Fig. 1 and 2.

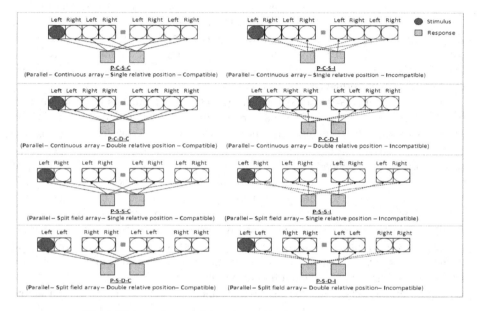

Fig. 1. Eight testing conditions in parallel S-R spatial orientation

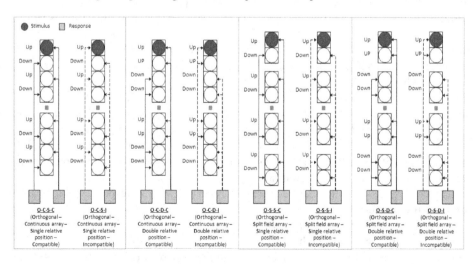

Fig. 2. Eight testing conditions in orthogonal S-R spatial orientation

It was hypothesized that: a) parallel configurations between displays and controls were better than orthogonal configurations as a result of the congruent spatial dimensions (both in horizontal dimension) of the stimulus and response sets; b) the performance under the split array – with only two boxes connected – surpassed that under the continuous array – with four boxes connected, as the relative position of right-left (up-down) was more salient in the split field setting, providing a strong cue for producing responses; c) the mappings under compatible conditions were superior to those under incompatible ones in terms of reaction time and accuracy due to the less recoding and higher rate of information transfer during the responding process [10]; d) the response performance on the single relative position alignment was better than the double one as the right-left (up-down) cue (reference frame) was more prominent.

2   Method

2.1   Design

In this study, two stimulus-response orientations (parallel and orthogonal) were tested. For the parallel orientation, the stimulus and response sets were placed horizontally and in parallel to each other, while for the orthogonal orientation, the stimulus array was vertically presented and perpendicular to the response keys. In each spatial orientation, there were eight testing conditions combining the factors of stimulus grouping (continuous array vs. split field array), alignment (single vs. double) and S-R compatibility (compatible vs. incompatible). Eight code names were defined to represent the eight testing conditions that to be tested for each participant in the parallel orientation: P (Parallel)-C (Continuous array)-S (Single relative position alignment)-C (Compatible), P-C-S-I (Incompatible), P-C-D (double relative position alignment)-C, P-C-D-I, P-S (Split field array)-S-C, P-S-S-I, P-S-D-C and P-S-D-I. For testing of the orthogonal orientation, eight similar code names were also defined, which were O (Orthogonal)-C-S-C, O-C-S-I, O-C-D-C, O-C-D-I, O-S-S-C, O-S-S-I, O-S-D-C and O-S-D-I. 30 participants were recruited and randomly divided into five groups of six participants each, and the test sequence of each group was in a quasi-random order so that each participant was tested with all the sixteen testing conditions. In a trial, the visual stimulus was lit up in red randomly in one of the eight possible signal locations. Each signal position was tested four times in a random order for each testing condition. Participants needed to respond to the lit up signal with the two square response keys under the stimulus array. The 16 testing conditions were explicitly shown in Fig.1 and 2.

2.2   Apparatus and Stimuli

This experiment was carried out using a personal computer with a 17-inch touch-screen display. The computer language Visual Basic 2010 was employed for stimulus preparation and response data collection. The touch-screen display was tipped at an angle of 15 degree from horizontal for ensuring comfortable responses made by participants. Eight identical 15-mm diameter stimulus circles with each embedded in a square box were presented in two linear array types (continuous array vs. split field array) (Fig. 1). During the stimulus presentation, one of the stimulus circles would be lit up in red. Each stimulus array type was tested in both parallel and orthogonal orientations relative to two horizontally aligned response keys positioned underneath. A green square of 10-mm side length was shown at the center of the stimulus array serving as a fixation point as well as a warning signal before stimulus presentation. Two grey square-shaped response keys of 20-mm side length each were positioned below the stimulus array on the immediately left and right sides of the midline of the display, and to be responded by participants' index and ring fingers of their right hand, respectively.

2.3   Participants

Thirty Chinese students of City University of Hong Kong (22 males and 8 females) of ages 21-25 participated in this experiment. They were all right-handers as tested with the Lateral Preference Inventory [22]. All of them had normal or corrected-to-normal vision (Optical Co., Inc., Model 2000P Orthorator) and normal color vision (Ishihara Pseudo isochromatic Plates). They all gave informed consent before the start of the experiment and did not report any physical or health problems for the hands (fingers) they used for the test.

2.4   Procedure

There were 16 testing conditions for each participant. Each condition contained 15 practice trials and 32 test trials. Participants were required to have at least 13 correct trials in the practice session prior to the start of test trials in each test condition. Before testing, participants were asked to position their left index and right ring fingers of the right hand above the two virtual keys with their wrists supporting by a soft cushion. They were instructed about the spatial mappings being tested in that particular condition. At the beginning of each trial, the participant fixated a lit up green square signal. After a delay of 1-3 s, one of the eight visual stimuli lit up in red. Participants then touched the control key according to the condition being tested. The fixation green square and red stimulus remained lit for 1 s or until the participant made a response. Responses made with the wrong keys were counted as errors and those made before 150 ms or after 1100 ms were considered to be misses (errors). The green square was then reset and lit up again after 1 s, indicating the start of another trial. Participants were asked to react as fast and accurately as they could. No feedback on speed or accuracy was given. There was a 2-min break for participants after testing each mapping condition. Participants' reaction times and errors were recorded for further analysis.

3   Results

A total of 16,042 (30 participants x 16 conditions x 32 trials + 682 make-up trials) responses were collected in this study. Overall, 682 (4.25%) responses were incorrect or made after the time limit. Therefore, a total of 15,360 (95.75%) correct responses were thus used for further analysis.

3.1   Mean Reaction Time

The 15,360 correct RTs were within the range of 356-1014 ms, with a mean of 791 ms and a standard deviation of 118 ms. Individual participants' mean RT ranged from 654 to 918 ms. The mean RTs for different testing conditions are summarized in Table 1. Amongst the 16 testing conditions, the shortest value (745 ms) was obtained for the condition 'P-S-S-C', while the longest value (817 ms) was for the condition 'O-C-S-C'. The average mean RTs computed for orientations of 'Parallel' and 'Orthogonal' were 786 and 795 ms respectively. It can also be seen that the effect of grouping influenced RTs such that conditions with split field array had better RTs than with continuous array regardless of the stimulus orientation. As to the alignment effect, the single relative position alignment (781 ms) was responded to faster than the double one (791 ms) in the parallel orientation, while there was no marked difference between the two alignments in the orthogonal orientation. Interestingly, the effect of spatial compatibility existed only in the parallel orientation that compatible mappings were always responded to faster than incompatible mappings, whereas the opposite results were obtained in the orthogonal orientation.

Further examination of RT was performed with repeated-measures ANOVA. The main factors considered were stimulus orientation, grouping, alignment and S-R compatibility. The results showed that the main factors of orientation [$F_{(1, 29)} = 4.71$, $p < 0.05$] and grouping [$F_{(1, 29)} = 23.18$, $p < 0.001$] were significant, as were the two-way interactions of grouping x alignment [$F_{(1, 29)} = 43.89$, $p < 0.001$] and orientation x S-R compatibility [$F_{(1, 29)} = 19.32$, $p < 0.001$]. There were no significant differences for the effect of alignment and S-R compatibility as well as other two-way and three-way interactions (p's > 0.05). As suggested by the sparsity-of-effects principle that a system or process is driven primarily by some of the main effects and low-order interactions [23], only the interactions of up to three factors were considered here. Regarding the two significant main factors, responding to the parallel orientation was found to be significantly faster than to the orthogonal orientation, and the split array led to significant RT advantage than did the continuous one. In respect of the two-way interaction effects of grouping and alignment, an interaction plot is shown in Fig. 3. It shows that there was no obvious RT difference between the continuous and the split array for the double relative position alignment. However, for the single relative position alignment, with the split array, a marked reduction in RT was resulted. As for the interaction effect of orientation and S-R compatibility, Fig. 4 illustrates that the effect of spatial compatibility affected participants' response performance oppositely under the different stimulus orientations. For the parallel orientation, as expected, compatible mappings resulted in faster RTs, while incompatible mappings in slower RTs. However, for the orthogonal orientation, the opposite result was obtained that compatible and incompatible mappings contributed to slower and faster RTs, respectively. This somewhat unexpected result provides a good piece of evidence that mapping a right key to an up stimulus and a left key to a down stimulus does not always lead to better response performance or even degrades the performance, at least for the stimulus-response sets used here.

Table 1. Mean reaction times (RT) (ms) and error percentage (EP) (%) computed for different testing conditions

Orientation	Array	Alignment	Condition	Mean (SD)
Parallel (RT: 786, EP: 4.64)	Continuous array (RT: 797, EP: 4.92)	Single (RT: 800, EP: 5.42)	P-C-S-C	RT: 793 (118), EP: 2.60 (2.73)
			P-C-S-I	RT: 807 (109), EP: 8.23 (12.70)
		Double (RT: 794, EP: 4.43)	P-C-D-C	RT: 787 (123), EP: 1.98 (2.78)
			P-C-D-I	RT: 800 (113), EP: 6.88 (8.93)
	Split field array (RT: 775, EP: 4.35)	Single (RT: 762, EP: 1.67)	P-S-S-C	RT: 745^A (124), EP: 0.73^A (2.12)
			P-S-S-I	RT: 779 (108), EP: 2.60 (3.19)
		Double (RT: 788, EP: 7.03)	P-S-D-C	RT: 786 (129), EP: 5.00 (4.83)
			P-S-D-I	RT: 790 (116), EP: 9.06^B (8.06)
Orthogonal (RT: 795, EP: 4.23)	Continuous array (RT: 803, EP: 3.88)	Single (RT: 810, EP: 3.96)	O-C-S-C	RT: 817^B (116), EP: 5.42 (4.99)
			O-C-S-I	RT: 803 (105), EP: 2.50 (3.32)
		Double (RT: 795, EP: 3.81)	O-C-D-C	RT: 812 (120), EP, 4.90 (5.90)
			O-C-D-I	RT: 778 (108), EP: 2.71 (4.84)
	Split field array (RT: 788, EP: 4.58)	Single (RT: 777, EP: 3.07)	O-S-S-C	RT: 808 (120), EP: 3.33 (4.26)
			O-S-S-I	RT: 746 (112), EP: 2.81 (8.93)
		Double (RT: 799, EP: 6.10)	O-S-D-C	RT: 812 (120), EP: 7.19 (6.04)
			O-S-D-I	RT: 786 (116), EP, 5.00 (4.96)

^{A} The shortest RT / ^{B} The longest RT.

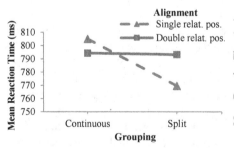

Fig. 3. Interaction plots of mean reaction times (RTs) for stimulus grouping and alignment

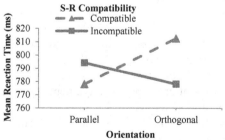

Fig. 4. Interaction plots of mean reaction times (RTs) for stimulus orientation and S-R compatibility

3.2   Mean Response Error

Altogether participants made a total of 682 (4.25%) incorrect or missing responses. The mean error percentages (EP) for the 16 testing conditions are shown in Table 1. The most accurate condition was 'P-S-S-C' (EP = 0.73%), while the least was 'P-S-D-I' (EP = 9.06%). Further analysis of the mean EP was performed with the non-parametric Friedman Test, and it showed there were significant differences among the 16 testing conditions (χ^2 (15) = 104.72, p < 0.001). Wilcoxon signed-rank test was then conducted to investigate the differences in EPs between each factor. The results showed there were no significant differences in EPs (p's > 0.05) between the parallel (EP = 4.64%) and orthogonal (EP = 4.23%) orientations, continuous (EP = 4.40%) and split (EP = 4.47%) groupings, as well as compatible (EP = 3.89%) and incompatible (EP = 4.97%) mappings. Only the factor of stimulus alignment was found to be significant (p < 0.001) that the EP for the double relative position alignment (EP = 5.34%) was significantly larger than that for the single one (EP = 3.53%). The results suggest that the conditions that provided salient relative spatial correspondence between stimulus and response were less prone to error responses, and although not significant, less error responses were made for mapping a left key with up stimuli and a right key with down ones.

4   Discussion

In this study, two control keys were used to respond to eight visual signals arranged in parallel and orthogonal orientations. It was found that participants responded significantly faster to the horizontally presented stimulus arrays than to the vertically presented ones. It may be due to the fact that the parallel orientation could provide congruent spatial dimension and obvious spatial correspondence between the stimulus and response sets, thereby resulting in faster responses. However, for the orthogonal orientation, the mapping between the stimulus and response sets depended upon their relative salience, requiring an additional translation step for stimulus-response mapping and thus resulting in longer reaction time. Moreover, faster reaction times were obtained for the conditions with the split field array than that with the continuous array in both parallel and orthogonal orientations. It is believed that the split field array could provide participants with more salient right-left and up-down reference frames for the parallel and orthogonal orientations, respectively, leading to better response performance. The main factor of alignment alone was nonsignificant, but its interaction effect with grouping was significant such that the single relative position alignment with the split grouping resulted in much faster RT than that with the continuous grouping, while no much difference in RT was observed for the double relative position alignment between the two different groupings. This finding suggests that if stimulus signals cluster together, the salience of left (up) and right (down) coding will be weakened, probably due to the influence of adjacent stimuli. Overall, the result showed that the condition 'P-S-S-C', which had the clearest relative spatial correspondence, yielded the best performance amongst all the test conditions. From the reaction time examination, it is noted that there was no significant differences between compatible and incompatible conditions. However, with the significant interaction effect of orientation and S-R compatibility, for the conditions with orthogonal orientation, the mean reaction times for compatible conditions (i.e. the left key for up signals and the right key for down signals) were significantly faster than that for incompatible conditions (i.e. the left key for down signals and the right key for up signals). This finding of preferable left-up and right-down mapping was consistent with the previous study of Bauer and Miller [17] (experiment 3) showing different mapping preferences for the left and right hands towards vertical stimuli and horizontal responses. They found that left-up and right-down mapping was preferable for the right hand, whereas right-up and left down for the left hand. However, the response preferences towards orthogonal mapping are rather mixed that some other studies reported that right-up and left-down mapping was of greater preference, seemingly due to salient features coding between the stimulus and response directions [4]. Nevertheless, the finding of this study demonstrated that left-down and right-up mapping relationship responding with right hand was very robust.

5   Conclusion

For the eight visual signals and two controls interacted horizontally and vertically with different S-R mapping types, it was found that the conditions in the parallel S-R orientation resulted in better response performance than in the orthogonal orientation. Besides, for stimulus grouping, visual signals split into two rather than four in a group could provide salient reference frames for the stimulus and response set and thus achieving faster reaction time. For the different stimulus alignments, the single relative position alignment was less prone to error responses than the double one, but no significant difference in reaction times was found between the two alignments. An interaction effect of grouping and alignment was observed that participants responded very differently towards the continuous and split arrays with the single relative position alignment. Also, with the orthogonal orientation, the left-up and right-down mapping yielded better response performance, which was different from the results of some previous studies showing the better response performance of right-up and left-down mappings, implying the intricate stimulus-response mappings here and cultural factors might affect the compatibility relations in this orientation [24].

Acknowledgements. The work described in this paper was fully supported by a grant from City University of Hong Kong (Project No. 7002820). The authors thank for the data collection done by YP Yau.

References

1. Fitts, P.M., Deininger, R.L.: S-R compatibility: Correspondence among paired elements within stimulus and response codes. Journal of Experimental Psychology 48, 483–492 (1954)
2. Fitts, P.M., Seeger, C.M.: Spatial characteristics of stimulus and response codes. Journal of Experimental Psychology 46, 199–210 (1953)
3. Proctor, R.W., Reeve, T.G.: Stimulus-Response Compatibility: An Integrated Perspective. North-Holland, Amsterdam (1990)
4. Proctor, R.W., Vu, K.–P.: Stimulus-Response Compatibility Principles: Data, Theory, and Application. CRC Press, Boca Raton (2006)

5. Chan, A.H.S., Chan, K.W.L.: Design implications from spatial compatibility on parallel and orthogonal stimulus-response arrays. Asian Journal of Ergonomics 5(2), 111–129 (2004)
6. Chan, K.W.L., Chan, A.H.S.: Three-dimensional spatial stimulus-response (S-R) compatibility for visual signals with hand and foot controls. Applied Ergonomics 41(6), 840–848 (2010)
7. Chan, K.W.L., Chan, A.H.S.: Spatial stimulus response compatibility for a horizontal visual display with hand and food controls. Ergonomics 54(3), 233–245 (2011)
8. Tsang, S.N.H., Chan, A.H.S.: Correspondence and non-correspondence of spatial and anatomical finger distance on spatial compatibility. Engineering Letters 19(2), 119–124 (2011)
9. Tsang, S.N.H., Chan, A.H.S.: Spatial S-R compatibility studies on fingers: A review and promising directions of further research. In: Ao, S.I., et al. (eds.) IAENG Transactions on Engineering Technologies - Special Edition of the International MultiConference of Engineers and Computer Scientists 2011, vol. 7, pp. 284–293. World Scientific (2012)
10. Umilta, C., Nicoletti, R.: Spatial stimulus-response compatibility. In: Proctor, R.W., Reeve, T.G. (eds.) Stimulus-response Compatibility: an Integrated Perspective, pp. 89–116. North-Holland, Amsterdam (1990)
11. Thurlings, M.E., van Erp, J.B.F., Brouwer, A.M., Blankertz, B., Werkhoven, P.: Control-display mapping in brain-computer interfaces. Ergonomics 55(5), 564–580 (2012)
12. Li, X., Ruan, D.: Comparative study of fuzzy control, PID control, and advanced fuzzy control for simulating a nuclear reactor operation. International Journal of General Systems 29, 263–279 (2000)
13. Yamaguchi, M., Proctor, R.W.: Stimulus-response compatibility with pure and mixed mappings in a flight task environment. Journal of Experimental Psychology: Applied 12, 207–222 (2006)
14. Mulder, M., Winterberg, R., Van, M.M.: Direct manipulation interfaces for in-flight four-dimensional navigation planning. The International Journal of Aviation Psychology 20(3), 249–268 (2010)
15. Liu, Y.C., Jhuang, J.W.: Effects of in-vehicle warning information displays with or without spatial compatibility on driving behaviors and response performance. Applied Ergonomics 43(4), 679–686 (2012)
16. Andre, A.D., Haskell, I., Wickens, C.D.: S-R compatibility effects with orthogonal stimulus and response dimensions. In: Proceedings of the Human Factors Society 35th Annual Meeting, pp. 1546–1550. Human Factors Society, Santa Monica (1991)
17. Bauer, D.W., Miller, J.: Stimulus–response compatibility and the motor system. Quarterly Journal of Experimental Psychology 34A, 367–380 (1982)
18. Weeks, D.J., Proctor, R.W.: Salient-features coding in the translation between orthogonal stimulus-response dimensions. Journal of Experimental Psychology: General 119, 355–366 (1990)
19. Lamberts, K., Tavernier, G., d'Ydewalle, G.: Effects of multiple reference points in spatial stimulus-response compatibility. Acta Psychologica 79, 115–130 (1992)
20. Roswarski, T.E., Proctor, R.W.: Multiple spatial codes and temporal overlap in choice-reaction tasks. Psychological Research 59, 196–211 (1996)
21. Lleras, A., Moore, C.M., Mordkoff, J.T.: Looking for the source of the Simon effect: Evidence of multiple codes. American Journal of Psychology 117, 531–542 (2004)
22. Coren, S.: The lateral preference inventory for measurement of handedness, footedness eyedness, and earedness: norms for young adults. Bulletin of the Psychonomic Society 31(1), 1–3 (1993)
23. Montgomery, D.C.: Design and Analysis of Experiments, 4th edn. John Wiley and Sons, New York (1997)
24. Proctor, R.W., Vu, K.-P.: Cumulative knowledge and progress in human factors. Annual Review of Psychology 61, 623–651 (2010)

The Influence of Password Restrictions and Mnemonics on the Memory for Passwords of Older Adults

Kim-Phuong L. Vu and Martina M. Hills

Department of Psychology,
California State University Long Beach,
1250 N Bellflower Blvd, Long Beach CA 90840
Kim.Vu@csulb.edu,
martinirox99@gmail.com

Abstract. Accessing Internet accounts can provide convenient services to users, regardless of age. However, these online services typically require that users enter a username and password. Forgetting one's password, then, often results in the inconvenience of having to reset your password. Although there has been research on the memorability of passwords, this research often focuses on younger adults. Little research has taken older adults into consideration when designing password requirements. Older adults show cognitive decline in memory, which can make the task of remembering passwords especially difficult. However, older adults experience less difficulty in memory for familiar pictures, making the use of pictures an ideal candidate for cuing passwords. Participants in this study were asked to generate passwords for five different fictitious online accounts using a text-based or image-based mnemonic technique. Older adults were less likely to forget passwords that were generated using image-based mnemonic technique compared to the text-based one, implying that pictures can be used as cues for password recall for older adults.

1 Introduction

The advantage of relying on online services is quite clear in that it allows users to access web-based services at almost any time and from any place where there is an internet connection. However, accessing online accounts requires that users enter a username and password [1, 2]. With the increased use of the internet, the number of passwords per user has grown [3], making it a difficult task to remember unique passwords for each account. The use of unique passwords is preferred because recycled passwords can result in unauthorized access to multiple accounts of a particular user if one account is compromised. Techniques for helping users to remember secure passwords are needed because even with the fast growth of alternative authentication tools such as tokens, smart cards, and biometric devices, the username-password technique has continued to be the main choice for security systems because of its ease of implementation [4].

Companies that use internet services have the option of providing users with a secure password to use. However, these passwords tend to be random strings of

S. Yamamoto (Ed.): HIMI/HCII 2013, Part I, LNCS 8016, pp. 660–668, 2013.

characters that are difficult for users to remember. As a result, users tend to write these types of passwords down, decreasing their effectiveness in terms of security. Companies can also add password requirements to improve the security of user-generated passwords. These password restrictions often require the use of both upper-case and lowercase letters, digits and/or special characters, and a minimum password length [5]. Although the addition of these restrictions can also cause difficulty in password memorability for many users [2], these generated passwords tend to be more memorable than computer-generated ones. The forgetting of passwords is likely to be more pronounced among older adults due to the decline in memory that is associated with the normal aging process [6].

This issue of increasing older adults' ability to remember passwords needs to be examined promptly due to the rapidly increasing age of the American population [7]. According to a report from The United States Census Bureau entitled, "Expectation of Life and Expected Deaths by Race, Sex, and Age: 2006," the average life span of adults has increased by eight years from 1970 to 2010. This means that adults are living longer than they were 40 years ago. The number of older adults using the internet has also increased over the years. In 1996, only 2% of older adults age 65 and older used the internet, but this percentage increased to 22% by 2004 [8] and 53% of by 2012 [9]. Due to the escalating number of tasks that can be completed online, the number of accounts and passwords that need to be remembered can put a toll on older adults' memory capabilities. Thus, it is vital to consider the population of older adult users when it comes to password recall.

A couple of studies have shown that memorability of passwords can be improved with the use of mnemonic techniques [2, 10]. Mnemonic strategies encourage deeper processing of information by relating new knowledge with knowledge already established in memory [11]. One of the most effective password generation mnemonic techniques is the image-based one [2]. The image-based mnemonic allows users to generate their own passwords using well-known pictures instead of generating complex words or letter/character combinations to abide by required website guidelines. However, the effectiveness of the image-based mnemonic technique has been examined only with a sample of younger adults.

Teaching older adults how to create passwords that are both secure and easier to remember is crucial for their ability to take advantage of the services provided by the online world. Images can be stored in memory and retrieved more easily than words [12], a phenomenon known as the "picture superiority effect." This is so, even with the deterioration of cognitive processing [12]. Thus, the image-based mnemonic method has the potential to be employed by both older and younger adults.

The goal of the present study was to determine whether teaching older adults how to create passwords using image-based mnemonics can lead to better memory for those passwords. Teaching older adults how to memorize strong passwords through use of the image-based mnemonic technique will not only help them secure their accounts, but may also reduce the expense associated with resetting lost passwords.

2   Current Study

This study examines the effectiveness of two different password generation methods for older adults (i.e., age 55 and over) and younger adults (age 18 to 30). All participants in each group were responsible for creating their own passwords for each of five different fictitious online accounts. Participants were then tested on their ability to recall the passwords at a 10-min and 1-wk delay interval. Cracking software was used to analyze the strength of each password, and differences in password length and complexity were examined for each age group by password generation technique.

2.1   Method

Participants. Thirty-seven older adult participants and 40 younger adult participants were recruited from California State University Long Beach (CSULB) and its surrounding communities. Older adult participants ranged from 55-86 years old (M = 71.06, SD = 8.78; 25 female and 9 male). Younger adult participants ranged from 18-25 years old (M =19.3, SD = 1.57; 34 female and 6 male).

Older adults were paid \$15 to participate in the entire experiment, which consisted of two sessions lasting less than 1 hour each. The younger adults were recruited from the university's Introductory Psychology Participant pool, and the students received experimental credits for participating in the study. At the time participants signed up, they were informed that they were taking part in a study examining password generation and memorability. All participants were asked to bring to the first session of the experiment five different personal pictures that they knew well and could put into five different categories. For the older adult group, 18 participants were randomly assigned to the image-based mnemonic group and 19 to the text-based mnemonic group. For the younger adult group, 20 participants were randomly assigned to the image-based mnemonic group and 20 to the text-based mnemonic group.

Design, Apparatus, and Procedure. The methods and procedures were closely modeled after Nelson and Vu [2]. A 2 (Password generation technique: image-based mnemonic or text-based mnemonic) by 2 (Recall delay: 5-min or 1-wk delay) by 2 (Age: Older adults or Younger adults) mixed design was used. Password generation technique and age were the between-subjects variables and recall delay was the within-subject variable.

A Java program was used to present the experiment on a laptop computer with a 14" screen. Participants were presented instructions on what type of generation technique they were employing. The program also checked that each password met the set criteria for each generation technique. It also recorded the generated password and the amount of time it took the participant to recall their passwords at both the 10-min interval and the 1-wk interval.

All participants were tested individually in a quiet, well-lit room. The experiment consisted of two sessions, held one week a part. The first session consisted of two parts, and the second session only consisted of one part. At the beginning of the first session, participants were introduced to the experiment, asked to sign a consent form and provided the five personal pictures to the experimenter. The pictures were added to a multimedia storage device and kept for the duration of the experiment. In the first session, participants generated five different passwords that satisfied a set of password restrictions for five different fictitious accounts. The password restrictions included: being generated from a sentence that made sense; being at least eight characters; use of a capital letter; use of a special character (e.g. @, #, $, or %); use of a digit; being generated from a sentence that had the special character and digit embedded in the way that it makes sense relative to the context of the sentence; being unique for each account. The five different accounts consisted of: E-mail, bank, computer, social networking, and bookstore.

Even though all participants provided the five personal pictures to the experimenter, only those randomly assigned to the image-based mnemonic group used their pictures in the experiment. The image-based mnemonic group was taught how to use this technique by giving participants examples of two different pictures used to create two different passwords. One example used a picture of a skateboard with the phrase "I like to skateboard" written underneath the image (see *Figure 1*). The participant was given 10 s to look at the image and the statement. The participant was informed as to the relationship the picture might have with personal knowledge and how to incorporate that knowledge into a password. For example, the person likes to skateboard so "I like to skateboard" could be used as a basis for the password.

I like to skateboard

Fig. 1. Example picture shown to participants in the image-based mnemonic group

As part of their training, the experimenter explained how pieces of information gathered from the picture could become more complex and meaningful to the participant. The experimenter pointed out that the skateboard was red and reminded her of learning her first trick on the red curb at school. The experimenter then demonstrated how the red color could be translated into the password by replacing "I" with "Eye" and capitalizing it because the red curb really caught her eye when she first learned to skate. The word "to" could be changed to number "2" and "skateboard" could be changed to "sk8board" by transforming part of the sound associated with the word to the number "8." The experimenter also pointed out that the letter "s" could be substituted for "$" to denote the money she spent buying her skateboard. The final transformation of the combination of letters to create the complex password of "EyeLike2$k8board." A second example was also provided to the participants.

For the text-based mnemonic technique group, participants were instructed to generate passwords based on self-generated phrases using the same examples employed in the image-based mnemonic technique but without the added benefit of the personal pictures.

After generating a password for each account, participants were tested for their recall of the passwords after a 5-min delay, and again after a 1-wk delay. For the recall session, participants were asked to recall each of the five passwords they created. The participants were instructed to enter the correct password for each account name that was prompted. The fictitious account names were displayed on the computer screen in a random order for four times each. The number of passwords forgotten at each interval was recorded as a measure of password memorability.

3   Results

3.1   Generation Time and Number of Attempts

The amount of time (in seconds) taken by a participant to generate a password that satisfied the password restrictions for each of the five fictitious accounts was recorded and averaged across the five accounts to determine a mean password generation time for each participant. A 2 (Password generation technique: image-based mnemonic or text-based mnemonic) by 2 (Age: Older adults or Younger adults) mixed analysis of variance (ANOVA) was run on mean generation time as a function of password generation technique and age group. There was a significant effect of age, $F(1,73) = 13.48$, $p < .001$ (see Figure 2). Older adults took over 1-min longer to generate an acceptable password than did younger adults. No other effects were significant for generation time.

The number of attempts needed by a participant to generate an acceptable password was also recorded and then averaged across the five accounts. The same two-way ANOVA was conducted as for mean generation time on the mean number of attempts. However, this analysis did not yield any significant effects.

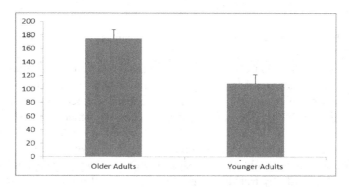

Fig. 2. Mean Password Generation Time (in Seconds) for Older and Younger Adults

3.2   Memorability of Passwords

The mean number of passwords forgotten by each participant was analyzed using a 2 (Password generation technique: image-based mnemonic or text-based mnemonic) by 2 (Recall delay: 10-min or 1-wk delay) by 2 (Age: Older adults or Younger adults) ANOVA. There was a significant main effect of delay on forgetting, $F(1, 73) = 12.08$, p < .01. Participants forgot more passwords ($M = 1.94$) after the 1-wk delay when compared to the 10-min delay ($M = 1.44$). There was also a main effect of age on forgetting, $F(1, 73) = 13.40$, $p < .01$, where older adults forgot ($M= 2.24$) more passwords than younger adults ($M = 1.14$).

Recall delay also interacted with age, $F(1, 73) = 8.68$, $p = .004$. Older adults showed a larger increase in the number of passwords forgotten from the 10-min to 1-wk delay compared to younger adults (.91 vs. 0.18 increase, respectively). This two-way interaction was qualified by a significant three-way interaction between age, recall delay, and password generation technique, $F(1, 73) = 4.25$, $p = .04$ (see Figure 3).

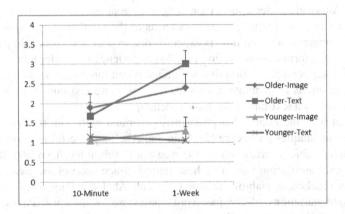

Fig. 3. Mean Number of Passwords Forgotten for Older and Younger Adults at the 10-Minute and 1-Week Interval

To determine the nature of these differences, simple effects analyses of participants' forgetting were conducted separately in the image-based mnemonic and text-based mnemonic conditions. In the image-based mnemonic condition, there was no statistically significant interaction between age and delay, $F < 1.0$. In the text-based mnemonic condition, though, a significant age × recall delay interaction was obtained, $F(1, 37) = 10.05$, $p = .003$. To characterize these differences, a comparison of the number of text-generated passwords forgotten by younger and older adults at each recall delay was performed. With a 10-min recall delay, there was no difference in older and younger adults' short term forgetting, $F(1, 38) = 1.16$, $p = .29$. However, with a 1-wk delay older adults forgot significantly more text-based mnemonic passwords ($M = 3.00$) than did younger adults ($M = 1.05$), $F(1, 38) = 15.77$, $p < .001$.

3.3   Password Security

The security of the generated passwords was assessed by the ability of the Cain and Abel software to crack the passwords. Each password was encrypted and turned into a HASH file. The document was then submitted to the Cain and Abel Cracking software in an attempt to recover the password. All passwords generated in this study were submitted to the cracking software for a 12-hour period. The software was not successful in cracking any of the passwords submitted. Thus, the passwords generated in both the image based and text-based groups were somewhat secure.

4   Discussion

Since accessing online services is important for all age groups, using mnemonic techniques to generate secure passwords can be very useful. The present study showed that older adults can generate passwords that are more resistant to being forgotten by using the image-based mnemonic technique compared to the text-based mnemonic technique. Although, older adults took longer to generate an acceptable password, they did not differ from younger adults in terms of the number of attempts needed to do so. The longer generation time is expected due to decreased processing speed and slower rates of information activation [13, 14] experienced by older adults. Thus, the present study supports the notion that the image-based mnemonic technique could be used by older adults to generate passwords that are more resistant to forgetting than those generated by a text-based mnemonic technique.

Consistent with the notion that passwords generated with both the text-based and image-based techniques are secure [2], Cain and Abel, a powerful password cracking system, was not able to crack any of the passwords submitted from both the image-based and text-based groups for a 12 hour period. Since none of the passwords were successfully cracked, a viability test of Cain and Abel cracking software was performed. Eight variations of the password "password" (password; Password; password1; Password1; p@ssword; P@ssword; p@ssword1; P@ssword1) were submitted to the Cain and Abel cracking software to test the cracking rate for each word. All variations were cracked by the software, indicating that the software is viable cracking tool. It is likely that the software needed more time for the brute-force attack to be successful in cracking passwords generated with the mnemonic techniques used in the present study.

5   Limitations of the Study and Recommendations for Future Research

The study was limited by a couple factors. The first factor was that the Java program used in this study was the same one we have previously used in our lab to study passwords generated by younger adults. Many of the older adult users, though, were confused by how the program functioned given its text-based interface. Using a more graphic interface may have facilitated the older adult's performance. The second limitation of the study was in regards to the use of the images for generating passwords. With limited directions to participants to bring in five significantly different images for five categories, some users reported not being able to make a good connection between the picture and account name. Many of the participants stated that they would have chosen different pictures for the study if they understood the significance of linking the pictures to the different accounts beforehand. Finally, participants also reported that there was some additional interference associated with having to generate five passwords for different accounts at the same time. Generally speaking, online account users are only responsible for generating one username and one password for an account at a time. The requirement to generate five unique passwords that met all the requirements at once may have been overwhelming to participants, especially the older ones. Despite these limitations, though, the older adults in this study still showed a benefit for generating passwords using the image-based mnemonic technique.

Future research should focus on helping users make better connections with the images and the different accounts. Improving such connections would enable users to have a better understanding of the password technique as well as be able to process the pictures along with the account name at a deeper level.

References

1. Renaud, K., Ramsay, J.: Now what was that password again? A more flexible way of identifying and authenticating our seniors. Behaviour and Information Technology 26, 309–322 (2007)
2. Nelson, D., Vu, K.P.L.: Effectiveness of image-based mnemonic techniques for enhancing the memorability and security of user-generated passwords. Computers in Human Behavior, 1–11 (2010)
3. Renaud, K., De Angeli, A.: My password is here! An investigation into visuo-spatial authentication mechanisms. Interacting with Computers 16, 1017–1041 (2004)
4. Brown, A.S., Bracken, E., Zoccoli, S., Douglas, K.: Generating and remembering passwords. Applied Cognitive Psychology 18, 641–651 (2004)
5. Gehringer, E.F.: Choosing passwords: Security and human factors. Department of Electrical and Computer Engineering, Department of Computer Science, North Carolina State University, pp. 369–373 (2002)
6. Luo, L., Craik, F.I.M.: Age differences in recollection: specificity effects at retrieval. Journal of Memory and Language 60, 421–436 (2009)
7. Wagner, N.L., Hassanein, K., Head, M.M.: Computer use by older adults: A multidisciplinary review. Computers in Human Behavior 26, 870–882 (2010)
8. Gatto, S.L., Tak, S.H.: Computer, internet, and e-mail use among older adults: Benefits and barriers. Educational Gerontology 34, 800–811 (2008)
9. Zickuhr, K., Madden, M.: Older adults and internet use: For the first time, half of adults ages 65 and older are online. Pew Research Center's Internet & American Life Project Report (2012),
   http://pewinternet.org/Reports/2012/
   Older-adults-and-internet-use.aspx

10. Vu, K.P.L., Proctor, R.W., Bhargav-Spanzel, A., Tai, B.-L., Cook, J., Schultz, E.E.: Improving password security and memorability to protect personal and organizational information. International Journal of Human-Computer Studies 65, 744–757 (2007)
11. Roediger, H.L.: The effectiveness of four mnemonics in ordering recall. Journal of Experimental Psychology: Human Learning and Memory 6, 558–567 (1980)
12. Renaud, K., De Angeli, A.: Visual passwords: Cure-all or snake-oil? Communications of the ACM 52, 135–140 (2009)
13. Bailey, H., Dunlosky, J., Hertzog, C.: Does differential strategy use account for age-related deficits in working-memory performance? Psychology and Aging 24, 82–92 (2009)
14. Hertzog, C., Dixon, R.A., Hultsch, D.F., MacDonald, W.S.: Latent change models of adult cognition: Are changes in processing speed and working memory associated with changes in episodic memory? Psychology and Aging 18, 755–769 (2003)

Word Classification for Sentiment Polarity Estimation Using Neural Network

Hidekazu Yanagimoto, Mika Shimada, and Akane Yoshimura

School of Engineering, Osaka Prefecture University
Osaka, Japan, 599-8531
{hidekazu,shimada,yoshimura}@cs.osakafu-u.ac.jp

Abstract. Though there are many digitalized documents in the Internet, the almost all documents are unlabeled data. Hence, using such numerous unlabeled data, a classifier has to be construct. In pattern recognition research field many researchers pay attention to a deep architecture neural network to achieve the previous aim. The deep architecture neural network is one of semi-supervised learning approaches and achieve high performance in an object recognition task. The network is trained with many unlabeled data and transform input raw features into new features that represent higher concept, for example a human face. In this study I pay attention to feature generation ability of a deep architecture neural network and apply it to natural language processing. Concretely word clustering is developed for sentiment analysis. Experimental results shows clustering performance is good regardless of an unsupervised learning approach.

Keywords: Natural Language Processing, Deep Architecture Neural Network, Feature Extraction.

1 Introduction

Though there are many digitalized documents in the Internet, the almost all documents are unlabeled data. To label data much human power is needed since now only human understands information and classify them into appropriate clusters. Though a classifier is constructed to classify them automatically, many labeled data is needed to construct a high performance classifier. If you construct a classifier using such numerous unlabeled data, this problem vanishes. This approach is a semi-supervised learning approach.

In pattern recognition research field many researchers pay attention to a deep architecture neural network. The deep architecture neural network is one of semi-supervised learning approaches and achieves high performance in an object recognition task. The network is trained with many unlabeled data and transforms input raw features into new features, which show higher concept, for example a human face. Since the pattern recognition simulates one of human activities using a deep architecture neural network, in this study the neural network is applied to language understanding.

S. Yamamoto (Ed.): HIMI/HCII 2013, Part I, LNCS 8016, pp. 669–677, 2013.

Word classification for sentiment analysis is developed as a task of language understanding. The sentiment analysis determines article polarity using natural language processing. The polarity means positive, negative, or neutral from the viewpoint of an author. A polarity dictionary is used to develop the sentiment analysis system and it is important to construct a high quality polarity dictionary. Since the dictionary construction needs much human power to judge many words polarities, an automatic dictionary construction method is desired. Hence, my aim is that a deep architecture neural network is applied to the polarity dictionary construction. Before the goal this study checks whether a neural network can be applied to the dictionary construction or not constructing word classification system.

In Section 2 related works are explained. In Section 3 the proposed method is described from the viewpoint of neural network architecture and learning methodology. In Section 4 some experiments are explained and performance of the proposed method is discussed.

2   Related Works

A proposed method is related to neural network researches and feature extraction researches. Hence, in this section related works, that is neural network approaches and kernel methods, are explained.

A neural network is one of models to simulate a brain simply and was proposed by Rosenblatt[1]. Then Rumelhart et al. proposed backpropagation algorithm to train multi-layer feedforward neural network[2]. Because of a backpropagation algorithm neural network are used in various kind of research fields. The neural networks are generally shallow architecture neural networks, for example three-layer or four-layer neural networks but deeper neural networks are not used. Vanishing gradient problem[3] limits the number of layers in neural networks. The vanishing gradient problem means the backpropagation algorithm cannot propagate error in deeper layer's weight. Hence, though you use a deep architecture neural network, you cannot achieve good performance since you cannot adjust weights in the neural network.

To overcome this problem deep learning[4] was proposed. The deep learning is a methodology to train a deep neural network, which is many layers neural network. To solve the vanishing gradient problem the deep learning approach uses a layer-wise learning approach. These days the deep learning is applied to pattern recognition and natural language processing.

In pattern recognition researches Lee et al.[5] applied a deep architecture neural network to object recognition and could extract good characteristics from unlabeled enormous image data. The architecture of their neural network integrated local image features into high-level features, for example outline of cat face and human's back shot. In ILSVRC2012 Large Scale Visual Recognition Contest a deep convolutional neural network achieved the highest performance by Hinton et al[6].

In natural language processing researches deep architecture neural networks are used to construct a language model. Since a hidden Markov model is generally used as a language model, conditional probabilities is determined from training data in the neural network. This approaches are called a neural network language model and proposed by Bengio and Arisoy[7,8]. In natural language processing a document is represented as a discrete vector based on term frequency. On the other hand in neural network language model a document is represented as a continuous vector transforming discrete vectors into continuous vectors using a neural network. After then documents are classified for text classification, information retrieval, and information filtering.

A deep architecture neural network creates new features from primitive raw input data essentially. This characteristic is similar to a kernel method[9]. The kernel method maps features in input space onto features in higher-dimension space using nonlinear function, which is called a kernel function. In the kernel method the kernel functions are defined previously since the functions have to satisfy Mercer's theorem. On the other hand, the deep architecture neural network makes more complex features from input raw features according to a training data distribution.

Finally Restricted Boltzmann Machine (RBM)[10] and Sparse Autoencoder[11] are described. A deep architecture neural networks uses RBM and Sparse Autoencoder as a part of the network. To train hidden layers in a deep architecture neural network it is not realistic to use labeled data because of the vanishing gradient problem. They are trained without labeled data since their cost functions are errors between an input patten and an output pattern. In RBM neurons in a hidden unit are independent each other in determining outputs of neurons in a visible unit since their connections in RBM is restricted. Sparse Autoencoder is trained as fire of neurons in a hidden layer is sparse.

3   Feature Generation Using Neural Network

In this section the proposed method is described from the viewpoint of neural network architecture and learning methodology.

3.1   Neural Network Architecture

The proposed method uses a deep architecture neural network to generate a continuous feature vector from a discrete feature vector. The neural network cannot be trained with a backpropagation approach since the network has deep architecture.

Fig. 1 shows an example of a deep architecture neural network used in this study. The network is constructed combining some Restricted Boltzmann Machines (RBMs). A hidden layer in a previous RBM is a visible layer in the following RBM.

3.2   Learning Methodology

RBM is trained using a Contrastive Divergence k alrogithm[12,13].

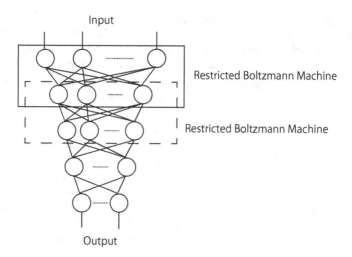

Fig. 1. This figure shows a deep architecture neural network in the proposed method. Each layer is regarded as a Restricted Boltzmann Machine and trained with RBM training method.

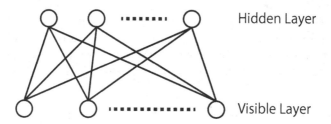

Fig. 2. This figure shows a typical Restricted Boltzmann Machine

In Fig 2 general RBM is illustrated. The RBM has 2-layer architecture, which is a hidden layer and a visible layer. Since neurons in the hidden layer are not observed outside, nobody cannot control them. The RBM obtains input data from neurons in the visible layer and keeps processing input data until the RBM is stable. Moreover, the RBM has no connection among neurons in the same layer. States of neurons in the same layer is defined independently when all states of neurons in another layer are known. Hence, neurons in the same layer is called conditional independence.

To introduce Contrastive Divergence k (CD-k) an energy function is defined. States of each neurons in the visible layer denotes $\mathbf{x}$ and states in the hidden layer denotes $\mathbf{h}$. A weight between h_i and x_j is W_{ij}. $\mathbf{b}$ and $\mathbf{c}$ denote weights of visible neurons and hidden neurons respectively. Hence, the energy function is defined below.

$$\text{Energy}(\mathbf{x}, \mathbf{h}) = -\mathbf{b}^{\mathrm{T}}\mathbf{x} - \mathbf{c}^{\mathrm{T}}\mathbf{h} - \mathbf{h}^{\mathrm{T}}W\mathbf{x} \qquad (1)$$

And using the energy function, a joint distribution of RBM is defined.

$$P(\mathbf{x}, \mathbf{h}) = \frac{e^{-\mathrm{Energy}(\mathbf{x}, \mathbf{h})}}{Z} \tag{2}$$

The Z is a normalized parameter. Moreover, since nobody can observe states in the hidden layer, $\mathbf{h}$ is marginalized out.

$$P(\mathbf{x}) = \frac{e^{-\sum_{\mathbf{h}} \mathrm{Energy}(\mathbf{x}, \mathbf{h})}}{Z} \tag{3}$$

To adjust a parameter W, gradient of $P(\mathbf{x})$, $\frac{\partial \log P(\mathbf{x})}{\partial W}$, has to be calculated. However, it is intractable to calculate $\frac{\partial \log P(\mathbf{x})}{\partial W}$ analytically. The CD-k algorithm approximates the gradient using difference between Kullback-Leibler divergences [12]. Since the CD-k algorithm needs states of every neurons after RBM carries out k times, the states are estimated using Gibbs sampling. Fig. 3 shows CD-1 algorithm, which is special version of CD-k, using a pesudocode. In this study CD-1 algorithm is used.

```
Initialize weights W randomly
for each epoch do
    for each data x_i of size D do
        Compute μ_i = E[h|x_i, W]
        Sample h_i ~ p(h|x_i, W)
        Sample x'_i = p(x|h_i, W)
        Compute μ'_i = E[h|x^i_i, W]
        Accumulate g = g + x_i μ_i^T - x'_i h'_i^T
        Update parameters W = W + α/D g
```

Fig. 3. The pseudocode shows CD-1 algorithm. When you use CD-k algorithm, you repeat sampling process k times.

A deep architecture neural network is constructed combining trained RBMs hierarchically. After a deep architecture neural network is trained using CD-1 algorithm, discrete feature vectors are transformed into continuous feature vectors. Hence, the outputs of the network are regarded as new feature vectors of input data. When an aim is classification, outputs of the network is inputs of a classifier.

The feature vectors are transformed based on a function constructed with numerous unlabeled data. Using RBM especially, input data are generally mapped onto lower-dimension feature space. Hence, since relevant data are located in neighborhood of lower-dimension feature space, the network is applied to classification task.

4 Experiments

Experiments are carried out using real stock market news, T&C news to evaluate performance of the proposed method.

4.1   Dataset

In experiments T&C news, which is one of stock market news delivery services in Japan, are used as a corpus. The corpus consists of 62,478 articles in 2010 including stock price news, business performance reports, comments of analysts and so on. 100 articles are labeled as positive, negative, or neutral by a stock market specialist. Positive articles include information on increasing stock price. On the other hand, negative articles includes information on decreasing stock price. Neutral articles do not affect stock price.

Since my aim is to estimate sentiment polarity of words, adjectives and some kinds of noun are extracted from the all articles as features. These words include author's intent and are used in sentiment analysis frequently. The number of features is 2,604. All articles are represented as a binary vector which denotes whether the articles include the selected words or not. If you use term occurrence frequency, almost all vectors are binary vectors since the news is very short.

After word extraction 39,269 articles are represented as feature vectors using extracted words and 71 labeled articles are included. To train a deep architecture neural network we use the 71 labeled articles and 10,000 articles that are selected from 39,198 randomly. Hence, 10,071 articles are used to train the network. Since in training phase label is not used at all, the network is trained with an unsupervised learning approach. The 71 articles are used to evaluate performance of classification with a deep architecture neural network. To evaluate performance of word classification clusters are checked manually and discussed from the viewpoint of understandability of clusters for human.

4.2   Results

A deep architecture neural network has 2,604 neurons in an input layer, 3 hidden layers, which have 1,000 neurons, 500 neurons, and 250 neurons respectively, and 100 neurons in an output layer. Hence, the network consists of 4 RBMs.

After applying the trained neural network to binary vectors of the training articles, a similarity distribution among 10,071 articles changes. Fig. 4 shows two distributions of similarity among all articles. You find the two distributions are very different. The left distribution with binary vectors shows all articles are less relevant each other though there are many articles with the same polarity.

First, clusters constructed with new feature vectors are discussed with the 71 labeled articles. Table 1 shows how many articles the proposed method improves. This result shows the proposed method improves many relevance rankings though in some of articles the proposed method worsens relevance ranking.

Finally, word clusters are discussed. The word clusters are constructed analyzing the first hidden layer. The highest weights among a neuron in hidden layer and all neurons in input layer denotes strong relevance among words. Hence, the clusters are constructed the weights between the input layer and the hidden layer. Cluster A is a cluster of positive words and Cluster B is a cluster of negative words.

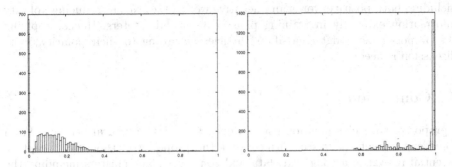

Fig. 4. The left graph shows a distribution of similarity among all articles using binary vectors for the articles. The right graph shows a distribution of similarity among all articles using continuous vectors generated with the proposed method.

Table 1. The table shows the number of ranking improvement for top 10 relevant articles between original features and new features the proposed method generated. Increasing the number of the same polarity articles in top 10 relevant ones, increase a score in "Improvement".

Improvement	Worsening	No change
36	17	18

Table 2. The table shows some clusters obtained with the proposed method. Original data is written in Japanese.

Cluster A	Cluster B
accounting	upswing
press release	average
adjustment	evolution
significant	drop-off
prediction	not(negation)
increased profit	trade
progress	caution
excellent condition	attention

4.3 Discussion

The proposed method can capture more essential relevance among articles than existing bag-of-words approach from Fig. 4 and Table 1. Since the proposed method trains the neural network with numerous unlabeled data and transform input data into lower dimension space, the neural network has a function gathering relevant words in the same neuron. The function affects performance of word clustering. From Table 2 the function works well in this network since some clusters include the same polarity words. However, there are many clusters including both positive words and negative words, too. Not introducing polarity information expressly in training phase causes bad clusters. Hence, applying the proposed method to classifying articles according to their polarity, more discussion is needed.

5   Conclusion

I proposed word classification using a deep architecture neural network. From some experiments it was confirmed that the proposed method could capture essential relevance among text data and construct some clusters including the same polarity words. The result shows a deep architecture neural network can be applied to natural language processing, too.

Since this study is the first step to apply a neural network to sentiment analysis, a classifier to estimate article polarity will be constructed or be applied to polarity dictionary construction. And I would like to discuss performance of the proposed method from the viewpoint of their applications.

Acknowledgement. I would like to thank Centillion Japan Co. Ltd. for giving us market news for our experiments.

References

1. Rosenblatt, F.: The Perceptron: A Probabilistic Model for Information Storage and Organization in the Brain. Psychological Review 65(6), 386–408 (1958)
2. Rumelhar, D.E., Hinton, G.E., Williams, R.J.: Learning representations by back-propagation errors. Nature 323, 533–536 (1986)
3. Hochreiter, S.: The Vanishing Gradient Problem During Learning Recurrent Neural Nets and Problem Solutions. Int. Journal of Uncertainty, Fuzzines and Knowledge-Based Systems 6(2), 107–116 (1998)
4. Bengio, Y.: Learning Deep Architecture for AI. Foundations and Trends in Machine Learning 2(1), 1–127 (2009)
5. Lee, Q.V., Ranzato, M., Monga, R., Devin, M., Chen, K., Corrado, G.S., Dean, J., Ng, A.Y.: Building High-level Features Using Large Scale Unsupervised Learning. In: Proc. of the 29th Int. Conference on Machine Learning (2012)
6. Krizhevsky, A., Sutskever, I., Hinton, G.E.: ImageNet Classification with Deep Convolutional Neural Networks. In: Advances in Neural Information Processing, vol. 25. MIT Press, Cambridge (2012)
7. Bengio, Y., Ducharme, R., Vincent, P., Jauvin, C.: A Neural Probabilistic Language Model. Journal of Machine Learning Research 3, 1137–1155 (2003)
8. Arisoy, E., Sainath, T.N., Kingsbury, B., Ramabhadran, B.: Deep Neural Network Language Model. In: Proc. of NAACL-HLT 2012, pp. 20–28 (2012)
9. Shoelkopf, B., Smola, A.J.: Learning with Kernels: Support Vector Machines, Regularization, Optimization, and Beyond. The MIT Press (2001)

10. Hinton, G.E., Salakhutdinov, R.R.: Reducing the Dimensionality of Data with Neural Network. Science 313, 504–507 (2006)
11. Lee, H., Battle, A., Raina, R., Ng, A.Y.: Efficient Sparse Coding Algorithm. In: Advances in Neural Information Processing Systems, vol. 19, pp. 801–808 (2006)
12. HInton, G.E., Osindero, S., Teh, Y.W.: A Fast Learning Algorithm for Deep Blief Nets. Neural Computation 18, 1527–1554 (2006)
13. Muraphy, K.P.: Machine Learning: A Probabilistic Perspective. The MIT Press (2012)

Author Index